New Perspectives on

Macromedia® Dreamweaver® MX 2004

Comprehensive

Kelly Hart

Mitch Geller

Ruth Guthrie
Contributing Author

THOMSON
COURSE TECHNOLOGY

Australia • Canada • Mexico • Singapore • Spain • United Kingdom • United States

New Perspectives on Macromedia® Dreamweaver® MX 2004— **Comprehensive** is published by Course Technology.

Managing Editor:
Rachel Goldberg

Senior Product Manager:
Kathy Finnegan

Senior Technology Product Manager:
Amanda Young Shelton

Product Manager:
Karen Stevens

Contributing Author:
Ruth Guthrie

Product Manager:
Brianna Germain

Associate Product Manager:
Emilie Perreault

Editorial Assistant:
Shana Rosenthal

Senior Marketing Manager:
Joy Stark

Developmental Editor:
Robin Romer

Production Editor:
Custom Editorial Productions, Inc.

Composition:
GEX Publishing Services

Text Designer:
Steve Deschene

Cover Designer:
Nancy Goulet

Cover Artist:
Ed Carpenter
www.edcarpenter.net

COPYRIGHT © 2004 Course Technology, a division of Thomson Learning, Inc. Thomson Learning™ is a trademark used herein under license.

Printed in the United States of America

2 3 4 5 6 7 8 9 BM 08 07 06 05

For more information, contact Course Technology, 25 Thomson Place, Boston, Massachusetts, 02210.

Or find us on the World Wide Web at: www.course.com

ALL RIGHTS RESERVED. No part of this work covered by the copyright hereon may be reproduced or used in any form or by any means—graphic, electronic, or mechanical, including photocopying, recording, taping, Web distribution, or information storage and retrieval systems—without the written permission of the publisher.

For permission to use material from this text or product, submit a request online at www.thomsonrights.com

Any additional questions about permissions can be submitted by e-mail to thomsonrights@thomson.com

Disclaimer
Course Technology reserves the right to revise this publication and make changes from time to time in its content without notice.

Disclaimer
Any fictional URLs used throughout this book are intended for instructional purposes only. At the time this book was printed, any such URLs were fictional and not belonging to any real persons or companies.

Some of the product names and company names used in this book have been used for identification purposes only and may be trademarks or registered trademarks of their respective manufacturers and sellers.

"Avon," an essay from a collection of writings entitled *Punch* appears in Case Problem 3 in all tutorials courtesy of Kelly Hart. Avon and Punch are © Copyright Kelly Hart, 2004. All rights reserved.

The following images, which are included with the Data Files and used in Case Problem 2 in all tutorials, are provided courtesy of the Sid Richardson Museum of Western Art (www.sidrmuseum.org), Fort Worth, Texas:

"A Quiet Day in Utica" by Charles M. Russell, 1907, Oil on canvas.

"Cow Punching Sometimes Spells Trouble" by Charles M. Russell, 1889, Oil on canvas.
"Indians Hunting Buffalo" by Charles M. Russell, 1894, Oil on canvas.
"The Bucker" by Charles M. Russell, 1904, Pencil, watercolor, and gouache on paper.
"Deer in Forest" by Charles M. Russell, 1917, Oil on canvas.
"Buffalo Runners—Big Horn Basin" by Frederic Remington, 1909, Oil on canvas.
"The Sentinel" by Frederic Remington, 1908, Oil on canvas.
"The Cow Puncher" by Frederic Remington, 1901, Oil (black and white) on canvas.
"The Love Call" by Frederic Remington, 1909, Oil on canvas.
"Among the Led Horses" by Frederic Remington, 1909, Oil on canvas.
"The Luckless Hunter" by Frederic Remington, 1909, Oil on canvas.
"The Riderless Horse" by Frederic Remington, 1886, Pencil, pen and ink, and watercolor on paper.

All media elements used in Case Problem 1 are provided courtesy of Dr. Jerold A. Edmondson and are © Copyright Dr. Jerold A. Edmondson, 2004. All rights reserved.

ISBN 0-619-21420-1

Preface

Real, Thought-Provoking, Engaging, Dynamic, Interactive—these are just a few of the words that are used to describe the New Perspectives Series' approach to learning and building computer skills.

Without our critical-thinking and problem-solving methodology, computer skills could be learned but not retained. By teaching with a case-based approach, the New Perspectives Series challenges students to apply what they've learned to real-life situations.

Our ever-growing community of users understands why they're learning what they're learning. Now you can too!

See what instructors and students are saying about the best-selling New Perspectives Series:

> "First of all, I just have to say that I wish that all of my textbooks were written in the style of the New Perspectives series. I am using these titles for all of the courses that I teach that have a book available."
> — Diana Kokoska, University of Maine at Augusta

> "The New Perspectives format is a pleasure to use. The Quick Checks and the tutorial Review Assignments help students view this complex topic from a real work perspective."
> — Craig Shaw, Central Community College, Hastings

> "We have been using the New Perspectives Series for several years and are pleased with it. Step-by-step instructions, end-of-chapter projects, and color screenshots are positives."
> — Mike Losacco, College of DuPage

www.course.com/NewPerspectives

Why *New Perspectives* will work for you

Context

Each tutorial begins with a problem presented in a "real-world" case that is meaningful to students. The case sets the scene to help students understand what they will do in the tutorial.

Hands-on Approach

Each tutorial is divided into manageable sessions that combine reading and hands-on, step-by-step work. Screenshots—now 20% larger for enhanced readability—help guide students through the steps. **Trouble?** tips anticipate common mistakes or problems to help students stay on track and continue with the tutorial.

Review

In New Perspectives, retention is a key component to learning. At the end of each session, a series of Quick Check questions helps students test their understanding of the concepts before moving on. And now each tutorial contains an end-of-tutorial summary and a list of key terms for further reinforcement.

Assessment

Engaging and challenging Review Assignments and Case Problems have always been a hallmark feature of the New Perspectives Series. Now we've added new features to make them more accessible! Colorful icons and brief descriptions accompany the exercises, making it easy to understand, at a glance, both the goal and level of challenge a particular assignment holds.

Reference

While contextual learning is excellent for retention, there are times when students will want a high-level understanding of how to accomplish a task. Within each tutorial, Reference Windows appear before a set of steps to provide a succinct summary and preview of how to perform a task. In addition, a complete Task Reference at the back of the book provides quick access to information on how to carry out common tasks. Finally, each book includes a combination Glossary/Index to promote easy reference of material.

www.course.com/NewPerspectives

New Perspectives offers an entire system of instruction

The New Perspectives Series is more than just a handful of books. It's a complete system of offerings:

New Perspectives catalog
Our online catalog is never out of date! Go to the catalog link on our Web site to check out our available titles, request a desk copy, download a book preview, or locate online files.

Coverage to meet your needs!
Whether you're looking for just a small amount of coverage or enough to fill a semester-long class, we can provide you with a textbook that meets your needs.
- Brief books typically cover the essential skills in just 2 to 4 tutorials.
- Introductory books build and expand on those skills and contain an average of 5 to 8 tutorials.
- Comprehensive books are great for a full-semester class, and contain 9 to 12+ tutorials.
- Power Users or Advanced books are perfect for a highly accelerated introductory class or a second course in a given topic.

So if the book you're holding does not provide the right amount of coverage for you, there's probably another offering available. Go to our Web site or contact your Course Technology sales representative to find out what else we offer.

Instructor Resources
We offer more than just a book. We have all the tools you need to enhance your lectures, check students' work, and generate exams in a new, easier-to-use and completely revised package. This book's Instructor's Manual, ExamView testbank, PowerPoint presentations, data files, solution files, figure files, and a sample syllabus are all available on a single CD-ROM or for downloading at www.course.com.

How will your students master Computer Concepts and Microsoft Office?
Add more muscle and flexibility to your course with SAM (Skills Assessment Manager)! SAM adds the power of skill-based assessment and the award-winning SAM classroom administration system to your course, putting you in control of how you deliver exams and training.

By adding SAM to your curriculum, you can:
- Reinforce your students' knowledge of key computer concepts and application skills with hands-on exercises.
- Allow your students to "learn by listening," with access to rich audio in their training.
- Build hands-on computer concepts exams from a test bank of more than 200 skill-based concepts, windows, and applications tasks.
- Schedule your students' training and testing exercises with powerful administrative tools.
- Track student exam grades and training progress using more than one dozen student and classroom reports.

Teach your introductory course with the simplicity of a single system! You can now administer your entire Computer Concepts and Microsoft Office course through the SAM platform. For more information on the SAM administration system, SAM Computer Concepts, and other SAM products, please visit www.course.com/sam.

Distance Learning
Enhance your course with any of our online learning platforms. Go to www.course.com or speak with your Course Technology sales representative to find the platform or the content that's right for you.

www.course.com/NewPerspectives

About This Book

Students will gain confidence as they learn how to use Dreamweaver MX 2004 to create and manage complex Web sites.

- Updated for the Dreamweaver MX 2004 software, including enhanced CSS features!
- New to this edition! New tutorial on database integration teaches students how to develop Web pages that interact with a server-side database. This tutorial was written for two database configurations—Windows IIS and X—to accommodate most lab situations.
- New to this edition! New appendix introduces students to working with graphics files in Macromedia® Fireworks®!
- In addition to teaching how to use Dreamweaver, this book provides extensive information about planning and designing a Web site, including information architecture, marketing and target audience research, and end-user analysis and profiling.
- Each tutorial includes a section in which students review the HTML code of the pages they built.

Acknowledgments

The authors wish to thank:

Robin Romer, our editor extraordinaire, for skillfully guiding us to shape our ramblings into a "real book" while also managing the increasingly complex "Jake Project." Thank you for all your hard work and dedication.

Contributing author Ruth Guthrie for her generosity and hard work on the Fireworks MX 2004 appendix.

Charlie Lindahl (aka CyberChuck) for introducing us to an *amazing new thing* called the Web on his new Mosaic Version 0.2A browser (1993), helping us to keep up with the latest developments ever since, and for his never-ending encouragement and enthusiasm.

Richard Strittmatter of Computeam.com for his insightful and practical guidance through the maze that is contemporary database design and for continuing to provide definitive answers for the complex and often misunderstood technologies of the Internet.

The staff and management of Meshnet.com for graciously providing hosting and support (and for once again rebuilding our servers).

The staff of the Sid Richardson Museum and Store (www.sidrmuseum.org/store) for their support and generosity in allowing us to use images from the Sid Richardson Collection of Western Art.

The Course Technology team—Rachel Crapser, Managing Editor; Karen Stevens, Product Manager; John Freitas and his team of Quality Assurance testers; Megan Smith-Creed, Production Editor; and Emilie Perreault, Associate Product Manager—for all their support during this second go-around.

Mitch would like to thank Edyie and Joe Geller, Pam, Gregg, and the rest of the family for their love and support…you guys are the greatest! He would also like to thank John Knecht, John Orentlicher, and Don Little.

Kelly would like to thank Mary O'Brien for her culinary, caffeination, and grammatical assistance along with the rest of the Nu-Design.com team, Tika, Brian, and Matt, for their support.

www.course.com/NewPerspectives

Brief Contents

Dreamweaver

Macromedia® Dreamweaver® MX 2004—Level I Tutorials — DRM 1

Tutorial 1 .... DRM 3
Introducing Dreamweaver MX 2004
Exploring an Existing Web Site

Tutorial 2 .... DRM 47
Planning and Designing a Successful Web Site
Developing a Web Site Plan and Design

Tutorial 3 .... DRM 103
Adding and Formatting Text
Using the Property Inspector, CSS Styles, and HTML Tags

Tutorial 4 .... DRM 167
Organizing Page Content and Layout
Working with Graphics, Rollovers, and Tables

Tutorial 5 .... DRM 245
Adding Shared Site Elements
Creating a Navigation Bar and Using Frames

Tutorial 6 .... DRM 309
Creating Dynamic Pages
Inserting Layers and Adding Behaviors

Macromedia® Dreamweaver® MX 2004—Level II Tutorials — DRM 369

Tutorial 7 .... DRM 371
Adding Rich Media to a Web Site
Inserting Flash, Shockwave, Sound, and Video Elements

Tutorial 8 .... DRM 421
Creating Reusable Assets and Forms
Creating Meta Tags, Library Items, Templates, and Forms

Tutorial 9 .... DRM 481
Adding Database Functionality
Collecting and Viewing Form Data in a Database

Additional Cases .... ADD 543
Building a Web Site with a Form
Building a Web Site with Database Functionality

Appendix A .... DRM 549
Introduction to Fireworks MX 2004

Appendix B .... DRM 585
Guide to Using Dreamweaver on the Macintosh

Table of Contents

Preface iii
Macromedia® Dreamweaver® MX 2004
Level I Tutorials 1
    Read This Before You Begin 2

Tutorial 1   3

Introducing Dreamweaver MX 2004 3
Exploring an Existing Web Site 3

Session 1.1 4
Dreamweaver and the Internet 4
    The Internet and the World Wide Web 4
    Web Servers and Clients 5
    Web Pages and Web Sites 6
Session 1.1 Quick Check 14

Session 1.2 14
Evolving Web Design Tools 14
    Comparing Page-Centric and Site-Centric Design Tools 15
Starting Dreamweaver and Selecting a Workspace Layout Configuration 15
Creating a Site Definition 18
    Configuring a Local Site Definition 19
Exploring the Dreamweaver Environment 22
    Files Panel 22
    Document Window 26
    Property Inspector 30
    Insert Bar 33
Getting Help in Dreamweaver 35
Exiting Dreamweaver 39
Session 1.2 Quick Check 39
Tutorial Summary 40
Key Terms 40
Review Assignments 40
Quick Check Answers 45

Tutorial 2   47

Planning and Designing a Successful Web Site 47
Developing a Web Site Plan and Design 47

Session 2.1 48
Creating a Plan for a New Web Site 48
    Determining Site Goals 48
    Identifying the Target Audience 50
    Conducting Market Research 52
    Creating End-User Scenarios 54
Session 2.1 Quick Check 56

Session 2.2 56
Creating Information Architecture 56
    Creating Categories for Information 56
    Creating a Flowchart 57
    Gathering and Organizing Information 59
Designing a Web Site 59
    Creating a Site Concept and Metaphor 59
    Considering Accessibility Issues 60
    Selecting Colors 61
    Selecting Fonts 64
    Choosing a Graphic Style and Graphics 66
    Sketching the Layout 68
    Checking the Design for Logic 69
Session 2.2 Quick Check 69

Session 2.3 70
Creating a New Site 70
    Creating a Local Site Definition 70
    Creating a Remote Site Definition 71
Creating and Saving Pages in a Defined Site 74

Adding New Pages	74
Saving New Pages	76
Setting Page Titles	76
Resaving Pages	77
Reviewing the HTML Tags	78
Setting Page Properties	80
Previewing a Site in a Browser	87
Uploading a Web Site to a Remote Location	89
Previewing on the Web	91
Session 2.3 Quick Check	93
Tutorial Summary	93
Key Terms	93
Review Assignments	94
Quick Check Answers	100

Tutorial 3 103

Adding and Formatting Text **103**

Using the Property Inspector, CSS Styles, and HTML Tags 103

Session 3.1 .... **104**

Adding Text to a Web Page	104
Checking the Spelling in Web Pages	106
Using the Find and Replace Tool	107
Formatting Text Using the Property Inspector	108
Creating Text Hyperlinks	111
Adding and Formatting Hyperlink Text	111
Creating Links from Text	112
Exploring HTML Tags for Hyperlinks	115
Exploring HTML Tags that Apply to Hyperlinks	116
Session 3.1 Quick Check	119

Session 3.2 .... **119**

Understanding Cascading Style Sheets	119
Creating CSS Styles	120
Modifying HTML Tags	121
Creating and Applying Custom Style Classes	125
Using the Advanced CSS Type to Customize Anchor Tag Pseudoclasses	127
Session 3.2 Quick Check	130

Session 3.3 .... **130**

Using External Style Sheets	130
Exporting Styles to an External Style Sheet	130
Deleting Styles from a Style Sheet	132
Attaching a Style Sheet to Web Pages	133
Creating a Style in an External Style Sheet	135
Examining Code for CSS Styles	137
Viewing Code for Internal Style Sheets	138
Viewing Code for External Style Sheets	139
Viewing Style Tags	141
Editing CSS Styles	144
Editing Styles in the CSS Style Definition Dialog Box	144
Editing Styles with the Tag Inspector	146
Changing Text Appearance in the Property Inspector	148
Exploring HTML Tags Used with Text	149
Formatting Text in HTML Mode	153
Updating a Web Site on a Remote Server	154
Session 3.3 Quick Check	155
Tutorial Summary	156
Key Terms	156
Review Assignments	156
Quick Check Answers	165

Tutorial 4 167
Organizing Page Content and Layout 167
Working with Graphics, Rollovers, and Tables 167

Session 4.1 168

Understanding Graphics and Compression 168
    Using GIF 169
    Using JPEG 169
    Using PNG 170

Adding Graphics to Web Pages 171
    Using the Insert Bar to Add Graphics 171
    Using the Assets Panel to Insert Graphics 173

Formatting Graphics Using CSS Styles and the Property Inspector 175

Editing Graphics from Within Dreamweaver 178

Creating Graphic Hyperlinks 183
    Linking an Image 183
    Creating an Image Map 184

Creating Rollovers 187
    Inserting Rollovers 187
    Editing a Rollover 191

Session 4.1 Quick Check 191

Session 4.2 191

Creating Tables 191
    Inserting a Table 192
    Adding Content to Cells 195

Selecting Tables and Table Elements 196
    Selecting a Table 197
    Selecting a Table Cell 198
    Selecting Columns and Rows 199
    Using Expanded Tables Mode 200

Working with the Entire Table 201

Modifying Table Attributes 201
Resizing and Moving a Table 203
Deleting a Table 205

Working with Table Cells 205
    Modifying Cell Formatting and Layout 205
    Adjusting the Row Span and Column Span of Cells 207

Working with Rows and Columns 208
    Modifying Rows and Columns 208
    Resizing Columns and Rows 208
    Adding and Deleting Columns and Rows 209

Using Preset Table Designs 210

Exploring the HTML Code of Tables 212
    Redefining Table Tags Using CSS Styles 215

Session 4.2 Quick Check 215

Session 4.3 215

Planning a Table in Layout Mode 215

Creating a Table in Layout Mode 218
    Drawing Cells in Layout Mode 218
    Drawing a Table in Layout Mode 220

Selecting Tables and Cells in Layout Mode 221
    Selecting Tables in Layout Mode 222
    Selecting Cells in Layout Mode 222

Working with Tables in Layout Mode 223
    Resizing Tables in Layout Mode 224
    Modifying Table Attributes in Layout Mode 225
    Deleting a Layout Table 227

Working with Cells in Layout Mode 228
    Moving and Resizing Cells in Layout Mode 228
    Modifying Cell Attributes in Layout Mode 229
    Adding Content to Cells in Layout Mode 231

Updating the Web Site on the Remote Server 233

Session 4.3 Quick Check 235
Tutorial Summary 235
Key Terms 235
Review Assignments 235
Quick Check Answers 243

Tutorial 5 245
Adding Shared Site Elements 245
Creating a Navigation Bar and Using Frames 245

Session 5.1 246
Creating a Navigation Bar Object 246
   Inserting a Navigation Bar 249
   Copying a Navigation Bar 255
Modifying the Navigation Bar 257
Session 5.1 Quick Check 259

Session 5.2 259
Understanding Frames and Framesets 259
Creating a Web Page That Uses Frames 262
   Creating Frames by Splitting a Web Page 263
   Creating Frames by Dragging Borders 265
   Using a Predefined Frameset 267
   Selecting and Saving Frames 269
   Selecting and Saving the Frameset 270
Adjusting Page Properties for Frames 271
Adjusting Frame and Frameset Attributes 274
   Adjusting Frame Attributes 275
   Adjusting Frameset Attributes 277
Session 5.2 Quick Check 279

Session 5.3 279
Inserting Frames and NoFrames Content 279
   Adding Content to Frames 279
   Adding NoFrames Content 282
Using Hyperlinks with Frames 283

Reviewing HTML Associated with Frames and Targets 289
Finding Solutions to Common Frame Problems 291
Updating the Web Site on the Remote Server 294
Session 5.3 Quick Check 296
Tutorial Summary 296
Key Terms 296
Review Assignments 296
Quick Check Answers 307

Tutorial 6 309
Creating Dynamic Pages 309
Inserting Layers and Adding Behaviors 309

Session 6.1 310
Using Layers 310
   Inserting Layers 310
Selecting, Resizing, and Moving a Layer 311
Adding Content to a Layer 315
Adjusting Layer Attributes 320
Examining the Code for Layers 323
Session 6.1 Quick Check 325

Session 6.2 325
Modifying Layers 325
   Adjusting Layer Stacking Order 325
   Aligning Layers 329
   Positioning Layers and Other Elements Using the Grid 330
   Creating Nested Layers 331
Using the Netscape Resize Fix 333
Converting Layers to Tables 334
Session 6.2 Quick Check 336

Session 6.3 337
Understanding Behaviors 337
   Adding Behaviors Using the Behaviors Panel 338
   Adding an E-mail Link to a Page 348

    Adding a Custom Script to a Page 348

    Editing and Deleting Behaviors 353

Updating the Web Site on the Remote Server 354

Session 6.3 Quick Check 356

Tutorial Summary 356

Key Terms 356

Review Assignments 356

Quick Check Answers 366

Macromedia® Dreamweaver® MX 2004
Level II Tutorials 369
    Read This Before You Begin 370

Tutorial 7 371
Adding Rich Media to a Web Site 371
Inserting Flash, Shockwave, Sound, and Video Elements 371

Session 7.1 372

Adding Media to a Web Site 372

Understanding Macromedia Flash 372

Adding Flash Movies to Web Pages 375

    Adjusting Attributes of a Flash Movie 378

Adding Flash Text to Web Pages 380

Using Flash Buttons 383

Session 7.1 Quick Check 385

Session 7.2 385

Understanding Macromedia Shockwave 385

Adding Shockwave Movies to Web Pages 389

    Adjusting Attributes of a Shockwave Movie 393

Understanding Sound 394

Embedding a Sound-only Flash Movie 396

    Adjusting Attributes of a Sound-only Flash Movie 399

    Embedding Other Sound Formats 399

Creating a Link to an MP3 Sound File 399

    Creating Links to Other Sound Files 401

Session 7.2 Quick Check 402

Session 7.3 402

Understanding Digital Video 402

    Reviewing Video File Formats 403

Adding Video to a Web Page 404

    Downloading the RealMedia Suite Extension for Dreamweaver 404

    Adding a RealMedia Video Clip to a Web Page 406

    Adjusting the Attributes of a Video Clip 408

    Downloading the RealPlayer for Internet Explorer 409

Adjusting a RealMedia Video Clip to Display over the Internet 412

Updating the Web Site on the Remote Server 413

Session 7.3 Quick Check 414

Tutorial Summary 414

Key Terms 414

Review Assignments 415

Quick Check Answers 419

Tutorial 8   421
Creating Reusable Assets and Forms 421
Creating Meta Tags, Library Items, Templates, and Forms 421

Session 8.1 422

Reviewing Head Content 422

Optimizing Web Pages for Search Engine Placement 422

Adding and Editing Keywords 423

    Adding Keywords and Examining the Code 424

    Editing Keywords 425

Adding and Editing a Meta Description 426

    Adding a Meta Description and Viewing the Code 427

    Editing a Meta Description 428

Understanding Library Items 428	Updating the Web Site on the Remote Server 472
Creating and Using a Library Item 429	Session 8.3 Quick Check 473
Adding a Library Item to Web Pages 432	Tutorial Summary 473
Examining the Code for a Library Item 432	Key Terms 473
Editing a Library Item 434	Review Assignments 473
Deleting a Library Item 436	Quick Check Answers 479
Session 8.1 Quick Check 437	

Session 8.2 437

Understanding Templates 437	
Creating a Template 438	

Tutorial 9 481
Adding Database Functionality 481
Collecting and Viewing Form Data in a Database 481

Session 9.1 482

Adding Regions to a Template 440	Exploring Databases and Dynamic Page Content 482
Creating Web Pages from a Template 444	Creating Database-Driven Pages Using MySQL and PHP 483
Creating a New Template-Based Page 444	Modifying the Form 484
Applying a Template to an Existing Web Page 447	Creating New Pages 485
Editing a Template 448	Creating a Database on a Remote Server 487
Deleting a Template 450	Connecting a Web Site to a Database 489
Creating Nested Templates 450	Adding Server Behaviors 491
Session 8.2 Quick Check 453	Creating Backend Pages for Viewing Data in a Database 495
	Creating a Login Page to Protect Backend Pages 500

Session 8.3 453

Understanding Forms 453	Session 9.1 Quick Check 505

Session 9.2 506

Creating a Form 454	Creating Database-Driven Pages Using Access and ASP 506
Adding a Form to a Web Page 454	Modifying the Form 506
Setting Form Attributes 455	Creating New Pages 508
Adding Form Objects 457	Uploading a Database to a Remote Server 510
Creating the Form Structure 458	Connecting a Web Site to a Database 512
Inserting Text Fields and Areas into a Form 460	Add Server Behaviors 514
Inserting Checkboxes into a Form 462	Creating Backend Pages for Viewing Data in a Database 519
Adding Radio Buttons to a Form 463	Creating a Login Page to Protect Backend Pages 523
Adding Lists to a Form 465	Session 9.2 Quick Check 528
Adding Buttons to a Form 466	Tutorial Summary 528
Validating Form Data 468	
Testing a Form 470	

Key Terms	529
Review Assignments	529
Quick Check Answers	542

Additional Cases — 543

Building a Web Site with a Form **543**

Building a Web Site with Database Functionality **546**

Appendix A — 549

Introduction to Fireworks MX 2004 .... **549**

Fireworks MX 2004 Editing Tools and File Creation 550
   Previewing the Tools Panel 552
   The Main and Modify Toolbars 552
   The Property Inspector 553
   Creating a New Document 554
   Saving and Exporting Files 556

Using the Tools Panel 558
   Selection Tools 558
   Bitmap Tools 561
   Vector Tools 568
   Web Tools 574
   Colors Tools 574
   View Tools 575

Working with Panels 575
   The Optimize Panel 575
   The Layers Panel 576

   The Assets Panel Group 579

Working with Images in Other Applications 579
   Editing Options from the Dreamweaver Workspace 580
   Working with Fireworks and Other Applications 580
   Working with the Quick Export Button 581

Quick Check 581
Appendix Summary 582
Key Terms 582
Review Assignments 582
Quick Check Answers 583

Appendix B — 585

Guide to Using Dreamweaver on the Macintosh ... **585**

Global Alternate Instructions for Working on a Macintosh 586
   Windows Instructions for Macintosh Users 586
   Previewing or Viewing Web Pages in a Browser 586
   File Navigation and Selection 587

Using Dreamweaver MX 2004 on the Macintosh 587
   Starting Dreamweaver 587
   Importing a Word Document into Dreamweaver 587
   Dreamweaver Preferences 588
   Files Panel Menu Bar 588
   Getting Help in Dreamweaver 588

Task Reference .... **REF 589**

Glossary/Index .... **REF 595**

New Perspectives on
Macromedia® Dreamweaver® MX 2004

Tutorial 1   DRM 3
Introducing Dreamweaver MX 2004
Exploring an Existing Web Site

Tutorial 2   DRM 47
Planning and Designing a Successful Web Site
Developing a Web Site Plan and Design

Tutorial 3   DRM 103
Adding and Formatting Text
Using the Property Inspector, CSS Styles, and HTML Tags

Tutorial 4   DRM 167
Organizing Page Content and Layout
Working with Graphics, Rollovers, and Tables

Tutorial 5   DRM 245
Adding Shared Site Elements
Creating a Navigation Bar and Using Frames

Tutorial 6   DRM 309
Creating Dynamic Pages
Inserting Layers and Adding Behaviors

New Perspectives Series

Read This Before You Begin: Tutorials 1–6

To the Student

Data Files

To complete Tutorials 1–6 of this text, you will need the starting student Data Files. Your instructor will either provide you with these Data Files or ask you to obtain them yourself.

Tutorials 1–6 require the folders shown to complete the Tutorials, Review Assignments, and Case Problems. You will need to copy these folders from a file server, a standalone computer, or the Web to the drive and folder where you will be storing your Data Files. Your instructor will tell you which computer, drive letter, and folder(s) contain the files you need. You can also download the files by going to www.course.com; see the inside back or front cover for more information on downloading the files, or ask your instructor or technical support person for assistance.

▼ **Dreamweaver MX 2004**
Tutorial.01
Tutorial.02
Tutorial.03
Tutorial.04
Tutorial.05
Tutorial.06

Recommend MM 352

To the Instructor

The Data Files are available on the Instructor Resources CD for this title. Follow the instructions in the Help file on the CD to install the programs to your network or standalone computer. See the "To the Student" section above for information on how to set up the Data Files that accompany this text.

You are granted a license to copy the Data Files to any computer or computer network used by students who have purchased this book.

System Requirements

If you are going to work through this book using your own computer, you need:

- **System Requirements** This text assumes a default installation of Macromedia Dreamweaver MX 2004. A text editor and a Web browser (preferably Internet Explorer or Netscape Navigator, versions 4.0 or higher) must be installed on your computer. If you are using a nonstandard browser, it must support frames and HTML 6.0 or higher.

  The screenshots in this book were taken using a computer running Windows XP Professional and, when showing a browser, Internet Explorer 6. If you are using a different operation system or a different browser, your screen might differ from the figures shown in the book.

  Macromedia recommends the following Windows system configuration: 600 MHz Intel Pentium III processor or equivalent; Windows 98 SE (4.10.2222 A), Windows 2000, or Windows XP; 128 MB RAM (256 MB recommended); and 275 MB available disk space. Dreamweaver MX 2004 does not support monitor resolutions below 1024 × 768 pixels.

- **FTP Trouble?** With some Windows servers, the Dreamweaver built-in FTP client does not work properly and may give continuous or intermittent errors. If FTP/connection errors occur, first double-check all the remote and testing server configuration settings. Next, review the following support documents on the Macromedia Web site: http://www.macromedia.com/support/dreamweaver/ts/documents/emerging_issues.htm
http://www.macromedia.com/support/dreamweaver/ts/documents/troubleshooting_ftp.htm

  If you cannot resolve the problem, you may need to utilize a separate FTP program (see www.ipswitch.com).

- **Server Requirements** Tutorial 9 requires you to create or upload a database to a server. This text was written to and tested on both a Linux server and Windows server. The recommended server configurations are listed below.

  For a Linux server:
  - Apache 1.3.26 or above
  - PHP 4.3.2 or above
  - MySQL 3.23 or above
  - Any current distribution of Linux

  For a Windows server:
  - Windows 2000 IIS 5.0 or above
  - Running .net 1.1 framework
  - The IIS User must have write permissions for the database directory

- **Data Files** You will not be able to complete the tutorials or exercises in this book using your own computer until you have the necessary starting Data Files.

www.course.com/NewPerspectives

Dreamweaver | DRM 3

Tutorial 1

Objectives

Session 1.1
- Explore the structure and history of the Internet and the World Wide Web
- Become familiar with the roles of Web servers and Web clients
- Learn the basic components of a Web page
- Open a Web page in a browser
- Use hyperlinks

Session 1.2
- Review the history and design approaches of Web design software
- Start Dreamweaver and select a layout
- Create a local site definition
- Explore the Dreamweaver tool set
- Investigate the Dreamweaver Help features
- Exit Dreamweaver

Introducing Dreamweaver MX 2004

Exploring an Existing Web Site

Case

Catalyst

Catalyst is an independent record label in Denton, Texas, just north of Dallas, that was started by Sara Lynn in 2000. Most of the groups affiliated with the label originated as part of the underground Denton music scene, which centers around the University of North Texas. A year ago, Catalyst created a Web site to promote its bands. Since that time, some of the bands have developed a national following. Sara believes that this success is due, in part, to the exposure from the Catalyst Web site. She also believes that further development of the Web site will generate more national publicity as well as increase CD sales. Therefore, she wants to redesign and expand the Web site.

Brian Lee, who is responsible for public relations and marketing at Catalyst, has a background in multimedia development and will head the Web development team. The new Catalyst Web site will be developed using Macromedia Dreamweaver MX 2004. Brian's team will research the current market trends as well as design and create a new Web site for Catalyst. You will work with Brian and his team to develop this site.

Student Data Files

▼**Tutorial.01 folder**

▽ **Tutorial folder**
▽ **Catalyst folder**
   bands.htm
   contact.htm
   index.htm
   products.htm
   ▽ **graphics folder**
      DizziedConnectionCDcover.jpg
      LifeInMinorChordsCDcover.jpg
      SlothChildCDcover.jpg
      SurfaceSuctionCDcover.jpg
   ▽ **Library folder**
      styles.xml

▽ **Review folder**
   (no starting Data Files)

▽ **Cases folder**
▽ **Museum folder**
   ▽ **Dreamweaver folder**
      contact.htm
      index.htm

You'll start by reviewing the history and structure of the Internet and the World Wide Web. Then you'll explore the components of a basic Web page. Finally, you'll examine the Dreamweaver tool set and learn how to use the Dreamweaver Help features.

Session 1.1

Dreamweaver and the Internet

Dreamweaver is a Web site creation and management tool. To better understand what this means, you'll need to review some basic terms and concepts associated with Web sites.

The Internet and the World Wide Web

The **Internet** is a huge global network made up of millions of smaller computer networks that are all connected together. A **network** is a series of computers that are connected together to share information and resources. Within each network, one or more computers is designated as the server. A **server** is the computer that stores and distributes information to the other computers in the network. The Internet provides a way for people to communicate and exchange information via computer, whether they are across the street or across the globe. All of the computers connected to the Internet can communicate and exchange information. Figure 1-1 illustrates the Internet, using a series of roadways to represent the interconnecting networks that make up the Internet.

Figure 1-1   **Illustration of the Internet**

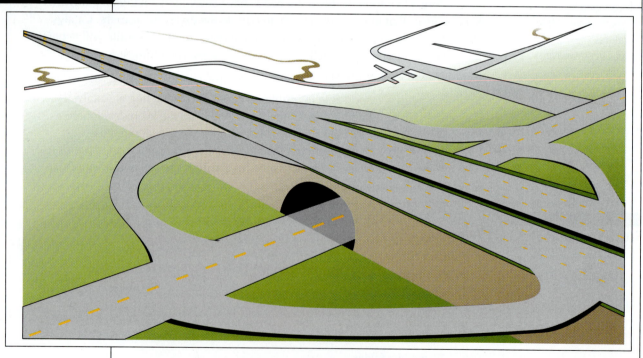

As the Internet has evolved, different protocols have been developed to allow information to be shared in different ways. A **protocol** is a set of technical specifications that define a format for sharing information. Creating an agreed-upon protocol enables a programmer to create software that can interact with all the other software that uses the same protocol. For example, **Simple Mail Transfer Protocol (SMTP)** is an agreed-upon format used by some e-mail software. Without this standard protocol, there would be many incompatible e-mail formats, and you would be able to exchange e-mail only with people who were using the same e-mail software. Another common Internet protocol is **File Transfer Protocol (FTP)**, which is used to copy files from one computer to another over the Internet.

In 1989, Timothy Berners-Lee and his team of scientists at CERN (the European Organization for Nuclear Research) created what we call the World Wide Web as a means for scientists to more easily locate and share data. The **World Wide Web (WWW or Web)** is actually a subset of the Internet with its own protocol, **HTTP (Hypertext Transfer Protocol)**, and its own document structure, called **HTML (Hypertext Markup Language)**. HTTP controls the transfer of Web pages over the Internet, whereas HTML provides instructions on how to format Web pages for display. **Web pages** are the electronic documents of information on the Web; a group of related and interconnected Web pages is referred to as a **Web site**. Figure 1-2 shows how the Web page vehicles must follow the HTTP rules of the road to travel the Internet roadways. Notice that other vehicles, following other protocols, share the Internet as well.

Illustration of the World Wide Web — Figure 1-2

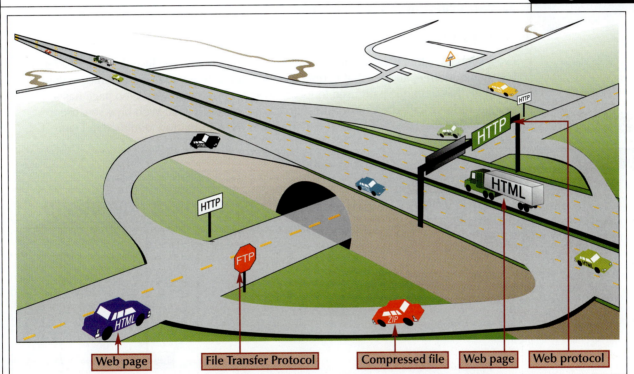

In addition to standards for transfer and display of information, the Web introduced the technology for hyperlinks to the Internet. **Hyperlinks** (or **links**) are nodes that provide the ability to cross-reference information within a document or a Web page and enable the user to move from one document or Web page to another.

Web Servers and Clients

There are two general categories for the computers involved in accessing Web pages: Web servers and Web clients. When you create a Web page or a Web site, you must post a copy of your work to a Web server to share the page with the world. A **Web server** is a specialized server that stores and distributes information to computers that are connected to the Internet.

A **Web client** (or client) is the computer an individual uses to access information, via the Internet, that is stored on Web servers throughout the world. A home computer with Internet access is considered a Web client. You must have access to the Internet to view a Web site. Most people connect to the Internet through an Internet service provider. An **Internet service provider (ISP)** is a company that has direct access to the Internet and sells access to other smaller entities. Some large institutions, such as universities, have direct links to the Internet and are, in essence, their own ISPs.

In addition to being connected to the Internet, to view a Web site you must have a Web browser installed on your client computer. A **Web browser** is the piece of software that interprets and displays Web pages. The Web browser enables users to view Web pages from their client computer. Two of the most common Web browsers are Microsoft Internet Explorer and Netscape Navigator.

Web Pages and Web Sites

Now that you understand what a Web page is and how your computer accesses a Web page on the Internet, you'll examine some elements that are common to all Web pages: the Web address, hyperlinks, and content.

Web Address

Every Web page that is posted to the Internet has a Web address. Just like your residence has a unique street address that people use to locate where you live and a file on your computer has a unique path used to locate where it is stored, every Web page has a unique address, called a **Uniform Resource Locator (URL)**, that Web browsers use to locate where that page is stored. A URL includes the information identified in Figure 1-3.

Figure 1-3   **Parts of a URL**

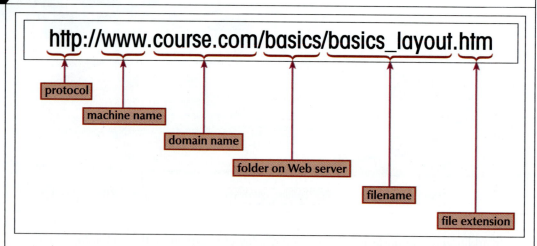

The first portion of the URL indicates the protocol, which is usually HTTP but can be **HTTPS (Hypertext Transfer Protocol Secure)**. HTTPS means that the site is secure because it encrypts data transferred between a user's browser and the server. **Encryption** is the process of coding data so that only the sender and/or receiver can read it, preventing others from being able to understand it. This is important when a user submits confidential or credit card information over the Web.

The protocol is immediately followed by "://" which originated from UNIX (a server operating system) and essentially says, "what follows should be interpreted according to the indicated protocol." When typing a URL into a browser, if you omit the protocol, the browser assumes you mean *http://*.

The next part of the URL is the **machine name**, which is a series of characters that the server administrator assigns to the Web server. Often, the machine name is *www*, but it can be any word, phrase, or acronym. It can even be omitted entirely. For example, the URL *shop.macromedia.com* for the Macromedia Worldwide Store uses *shop* as the machine name, and the URL *CNN.com* for CNN omits the machine name entirely. Many servers are configured to route the URL both with and without a *www* to the same location. For example, *www.course.com* and *course.com* both go to the same place. Because so many sites use *www* as the machine name, it is better to include it if you are not sure of the exact URL for a site.

The machine name is followed by the domain name. The **domain name** is a name that identifies a Web site and is chosen by the site owner. Domain names are often a word or phrase related to an organization or individual. For example, *course* is the domain name for Course Technology, the publisher of this book. What is commonly referred to as the domain name of a Web site is actually the domain name combined with a top-level domain. A **top-level domain** is the highest category in the Internet naming system. The top-level domain may indicate the Web site's type of entity or country of origin. Common top-level domains are commercial (.com), organization (.org), network (.net), U.S. educational (.edu), and U.S. government (.gov). Although .com and .org are generally available to anyone, .edu must be some type of educational entity in the United States and .gov is reserved for the United States government. Some top-level domains for countries are United States (.us), Canada (.ca), United Kingdom (.uk), and Japan (.jp). The domain name and top-level domain are combined to create a name that is unique to a Web site. No two Web sites can have the same domain name and top-level domain. For example, *course.com* is the domain name/top-level domain for Course Technology, the publisher of this book. No other Web site can use this exact combination of names. However, another site might use *course.org*, or *course.uk*. This is why many companies will purchase all possible domain name/top-level domain combinations and point them all to the same site. What makes this confusing is that people commonly refer to the domain name/top-level domain combination as the domain name. To ensure that each domain/top-level domain combination is only used once, domain names must be registered for a fee with a domain registrar and are regulated by ICANN (Internet Corporation for Assigned Names and Numbers). Domain names can be purchased for a period of 1 to 5 years, and the owner has the opportunity to renew before anyone else can buy the name. Once you own a domain name, no one else can use it. As of February 2004, there were more than 46 million domain names.

The top-level domain might be followed by nested directories (or folders), which indicate the location of the file on the Web server. The last name in the series is usually the filename, as indicated by the .html or .htm extension. The folders and filenames are separated by slashes (/).

By knowing the parts of a URL and what they indicate, you can gather some information about the site you are visiting. You can also make an educated guess when trying to determine the correct URL for a site you want to visit.

Opening a Remote Web Page in a Browser

Reference Window

- Double-click the Internet Explorer icon or your Web browser icon on the desktop (*or* click the Start button, and then click Microsoft Internet Explorer or your Web browser).
- Type the URL of the Web page you want to open in the Address text box at the top of the browser window, and then press the Enter key.

You'll use a URL to open the main page of the Course Technology Web site. You enter a URL because you are accessing the site over the Internet from a remote server.

To open a remote Web page in a browser:

1. Verify that your computer is on and that the Windows desktop is running. See Figure 1-4.

Figure 1-4   **Windows desktop**

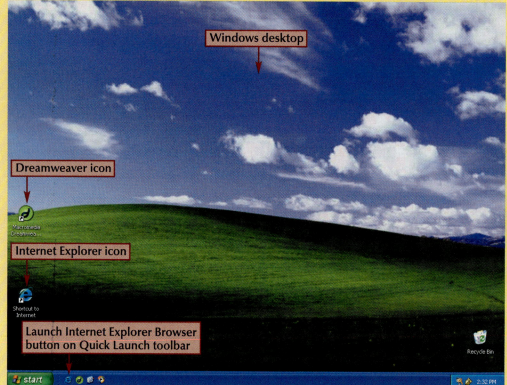

Trouble? If the icons or the background on your desktop differ from those in Figure 1-4, your computer is configured differently. However, you should be able to perform the steps accurately. Continue with Step 2.

2. Click the **Start** button, point to **All Programs**, and then click **Internet Explorer**. The Web browser opens and displays the default page. You'll open the Course Technology Web site by entering its URL.

Trouble? If you don't see the Internet Explorer on the All Programs menu, then click the Launch Internet Explorer Browser button on the Quick Launch toolbar or the Internet Explorer icon on the desktop. If you are using Netscape Navigator or a different Web browser, use the desktop icon or Start menu to open that browser.

3. Click in the **Address** text box at the top of the window to select its contents.

4. Type **www.course.com** in the Address text box, and then press the **Enter** key. The main page for the Course Technology Web site opens.

Trouble? If you do not have Internet access, you will not be able to view the Course Technology Web site. Continue with Step 5.

Trouble? If you are using Netscape Navigator, type the URL into the Location text box, and then press the Enter key.

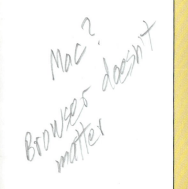

5. If necessary, click the **Maximize** button on the Internet Explorer title bar to maximize the window. See Figure 1-5.

Figure 1-5

Course Technology home page

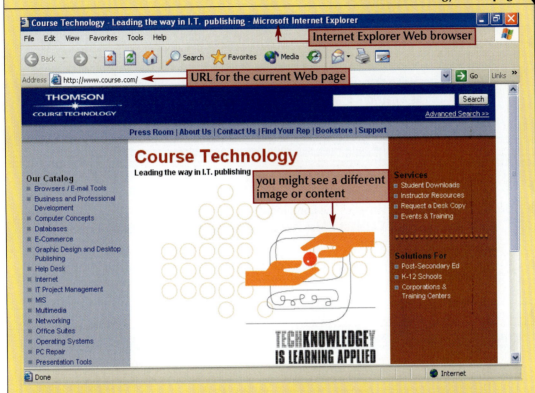

Trouble? If the Web page you see looks different from the one shown in Figure 1-5, the content or layout of the page has changed since this book was printed. Web pages are constantly being changed and updated.

Sometimes you'll need to view a Web page that is not posted to the Web. For example, a client may hand you files on a disk or a coworker may ask you to view a Web page from a local source such as a removable storage disk (for example, a floppy disk, a Zip disk, or a CD-ROM), a computer hard drive, or a local network server before the Web page is posted to the Web. You can view a local copy of a Web page in your browser by typing the file path instead of the URL.

Reference Window

Opening a Local Web Page in a Browser

- Type the file path in the Address text box, and then press the Enter key.

or

- Click File on the menu bar, and then click Open.
- Click the Browse button, click the Look in list arrow, and then navigate to the location where the Web page is stored.
- Click the Web page filename to select it, and then click the Open button.
- Click the OK button in the Open dialog box.

Brian asks you to view a copy of the existing Catalyst Web site. You'll start by opening the site's **home page**, which is the main page of a Web site. You can type the file path in the Address text box or browse to locate the file.

To open a local Web page in a browser:

1. Make sure your computer can access your Data Files for this tutorial.

   Trouble? If you don't have the Data Files, you need to get them before you can proceed. Your instructor will either give you the Data Files or ask you to obtain them from a specified location (such as a network drive). In either case, be sure that you make a backup copy of your Data Files before you start using them, so that the original files will be available on your copied disk in case you need to start over because of an error or problem. If you have any questions about the Data Files, see your instructor or technical support person for assistance.

2. Click **File** on the menu bar of the browser, and then click **Open**. The Open dialog box opens.

3. Click the **Browse** button, click the **Look in** list arrow, navigate to the **Tutorial.01\Tutorial\Catalyst** folder included with your Data Files, click **index.htm**, and then click the **Open** button.

4. Click the **OK** button in the Open dialog box. The home page for the Catalyst Web site opens. See Figure 1-6.

Figure 1-6   Catalyst home page

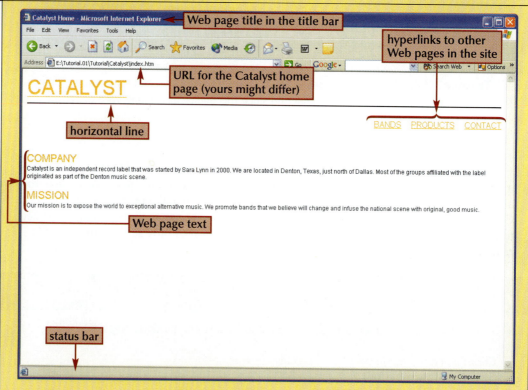

Trouble? If a Dial-up Connection dialog box opens, the browser is trying to connect to the Internet. Click the Work Offline or Cancel button to close the dialog box. It is not necessary to connect to the Internet to complete these steps.

Web sites are **nonlinear**, which means that information branches out from the home page in many directions much like railroad tracks branch out from a train station. You can think of the home page as the hub or "train station" of a Web site. Just as people go to a train station to begin a train trip, the home page is where most people start when they want to explore a Web site. The major categories of information contained in the Web site branch out from the home page. Just as different sets of train tracks overlap, the branches of a Web site interconnect (through links), and just as one train station is connected to other train stations, your Web site can be linked to other Web sites.

Hyperlinks

Hyperlinks can be graphics, text, or buttons with hotspots (active areas) that, when clicked with a mouse, take you to another related section. The related section can be on the same Web page, another Web page on the same site, or on another Web site altogether. This interlinking of information from various places gives the Web its nonlinear nature and even its name. There are several ways that links are indicated on a Web page. When positioned over a link, the mouse pointer will change from an arrow to a hand with a pointing finger.

Text links are often underlined and appear in a different color to distinguish them from other text. A **graphic** is a visual representation, such as a drawing, painting, or photograph. Images, such as the CD covers on the Products page, are a type of graphic. Graphic links are not usually visually distinguishable from graphics that are not links, although the mouse pointer changes to the pointing finger when it is positioned over a graphic link.

The Catalyst company logo, located at the upper-left corner of the Web page, is also a link. A **logo** is usually a graphic used by a company for the purposes of brand identification. In this case, the company logo is actually formatted text. A company logo is often used as a link to the Web site home page.

You need to become familiar with the artists that Catalyst represents and the CDs that they sell, so Brian asks you to review the Bands and Products pages of the Web site. You'll use links to move between the pages.

To use a link:

1. Point to the **BANDS** hyperlink, but do not click it. The pointer changes to to indicate that you are pointing to a hyperlink. The URL for the new page appears on the left side of the status bar, a banner of details about the window's contents that appears at the bottom of the browser window.

2. Click the **BANDS** hyperlink. The Bands page replaces the home page in the browser window. See Figure 1-7.

Figure 1-7   **Bands page**

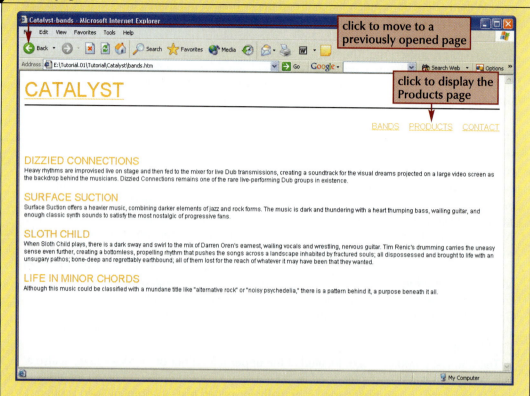

3. Click the **PRODUCTS** hyperlink. The Products page replaces the Bands page in the browser window. See Figure 1-8.

Figure 1-8   **Products page**

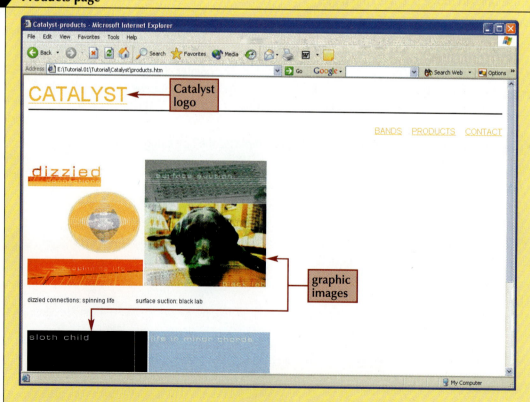

4. Point to the **Catalyst logo** on the Products page, but do not click it. The pointer changes to 👆 and the home page URL appears in the status bar.

5. Click the **Catalyst logo**. The home page reappears in your browser.

After you view two or more Web pages, you can quickly move between the pages you have opened by using buttons on the browser toolbar. Rather than reloading the home page, you can use the Back button to return to the previous page. Once you return to a previously opened page, the Forward button becomes active so you can redisplay a later page.

To go back and forward between previously viewed pages:

1. Click the **Back** button ⬅ on the browser toolbar. The Products page reappears in the browser window.

2. Click the **Forward** button ➡ on the browser toolbar. The Catalyst home page reappears in the browser window.

You have used links to move through the Catalyst Web site and see the content.

Content

The main purpose of most Web sites is to provide information, which is conveyed through the content. **Content** is the information presented in a Web page. A Web page usually contains a combination of text, graphics, and possibly multimedia elements such as video, animation, or interactive content. The blend of these elements is determined by deciding what will most effectively convey the intended message or information. Ignoring the content of a Web site is a common mistake made by inexperienced designers.

Brian asks you to review the content of the Catalyst Web site, looking for content and design elements that should be added or changed when you redesign the site.

To review site content:

1. Read the content on the home page of the Catalyst Web site, considering what information might be appropriate to add and what design changes you would like to see.

2. Click the **BANDS** hyperlink.

3. Review the content of the Bands page, considering what information might be appropriate to add and what design changes you would like to see.

4. Click the **PRODUCTS** hyperlink, and then review the content of the Products page, considering what information might be appropriate to add and what design changes you would like to see.

5. Click the **CONTACT** hyperlink, review the content on the Contact page, considering what information might be appropriate to add and what design changes you would like to see.

From your review of the site content, you might have a list of changes you would suggest to Brian. For example, you might want to add more information to the descriptions in the Bands page. The Products page might also include song titles for each CD. You're done looking at the Catalyst site from the browser, so you'll close the site and the browser for now.

> **Reference Window**
>
> ### Closing the Browser Window
>
> - Click File on the menu bar.
> - Click Close.
>
> or
>
> - Click the Close button in the browser program window title bar.

To close the browser window:

1. Click the **Close** button ☒ in the browser window title bar to exit your browser. The browser window closes.

In this session, you learned about the Internet, the Web, Web servers, and clients. You explored different components of a Web page. Also, you opened the existing Catalyst Web site in a browser, navigated between the Web pages, and reviewed the site's content. In the next session, you will view the existing Catalyst Web site from within Dreamweaver.

Review

Session 1.1 Quick Check

1. What is the Internet?
2. What is the World Wide Web?
3. Explain the difference between a Web server and a Web client.
4. What is a Web browser?
5. What is a URL?
6. In the following URL, what is the domain name: *http://www.course.com/index.html*
7. Define hyperlinks.
8. Explain the purpose of content on a Web site.

Session 1.2

Evolving Web Design Tools

In the early days of Web design, most Web pages contained only text and were created by typing HTML into documents using a simple text editor (such as Notepad or Simple Text). To create a Web page, you had to know how to write HTML from scratch. As the Web evolved, Web authors began to create more complex graphical interfaces. This made creating Web pages from scratch cumbersome. HTML was designed by scientists as a means of sharing information. Using HTML for graphically complex interfaces involves complex HTML structures that are not practical (for most people) to type. Furthermore, artists, graphic designers, business people, and nonprogrammers who wanted to create Web pages did not necessarily want to learn all the intricacies of HTML. This led to the development of software packages that allowed people to design Web pages by typing, placing, and manipulating content in an environment that more closely approximated the look of the Web page they wanted to create. The software actually wrote the HTML for them. These software packages were originally referred to as **WYSIWYG** (What You See Is What You Get) programs, because the Web page is displayed in the program window as it will appear to the end user and the code is hidden from sight. Today, the acronym WYSIWYG is not often used because almost all software is designed to show you what you will get as you work. Also, this has been critiqued as a bit of a misnomer with Web software because what you get really depends on the specific browser and version used to view the page.

With these Web software packages, people who were not programmers were able to design Web pages, and designers gained even more control over the look of their sites across the various browsers. Dreamweaver grew out of this need for easy-to-use, visual tools that allow Web authors to rapidly develop reliable and well-coded Web pages. Dreamweaver has become one of the most widely used site development and management tools because of its ease of use, accurate HTML output, and powerful tool set. With Dreamweaver, you can create a successful Web site without knowing any HTML. However, some familiarity with HTML enables you to make the site work better, fix problems that arise, and create elements that are complex or impossible to create in Dreamweaver.

Comparing Page-Centric and Site-Centric Design Tools

There are two popular ways that Web development programs approach Web site design: page-centric design and site-centric design. Many software packages use a **page-centric design** approach, which concentrates on designing and creating individual Web pages and then linking them together, rather than concentrating on the Web site as a whole. Designers create one page, then they create a second page and attach it to the first page, then they create a third page to attach to the first two, and the site grows from there.

Dreamweaver takes the opposite approach: site-centric design. A **site-centric design** approach focuses on planning the Web site structure and design before creating any pages. Designers associate the parameters with the site, and the parameters are then used by all the pages of the site. One benefit of site-centric design is that if the designer wants to change some aspect of the site, such as a heading color or page background color, the change is made once and all the pages associated with the site reflect the change.

Professional Web designers tend to prefer site-centric design tools, like Dreamweaver, which are more comprehensive than page-centric design tools.

Starting Dreamweaver and Selecting a Workspace Layout Configuration

To get started you will need to open Dreamweaver, set the workspace environment, and make sure that it is in the default layout configuration. The Dreamweaver program window consists of several smaller windows, toolbars, and panels. There are two preset workspace environments from which to choose:

- **Designer.** The Designer workspace environment, recommended for most users, is an integrated workspace that uses multiple document interface. **Multiple document interface (MDI)** enables all the document windows and panels to be integrated in one large application window. In this environment, the Document window shows Design view by default, and the panels are docked to the right and below the Document window. You will use Designer workspace environment in these tutorials.
- **Coder (HomeSite).** The Coder workspace environment uses the same integrated workspace as the Designer workspace layout, but the panels are arranged similarly to two other Macromedia software products, HomeSite™ and ColdFusion® Studio. Also, the Document window shows the Code view by default. The Coder workspace environment is used primarily by people who are familiar with HomeSite and ColdFusion.

Once you select a work environment, you can move windows and adjust the workspace to suit your work style. Dreamweaver opens in the same state it was in when it was last closed, so—depending on the working method of the person who last used the computer that you are working on—Dreamweaver could open in either environment and in any number of configurations.

You will use the Designer workspace environment in the default layout configuration for these tutorials. If someone else has used your computer and rearranged the position of panels, you can reset Dreamweaver to the default Designer workspace environment by selecting the Coder environment, and then reselecting the Designer environment. You must close Dreamweaver and restart in order for the new preferences to take effect.

Reference Window

Selecting a Workspace Environment

- Click Edit on the menu bar, and then click Preferences.
- Make sure General is selected in the Category list, and then click the Change Workspace button.
- Click the Coder option button or click the Designer option button, and then click OK.
- Click the OK button in the Preferences dialog box.
- Click File on the menu bar, and then click Exit to exit Dreamweaver.
- Start Dreamweaver.

The figures in this book show Dreamweaver in the default layout of the Designer workspace environment. As you become more proficient with Dreamweaver, you may find that you prefer a different setup, but for now you should use the default layout.

To start Dreamweaver and select the Designer workspace environment:

1. Click the **Start** button on the taskbar, point to **All Programs**, point to **Macromedia**, and then click **Macromedia Dreamweaver MX 2004**. Dreamweaver starts with various windows and toolbars displayed.

    Trouble? If you do not see the Macromedia folder, click Macromedia Dreamweaver MX 2004 on the All Programs menu. If you can't find Macromedia Dreamweaver MX 2004 on the All Programs menu, press the Esc key to close the Start menu, and then double-click the Macromedia Dreamweaver MX 2004 program icon on your desktop.

    Trouble? If this is the first time Dreamweaver has been started on this computer, the Workspace Setup dialog box opens. Make sure the Designer Workspace option button is selected, click the OK button, and then continue with Step 2.

2. Click **Edit** on the menu bar, and then click **Preferences**. The Preferences dialog box opens.

3. Click **General** in the Category list, if necessary, and then click the **Change Workspace** button. The Workspace Setup dialog box opens. See Figure 1-9.

Figure 1-9

Workspace Setup dialog box

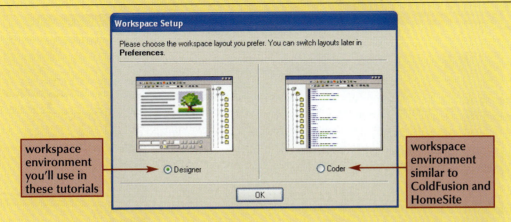

workspace environment you'll use in these tutorials → Designer

workspace environment similar to ColdFusion and HomeSite ← Coder

▶ 4. Click the **Coder** option button, and then click the **OK** button. A dialog box opens, warning that the change in the workspace environment will take effect the next time you start Dreamweaver.

▶ 5. Click the **OK** button in the warning dialog box.

Before you restart Dreamweaver, you'll select the Designer workspace environment. This clears any configuration changes that might have been made by another user, and returns the workspace layout to its default position.

▶ 6. Click the **Change Workspace** button, click the **Designer** option button, click the **OK** button in the Workspace Setup dialog box, and then click the **OK** button in the warning dialog box.

▶ 7. Click the **OK** button to close the Preferences dialog box. The Dreamweaver workspace will not change configurations until the program has been closed and reopened.

▶ 8. Click **File** on the menu bar, and then click **Exit** to exit Dreamweaver.

▶ 9. Start Dreamweaver again.

▶ 10. Click the **Maximize** button □ in the program window title bar, if necessary. See Figure 1-10.

Figure 1-10 Dreamweaver in Designer workspace environment

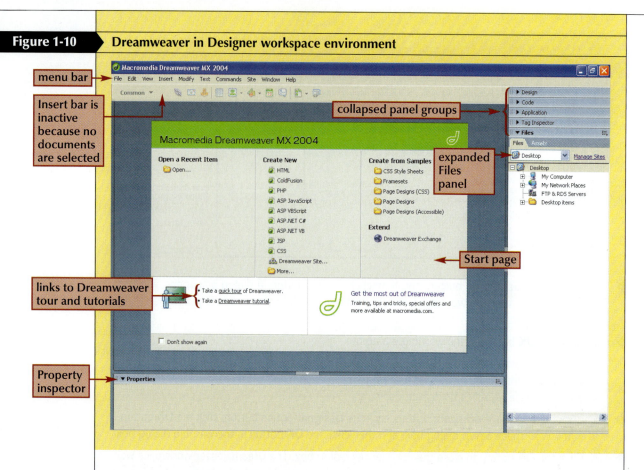

The basic elements of the Designer environment in the default view of the workspace layout are labeled in Figure 1-10. The **menu bar**, located at the top of the work area, is a categorized series of menus that provide access to all the tools and features available in Dreamweaver. The Text menu, for example, has commands for creating and formatting text.

Each **panel group** on the right side of the screen contains related panels. A **panel** contains related commands, controls, and information about different aspects of working with Dreamweaver. The Start page, which appears when you initially open Dreamweaver, enables you to create a new document, open an existing document on which you have recently worked, take a Dreamweaver product tour, or complete a Dreamweaver tutorial. You will learn about the other Dreamweaver elements as you use them.

Before you can open the Catalyst Web site in Dreamweaver, you must create a local site definition for the Catalyst Web site.

Creating a Site Definition

Working on a Web site is a lot like working on a report. Usually you keep the original report locally on your computer and distribute a copy of the report to others to review. In the case of a Web site, you work on the original site on your computer and then have Dreamweaver post a copy to a publicly viewable space, such as a Web server. The original site stored on your computer is the local version, and the copy Dreamweaver posts is the remote version. You make all changes and revisions to the local site and then have Dreamweaver update the remote site. A **site definition** is the information that tells Dreamweaver where to find the local and remote files for the Web site, along with other parameters that affect how the site is set up within Dreamweaver. Dreamweaver stores a local Web site in the same format as it will be posted on the Web.

The site definition is *not* kept as part of the site. Instead the site definition is stored in the Windows registry. If you move to another computer to work, you must re-create the site definition on that computer.

There are two main categories in a site definition—local information and remote information. You should create the local information for the site definition (referred to as the local site definition) before you begin working on a Web site. It is acceptable to wait to create the remote information for the site definition (referred to as the remote site definition) until you are ready to post a copy of the site to a Web server.

Configuring a Local Site Definition

A **local site definition** is the information stored on the computer that you are using that tells Dreamweaver where the local root folder is located. A **local root folder** is the location where you store all the files used by the local version of the Web site. You can use files stored anywhere on your hard drive or network to create your site; Dreamweaver prompts you to copy these files into the local root folder so that everything you need will be located in one convenient location. If you use a different computer for a later work session, you'll need to re-create the local site definition on that computer.

You can place the local root folder on a hard drive or on a removable disk. Be aware, however, that working on a site stored on a removable disk can be slower than working on a site stored on a hard drive. Also, when you create the local site definition, you need to be sure to use the most recent version of the site.

There are two ways to create a local site definition. You can click the Basic tab in the Site Definition dialog box and use the Site Definition Wizard to walk you through the process of setting up a site. However, using the Site Definition Wizard prompts you to set the remote site definition as well. The second method is to click the Advanced tab in the Site Definition dialog box and input the information manually. For these tutorials, you will input the information manually so that you can better understand the process of creating a local site definition.

Creating a Local Site Definition

Reference Window

- Click Site on the menu bar, and then click Manage Sites (*or* click the Site list arrow in the Files panel, and then click Manage Sites).
- Click New in the Manage Sites dialog box, and then click site.
- Click the Advanced tab in the Site Definition dialog box.
- Click Local Info in the Category list.
- Type a name in the Site Name text box.
- Type a path in the Local Root Folder text box (*or* click the Browse button, navigate to the Web site's folder, and then click the Select button).
- Click the Refresh Local File List Automatically check box to check it.
- Click the Enable Cache check box to check it.
- Click the OK button.

You'll need to enter several pieces of information and select a few options to set up a local site definition. The following list explains the parts of a local site definition:

- **Site Name.** An internal name you give the Web site for your reference. This name appears on the Site menu in the Document window and in the Files panel, but is not used outside the Dreamweaver environment. You'll use "Catalyst" as the site name for the existing Catalyst site.
- **Local Root Folder.** The location where you want to store all the files used by the local version of the Web site. You choose where to place the local root folder on your computer, network, or removable disk.

When creating the local root folder, use a logical folder structure and a descriptive naming system. A logical folder structure helps keep the Web site files organized. For example, it is a good idea to store each project in its own folder and to create a Dreamweaver subfolder within each project folder so that the Dreamweaver files remain separate from any original, uncompressed artwork and working files that you have not yet added to the Web site. You might, for instance, create a Catalyst project folder that contains a Dreamweaver subfolder. Any text files or graphics that you have not yet added to the Web site would be stored in the Catalyst folder. The Dreamweaver subfolder would be the local root folder for the new Catalyst Web site project. Remember that folder names can include any series of letters, numbers, hyphens, and underscores. They should not include spaces, symbols, or special characters, which can cause problems on some servers. Symbols and special characters can also have different meanings on different platforms.

- **Refresh Local File List Automatically.** An option that enables Dreamweaver to update the list of local files any time you add, delete, move, or rename a file used in the Web site. You'll usually leave this option checked.
- **HTTP Address.** The URL of your Web site, which Dreamweaver uses to verify links. You will enter this URL in a later tutorial when you publish the Catalyst Web site.
- **Cache: Enable Cache.** An option that enables Dreamweaver to use a **cache**, a temporary local storage space, to speed up the processing time needed to update links when you move, rename, or delete a file. You'll usually leave this option checked.

You must create a local site definition before you can view the Catalyst Web site from within Dreamweaver on your computer.

To create the local site definition:

1. Click **Site** on the menu bar, and then click **Manage Sites**. The Manage Sites dialog box opens. See Figure 1-11.

Figure 1-11 Manage Sites dialog box

2. Click the **New** button, and then click **Site**. The Site Definition for Unnamed Site 1 dialog box opens.
3. Click the **Advanced** tab, and then click **Local Info** in the Category list, if necessary. See Figure 1-12.

Site Definition for Unnamed Site 1 dialog box   Figure 1-12

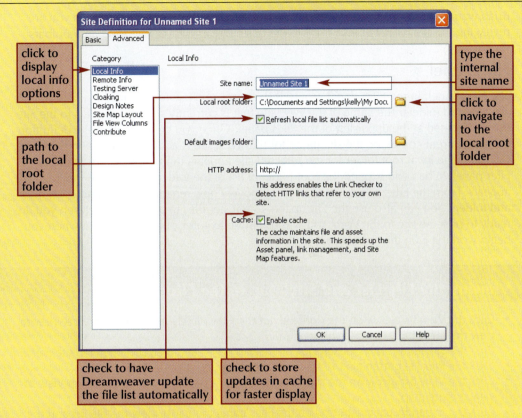

4. Select the text in the Site Name text box, if necessary, and then type **Catalyst**. Catalyst is the name you will use to reference the site; this name will not be used outside the Dreamweaver environment.

5. Click the **Local Root Folder Browse** button to open the Choose Local Root Folder for Site Catalyst dialog box, navigate to the **Tutorial.01\Tutorial\Catalyst** folder included with your Data Files (the location where the Catalyst Web site is stored), and then click the **Select** button to open the folder.

6. Click the **Refresh Local File List Automatically** check box to check it, if necessary. Dreamweaver will update your file list whenever you add, move, delete, or rename a file in this Web site.

7. In the Cache section, click the **Enable Cache** check box to check it, if necessary. Dreamweaver will quickly update links whenever you move, rename, or delete a file.

8. Click the **OK** button to close the Site Definition dialog box. The site name "Catalyst" appears in the Manage Sites dialog box.

9. Click the **Done** button to close the Manage Sites dialog box. Dreamweaver scans the existing files and creates the file list for the site, which is visible in the Files panel.

   Trouble? If a dialog box opens with the message that the initial site cache will now be created, click the OK button.

Next, you will explore the Catalyst Web site from within Dreamweaver.

Exploring the Dreamweaver Environment

Brian wants you to explore the Catalyst Web site from within Dreamweaver. As you are reviewing the site, you will also explore the basic Dreamweaver windows and toolbars.

Files Panel

The Files panel, in the Files panel group, is the panel you use to manage local and remote site files and folders. The name of the Web site that is currently selected appears in the Site list box located at the upper-left of the Files panel. Once you create a local site definition on your current computer, the site name for that Web site is added to the list (in this case, Catalyst). The local root folder for the selected site appears in the lower portion of the Files panel. When you expand the root folder, a list of the folders and files in the local site appears. From the Files panel, you can view, move, copy, rename, delete, and open files and folders. You can also use the Files panel to transfer files to a remote site when you are ready to post the site to the Web. You will use these features of the Files panel when you begin working with the remote site.

Reference Window | **Viewing the File List and Site Map in the Files Panel**

- Click the View list arrow on the right side of the Files panel, and then click Local View to view the file list.
- Click the Site list arrow on the left side of the Files panel, and then click the Web site name.
- Click the Plus (+) button next to the Web site folder in the list.
- Click the View list arrow on the right side of the Files panel, and then click Map View to view the site map.
- Click the Expand/Collapse button on the Files panel toolbar to view the file list and the site map simultaneously.
- Click the Expand/Collapse button on the Files panel toolbar again to collapse the view.

The Files panel also includes an **integrated file browser** that enables you to browse files that are located outside of your site. Once you set up a remote site, you can select Remote View from the View list, and a list of the files and folders in the remote site will appear in the lower portion of the Files panel. You can expand the Files panel to fill the work area. When the Files panel is expanded, the lower portion of the panel is divided vertically into two panes so you can display both the local and remote views of your site simultaneously.

To view the file list of a local Web site in the Files panel:

1. Click the **View** list arrow on the right side of the Files panel, and then click **Local View**, if necessary.

2. Click the **Site** list arrow on the left side of the Files panel, and then click **Catalyst**, if necessary. The Catalyst Web site appears in the list below the toolbar.

3. Click the **Plus (+)** button 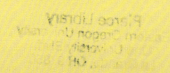 next to the Site - Catalyst folder, if necessary. The graphics folder, the Library folder, and the Catalyst Web page files appear in the list. See Figure 1-13.

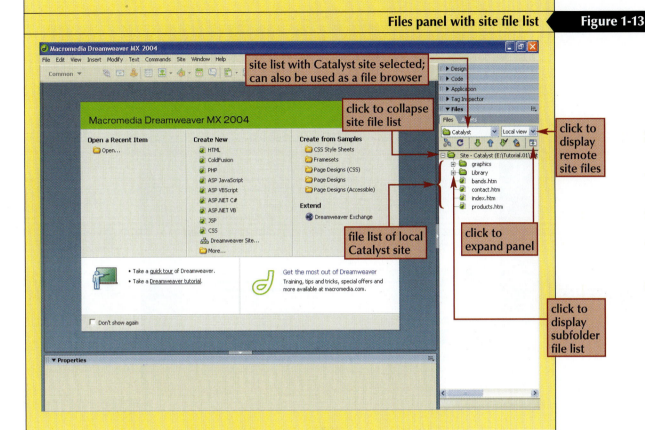

Figure 1-13 Files panel with site file list

When a Web site is selected, the folders and pages in the local root folder of that site are displayed. Currently, the folders and pages in the local root folder of the Catalyst Web site are visible. A folder icon precedes the folder name, whereas a Dreamweaver Web page icon precedes the Web page filenames. Each filename is followed by a **file extension**, which is used by Windows to determine the file type. The file extension for Web pages can be either .htm or .html. Depending on how your Web server is set up, you might be required to use one or the other for the entire site or for only the default page.

Another way to view the files and folders in a Web site is with the site map. A **site map** is a visual representation of how the pages in a Web site are interrelated. You can display the site map in the Files panel by selecting Map View from the View list. You might need to resize the Files panel to view the entire site map. The Expand/Collapse button on the Files panel toolbar toggles the Files panel between a one-pane view and a two-pane view.

You'll view the site map for the Catalyst Web site.

To view the site map alone and with the local file list simultaneously:

1. Click the **View** list arrow on the right side of the Files panel, and then click **Map View**. The site map appears in the Files panel. See Figure 1-14.

Figure 1-14   **Files panel with site map**

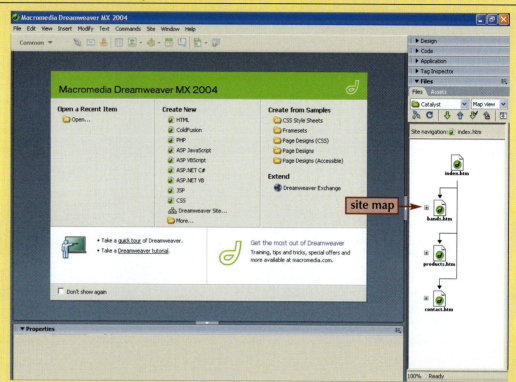

2. Click the **Expand/Collapse** button on the Files panel toolbar. The Files panel expands to fill the program window and displays both the site map (Map view) and the site list (Local view) simultaneously. See Figure 1-15.

Figure 1-15   **Files panel with file list and site map**

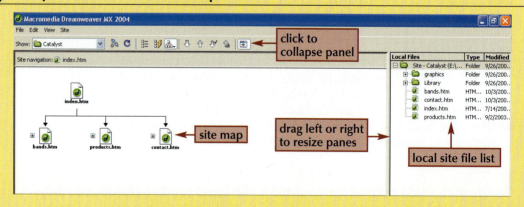

3. Click the **Expand/Collapse** button on the Files panel toolbar. The Files panel collapses to its original size.

4. Click the **View** list arrow, and then click **Local View** to return to Local view.

You can open any page in the Web site by double-clicking its filename in the file list or the site map. Each page opens in the Document window. You can open multiple pages at one time. Although there are other methods for opening Web pages in Dreamweaver, this method ensures that you always open the file from the root folder (rather than from a backup copy or another location). You can move between the open pages by clicking the page name for the page you want to make active. The page names of all of the open pages are located at the top of the Document window above the Document toolbar. The active page is displayed in the Document window, the name of the active page is displayed on the active tab, and information for the active page appears in brackets beside the software information in the blue title bar at the top of the Dreamweaver window.

You'll use the Files panel to open the Bands and Products pages.

To open Web pages from the Files panel:

1. Double-click **bands.htm** in the Files panel. The Bands page opens in the Document window to the left of the Files panel.

2. Double-click **products.htm** in the Files panel. The Products page opens in the Document window, and now is the active page. See Figure 1-16.

Open Web pages — Figure 1-16

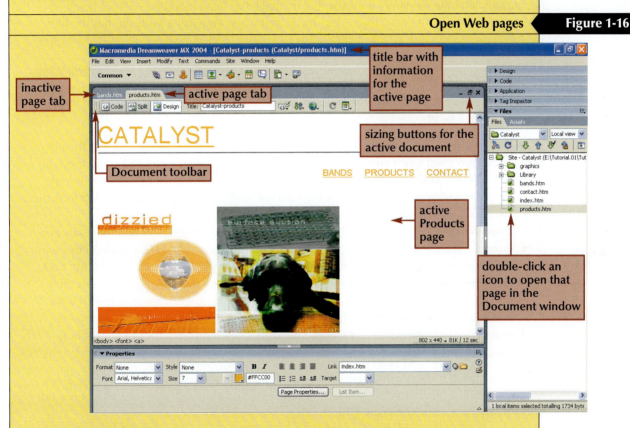

3. Click the **bands.htm** tab at the top of the Document window. The Bands page window becomes the active page and appears in the Document window. The Bands page information appears in the title bar at the top of the Dreamweaver window, and bands.htm is displayed in the active tab.

4. Click the **Close** button ✖ on the Document window title bar. The Bands page closes, and the Products page is the active page.

5. Click the **Close** button ✖ on the Document window title bar to close the Products page.

Next, you'll review the Document window.

Document Window

The **Document window** is the main workspace where you create and edit Web pages. You use tools from the various panels, toolbars, and inspectors to manipulate the page that is open in the Document window.

The Document toolbar, located below the active page tab, includes buttons for the most commonly used commands related to the Document window.

At the top of the Dreamweaver window, beside the Dreamweaver information is the title bar information for the active document. The **title bar** information includes the page title and the filename of the selected document or Web page. The **page title** is the name you give a Web page; when the Web page is displayed in a browser, the page name will appear in the browser's title bar. The **filename**, the name under which a Web page is saved, appears in parentheses to the right of the page title in the title bar. If an asterisk (*) appears after the filename, it means that the page has been modified without being resaved. Usually, the page that opens by default when you visit a Web site has the filename index.htm, index.html, default.htm, or default.html. A Web server will display this page if the viewer has not requested a specific file in the URL.

The middle of the Document window is the workspace where you create and edit Web pages. There are three ways to display the information in the Document window: Design view, Code view, and Split view. The buttons that control the views are located on the Document toolbar.

- **Design view.** Displays the page as it will appear in a browser. Design view is the primary view used when you are designing and creating a Web page. In Design view, all of the HTML code is hidden so you can focus on how the finished product will look. When you view the home page of the Catalyst Web site in Design view, it will look the same as it does in a browser.
- **Code view.** Displays the underlying HTML code that Dreamweaver automatically generates as you create and edit a page. You can also enter or edit HTML code in this window. This view is used primarily when you want to work directly with the HTML code.
- **Split view.** Splits the Document window into two panes: the upper pane shows the underlying code and the lower pane shows the page as it will appear in the browser. You can easily move between the panes to either edit the HTML code or change the design using the Dreamweaver tools. This view is used primarily when you want to debug or troubleshoot a page.

You'll look at the Catalyst home page in the different views. The filename of the home page is index.htm, because it is the page that displays by default when the viewer has not requested a specific file in the URL.

To display a Web page in different views:

1. Double-click **index.htm** in the Files panel. The Catalyst home page opens in the Document window workspace.
2. Click the **Show Design View** button on the Document toolbar, if necessary. The home page appears in Design view. See Figure 1-17.

Figure 1-17 Home page in Design view

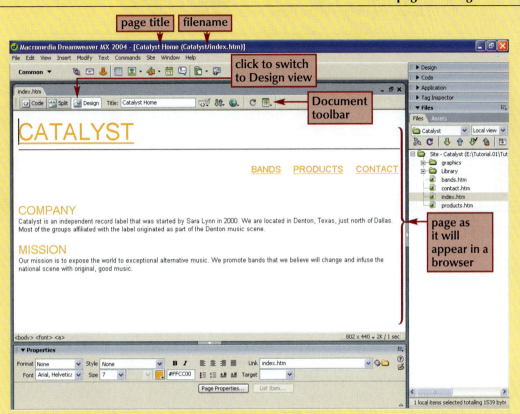

3. Click the **Show Code View** button on the Document toolbar to view the HTML code for the home page. See Figure 1-18.

Figure 1-18 Home page in Code view

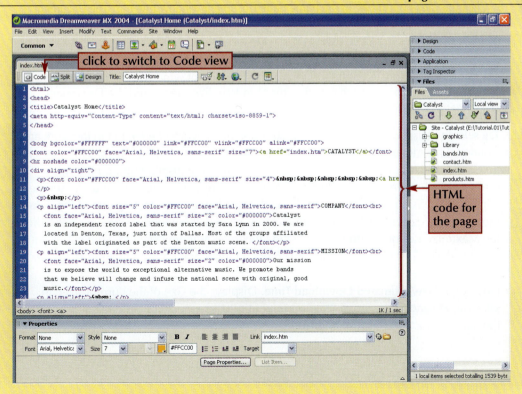

4. Click the **Show Code and Design Views** button on the Document toolbar to view both the code and the design of the home page. See Figure 1-19.

Figure 1-19   Home page in Split view

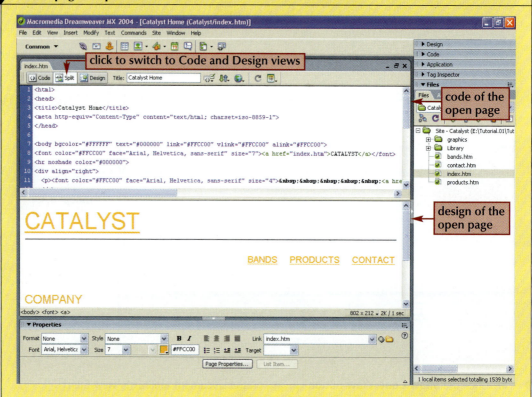

5. Click the **Show Design View** button on the Document toolbar. The home page returns to Design view.

6. Click the **Close** button in the home page Document window title bar. The Document window closes.

The **status bar** is located at the bottom of the Document window. Three things always appear in the status bar: the tag selector, the Window Size menu, and the Document Size/Estimated Download Time.

- **Tag selector.** Displays all the HTML tags surrounding the current selection in the work area.
- **Window Size menu.** Displays the Document window's current dimensions in pixels. A **pixel**, which stands for picture element, is the smallest adjustable unit on a display screen. The numbers change when you resize the Document window. You can set the window dimensions by manually resizing the window or by selecting one of the common monitor sizes from the menu. Before you change the window size, you must click the Maximize/Restore button to make the Document window sizable. Sometimes you may need to adjust the size of the Document window manually so that the status bar is displayed.
- **Document Size/Estimated Download Time.** Displays the size of the current page in kilobytes (K) and the approximate amount of time in seconds it would take to download the page over a 28-Kbps modem.

You'll review the status bar items as you explore and modify the Bands page.

To explore the status bar:

1. Open the **bands.htm** page in the Document window.
2. Drag to select the **Catalyst logo** at the top of the Bands page. The status bar tag selector shows the HTML tags associated with the selected text. See Figure 1-20.

Figure 1-20   Status bar items

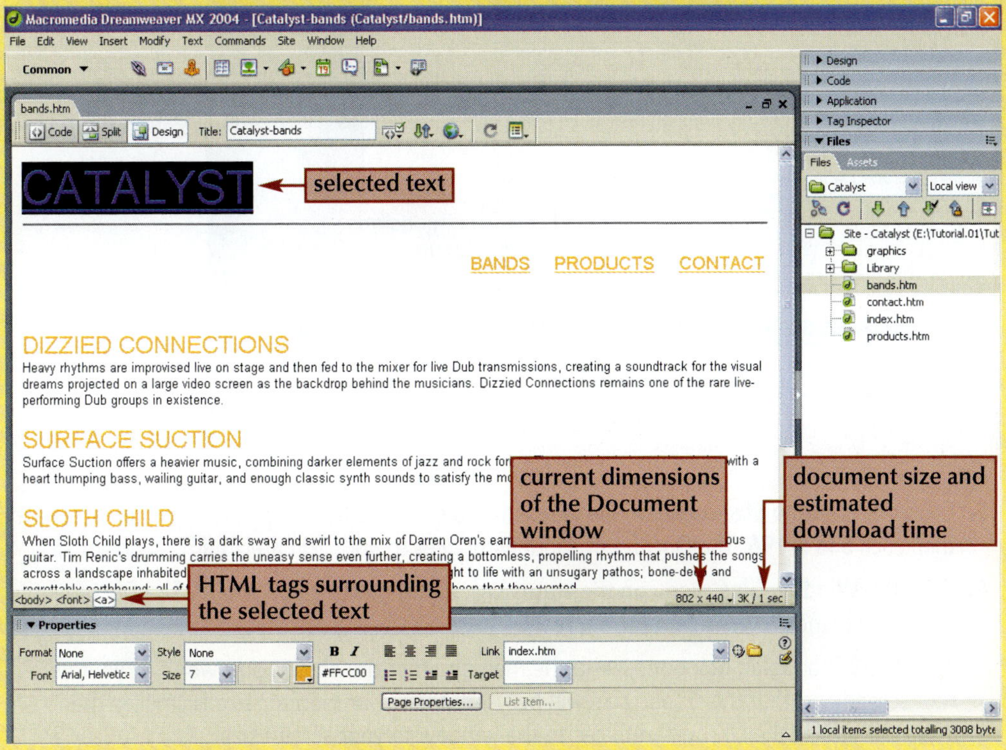

Trouble? If you don't see the <font> tag in the status bar, the tag isn't selected in the underlying code. Continue with Step 3.

3. Drag to select some of the text below the Dizzied Connections heading. The following HTML tags now appear in the tag selector: <body>, <div>, <p>, and <font>.
4. Click the **Restore** button on the Document window to make the Document window sizable. See Figure 1-21.

| Figure 1-21 | Resized Document window |

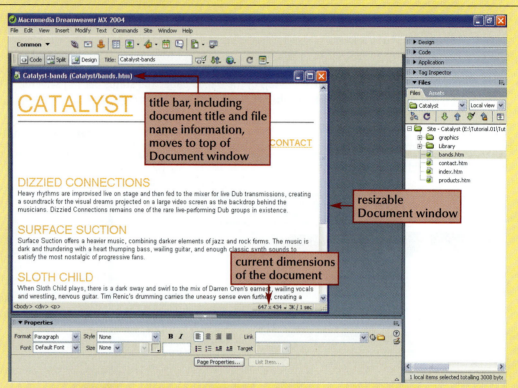

5. Click the **Window Size** menu on the status bar to display a list of common monitor sizes, and then click **536 x 196**. The Document window reduces to approximately half its current size.

6. Click the **Window Size** menu on the status bar, and then click **955 x 600**. The Document window expands to fill most of the screen.

    Trouble? If a dialog box opens with the message that the chosen size won't fit your current screen and that the screen size will be used, then your monitor size is smaller than 955 x 600. Click the OK button to resize the window to your screen size.

7. Click the **Maximize** button on the Document window to return the Document window to its maximized state.

    Trouble? If you can't see the Maximize/Restore button, click Window on the menu bar, click Tile Horizontally to have the Document window automatically fill the workspace, and then repeat Step 7.

8. Review the **Document Size/Estimated Download Time** for the Bands page.

9. Close the Bands page.

    Trouble? If a dialog box opens, asking you to save changes, click the No button.

Next, you'll explore the Property inspector.

Property Inspector

The most frequently used tool is the **Property inspector**, a toolbar with buttons for examining or editing the attributes of any element that is currently selected on the page displayed in the Document window. A **page element** is either an object or text. The Property inspector buttons and options change to reflect the attributes of the selected element.

You'll use the Property inspector to explore the attributes of different objects on the Catalyst site.

To explore object attributes using the Property inspector:

1. Open the **index.htm** page in the Document window. The home page opens.
2. Drag to select the text in the paragraph below the Company heading in the Document window. The Property inspector attributes reflect the selected text. The attributes associated with text are similar to those in a word processing program, such as text size, color, styles (bold and italics), alignment, and indent. See Figure 1-22.

Property inspector with text attributes **Figure 1-22**

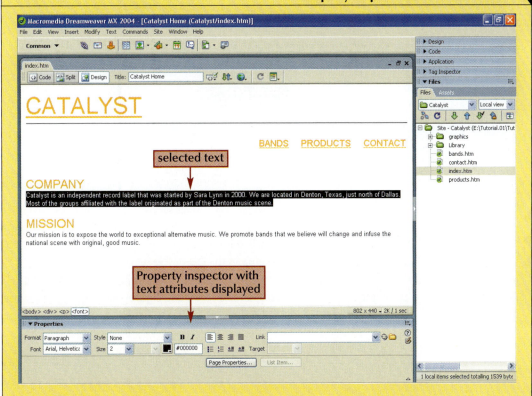

3. Drag to select the **BANDS** link at the top of the page in the Document window. The Property inspector attributes change to reflect the selected text and include the link information. See Figure 1-23.

Figure 1-23 Property inspector with text link attributes

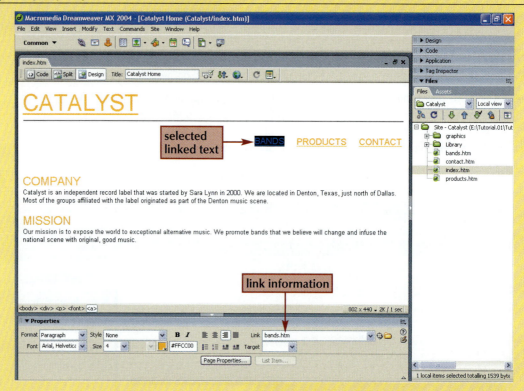

▶ 4. Close the home page.

▶ 5. Open the **products.htm** page in the Document window.

▶ 6. Click the **Dizzied Connections CD cover image** in the Document window to select it, and then observe the attribute changes in the Property inspector. Notice the attributes related to images, such as height and width, borders, and so forth. See Figure 1-24.

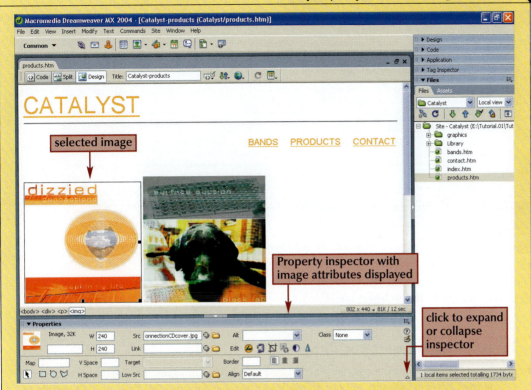

Figure 1-24 Property inspector with image attributes

Trouble? If the Property inspector is not expanded to show a second row of attributes, you need to expand the Property inspector. Click the expander arrow in the lower-right corner of the Property inspector.

Next you'll explore the Insert bar.

Insert Bar

In Dreamweaver, anything that you create or insert into a page is called an **object**. For example, tables, images, and links are objects. Whenever you want to create a new object, you use the Insert bar. The **Insert bar**, located directly below the menu bar, contains buttons that are used to create and insert objects. The buttons on the Insert bar are organized into categories. You use the Category list, located at the left of the Insert bar, to choose another category of buttons. When a category is selected, it appears at the top of the Category list and the buttons in that category are displayed on the Insert bar. When you place the pointer over a button, a tooltip with the button name is displayed. Some buttons contain menus of additional buttons with common commands. Clicking a button on the Insert bar either enables you to insert or create the associated object or opens a menu containing additional, related buttons. For example, when you click the Image button, a menu of image-related buttons is displayed. Buttons that have menus containing additional choices display an arrow at the right of the button. Figure 1-25 describes the Insert bar categories and the task associated with each category.

Figure 1-25   Insert bar categories

Category	Description of tasks
Common	Create and insert the most frequently used objects, such as images, templates, media elements, and tables.
Layout	Draw and insert tables, layers, div tags, and frames as well as switch between Standard view, Layout view, and Expanded Tables view.
Forms	Create and insert form elements in pages that include interactive forms.
Text	Insert text and list formatting tags such as bold (b), unorder list (ul), and paragraph (p) or open the Font Tag Editor.
HTML	Insert HTML tags, including tags for elements that are found in the head section of the page, tags for horizontal rules, tags for tables and tags for frames as well as scripts.
Application	Insert dynamic elements, such as recordsets and repeated regions.
Flash elements	Insert Flash elements.
Favorites	Organize the most commonly used Insert bar buttons in one convenient location.

The Insert bar displays the Common category of buttons by default. You'll explore some of the categories in the Insert bar.

To explore the Insert bar categories:

1. Click the Insert bar **Category** list arrow, and then click **Common**, if necessary. The buttons in the Common category appear on the Insert bar. See Figure 1-26. You can add objects to the Insert bar, so your Insert bar might include additional items.

Figure 1-26   Insert bar

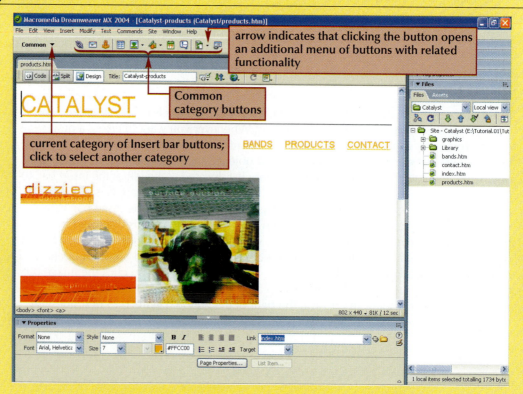

▶ 2. Point to each button to display a tooltip with its name, and then click the **Image** list arrow on the Insert bar. The Image menu opens.

▶ 3. Click the **Category** list arrow, and then click **Layout**. The buttons for creating commonly used layout elements appear on the Insert bar.

▶ 4. Click the **Category** list arrow, and then click **Forms**. The buttons for creating a form and inserting form elements such as buttons, menus, checkboxes, and images appear on the Insert bar.

▶ 5. Point to each button to display a tooltip with its name.

▶ 6. Click the **Category** list arrow, and then click **Common**.

▶ 7. Close the Products page.

As you are working in Dreamweaver, you may find that you need some help.

Getting Help in Dreamweaver

As you develop a Web site, you might run into a question about the purpose of a certain feature or want to review the steps for completing a specific task. Dreamweaver has a comprehensive Help system that provides a variety of ways to get the information you need.

Dreamweaver includes a Help command called Using Dreamweaver that provides information about all the Dreamweaver features. To open this Help window, you click Help on the menu bar, and then click Using Dreamweaver to open the Using Dreamweaver window. Once open, three tabs give you access to the Help topics: Contents, Index, and Search. The Contents tab arranges the information by subject categories, similar to the table of contents in a printed book. The Index tab arranges the information alphabetically by topic. The Search tab allows you to look up information by typing a keyword or phrase. The relevant Help topic appears in the right pane of the browser window and can include explanations, descriptions, figures, and links to related topics.

Getting Help in Dreamweaver

Reference Window

- Click Help on the menu bar, and then click Using Dreamweaver.
- Click the Contents tab, and then click a topic or subtopic in the Contents list to display that Help topic.
- Click the Index tab, type a letter or word into the text box, and then double-click a topic or subtopic in the Index list (*or* click a topic or subtopic, and then click the Display button).
- Click the Search tab, type keywords into the text box, click the List Topics button, click a topic in the Select topic to display list, and then double-click a topic and/or subtopic in the Topic list (*or* click a topic or subtopic, and then click the Display button).
- Click the Close button in the Help window title bar and, if necessary, click the Close button in the Search window.

or

- Click the Help button in any window *or* toolbar (*or* right-click any panel tab, and then click Help on the context menu to open the Using Dreamweaver window to a context-sensitive Help topic).
- Click the Close button in the Help window title bar.

You'll open the Using Dreamweaver window features to look up information about the Document window, the Insert bar, and the Property inspector.

To look up information in Using Dreamweaver:

1. Open the **index.htm** page in the Document window.

2. Click **Help** on the menu bar, and then click **Using Dreamweaver**. The Using Dreamweaver window opens.

3. Click the **Contents** tab, if necessary, click **Dreamweaver Basics** in the Contents list, click **Exploring the Workspace**, click **About the Dreamweaver Workspace**, and then click **The Document Window**. The Document Window Help topic appears in the right pane of the Using Dreamweaver window.

4. Click the **Maximize** button 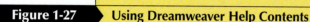 in the Using Dreamweaver window, if necessary. Notice the links to a related topic. See Figure 1-27.

Figure 1-27   **Using Dreamweaver Help Contents**

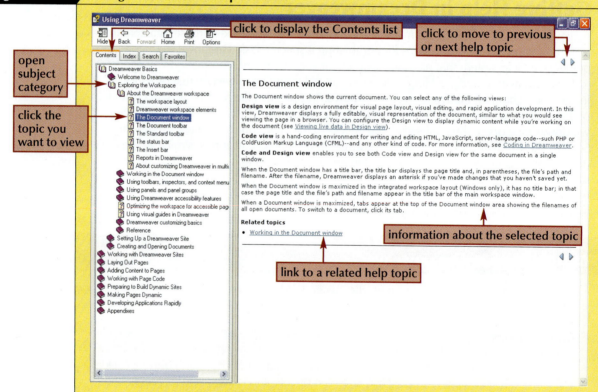

5. Read the information about the Document window.

6. Click the **Index** tab to display an alphabetical list of Help topics.

7. Type **insert** in the keyword text box to display a list of Help topics that begin with "insert," and then double-click **categories** under the Insert bar heading in the list. The Using the Insert Bar Help topic appears in the right pane. See Figure 1-28.

Using Dreamweaver Help Index | Figure 1-28

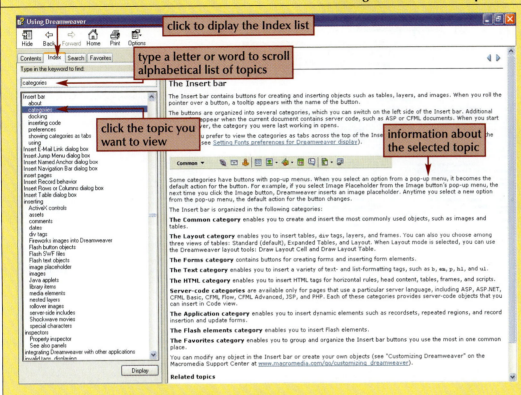

8. Read the information about using the Insert bar.

9. Click the **Search** tab, type **Property inspector** in the text box at the top of the Search pane, and then click the **List Topics** button. A list of Help topics that contain the keywords "Property inspector" appears in the list. See Figure 1-29. The list is sorted alphabetically.

Figure 1-29 Using Dreamweaver Help Search window

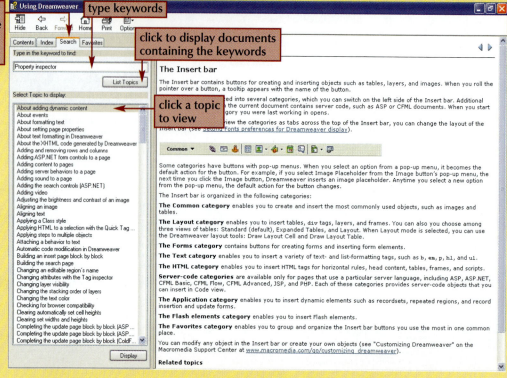

10. Scroll the Select Topic to Display list to **Using the Property Inspector**, then double-click that topic. The Using the Property Inspector Help topic appears in the right side of the window with the keywords highlighted everywhere they appear in the pane.

11. Read the information about using the Property inspector.

12. Click the **Close** button ⊠ in the Using Dreamweaver window title bar.

Another way to access Dreamweaver Help topics is by using context-sensitive help, which opens the Help topic related to the feature you are using. You access context-sensitive Help by clicking the Help button in any dialog box or toolbar about which you have a question, or by right-clicking any panel tab and then clicking Help.

You'll use context-sensitive Help to learn more about the text-formatting features of the Property inspector.

To use context-sensitive Help:

1. Select the block of body text below the Company heading on the home page.

2. Click the **Help** button ⓘ in the upper-right corner of the Property inspector. The Using Dreamweaver window opens.

3. Read the Help information about setting text property options.

4. Close the Help window.

Dreamweaver also provides you with additional information about the program with a quick tour and Tutorials. These features are accessed from the Help menu or the Start page. The quick tour contains animations that provide overviews of the Web development process and Dreamweaver features. The Getting Started and Tutorials provide hands-on experience in creating a sample Web site in Dreamweaver.

Finally, Macromedia provides additional Dreamweaver product support and Help features on its Web site (www.macromedia.com). You can also access the Dreamweaver help section of the Macromedia Web site by clicking **Dreamweaver Support Center** in the Help menu. The Web site provides you with the latest information on Dreamweaver, advice from experienced users, and advanced Help topics, as well as examples, tips, and updates. You can also join a discussion group to converse with other Dreamweaver users.

Exiting Dreamweaver

When you are finished working, you need to close the Web site and exit the Dreamweaver program. The Exit command on the File menu exits Dreamweaver and closes all open windows. You can also use the Close command or the Close button on the window title bars to close each open window until the program exits. Dreamweaver will prompt you to save any Web pages that you haven't yet saved.

Exiting Dreamweaver | Reference Window

- Click File on the menu bar, and then click Exit.

or

- Click the Close button in the Dreamweaver program window title bar.

Because you haven't made any changes to the Catalyst site, you can close any open pages without saving, and then exit the site.

To exit Dreamweaver:

1. Close the home page.
2. Click **File** on the menu bar, and then click **Exit**. Dreamweaver exits.

You've reviewed the existing Catalyst site and are ready to begin planning the new Web site.

Session 1.2 Quick Check | Review

1. Do you need to know HTML to create a successful Web site in Dreamweaver? Why or why not?
2. Explain the difference between a page-centric design approach and a site-centric design approach.
3. What is the difference between the local site and the remote site in Dreamweaver?
4. What is a site definition, and where is it stored?
5. What is the local root folder?
6. Which window or panel do you use to manage local and remote site files?
7. Which view in the Document window displays only the underlying HTML code that Dreamweaver automatically generates as you create and edit a Web page?
8. Where would you turn for information about all of the Dreamweaver features?

Review

Tutorial Summary

In this tutorial, you learned about the Internet and the World Wide Web. You explored the relationship between Web servers and Web clients, and you opened and reviewed a Web site in a browser, examining the components of a basic Web page. You reviewed the history of Web design tools. You started Dreamweaver, arranged the work environment, and created the local portion of a site definition. Finally, you explored the Dreamweaver tool set and help system.

Key Terms

cache
content
Document window
domain name
Dreamweaver
Dreamweaver Support Center
encryption
file extension
File Transfer Protocol (FTP)
filename
graphic
home page
HTML (Hypertext Markup Language)
HTTP (Hypertext Transfer Protocol)
HTTPS (Hypertext Transfer Protocol Secure)
hyperlink (or link)
Insert bar

integrated file browser
Internet
Internet service provider (ISP)
local root folder
local site definition
logo
machine name
menu bar
multiple document interface (MDI)
network
nonlinear
object
page element
page title
page-centric design
panel
panel group
pixel
Property inspector
protocol

server
Simple Mail Transfer Protocol (SMTP)
site definition
site map
site-centric design
status bar
title bar
top-level domain
Uniform Resource Locator (URL)
Web browser
Web client (or client)
Web page
Web server
Web site
World Wide Web (WWW or Web)
WYSIWYG

Practice

Practice the skills you learned in the tutorial.

Review Assignments

There are no Data Files needed for the Review Assignments.

Brian Lee is getting ready to have his team begin planning the new Catalyst Web site. In preparation, he wants you to review the Web sites of bands that you like. While looking, keep your eyes open for possible improvements that could be incorporated into the new Catalyst site.

1. Start your Web browser.
2. Type the URL for the Web site of a favorite band in the Address text box, and then press the Enter key. (*Hint:* If you don't know the URL for the band's Web site, try typing "*www.thenameoftheband.com*" in the Address text box, using the actual band name.)
3. Review the home page of the band's Web site to see what information is included and how the information is arranged.
4. Use hyperlinks to explore the site. Look at how information is presented and whether you can move easily between sections.

5. Click the band's logo, if there is one. Notice whether the logo is a hotspot, and, if it is, where it takes you.
6. Repeat Steps 2 through 5 to explore the Web site for another band and review the information the site contains.
7. Compare the two sites that you explored. Write down your responses to the following questions:
   a. What are the similarities and the differences between the sites?
   _____
   _____
   _____

   b. Which features do you prefer? Why?
   _____
   _____
   _____

   c. Can any of the features from these sites be incorporated into the Catalyst Web site? If so, which features?
   _____
   _____
   _____

   d. How would the changes improve the Catalyst site?
   _____
   _____
   _____

8. Close the browser window.
9. Start Dreamweaver.
10. Click Help on the menu bar, click Using Dreamweaver to open the Using Dreamweaver window, and then click the Contents tab.
11. Click Dreamweaver Basics in the Contents list, and then click Welcome to Dreamweaver.
12. Read the information in the Welcome to Dreamweaver pane, and then click the Next arrow link (the right arrow) at the end of the overview to move to the next topic. (*Hint:* The left and right arrows are links that move you consecutively through the Help topics.)
13. Read the next three Help topics, using the Next arrow link to move to the consecutive pages, and then close the Using Dreamweaver window.
14. View the quick tour. Click the quick tour link on the Start page, and then listen to the presentation. (*Hint:* If you do not have audio capabilities, click the slide notes check box and read the text.)
15. Click Product Overview when the selection appears and listen to the presentation.
16. When the movie ends, click the Close button to close the tour.
17. Exit Dreamweaver.

Research

Research existing Web sites in preparation for creating a Web site to present the data on small rural communities in northern Vietnam.

Case Problem 1

There are no Data Files needed for this Case Problem.

Hroch University Anthropology Department Dr. Matt Hart is a social anthropologist at Hroch University, which has an internationally acclaimed anthropology department renowned for its research. Matt has lived in Asia for the last two years collecting data on small rural communities in northern Vietnam. He wants to create a Web site to present his research findings and accompanying graphics. He asks you to review existing Web sites that deal with social anthropology and northern Vietnam in preparation for designing his Web site. He also asks you to find out what image file formats are compatible with Dreamweaver.

1. Start your Web browser.

Explore

2. Use a search engine to find Web sites related to social anthropology. Type the URL for a search engine into the Address text box, and press the Enter key to open the search engine. (Two popular search engines are *www.google.com* and *www.dogpile.com*.)

Explore

3. Search for relevant Web sites by typing the term "social anthropology" into the search text box and then clicking the Search button. The search engine displays a list of pages that contain the words in your search. (*Hint:* If too many unrelated choices appear, narrow the search by typing quotation marks around the keywords and clicking the Search button. If no matches appear, check your spelling and try again.)
4. Click the link for an appropriate page to open the Web site, and then explore the Web site, making notes about what information is included, how the material is organized, and what images are included.
5. Click the Back button on the browser toolbar until you return to the search engine results. Then investigate a second Web site, taking notes about its content and organization.
6. Return to the search engine and search for Web sites related to "northern Vietnam." Explore at least one Web site, taking notes about its content and organization.

Explore

7. Write a memo to Matt giving a brief description of the sites' similarities and differences, and list features you would like to incorporate into the new Web site. Include the URL for each site you analyzed.
8. Close the browser window.
9. Start Dreamweaver, and then select the Design workspace environment.
10. Click Help on the menu bar, and then click Using Dreamweaver.
11. Use the Contents tab to display the Inserting Images topic from the Adding Content to Pages category.
12. Read the About Images topic to learn about the image file formats that Dreamweaver uses.
13. Add to your memo a brief explanation of which image file formats are compatible with Dreamweaver.
14. Exit Dreamweaver.

Challenge

Extend what you've learned to explore an art museum Web site from within Dreamweaver.

Case Problem 2

Data Files needed for this Case Problem: Museum\Dreamweaver\index.htm, Museum\Dreamweaver\contact.htm

Museum of Western Art The Fort Worth Museum of Western Art has been a premier gallery for many years. As part of the museum's plan to further community education about western art, Tika Hagge, the museum manager and curator, wants to expand the museum Web site. She has contracted C. J. Strittmatter to design and maintain the new site. You'll work with C. J. on the site. To start, you'll review the museum's current Web site.

1. Start Dreamweaver, and then select the Design workspace environment, if necessary. (*Hint:* If the panels in your workspace have been rearranged, select the Code environment, click the OK button, select the Design environment, click the OK button, and then close and reopen the software to reset the panels to the default view.)
2. Create a local site definition for the museum's Web site. Use "Museum of Western Art" as the site name, set the path to the **Tutorial.01\Cases\Museum\Dreamweaver** folder included with your Data Files as the local root folder, check the Refresh Local File List Automatically check box, and check the Enable Cache check box, if necessary.
3. Select Museum of Western Art in the Site list in the Files panel in Local view.
4. Expand the folder list, if necessary. How many pages are in the site? _____
5. Display the site map in the Files panel. How are the pages connected? _____ _____

Explore
6. Click the Plus (+) button next to the contact.htm page. Notice the globe icon, which indicates a file on another site or a special link (such as an e-mail link).

Explore
7. Display the page titles in the site map by clicking View on the Files panel menu bar, and then clicking Show Page Titles.

Explore
8. Display the filenames by turning off the Show Page Titles command.
9. Right-click the Files panel group name, and then click Help on the context menu to open context-sensitive Help.
10. Read the Using the Files Panel Help topic, and then close the Help window.

Explore
11. Display the site map and the files list in the Files panel. (*Hint:* Click the Expand/Collapse button and select Map and Files to display both the site map and the file list.)
12. Collapse the Files Panel, and then display only the local files list.
13. Open the site's home page (index.htm) from the Files panel, and then read the page's content.
14. Open the site's Contact page (contact.htm) from the Files panel, and then read the contents of the page.
15. Make the home page the active page.
16. Change the view to Split view.
17. Close all open pages, and then exit Dreamweaver.

Case Problem 3

Research

Find and review competing Web sites for an independent publisher of fringe writing.

There are no Data Files needed for this Case Problem.

NORM NORM is an independent publishing company in California that concentrates on cultivating fringe writings of all sorts. Norman Blinkered started the company in 1988, using his kitchen as an office. Since then, NORM has grown and prospered. Norman recently hired Mark Chapman to design and maintain a Web site for the company in hopes of expanding NORM's market through Internet exposure. Mark asks you to research the Web sites of other independent publishing companies. Norman has provided a list of some competitors: Seven Stories Press, Akashic Books, Soft Skull Press, and Verso. You'll use a search engine to find the Web sites of NORM's competitors. Then you'll investigate the sites you find.

1. Start your Web browser.

Explore
2. Use a search engine to find the Web sites for NORM's competitors. Type the URL for a search engine into the Address text box, and press the Enter key to open the search engine. (Two popular search engines are *www.google.com* and *www.dogpile.com*.)
3. Search for a competitor's Web site by typing the company's name in the search text box and then clicking the Search button. The search engine displays a list of pages that contain the words in your search.

Explore

Explore

4. Click the link for an appropriate page to open the Web site. Then explore the Web site, making notes about the site's design, what information is included, how the material is organized, and to whom the site would appeal.
5. Click the Back button on the browser toolbar until you return to the search engine results.
6. Repeat Steps 3 through 5 for each of NORM's competitors.
7. Return to the search engine and search for Web sites for independent publishing companies. Explore at least one Web site, taking notes about its content and organization.
8. Write a brief description of the sites' similarities and differences, listing both content and design features you would like to incorporate into the new Web site. Include the URL for each site.
9. Close the browser window.

Case Problem 4

Research

Find and review competing sushi restaurant Web sites and find information about basic HTML in preparation for creating a Web site for a newly opening sushi restaurant.

There are no Data Files needed for this Case Problem.

Sushi Ya-Ya Sushi Ya-Ya is a small sushi restaurant that will be opening soon in the French Quarter of New Orleans. Charlie Lindahl, the store's owner, has decided that a Web site with online ordering features would help create publicity for the new restaurant and garner lunch sales by encouraging carry-out orders from local businesses. Charlie hired Mary O'Brien to create and design the site. You will assist Mary in building the site. Mary asks you to research what other sushi restaurants have done with their Web sites. Then she asks you to use Dreamweaver to find information about basic HTML.

1. Start your Web browser.

Explore

2. Use a search engine to find the Web sites for sushi restaurants. Type the URL for a search engine into the Address text box, and press the Enter key to open the search engine. (Two popular search engines are *www.google.com* and *www.dogpile.com*.)

Explore

3. Search for sushi restaurant Web sites by typing the appropriate keywords in the search text box and then clicking the Search button. The search engine displays a list of pages that contain the words in your search.
4. Explore at least three sushi restaurant sites. For each site, write down the site's URL and any useful information about the site's content, organization, and design. (*Hint:* Use the Back button on the browser toolbar to return to the search results and link to a different restaurant.)
5. Write a brief description of the sites' similarities and differences, listing both content and design features you would like to incorporate into the new Sushi Ya-Ya Web site. Include the URL for each site.
6. Close your browser.
7. Start Dreamweaver, and then select the Designer workspace layout.
8. Open the Using Dreamweaver window.

Explore

9. Select Search and type "Property inspector" into the Type in the Keyword to Find text box, and then click the List Topics button.
10. Open the Editing Code with the Property Inspector topic, and read it.
11. Type "text properties" into the Type in the Keyword to Find text box, and then click the List Topics button.

Explore

12. Open the About Formatting Text topic, and read it.
13. Close the Help window, and then exit Dreamweaver.

Review

Quick Check Answers

Session 1.1

1. the world's largest computer network used for communicating and exchanging information via computer
2. a subset of the Internet with its own protocol (HTTP) and document structure (HTML)
3. A Web server is a specialized server that stores and distributes information to computers that are connected to the Internet. A Web client is a computer that an individual uses to access Internet information via a Web server.
4. the software installed on a client computer that allows users to view Web pages
5. a unique address that Web browsers use to locate where a specific Web page is stored
6. course.com
7. graphics, text, or buttons with hotspots that, when clicked with a mouse, take you to another related section on the same Web page, another Web page on the same site, or another Web site entirely
8. to effectively convey the Web site's intended message or information—usually with a combination of text, graphics, and possibly multimedia elements such as video, animation, or interactive content

Session 1.2

1. No. However, some familiarity with HTML enables you to make the site work better, fix problems that arise, and create elements that are complex or impossible to create in Dreamweaver.
2. Page-centric design concentrates on designing and creating Web pages individually and then linking them. Site-centric design focuses on planning the Web site structure and design before creating any pages.
3. The local site is stored on your computer and is the version you work on; the remote site is a copy of the local site that Dreamweaver posts to a publicly viewable space, such as a Web server.
4. A site definition is the information that tells Dreamweaver where to find the local and remote files for the Web site. It also defines other parameters that affect how the site is set up within Dreamweaver. It is stored in the Windows registry. If you move to another computer to work, you must re-create the site definition on that computer.
5. the location where you want to store all the files used by the local version of the Web site
6. Files panel
7. Code view
8. Using Dreamweaver Help

Dreamweaver DRM 47
Tutorial 2

Objectives

Session 2.1
- Determine the site goals
- Identify the target audience
- Conduct market research
- Create end-user scenarios

Session 2.2
- Design the information architecture
- Create a flowchart and site structure
- Create a site concept and metaphor
- Design the site navigation structure
- Develop the aesthetic concept for the site

Session 2.3
- Create a site definition for a new site
- Add pages to a site
- Review basic HTML tags
- Set page properties
- Preview the site in a browser
- Upload the site to a remote server, and preview it on the Web

Planning and Designing a Successful Web Site

Developing a Web Site Plan and Design

Case

Catalyst

Because Dreamweaver uses a site-centric approach for designing Web sites, a considerable amount of planning must take place before you can create a Web site in Dreamweaver. Although planning might seem like a lot of work, it will help you avoid reworking site elements. In the end, planning will save you time and frustration. Also, it is almost impossible to create an effective Web site without having a clear idea of the site's goals. Planning enables you to determine what you need from a Web site and how the site will meet those needs.

Brian Lee, the public relations and marketing director at Catalyst, asks you to work with him to plan the new Web site for Catalyst. First, you will determine site goals and identify the target audience. To do this, you will conduct market research and create end-user scenarios. Then, you will design the information architecture, create a flowchart and site structure, design the site navigation structure, and develop the aesthetic concept for the site. Finally, you will create the new site.

Student Data Files

▼**Tutorial.02 folder**

▽ Tutorial folder
   Background.gif

▽ Catalyst folder
   bands.htm
   contact.htm
   index.htm
   products.htm

     ▽ graphics folder
       DizziedConnectionCDcover.jpg
       LifeInMinorChordsCDcover.jpg
       SlothChildCDcover.jpg
       SurfaceSuctionCDcover.jpg

         ▽ Library folder
           styles.xml

▽ Review folder
   (no starting Data Files)

▽ Cases folder
   HartBackground.gif
   HartMemo.doc
   NORMBackground.gif

Session 2.1

Creating a Plan for a New Web Site

Whether you are part of an in-house Web team or an independent designer hired to create a Web site, the first order of business for designing a professional Web site is to determine the goals, the target audience, and the expectations for the site. You obtain this information from the **client**, the person or persons for whom you are creating the site. This process usually requires a series of meetings and a considerable amount of time.

These client meetings and initial time are a crucial part of the planning process, because it is impossible to design a Web site that will effectively meet the client's needs until you determine exactly what those needs are. You should explain clearly to the client what information you will need from him or her and what value his or her contribution will make to the final Web site. By making the client aware of what to expect and by communicating effectively with the client throughout the process, you help to ensure a successful project and a satisfied client.

It is important to understand that there are many possible paths in any creative process. However, as you gain experience in planning, designing, and creating Web sites, you will find that some things work better than others. You will come up with your own ideas about the new Catalyst site's goals, the target audience, and so forth, and then compare them to those approved by Brian. You will then evaluate how your plan is similar to and different from the final Catalyst Web site plan, and consider the benefits and drawbacks of each plan.

Reference Window | **Creating a Plan for a New Web Site**

- Determine the site goals.
- Identify the target audience.
- Conduct market research.
- Create end-user scenarios.

Determining Site Goals

The first question you should ask when you begin to plan a site is: What are the primary goals for the Web site? A Web site can have one goal or many goals. It is a good idea to brainstorm with the client, in this case Brian, and create a list of all the goals you can think of for the site. For example, the goals of a commercial Web site might be to:

- Provide information about a product
- Sell a product
- Increase brand recognition
- Provide help or operational instructions

This list, which could go on and on, is very general. The goal list for an actual site should be much more specific. For example, it should state what the product or products are.

There are a few guidelines to keep in mind as you develop the list of site goals. First, write site goals in an active voice rather than passive. Second, use action verbs to help you select achievable goals rather than concepts. For example, brand recognition is a concept, not a goal; *increase* brand recognition is a goal. Action verbs include words such as achieve, increase, and provide. Third, think about the different aspects of the site. For example, in addition to selling products, you may want to provide reliable support. Finally, make a comprehensive list. You should have at least 10 goals in your original list.

Once you have a list of possible site goals, review the list and place the goals in order of importance from most important to least important. For example:

- Sell a product
- Increase brand recognition
- Provide information about a product
- Provide help or operational instructions

Review your list and, if possible, combine goals; then reprioritize if necessary. Some of the lower-priority goals might actually be part of higher-priority goals. For example, in some cases, providing help or operational instructions may be incorporated into the general goal of providing information about the product. There is a limit to the number of goals that a Web site can effectively achieve; therefore, the first four or five goals are probably the ones you will want to focus on. Remember, site goals are most effective if they are the result of collaboration with the client. After all, just as you are an expert on Web design, the client is an expert concerning his or her business.

Brian asks you to develop a list of goals for the new Catalyst site. As you gain experience in designing Web sites, your ability to identify and articulate goals will continue to improve.

To create a list of goals for the new Catalyst site:

1. Write down at least 20 possible site goals.
2. Review the list to be sure that all statements are in the active voice and use action verbs.
3. Prioritize the goals in order of importance.
4. Review your list, combining goals if possible and reprioritizing them if necessary.
5. Review the top five goals. Think about what you want to accomplish with the site and make sure that your list of goals will help achieve a successful site.

   Brian created a list of goals for the new Catalyst Web site, and then prioritized and combined them.

6. Compare your list to Brian's goal list shown in Figure 2-1.

Figure 2-1   Catalyst Web site goals

1. Enhance label identity.
2. Increase band recognition.
3. Promote band image.
4. Boost sales of CDs and promotional products.
5. Provide tour date information.
6. Provide information about individual band members.
7. Provide press information.
8. Create cross interest between bands with similar sounds.
9. Link to fan sites.
10. Produce a sound library (long-term, not immediate).
11. Construct and link to individual band sites (long-term, not immediate).
12. Create a photo library for each band (long-term, not immediate).
13. Create other materials (such as Flash animations) to increase interest (long-term, not immediate).

You will use the site goals to make decisions about the site organization and structure. The site's primary goal is to enhance label identity—in other words, to make people aware of Catalyst and to associate the label with certain types of bands. The site will be organized to emphasize the Catalyst name and logo. The home page will include information about the label followed by band information. The label logo will appear at the top of every page, and the site navigation will be organized so that a "label information" category is included in the top level of the site.

The priority of the goals helps to determine the site's layout. If the first two goals were switched, and increased band recognition was the primary goal, the site structure might be organized differently. The band information could appear above the label information. The band logos could appear at the top of all of the pages instead of the label logo. The individual bands could be placed in their own categories in the top level of navigation. This is just one set of many possible changes.

When you start to examine the way that site goals can affect the structure of the final site, you can see just how important it is to carefully consider what you want to accomplish. Taking the time to establish goals and expectations from the very beginning will make a world of difference in the final site.

Identifying the Target Audience

The **target audience** for a Web site is the group of users that you would *most* like to visit the site. You identify the target audience by creating a user profile. A **user profile** is the information that you gather from a list of questions, as shown in Figure 2-2. The user profile is a tool designed to help you determine the characteristics of the group of people you are trying to reach—the target audience. (In this case, the word "user" refers to the target user group, not an individual user.)

You can also use other resources to help you create a user profile. If the client has an existing Web site, you may be able to obtain specific data about current users from usage logs and user registration data. Usage logs are exact records of every visit to the site; they include information such as the time and date of the visit, the visitor's ISP, the visitor's pathway through the site, the visitor's browser and operating system, and so forth. Some sites require visitors to register by creating a user ID and providing personal information before being allowed access. You can analyze this registration information when it is available to further define the target audience.

Figure 2-2 General user profile questions

1. **What is the age range of the user?** Sites can appeal to a range of ages. The age range will depend on the site goals. Generally, the group members are linked because they share a commonality, such as a habit, a characteristic, or a developmental stage.

2. **What is the gender of the user?** Sites can be targeted to males only, females only, or males and females. Not all sites are targeted to a specific gender.

3. **What is the education level of the user?** Education level will be a range. Designate education level either by the current year in school (e.g., senior in high school) or the degree earned if out of school (e.g., associates degree).

4. **What is the economic situation of the user?** Economic situation refers to the annual income level of the user as well as other extenuating economic factors like parental support or student loans. For example, the user may be a student who has only a part-time job. As a student, the user may have a lower income bracket, earning only $20,000 a year, but extenuating economic factors like parental support and student loans may affect the user's buying power. All of this information should factor into the user's economic situation.

5. **What is the geographic location of the user?** Is the site targeted at users in a specific city, a specific region, or a specific country?

6. **What is the primary language of the user?**

7. **What is the ethnic background of the user?** Most sites are targeted at a user group with diverse cross-sections of ethnic backgrounds; however, sometimes ethnicity is a factor in your target audience. For example, *Jet Magazine* is targeted at African-American users.

8. **Are there other unifying characteristics that are relevant to the user?** If you know that the target group has a common characteristic that may be of use in designing the Web site, list it here. Unifying characteristics are useful if they are related to the topic of the Web site or if they could affect the goals of the site. For example, unifying characteristics might include things such as: target users have diabetes (for a diabetes disease-management site), target users ride dirt bikes (for a BMX motocross site), target users listen to club music (for an alternative music site), and so forth.

Brian asks you to create a user profile that identifies the target audience of the Catalyst Web site.

To identify the target audience for the new Catalyst Web site:

1. Answer the User Profile Questions listed in Figure 2-2.
2. Review your answers to ensure that the target audience you identified reinforces the final site goals listed in Figure 2-1. If it does not, you will need to re-evaluate your site goals or adjust your target audience so that the two are compatible.
3. Compare your answers to the User Profile Questions to those compiled by Brian, shown in Figure 2-3.

Figure 2-3 | **User profile for the Catalyst site**

1. Age: 18 to 29
2. Gender: male and female
3. Education level: late high school to college
4. Economic situation: students with expendable income from parental support/financial aid; recent college graduates entering the workplace
5. Geographic location: United States and Canada; the label has concentrated on signing bands from the Denton, Texas area but wants to target a larger area with its Web site
6. Primary language: target user will speak/read English
7. Ethnic background: the Catalyst Web site will not target a specific ethnic background
8. Other unifying characteristics: participation in the "indie" (independent) college music scene

Sometimes clients and designers are hesitant to identify the target audience because they think it will limit the reach of the Web site. However, a very broad target audience can be even more restrictive than having a very narrow target audience. A site that must appeal to many different groups of people must be more generic in some ways. For example, if the new Catalyst Web site is intended to appeal to an older audience (50 to 60 years of age) as well as to a college-aged audience (18 to 29 years of age), you can include only elements that will be attractive and communicate effectively with both age groups. You can see how this might limit some stylistic options (such as graphic choice, word choice, and color choice) that would be available to a Web site with a target audience that included only a college-aged group.

Some sites are intended to appeal to a broad target audience. Consider the Internal Revenue Service (IRS). The IRS Web site (*www.irs.gov*) is designed to be an informational site available to a diverse group of people. The site contains a huge amount of information about U.S. tax laws and tax preparation. Knowing that the target audience for the IRS site is broad and that the goal of the site is to dispense information, designers chose to create a text-based site with very few graphic elements that will be accessible to the broadest possible group of users. The IRS site is very effective at achieving its goals. However, this primarily text-based design would not be effective if the main goal was entertainment because—although rich in informational content—the site is not very entertaining.

Once you have identified a target audience, you can use the general information from the user profile as a basis to research and make more advanced decisions about user wants, needs, technical proficiencies, and so forth. When used appropriately, the target audience information is a great tool for focusing a Web site to achieve the site goals. However, be careful not to get lost in stereotypes. It is easy to draw general conclusions about the target audience without backing up those assumptions with research. This can lead to a Web site that seems targeted to your intended audience, but, in fact, does not actually appeal to them. For example, we have all been sitting in front of the television when a commercial that is supposed to appeal to our gender and/or age group comes on the screen. Think about your reaction to a commercial that has the right look but underestimates your intelligence or misinterprets your styles, habits, and so forth. Use the target audience information as a starting point for your research.

Conducting Market Research

Market research is the careful investigation and study of data about the target audience's preferences for a product or service. It also includes evaluating the products or services of competitors. The user profile provides information about your target audience. Once you've created the user profile, you need to investigate the habits, interests, likes, and dislikes of that group of people, as well as what Catalyst's competitors are doing to attract them.

Advertising and design agencies spend a substantial amount of money subscribing to services that provide in-depth market analysis of products or services and their target audiences (like www.ipsos-asi.com or www.imarketinc.com), but the average designer has to rely on his or her own research. You will look for information that will help you to build a Web site tailored to the target audience Catalyst wants to attract. Technical information—such as the screen size and the speeds of the computer and Internet connection that the target audience uses—tells you the technical limitations of an effective site. Information on the spending habits of the target audience tells you the potential profitability of the Web site. Information on the interests of the target audience tells you what will appeal to the target audience and what elements you might include in the site to draw them in. Information about the culture and the customs of the target audience tells you what colors, symbols, fashions, styles, and so forth will be effective in communicating with the target audience. Finally, information about competing Web sites tells you what the competition believes is effective in attracting and communicating with the target audience.

The fastest way to obtain information about the habits, interests, and likes of a target audience is to use a search engine, such as www.altavista.com or www.google.com, to locate Web sites with statistics and other data about the target audience's lifestyle and preferences. A **search engine** is a Web site whose primary function is to gather and report what information is available on the Web related to specified keywords or phrases. Brian spent some time online and compiled the information shown in Figure 2-4.

Catalyst target audience information   Figure 2-4

- 78% of college students own computers.
- Student shoppers tend to go off-campus or online to find the most competitive pricing.
- 72% of students use online services on a daily basis. 52% use search engines to locate stores online. (Yahoo and Google are among the most frequently used.)
- College students spend an average of $480 online annually. Among the most commonly purchased items are music (46% of students buy their music online), books (37%), tickets for air travel (32%), concert and other event tickets (22%), and computer software (14%).
- 58% of college students downloaded music from the Internet in the last year.
- 65% of college students have and use credit cards.

You'll look for additional information about the target audience for the Catalyst Web site. Make sure that you note the source of the information and the URL of the Web page in case you need to refer to that source in the future.

To gather information on your target audience:

1. Start your browser, type **www.dogpile.com** in the Address text box, and then press the **Enter** key. The Dogpile home page opens.

    Trouble? If the Dogpile search engine is unavailable (sometimes sites go down), you can try another search engine. Type "www.google.com" (or the URL for your favorite search engine) in the Address text box, and then press the Enter key.

2. Type **market research student spending** into the text box at the top of the page, and then click the **Google Search** button to start the search.

3. Review the list of Web sites, click the link for a Web site that looks promising, and then explore that Web site.

4. Write down any pertinent information. Make sure to note the source of the information and the URL of the Web page in case you need to refer to that source in the future.

5. Click the **Back** button on the toolbar to return to the search results.
6. Repeat Steps 3 and 4 to gather information from another Web site.

By now you should have an understanding of the target audience's habits and likes. It is time to switch your focus from the habits of the target audience to what you can do with the Web site to attract the target audience. Next, you'll investigate Web sites that the target audience frequents as well as the Web sites of Catalyst competitors. You will have to make assumptions about which sites are popular with the target audience based on the information that you gathered about its habits and preferences. By exploring sites that are popular with the target audience and the sites of competitors, you can familiarize yourself with graphic styles to which the target audience is accustomed as well as the colors, symbols, fashions, styles, and slang terms that have been effective in communicating with the target audience.

While you are exploring Web sites, pay close attention to their designs. What colors do the sites use? How is the information laid out? What are the navigation systems like? Is there anything unique about the sites? What aspects of the sites might appeal to the target audience? How is the space used? Can you ascertain what the sites' goals might be? Is the content presented in straightforward language or in slang specific to the target audience? Is there a lot of text on each page or is the text broken into smaller segments?

Brian asks you to explore some music-related Web sites.

To explore other music Web sites:

1. Type **www.mtv.com** in the Address text box, and then press the **Enter** key. The MTV home page opens.
2. Navigate through the Web site, evaluating the colors, information layout, navigation system, use of space, content, language style (formal, conversational, slang, etc.), and so forth.
3. Record your findings and make notes about anything you feel is important about the site.
4. Repeat Steps 1 through 3 for **www.altpress.com**, the Web site for *Alternative Press Magazine*.
5. Search for and explore other sites that the target audience might frequent.
6. Look at the Web site for two other music labels, such as **www.fatwreck.com**, **www.4ad.com**, or **www.dischord.com**. What information do they include? Does the information change when the label is trying to target a different audience? Think about what you like and dislike about the sites.

By this point, you should have a clear idea of the target audience, including the users' habits, interests, and so forth. You should also have an understanding of what you can do with the Web site to attract the target audience. You will use this information to develop end-user scenarios.

Creating End-User Scenarios

End-user scenarios are imagined situations in which the target audience might access a Web site. End-user scenarios are used to envision actual conditions that an end user will be in while experiencing the Web site. Scenarios enable you to visualize an abstract target audience as real people. By placing characters in realistic situations, you can get a better sense of what factors might affect the users' experience with the Web site. Then, you can anticipate the end users' needs and build a Web site that incorporates these factors into its design.

Brian created two scenarios for the Catalyst Web site, as shown in Figure 2-5. The scenarios provide insights that go beyond statistics and facts. For example, from Scenario 1, you learn that there is a good chance that the target audience will not have access to audio on the Web site; therefore, you can conclude that the audio should not be a primary component.

End-user scenarios for the Catalyst site | Figure 2-5

Scenario 1

Tim Roth is a junior at the University of North Texas in Denton, Texas. He is 21 and lives on campus in one of the older dorms. Tim has a computer, but the dorms are not equipped with high-speed Internet connections; therefore, when Tim wants to surf from his room, he must do it via a 56k modem. He does most of his surfing late at night in the computer science lab that has 24-hour access. Because the lab computers have no speakers, Tim can listen to sound only if he brings his headphones.

Tim is a fan of Surface Suction and attends the band's shows regularly. He visits the Catalyst site frequently to check out new bands. The feature that he would most like to see added to the Catalyst site is a regularly updated list of live shows. Tim's other favorite sites are the Rubber Gloves Rehearsal Studio Web site and The Good Records Web site.

Scenario 2

Sita Owanee, 26, is a recent graduate of Syracuse University's art media studies MFA program. She is now living in New York City and is working as a graphic designer. Because Sita has just started her career and has little expendable income, she has access to the Web via only a 56k modem and a moderately equipped computer.

Sita has a passion for dub music. Dizzied Connections is one of her favorite bands. She discovered the Catalyst Web site when Dizzied Connections moved to the label and has since become a regular visitor. She visits the site to keep up with Dizzied Connections and to see if Catalyst has signed other bands with the same sound. Sita would most like to see an expanded section featuring her favorite band. Regularly updated news about the band would keep her interested in the site. Sita's other favorite sites include the Knitting Factory Web site and the Village Voice Web site.

Brian asks you to create a third scenario for the Catalyst site.

To create an end-user scenario:

1. Review the Catalyst site goals, user profile, and market research.
2. Create a character who might visit the Catalyst Web site. Give the character a name and attributes, such as age, gender, location, and so forth.
3. Place the character in a situation where he or she is accessing the Web site. Describe the user's surroundings and the user's experience with the site.

Planning might seem time-consuming and difficult, but a few hours of advanced preparation will save you many hours of redesign work later. In the next session, you will work on the Catalyst site's informational structure and aesthetic design.

Review

Session 2.1 Quick Check

1. True or False? There is only one plan and design for a Web site.
2. What is the purpose of listing site goals?
3. How many goals can a Web site achieve effectively?
4. What is a target audience for a Web site?
5. Why would you create a user profile?
6. What happens if you draw general conclusions about the target audience without backing up those conclusions with research?
7. Why would you conduct market research?
8. What are end-user scenarios?

Session 2.2

Creating Information Architecture

Creating an **information architecture** is the process of determining what you need a site to do, and then constructing a framework that will allow you to accomplish those goals. It applies the principles of architectural design and library science to Web site design by providing a blueprint for Web page arrangement, Web site navigation, and page content organization. The basic process for creating the information architecture for a site is to construct information categories, draw a flowchart, and organize the available information into pages. You'll work on the information architecture for the new Catalyst site.

Creating Categories for Information

Categories provide structure for the information in a Web site and are used to create the main navigation system. The main **navigation system** is the interface that visitors use to move through a Web site. This interface appears on every page in the site. The main categories of a Web site are like the subject sections of a library or bookstore (fiction, poetry, reference material, etc.); they show the user what types of information are included in the Web site. The categories should be based on the site goals and the information gathered during the preliminary planning stages. When you create the Catalyst categories, think about how the information should be organized to achieve the site goals, then use what you learned from visiting other sites to create logical groupings of information. You should include no more than five main categories on a Web site, because more than five main categories make the pages seem cluttered.

Categories can be divided into subcategories, just like the fiction section in a library or bookstore might be divided into historical novels, mysteries, literature, science fiction, and so forth. Subcategories should be arranged in hierarchical order, placing the most important subcategories first. Once you know the major categories for the Catalyst site, you can list all the subcategories that will fall under each category in a hierarchical order. You should include no more than five subcategories for each main category, because fragmenting information into too many subcategories makes the Web site more difficult to navigate.

For more complex sites, individual subcategories can be divided into third-level subcategories. Before creating third-level subcategories, make sure that there is enough information to warrant the breakdown. Visitors dislike having to link too far down into a site to find relevant information. Third-level subcategories are appropriate only when a Web site is incredibly information intensive, such as a research site, and there is no other means to effectively convey the information.

The best way to present the major categories and the subcategories for a Web site is in a standard outline format. Brian created the outline shown in Figure 2-6 to show how the Catalyst site content can be structured.

Catalyst Web site categories Figure 2-6

```
                 Catalyst Web Site Category Outline

           I. Home Page
                a. Label
                     i.   News
                     ii.  Mission statement
                     iii. Company history
                     iv.  Employee biographies
                b. Bands
                     i.   Dizzied Connections
                     ii.  Sloth Child
                     iii. Life in Minor Chords
                c. Catalogue
                     i.   CDs
                     ii.  Vinyl
                d. Tour Dates
                     i.   Tour schedules
                     ii.  Venues and ticket information
                e. Contact
                     i.   Company contact information
                     ii.  Directions
                     iii. E-mail form
```

Brian asks you to create an alternate outline with another possible version of the categories and subcategories for the Catalyst Web site.

To create an information category outline:

▸ 1. Review the site goals and your research, and then use that information to create a list of five categories of information for the Catalyst Web site.

▸ 2. Start an outline using the categories you listed in Step 1 as section headings.

▸ 3. List all the subcategories that will be included in the first section of your outline, and then arrange them in hierarchical order.

▸ 4. Break the subcategories into their respective subcategories, where applicable, and arrange them in hierarchical order.

▸ 5. Repeat Steps 3 and 4 for each section of your outline.

▸ 6. Compare your outline to Brian's outline, shown in Figure 2-6.

Next you'll work on the flowchart for the Catalyst site.

Creating a Flowchart

A **flowchart** is a diagram of geometric shapes connected by lines that shows steps in sequence. The shapes represent steps, decision points, and dead ends. The lines represent the connection of steps. If steps must be followed in a particular order or direction, then arrows are attached to the lines. In Web design, a flowchart provides a visual representation of the hierarchical structure of the pages within the site. The shapes represent pages and the lines represent their connection.

You create a flowchart from the information category outline. The main categories become the major branches of the flowchart and the subcategories become the sub-branches. Most of the time, visitors can move between pages of a Web site in any direction, so arrows are usually not included. You can use shapes to designate different types of pages in the Web site. For example, all form pages can be hexagons while regular pages can be squares. There is no widely recognized standard for the shapes used to designate different Web pages; therefore, a key or legend for deciphering what the shapes represent is often included in the chart. Figure 2-7 shows the flowchart that Brian created for the new site.

Figure 2-7   **Catalyst Web site flowchart**

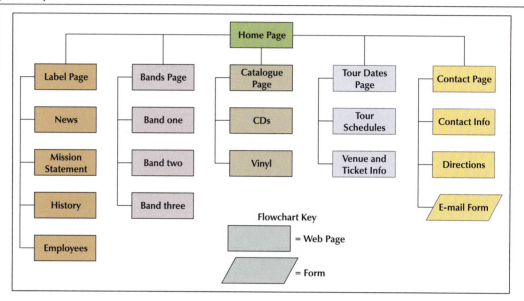

Brian asks you to create a flowchart using the outline that you created. You can create a flowchart using flowcharting software or sketch a flowchart using pen and paper.

To create a flowchart:

1. Draw a square at the top of the page and label it **Home Page**.
2. Draw five squares in a horizontal row below the Home Page square for each of the main categories of your outline, and label each square with one category.
3. Draw a line from each main category page to the home page to connect them.
4. Repeat Steps 2 and 3 to add the subcategory pages below the category pages. Continue until all of the information from your outline is represented in the flowchart.
5. Create a key for your flowchart by drawing and labeling the shapes you used.
6. Compare your flowchart to the flowchart Brian created, shown in Figure 2-7.

Next, you'll work on the page content for the Catalyst site.

Gathering and Organizing Information

The next step in the process of creating an information architecture is to gather and organize all possible sources of information. The materials that you collect will be used to create the content for the site. It is best to err on the side of excess at this stage, because the more raw materials you have to work with, the better job you can do once you actually start to create content.

Gathering information is often like detective work; you'll need to use your instincts, follow leads, do research, and talk to others to gather everything you can. Based on the site goals, the market research, the information outline, and the flowchart, you and Brian will need information about:

- the company and the management team
- the bands and the band members
- the products (CDs and vinyl)

You will find this information in a variety of places. Much of the information you need can be found in promotional materials such as brochures, flyers, press releases, reviews, and articles. Gather all of the available graphic materials and any pertinent company documents (such as the company's mission statement and employee biographies). Outside resources can also provide some information. Outside resources include reviews, articles, and other Web sites that reference the product or service. You'll want a paper copy of all the information for ease of organization. Once all the information is compiled and printed, you are ready to start organizing it.

Organizing the data lets you see exactly what you have gathered about each relevant topic. You need to sort the collected materials, piece by piece, into the categories and subcategories you established earlier. You may need to split some items, such as a brochure, into more than one category. Information that fits more than one category should be placed in the category that seems most appropriate. Review any information that is relevant but doesn't fit the planned pages. Try to find a place in the existing structure where the information might fit. You might also consider whether it warrants creating a separate section or a new page.

Next you will create the aesthetic design for the site. After you have designed the aesthetic structure of the pages, you will create page content out of the materials that you have assembled and organized.

Designing a Web Site

The phrase "look and feel" is used to describe the overall impact of the external characteristics of a Web site. It refers to the way that all the elements of the site design interact to create an experience for the user. The look and feel is achieved from a mixture of many smaller choices, including which colors, fonts, graphic style, and layout are selected for the design. To combine all these elements effectively, you start by creating a concept and metaphor for the site.

Creating a Site Concept and Metaphor

A good concept is the basis for developing an aesthetically cohesive Web site. A **site concept** is a general underlying theme that unifies the various elements of a site and contributes to the site's look and feel. To develop a site concept, review some of the artwork and Web sites that appeal to the target audience and look for common underlying themes. Next, make a list of words that describe what you would like the site to convey. Try to think of words that will reinforce the site goals and words that will communicate something to the target audience. Finally, write the concept out on a piece of paper.

Once you have developed a site concept, you create a metaphor for the site. A **metaphor** is a comparison in which one object, concept, or idea is represented as another. For example, the expression "at that moment, time was molasses" and Shakespeare's famous observation that "all the world's a stage" are metaphors. The site metaphor should be a visual extension of the site concept, thereby reinforcing the site message and the site goals. The metaphor helps to create a unified site design. It does not have to be concretely represented in the site. For example, if the site concept is fluidity, the metaphor might be a river. In this case, the site might not be designed to look like a river, but instead would integrate elements that are commonly identified with rivers: a series of small, partially transparent, wavy lines in the page background; a flowing theme in the graphic design; and colors that are cool, such as muted blues and silvers. The river metaphor is an instrument to focus the aesthetic choices.

For the new Catalyst Web site, Brian came up with a list of words to describe the site: *hip, retro, logical, underground, alternative, minimalist,* and *intuitive*. Some words apply to a look that is popular with the target audience (hip, retro); other words apply to the flow of information (logical, intuitive). Next, he reviewed the CD cover art on the current Catalyst Web site as well as the CD cover art of other bands in the same genre of music to get a feel for the artwork styles that are popular with the Catalyst target audience. Finally, he decided on the site concept—appropriation of items from the past to create a new look—and the metaphor—recycling. In later sections, you will see how the recycling metaphor helps to shape the site design by providing a foundation for color choice, font choice, graphics choice, and layout.

Brian asks you to develop another concept and metaphor for the new Catalyst Web site.

To develop a site concept and metaphor:

1. List at least five words that describe the site.
2. Click **File** on the browser menu bar, click **Open**, click the **Browse** button, click the **Look in** list arrow, navigate to the **Tutorial.01\Tutorial\Catalyst** folder included with your Data Files, double-click **index.htm**, and then click the **OK** button. The current Catalyst Web site opens in your Web browser.
3. Click the **PRODUCTS** link, review the CD cover art on the Products page, and then close the Catalyst Web site.
4. Review other artwork that appeals to the target audience.
5. Choose a site concept.
6. Choose a site metaphor.
7. Write a paragraph that explains how you could integrate the concept and the metaphor into the site.

Next, you will learn how to make your site accessible to people with disabilities.

Considering Accessibility Issues

The Web is a public venue used by a variety of people, including people with disabilities. With regard to Web design, **accessibility** refers to the quality and ease of use of a Web site by people who use assistive devices or people with disabilities. (An **assistive device** is an apparatus that provides a disabled person with alternate means to experience electronic and information technologies.) Some ways you might enhance the accessibility of a Web site include providing alternate text descriptions that can be read by audio assistive devices for any graphics on the site, and establishing basic text links in addition to graphical navigation structures.

Effective June 21, 2001, Section 508 of the federal Rehabilitation Act requires all United States federal government agencies, as well as public colleges and universities, to make their electronic and information technology accessible to people with disabilities. Although private companies are under no legal obligation to make their sites accessible, many try to ensure that their sites are at least partially in line with current federal guidelines. Because technologies change rapidly, the Web is the best source for current accessibility guidelines and accessibility-checking tools.

Macromedia offers a number of tools to help you develop accessible Web sites, including templates and checking utilities. Search the Macromedia Web site (*www.macromedia.com*) using the keyword "accessibility" for information. You can also activate Accessibility dialog boxes within Dreamweaver so that every time you insert an object into a Web page, Dreamweaver will prompt you for the information you need to add accessibility.

The World Wide Web Consortium (W3C) also provides information about accessibility technology, guidelines, tools, education and outreach, and research and development. It has created a Web Accessibility Initiative (WAI) whose mission is to promote usability of the Web for people with disabilities. (For more information on this, go to its Web site at *www.w3.org/WAI.*)

Another place to find help in adding accessibility to a Web site is the Center for Applied Special Technology (CAST). CAST is a nonprofit organization whose mission is to expand opportunities for people with disabilities through innovative uses of computer technology. CAST developed Bobby, a tool that checks Web pages for accessibility issues and returns a detailed report with suggestions for improvement. Bobby is now owned by Watchfire. (Go to *bobby.watchfire.com* for more information about Bobby.)

For now, Brian wants to adjust the new Web site design for accessibility without changing the site's look and feel. This will make the site available to as wide an audience as possible while maintaining a look and feel that appeals to the target audience. Brian plans to implement basic accessibility modifications into the design for the new site, and then create a parallel site next year that will meet all the current accessibility guidelines.

Based on a review of the current guidelines, Brian has decided to include alternate text descriptions for graphics and graphic links. This alternate text can be "read" by audio assistive devices. Depending on the browser, this information will appear in place of a graphic or when the user points to an image or link. Brian wants to make the alternate text as descriptive as possible so that anyone can appreciate the site content even without seeing it. He also wants to run the completed site through Bobby. Based on the suggestions made in that report, Brian will begin to plan the parallel site that Catalyst will build next year.

Selecting Colors

Color is an interesting component of design because it affects the emotional response that a user has to the site. The colors you choose set the tone of the site. Before selecting colors for a Web site, you'll need a basic understanding of how color applies to Web design.

There are two major systems of color. The traditional **subtractive color system** uses cyan, magenta, and yellow as its primary colors; all other colors are created by mixing these primary colors. It is called the subtractive color system because new colors are created by adding pigment such as ink and paint and removing light. If the primary colors of the subtractive color system were combined in equal amounts, they would make black, the absence of light. The **additive color system** uses red, green, and blue as its primary colors. This system is also called the **RGB system** (for red, green, and blue). As with the subtractive color system, all other colors are created by combining these primary colors. It is called the additive color system because it works like a prism—new colors are created by adding varying amounts of light. If all of the primary colors of the additive system are combined in equal amounts, they create pure white light. Figure 2-8 shows how the primary colors (red, green, and blue) can be mixed in various combinations to create secondary colors (cyan, magenta, and yellow), and how the primary colors can be combined equally to create white.

Figure 2-8 RGB color system

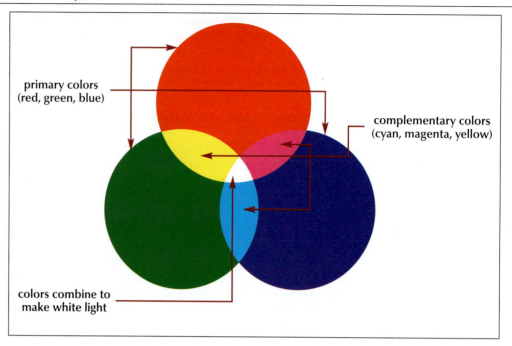

Web sites are a digital media designed to be viewed on monitors. A monitor combines hundreds of thousands of pixels (tiny dots of light that glow in different color intensities) to create images. Because monitors work with light, they use the additive RGB color system. When creating or saving graphics for the Web, you should use RGB color.

Color is a good tool for emphasizing information, such as headlines from body text, or for drawing the eye to a specific area of the page. Color can also be used to distinguish segments of the Web site (when you use a different color for each major category, for example).

Choosing a color palette can be difficult. There is no precise scientific method to ensure that you choose the perfect colors. This is why most design teams include a graphic artist who is trained in color theory. However, even without extensive color training, you can select attractive and effective colors for a Web site. Keep in mind the following basic color concepts and strategies:

- **Keep it simple.** With color choice, more is definitely not better. Everyone has seen a Web site that looks as if it erupted from a rainbow. Too many competing colors cause the eye to race around the page, leaving the user dazed and confused.
- **Include three to six colors per site.** You'll use these same colors for all of the site's elements, including the text, background, links, logo, buttons, navigation bar, and graphics. Black and white count as colors when selecting a palette. (This rule does not apply to the use of photographic images, which have many colors and can enhance your site.)
- **Consider the mood you want to create.** Colors create a mood. Studies have shown that colors have a psychological effect on people. For example, blue is calming, whereas red is hot or intense. Think about what things your target audience might associate with a color when choosing a palette for a Web site.
- **Keep the target audience in mind.** Different cultures do not always have the same psychological associations with specific colors. For example, the United States associates white with purity and red with danger, whereas some countries associate white with death and red with marriage. If a Web site has a global or foreign target audience, you might need to research the customs and symbols of the target culture.

One way to develop a color palette is to look to other works of art for inspiration. Think of what emotions and feelings you want to evoke with the Web site, and then find a painting, photograph, or other work of art that stirs those feelings in you. Evaluate the colors the artist used. Consider how the colors interact. Try to pinpoint colors that are causing the emotion. Consider how the color palette works with your metaphor. Think about how you might use that color palette in the Web site.

Brian chose the colors shown in Figure 2-9 for the new Catalyst Web site. This color palette retains the two colors used in the current Catalyst site, and adds a third color. Black and white will be the other colors used in the site. Because the number one site goal is to increase label identity, Brian didn't want to discard the color palette that is currently identified with the Catalyst label. The first two colors, retained from the current Catalyst site, are used in the logo as well as other print materials. Brian decided to add a third color so that the designer can combine the colors in different ways, providing additional flexibility. The color palette also fits nicely into the recycling design metaphor because the varying shades of yellow and orange are reminiscent of colors popular in the early 1970s. In the site, all three colors will be used in the logo, Yellow-Yellow-Orange will be used in a strip across the top of the site, and Dark-Hard-Orange will be used in a smaller strip below the top strip. Font colors will be discussed in the next section.

Color palette for the new Catalyst Web site — **Figure 2-9**

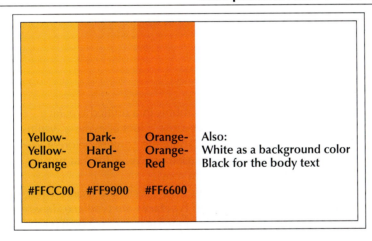

The figure refers to the colors by their color names as well as their hexadecimal color codes. Although color names are easy to remember and may have more meaning to the average person, they can be unreliable when trying to communicate specific color values. One person may use the word red to refer to the generic red family of colors, another person may be referring to the specific color designated as red in the Web Safe Color Palette, while still another person may be referring to a red in a different color palette. The color names used in these tutorials are the Web Safe Color Palette names. The **Web Safe Color Palette** consists of 216 colors and provides Web designers a reliable color palette to work with. The Web Safe Color Palette was created when many computers could display only 256 colors at a time. Because current computers can display 16+ million colors and many designers have disregarded the Web Safe Color Palette, many of the colors currently in use in Web sites do not have reliable color names. All colors, however, have hexadecimal color codes, and all well-coded HTML uses hexadecimal color codes instead of color names. **Hexadecimal color codes** are six-digit numbers in the form of #RRGGBB where RR is replaced by the hexadecimal color value for red, GG is replaced with the green value, and BB is replaced with the blue value. The specified amounts of each of these colors are mixed together by the system to create the color you specify. **Hexadecimal** is a number system that uses the digits 0 through 9 to represent the decimal values 0 through 9, plus the letters A through F to represent the decimal values 10 through 15. To ensure that the color you specify is understood by the browser and displayed properly, you will use the hexadecimal color codes to designate colors when you create the Catalyst Web site. However, you do not need to know the hexadecimal color codes when you are selecting colors in Dreamweaver. Instead, you can click the color you want to use and Dreamweaver will display the hexadecimal code for that color.

You'll select a color palette that will work with the site metaphor you developed. You can use a graphic program (such as Adobe Photoshop, Macromedia Fireworks, or Adobe Illustrator), crayons, markers, or colored paper to create your color palette.

To choose a color palette:

1. Envision a set of colors that will work with your site concept and metaphor.
2. Look at works of art for inspiration.
3. Think about the psychological associations of the colors. Are these in line with your site goals?
4. Draw a series of rectangles (one for each color in your palette) side by side, and then fill each with one color.
5. Write a brief explanation of your color choice and how it reinforces the site concept and metaphor. Describe where and how you intend to use the colors in the site.

Next, you'll work on font choice.

Selecting Fonts

Font refers to a set of letters, numbers, and symbols in a unified typeface. Font choice is important in creating an effective Web site because a font conveys a wealth of subtle information and often creates an impression about the content before it is even read. Think about the different fonts that might be used on Web sites that present current news and events, Far East travel, and science fiction movies.

There are three categories of typefaces: serif, sans serif, and mono. These categories are also referred to as **generic font families**. **Serif typefaces** are typefaces in which a delicate, horizontal line (called a serif) finishes off the main strokes of each character; an example would be the horizontal bars at the top and bottom of an uppercase M. The most common serif typeface is Times New Roman. **Sans-serif typefaces** are typefaces in which these lines, or serifs, are absent. (*Sans* means without in French, so *sans serif* means *without serif*.) The most common sans-serif typeface is Helvetica. A third category, mono, is sometimes used. *Mono* is short for *monospaced*. A **monospaced font** is one in which each letter takes exactly the same width in the line; for example, the letter *i* (a thin letter) would take the same amount of space as the letter *m*. A common monospaced font is Courier. Monospaced fonts are serif fonts, but they are considered a separate generic font family in Dreamweaver. Fonts that are not monospaced are **proportional fonts**, because each letter takes up a different width on the line proportional to the width of the letter—for example, the letter *i* takes less space than the letter *m*. Both the serif typeface Times New Roman and the sans-serif typeface Helvetica are proportional fonts.

A font must be installed on the end-user's computer for the page to be displayed using that font. If a font is not found on the client computer, the page will be displayed in the default font the end user has chosen for his or her browser. Dreamweaver arranges fonts into groups, which provide designers with the best chance for achieving the desired look for the page. Figure 2-10 lists the default Dreamweaver font groupings. Each group contains the most common names for the selected font; these common names include at least the most common PC name, the most common Mac name (when different), and the generic font family name. When you apply a font grouping to text, Dreamweaver places a

CSS style that contains all three choices around the specified text, thus ensuring maximum potential for aesthetic continuity across all platforms and all computers.

Figure 2-10

Default font groups in Dreamweaver

> Arial, Helvetica, sans-serif
> Times New Roman, Times, serif
> Courier New, Courier, mono
> Georgia, Times New Roman, Times, serif
> Verdana, Arial, Helvetica, sans-serif
> Geneva, Arial, Helvetica, sans-serif

Selecting a font also involves choosing a font color and font size, and sometimes a font style. **Font color** refers to the color that is applied to the font. The font color should be chosen from the colors you selected for the site's color palette. **Font size** refers to the size of the font. There are two types of font sizes: relative sizes and specific sizes. Relative font sizes define font size in respect to the default font size that the end user has set for his or her browser. Relative font sizes range from xx small to xx large, where xx small, x small, and small are smaller than the browser's default font size; medium is equal to the browser's default font size; and large, x large, and xx large appear bigger than the browser's default font size. Relative font sizes are often used as part of accessible design because the end user controls the default font size of the base font and can therefore change the size at which the text is displayed in the browser. Specific font sizes are fixed sizes. Using fixed font sizes enables the designer to decide exactly how a page will display in a user's browser. Pixels work well as a unit for defining a specific font size because the pixel unit is supported by both major browsers. **Font style** refers to the stylistic attributes that are applied to the font. Stylistic attributes include bold, italic, and underline.

As you select fonts for a Web site, keep in mind the following strategies:

- **Less is more.** In general, you should use no more than two fonts in a Web site so that the site will have a consistent look. You should use one font, one font size, and one font color for the general body text (although text links in the body text will be distinguished by a different color). You can use a second font, size, and color for headings.
- **Convert headings to images.** Sometimes headings and logos are actually text that has been converted to an image in a graphics program. By converting text into an image, the designer has greater control over the look of the final site, because the designer can choose a font that is not in the Dreamweaver font list and may not be found on every computer.
- **Consider what you are trying to convey.** Fonts create an impression about the content of the site. Different fonts are associated with specific types of content. For example, the titles of old horror movies always appeared in a gothic font; therefore, that font is usually associated with horror movies. Choose fonts that will support the concept and metaphor for the site.
- **Consider accessibility.** Visually impaired users of the Web site may have a hard time reading certain fonts or smaller sizes. Review accessibility Web sites to find guidelines about fonts and font size.

Brian decided to use black; size 14 pixels; and Arial, Helvetica, sans-serif for the general body text on the Catalyst Web site. Brian selected the Arial, Helvetica, sans-serif grouping because of its simplicity, which will help give the site a minimalist look. He used black text and the default font size because it is easy to read. The logo, headings, and site navigation categories will be graphics made from text using the Bauhaus Lt Bt font and a combination of the Web site palette colors. Brian selected the Bauhaus font, which was used prevalently on T-shirts and in advertising in the early 1970s, because it supports the site metaphor.

Although it is not necessary, designers often choose to have links formatted in different colors depending on their state. For example, Brian selected the following colors for links in the new Catalyst site. A **text link**, which is a hyperlink that has not yet been clicked, will be the color Yellow-Yellow-Orange. An **active link**, which is a text hyperlink that is in the process of being clicked, will be the color Dark-Hard-Orange. And a **visited link**, which is a text hyperlink that has been clicked, will be the color Orange-Orange-Red. See Figure 2-11.

Figure 2-11   **Font choices for the new Catalyst site**

Page Headings will be:
font group: Arial, Helvetica, sans-serif; size: heading 1; color: Dark-Hard-Orange

Subheadings will be:
font group: Arial, Helvetica, sans-serif; size: heading 2; color: Dark-Hard-Orange

linked text will be:
font group: Arial, Helvetica, sans-serif; color: Orange-Orange-Red

active links will be:
font group: Arial, Helvetica, sans-serif; color: Yellow-Yellow-Orange

visited links will be:
font group: Arial, Helvetica, sans-serif; color: Dark-Hard-Orange

body text will be:
font group: Arial, Helvetica, sans-serif; size: 14 pixels; color: Black

You'll select a set of fonts that will go with the concept and metaphor you developed for the Catalyst site.

To choose fonts:

1. Review accessibility Web sites for information about font choice, and then exit your browser.
2. Envision a font for the general body text that will work with the site concept and metaphor. Review the list in Figure 2-10 for a list of font grouping options.
3. Choose a font color from your site color palette for the body text.
4. Choose a color from your color palette for any text hyperlinks that will appear in the body text. Choose different colors for active links and visited links.
5. Choose a font size for the body text.
6. Choose a font, color, and size for the headings.
7. Write a brief explanation of your font choices.

Next, you'll select a graphic style.

Choosing a Graphic Style and Graphics

The graphics in a Web site provide the personality of the site. Recall that graphics can include images, photographs, buttons, logos, and so forth. **Graphic style** refers to the look of the graphic elements in the site. Designing a consistent look for all the graphics in a Web site is one of the keys to developing a cohesive, well-made Web site.

When selecting a graphic style, keep in mind the following strategies:

- **Be consistent.** If you use a cartoonish drawing for one button, then use cartoonish drawings for all the buttons. If you add a photographic image to the upper-right corner of one page, then consider adding photographic images to the upper-right corners of all the pages. Consistency in choosing graphics gives your site a cohesive look.
- **Design with purpose.** When you add a graphic to a page, ask yourself what the graphic adds to the page. Make sure that you have a reason for adding each graphic to the site.
- **Consider size.** Reduce all of the graphics to the smallest possible file size that you can get without sacrificing the quality of the image. The file size of each graphic contributes to the file size of the Web pages; and the smaller you can keep the file size of the Web pages, the faster they will load in the user's browser. You will have to use a graphics program such as Adobe Photoshop or Macromedia Fireworks to do this.
- **Consider the target audience.** Review the user profile and consider the technical capabilities of the target audience. Choose graphics that will not keep users from enjoying the site by making the pages load too slowly.
- **Support your concept and metaphor.** Choose graphics that reinforce the concept and metaphor of the site. Visual symbols are very powerful tools for conveying information. Make sure you consider what each graphic adds to the site, and make sure that each graphic reinforces the site metaphor.

Based on the Catalyst site goals, the CD cover art for the bands represented by the Catalyst label, the color palette, font choices, and site metaphor, Brian selected a graphic style that mimics the flat, traditional, two-dimensional style prevalent in magazine advertisements during the 1950s and 1960s. Any graphics used in the site will be combined with processed industrial photographs to create a "hip" recycled look. By juxtaposing design styles and images from an earlier time with modern music and content, the site will deconstruct both the old and the new, creating a style and depth that should appeal to the target audience. Figure 2-12 shows the new Catalyst logo as a sample of the graphic style that was chosen.

Sample of the graphic style for the new Catalyst site Figure 2-12

You should make a list of the graphics that you want to include in the site. Include logos, buttons, illustrations, and so forth.

You'll choose a graphic style for the site concept that you selected for the new Catalyst Web site.

To choose a graphic style and graphics:

1. Review the concept and metaphor for the site, the user profile, and the research that you gathered about sites that appeal to the target audience.
2. Make a list of the graphics that you want to include in the site (logos, buttons, illustrations, etc.).

3. Write a paragraph that describes the graphic style for your site. Explain how this graphic style supports your metaphor.

With the colors, fonts, and graphic style in place, you can determine the site's layout.

Sketching the Layout

The term *layout* comes from traditional print design. **Layout** is the position of elements, in this case, on the screen. When creating the layout, you decide where in the Web pages to place the navigation system, text, logo, artwork, and so forth. The layout should support the site goals and metaphor. It should be easy for a user to follow, and it should appeal to the target audience. Often, two or three effective layouts are possible. Initially, designers create rough sketches of possible layout designs. The client and design team then choose the sketch that they like best, and then create **comps** (comprehensive drawings) from the sketch. The comps are fully developed, detailed drawings that provide a complete preview of what the final design will look like.

Brian developed rough sketches of two possible layouts for the new Catalyst Web site, as shown in Figure 2-13. The first sketch places the site navigation system at the top of the page, whereas the second sketch places the site navigation system along the left side of the page. Although both layouts are effective, Brian decided to go with Layout 1. The top navigation system makes better use of the available space and appears to flow better with the selected graphic style.

Figure 2-13   **Layout sketches for the new Catalyst site**

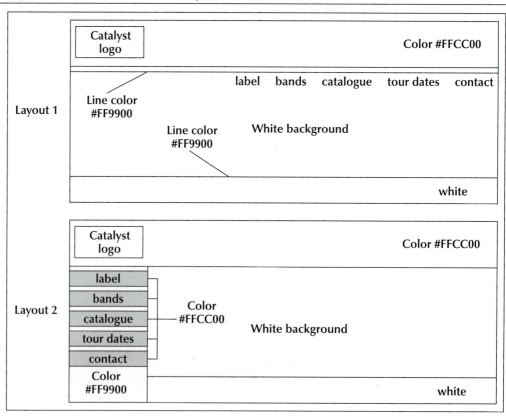

You'll draw a rough sketch of a layout that will support the site metaphor you have chosen.

To create a rough sketch of the site layout:

1. Draw a rough sketch of your site layout.
2. Add objects to represent items that you cannot draw, and label them. For example, draw a square the size of a photograph you plan to include and write a brief description of the photograph inside the square.
3. Add labels to identify the colors of each section and the lines (for example, write "white background" across the background).
4. Write a paragraph that explains why you selected this layout. Describe how the layout reinforces the site concept and metaphor and helps to achieve the site goals.

Before the design is considered complete, you need to review its logic.

Checking the Design for Logic

The final step of designing a site is to check the design for logic. It is important that the end user is able to navigate easily through the site. A Web site that is attractive to view but confusing to navigate is not well designed. When you check a design for logic, look at all of the elements of the site plan as though you were seeing them for the first time and answer the following questions:

- Is the navigation system easy to follow?
- Does the graphic style support the site metaphor?
- Do the individual elements flow together to create a consistent look for the site?

If you find problems or inconsistencies in any area, you'll need to work through the steps that pertain to the trouble area again, addressing the problems as you go. Brian has checked the new Catalyst Web site design and is satisfied that it is logical and consistent.

With the planning and design complete, you're ready to start building the site. You'll do this in the next session.

Session 2.2 Quick Check

1. What is information architecture?
2. What is the purpose of categories?
3. How is a flowchart used in Web design?
4. Why is gathering information similar to detective work?
5. What is a site concept?
6. Why would you want to consider accessibility issues when creating a Web site?
7. What are four color concepts and strategies?
8. True or False: Designing a consistent look for all the graphics in a Web site is one of the keys to developing a cohesive, well-made Web site.
9. What does the term *layout* mean?

Session 2.3

Creating a New Site

With the planning and design for the new Catalyst Web site complete, you're ready to create the site. You create a new site in Dreamweaver by setting up the site definition for the site. Remember that a site definition has two main parts—the local info and the remote info.

Creating a Local Site Definition

The process for creating the local site definition for a new site is the same as the process for creating one for an existing site. You need a site name and a local root folder to create the local site definition.

You'll use "NewCatalyst" as the site name to reference the site within Dreamweaver. Spaces are not used in site names, folder names, or filenames because they can cause problems with some operating systems. You can capitalize the first letter of each word to make each site or filename more readable. To keep your local root folder organized, it's a good idea to set up additional folders before you begin working on a site, and then to save all the site files to the folders you designated for them as you go. The local root folder for the site will be named "Dreamweaver," which will be stored in a project folder named "Catalyst" on the drive you select. Within the Dreamweaver folder, you will create a folder named "Graphics" so that you have a designated place within the local root folder to keep the copies of the graphics that you use in the site. This folder structure, Catalyst\Dreamweaver\Graphics, keeps the Dreamweaver files separate from original, uncompressed artwork and working project files that you have not yet added to the Web site.

You'll create the local site definition for the new Catalyst site.

To create the local site definition:

1. Start **Dreamweaver**, set your workspace environment to **Designer**, if it is not already set, and then close any pages that are open.

2. Click **Site** on the menu bar, and then click **Manage Sites**. The Manage Sites dialog box opens.

3. Click the **New** button, and then click **Site**. The Site Definition for Unnamed Site 1 dialog box opens.

4. Click the **Advanced** tab, if necessary, and then click **Local Info** in the Category list, if necessary.

5. Select the text in the Site Name text box, if necessary, and then type **NewCatalyst** (do not type a space between the words). NewCatalyst is the name you will use to reference the site.

   Filenames, folder names, and paths are often case-sensitive. Make sure you type the names exactly as shown in the steps.

6. Click the **Browse** button next to the Local Root Folder text box to open the Choose Local Root Folder for Site NewCatalyst dialog box, and then navigate to the location where you will store your Web site files.

   Trouble? If you are unsure of the location in which to store the Catalyst Web site, ask your instructor or technical support person for help.

7. Click the **Create New Folder** button in the Choose Local Root Folder for Site NewCatalyst dialog box, type **Catalyst** as the folder name, and then press the **Enter** key. The Catalyst folder is created.

8. Double-click the **Catalyst** folder to open it, click the **Create New Folder** button 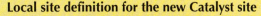 to create the new folder, type **Dreamweaver** as the folder name, press the **Enter** key to save the name, and then double-click the **Dreamweaver** folder to open it.

9. Click the **Select** button to set the path for the local root folder. You can also type the path to the local root folder in the Local Root Folder text box.

10. Click the **Refresh Local File List Automatically** check box to check it, if necessary.

11. Click the **Browse** button next to the Default Images Folder text box to open the Choose Local Images Folder for Site NewCatalyst dialog box, navigate to the **Catalyst\Dreamweaver** folder, which is the local root folder, click the **Create New Folder** button, type **Graphics** as the folder name, press the **Enter** key, click the **Open** button, and then click the **Select** button to set the path for the default images folder. You can also type the path to the Graphics folder in the Default Images Folder text box.

12. Click the **Enable Cache** check box to check it, if necessary. The information for the local site definition is complete. See Figure 2-14.

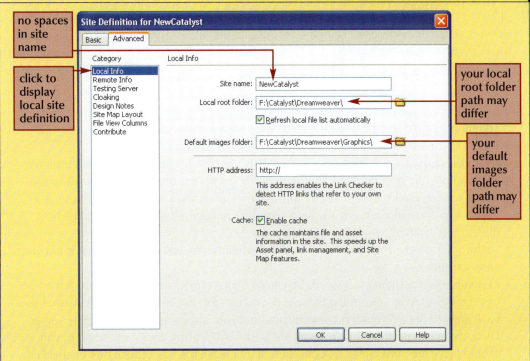

Figure 2-14 Local site definition for the new Catalyst site

Sometimes, Dreamweaver creates a folder in the local root folder named "_notes." Do not delete this folder, as it is necessary for Dreamweaver to display the site properly; however, you can ignore it.

Before you close the Site Definition dialog box, you'll create the remote site definition.

Creating a Remote Site Definition

A **remote site definition** is the information stored on the computer that you are using that tells Dreamweaver where the remote server is located and how to connect to it. Creating a remote site definition enables you to put the Web site on a Web server so that it can be seen on the Web. Viewing a site in a browser on the Web enables you to verify that the features of your Web site work in the browser and when viewed by others over the Web. You set the remote site definition in much the same way as you do the local site definition.

Reference Window

Creating a Remote Site Definition for FTP Access

- Click Site on the menu bar, and then click Manage Site.
- Click the site name in the list in the Manage Sites dialog box.
- Click the Edit button.
- Click the Advanced tab, if necessary, and then click Remote Info in the Category list.
- Click the Access list arrow, and then click FTP.
- Type the FTP host address where the public version of your Web site will be hosted in the FTP Host text box.
- Type the host directory name in the Host Directory text box.
- Type your login name in the Login text box.
- Type your password in the Password text box, and then check the Save check box if you want Dreamweaver to remember your password.
- Click the Use Passive FTP check box to check it.
- Verify that the Enable File Check In and Check Out check box is not checked.
- Click the OK button.
- Click the Done button in the Edit Sites dialog box.

First, you need to choose how you will access your Web server. Remote access is usually via FTP, although some larger organizations provide remote access through a local network. These tutorials use FTP in the remote site definition. The following list describes the FTP options you need to set:

- **FTP Host.** The full name of the FTP host, which is what you will use to access the Web server where the public version of your Web site will be stored. For example, the FTP host might be *www.domain.com* or *ftp.domain.com*. Do *not* include a protocol. (A common mistake is to precede the host name with a protocol, such as FTP:// or HTTP://.) The FTP host name is available from your hosting provider.
- **Host Directory.** The location where your Web site files are located on the Web server. For example, the host directory might be *public_html*. You often see more folders and files if you log on the host directory through FTP rather than with a Web browser; the Web folder is usually but not always a subfolder of your default FTP folder. The host directory is available from your hosting provider.
- **Login.** Your assigned login name. Be careful when typing your login name as it may be case-sensitive.
- **Password.** Your assigned password. Be careful when typing your password as it may be case-sensitive. After you set the password, you can use the Test button to verify that you have entered the information correctly and that you can connect to the remote server. Dreamweaver has the ability to save your password. During your work session, you should leave the Save check box checked. If you leave the Save check box unchecked, then you may have to re-enter your password periodically throughout your work session. If you are working on a public system, however, before ending your work session, open the Remote Info category in the Site Definition dialog box and uncheck the Save check box. This ensures that the next person to use the computer cannot load your site definition and log on to your account. *If you do not uncheck the Save check box, then your password remains on the computer.*
- **Use Passive FTP.** A server parameter. This information is available from your hosting provider. If you cannot obtain this information, leave the check box checked. If you have difficulties when you preview the site on the Web, reopen the Site Definition dialog box and uncheck the Use Passive FTP check box.
- **Use Firewall.** This option is relevant only if your computer includes a firewall that prevents outbound connections. (This is a rare occurrence, especially in schools, because

most firewalls restrict only inbound traffic.) A **firewall** is a hardware or software device that restricts access between the computer network and the Internet, thereby protecting the computer behind the firewall.
- **Use Secure FTP (SFTP).** This option is relevant only if you are using secure FTP. This information is available from your hosting provider. If you cannot obtain this information, leave the check box unchecked.
- **Automatically Upload Files.** This option automatically uploads files to the remote server when you save a page. Do not check this check box.
- **Check In/Out.** An option that enables multiple users to access files on the Web site.

You'll create a remote site definition so you'll be able to preview the Catalyst site on the Web. If you do not have access to FTP, then you will not be able to create and preview the remote Web site.

To create the remote site definition:

1. Click **Remote Info** in the Category list in the Site Definition for NewCatalyst dialog box.

   Trouble? If you do not have access to an FTP host on a Web server, you cannot create a remote site definition using these steps. Your instructor may provide you with directions for creating a remote site definition using a local network. If you do not have access to an FTP host on a Web server, continue with Steps 11 and 12 to save the local site definition.

2. Click the **Access** list arrow, and then click **FTP**. Additional options appear in the dialog box. See Figure 2-15.

Figure 2-15   Remote site definition for FTP access

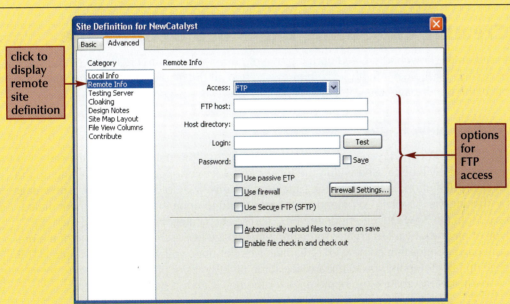

3. Click in the **FTP Host** text box and then type the address to the FTP Host, which enables you to connect to the server where the public version of your Web site will be hosted.
4. Press the **Tab** key to move the insertion point to the Host Directory text box, and then type the host directory name.
5. Press the **Tab** key to move the insertion point to the Login text box, and then type your login or user name. Remember that on many systems, the login ID is case-sensitive.

6. Press the **Tab** key to move the insertion point to the Password text box, and then type your password. Remember that on many systems, the password is case-sensitive.

7. Click the **Test** button. Dreamweaver tests the connection to ensure that you can connect to the remote server.

   Trouble? If the connection fails, you might have entered some of the information incorrectly. Verify the information you entered in Steps 3 through 6, and then repeat Step 7.

8. Click the **Save** check box to check it, if necessary. Dreamweaver will remember your password. If you are working on a public computer, remember to uncheck the Save check box before you end your work session.

9. Click the **Use Passive FTP** check box to check it.

10. If your computer uses a firewall that restricts outbound connections, click the **Use Firewall** check box to check it, and then enter the additional information.

11. Verify that the **Automatically Upload Files to Server on Save** and the **Enable File Check In and Check Out** check boxes are unchecked.

12. Click the **OK** button. The Site Definition for NewCatalyst dialog box closes and the site definition is saved.

    A dialog box might open with the message that the initial site cache will be created.

13. If necessary, click the **Done** button to close the dialog box. The site definition for the new Catalyst Web site is complete.

You will create pages for the new Catalyst site.

Creating and Saving Pages in a Defined Site

Based on the flowchart created during planning, Brian asks you to create, save, and set page titles for the new Catalyst site home page and all the first-level Web pages: the Label page, the Bands page, the Catalogue page, the Tour Dates page, and the Contact page.

Adding New Pages

Once a site is defined, you can create the pages that will be associated with the site. These pages will be located within the local root folder you specified when setting up the local site definition, in this case, the Catalyst\Dreamweaver folder. You create a new page by clicking the New File command on the File menu to open the New Document dialog box. From the New Document dialog box, you select a category of pages and then the type of page you want to create. You can create a page from scratch or use one of the prebuilt page designs that come with Dreamweaver. For now, you will create a simple HTML page. In later tutorials, you will learn about the other types of pages.

You'll start by creating the home page for the new Catalyst site.

To add a new page to a site:

1. Click **File** on the menu bar, and then click **New**. The New Document dialog box opens with the General tab selected.

2. Click **Basic Page** in the Category list, if necessary, and then click **HTML** in the Basic Page list. See Figure 2-16. You could also click HTML in the Create New list on the Start page to create a basic HTML page.

Figure 2-16 New Document dialog box

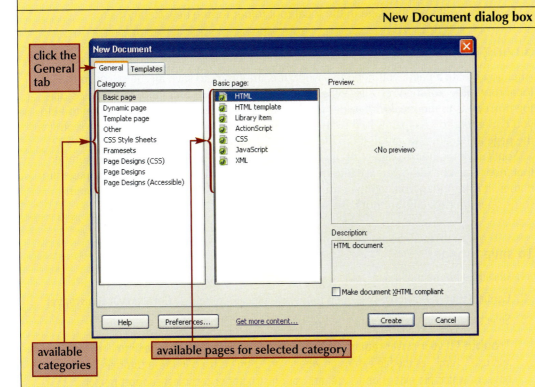

3. Click the **Create** button to create the page. The Untitled-1 page opens in the Document window. See Figure 2-17.

Figure 2-17 New page in the Document window

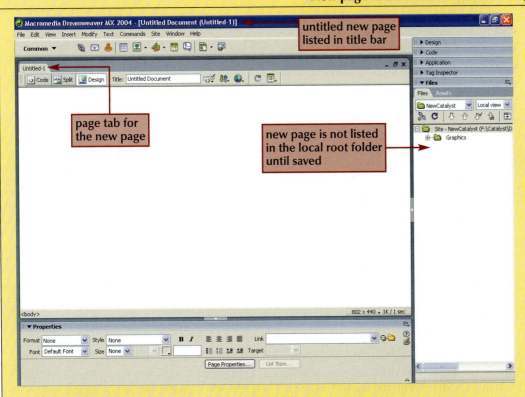

Trouble? If your Document window is restored down, you need to maximize it. Click the Maximize button on the Document window title bar.

Next, you will save the page in the local root folder for the new Catalyst site.

Saving New Pages

After you create a page, you need to save it. It is important to save all the pages in the local root folder for the Web site. When you use the Save As command, the Save As dialog box opens to the local root folder for the site that is selected in the Files panel to help you remember to save pages in the site's local root folder. When you save a page, you give the page a filename. Recall that the filename is the name under which a page is saved.

You'll save the home page with the filename of index.htm (or index.html); remember that *index* must be all lowercase letters. You'll use lowercase letters for all of the page filenames. It is important to keep the case of the filenames consistent because, although some operating systems are not case-sensitive, some are.

To save a page:

1. Click **File** on the menu bar, and click **Save As**. The Save As dialog box opens.
2. Confirm that the dialog box is open to the site's local root folder: **Catalyst\Dreamweaver**.
3. Select the text in the File Name text box, and then type **index.htm**.

   Trouble? If your server requires .html file extensions, then type "index.html" in Step 3 and use ".html" as the file extension whenever ".htm" is used in these tutorials. If you are not sure which file extension to use, ask your instructor or technical support person.

4. Click the **Save** button. The new filename appears in the page tab at the top of the Document window, in the title bar, and in the Files panel. See Figure 2-18.

| Figure 2-18 | Saved page in the Document window |

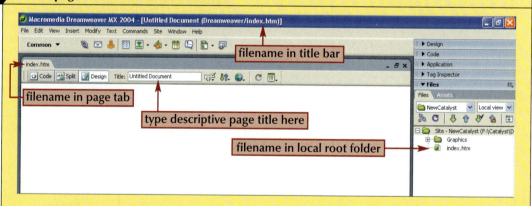

Trouble? If you don't see the new file in the Files panel, the Files panel is probably set to show Remote view. Click the View list arrow on the Files panel toolbar, and then click Local View.

Before you close the page, you'll set the page title for the page.

Setting Page Titles

Recall that the page title is the name that will appear in the browser title bar. You should use the name of the Web site and a descriptive word or phrase for each page so that users can quickly determine the overall page content. You add a page title by typing the text in the Title text box on the Document toolbar. The page title then appears in the title bar.

You'll enter "Catalyst - Home" as the page title for the home page.

To add a page title to a page:

1. Drag to select **Untitled Document** in the Title text box on the Document toolbar.
2. Type **Catalyst - Home** in the Title text box on the Document toolbar.
3. Press the **Enter** key. The title bar information for the page shows the new title. The asterisks next to the filename in the title bar and in the page tab at the top of the Document window indicate that changes have been made to the page since the last time it was saved. See Figure 2-19.

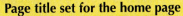

Figure 2-19 Page title set for the home page

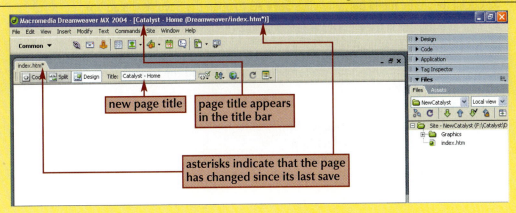

After you add the page title to a page, you should resave the page.

Resaving Pages

It is important to save frequently—at least every ten minutes—and whenever you have finished modifying a page. You should also make sure all pages in the site are saved before you preview the site. Anyone who has worked on a computer for any length of time can confirm that programs crash at the least opportune moment. Saving your work frequently prevents large losses.

There are a few measures built into Dreamweaver to help you keep your work safe. If you have not saved a page after you have edited it and you try to close the page or exit the program, Dreamweaver will ask if you want to save the changes you made to that page. If you use an element, such as a graphic, in a page, and that element is not yet part of the site, Dreamweaver will ask if you want to save a copy of the element in the local root folder. By including copies of all of the files associated with a site within its local root folder, you prevent a myriad of complications from occurring.

You'll resave the home page, and then you'll close the page.

To resave and close a page:

1. Click **File** on the menu bar, and then click **Save**. The asterisk next to the filename in the Document window title bar disappears.
2. Click the **Close Page** button ✖ on the Document window title bar to close the home page.

You'll use a similar process to create and save the remaining top-level pages for the new Catalyst site. Rather than opening the New Document dialog box each time, you'll use the HTML link on the Start page.

To create and save additional new pages:

1. Click **HTML** in the Create New list on the Start page.
2. Select **Untitled Document** in the Title text box on the Document toolbar, type **Catalyst - Bands**, and then press the **Enter** key. The title bar shows the new title for the page.
3. Click **File** on the menu bar, and click **Save As** to open the Save As dialog box.
4. Type **bands.htm** in the File Name text box, and then press the **Save** button.
5. Click the **Close Page** button ✖ on the Document window title bar to close the page.
6. Repeat Steps 1 through 5 for the remaining pages, using the following filenames and page titles:

Page Title	Filename
Catalyst - Catalogue	catalogue.htm
Catalyst - Contact	contact.htm
Catalyst - Label	label.htm
Catalyst - Tourdates	tourdates.htm

Now that you have created the pages of the Catalyst site, you will review the HTML tags in the pages.

Reviewing the HTML Tags

The most common language of the Web is Hypertext Markup Language (HTML), which provides instructions for how to format Web pages for display. Because many types of computers are connected to the Web and people use different operating systems and software on their computers, Web pages are not tied to any specific software package; rather they are created in a common markup language that is viewable by a variety of software packages (including Web browsers). HTML uses a series of tags to tell a browser what to do with the information on a Web page and how to display it.

Even though Dreamweaver provides a graphical interface for creating a Web site in HTML, it is important to have a basic understanding of HTML in order to gain a true sense of what is going on. Web pages are text documents that include specific markup tags that tell a Web browser how to display the elements. Tags almost always appear in sets, and each tag is included within angle brackets, < and >. The opening tag tells a browser that a certain type of information will be following. The opening tag also contains any parameters or attributes that are to be applied to that information. The closing tag always starts with a forward slash, /, which tells the browser that the type of information that had been started is now finished.

Some tags are required for every Web page. These tags—HTML, head, title, and body—are described in Figure 2-20.

Figure 2-20 Basic HTML tags

Name	Opening Tag	Closing Tag	Description
HTML	<html>	</html>	Signify where the HTML coding begins and ends; usually appear at the beginning and ending of a Web page. Everything inside the <html> and </html> tags is HTML unless specifically denoted as something else by another type of tag.
head section	<head>	</head>	Contain the page title, the descriptive information for the page which is not seen in the browser, and programming scripts.
title	<title>	</title>	Surround the page title, which appears in the title bar of the browser window when a viewer opens that page.
body	<body>	</body>	Surround all the content or visible elements on the page. Includes other tags to format the content. Also contains some scripts.

Many other tags appear within the body of a document to format the content. In addition, other code, such as JavaScript and Cascading Styles, are sometimes used within HTML to add additional functionality to pages. For example, you might include a JavaScript that will adjust the page to optimize display for the user's browser. You'll see these additional tags as you continue to build the pages for the new Catalyst Web site.

You'll review the HTML tags that Dreamweaver generated when you created the Web pages.

To review HTML tags:

1. Double-click **index.htm** in the Files panel. The home page opens in the Document window.
2. Click the **Show Code View** button on the Document toolbar. The Document window displays the underlying HTML coding for the home page. See Figure 2-21. The line numbers are only for the user's reference; the line numbers shown in the figure may not match the ones on your screen. Also, the lines of code on your screen may wrap differently than those in the figure.

Figure 2-21 HTML code for the home page

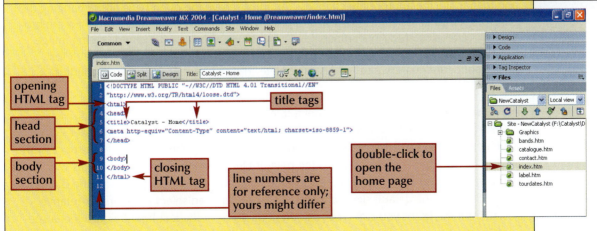

Trouble? If you cannot see all of the code, you may need to scroll the window. Drag the horizontal scroll box all the way to the left edge of the horizontal scroll bar.

3. Click the **Close Page** button ✖ on the Document window title bar to close the home page.

Although you will usually work in Design view, you can create and edit your pages in Code view. You'll use Code view to change the page title for the Tour Dates page from "Catalyst - Tourdates" to "Catalyst - Tour Dates."

To edit a page in Code view:

1. Double-click **tourdates.htm** in the Files panel to open the Tour Dates page in the Document window, and then click the **Show Code View** button [Code] on the Document toolbar, if necessary. The Tour Dates page is displayed in Code view.

2. Locate the title tags in the Document window.

3. Select the **Catalyst - Tourdates** text between the opening and closing title tags, and then type **Catalyst - Tour Dates**. The page title is updated. You'll switch to Design view to review the change.

4. Click the **Show Design View** button [Design] on the Document toolbar. The Tour Dates page is displayed in Design view. The text both in the Title text box on the Document toolbar and in the title bar show the revised page title, which you changed directly in the code.

5. Click **File** on the menu bar, and then click **Save** to save the change you made to the Tour Dates page.

6. Click the **Close Page** button ✖ on the Document window title bar to close the Tour Dates page.

Next, you will set the page properties for the pages in the new Catalyst site.

Setting Page Properties

Once you have created a page, the next step is setting the basic page properties. **Page properties** are attributes that apply to an entire page rather than to only an element in the page. To set page properties, you open the page for which you want to set page properties, and then make the appropriate changes. You must resave the open page after changing the page properties to associate the new properties with that page. The page properties are broken into five categories: Appearance, Links, Headings, Title/Encoding, and Tracing Image.

The Appearance category includes general page properties, such as the default text, background, and margin attributes for the page. The different Appearance properties include:

- **Text settings.** The page font is the default font that is used to display page text. Remember that fonts can be displayed only if they are installed on the end user's computer and that Dreamweaver groups fonts to ensure the highest possibility of successful display. The Page Font list contains the default Dreamweaver font groupings, as was shown in Figure 2-10. You will use the Arial, Helvetica, sans-serif group for the Catalyst site. Size sets the default size for text in the page. You can select a specific or relative size from the list or you can type a different font size in the text box. If you select a specific size, you must also choose a unit selection. Pixels are the most frequently used unit for specific font size. You'll use a variety of sizes in the Catalyst site. The text color sets the default color for text on the page. The initial default text color is black, which has the hexadecimal color code #000000. When you want to select a different color and do not know its hexadecimal color code, you use the color picker to select from a visual display in Dreamweaver, and Dreamweaver will insert the hexadecimal color code. It is best to use the hexadecimal color code, if you know it, to ensure that you always use the exact same color each time you insert the color. Figure 2-22 shows the color picker in the Page Properties dialog box.

Page Properties dialog box with the color picker open Figure 2-22

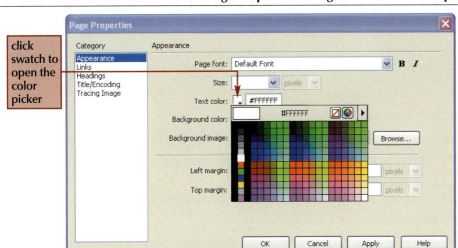

click swatch to open the color picker

- **Background settings.** You can set the Background color and the Background image for the page. A Web page background can be an image, a color, or both. If both are used, the color will appear while the image is downloading, and then the image will cover up the color. If the image contains transparent pixels, then the background color will show through. The default background is no color, and most browsers display an absence of color as white. You'll use white, which has the hexadecimal color code #FFFFFF, for the background color of the new Catalyst site. You will also use a background image for the new Catalyst site.
- **Margin settings. Margins** are measurements that specify where page content is placed in the page. You can specify left, right, bottom, and top page margin spaces. The new Catalyst site will have left and right margins of 5 and top and bottom margins of 0.

The Links category includes the page properties for hyperlinked text. You can select Same as Page Font from the Link Font list to use the page font for hyperlinked text or you can select a different Font group from the list if you want hyperlinked text to appear in another font. For the Catalyst site, you will use the same font for links and text and you will not set a size. You can set a default color for hyperlinked text in the page. If you do not specify a color for visited or active links, the browser's default colors will be used. The new Catalyst Web site will use Yellow-Yellow-Orange for the links, Orange-Orange-Red for the visited links, and Dark-Hard-Orange for the active links. The final attribute in the Links category is the Underline option. You can choose to always underline linked text, never underline linked text, show underline only on rollover, or hide underline on rollover. The Catalyst site will use the Always Underline option.

The Headings category enables you to set font, font size, and font color attributes for the headings in your page. You will set two headings for the Catalyst site. The top-level heading, Heading 1, will be 30 pixels in size and the color Dark-Hard-Orange. The second-level heading, Heading 2, will be 20 pixels in size and the color Dark-Hard-Orange.

The Title/Encoding category enables you to set the page title and document encoding type. The page title can also be set from the Document window, as you did earlier. **Document encoding** specifies how the digital codes will display the characters in the Web page. The default Western [Latin1] setting is the setting for English and other Western European languages.

Finally, the Tracing Image category enables you to select an image as a guide for re-creating a design or mock-up that was originally created in a graphics program. For example, if you created a mock-up of your site in Adobe PhotoShop, you could import a copy of that mock-up into Dreamweaver as a tracing image. Then you could use that image as a reference while re-creating the individual elements in Dreamweaver. The tracing image is visible only in the Dreamweaver environment.

You'll set the page properties for the pages you added to the new Catalyst site.

To set Appearance page properties:

1. Double-click **index.htm** in the Files panel to open the home page.
2. Click **Modify** on the menu bar, and then click **Page Properties**. The Page Properties dialog box opens with the Appearance category selected.
3. Click the **Page Font** list arrow, and then click **Arial, Helvetica, sans-serif**.
4. Click the **Size** list arrow, and then click **14**.
5. Click in the **Text Color** text box, type **#000000**, which is the hexadecimal color code for black, and then press the **Tab** key. The color box changes to black to match the color code you just entered.
6. Click the **Background Color** box to open the color picker, and then point to the **white swatch** in the pop-up color picker. The hexadecimal color code at the top of the color picker changes as you move the pointer over the color swatches.
7. Click the **white swatch** in the color picker to select white as the background color. The hexadecimal code #FFFFFF appears in the Background Color text box.
8. Click the **Browse** button next to the Background Image text box to open the Select Image Source dialog box, navigate to the **Tutorial.02\Tutorial** folder included with your Data Files, and then double-click **background.gif**. The image is selected as the background image. A copy of the image is placed in the Graphics folder and the file path is displayed in the Background Image text box.
9. Click in the **Left Margin** text box, and then type **5**.
10. Press the **Tab** key twice to move the insertion point to the Right Margin text box, and then type **5**.
11. Press the **Tab** key twice to move the insertion point to the Top Margin text box, and then type **0**.
12. Press the **Tab** key twice to move the insertion point to the Bottom Margin text box, and then type **0**. See Figure 2-23.

Figure 2-23

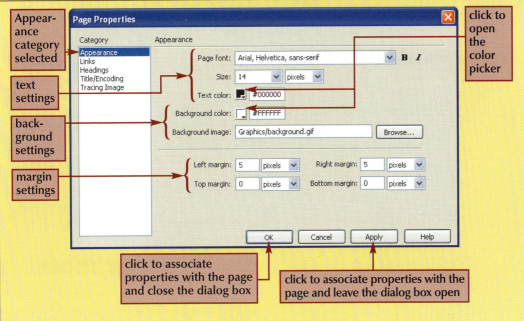

Completed Appearance category in the Page Properties dialog box

You've entered all the Appearance properties. Next, you'll set the page properties for the Links category.

To set Links page properties:

1. Click **Links** in the Category list. The Page Properties dialog box shows the settings for the Links category.

2. Click in the **Link Color** text box, and then type **#FFCC00**, which is the hexadecimal color code for Yellow-Yellow-Orange.

3. Press the **Tab** key four times to move the insertion point to the Visited Links text box, and then type **#FF6600**, which is the hexadecimal color code for Orange-Orange-Red.

4. Press the **Tab** key twice to move the insertion point to the Active Links text box, and then type **#FF9900**, which is the hexadecimal color code for Dark-Hard-Orange. See Figure 2-24.

| Figure 2-24 | Completed Links category in the Page Properties dialog box |

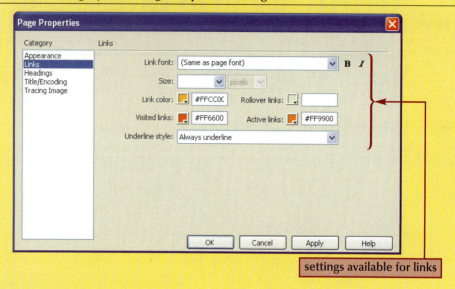

settings available for links

You've entered all the Links properties. Next, you'll set the page properties for the Heading 1 category.

To set Headings page properties:

1. Click **Headings** in the Category list. The Page Properties dialog box shows the settings for the Headings category.
2. Type **30** in the Heading 1 text box.
3. Press the **Tab** key three times to move to the Heading 1 color input text box, and then type **#FF9900**, which is the hexadecimal color code for Dark-Hard-Orange. See Figure 2-25.

| Figure 2-25 | Completed Headings category in the Page Properties dialog box |

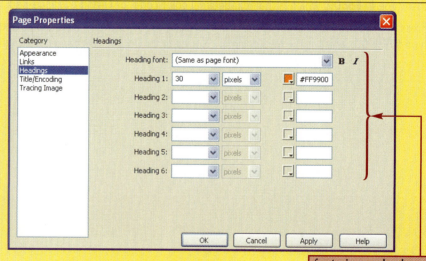

font, size, and color settings for each heading

You've entered all the page properties for the home page. You'll close the Page Properties dialog box, and then save and close the home page.

To save the page properties:

1. Click the **OK** button. The Page Properties dialog box closes, and the property settings are applied to the home page. See Figure 2-26.

Home page with the page properties set — Figure 2-26

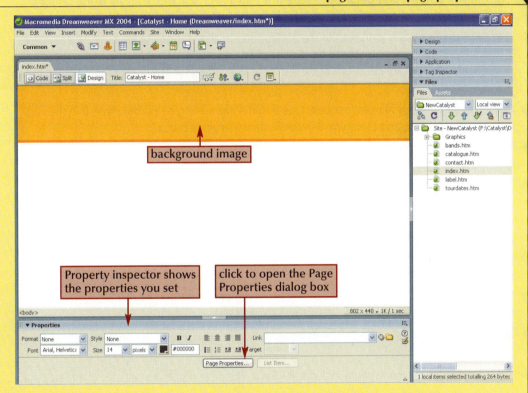

2. Click **File** on the menu bar, and then click **Save**. The page properties are saved with the page.
3. Click the **Close Page** button ✖ on the Document window title bar to close the home page.

Next, you'll set the page properties for the other pages you created for the new Catalyst site: bands.htm, catalogue.htm, contact.htm, label.htm, and tourdates.htm. Remember that you need to include only one copy of the background.gif image in the Graphics folder.

To set page properties for additional pages:

1. Double-click **bands.htm** in the Files panel to open the Bands page, and then click the **Page Properties** button in the Property inspector. The Page Properties dialog box opens with the Appearance category selected.
2. Click the **Page Font** list arrow, and then click **Arial, Helvetica, sans-serif**.
3. Click the **Size** list arrow, and then click **14**.
4. Type **#000000** in the Text Color text box to change the text color to black.
5. Click the **Background Color** box to open the color picker, and then click the **white swatch**. The hexadecimal code #FFFFFF appears in the Background Color text box.
6. Click the **Browse** button next to the Background Image text box to open the Select Image Source dialog box, navigate to the **Catalyst\Dreamweaver\Graphics** folder, and then double-click **background.gif**. You'll use this same image for the background image on all the pages.
7. Type **5** in the Left Margin text box, type **5** in the Right Margin text box, type **0** in the Top Margin text box, and then type **0** in the Bottom Margin text box.
8. Click **Links** in the Category list. The Page Properties dialog box shows the settings for the Links category.
9. Type **#FFCC00** (the hexadecimal color code for Yellow-Yellow-Orange) in the Link Color text box, type **#FF6600** (the hexadecimal color code for Orange-Orange-Red) in the Visited Links text box, and then type **#FF9900** (the hexadecimal color code for Dark-Hard-Orange) in the Active Links text box.
10. Click **Headings** in the Category list. The Page Properties dialog box shows the settings for the Headings category.
11. Type **30** in the Heading 1 text box, and then type **#FF9900** (the hexadecimal color code for Dark-Hard-Orange) in the Heading 1 color input text box.
12. Click the **OK** button. The Page Properties dialog box closes, and the property settings are applied to the page.
13. Click **File** on the menu bar, and then click **Save**. The page properties are saved with the page.
14. Click the **Close Page** button ✖ on the Document window title bar to close the page.
15. Repeat Steps 1 through 14 to set the page properties for the following pages: **catalogue.htm**, **contact.htm**, **label.htm**, and **tourdates.htm**.

You have finished creating the pages for the new Catalyst site and setting the page properties. Now you will preview the site.

Previewing a Site in a Browser

There are often variations in the way that different browsers display Web pages; there are even variations in the way that different versions of the same browser will display Web pages. That is why, once you have started building a Web site, you should preview it in the various browsers that you are planning to support. Catalyst plans to support both Internet Explorer and Netscape Navigator, the two most commonly used browsers.

You can preview your site in any browser that is in the Dreamweaver Preview list. You may need to add the browser in which you want to preview your Web pages to the Preview list. You should designate the two browsers that you consider most important as the primary and secondary browsers. Dreamweaver defaults to the primary browser when you preview your work, and both the primary and secondary browsers have keyboard shortcuts.

To make a browser your primary browser, you check the Primary Browser check box when adding the browser to your list. To make a browser the secondary browser you check the Secondary Browser check box. If you do not check either the Primary or Secondary check box, the browser will be added to the Preview in Browser list on the File menu but it will not have a keyboard shortcut. These tutorials use Internet Explorer version 6 as the primary browser.

To add a browser to the Preview list:

1. Click **File** on the menu bar, point to **Preview in Browser**, and then click **Edit Browser List**. The Preferences dialog box opens with Preview in Browser selected in the Category list. See Figure 2-27.

Figure 2-27 — Preferences dialog box

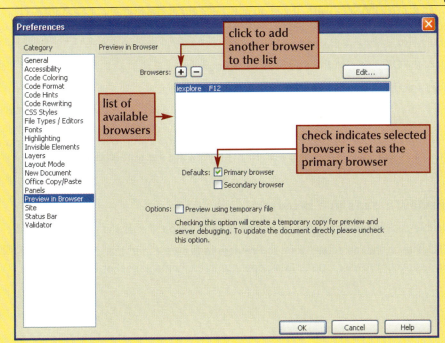

2. Look for the browser that you use in the Browsers list box. If the browser is listed, click the browser to select it, check the Primary Browser or Secondary Browser check box as needed, and then skip to Step 8. If the browser is not listed, continue with Step 3.

3. If you need to add a browser, click the Browsers **Plus (+)** button . The Add Browser dialog box opens. See Figure 2-28.

Figure 2-28   **Add Browser dialog box**

4. Type the name of the browser you are adding in the Name text box.

5. Click the **Browse** button to open the Select Browser dialog box, navigate to the folder containing the browser that you want to add, click the browser program icon, and then click the **Open** button. The path to the file that you selected appears in the Application text box.

   Trouble? If you cannot find the browser program icon on the computer that you are using, ask your instructor or technical support person for help.

6. Click the **Primary Browser** check box to insert a check mark if you want Dreamweaver to default to this browser when you preview your work. Check the **Secondary Browser** check box to check it if you want this to be the secondary browser choice that you can access when previewing your work. If you do not check either the Primary or Secondary check box, the browser will be added to the Preview in Browser list on the File menu, but it will not have a keyboard shortcut.

7. Click the **OK** button in the Add Browser dialog box.

8. Click the **OK** button in the Preferences dialog box.

Once a browser has been added to Dreamweaver, you can preview the pages you created for the new Catalyst site. You'll start by previewing the home page.

To preview a page in a browser:

1. Double-click **index.htm** in the Files panel. The home page opens in the Document Window.

2. Click **File** on the menu bar, point to **Preview in Browser**, and then click **iexplore** or the name of your browser. The browser opens with the home page. See Figure 2-29.

Figure 2-29 Home page previewed in Internet Explorer

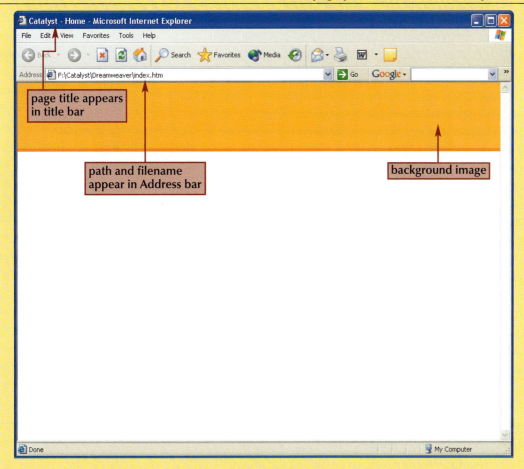

3. Review the page. The background image is displayed, the page title appears in the title bar, and the filename is shown in the Address bar.

4. Click the **Close** button ⊠ on the browser window title bar to close the browser window. The other pages should all look the same at this point, so you won't preview them yet.

5. Click the **Close Page** button ✖ on the Document window title bar to close the home page.

Next, you will preview your site from the Web.

Uploading a Web Site to a Remote Location

Once you have created pages in your Web site, you should upload the site to your remote location— either a Web server or your network server.

You upload a Web site to your server so that you can view the site over the Web as the end users will see it. Previewing the site from within Dreamweaver is a convenient way to check your site for problems while you are working, but you should also upload your site periodically (at least once a day) to make sure that it displays correctly. Sometimes there are differences in the way a page previews from within Dreamweaver and the way it actually looks when it is viewed on the Web.

You set the parameters when you created the remote site definition, so the rest is easy. You upload Web sites from the Files panel. First, you connect to the remote server where your site will be located, using the Connects to Remote Host button on the Files panel toolbar. Then, you select the files in the local root folder that you want to upload, pressing the Ctrl key as you select nonadjacent files or pressing the Shift key to select a block of adjacent files. Finally, you "put" the selected files on the server, using the Put File(s) button on the Files panel toolbar. When you are done, you should disconnect from the remote server using the Disconnects from Remote Host button on the Files panel toolbar.

All of the files that the remote version of a Web site will use must be located on the Web server. The first time you upload a site, you must include all the files and folders for the site, including the graphics located in the Graphics folder. From then on, you update the remote site by uploading only files that you have changed. When you upload a Web page or group of pages, Dreamweaver will ask you if you want to upload the dependent files. **Dependent files** are files such as the graphics files that are used in the Web page or pages. If you have not yet uploaded these files, or if you have modified them, you will need to upload these dependent files. However, if you have already uploaded them and you have not modified them, it is not necessary to upload them again.

When you upload the pages to the remote server, be careful to use the Put File(s) button on the Files panel toolbar, not the Get File(s) button. The Get File(s) button downloads the files from the remote server to your local root folder, and you might overwrite the more current files in your local root folder.

You will upload the new Catalyst site to the remote server so you can preview it on the Web.

To upload a site to the remote server:

1. Click the **Connects to Remote Host** button on the Files panel toolbar. When Dreamweaver is connected to the remote host, you see a green light on the Connects to Remote Host button. Dreamweaver connects to the remote host, and the Files panel changes to Remote view.

    Trouble? If you do not have access to a remote host, you cannot upload your site. Check with your instructor to see if he or she has alternate instructions. If not, skip to Step 9.

2. Click the **View** list arrow on the Files panel toolbar, and then click **Local View**.

3. Click the **Graphics** folder, press and hold the **Shift** key, and then click **tourdates.htm** to select all of the files in the local file list. These are the files you want to upload to the server.

4. Click the **Put File(s)** button on the Files panel toolbar. A dialog box opens, asking if you want to include dependent files. You have already selected all of the dependent files for the site—the Graphics folder—in addition to the pages.

5. Click the **No** button.

6. Click the **View** list arrow, and then click **Remote View**. The Files panel switches to Remote view and you see the list of files you uploaded to the remote server.

7. Click the **Expand/Collapse** button 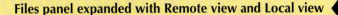 on the Files panel toolbar. The Files panel expands to display both the Remote and Local views. See Figure 2-30.

Figure 2-30 Files panel expanded with Remote view and Local view

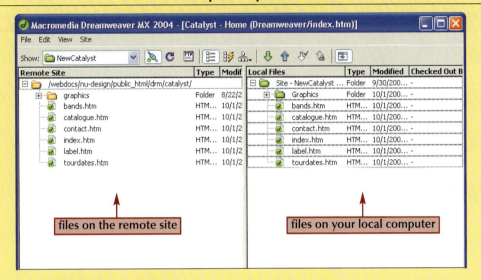

files on the remote site

files on your local computer

8. Click the **Disconnects from Remote Host** button on the Files panel toolbar, click the **Expand/Collapse** button on the Files panel toolbar to collapse the Files panel, click the **View** list arrow, and then click **Local View** to return to Local view.

 If you are working on a public computer, continue with Step 9; otherwise skip to Step 11.

9. If you are working on a public computer, click **Site** on the menu bar, click **Manage Sites** to open the Manage Sites dialog box, make sure **NewCatalyst** is selected in the list, and then click the **Edit** button. The Site Definition for NewCatalyst dialog box opens.

10. Click **Remote Info** in the Category list, click the **Save** check box to uncheck it, click the **OK** button, and then click the **Done** button in the Edit Sites dialog box. Now, the next person who uses the computer cannot load your site definition and log on to your account.

Next, you'll preview your Web site on the remote server.

Previewing on the Web

Once the files are uploaded to the remote site, you and others can view them in a browser. You'll explore the remote site using a browser to check if the page looks the same on the Web as it does in Dreamweaver. If you find differences, such as extra spaces, write them down and discuss them with your instructor. At this point, the only difference that you should see is in the site address. When you preview over the Web, the site will have an actual Web address instead of a file path.

To view a site from a remote location:

1. Start your browser, type the URL of your remote site into the Address bar on the browser toolbar, and then press the **Enter** key. The index.htm page of the NewCatalyst site from the remote server loads in the browser window. See Figure 2-31.

| Figure 2-31 | Catalyst home page viewed over the Internet |

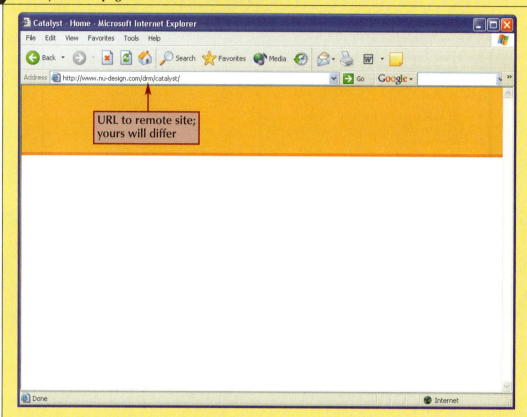

Trouble? If the browser window displays the list of files stored on the remote site, double-click the index.htm file to open the home page.

Trouble? If the browser displays a warning that the listing was denied, type the base URL of the remote site, type "/" (a forward slash), and then type "index.htm" into the Address bar in your browser's toolbar.

Trouble? If any pages or items are missing or do not display correctly, the files might have been corrupted during the upload process or you might not have uploaded all the dependent files. Repeat the previous set of steps to upload all of the files to the remote location. If you still have problems and your remote server is a Windows server, using an outside FTP program to upload all the files to your remote server may solve the problem (see the Read This Before You Begin page for more information). If you still have problems with your remote site, you might need to edit the remote site definition and click the Use Passive FTP check box to uncheck it. Ask your instructor or technical support person for help.

2. Click the **Close** button ✕ on the browser title bar to close the browser window.

You have finished creating the pages for the new Catalyst site, setting the page properties for the home page, and previewing the page. In the next tutorial, you'll add and format the text on each page.

Review

Session 2.3 Quick Check

1. What are the two main parts of the site definition?
2. What is the purpose of creating a remote site definition?
3. What happens when you click the New command on the File menu?
4. When should you save your work?
5. True or False? Web pages are created in a markup language that is viewable by only specific software packages.
6. Explain what page properties are.
7. What are two ways to preview a site you are creating?
8. What are dependent files?

Review

Tutorial Summary

In this tutorial, you planned the structure of the new Catalyst Web site. You determined the site's goals, defined a target audience, and created an end-user profile. Then you researched the intended market and created end-user scenarios. You used this information to make preliminary decisions about the new Catalyst Web site.

You also created the information architecture for the Catalyst Web site, which included creating a flowchart and organizing information categories. Then you designed the site by developing a site metaphor. You also established a color palette, a font set, a graphic style, and a layout design for the site.

Finally, you created a new site. You set up the site definition for both the local and remote information. You added all the top-level pages to the site, and then reviewed the HTML tags that Dreamweaver compiled. You set the page properties for each page. And you previewed the site in a browser and on the Web.

Key Terms

accessibility
active link
additive color system
assistive device
client
comp
dependent file
document encoding
end-user scenario
firewall
flowchart
font
font color
font size

font style
generic font families
graphic style
hexadecimal
hexadecimal color code
information architecture
layout
margin
market research
metaphor
monospaced font
navigation system
page properties
proportional font

remote site definition
RGB system
sans-serif typeface
search engine
serif typeface
site concept
subtractive color system
target audience
text link
user profile
visited link
Web Safe Color Palette

Practice

Practice the skills you learned in the tutorial.

Review Assignments

There are no Data Files needed for the Review Assignments.

Web design teams often develop two or three Web site layouts and designs for a client, who then chooses one concept for development. The alternate design can have a different metaphor, be based on reordered site goals, or geared for another target audience. Sara is considering expanding the Catalyst label to include Texas Blues bands. Brian asks you to plan and design an alternate Catalyst site for a band lineup devoted to Texas Blues bands.

1. Define a list of site goals for the alternate Catalyst site.
2. Do research and identify the target audience for the alternate Catalyst site.
3. Create a user profile for the alternate Catalyst site.
4. Conduct market research to gather information about Texas Blues music Web sites and other Web sites that cater to your target audience.
5. Develop two end-user scenarios for the alternate Catalyst site.
6. Create an information category outline arranged in hierarchical order for the alternate Catalyst site.
7. Create a flowchart for the alternate Catalyst site.
8. Develop a site concept and a metaphor for the alternate Catalyst site.
9. Choose a color palette, fonts, and a graphic style for the alternate Catalyst site.
10. Create a rough sketch of the layout for the alternate Catalyst Web site.
11. Create a local site definition using "CatalystBlues" as the site name and use the Browse button to identify the local root folder as a Dreamweaver folder that you create within a folder named "CatalystBlues" in the location where you are storing your Web site files. Refresh the local file list automatically, and enable cache.
12. Create a remote site definition using FTP access for the CatalystBlues site.
13. Add the home page to the CatalystBlues site (using "index.htm" as the filename). Open the index.htm page in the Document window, and then set an appropriate page title. In the Page Properties dialog box, set appropriate properties for the Appearance, Links, and Headings categories. Save the page.
14. Repeat Step 13 for all the first-level pages you need to add to the CatalystBlues site, based on your site plan.
15. Review the HTML tags for the home page in Code view.
16. Preview the pages in your browser, looking for consistency in display. Each page should have the same background, and each page should have the page title that you assigned to it displayed in the browser title bar. Close the browser window and any open pages.
17. Upload the site to your remote server, selecting all the files and the folder for upload.
18. Preview the pages on the Web, looking for consistency in display. Again, each page should have the same background and each page should have the page title that you assigned to it displayed in the browser title bar.

Research

Plan and design a Web site about small rural communities of northern Vietnam.

Case Problem 1

Data Files needed for this Case Problem: HartMemo.doc, HartBackground.gif

Hroch University Anthropology Department You are working with Dr. Matt Hart, a social anthropologist at Hroch University, to create a Web site to present his research findings and accompanying graphics about the small rural communities of northern Vietnam. To initiate the planning and design, you asked Dr. Hart to provide you with a list of site goals, ideas on a target audience, and the material that he wants to include on the site. Dr. Hart has responded with a memo that outlines the decisions he made. You'll use the information from the memo to plan the Web site. Dr. Hart, however, did not provide all the information that you requested (a common occurrence when working with clients). You'll use the information Dr. Hart provided as a starting point. It will be necessary for you to research and make some decisions on your own.

1. Open the **HartMemo.doc** document file located in the **Tutorial.02\Cases** folder included with your Data Files in Microsoft Word (or another word processing program), and then read the memo.
2. Review the goals that Dr. Hart listed, and then create a list of site goals for the Web site. Consider the order of importance and wording.
3. Define a target audience and a user profile for the site. (*Hint:* Search online sources to learn more about the groups of people listed in the memo.)
4. Conduct market research. Find and review at least four Web sites that deal with the lesser-known areas of northern Vietnam, provide information on social anthropology, or are targeted at presenting research online.

Explore

5. Write a paragraph documenting the findings from your market research. Include the URLs of the Web sites that you visited, as well as information about categories of information, graphic style, layout, and site metaphor.
6. Create three end-user scenarios for the site.
7. Develop an information category outline. Base the categories and hierarchy on the memo and your market research.
8. Create a flowchart for the site.
9. Develop a site concept and metaphor for the site. (Even sites that have minimal design can benefit from a site metaphor.)

Explore

10. Investigate usability guidelines that deal with text. Research these guidelines at *www.w3.org/WAI*. Write down your findings and use them when making font choices.
11. Design a color palette for the site. Write a paragraph explaining your choice.
12. Choose the fonts for the site. Write a paragraph explaining your choice.
13. Plan the graphic style of the site. Write a paragraph explaining your choice.
14. Create a rough sketch of the layout of the site. Write a paragraph explaining your choice.

Explore

15. Check the design for logic by reviewing the decisions that you have made. Make sure that your design reinforces the site goals and supports the site metaphor.
16. Create a local site definition, using "Hart" as the site name, and "Hart\Dreamweaver" as the local root folder in the folder and location where you are storing your Web site. Create a folder named "Graphics" in the local root folder and select that folder as the default images folder. Refresh the local file list automatically, and enable cache.

17. Create a remote site definition using FTP access for the Hart site.
18. Create an HTML page for the home page using "index.htm" as the filename. Open the page in the Document window, and then enter "Hroch University Anthropology Dept. - Prof. Hart - Home" as the page title. In the Page Properties dialog box, set the background image to the **HartBackground.gif** file located in the **Tutorial.02\Cases** folder included with your Data Files (remember, once you add a copy of the image to your Graphics folder, you can select it from the Graphics folder for the other pages), set the background color to white, and set the text color to black. Save the page.
19. Repeat Step 18 to create the remaining top-level pages for the Hart site, using the following filenames and page titles:

Filename	**Page Title**
contact.htm	Hroch University Anthropology Dept. - Prof. Hart - Contact
cultural_cross_pollination.htm	Hroch University Anthropology Dept. - Prof. Hart - Cultural Cross-pollination
linguistic_differences.htm	Hroch University Anthropology Dept. - Prof. Hart - Linguistic Differences
prof_hart.htm	Hroch University Anthropology Dept. - Prof. Hart
rituals_and_practices.htm	Hroch University Anthropology Dept. - Prof. Hart - Rituals and Practices

20. Preview the pages in your browser, looking for consistency in display. Each page should have the same background, and each page should have the page title that you assigned to it displayed in the browser title bar.
21. Review the HTML tags for the home page in Code view, and then close any open pages.
22. Upload the site to your remote server, selecting all the files and the folder for upload.
23. View the pages on the Web, looking for consistency in display. Again, each page should have the same background and each page should have the page title that you assigned to it displayed in the browser title bar.

Case Problem 2

There are no Data Files needed for this Case Problem.

Museum of Western Art   C. J. Strittmatter, who has been hired to design the Web site for the Fort Worth Museum of Western Art, asks you to work on the plan and design of the new Web site. To develop a feasible plan, you'll need to conduct marketing research on other western art museum sites. In addition, C.J. asks you to research the current accessibility guidelines for using alternate text descriptions on graphics. You'll then create the new site, add the home page and top-level pages to the site, and set page properties.

1. Define the goals for the site.
2. Define a target audience and a user profile for the site.
3. Conduct market research. Find and review at least four Web sites that deal with western art. (*Hint:* Use a search engine to search the keywords "western art," "cowboy art," and "Texas museums.")
4. Write a paragraph documenting the findings from your market research. Include the URLs of the Web sites that you visited, as well as information about categories of information, graphic style, layout, and site metaphor.

Research: Plan and design a Web site for an art museum.

Explore

5. Create two end-user scenarios for the site.
6. Develop an information category outline for the site.
7. Create a flowchart for the site.
8. Develop a site concept and metaphor for the site. Write a paragraph explaining your choices.

Explore

9. Investigate usability guidelines that deal with Alt messages. Alt messages are text messages that can be read by assistive devices. They are used with graphic buttons and so forth to make the site more accessible. Research these guidelines at *www.w3.org/WAI*. Write down your findings to use when working on the site's graphics.
10. Design a color palette, choose the fonts, and select a graphic style for the site. Write a paragraph explaining your choices.
11. Create rough sketches of two layouts for the site. Write a paragraph explaining which layout you prefer and why.

Explore

12. Check the logical layout of the design you prefer by reviewing the decisions that you have made. Make sure that your design reinforces the site goals and supports the site metaphor.
13. Create a local site definition, using "Museum" as the site name and "Museum\Dreamweaver" as the folder and location where you are storing your Web sites as the local root folder. Create a folder named "Graphics" in the local root folder and select that folder as the default images folder. Refresh the local file list automatically, and enable cache.
14. Create a remote site definition using FTP access for the Museum site.
15. Create the home page for the Museum site using "index.htm" as the filename and enter "Museum of Western Art - Home" as the page title.

Explore

16. Click the Page Properties button in the Property inspector. Set the page font to "Times New Roman, Times, serif," set the size to "medium," set the text color to "#ECB888," and then set the background color to "#CC6600." Set the links, visited links, and active links colors to "#ECB888." Set heading 1 to size "xxlarge" and color "#006666." Set heading 2 to size "large" and color "#006666." Save the page.
17. Repeat Steps 15 and 16 to create the top-level pages for the Museum site, using the following filenames and page titles.

Filename	Page Title
art.htm	Museum of Western Art - Art
artists.htm	Museum of Western Art - Artists
location.htm	Museum of Western Art - Location
museum.htm	Museum of Western Art - Museum

18. Preview the pages in your browser, looking for consistency in display. Each page should have the same background, and each page should have the page title that you assigned to it displayed in the browser title bar.
19. Upload the site to your remote server. Remember to select all the files and the folder for upload.
20. View the pages on the Web, looking for consistency in display. Again, each page should have the same background and each page should have the page title that you assigned to it displayed in the browser title bar.

Research

Plan and design a Web site for an independent publisher of fringe writing.

Case Problem 3

Data Files needed for this Case Problem: NORMBackground.gif

NORM You are working on the new Web site for NORM, an independent publishing company in California that concentrates on cultivating fringe writings of all sorts. The Web design team is in the initial planning phase of designing the new NORM Web site. Using your research on NORM competitors, you'll develop a plan for the new NORM site. Then you'll create the new site, add the home page and top-level pages to the site, and set the page properties.

1. Define a list of goals for the site.
2. Define a target audience and a user profile for the site.
3. Conduct market research as needed by visiting competitors' sites.
4. Compose two end-user scenarios for the site.
5. Develop an information category outline for the site.
6. Create a flowchart for the site.
7. Develop a site concept and metaphor for the site. Write a paragraph explaining your choices.
8. Design a color palette, choose the fonts, and select a graphic style for the site. Write a paragraph explaining your choices.
9. Create a rough sketch of the layout of the site. Write a paragraph explaining your choice.

Explore

10. Check the layout of the design for logic by reviewing the decisions that you have made. Make sure that your design reinforces the site goals and supports the site metaphor.
11. Create a local site definition, using "NORM" as the site name and "Norm\Dreamweaver" in the folder and location where you are storing your Web sites as the local root folder. Create a folder named "Graphics" in the local root folder and select that folder as the default images folder. Refresh the local file list automatically, and enable cache.
12. Create a remote site definition using FTP access for the NORM site.
13. Create a new HTML page for the home page using "index.htm" as the filename. Open the page in the Document window and set "NORM - Home" as the page title.

Explore

14. Click the Page Properties button in the Properties inspector. Set the page font to "Arial, Helvetica, sans-serif," set the font size to "14 pixels," set the text color to "#FFFFFF," and set the background image to the **NORMBackground.gif** file located in the **Tutorial.02\Cases** folder included with your Data Files (remember, once you add a copy of the graphic to the Graphics folder, you can select it from the Graphics folder as the background image for other pages). Set the background color to "#003366," set the left margin to "5," and set the right, top, and bottom margins to "0."
15. Set links, visited links, and active links color to "#FFFFFF," set rollover links to "#CCCFE6," and then click Show Underline Only on Rollover in the Underline Style list box. Set heading 1 to size "40 pixels" and color "#FFFFFF." Set heading 2 to "20 pixels" and color "#FFFFFF." Save and close the page.

Explore

16. Right-click index.htm in the Files panel, point to Edit, and then click Copy. Right-click a blank spot in the Files panel, point to Edit, and then click Paste. A page with the filename "Copy of index.htm" appears in the list.

Explore

17. Right-click Copy of index.htm in the Files pane, point to Edit, and then click Rename. Type "books.htm" as the new filename, and then press the Enter key. The copied page is renamed as you can see in the file list.

Explore

18. Open the new page in the Document window, and then change the page title to a name that corresponds to the filename. Open the Page Properties dialog box. Notice that the page properties for the page are already set. Click the OK button, and then save and close the page.

19. Repeat Steps 16 through 18 to create the following pages: company.htm, contact.htm, and links.htm.

20. Preview the pages in your browser, looking for consistency in display. Each page should have the same background, and each page should have the page title that you assigned to it displayed in the browser title bar.

21. Review the HTML tags for the home page in Code view, and then close any open pages.

22. Upload the site to the remote server. Remember to select all of the files and the folder for upload.

23. View the pages on the Web, looking for consistency in display. Each page should have the same background, and each page should display the page title you assigned it in the browser title bar.

Challenge

Plan and design a Web site for a newly opening sushi restaurant. Then begin to create the site based on your plan.

Case Problem 4

There are no Data Files needed for this Case Problem.

Sushi Ya-Ya You are working with Mary O'Brien to create and design a Web site for Sushi Ya-Ya, a small sushi restaurant that will be opening soon in the French Quarter of New Orleans. Mary asks you to develop a Web site plan and design to present to Charlie Lindahl, the restaurant's owner, for review at the next scheduled meeting. Because Sushi Ya-Ya is not yet open, there is no established customer base. You know that the client wants to attract the employees of local businesses for its lunch clientele. You will have to do further research to define the target audience as well as to develop content for the site, as the business has not yet generated any informational materials.

1. Research restaurant Web sites (sushi restaurants in particular) and the French Quarter in New Orleans. Make notes about your findings.
2. Construct a list of goals for the site.
3. Define a target audience and a user profile for the site.
4. Complete your market research. Review at least eight Web sites, including restaurant sites, sites geared at your target audience, sites about New Orleans and the French Quarter, and sites about sushi.
5. Write a paragraph documenting the findings from your market research. Include the URLs of the Web sites that you visited.
6. Compose two end-user scenarios for the site.
7. Develop an information category outline for the site.

8. Create a flowchart for the site.
9. Develop a concept and metaphor for the site. Be creative, but make sure that your metaphor will support the site goals.
10. Design a color palette, choose the fonts, and select a graphic style for the site. Write a paragraph explaining your choices.
11. Create rough sketches of two layouts of the site. Write a paragraph explaining which layout you prefer and why.

Explore 12. Check the layout of the design you prefer for logic by reviewing the decisions that you have made. Make sure that your design reinforces the site goals and supports the site metaphor.
13. Create a local site definition, using "SushiYaYa" as the site name and "SushiYaYa\Dreamweaver" in the folder and location where you are storing your Web sites as the local root folder. Create a folder named "Graphics" in the local root folder and select that folder as the default images folder. Refresh the local file list automatically, and enable cache.
14. Create a remote site definition using FTP access for the SushiYaYa site.

Explore 15. Create each of the first-level pages of the SushiYaYa site based on your site plan and flowchart. Name each page with a descriptive filename. Open each page in the Document window, and then set the appropriate page title, background, and colors in the Page Properties dialog box. Save each page.
16. Preview the pages in your browser, looking for consistency in display. Each page should have the same background, and each page should have the page title that you assigned to it displayed in the browser title bar.
17. Review the HTML tags for the home page in Code view, and then close any open pages.
18. Upload the site to the remote server. Remember to select all of the files and the folder for upload.
19. View the pages on the Web, looking for consistency in display. Again, each page should have the same background and each page should have the page title that you assigned to it displayed in the browser title bar.

Review

Quick Check Answers

Session 2.1

1. False; there are many possible paths in any creative process.
2. to make decisions about the site's organization and structure
3. four or five
4. the group of users that you would most like to visit the site
5. to help identify the target audience by determining the characteristics of the group of people you are trying to reach
6. You may create a Web site that seems targeted to the intended audience, but that does not actually appeal to them.

7. to find out the target audience's preferences for a product or service; investigate the target audience's likes, dislikes, and interests; and evaluate competitors' products or services
8. imagined situations in which members of the target audience might access a Web site

Session 2.2

1. the process of determining what you want a site to do and then creating a framework that will allow you to accomplish those goals
2. to provide structure for the information in a Web site and are used to create the main navigation system
3. to provide a visual representation of the hierarchical structure of the pages within the site
4. because you need to use your instincts, follow leads, do research, and talk to others to gather everything you can
5. a general underlying theme that runs through the site and is used as a unifying mechanism for various elements that contribute to the site's look and feel
6. because the Web is a publishing venue used by a variety of people, including people with disabilities
7. keep it simple; include three to six colors per site; consider the mood you want to create; and keep in mind the target audience
8. True
9. the position of elements (navigation system, text, logo, artwork, etc.) in a Web page

Session 2.3

1. local info and remote info
2. to put a Web site on a Web server so it can be seen on the Web, enabling you to verify that the Web site's features work in the browser and over the Web
3. The New Document dialog box opens.
4. at least every ten minutes and whenever you have finished modifying a page
5. False; HTML is a common markup language that is viewable by a variety of software packages, including Web browsers.
6. attributes that apply to an entire page rather than to an element on the page, such as a page title, background, text and link colors, and margins
7. in a browser; on the Web
8. files that are used in the Web pages

Adding and Formatting Text

Using the Property Inspector, CSS Styles, and HTML Tags

Objectives

Session 3.1
- Type text into a page
- Copy text from a document and paste it into a page
- Check for spelling errors
- Create hyperlinks
- Examine HTML tags for hyperlinks

Session 3.2
- Explore CSS styles and style sheets
- Modify HTML tags
- Create custom style classes
- Create styles for the <a> tag selectors

Session 3.3
- Create an external style sheet
- Attach an external style sheet to a Web page
- Edit styles
- Delete styles
- Examine the code for styles and style sheets
- Examine HTML tags used to format text

Case

Catalyst

Sara Lynn, the president of Catalyst, and Brian Lee, the public relations and marketing director, have approved the design plan for the new Catalyst Web site. The next step is to add text to the site's pages and to format the text by adding the appropriate styles, based on the design plan. Each page of the Catalyst site will contain at least three text elements—the page heading, subheadings, and body text—as well as hyperlink styles and so forth. Formatting provides a way to distinguish between these different types of text. Dreamweaver created styles for the body text, hyperlinks, and page heading elements when you set the page properties. You'll create additional elements in this tutorial.

In this tutorial, you will type some of the text directly into a Web page, and import some of the text from text files. You will use the spelling checker and Find and Replace tools to correct typing errors and capitalization errors in the text. You will create hyperlinks to navigate among the pages in the site. You will create and apply different types of CSS styles. Finally, you will create an external style sheet and attach the external style sheet to all the Web pages to make the formatting consistent from one page to another.

Student Data Files

▼**Tutorial.03 folder**

▽ Tutorial folder
    Bands.doc

▽ Review folder
    Catalogue.doc
    Contact.doc
    Label.doc

▽ Cases folder
    Artists.doc
    Company.doc
    HartContact.doc
    Home.doc
    Links.doc
    Location.doc
    Museum.doc
    NORMContact.doc
    Overview.doc
    ProfHart.doc
    SushiYa-YaContent.doc
    Welcome.doc

Session 3.1

Adding Text to a Web Page

Almost every Web page includes text elements. In fact, text is the basis of most Web sites. To ensure maximum readability, you want to be sure that the text you add to a Web page is clearly written and free from spelling, punctuation, and grammatical errors. Well-written Web content is concise, effectively communicates the point, and is written with the end users in mind. By the time you are ready to add the content to a Web site, you will already have the information architecture, which will tell you what you need to include in each page. You will also have all the raw materials, including the text and the graphics, so that you are not composing on the fly. In addition, you will have set the page properties for the pages so that basic text formatting attributes are set.

There are two ways to add text to a page in Dreamweaver. You can simply type in the workspace of the Document window to add text to the page. This is a good method for adding small amounts of text or text that will be heavily formatted. You can also copy existing text from another file (whether a text document or a Web page) and paste it into the workspace of the Document window in Design view. This is a good method for adding text to a site if there is a great deal of text to contend with; most word processing programs have better spell checking and grammar checking features as well as a built-in thesaurus. However, sometimes there are errors—such as extra spaces, oddly positioned text, or misinterpreted symbols—that appear in the Web page when text is imported from another program. Whenever you copy text from another source, it is important to read the text and correct any errors that have been introduced. Note that when you copy text from a text file, any formatting from the original file is lost when you paste the text into Dreamweaver. Line breaks, however, are maintained.

Brian asks you to add text to the Bands page in the Catalyst site. He has already typed the text into a Word document.

To add text to a Web page:

1. Open the **NewCatalyst** site you modified in Session 2.3, click the **View** list arrow in the Files panel, and then click **Local View**.

   Trouble? If you are working on a different computer than you did in Session 2.3, you will need to re-create the site definition on this computer (both the local info and the remote info).

2. Double-click **bands.htm** in the Files panel to open the Bands page in the Document window, and then click the **Show Design View** button on the Document toolbar, if necessary, to switch to Design view.

3. Press the **Enter** key four times to move the insertion point a few lines below the colored portion of the page background, and then type **CATALYST BANDS**. The text you typed appears in the Document window. See Figure 3-1.

Text typed in the Bands page — **Figure 3-1**

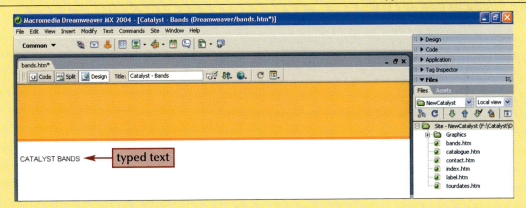

4. Open the **Bands.doc** file located in the **Tutorial.03\Tutorial** folder included with your Data Files in Word or another word processing program. This document contains the rest of the text you want to add to the Bands page. Notice that the paragraph headings are bold and that the text is displayed in the Times New Roman font.

5. Press the **Ctrl+A** keys to select all the text in the document, press the **Ctrl+C** keys to copy the text to the Windows Clipboard, and then click the **Close** button ⊠ on the title bar of the program window to close the document and exit the word processing program.

6. Click the Document window to place the insertion point after the text you typed in the Bands page, if necessary, and then press the **Enter** key twice to move the insertion point down two lines.

7. Click **Edit** on the menu bar, and then click **Paste Text**. The text you copied from the Bands.doc document is pasted into the Bands page.

8. Scroll to the top of the page. See Figure 3-2.

Text copied from the Bands document — **Figure 3-2**

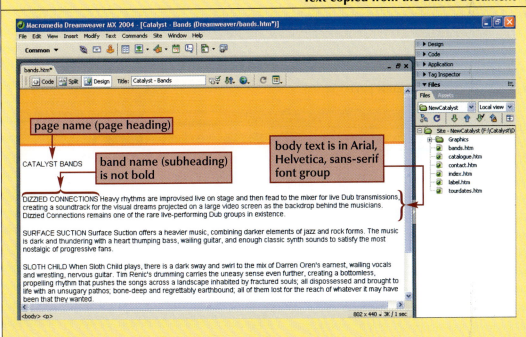

9. Scroll as needed and read the Bands page text. Notice that the paragraph headings are not bold, as they were in the text document. Also notice that the text is displayed in the Arial, Helvetica, sans-serif font group that you selected when you set the page properties and not in the font from the text document. Before you continue, you'll save the page with the text.
10. Click **File** on the menu bar, and then click **Save**.

Next, you will check the text for spelling errors.

Checking the Spelling in Web Pages

It is important to proofread all of the text that you add to Web pages, whether you typed it directly into the Web page or you copied it from another file. You cannot assume that text you receive from someone else has been proofed and corrected. You should also use Dreamweaver's built-in spell checker to double-check for errors. Errors in spelling and grammar can detract from the overall impression of the site. They can make the company, product, or service seem unprofessional.

Brian asks you to use the spell-checker tool and then proofread the Bands page to double-check for spelling errors. The spell checker is not foolproof, so when you proofread the page, it is a good idea to look for errors that a spell checker won't catch, such as incorrectly used homonyms (for example, *there*, *their*, and *they're*), a correctly spelled word that is wrong in context (such as *from* versus *form*), or missing words.

To check a page for spelling errors:

1. Scroll to the top of the Bands page, click to place the insertion point above the text, click **Text** on the menu bar, and then click **Check Spelling**. The Check Spelling dialog box opens, displaying the first word that it finds that does not match any words in the built-in dictionary, in this case the word "fead."
2. Drag the Check Spelling window by its title bar so that you can see the sentence with the highlighted word in the Document window. The word should be "fed."
3. Click **fed** in the Suggestions list. See Figure 3-3.

Figure 3-3 Spell checking the Bands page

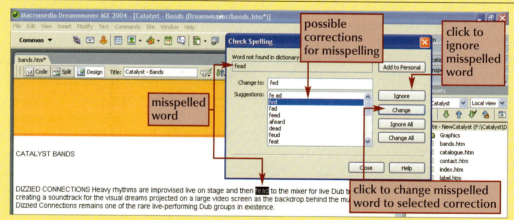

4. Click the **Change** button to replace the highlighted word with the selected word in the Suggestions list. The spell checker stops at the next "misspelled" word it finds, "synth."

5. Read the sentence containing the highlighted word in the Document window. In this case, the word "synth" is an abbreviation for "synthesizer" and it is not misspelled. Although the spell checker does not recognize this abbreviation, it is a slang term that will be recognized by the target audience.

6. Click the **Ignore** button to leave the word as it is and continue checking the spelling.

7. Continue checking the rest of the page, ignoring the rest of the words the spell checker flags as misspelled, and then click the **OK** button in the dialog box that opens telling you that the spelling check is complete.

8. Proofread the Bands page one last time, and then save the page.

If necessary, you can globally find and replace text in the page.

Using the Find and Replace Tool

Like word processing programs, Dreamweaver has a Find and Replace tool that enables you to locate text or tags and then to replace the located elements with other text or tags. When using this tool you can specify the area in which the search will occur (Current Document, Open Documents, Entire Current Local Site, Selected Files in Site, Folder, or Selected Text) as well as the kind of search that will be performed. A Source Code search locates instances of the designated text string within the HTML source code. A Text search locates instances of the designated text string within the document text. A Text (Advanced) search enables you to further specify the parameters of the search. For example, you can set the search to locate instances of the designated text string within only a specified tag and so forth. Finally, a Specific Tag search locates specific tags, attributes, and attribute values and enables you to replace the designated tag, attribute, or attribute value with a new tag, attribute, or attribute value.

You will use the Find and Replace tool to locate all of the instances of the word "Dub" in the Bands page and to replace it with the word "dub" (all in lowercase).

To find and replace text:

1. Click to the left of the CATALYST BANDS page heading to position the insertion point at the top of the page.

2. Click **Edit** on the menu bar, and then click **Find and Replace**. The Find and Replace dialog box opens. See Figure 3-4.

Find and Replace dialog box — **Figure 3-4**

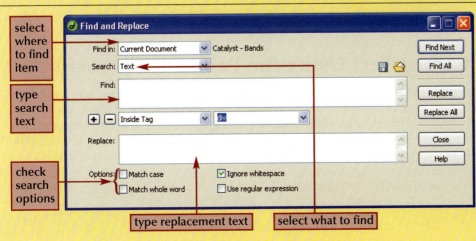

3. Click the **Find in** list arrow, click **Current Document**, click the **Search** list arrow, and then click **Text**, if necessary.

4. Click in the **Find** text box, and then type **Dub**. This is the word you want to search for.

5. Click in the **Replace** text box, and then type **dub**. This is the word you want to use.

6. Click the **Match Case** check box to insert a check mark, and then make sure the other check boxes are unchecked. This instructs Dreamweaver to look for words with the exact capitalization as in the Find text box and insert words with the exact capitalization as in the Replace text box.

7. Click the **Find Next** button. The first instance of the word *Dub* is selected in the Bands page. See Figure 3-5.

Figure 3-5   First instance of search text in the Bands page

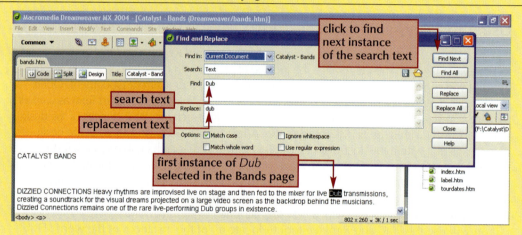

8. Click the **Replace** button in the Find and Replace dialog box. The selected instance of *Dub* is replaced with *dub*, and then the next instance of *Dub* is selected. Rather than finding and replacing one instance of the search text at a time, you can replace all the instances at one time.

9. Click the **Replace All** button in the Find and Replace dialog box. Dreamweaver replaces the remaining instances of the text string in the page. The Results panel group expands to the Search panel and lists all instances where the search text was replaced in the page.

10. If necessary, collapse the Results panel group.

Now you will format the text in the Bands page using the Property inspector.

Formatting Text Using the Property Inspector

The simplest way to format text in Dreamweaver is to select the text in the Document window and set the attributes for the text in the Property inspector. You can set the attributes for a single letter, a word, a line of text, or an entire block of text. The attributes for text formatting are similar to those you will find in a word processing program; however, when text is formatted in Dreamweaver, CSS styles that control the look and layout of the text are added in the background. Text formatting attributes included in the Property inspector are format, font, style, size, color, emphasis, alignment, lists, and indents.

The format attributes are a list of standardized HTML tags used for text formatting. These include the paragraph tag and a variety of heading tags. When you select fonts, sizes, and colors for headings in the Page Properties dialog box, Dreamweaver creates CSS styles that customize the appearance of the heading tags in the Format list. In the Catalyst site, selecting text and clicking the Heading 1 tag in the Format list will cause the selected text to be displayed in Arial, Helvetica, sans-serif; 30 pixels; and #FF9900 (Dark-Hard-Orange), which are the attributes you selected for the Heading 1 tag when you set the page properties. You did not select attributes for the other heading tags when you set the page properties. As a result, if you select text and click the Heading 2 or other heading tags, Dreamweaver will apply the default attributes for that tag to the selected text.

The font attributes are a list of the standard font groups available for use in Web pages. The default font group for the page is the font group that you selected for the page font in the Page Properties dialog box. The page font for the Catalyst site is Arial, Helvetica, sans-serif. To select a different font group for a section of text, you simply select the text in the Document window and then choose the desired font group from the Font list in the Property inspector. If you do not select a font group in the Property inspector, the text will be displayed in the selected page font. The Default Font option displays the text in the default font of the end-user's browser. When a font group is selected, Dreamweaver creates a CSS style containing all the choices in the font group and places a tag containing the CSS style around the specified text. You can add fonts to the list, but it is recommended that you use caution when doing this because a font must be installed on the end-user's computer to display the text in that font. If the font is not installed on the end-user's computer, the text will be displayed in the browser's default font.

Size attributes are a list of available font sizes. You can select a specific or relative size from the list or you can type a different font size in the text box. If you select a specific size, you must also choose a unit selection. Pixels are the most frequently used unit for specific font size. The default size is the size that you selected in the Page Properties dialog box.

The font color attributes enable you to change the color of selected text. The default font color for a page is the color you selected in the Page Properties dialog box. To change the color of a selected block of text, you can type the hexadecimal color code into the color text box or select a color with the color picker.

The buttons in the Property inspector enable you to change the emphasis of selected text with boldface and italics; apply a left, center, or right alignment to a paragraph; turn paragraphs into items in an unordered (bulleted) or ordered (numbered) list; and apply or remove indents from paragraphs. You can also change the default text attributes for the page by clicking the Page Properties button in the Property inspector and changing the selections in the Page Properties dialog box.

Formatting Text Using the Property Inspector

- Select the text that you want to format in the Document window.
- Click the Font list arrow in the Property inspector, and then click the font grouping you want.
- Click the Size list arrow in the Property inspector, and then click the size you want.
- Click in the color text box in the Property inspector and type the hexadecimal color code of the color you want (*or* click the color box in the Property inspector and click the color swatch you want in the color picker).
- Click the Bold button and/or the Italic button in the Property inspector.
- Click one of the alignment buttons in the Property inspector.
- To create a text hyperlink, select the text, click the Browse for File button in the Property inspector, and then navigate to the file to which you want to link (*or* click the Point to File button in the Property inspector and then drag to the file to which you want to link, *or* type the external URL in the Link text box).

Reference Window

Next, you'll format the text in the Bands page. The page heading—CATALYST BANDS—will be formatted using Heading 1 in the Format list. (Remember you set the Heading 1 attributes when you set the page properties.) You will format the band names in the paragraph headings—Dizzied Connections, Surface Suction, Sloth Child, and Life in Minor Chords—as subheadings using Heading 2 in the Format list. (You did not set the Heading 2 attributes when you set the page properties so text formatted with this tag will display the tag's default formatting.) You can make these changes in the Property inspector.

To format the text with the Property inspector:

1. Select **CATALYST BANDS** in the Document window, click the **Format** list arrow in the Property inspector, and then click **Heading 1**. See Figure 3-6.

Figure 3-6   **Property inspector for unformatted page name text**

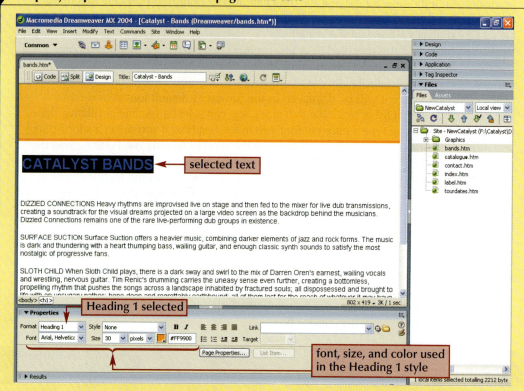

2. Place the insertion point after DIZZIED CONNECTIONS, and then press the **Enter** key. The text to the right of the heading moves to the next line in the page.

3. Select **DIZZIED CONNECTIONS**, click the **Format** list arrow in the Property inspector, click **Heading 2**, and then press the **Right Arrow** key to deselect the text. See Figure 3-7.

Formatted page name — Figure 3-7

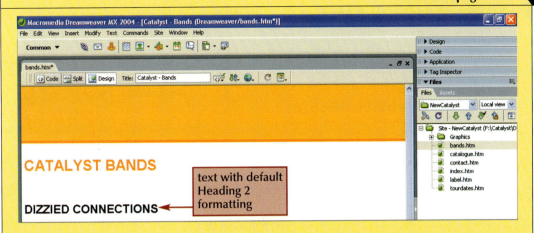

Trouble? If the text in the paragraph above the DIZZIED CONNECTIONS heading text displays the attributes of the heading, the opening <h2> tag has been placed before the affected text. Select the text that you wanted to change, click the Show Code and Design Views button on the Document toolbar, select the <h2> tag in the Code pane, drag the tag directly in front of the DIZZIED CONNECTIONS text, and then click the Show Design View button on the Document toolbar.

4. Repeat Steps 2 and 3 to format the three other paragraph subheadings on the page: **SURFACE SUCTION**, **SLOTH CHILD**, and **LIFE IN MINOR CHORDS**.

5. Save the page.

The Catalyst site plan calls for text hyperlinks at the top of each page. You'll add these next.

Creating Text Hyperlinks

Hyperlinks enable users to move between pages in a Web site and to connect to pages on other Web sites. For the Catalyst site, you will create text hyperlinks for the main navigation system as called for in the site plan. First, you'll add the link text to one of the pages in the site and format it. Then, you'll create the hyperlinks. Finally, you will copy the links to the rest of the pages in the site.

Adding and Formatting Hyperlink Text

You'll insert the text for the hyperlinks—label, bands, catalogue, tour dates, and contact—on a blank line just below the colored part of the page background. You want to separate each word with two **nonbreaking spaces**, which are special, invisible characters used to create more than one space between text and other elements. In HTML, only one regular space will display between items no matter how many spaces you type using the spacebar. Using nonbreaking spaces enables you to separate items with more than one space between them.

After you insert the link text, you'll format it by setting the size and alignment. You won't set any colors for the link text because you specified them when you set the page properties.

To add and format text for hyperlinks on a Web page:

1. Click just below the colored portion of the background to position the insertion point; if necessary press the **Shift+Enter** keys to move the pointer down one line.

2. Type **label**, click the **Category** button on the Insert bar, and then click **Text**. The buttons in the Text category appear on the Insert bar.

3. Click the **Characters** list arrow on the Insert bar, click the **Non-Breaking Space** button , and then click the **Non-Breaking Space** button again. Two nonbreaking spaces are inserted after the text. (A breaking space and a nonbreaking space look the same in Design view.)

   You can also insert nonbreaking spaces using the keyboard.

4. Type **bands**, and then press the **Ctrl+Shift+Spacebar** keys twice to insert two nonbreaking spaces.

   You'll repeat this process to enter the rest of the link text.

5. Type **catalogue**, press the **Ctrl+Shift+Spacebar** keys twice, type **tour dates**, press the **Ctrl+Shift+Spacebar** keys twice, type **contact**, and then press the **Ctrl+Shift+Spacebar** keys twice. The text for each link is followed by two nonbreaking spaces. See Figure 3-8.

Figure 3-8   Link text typed in the Bands page

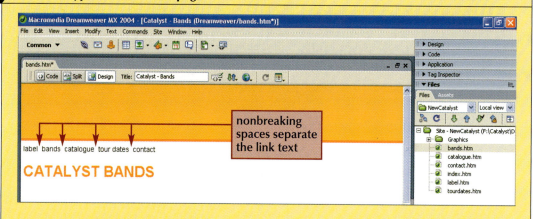

6. Click the **Align Right** button in the Property inspector. The link text moves to the right side of the page.

7. Save the page.

Now you will create the text hyperlinks.

Creating Links from Text

You can create text hyperlinks using the Property inspector to associate the text with a specific file or Web page. The first time you link to a file, you select the link text, then you use the Browse for File button or the Point to File button next to the Link text box in the Property inspector to select the appropriate file. Dreamweaver will then create the link for you. (You can also type the URL into the Link text box in the Property inspector, but if you mistype the URL or path, the link will not work.) If the page you link to is outside the local root folder, Dreamweaver prompts you to include a copy of the page in the site (that is, in the local root folder). Remember to keep all the elements you use in your site within the site's local root folder so that these elements will be accessible when you publish the site and Dreamweaver can manage the site and its elements for you.

Once you link to a file, it will appear in the Link list in the Property inspector. If you need to add another link to that file, first select the new link text, and then click the Link list arrow and select the file from the list.

There are two types of links—relative links and absolute links. Relative links can be relative to the document or to the site's root folder. **Document relative links** don't specify the entire URL of the Web page you are linking to; instead, they specify a path from the current page. You use document relative links when you are linking to pages within your site, because you can move the site to a different server location or different domain, and the links will still work. In addition to standard document relative links, Dreamweaver includes an option to create site root relative links. **Site root relative links** specify a path from the site's root folder to the linked document. You can use site root relative links when you work on large sites with complex folder structures that change frequently. When you link to a page anywhere within your local root folder, Dreamweaver creates a relative link. In these tutorials, you will use document relative links.

When you link to a page in another site, you use an absolute link. An **absolute link** contains the complete URL of the page you are linking to, which includes *http://www.domainname.com/* plus the filename of the page to which you are linking. You use an absolute link when you want to link to Web pages outside of a site.

Next, you'll create hyperlinks from the link text you just added. Each link connects to the appropriate existing Web page. You will also create a link from the link text for the current page to itself (for example, on the Contact page, you will link the link text "contact" to the Contact page). Although the link will not go anywhere, formatting it as a link will maintain consistency in the look of the text in the navigation system, and, when you copy the navigation system to other pages of the site, you will not have to create additional links. Remember, when you set the page properties, you designated various colors for four states of links (text links, rollover links, active links, and visited links).

To create hyperlinks from text:

1. Select **label** in the Bands page.
2. Click the **Browse for File** button in the Property inspector. The Select File dialog box opens. The Look in list box lists folders and pages in the local root folder for the site that is currently selected in the Files panel.
3. Click **label.htm** in the Look in list box. See Figure 3-9.

Select File dialog box — **Figure 3-9**

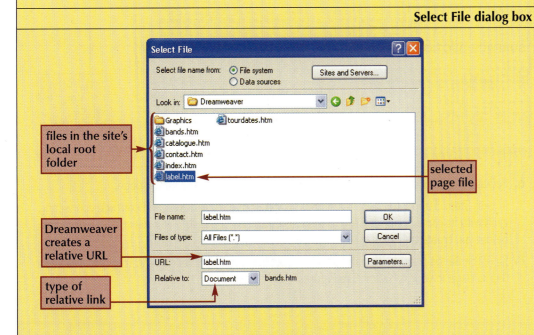

- files in the site's local root folder
- selected page file
- Dreamweaver creates a relative URL
- type of relative link

4. Click the **OK** button, and then press the **Right Arrow** key to deselect the text. The word *label* is now a hyperlink to the Label page in the NewCatalyst site. See Figure 3-10.

Figure 3-10 | Label text converted to a hyperlink

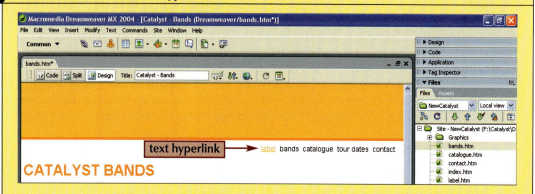

5. Select **bands** in the Document window, click the **Point to File** button in the Property inspector (do not release the mouse button), and then drag the pointer to the **bands.htm** file in the Files panel, as shown in Figure 3-11.

Figure 3-11 | Creating a hyperlink using the Point to File button

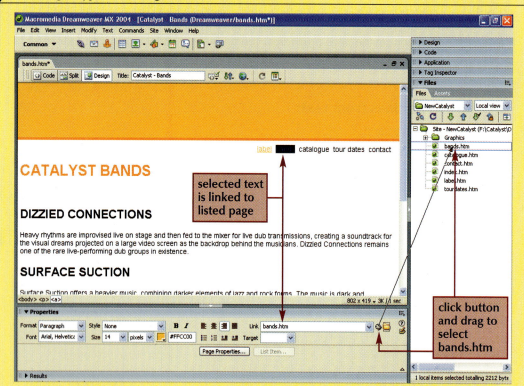

6. Release the mouse button. The word *bands* is now linked to the Bands page.

7. Repeat Steps 5 and 6 to create hyperlinks for **catalogue**, **tour dates**, and **contact**, connecting each with its corresponding file. (For the tour dates link, make sure you select both words before you create the link.)

8. Save the Bands page, click **bands.htm** in the Files panel to select it, and then preview the Bands page in your browser. See Figure 3-12.

Figure 3-12

Bands page previewed in a browser window

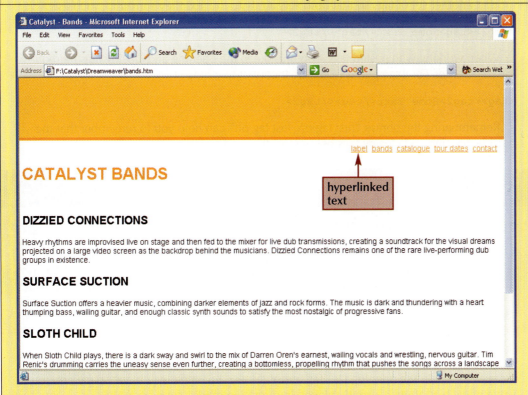

9. Place the pointer over the **label** link. The pointer changes to 👆.
10. Click the **label** link. The Label page is displayed in the browser window.
11. Click the **Back** button ⬅ on the browser toolbar. The home page is displayed in the browser window and the label link text is a different color.
12. Close the browser window.

Next, you'll look at the HTML tags that Dreamweaver inserted when you formatted text and created hyperlinks.

Exploring HTML Tags for Hyperlinks

HTML tags, whether they apply to text, hyperlinks, or other elements, follow a specific format. As you have already seen, most HTML tags come in pairs with an opening and closing tag that surrounds the text to which the tag is applied, as in the following example:

`<tag>Some Text</tag>`

Opening tags are placed before the text, or other element, to which they are applied, and take the form <tag>, where "tag" is replaced by the HTML tag you are using. There is an opening bracket, the tag, and a closing bracket. Closing tags are placed after the text, or other element, to which they are applied, and take the form </tag>. Again, there are opening and closing brackets, but in a closing tag, a forward slash is included inside the opening bracket, before the tag name.

Tags can also be used together, or nested. With **nested** tags, one set of tags is placed around another set of tags so that both sets apply to the text they surround, such as:

`<tag2><tag>Some Text</tag></tag2>`

When working with nested tags, you must keep the opening and closing tags paired in the same order. For example, it would be incorrect to write:

`<tag><tag2>Some Text</tag></tag2>`

Remembering the phrase "first tag on, last tag off" can help you to remember that the outside opening and closing tags belong together and so forth.

Reference Window | Examining HTML Tags

- Click the Show Code View button or the Show Code and Design Views button on the Document toolbar.
- If the lines of code do not wrap in the Document window, click the Code View Options button on the Document toolbar, and then click Word Wrap.
- Expand the Code panel group, click the Reference tab, right-click the tag you want to examine in the Code pane, and then click Reference to display a description of the tag in the Reference panel.

Some tags also contain attributes, such as size, color, and alignment. These attributes are placed within the opening tag. Tag attributes are separated by a blank space and the value of each attribute is usually placed in quotation marks, such as:

`<tag color="x" size="x">Some Text</tag>`

The specific tags that are used depend on the applied formatting and the type of element, such as a hyperlink. Some helpful reference sites for HTML tags include *hotwired.lycos.com/webmonkey* (try the HTML Cheatsheet) and *www.w3.org*.

You will look at the HTML tags for hyperlinks.

Exploring HTML Tags that Apply to Hyperlinks

Hyperlinks are created in HTML with the **anchor tag**, which has the general format:

`<a href="absolute or relative path">Link Text</a>`

where "href" is short for hypertext reference, "absolute or relative path"—the URL or page for the link—is the value for href, and "Link Text" indicates the text on the Web page that users click to use the link. Absolute, document relative, and site root relative links have different path information in the href attribute. Figure 3-13 lists the anchor tag with the three types of links.

Figure 3-13 Anchor tags for absolute and relative links

Link	Anchor tag	Description
Absolute	`<a href="http://www.websitename.com">`Text link to a Web page outside current site`</a>`	Specifies the absolute or complete path to the linked page.
Document Relative	`<a href="anotherpage.htm">`Text link to another page within current site`</a>`	Specifies the location of the linked page relative to the current page. Commonly used.
Site Root Relative	`<a href="/subfolder/anotherpage.htm">`Text link to another page within current site`</a>`	Specifies the location of the linked page relative to the root folder. Used sometimes when sites have a lot of subfolders within the root folder and change frequently.

One of the attributes you can specify with an anchor link is the target attribute. The **target** attribute specifies where the link opens—in the current browser window or a new browser window. The default is for the new page to be opened in the current browser window, replacing the page from which you linked. If you want the new page to replace the current page, you do not need to include a target attribute. If you specify "_blank" as the target attribute, the linked page opens in a new browser window. The complete anchor tag for opening a page in a new browser window takes the format:

```
<a href="absolute or relative path" target="_blank">Link Text</a>
```

Another anchor tag attribute is the name attribute. The name attribute associates a name with a specific named location within a Web page. With the name attribute, you can link to the named location on the current page or another page, much like a bookmark. You use the anchor tag with the name attribute in the format:

```
<a name="anchor_name">Some Text</a>
```

where "anchor_name" is the name you give the anchor, and "Some Text" is the text that is being named as the anchor. Anchor names are case-sensitive. When you create a named anchor, Dreamweaver inserts an anchor icon into the Document window beside the text. The anchor icon is not visible in a browser.

Once a location on a page has a named anchor, you can create links to it from other locations in the same page or from other pages. For example, you can select the page heading and create an anchor to the text named "top," then type "back to the top" at the bottom of the page and create a link from that text to the "top" anchor. This enables the user to jump from the bottom to the top of the Web page by clicking the "back to the top" link. The format for an anchor tag that links to a named anchor on the same page is:

```
<a href="#anchor_name">Link Text</a>
```

If you are linking to a named anchor in a different page, you need to include the path and filename to the page containing the named anchor in the following general format:

```
<a href="absolute or relative path#anchor_name">Link Text</a>
```

The # symbol always precedes the anchor name when it is used in a link.

You'll look at the HTML for the hyperlinks you created in the Bands page.

To examine HTML tags for hyperlinks:

1. Select the **contact** link in the Bands page then click the **Show Code and Design Views** button on the Document toolbar. The page is displayed in Split view.

2. Examine the anchor tag that surrounds the selected text in the Code pane of the Document window. See Figure 3-14.

Figure 3-14   Anchor tag in the Bands page

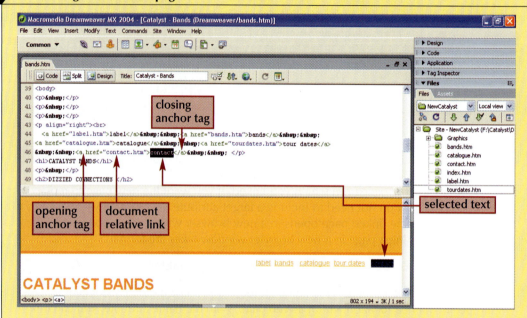

Trouble? If the lines of code do not wrap in the Document window, you need to turn on word wrap. Click the View Options button on the Document toolbar, and then click Word Wrap.

3. Select **a href=** (the entire opening anchor tag) in the Code pane, right-click the selected tag, and then click **Reference**. The Reference panel in the Code panel group expands. The O'Reilly HTML Reference description of the Anchor tag is visible.

4. Read the description of the anchor tag in the Reference panel.

5. Click the **Select Attribute** list arrow, click **href**, read the description of the href attribute in the Reference panel, and then click the **Collapse** arrow at the top of the Code panel group to minimize it.

6. Click the **Show Design View** button on the Document toolbar. The page is displayed in Design view.

So far, you have added text to a Web page, used the spell checker and proofed the page, used the Find and Replace tool to change all instances of the capitalization of a word on the page, and then formatted text with the Property inspector. You also created text hyperlinks and reviewed the HTML tags used for the hyperlinks. In the next session, you'll work with Cascading Style Sheets.

Session 3.1 Quick Check

1. What are two ways to add text to a page in Dreamweaver?
2. True or False? It is not necessary to read a page and look for errors if you use the spell checker.
3. To format text, select the text in the Document window and select formatting options in the _____.
4. _____ enable users to move between pages in a Web site and to connect to pages on other Web sites.
5. When you link to a page in the site's local root folder, what type of link is created by default?
6. What is the general format for the HTML code for the bold tag?
7. Which tag is used to create hyperlinks?

Session 3.2

Understanding Cascading Style Sheets

The way that HTML displays and formats text has evolved over time. Each evolutionary step has provided better control over the way text is formatted and displayed.

The World Wide Web Consortium (W3C) publishes recommendations for HTML standards. As new versions of HTML are developed and then accepted, the W3C assigns version numbers to these standards (a lower number equals an older standard). New HTML versions contain new elements, tags, and updated methods of doing things. Tags that have been replaced in new versions of HTML are kept around for compatibility with older browsers. These older tags that are in the process of becoming obsolete are called **deprecated**. Because many people use older browsers that rely on the earlier versions of HTML, deprecated tags are phased out slowly. Specifications and standards change rapidly, so there is no easy way to predict exact adoption rates for newer standards and technologies. The W3C Web site (*www.w3c.org*) is a good reference for current trends and changes.

In the earliest days of the Web, designers had limited control over the way text was displayed in a browser. Text was displayed in the default font and size set by the user's browser. The way it looked was also affected by the user's operating system. Designers had no font control within a Web page except for the six predefined heading tags that could be used to denote importance of text by changing the relative size of the headings. In HTML 2, bold, italic, and underline attributes were added. In HTML 3.2, another milestone in controlling the display of text was added—the HTML font tag (or just font tag). The **font tag** allowed designers to designate which font and which relative font size the Web page should be displayed in (as long as the designated font was installed on the user's computer). In HTML 4.01, font tags were deprecated and their functions replaced and expanded upon by Cascading Style Sheets.

Cascading Style Sheets were created as the answer to the limitations of HTML and they are the current standard for layout and formatting in Web pages. A **Cascading Style Sheet (CSS)** is a collection of styles that is either inserted in the head of the HTML of a Web page and used throughout that page (an internal style sheet), or is attached as an external document and used throughout the entire Web site (an external style sheet). A **CSS style** is a rule that defines the appearance of an element in a Web page either by redefining an existing HTML tag or by creating a custom style (also called a class style or a custom style class). CSS styles define text appearance, position, and many other aspects of Web page layout. They allow you to specify more parameters of the design than earlier HTML specifications; for example, you can create custom list bullets.

Dreamweaver uses CSS styles by default to format page elements. When you defined the page properties for the Catalyst site, Dreamweaver added CSS styles, which control the appearance of the text placed in the page. For example, the text that you pasted in the Bands page is displayed in the Arial, Helvetica, sans-serif font group, which you defined as the page font when you set the page properties for the Bands page. You can also create CSS styles yourself.

A CSS style sheet provides a convenient way to store styles that can be defined in one location and then applied to content residing in many other locations. This ability to separate the look of the site from the content of the site enables the designer to more easily update the Web site's appearance. In addition, designers can redefine an existing CSS style, and any content to which that style has been applied is updated to reflect the changes. This makes changing the font for all headings in a site or changing the color of body text on all the pages a simple task.

Although CSS styles are the current standard for formatting the look and layout in Web pages, some limitations still exist. CSS styles were adopted as part of HTML 4 and are not fully compatible with older browsers. If you are working on a Web site that supports browser versions 3.0 and older, you will need to use the pre-CSS formatting alternatives (which you will learn about in Session 3.3). Previewing the Web site in every browser and browser version you are planning to support before making the site public is the best way to verify that all aspects of the site work and display as you expect.

Creating CSS Styles

You can create styles yourself using the CSS Styles panel. When you create a CSS style, first you choose the type of style you want; then you choose the name, tag, or selector of the style; and finally, you choose the location of the style. There are three types of CSS styles: redefined HTML tags, custom styles, and advanced. A **redefined HTML tag** is an existing HTML tag that you modify. You can change and remove existing attributes or add new attributes to any HTML tag to make the tag more useful. This is probably the most common type of CSS style. When you redefine an HTML tag, the modified CSS style is used in every instance of that tag. A **custom style** (also called a **custom style class**) is a style you create from scratch and apply to the element you have selected in the page. A custom style can be applied to any tag. The **advanced style** is used to redefine formatting for a group of tags or for all tags that contain a particular ID attribute. This type of style is most commonly used to customize the appearance of text links.

After you decide on a type of style, you choose a Name/Tag/Selector, depending on the type of style you selected. If you are redefining an HTML tag, you must select the tag you want to modify. If you are creating a custom style class, you must type a name for the new style. If you are creating an advanced style, you must select the appropriate **selector**, the name of the style. In actuality, a selector can be a tag (if you are redefining an HTML tag), a period followed by a name you choose (if you are creating a custom style class), or a combination of tags separated by commas or a pseudoclass (if you are using an advanced style). When you create a new style, Dreamweaver refers to the name of the style as selector only when you create an advanced style.

Finally, you must select the location in which you will define the style. You can save the style you are creating in a new (external) style sheet file, in an existing external style sheet file, or only within the current document. When you save the file in the current document, Dreamweaver creates an **internal style sheet** that embeds (or inserts) the styles in the head of the current Web page and applies them only throughout that document. Creating an internal style sheet is useful because it enables you to update the look of all elements on which a style is used throughout the page. For example, if you wanted to change the look of all the subheadings in a page, you could change the subheading style instead of selecting and modifying each subheading individually. An **external style sheet** is a separate file that contains all the CSS styles used in a Web site. When you define styles in an external style sheet, you can use the styles in any page in the Web site to which you connect that style sheet. Editing a style in the external style sheet will update all instances in which that style is used throughout the site. This is the most powerful way to use styles.

Every CSS style (or rule) consists of two parts: the selector and the declaration. The **declaration** defines the attributes that are included in the style. Once you select the type, the name (selector), and the location of the style, you can choose the various attributes to be included in the declaration for the style. The eight categories of attributes that you can combine to create a style are:

- **Type.** Font and type settings and attributes such as font family, font size, color, decoration, weight, and so forth. More type attribute choices are available here than in the Property inspector when text is selected.
- **Background.** A color or an image, fixed or scrolling, that can be placed behind a page element, such as a block of text. CSS background attributes overlay the Web page background designated with the page properties and can be added behind any page element.
- **Block.** Spacing and alignment settings for tags and attributes. Examples include the spacing between words, letters, and lines of text; the horizontal and vertical alignment of text; and the indent applied to the text.
- **Box.** Attributes that control the placement of elements in the page. When you select a letter, a word, a group of words, or any other element, a selection box surrounds all the selected elements. Box attributes control the characteristics of the selection box, enabling you to set margins, padding, float settings, and so forth.
- **Border.** The dimensions, color, and line styles of the borders of the selection box that surrounds elements.
- **List.** The number format or the bullet shape or image and its position used with ordered and unordered lists.
- **Positioning.** Layer positioning attributes. Applying positioning attributes to a tag or selected text will change the selected item into a new layer using the default tag for defining layers which is set in Layer preferences.
- **Extensions.** Attributes that control page breaks during printing, the appearance of the pointer when positioned over objects in the page, and special effects to objects. Most browsers do not support some extensions' attributes.

On occasion, CSS styles are not visible within the Dreamweaver environment. You must preview the page in a browser to view the page with all attributes of the styles applied.

Modifying HTML Tags

The simplest way to create a CSS style is to redefine an existing HTML tag. Often modifying an existing HTML tag can make it more useful. For example, The Heading 1 tag, <h1>, is an HTML tag that was introduced in an early version of HTML. It was created to give designers some control over the size at which text was displayed. Because designers did not have a lot of control over text size at the time, the format of the Heading 1 tag changes based on how each user's browser interprets the tag, making the heading's layout and appearance inconsistent and limited. However, when you set page properties, you selected size and color attributes for the Heading 1 tag, <h1>, and Dreamweaver created a style that customized the appearance of that tag. Customizing the existing Heading 1 tag gives you a consistency that the <h1> tag would otherwise lack and makes the tag useful.

| Reference Window | **Modifying an Existing HTML Tag** |

- Click the New CSS Style button in the CSS Styles panel to open the New CSS Style dialog box.
- Click the Redefine HTML Tag option button.
- Click the Tag list arrow, and then click the tag you want to modify.
- Click the appropriate Define In option button.
- Click the OK button to open the CSS Style Definition dialog box.
- Click a category in the Category list, and then set the options you want.
- Click the OK button.

Many designers prefer to redefine HTML tags when creating CSS styles because tags often are automatically inserted for them, and older browsers that don't support CSS styles will apply the standard formatting of the HTML tags. For example, Dreamweaver applies the paragraph tag whenever you press the Enter key. If you modify the paragraph tag, Dreamweaver will automatically insert the new formatting attributes anywhere a paragraph tag is found in the Web page. A redefined HTML tag is applied in the same way that the tag would normally be applied.

When you create a CSS style to modify an HTML tag, Dreamweaver provides you with an extensive list of tags from which to choose. You can change and remove existing attributes or add new attributes to any tag. When you modify the attributes associated with a tag, the changes you make will apply to every instance of that tag.

Brian asks you to customize the look of the Heading 2 tag so that the subheadings in the Bands page will be displayed in accordance with the approved Catalyst style: font—Arial, Helvetica, san-serif; size—20 pixels; color—#FF9900; and case—uppercase. You will not specify a font because the style uses the page font you selected when you defined the page properties for the Bands page.

Styles **inherit** the attributes of higher-level tags when those attributes are not also specified in the current style. Because the attribute that specifies the page font was placed in the body tag, which surrounds all the other tags that format content in a Web page, the specified font family applies to the Heading 2 tag by default, unless you specify another font for this tag when you create the style. If you do specify a font in the Heading 2 tag style, it will override what was specified in the body tag; text to which the Heading 2 tag is applied will display that font in the body tag. This happens because style sheets are **cascading**; if an attribute is defined in two styles that affect the same object, the style that is "closer" to the object in the code will override the value of the attribute in the tag that is farther away from the object in the code. The cascading effect of style sheets is very powerful because it enables you to create general styles that affect the entire page. You create additional styles only for items that are exceptions to the general style.

In addition, Brian wants the subheadings to be placed directly above the description paragraphs. Heading tags are block level tags, which means they always affect the entire block of text even if they are applied only to a few words in the block of text. Placing the heading tags directly above the paragraphs would cause the paragraphs to be displayed with the heading formatting. You will change the Heading 2 tag style by selecting Inline from the Display list in the Block category of the CSS Style Definition dialog box. This will enable you to place the subheadings directly above the paragraphs.

To modify an existing HTML tag:

1. If you took a break after the last session, make sure the **NewCatalyst** site is open, the **bands.htm** page is open in the Document window, and the page is displayed in Design view.
2. Click the **Expand** arrow on the Design panel group to open the Design panel group, and then click the **CSS Styles** tab. The CSS Styles panel opens and lists the styles that Dreamweaver created. See Figure 3-15.

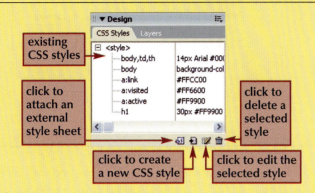

Figure 3-15 CSS Styles panel

3. Click the **New CSS Style** button in the CSS Styles panel. The New CSS Style dialog box opens. See Figure 3-16.

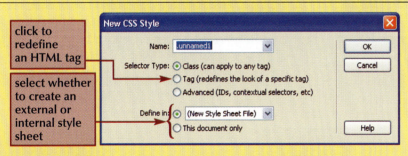

Figure 3-16 New CSS Style dialog box

4. Click the **Tag** option button in the Selector Type section. A list of tags is now available in the Tag list at the top of the dialog box.
5. Click the **Tag** list arrow, and then click **h2**. This specifies that you'll modify the <h2> tag.
6. Click the **This Document Only** option button, if necessary. This creates an internal style sheet.
7. Click the **OK** button. The CSS Style Definition for h2 dialog box opens.
8. Click **Type** in the Category list box, if necessary.
9. Click in the **Size** text box, type **20**, and then, if necessary, click the right **Size** list arrow, and then click **pixels**.
10. Click the **Case** list arrow, and then click **Uppercase**.
11. Click in the **Color** text box, type **#FF9900**, and then press the **Tab** key. See Figure 3-17.

| Figure 3-17 | CSS Style Definition for h2 dialog box |

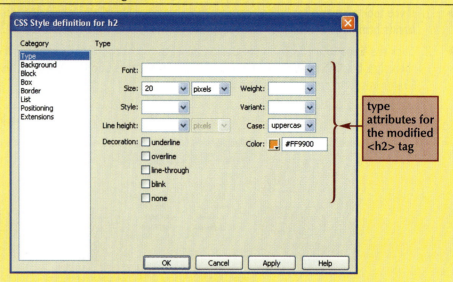

12. Click **Block** in the Category list, click the **Display** list arrow, and then click **Inline**.
13. Click the **OK** button. The style appears in the style list in the CSS Styles panel and the sub-headings in the Bands page reflect the new style. See Figure 3-18.

| Figure 3-18 | Formatted Bands page |

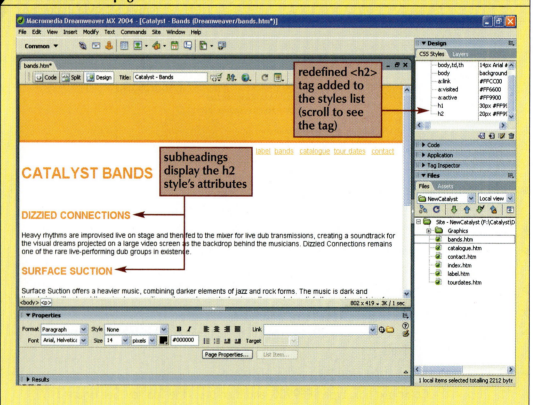

Now that you've created a style by modifying an existing tag, you'll remove the formatting from the paragraph text that follows each subheading in the Bands page.

To remove formatting from text:

1. Place the insertion point after the DIZZIED CONNECTION paragraph text, and then press the **Enter** key. The SURFACE SUCTION subheading moves down two lines.

2. Place the insertion point before the DIZZIED CONNECTION paragraph text, click the **Format** list arrow in the Property inspector, and then click **None**. The formatting is removed from the paragraph text and the text moves to the same line as the subheading.

3. Press the **Shift+Enter** keys to insert one line break. The paragraph text moves directly below the subheading.

4. Repeat Steps 1 through 3 to format the other subheadings in the page.

5. Save the Bands page.

Next, you'll create a custom style class.

Creating and Applying Custom Style Classes

Modifying text attributes is not limited to the redefinition of existing HTML tags. You can also create custom style classes, which are styles you build from scratch and give a unique name. The process for creating a custom style class is similar to redefining an HTML tag, except that you name the style and specify all the attributes you want the style to include. Some designers prefer to create custom style classes instead of redefining existing tags (such as the heading tags) when they are creating styles for an element that will be used in a limited way, or as an exception to the norm. For example, when you selected the page font in the Page Properties dialog box, Dreamweaver redefined the body tag to include the selected font group. This ensures that all the text in the Web page will be displayed in the selected font group because the body tags are always included in the code for a Web page. If you decide to display a small section of text in a different font, a good way to do this would be to create a custom style and apply the custom style only to that text.

Creating a Custom Style Class

Reference Window

- Click the New CSS Style button in the CSS Styles panel to open the New CSS Style dialog box.
- Click the Class option button.
- Click the Name text box to select the text, and then type the name of the new custom style class.
- Click the appropriate Define In option button.
- Click the OK button to open the CSS Style Definition dialog box.
- Click a category in the Category list, and then set the options you want.
- Click the OK button.

Sara has signed a new band to the Catalyst label, and Brian wants to use an alternate subheading style for new bands to promote them and draw attention to them in the Web site.

You will add the name of the new band to the bottom of the Bands page, and you will create a custom style class for the new band subheading. Finally, you will apply the custom style to the new heading text. You'll name the style ".NewBandSub." By convention, the name of a custom style class always begins with a period, has no spaces, and cannot contain any special characters. (If you forget to add the period, Dreamweaver will add it for you.) In addition to a font, size, and color, you'll include a background color in the custom style class.

To create a custom style class:

1. Click the **New CSS Style** button in the CSS Styles panel. The New CSS Style dialog box opens.
2. Click the **Class** option button in the Type category.
3. Click the **Name** text box to select the text, and then type **.NewBandSub** (including the period before the name).
4. Click the **This Document Only** option button in the Define In section, and then click the **OK** button. The CSS Style Definition for .NewBandSub dialog box opens.
5. Click **Type** in the Category list box, if necessary.
6. Type **20** in the Size text box, click the right **Size** list arrow, and then select **pixels**, if necessary.
7. Click the **Case** list arrow, click **Uppercase**, click in the **Color** text box, and then type **#FF9900**.

   Next, you will change the category so you can add the background color.
8. Click **Background** in the Category list.
9. Click in the **Background Color** text box, type **#FFCC00**, and then click the **OK** button. The name of the new style appears at the bottom of the list in the CSS Styles panel.

Once you create a custom style class, you must apply it to the text you want to format. You apply a custom style class to selected text from the Property inspector. When you create a new custom style class style, the name of that style will appear in the Style list in the Property inspector as well as the style list in the CSS Styles panel. You apply the style to selected text by selecting the style from the Style list in the Property inspector. To help you remember what a style looks like, when possible, each style name in the Style list in the Property inspector is formatted with the attributes for that style.

You'll type the name of the new band, FireFly, at the bottom of the Bands page, and then you will apply the .NewBandSub style to the new band name.

To apply a custom style class:

1. Position the insertion point at the bottom of the Bands page, type **FireFly**, and then press the **Shift+Enter** keys to insert one line break.
2. Type **The newest band on the Catalyst label. More info. coming soon.**
3. Select the band name, click the **Style** list arrow in the Property inspector, and then click **NewBandSub**. The style is applied to the text. See Figure 3-19.

Custom .NewBandSub style created and applied | Figure 3-19

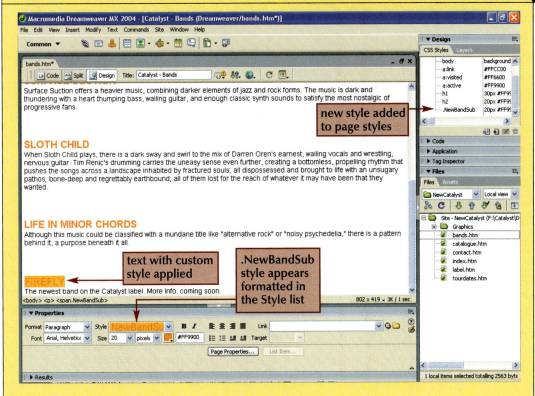

4. Save the page, and then preview the page in a browser.

You can also create CSS styles to format the text links for the site.

Using the Advanced CSS Type to Customize Anchor Tag Pseudoclasses

When you set the page properties for the Catalyst site, Dreamweaver created CSS styles to customize the appearance of hyperlinks for the site. You can also create these styles manually using the advanced style. When you create an advanced style, you redefine the formatting for a group of tags or for tags containing a specific ID attribute. In this case, you would create a CSS style for each part, or pseudoclass, of the <a> tag. According to style sheet standards, a **pseudoclass** is any class that is applied to entities other than HTML Specifications Standard tags. For example, the anchor tag <a> is broken into four parts (pseudoclasses): a:link, a:hover, a:active, and a:visited. Each of these pseudoclasses controls a portion of the hyperlink functionality of the anchor tag. The a:link portion of the tag controls the way the link text looks before the link has been visited. The a:hover portion of the tag controls the way the link text looks while the pointer is over the link text. (The a:hover portion of the tag is not supported by Netscape Navigator version 4.) The a:active portion of the tag controls the way the link text looks as it is being clicked. The a:visited portion of the tag controls the way the link text looks after the link has been visited. You can use advanced styles to modify each part of the anchor tag in the same way you redefined an existing HTML tag.

When you set the page properties for the Bands page, Dreamweaver created styles a:link, a:visited, and a:active pseudoclasses of the anchor tag. Now you will set the style for the a:hover pseudoclass.

| Reference Window | **Using the Advanced CSS Type for Hyperlinks** |

- Click the New CSS Style button in the CSS Styles panel to open the New CSS Style dialog box.
- Click the Advanced option button.
- Click the Selector list arrow, and then click the selector you want to modify.
- Click the appropriate Define In option button.
- Click the OK button to open the CSS Style Definition dialog box.
- Click a category in the Category list, and then set the options you want.
- Click the OK button.

When you define the parts of the anchor tag manually, you must define them in the order in which they appear in the CSS Selector list: a:link, a:visited, a:hover, a:active. The a:hover style must be placed after the a:link and a:visited styles so they don't hide the color property of the a:hover style. Similarly, the a:active style must be placed after the a:hover style, or the a:active color property will display when a user both activates and hovers over the linked text. When you set the hyperlink attributes in the Page Properties dialog box, Dreamweaver creates the CSS styles for the pseudoclasses of the anchor tag and automatically places the styles in the correct order in the style sheet.

You'll finish customizing the appearance of the text links in the Bands page using the advanced type to create a style for the a:hover pseudoclass of the anchor tag. Because Dreamweaver always adds new styles at the bottom of the style list and because the a:hover selector must be placed before the a:active selector in the list, you need to delete the existing a:active style from the style list. Then you can create the a:hover style and re-create the a:active style.

To delete a style from the CSS Styles panel:

1. Click the **a:active** style in the style list in the CSS Styles panel to select it.
2. Click the **Delete CSS Style** button 🗑 in the CSS Styles panel. The style is removed from the list.

Now you will create the new selector styles.

To customize the appearance of hyperlinks using the advanced type:

1. Click the **New CSS Style** button in the CSS Styles panel. The New CSS Style dialog box opens.
2. Click the **Advanced** option button in the Selector Type section.
3. Click the **Selector** list arrow, and then click **a:hover**.
4. Click the **This Document Only** option button in the Define In section, and then click the **OK** button. The CSS Style Definition for a:hover dialog box opens.
5. Click **Type** in the Category list, if necessary.
6. Type **#FF9900** in the Color text box, click the **None** check box in the Decoration section to check it, and then click the **OK** button. The a:hover style is customized for the Catalyst site and is added to the style list in the CSS Styles panel.

You'll repeat this process to re-create the a:active style.

7. Click the **New CSS Style** button in the CSS Styles panel to open the New CSS Style dialog box.

8. Make sure the **Advanced** option button is selected, click the **Selector** list arrow, click **a:active**, make sure the **This Document Only** option button is selected, and then click the **OK** button. The CSS Style Definition for a:active dialog box opens.

9. Click **Type** in the Category list, if necessary, type **#FF9900** in the Color text box, and then click the **OK** button. The a:active portion of the tag is customized.

10. Save the Bands page.

You'll preview the Bands page in a browser so you can test the links.

To preview the customized text links in a browser:

1. Preview the Bands page in a browser. The custom a:link style is visible.
2. Point to the **catalogue** link. The hover style is visible. See Figure 3-20.

Bands page with customized link styles previewed in a browser — Figure 3-20

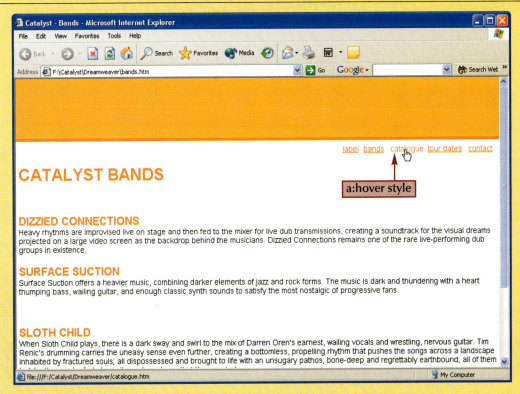

3. Click the **catalogue** link. The Catalogue page opens in the browser.
4. Click the **Back** button on the browser toolbar. The Bands page reloads.
5. Close the browser window.

In this session, you created CSS styles in the Bands page by redefining an HTML tag, creating a custom style, and creating an advanced style. In the next session, you will export the styles from the Bands page to an external style sheet, create CSS styles in an external style sheet, and attach the external style sheet to the pages of the Catalyst site.

Review

Session 3.2 Quick Check

1. What is a CSS style?
2. True or False? When you redefine a CSS style after it has been applied to text, the look of the content to which the style has been applied is also updated.
3. What is a CSS style that you create from scratch called?
4. True or False? You can save CSS styles in a style sheet that can be applied to all of the pages in a site.
5. How does modifying an HTML tag make it more useful?
6. When do some designers prefer to create custom style classes instead of redefining existing HTML tags?
7. With what letter or character do custom style class names start?

Session 3.3

Using External Style Sheets

Having all the styles for a Web site located in one place is one of the greatest advantages of using CSS styles. Using an external style sheet enables you to separate the style of your Web site from the content of your Web site, enabling you to make site-wide stylistic changes by updating a single file. So far, you have created and used styles within one document, or page, in the Catalyst site. To use the styles you created throughout a site, they must be located in an external style sheet, a file that contains the CSS styles defined for a Web site. This file has the file extension .css. You can have as many external style sheets as you would like for a site, but it is usually easier to incorporate all styles into one external style sheet. You can either create a style in an external style sheet or you can export the styles you created within a Web page to an external style sheet.

Exporting Styles to an External Style Sheet

If you've already created styles in a specific document or page, you can export those styles to an external style sheet rather than re-create them. This enables you to use those styles throughout the Web site. To keep the files in a Web site organized, you should create a folder in the local root folder of the Web site, such as a folder named "Stylesheets," and then save the external style sheet file with a descriptive name, such as "catalyst_styles," within that folder. In order to export CSS styles to an external style sheet, the Web page where the styles are currently located must be open.

Reference Window | Exporting Styles to an External Style Sheet

- Open the Web page whose styles you want to export.
- Click File on the menu bar, point to Export, and then click CSS Styles to open the Export Styles As CSS File dialog box.
- Navigate to the folder in which you are saving your style sheets in the local root folder.
- Type a name for the style sheet in the File Name text box.
- Click the Save button.

Because you want to use the styles you created for the Bands page in all the other pages in the Catalyst site, you'll export those styles to an external style sheet that you'll store in a new folder named "Stylesheets" in the local root folder. When you export the styles from the Bands page, all of the styles from the Bands page, including the styles that Dreamweaver created when you set the page properties, are exported to the external style sheet. In this case, you will create the style sheet when you export the styles from the Bands page.

To export styles to an external style sheet:

1. If you took a break after the last session, make sure the **NewCatalyst** site is open, and the **bands.htm** page is open in the Document window.
2. Make sure **bands.htm** is selected in the Files panel.
3. Click **File** on the menu bar, point to **Export**, and then click **CSS Styles**. The Export Styles As CSS File dialog box opens.

   You need to create a new folder in which to store the external style sheet.

4. Verify that the Save in list box displays the local root folder of your NewCatalyst Web site (the Dreamweaver folder).
5. Click the **Create New Folder** button on the dialog box toolbar, type **Stylesheets** in the Name text box, and then press the **Enter** key. The Stylesheets folder is created within the local root folder of your NewCatalyst Web site.
6. Double-click the **Stylesheets** folder to open the folder. You want to save the external style sheet in this folder.

   Next, you'll name the external style sheet with a descriptive name.

7. Click in the **File Name** text box, and then type **catalyst_styles**. See Figure 3-21.

Figure 3-21   Export Styles As CSS File dialog box

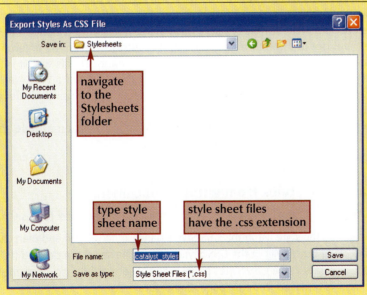

8. Click the **Save** button. The external style sheet file is saved within the folder you created.
9. Click the **Refresh** button on the Files panel toolbar to refresh the file list, and then click the **Plus (+)** button next to the Stylesheets folder to display the catalyst_styles.css file in the file list. See Figure 3-22.

Figure 3-22 External style sheet displayed in the Files panel

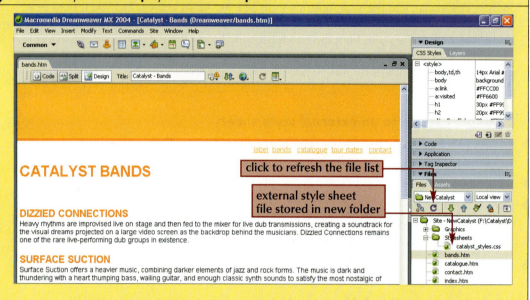

Once you have exported styles, you should remove them from the page.

Deleting Styles from a Style Sheet

You must delete all of the styles from within a page after you export those styles to an external style sheet. Otherwise, you will end up with multiple sets of styles with the same names, which can cause styles to conflict and lead to confusion. Using both sets of styles can negate some of the benefits of using style sheets because you don't have one centralized set of styles that is easily updated and used throughout the site. Also, because style sheets are cascading, the styles in an internal style sheet will override styles in an external style sheet wherever a style conflict exists. And when an attribute is defined in the external style sheet, but not in the internal style sheet, the attribute from the external style sheet will be displayed. You can see how this could get out of hand. This is why it is important to maintain an organized file structure and to keep all the styles for a Web site in one location. When you delete the styles from a page, the text will return to its default formatting and the background image will disappear.

Because you exported the styles from the Bands page to the external style sheet, you can delete all the styles located within the Bands page.

To delete all of the styles from within a document:

1. Click the **Minus (–)** button next to <style> in the CSS Styles panel to close the style list.
2. Select **<style>** in the style list in the CSS Styles panel, if necessary, and then click the **Delete CSS Style** button in the CSS Styles panel. The styles are deleted from the page, "(no styles)" appears in the CSS Styles panel, and the formatting (including the background image) is removed from the page. See Figure 3-23

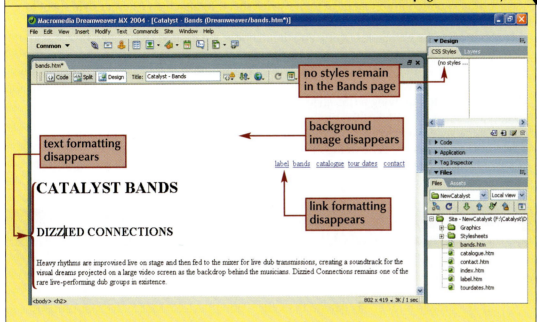

Figure 3-23 Bands page without styles

3. Save the Bands page.

You can also delete a single style if you are not going to use it in the site. Deleting styles that you are not using in a site helps to keep the site's files organized and lean. You delete a single style in the same way that you deleted all the styles, except that you select only the style that you want to delete from the page. External style sheets are uploaded to the Web server along with the Web pages, graphics, and other files associated with the site. By deleting unused styles, you are eliminating unnecessary materials from the site, reducing the size of the files, and eliminating clutter. Next, you'll attach the external style sheet to the Bands page.

Attaching a Style Sheet to Web Pages

When the styles for formatting a Web site are located in an external style sheet, you must attach the style sheet to each Web page that you want to format with those styles. You can attach an existing style sheet to each Web page when you create the pages, or you can attach an existing style sheet to each page when you need the styles. If you exported the styles in the external style sheet from a page in the Web site, the styles are automatically applied to the page content when you attach the external style sheet to that page.

The process for attaching a style sheet to a Web page is the same whether or not the styles were exported from that page to the styles sheet. To attach an external style sheet to a Web page, you must open the page in the Document window, click the Attach Style Sheet button in the CSS Styles panel, and then choose the desired style sheet. Before you attach the style sheet, you need to remove the current formatting; otherwise, the older formatting might override the CSS style you apply or combine with the CSS style, causing the text to display differently than you had intended.

The process for applying a CSS style saved in an external style sheet to the rest of the pages in a site is the same as the process for applying CSS styles created within a document. If the style is a custom style, you select the text to which you want to apply the style, and then click the style in the Property inspector. If the style is a modified HTML tag or an advanced type, you apply the tag in the regular way and the modified attributes of the tag will be included.

Reference Window

Attaching an External Style Sheet to a Web Page

- Open the Web page in Design view.
- Click the Attach Style Sheet button in the CSS Styles panel to open the Link External Style Sheet dialog box.
- Click the Browse button, navigate to the folder within the local root folder that contains the style sheets, click the name of the style sheet you want to attach to the Web page, and then click the OK button.
- Click the Link option button.
- Click the OK button.

You'll attach the catalyst_styles style sheet to the Bands page.

To attach an external style sheet to a Web page:

1. Click the **Attach Style Sheet** button in the CSS Styles panel. The Attach External Style Sheet dialog box opens. See Figure 3-24.

Figure 3-24 | **Attach External Style Sheet dialog box**

2. Click the **Browse** button, double-click the **Stylesheets** folder in the local root folder of your NewCatalyst site, click **catalyst_styles.css**, and then click the **OK** button to select the external style sheet you want to attach to the page.

3. Click the **Link** option button, if necessary, and then click the **OK** button. The external style sheet is attached and its name appears in the CSS Styles panel. Also, the styles in the external style sheet are applied to the content in the Bands page. The background image is not redisplayed in the page; you will correct this when you learn to edit styles. See Figure 3-25.

Figure 3-25 External style sheet attached to the Bands page

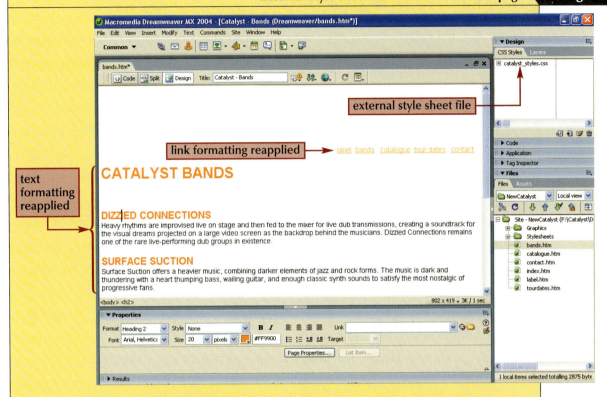

4. Click the **Plus (+)** button beside the style sheet name to view the styles. (If more than one style sheet is attached to the page, you can move between style sheets using the Plus (+) and Minus (–) buttons to open or close the desired style sheets.)

5. Save the Bands page.

Next, you'll add a new style to the external style sheet.

Creating a Style in an External Style Sheet

Once an external style sheet is created, you can add new styles to it at any time. The process of creating a style in an external style sheet is exactly the same as the process of creating a style in an internal style sheet. The only difference is that you choose the style sheet by name in the Define In list when you create the new style.

Defining a Style in an External Style Sheet — Reference Window

- Click the New CSS Style button in the CSS Styles panel to open the New CSS Style dialog box.
- Click the appropriate style type option button.
- Click the Name text box, and then type a name for the new style.
- Click the top option button in the Define In section, and then select the appropriate style sheet name from the list box.
- Click the OK button to open the CSS Style Definition dialog box.
- Click a category in the Category list, and then set the options you want.
- Click the OK button.

You need to create a style for the copyright information that will appear at the bottom of each page as a footer. Because this style will be used on each page in the Catalyst site, you'll define the new style in the catalyst_styles.css external style sheet. When you add a new style to the style sheet, the style sheet will open in the Document window. You must save the style sheet to save the new style. You will examine the styles later.

To define a style in an external style sheet:

1. Click the **New CSS Style** button in the CSS Style panel. The New CSS Style dialog box opens.

2. Click the **Class** option button, if necessary, select any text in the **Name** text box, and then type **.catalyst_footer**.

3. Click the top option button in the Define In section, make sure **catalyst_styles.css** is listed in the Define In list box, and then click the **OK** button to open the CSS Style Definition for .catalyst_footer in catalyst_styles.css dialog box.

4. Click **Type** in the Category list, if necessary, and then set the size to **10 pixels.**

5. Click **Block** in the Category list, click the **Text Align** list arrow, and then click **Center**.

6. Click the **OK** button. The .catalyst_footer style appears in the CSS Styles panel and in the Style list in the Property inspector. The catalyst_styles page opens in the Document window and an asterisk appears in the page tab.

    The style was added to the style sheet, and you must save the style sheet to save the changes.

7. Click the **catalyst_styles.css** tab in the Document window, save the page, and then click the **bands.htm** tab.

You'll add copyright text to the Bands page, and then apply the .catalyst_footer style to it.

To add text and apply an external style:

1. Press the **Ctrl+End** keys to move the insertion point to the end of the text in the Bands page, and then press the **Enter** key twice. This is the location where you'll type the copyright information.

2. If necessary, click the **Category** button on the Insert bar, and then click **Text**.

3. Click the **Characters** list arrow on the Insert bar, and then click the **Copyright** button © in the Characters list. The copyright symbol © is inserted at the beginning of the line.

4. Press the **Right Arrow** key to deselect the copyright symbol, press the **spacebar**, and then type **Catalyst, Inc. 2006**.

    Next, you'll apply the .catalyst_footer style to the copyright line.

5. Select the copyright symbol and text, click the **Style** list arrow in the Property inspector, click **catalyst_footer,** and then press the **Right Arrow** key to deselect the text. The style is applied to the text. See Figure 3-26.

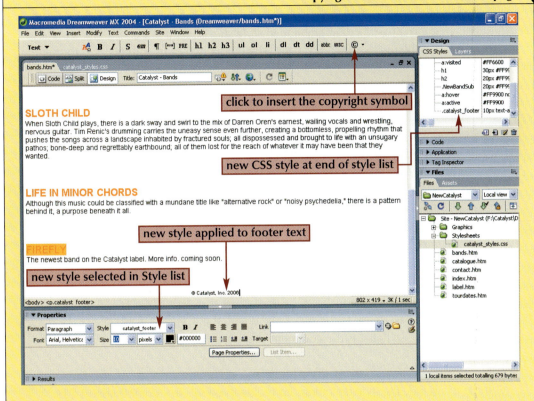

Figure 3-26 Copyright text added to the Bands page

6. Save the page.

Next, you will examine the code associated with style sheets. Once you are familiar with the code, you will learn to edit styles.

Examining Code for CSS Styles

As you created and applied CSS styles to format the text in the Bands page and when Dreamweaver created styles in the other pages of the site, Dreamweaver added the appropriate HTML code within the head of each page. The **head** of a Web page is the portion of the HTML between the head tags. The actual code included within the head differs based on whether you created an internal style sheet or an external style sheet.

When you create styles that apply only to the document in which you are working, the code for those styles is placed in the head of that page. If you attach an external style sheet to a Web page, a link tag to the style sheet is placed in the head of the HTML code for that page. The link tag allows the Web page to access the content of the external style sheet.

You will examine the HTML code in the head of the Bands page as well as the additional tags that appear throughout the Web page.

Viewing Code for Internal Style Sheets

When styles are defined in the current document only, the code is stored in an internal style sheet, which is also called an **embedded style sheet** because the styles are embedded (or placed) in the head of the Web page. The embedded styles can be used throughout the current Web page, but not in any other page. The code usually takes the format:

```
<style type="text/css">
<!--
name {
   attribute-name: attribute value;
   attribute2-name: attribute2 value;
}
-->
</style>
```

where name is the style name, the HTML tag name, or the tag and pseudoclass name.

The style definitions (or rules) all appear inside the style tags, which are in the format:

```
<style type="text/css">style definitions</style>
```

where type="text/css" indicates the format of the styles that will follow. Currently "text/css" is the only style type; however, the current HTML guidelines recommend that you include the style type to prevent problems if other style types are introduced in the future.

Nested within the style tag is the **comment tag**, which is in the format:

```
<!-- style definitions -->
```

Comment tags hide the style definitions from older browsers that do not support CSS styles. Browsers tend to ignore tags that they do not understand. Browsers that do not understand CSS style tags will ignore the tags, but the content of the style tag (the style definitions) will be displayed in the Web page as text. To avoid this problem, comment tags are placed around the style definitions to prevent older browsers from displaying them in the Web page.

Remember, every CSS style (or rule) consists of two parts: the selector and the declaration. The selector is the style name and the declaration defines the attributes that are included in the style. The format for the style definition is:

```
name {
   attribute-name: attribute value;
   attribute2-name: attribute2 value;
}
```

In Dreamweaver, the selector and opening bracket are located on the first line of code for the style and are displayed in pink. You can tell by the style name whether the style is a custom style, a redefined tag, or an advanced style tag. When a custom style class is created, a period precedes the name of the new style (for example, .catalyst_footer). If an existing tag is redefined, the tag name appears at the beginning of the style (for example, h1). If you use the advanced style, the tag name is followed by a colon and the pseudoclass (for example, a:active) or a number of tags separated by commas may appear if the advanced style is being created for a certain combination of tags. The style declaration is a series of attribute/value pairs. The attribute and value are separated by a colon and a space. Each attribute/value pair is displayed in blue on a separate line that ends with a semicolon and is indented under the selector. The closing bracket appears on a separate line after the final attribute/value pair and is displayed in pink. Styles follow this same format whether they are embedded within a page or located within an external style sheet.

You can view the embedded style sheet for a page by opening the page in the Document window and switching to Code view. You will open the Catalogue page and examine the internal style sheet code that Dreamweaver created when you defined the page properties.

To view the code for an internal style sheet:

1. Double-click **catalogue.htm** in the Files panel to open the Catalogue page, click the **Show Code View** button <code> on the Document toolbar, and then scroll to the top of the page. The code for the Catalogue page is displayed in the Document window. See Figure 3-27.

Figure 3-27   Code for the internal style sheet in the Catalogue page

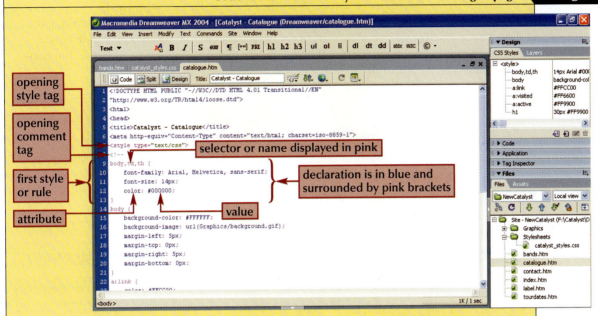

Trouble? If the code on your screen does not match the code in the figure, you do not have code wrap, word wrap, line numbers, syntax coloring, and/or auto indent turned on. Click the View Options button on Document toolbar, and then click Word Wrap, Line Numbers, Syntax Coloring, and/or Auto Indent to check each option as necessary.

2. Examine the code associated with the styles. Locate the opening head tag, and then locate the opening style tag.

3. Locate the opening comment tag, and then locate the first rule. Notice that each rule starts with the selector displayed in pink followed by the opening bracket. The declaration is indented beneath the selector and is displayed in blue. Each attribute/value pair is on a separate line ending with a semicolon. The attribute is separated from the value by a colon and a space. Finally, the closing bracket is displayed in pink on a separate line.

4. Close the Catalogue page.

Next, you will view the code for an external style sheet.

Viewing Code for External Style Sheets

When an external style sheet is attached to a page, a link tag appears within the head of the Web page and the styles are located in the style sheet, not in the head of the Web page. External style sheets are also called **linked style sheets**. Link tags do not include a closing tag or any style content information; they only convey relationship information about the linked document. Link tags can appear only within the head of a Web page and should not be confused with the anchor tag that is used to create hyperlinks in the body of a Web page.

Link tags appear in the following general format:

`<link rel="stylesheet" href="stylesheeturl.css" type="text/css">`

The first part of the tag, link, identifies the type of tag. The second part of the tag, rel=, indicates the relationship between the linked document and the Web page. The relationship itself appears within quotation marks; in this case, the relationship is "stylesheet," meaning that the linked document contains the CSS style for the page. Next, href="stylesheeturl.css" is the URL of the linked document. The URL appears within quotation marks. Finally, type= indicates the form of the content that will follow. MIME type is the standard for identifying content type on the Internet. The type also appears within quotation marks.

You'll look at the link to the external style sheet in the Bands page.

To view the code in the Bands page:

1. Click the **Show Code View** button on the Document toolbar, and then scroll to the top of the Bands page in the Document window.

2. Locate the link tag in the head of the Bands page. See Figure 3-28.

Figure 3-28 Code for the external style sheet in the Band page

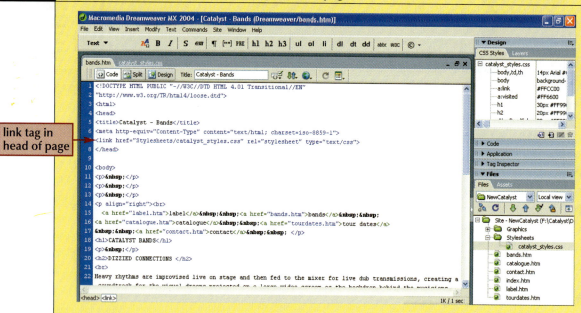

3. Locate the closing head tag. Notice that no styles are displayed in the head of the Bands page.

When styles are located in an external style sheet, you must open the style sheet to view the code for the styles. If you know how to enter code manually, you can edit the styles for the page by changing the code in the style sheet. You will open the catalyst_styles.css style sheet in the Document window and view the styles. Style sheets will open only in Code view.

To view the external style sheet:

1. Click the **catalyst_styles.css** tab in the Document window, and then scroll to the top of the page. The external style sheet appears in the Document window. See Figure 3-29.

Figure 3-29   External style sheet page

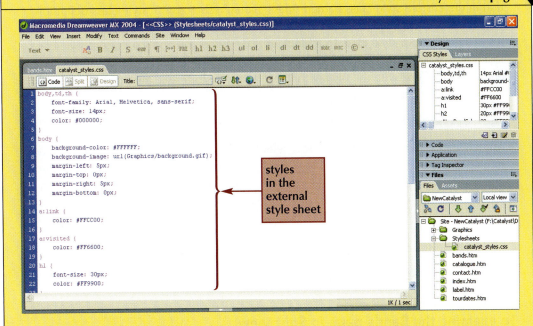

Trouble? If you don't see the catalyst_styles.css tab in the Document window, the external style sheet is not displayed. Click the Plus (+) button next to the Stylesheets folder in the Files panel to display its content, and then double-click catalyst_styles.css to open the external style sheet page.

2. Notice that the style format is the same as in the internal style sheet.
3. Close the catalyst_styles.css page.

Next, you will view style tags.

Viewing Style Tags

Whether styles are located in an internal or external style sheet, using CSS styles affects the code in the body of a Web page in the same way. When you use CSS styles to modify or customize HTML tags, you will not see any additional code in the body of the Web pages. The existing tags simply reference the new definitions, which are located either in the head portion of the Web page or in an external style sheet.

When you select text and apply a custom style class, Dreamweaver adds the attributes of that custom style class to the text by inserting additional code within the Web page in one of three ways:

- **Adding attributes to an existing tag.** When you apply a custom style class to text that is already surrounded by a tag, Dreamweaver adds the additional attributes of the custom style class to the existing tag. For example, if you apply a custom style class named "class_name" to a block of text that is already surrounded by a paragraph tag, <p>, Dreamweaver adds the attributes of the custom style to that paragraph tag in the following manner:

```
<p class="class_name">Content of text block</p>
```

where class="class_name" tells the browser to format the text according to the definition in the custom style class named "class_name." (The custom style class definition will be located either in the head of the Web page or in an external style sheet.)

- **Applying a custom style class to a block of text.** When you apply a custom style class to a block of text that is not already encompassed by a tag, Dreamweaver surrounds the entire block of text with the div tag that inserts the custom style attributes. The div tag appears in the general format

```
<div class="class_name">Content of text block</div>
```

- **Applying a custom style class to a text selection.** When you apply a custom style class to a selection smaller than a text block (such as a word, a phrase, or a portion of a text block), Dreamweaver surrounds the selection with a span tag that inserts the custom style attributes. The span tag appears in the following general format:

```
<span class="class_name">Content of text selection</span>
```

You will view the subheadings and footer in the Bands page in Split view to examine the code that Dreamweaver inserted into the page.

To examine the Bands page in Split view:

1. Click the **Show Code and Design Views** button [Split] on the Document toolbar, and then select **DIZZIED CONNECTIONS** in the Design pane. The text is also selected in the Code pane.

2. Examine the code around the selected text in the Code pane. The text is surrounded by the Heading 2 tag, <h2>. No extra code appears in the page because the <h2> tag simply references the style located in the style sheet and displays the text according to the rule that was defined. See Figure 3-30.

Figure 3-30 | **Code for a redefined HTML tag**

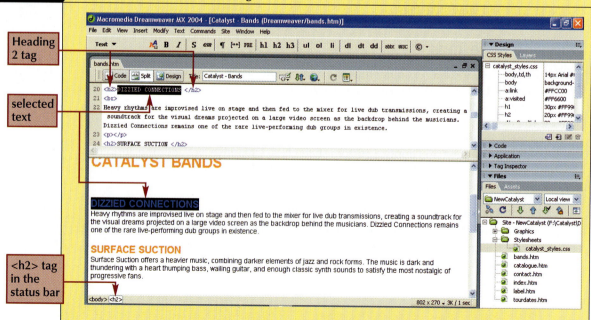

3. Scroll to the bottom of the page in the Design pane, select **FIREFLY**, and then examine the code surrounding the selected text in the Code pane. The custom style class information is inserted into a span tag because the paragraph tag that surrounds the subheading also surrounds the following paragraph text, but the style is applied to only the heading. See Figure 3-31.

Figure 3-31 Custom style class applied with a span tag

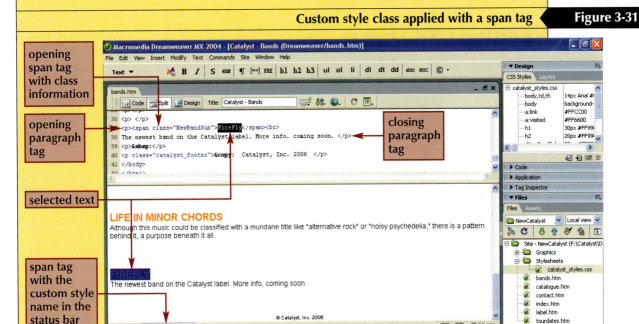

4. Select the footer text in the Design pane and examine the code surrounding the selected text in the Code pane. The custom style class information is inserted into the paragraph tag this time because the paragraph tag is only surrounding the affected text. See Figure 3-32.

Figure 3-32 Custom style class applied to the paragraph tag

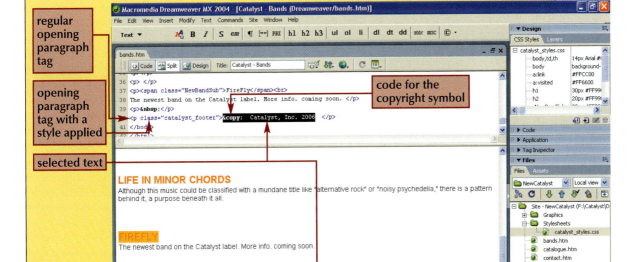

> **5.** Click the **Show Design View** button [Design] on the Document toolbar, and then scroll to the top of the page.

Next, you will edit CSS styles.

Editing CSS Styles

One of the most powerful aspects of Cascading Style Sheets is the ability to edit styles. You edit a style by adding or removing formatting attributes from an existing style. When you edit a style, any element to which the style is applied is updated automatically to reflect the changes you made. This helps you to maintain a consistent look throughout a Web site, whether it includes a few pages or many. It also enables you to control the look of an entire Web site from one centralized set of specifications. Dreamweaver includes several tools to help you manage and edit your styles, including the CSS Style Definition dialog box, the Tag inspector, and the Property inspector. You will explore each tool.

Editing Styles in the CSS Style Definition Dialog Box

You can edit styles in the CSS Style Definition dialog box. This is the same dialog box that you used to create the definitions. You open the CSS Style Definition dialog box by right-clicking the style name in the style list in the CSS Styles panel and clicking Edit or by selecting a style in the CSS Styles panel and clicking the Edit Style button. The changes you make will override the original style attribute selections. Once you have selected attributes for the style, you can view the style in the page by clicking the Apply button in the CSS Style Definition dialog box and viewing the page in the Document window.

Reference Window | **Editing a Style**

- Select the style that you want to edit in the CSS Styles panel.
- Right-click the name of the style, and then click Edit (*or* click the style name, and then click the Edit CSS Style button in the CSS Styles panel).
- Make the desired changes in the CSS Style Definition dialog box.
- Click the OK button.

When you exported the styles from the Bands page to the external style sheet, the background image stopped displaying. This is because the style specified a relative path from the image to the Bands page. The relative path must now be updated because the style sheet is now located in a subfolder rather than in the top level of the site's local root folder. Dreamweaver should have changed the path automatically, but did not. Instead, you will edit the style and change the path yourself.

To edit a style:

> **1.** Right-click the **body** style in the CSS Styles panel, and then click **Edit** on the context menu. The CSS Style Definition for body in catalyst_styles.css dialog box opens.
>
> **2.** Click **Background** in the Category list. See Figure 3-33.

Figure 3-33 CSS Style Definition for body in catalyst_styles.css dialog box

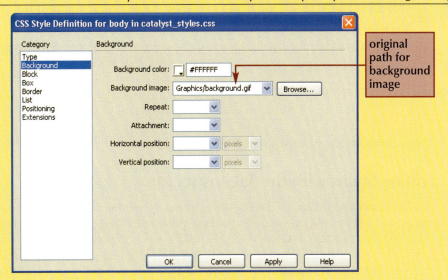

3. Click the **Browse** button to the right of the Background Image text box. The Select Image Source dialog box opens.

4. Navigate to the **Graphics** folder, click the **background.gif** image, and then click the **OK** button. The path now has two dots and a backslash before the (Graphics) folder name. The browser interprets these symbols to move up a level (out of the Stylesheets folder) and then look for the Graphics folder.

5. Click the **Apply** button. The Bands page displays the updated style so the background image appears. See Figure 3-34.

Figure 3-34 Bands page with updated body style

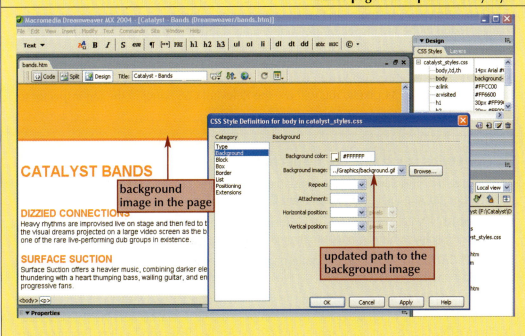

6. Click the **OK** button. The changes you made to the styles are accepted and the external style sheet opens.

   You must save the external style sheet to save the changes you made to the style. If the style were in an internal style sheet, you would save the page to save the changes to the style.

7. Save the catalyst_styles page, and then close it.
8. Preview the Bands page in a browser.

You can also edit styles with the Tag inspector.

Editing Styles with the Tag Inspector

The Tag inspector, located in the Tag panel group, is another tool you can use to examine and edit CSS styles. When you select a page element in Design view or when you select a tag (or portion of a tag) in Code view, all the CSS styles affecting the selection and the tags to which those rules are relevant appear in the Relevant CSS panel of the Tag inspector. Styles are listed in hierarchical order; styles that are closer to the text are displayed at the bottom of the list. This is useful because styles sometimes inherit attributes from higher-level styles and because, when an attribute value is selected in more than one style, the value that is located in the style closest to the element in the code will override the value of the higher-level style. Viewing a hierarchical list enables you to see all the styles that affect the selection and to determine where conflicts occur if something does not display correctly. When you select a style, the name and location of the document containing the style and all the attributes that can be associated with that style appear below the style list. You can display the attributes in alphabetical order or by category. (You will view the attributes in alphabetical order.) Attributes that have values are displayed in blue at the top of the list. When a style contains an attribute that is being overridden by another style for the selected element, the attribute appears in the list with a red line through it. Attribute names are displayed at the left of the list and values are displayed at the right. You can change or add values by typing in the value area or by selecting a value from a list. Any changes made in the Tag inspector are immediately applied to the page. You must save the page or any relevant style sheets to save the changes.

Brian has decided that the page head and subheadings should be larger. You will change the page heading size to 44 pixels, the subheading to 32 pixels, and the new bands subheading to 34 pixels. You will use the Relevant CSS panel in the Tag inspector to make the changes.

To edit styles using the Tag inspector:

1. Collapse the **Files** panel group, collapse the **Design** panel group, expand the **Tag Inspector** panel group, and then click the **Relevant CSS** tab. The Relevant CSS panel appears.

   Trouble? If you do not see the Tag Inspector panel group at the right of the screen, you need to display it. Click Window on the menu bar, and then click Tag Inspector.

2. Select **CATALYST BANDS** in the Bands page. The styles relevant to the page heading are listed in the Tag inspector.

3. Click the **Show Category View** button in the Tag inspector, and then click **h1** in the Applied Rules list, which is the style associated with the <h1> tag. Because the style is a redefined HTML tag, the tag name appears in both the Applied Rules and Tag lists. Dreamweaver uses the tag name as the style name for redefined HTML tags. See Figure 3-35.

Tag inspector with page heading styles listed — **Figure 3-35**

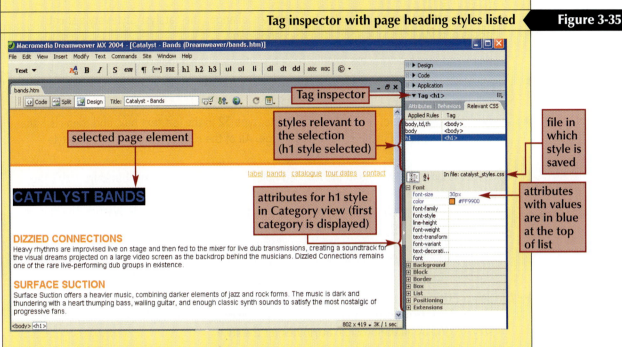

4. Click the **Show List View** button in the Tag inspector to show the attribute list in alphabetical order.

5. Click the value side of the font-size attribute, and then type **44** into the left text box. See Figure 3-36.

Updated font-size attribute in the Tag inspector — **Figure 3-36**

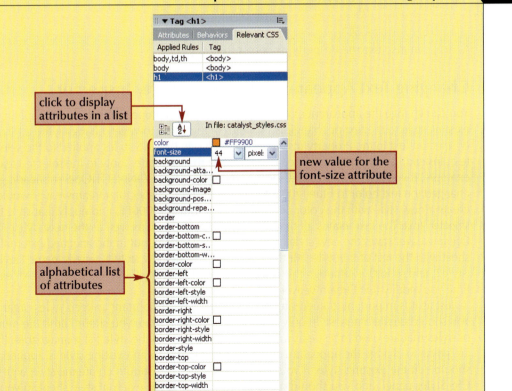

6. Click the attribute side of the list to accept the change. The catalyst_styles style sheet opens and the change is applied to the Bands page.

   You'll use the same process to edit the subheadings in the Bands page.

7. Select **DIZZIED CONNECTIONS** in the Bands page. The relevant styles are displayed in the Tag inspector with the h2 style selected.

8. Click the value side of the font size attribute, type **32** in the left text box, and then click the attribute side of the list to accept the change. All of the subheadings with the h2 style change size.

9. Click the **body,td,th** style in the Applied Rules list to see how the attributes from this tag affect the current selection. The color and font-size attributes have red lines through them because you set color and font size in the h2 style and those attributes override the ones in this higher-level style. The font-family attribute has a value in this style because the body tag affects all the elements in the body of your HTML code and you did not select a font family in the h2 style; the subheading text is displayed in the font family value selected in the body tag.

10. Select **FIREFLY** in the Bands page to display all the styles that are relevant to the selected text in the Tag inspector, and then click **.NewBandSub** in the Applied Rules list, if necessary, to display all the possible attributes for the style.

11. Click the value side of the font-size attribute, type **32** in the left text box, and then click the attribute side to accept the change. The new band subheading changes size in the Bands page.

12. Click the **catalyst_styles.css** tab in the Document window, save the catalyst_styles.css page, and then close the page. (You do not need to save the Bands page because you made all the changes to styles in the style sheet.)

13. Collapse the Tag Inspector panel group.

You can also use the Property inspector to apply styles.

Changing Text Appearance in the Property Inspector

You can change the appearance of selected text with the Property inspector by applying an existing style to the text or changing attributes of the text. However, changing the attributes of selected text in the Property inspector does not edit the CSS styles applied to the selected text. Instead, it will sometimes create a new style that is applied only to the selected text. For example, if you selected CONNECTIONS in the DIZZIED CONNECTIONS subheading and changed the text color to blue (#0000FF) in the Property inspector, Dreamweaver would create a new style with the color attribute value of blue (#0000FF) and apply that style to the selected text. The text retains all the other styles applied to it as well as the new style. Dreamweaver saves the new style in an internal style sheet, not in the attached external style sheet with the rest of the styles for the site, and gives the new style a generic name (.style1, .style2, and so forth). Although this is a simple way to modify the appearance of text, each time you modify text Dreamweaver creates a new style.

Just as it is important to keep site files organized, it is important to keep styles organized. You should create a new style only when it is necessary. Also, you should limit the number of styles that are used in a site as much as possible to keep the style list manageable. If you are going to change the appearance of all the text to which an existing style is applied, you should edit the existing style. If you need a new style, you should create the style with the CSS Styles panel, and you should place the new style in the external style sheet so you can use it throughout the site.

However, you can change text alignment in the Property inspector without creating a new style because Dreamweaver will simply add HTML tags around the selected text. You can also indent text, create order and unordered lists, and bold or italicize text in this way. You will create styles (redefined HTML tags) to customize the HTML tags mentioned above as needed. In this way, these tags become more useful just as the Heading tags became more useful when you customized their appearance. In addition, you can create custom styles that specify any of the above attributes as part of the style. As designers become more comfortable and proficient using style sheets, it is becoming good practice to use CSS styles for all Web page formatting, not just to define some display attributes. You should get in the habit of creating CSS styles for all formatting you want to add to a site.

Exploring HTML Tags Used with Text

Several HTML tags are used with text. You worked with a few, such as the body tag <body> and the Heading 1 tag <h1>, when you created styles by modifying the existing tags. Now you will learn about some other tags that affect text. In addition, you will learn about some deprecated tags, such as the font tag <font>, that are still in common use. Although these tags are being phased out and Dreamweaver no longer uses them by default, there are several important reasons to learn about them:

1. You will, most likely, need to update older HTML pages. Familiarity with the version of HTML in which the older pages were created makes the task easier and more efficient.
2. Your target audience may include users of older browsers or technology. It is impossible for these people to reliably view HTML pages that use the latest specifications. (We all know someone who has a five-year-old computer that they use but never update.)
3. Some new portable devices, specialized Web access tools, Web appliances and devices, and other programs are not compliant with the latest specifications and still rely on HTML 3.2 or earlier.
4. Some Web content management systems (for example, systems that dynamically create educational pages for online courses) do not support current formats.

When you create Web pages in Design view, Dreamweaver places the appropriate HTML tags around the text for you. To see the HTML tags, you need to switch to either Code view or Split view. Some of the more common text tags are described in Figure 3-37.

Common HTML tags for text   **Figure 3-37**

Tag Name	Tag Description	Tag Sample	Browser Display
Font	Contains the font face grouping, font size, and font color attributes. When you format text using the HTML mode in the Property inspector, Dreamweaver uses font tags to format the text.	`<color="#000000", size="3", font face="Arial, Helvetica, sans-serif"> Some text</font>`	Some text
Italic	Adds italic style to text. Accessibility guidelines recommend that you use the emphasis tag instead of the italic tag because the italic tag is used to create a visual presentation effect while the emphasis tag is used to indicate structural emphasis.	`<i>Some text</i>`	*Some text*

Figure 3-37   Common HTML tags for text (continued)

Tag Name	Tag Description	Tag Sample	Browser Display
Emphasis	Adds structural meaning to text and is to be rendered differently from other body text to designate emphasis. When you use the Italic button, Dreamweaver places emphasis tags around the selected text because accessibility guidelines recommend using the emphasis tag in place of the italic tag. Both Internet Explorer and Netscape Navigator italicize text that is surrounded by the emphasis tag.	`<em>Some text</em>`	*Some text*
Bold	Adds bold style to text. Accessibility guidelines recommend that you use the strong tag instead of the bold tag because the bold tag is used to create a visual presentation effect while the strong tag is used to indicate structural emphasis.	`<b>Some text</b>`	**Some text**
Strong	Adds structural meaning to text and is to be rendered differently from other body text to designate a stronger emphasis than the emphasis tag. When you use the Bold button, Dreamweaver places strong tags around the selected text because accessibility guidelines recommend using the strong tag in place of the bold tag. Both Internet Explorer and Netscape Navigator bold text that is surrounded by the strong tag.	`<strong>Some text </strong>`	**Some text**

Unordered List	Creates a list of bulleted items.	`<ul>`
		`<li>Item1</li>`
		`<li>Item2</li>`
		`</ul>`
			• Item1
			• Item2

Ordered List	Creates a list of numbered items.	`<ol>`
		`<li>Item1</li>`
		`<li>Item2</li>`
		`</ol>`
			1. Item1
			2. Item2

Paragraph	Designates a block of text that starts and ends with a break (a skipped line) and by default is left aligned with a ragged right edge. Dreamweaver places paragraph tags around blocks of text when you press the Enter key.	`<p>Some text in a paragraph.</p>` `<p>Another paragraph.</p>`	Some text in a paragraph. Another paragraph.

Blockquote	Usually indents text from both the left and right margins, and can be nested for deeper indents. Added in Dreamweaver with the Text Indent button; the Outdent button removes a blockquote tag.	`<p>Introductory text </p>`
		`<blockquote><p>Some text</p></blockquote>`
		`<p>Closing text</p>`
			Introductory text
			
			  Some text
			
			Closing text

Div	Divides a page into a series of blocks; for example, applying the Align attribute in the Property inspector sometimes creates a div tag with a value of left, center, or right to align the text.	`<div align="right">Some text, a paragraph, or other element</div>`	Some text, a paragraph, or other element

Common HTML tags for text (continued) — Figure 3-37

Tag Name	Tag Description	Tag Sample	Browser Display
Pre	Preserves the exact formatting of a block of text when it is displayed in a Web page by rendering text in a fixed pitch font and by preserving the associated spacing with white space characters. For example, a poem with pre tags around it would maintain indents, multiple spaces between words, and new lines that would otherwise be discarded when it was rendered in a browser.	`<pre>` Some preformatted text might look like this. `</pre>`	Some preformatted text might look like this.
Break	Forces a line break on a page. Used singly without a closing tag because it does not surround text and add attributes. Add by pressing the Shift+Enter keys or clicking the Break button in the Characters list in the Text category on the Insert bar.	`Some text`	Some text
Nonbreaking space	Inserts a space that will be displayed by the browser. (Browsers will display only one regular space between items in a Web page, regardless of how many regular spaces are entered.) Use nonbreaking spaces when you want to add more than one visible space between items. The nonbreaking space is a special character (not a tag) that is often used like a tag to format text. Insert by pressing the Ctrl+Shift+Spacebar keys or by clicking the Non-Breaking Space button in the Characters list in the Text category on the Insert bar.	`Some   text`	Some text
Basefont	Changes the attributes of the default font on which all the text contained in the Web page is based and overrides the default font settings in the user's browser. The basefont tag is placed in the head or body of the page and is used with the size attribute to change the size of the base font for the page. (When an absolute font size is used as the size value in the font tag, it overrides the basefont tag. When a relative font size is used as the size value in the font tag, it adds or subtracts from the size value you designate in the basefont tag.) This tag is used in conjunction with the font tag and does not apply to CSS styles.	`<basefont size="6">` Text at basefont size	Text at basefont size

Now you will examine the code for HTML tags that apply to text in the Bands page. You will also use the References tab in the Code panel group to gather additional information about some of the tags.

To examine the code for HTML tags that apply to text:

1. Click the **Show Code View** button on the Document toolbar. The Bands page displays in Code view.

2. Scroll to the top of the page, locate the body tag, and then locate the first paragraph tag <p> below the body tag.

3. Right-click the paragraph tag, and then click **Reference** on the context menu. The Code panel group opens to the Reference panel, which displays information about the paragraph tag. See Figure 3-38.

Figure 3-38   Reference panel for selected HTML paragraph tag

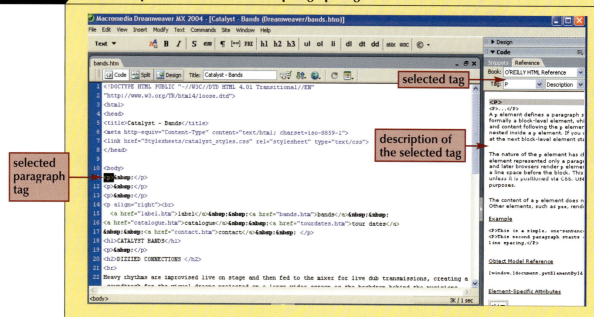

4. Read the information in the Reference panel, and then look at the code. There are four sets of paragraph tags in a row. The top three sets of tags contain a nonbreaking space character and are included in the code to display blank lines. The fourth has an align attribute with a value of right. This tag surrounds the linked text that is displayed in the upper-right corner of the Bands page.

5. Select the entire fourth paragraph tag, including the text and anchor tags, and then click the **Show Code and Design Views** button on the Document toolbar. The linked text is selected in the Design pane of the Document window.

6. Select the **CATALYST BANDS** text in the Design pane. The text is also selected in the Code pane.

7. Click in the opening h1 tag that is before the selected text in the Code pane, right-click the selected tag, and then click **Reference** on the context menu. A description of the Heading 1 tag appears in the Reference panel. Read the description.

8. Select the line break tag **
** in the Code pane, right-click the selected tag, and then click **Reference** on the context menu. Read the description of the <br> tag.

9. Examine the code for the rest of the page, using the Reference panel to learn about any tags that you do not recognize.

10. Collapse the Code panel group, click the **Show Design View** button on the Document toolbar, and then close the Bands page.

You can use these same HTML tags to format text.

Formatting Text in HTML Mode

At times, you might need to work on Web sites that were created in an older version of HTML. It is not a good idea to add CSS styles to these sites. You can modify the pages by creating the code manually in Code view, you can set preferences so that Dreamweaver uses only HTML tags to format pages, or you can select text and use the Font Tag Editor located in the Text category on the Insert bar to edit selected text with font tags. To change Dreamweaver to HTML mode, you click Edit on the menu bar, click Preferences, and then uncheck the Use CSS Instead of HTML Tags check box in the Preferences dialog box. Once the preference has been changed, formatting text using the Property inspector will add only HTML tags to the code of Web pages. Remember to change the preference back when you are finished.

The attributes and process for formatting text using the HTML font tag are not the same as the ones you have learned for formatting text using CSS styles. The following overview describes the attributes associated with the font tag. To format text in HTML mode, you select the text in the Document window and set the attributes for the selected text in the Property inspector. You can set the attributes for a single letter, a word, a line of text, or an entire block of text. The attributes for text formatting are similar to those in a word processing program; however, when text is formatted, HTML tags are added in the background. Text formatting attributes include format, font, font size, font color, emphasis, alignment, lists, and indents.

The format attributes are a list of standardized HTML tags used for text formatting. These include the paragraph tag and a variety of heading tags.

The font attributes are a list of the fonts available for use. The Default Font option displays the text in the default font of the end-user's browser. To maintain greater control of the aesthetic look of a page, you can choose a font group from the list. When a font group is selected, Dreamweaver places a font tag containing all of the choices in the font group around the specified text. You can also add fonts to the list, but it is recommended that you use caution when doing this because a font must be installed on the end-user's computer to display the text in that font. If the font is not installed on the end-user's computer, the text will be displayed in the browser's default font.

The font size attributes are a list of available font sizes. Unlike word processing programs, HTML has no fixed font size. Instead, when you choose a font size from the list, you are choosing from a scalable range of sizes relative to a **base font size**. The default base font size is 3; however, you can set the base font size for the Web page to a different value by inserting a base font tag designating a different base font size into the head portion of a Web page. If you do not choose a value from the font size list, text will be displayed at the base font size you selected for that page. If you have not added a base font tag, the text will be a 3. If you have added a base font tag, the text will be displayed at the designated size.

When you choose a value from the font size list, Dreamweaver inserts a font size tag into the HTML of your page. The first seven choices in the font size list are absolute font sizes (1 to 7). **Absolute font sizes** are based on the standard default base size of 3. Sizes 1 and 2 are smaller than 3, while sizes 4 through 7 appear progressively larger than 3. If you choose an absolute font size, the font size tag will override the base font tag and the text you select will be displayed at the designated size regardless of the base font size. The remaining choices in the font size list are relative font sizes (–7 to +7). **Relative font sizes** add or subtract from the base font size. For example, a +2 value increases the base font size by two sizes, and a –2 value reduces the base font size by two sizes. Relative font sizes are the best choice because they ensure that text will be proportionately scaled in the browser window. For example, if you change the base font size for the page to the absolute size 4, a +2 value adds 2 sizes to size 4; if you later change the base font size for the page to the absolute size 3, the +2 value adds 2 sizes to size 3.

In addition to the font sizes that you create for a Web page, users can change the overall size of text that appears in their browser—essentially scaling the size that text appears in their browser. For example, a visually impaired user might set the browser text to Larger to increase the readability of text on Web pages.

The font color attributes enable you to change the color of selected text. The default font color for a page is the color you selected in the Page Properties dialog box. To change the color of a selected block of text, you can type the hexadecimal color code into the color text box or select a color with the color picker.

The buttons in the Property inspector enable you to change the emphasis of selected text with boldface and italics; apply a left, center, or right alignment to a paragraph; turn paragraphs into items in an unordered (bulleted) or ordered (numbered) list; and apply or remove indents from paragraphs.

| Reference Window | **Formatting Text in HTML Mode** |

- Click Edit on the menu bar, click Preferences, uncheck the Use CSS Instead of HTML Tags check box, and then click the OK button.
- Select the text you want to format in the Document window.
- To change the font, click the Font list arrow in the Property inspector, and then click the font grouping you want.
- To change the font size, click the Size list arrow in the Property inspector, and then click the size you want.
- To change the color, click in the Text Color text box in the Property inspector and type the hexadecimal color code of the color you want, *or* click the Text Color box in the Property inspector and click the color swatch you want using the color picker.
- To change the style, click the Bold button and/or Italic button in the Property inspector.
- To change the alignment, click one of the alignment buttons in the Property inspector.

You'll post the updated files for the Catalyst site to your remote location.

Updating a Web Site on a Remote Server

As a final review of your work, you'll update the files on the remote server. Because you have uploaded the entire site already, you need to upload only the files that you have changed to update the remote site. This includes the Bands page and the external style sheet located in the Stylesheets folder.

| Reference Window | **Uploading a Site to the Remote Server** |

- Click the Connects to Remote Host button on the Files panel toolbar.
- Click the View list arrow on the Files panel toolbar, and then click Local View.
- Press and hold the Ctrl key, and then click all of the files and folders on the local site that have been modified or added.
- Click the Put File(s) button on the Files panel toolbar.
- Click the No button in the dialog box that opens asking if you want to include dependent files.
- Click the View list arrow on the Files panel toolbar, and then click Remote View.
- Click the Disconnects from Remote Host button on the Files panel toolbar.

You will upload the modified pages and new dependent files in the Catalyst site to the remote server. Then you'll preview the site on the Web.

To upload a site to the remote server:

1. Expand the **Files** panel group, and then click the **Connects to Remote Host** button on the Files panel toolbar. Dreamweaver connects to the remote host.
2. Click the **View** list arrow on the Files panel toolbar, and then click **Local View**.
3. Click the **Stylesheets** folder in the Files panel, press and hold the **Shift** key, click **bands.htm**, and then release the Shift key.
4. Click the **Put File(s)** button on the Files panel toolbar.
5. Click the **No** button when asked if you want to include dependent files. You already selected the new dependent file for the site when you selected the Stylesheets folder.
6. Click the **View** list arrow on the Files panel toolbar, and then click **Remote View**. A copy of the Stylesheets folder and the updated files appear in the remote file list in the Files panel.
7. Click the **Disconnects from Remote Host** button on the Files panel toolbar.
8. Click the **View** list arrow on the Files panel toolbar, and then click **Local View**.

Next, you'll preview the updated site in a browser. The site will include all of the new styles and text that you added to the local version.

To preview the updated site in a browser:

1. Start your browser, type the URL of your remote site into the Address text box on the browser toolbar, and then press the **Enter** key. The home page is displayed.
2. Place the pointer at the end of the URL and type **/bands**, and then press the **Enter** key. The Bands page opens in the browser window.
3. Read the text on the Bands page and examine the text to ensure that the formatting is displayed correctly.
4. Close the browser window.

In this session, you exported the styles from the Bands page to an external style sheet, created CSS styles in an external style sheet, and attached the external style sheet to the pages of the Catalyst site.

Session 3.3 Quick Check

Review

1. What is the file extension for an external style sheet?
2. True or False? You can apply CSS styles that you create in one Web page to text on another Web page in the same site.
3. Why is it a good idea to delete unneeded styles from a style sheet?
4. Why do you need to remove the current formatting from text in a Web page before attaching an external style sheet?
5. True or False? You cannot add new styles to an external style sheet.
6. What happens when you edit a CSS style?
7. Why is an internal style sheet also called an embedded style sheet?
8. True or False? A link tag has a closing tag.

Review

Tutorial Summary

In this tutorial, you learned how to add text to a page. You explored basic formatting techniques and learned to use the spell checking and find and replace tools. You created Cascading Style Sheets and used CSS styles to modify an existing HTML tag, to create a custom style class, and to customize the appearance of text links. You examined the styles in an internal style sheet, exported styles to an external style sheet, and attached an external style sheet to Web pages. You edited existing styles, examined the code for CSS styles, and learned about HTML tags that are associated with text. Finally, you uploaded your modified site to the Web server.

Key Terms

absolute font size	declaration	linked style sheet
absolute link	deprecated	nest
advanced style	document relative link	nonbreaking space
anchor tag	embedded style sheet	pseudoclass
base font size	external style sheet	redefined HTML tag
cascading	font tag	relative font size
Cascading Style Sheet (CSS)	head	selector
comment tag	inherit	site root relative link
CSS style	internal style sheet	target
custom style (or custom style class)		

Practice

Practice the skills you learned in the tutorial.

Review Assignments

Data Files needed for the Review Assignments: Contact.doc, Catalogue.doc, Label.doc

Brian wants you to continue adding and formatting the text on the Catalyst site. You'll open each page, delete the internal styles that were added, and then attach each page to the external style sheet. You will add text to the Contact, Company, Catalogue, and Label pages. You will add a navigation system to these pages by creating hyperlinks. You'll use existing CSS styles and create new styles to format the text you added, including a third-tier subheading style.

1. Open the NewCatalyst site that you modified in Tutorial 3, switch to Local view, if necessary, and then open the catalogue.htm page in the Document window in Design view.
2. Expand the CSS Styles panel, click the Minus (–) button next to style in the CSS Styles panel list to collapse the list, select <style>, if necessary, and then click the Delete CSS Style button in the CSS Styles panel. The page is blank.
3. Click the Attach Style Sheet button, browse to the Stylesheets/catalyst_styles.css page, if necessary, and then click the OK button to attach the external style sheet to the page. The background image is visible in the Document window.
4. Open the bands.htm page, place the insertion point at the top of the page, press and hold the Shift key, click after the contact text link, click Edit on the menu bar, click Copy, and then close the Bands page.
5. Click the catalogue.htm tab, place the insertion point at the top of the page, click Edit on the menu bar, and then click Paste. The formatted text links are pasted into the page. (*Hint:* If you cannot see the links, place the insertion point at the top of the page, and then press the Enter key. The links are the same color as the background image.)

6. Open the **Catalogue.doc** document located in the **Tutorial.03\Review** folder included with your Data Files in a word processing program, select all the text in the document, copy the selected text to the Windows Clipboard, and then close the document.
7. Place the insertion point after "contact" in the page, press the Enter key, click Edit on the menu bar, and then click Paste Text to paste the text into the page.
8. Select "Catalyst Catalogue," click the Format list arrow in the Property inspector, and then click Heading 1. (*Hint:* If the formatting is applied to additional text, click Edit on the menu bar and click Undo Text Formatting to undo the last step, switch to Code view, place paragraph tags around the heading text, switch to Design view and select the text, and then apply the Heading 1 style.)
9. Select "CDs," click the Format list arrow in the Property inspector, click Heading 2 to apply the style to the selected text, and repeat the process to apply the Heading 2 style to "VINYL." (*Hint:* If the formatting is applied to additional text, click Edit on the menu bar and click Undo Text Formatting to undo the last step, switch to Code view, place paragraph tags around the subheading text, switch to Design view and select the text, and then apply the Heading 2 style.)
10. Edit the Heading 1 style. Select the page heading in the Document window, open the Tag inspector to the Relevant CSS panel, select the h1 style if necessary, scroll to Text-transform in the attributes list, click in the value side of the list to display value options, select Uppercase, and then press the Enter key to accept the change. The style sheet opens and the page heading is displayed in uppercase in the Catalogue page.
11. Create a third-tier subheading CSS style to apply to the band names and CD titles. Click the New CSS Style button in the CSS Styles panel, click the Tag option button, click h3 in the Tag list, click the top Define In option button, select catalyst_styles.css in the Define In list, if necessary, and then click the OK button.
12. In the CSS Style Definition dialog box, click Type in the Category list, change the size to 14 pixels, change the color to #FF6600, click Background in the Category list, change the background color to #FFCC00, click Block in the Category list, click Inline from the Display list, and then click the OK button.
13. In the Catalogue page, select "Dizzied Connections: Spinning Life," and then click Heading 3 in the Format list in the Property inspector. (*Hint:* If the formatting is applied to additional text, click Edit on the menu bar and click Undo Text Formatting to undo the last step, switch to Code view, place paragraph tags around the text, switch to Design view and select the text, and then apply the Heading 3 style.)
14. Apply the Heading 3 style to the other band names and CD titles: "Surface Suction: Black Lab"; "Sloth Child: Them Apples"; and "life in minor chords: i believe in ferries."
15. Switch to Split view. In the Code pane, move the opening paragraph tag at the beginning of each numbered list to the end of that list directly before the closing paragraph tag, type a line break tag "<br>" at the beginning of each list, and then switch to Design view. Each list displays directly below its list heading.
16. Scroll to the bottom of the page, insert a blank line, switch the Insert bar to the Text category, click the Copyright button in the Characters list, press the Right Arrow key, press the spacebar, and then type "copyright Catalyst, Inc. 2006." Select the copyright line you just typed, and apply the catalyst_footer style from the Style list in the Property inspector.
17. Save the style sheet, save the Catalogue page, preview the page in a browser, and then close the page and the style sheet.
18. Open the contact.htm page in the Document window, and then repeat Steps 2 through 7 for the Contact page, using the **Contact.doc** document located in the **Tutorial.03\Review** folder included with your Data Files in Step 6.

19. Apply the Heading 1 style to the page heading, apply the Heading 2 style to "Contact" and "Directions," and then move the text to the line directly below the subheading. If necessary, switch to Code view, place a break tag "<br>" to the right of the closing h2 tag, and move the opening paragraph tag to the end of the text. Save and close the page.
20. Open the label.htm page in the Document window and repeat Steps 2 through 7 for the Label page, using the **Label.doc** document located in the **Tutorial.03\Review** folder included with your Data Files in Step 6.
21. Apply the Heading 1 style to "CATALYST LABEL" using the Property inspector. Apply the Heading 2 style to "News - HEY, look what they're saying!!!"; "Mission"; "History"; and "Employees." Apply the Heading 3 style to the following employee names: Sara Lynn, Enya Allie, Mark Salza, and Brian Lee.
22. Delete the blank lines below the Mission and History subheadings and below each employee name by moving the opening paragraph tag to the end of each block of text, and then adding a line break tag after the subheading or employee name.
23. Scroll to the bottom of the page, insert a blank line, switch the Insert bar to the Text category, click the Copyright button in the Characters list, press the Right Arrow key, press the spacebar, and then type "copyright Catalyst, Inc. 2006." Select the copyright line you just typed, and apply the catalyst_footer style from the Style list in the Property inspector.
24. Save the Label page, preview the page in a browser, and then close the page.
25. Open the tourdates.htm page, repeat Steps 2 through 5 for the Tour Dates page, and then save and close the Tour Dates page.
26. Upload the pages you modified and the updated style sheet to the remote site. Click the Connects to Remote Host button on the Files panel toolbar, switch to Local view, press the Ctrl key as you click the Stylesheets folder, catalogue.htm, contact.htm, label.htm, and tourdates.htm in the Local Files list, click the Put File(s) button on the Files panel toolbar, click the No button when asked to upload dependent files, and then click the Disconnects from Remote Host button on the Files panel toolbar.
27. Open a browser, type the URL for the remote NewCatalyst site into the Address text box on the browser toolbar, and then press the Enter key.
28. Navigate through the NewCatalyst site using the text links to open the other pages in the site.

Apply

Add and format text links and page content for a Web site about small rural communities of northern Vietnam.

Case Problem 1

Data Files needed for this Case Problem: Overview.doc, HartContact.doc, ProfHart.doc

Hroch University Anthropology Department Dr. Matt Hart has asked you to create a simple navigation system and to add text to the Web site you are creating to present his research about the small rural communities of northern Vietnam. Because his research papers are not complete, you'll add text stating that the papers are in process. Professor Hart has decided he wants minimal text formatting in the site so that his research will be accessible to the widest possible audience. Some of his colleagues live and work in remote areas and have access only to outdated computer systems.

1. Open the Hart site you created in Tutorial 2, Case 1, and then open the index.htm page in the Document window.
2. Move the insertion point below the color band at the top of the home page by pressing the Shift+Enter keys four times, type "Professor Hart," insert three nonbreaking spaces, type "Linguistic Differences," insert three nonbreaking spaces, type "Cultural Cross-pollination," insert three nonbreaking spaces, type "Rituals and Practices," insert three nonbreaking spaces, type "Contact Information," and then insert three nonbreaking spaces.

3. Use the Property inspector to create hyperlinks between each phrase you typed (Professor Hart, Linguistic Differences, Cultural Cross-pollination, Rituals and Practices, and Contact Information) and its corresponding page (prof_hart.htm, linguistic_differences.htm, cultural_cross_pollination.htm, rituals_and_practices.htm, and contact.htm).

Explore
4. Place the insertion point at the top of the page, select the blank lines and all the links, click Edit on the menu bar, and then click Copy HTML to copy the links from the page.
5. Save the home page, preview it in your browser, and then close it.

Explore
6. Open the contact.htm page in the Document window, move the insertion point to the top of the page, click Edit on the menu bar, and then click Paste HTML to copy the links onto the page.
7. Save the Contact page, preview the page in a browser, and then close the page.
8. Repeat Steps 6 and 7 to copy the links to each page in the site: cultural_cross_pollination.htm; linguistic_differences.htm; prof_hart.htm; and rituals_and_practices.htm.
9. Open the index.htm page in the Document window.
10. Copy the text in the **Overview.doc** document located in the **Tutorial.03\Cases** folder included with your Data Files, and then paste the text below the links on the home page. (*Hint:* Use the Paste Text command on the Edit menu.)
11. Apply the Heading 1 style to the "Brief History and Overview" heading using the Property inspector, and then save and close the page.
12. Open the contact.htm page, copy the text from the **HartContact.doc** document located in the **Tutorial.03\Cases** folder included with your Data Files, and then paste the text below the links on the Contact page.
13. Apply the Heading 1 style to the "Contact Information" heading using the Property inspector, and then save and close the page.
14. Open the prof_hart.htm page, copy the text from the **ProfHart.doc** document located in the **Tutorial.03\Cases** folder included with your Data Files, and then paste the text below the links on the Prof. Hart page.

Explore
15. Select all the contact information at the top of the Prof. Hart page, from the name through the e-mail address, and then click the Bold button and the Align Center button in the Property inspector.

Explore
16. Select the following text and then click the Bold button in the Property inspector to format the text with boldface: Higher Education, Academic Appointments, Editorial Work, Publications: Books, and Grants and Awards. Save and close the page.
17. Open the cultural_cross_pollination.htm page, move the insertion point below the text links at the top of the page, type "Cultural Cross-pollination," apply the Heading 1 style to the Cultural Cross-pollination heading using the Property inspector, and then save and close the page.
18. Open the linguistic_differences.htm page, move the insertion point below the text links, and then type "Linguistic Differences," apply the Heading 1 style to the Linguistic Differences heading using the Property inspector, and then save and close the page.
19. Open the rituals_and_practices.htm page, move the insertion point below the text links, and then type "Rituals and Practices," apply the Heading 1 style to the Rituals and Practices heading using the Property inspector, and then save and close the page.
20. Open the prof_hart.htm page, and switch to Split view. Select the first link and review the code. Select the bold text and find the strong tag and align attribute in the paragraph tag. Select the strong tag, right-click the selected tag, and then click Reference in the context menu. Read about the strong tag in the Reference panel, and then close the page.

21. Connect to your remote server, select the Graphics folder and all the pages in the Local Files list, and upload them to the remote folder.
22. View the remote Hart site in a browser. Test all the links and read the text on each page.

Challenge

Add and format text links, and then create an external style sheet and apply styles to text you add to a Web site for an art museum.

Case Problem 2

Data Files needed for this Case Problem: Welcome.doc, Museum.doc, Artists.doc, Location.doc

Museum of Western Art   C. J. Strittmatter asks you to add text to the Web site you are creating for the Museum of Western Art. He also asks you to create a navigation system on all of the pages. After looking over the pages in the site, you also decide to add a horizontal rule to each of the pages. You'll create an external style sheet and create CSS styles for the site. You will delete the styles from the pages of the site and attach the external style sheet to the pages, then you will use these styles to format the text. Finally, you'll upload the site to a remote location and preview it.

1. Open the Museum site you created in Tutorial 2, Case 2, and then open the index.htm page in the Document window.
2. Click File on the menu bar, point to Export, and then click CSS Styles to open the Export Styles As CSS File dialog box.
3. Browse to the local root directory of your Museum site, click the Create New Folder button, name the new folder "Stylesheets," open the Stylesheets folder, type "museum_styles" in the File Name text box, and then click the Save button to save the external style sheet.
4. Delete the styles from the home page, attach the external style sheet to the page, and then save and close the page.
5. Open each of the following pages (art.htm, artists.htm, location.htm, and museum.htm), delete the styles from the page, attach the external style sheet to the page, and then save and close the page.
6. Open the index.htm page, type "The Museum of Western Art" at the top of the page, apply the Heading 1 style to the text, select the text and create a hyperlink from the text to the index.htm page. (You will copy the linked text to the other pages in the site and you want it to have the same formatting in all the pages.)

Explore

7. Select the h1 style in the CSS Styles panel, click the Edit Style button, click Border in the Category list, and uncheck the Same for All check boxes in the Style, Width, and Color sections. Click Solid in the Bottom list box in the Style section, click Thin in the Bottom list box in the Width section, type "#006666" in the Bottom text box in the Color section, and then click the OK button. A horizontal line appears in the index page.

Explore

8. Open the Tag Inspector panel group, select the a:link style in the CSS Styles panel to open the Relevant CSS panel and display the attributes for a:link, scroll to the Text-decoration attribute, click in the value column, and then select None from the list to remove the underline from the a:link style. Repeat this process for the a:visited style to remove the underline from the style. The underline disappears from the text in the home page.
9. Move the insertion point directly below the horizontal line, and type the following text for the menu bar links with three nonbreaking spaces after each word: "Museum," "Art," "Artists," and "Location."

10. Create a custom style to format the menu bar text; name the style ".menustyle" and save it in the museum_styles.css style sheet. Click the Type category, select Bold from the Weight list, click the Block category, select Right from the Text Align list, select Block from the Display list (styles must be applied to block level tags for the align attribute to work), and then click the OK button. Select the menu bar link text and apply the new .menustyle from the Property inspector.
11. Create a hyperlink between each word (Museum, Art, Artists, and Location) and its corresponding page (museum.htm, art.htm, artists.htm, and location.htm).
12. Save the page, preview the page in a browser, and then save and close the museum_styles.css page.

Explore 13. Switch to Code view, select all the code between the body tags, click Edit on the menu bar, click Copy to copy the content from the home page, and then switch to Design view.

Explore 14. Open the art.htm page, switch to Code view, place the insertion point to the right of the opening body tag, press the Enter key, click Edit on the menu bar, and then click Paste to paste the code from the home page into the Art page.

15. Switch to Design view to view the copied content in page, and then save and close the page.

Explore 16. Repeat Steps 14 and 15 for the following pages: artists.htm, location.htm, and museum.htm.

17. Copy the text from the **Welcome.doc** document located in the **Tutorial.03\Cases** folder included with your Data Files, and then paste it below the links in the home page.
18. Select the h2 style in the CSS Styles panel, click the Edit Style button to edit the style, select Xx-large from the Size list in the Type category, and then click the OK button.
19. Select the WELCOME text, apply the Heading 2 style, save and close the page, and then save and close the style sheet.
20. Open the museum.htm page, copy the text from the **Museum.doc** document located in the **Tutorial.03\Cases** folder included with your Data Files, paste the text in the Museum page below the links, and apply the Heading 2 tag to THE MUSEUM heading, and then save and close the page.
21. Open the artists.htm page, copy the text from the **Artists.doc** document located in the **Tutorial.03\Cases** folder included with your Data Files, paste the text in the Artists page below the links, apply the Heading 2 tag to THE ARTISTS heading.
22. Create a custom style for the subheadings, name the style ".sub_headings" and add the style to the external style sheet. In the Type category, select X-large from the Size list, type "#006666" in the Color text box, and then click the OK button.
23. Place the insertion point after "Fredric Remington," press the Delete key to move the following paragraph onto the Fredric Remington line, and then press the Shift+Enter keys to move the text directly below the subheading.
24. Select the "Fredric Remington" subheading and apply the .sub_headings style using the Property inspector. The style is applied only to the selected text; you do not need to add line breaks or move paragraph tags because the style you created is applied using a span tag.
25. Repeat Steps 23 and 24 for the "Charles M. Russel" subheading, and then save and close the page and the style sheet.
26. Open the location.htm page, copy the text from the **Location.doc** document located in the **Tutorial.03\Cases** folder included with your Data Disk, paste the text in the Location page below the links, apply the Heading 2 tag to THE LOCATION heading, apply the .sub_headings style to HOURS: and LOCATION: subheadings, and then save and close the page.

Explore

27. Connect to your remote server, upload the Graphics folder, the Stylesheets folder, and all the pages to the remote server, and then disconnect from the remote server.
28. View the remote Museum site in a browser. Visit each page of the site, read the text, and test each link. Remember to click the logo text.
29. Click View on the browser's menu bar, point to Text Size, and then click Largest. The text in the page changes size because you used a relative font size in the page. Using a relative font size helps to make a page more accessible to users with disabilities. Click View on the menu bar, point to Text Size, and then click Medium.

Challenge

Create an external style sheet, and then create, edit, and apply new CSS styles to text you add to a Web site for an independent publisher of fringe writing.

Case Problem 3

Data Files needed for this Case Problem: Home.doc, Company.doc, NORMContact.doc, Links.doc

NORM With a plan and design in place for the NORM Web site, you're ready to add and format the text for the site. Norm Blinkered, the CEO of NORM, has already written the text for the site. You need to create an external style sheet, export the existing styles from the home page, delete the CSS styles from the pages of the site and attach the style sheet to the pages. You will also edit the existing CSS styles and create new styles as needed, then you will include the text on the pages and format the text.

1. Open the NORM site you created in Tutorial 2, Case 3, and then open the indcx.htm page.
2. Click Files on the menu bar, point to Export, and then click CSS Styles. Browse to the local root directory for the NORM site, create a folder named "Stylesheets" and name the external style sheet "norm_styles." View the new folder in the Files panel, clicking the Refresh button, if necessary.
3. Delete the existing styles from the home page, and then attach the norm_styles.css style sheet to the page. The background image disappears from the page because the relative path is incorrect in the body style.

Explore

4. Open the Tag Inspector panel group, select the body style in the CSS Styles panel, click the Show List View button in the CSS Properties panel, locate the Background-image attribute, click in the value column, click the Browse button, navigate to the NormBackground.gif file located in the Graphics folder, and then click the OK button. The background image appears in the page.
5. Save and close the style sheet, and then save and close the page.
6. Open the books.htm page, delete the styles from the page, attach the norm_styles.css style sheet to the page, and then save and close the page. Repeat this process for the company.htm, contact.htm, and links.htm pages.

Explore

7. Open the norm_styles.css style sheet. Create a custom style class with the name ".norm_headings" and defined in this document only because you are in the norm_styles.css external style sheet. In the CSS Style Definition dialog box, click Type in the Category list, change the size to 55 pixels, and then change the case to Uppercase.
8. Create a custom style class named ".norm_sub_headings" defined in this document only. In the CSS Style Definition dialog box, click Type in the Category list, change the size to 18 pixels, change the case to Uppercase, and change the decoration to Underline.
9. Create a custom style class named ".norm_book_titles" defined in this document only. In the CSS Style Definition dialog box, click Type in the Category list, change the style to Italic, and then change the color to #FFCC00.
10. Save and close the style sheet.

Tutorial 3 Adding and Formatting Text | Dreamweaver | DRM 163

11. Open the index.htm page, type "NORMbooks on the edge," highlight "NORM," and then apply the .norm_headings style from the Style list in the Property inspector. (The style is only applied to the selected text because the style is applied with a span tag.)
12. Select the "NORMbooks on the edge" text, and then use the Property inspector to create a hyperlink to the home page.
13. Move the insertion point one line below the horizontal line, and then type the following words separated by three nonbreaking spaces between each word: "company"; "books"; "links"; and "contact." (*Hint*: To move the insertion point down one line instead of two lines, press the Shift+Enter keys instead of just the Enter key.)
14. Use the Property inspector to create a hyperlink between each word (company, books, links, and contact) and its respective page (company.htm, books.htm, links.htm, and contact.htm).

Explore
15. Select all the text on the page, click Edit on the menu bar, click Copy HTML to copy the selected text, and then save and close the page.

Explore
16. Open the company.htm page, click Edit on the menu bar, click Paste HTML to paste the copied text at the top of the page, and then save and close the page.
17. Repeat Step 16 for the books.htm, contact.htm, and links.htm pages.
18. Preview the site in a browser and test the links to make sure they work.
19. Copy the text in the **Home.doc** document located in the **Tutorial.03\Cases** folder included with your Data Files, open the index.htm page, move the insertion point below the text links, click Edit on the menu bar, and then click Paste Text to paste the text into the page.
20. Apply the .norm_sub_headings style to "NORM book list" and "News," apply the .norm_book_titles style to each book title on the page, and then save and close the page.
21. Open the books.htm page, move the insertion point directly below the text links, type "Coming Soon," apply the .norm_sub_headings style to the text you typed, and then save and close the page.
22. Copy the text in the **Company.doc** document located in the **Tutorial.03\Cases** folder included with your Data Files, open the company.htm page, move the insertion point below the text links, click Edit on the menu bar, click Paste Text to paste the text into the page, apply the .norm_sub_headings style to "Mission" and "Staff," and then save and close the page.
23. Copy the text in the **NORMContact.doc** document located in the **Tutorial.03\Cases** folder included with your Data Files, open the contact.htm page, move the insertion point below the text links, click Edit on the menu bar, click Paste Text to paste the text into the page, apply the .norm_sub_headings style to "Contact," and then save and close the page.
24. Copy the text in the **Links.doc** document located in the **Tutorial.03\Cases** folder included with your Data Files, open the links.htm page, move the insertion point below the text links, click Edit on the menu bar, click Paste Text to paste the text into the page, and then apply the .norm_sub_headings style to "Links."

Explore
25. Select Ludlow Press, type "http://www.ludlowpress.com" in the Link text box in the Property inspector to create an absolute link to that Web site, and then delete the URL located beside "Ludlow Press" in the Document window. (*Hint:* Make sure to include "http://" when you type the link because it is an offsite hyperlink.) Repeat for the rest of the links using the URLs listed in the page.
26. Select Ludlow Press, switch to Split view, examine the code for an absolute link, switch to Design view, and then save and close the page.
27. Connect to your remote server, upload the Graphics folder, the Stylesheets folder, and the pages to the remote server, and then disconnect from the remote server.

Create

Create a navigation system, and then create and apply CSS styles to text in a Web site for a newly opening sushi restaurant.

28. View the remote site in a browser. Read each page of the site, check each link, and visit each page to make sure everything uploaded correctly.

Case Problem 4

Data File needed for this Case Problem: SushiYa-YaContent.doc

Sushi Ya-Ya Mary O'Brien wants you to start working on the navigation system and the styles for the Sushi Ya-Ya Web site. She asks you to create CSS styles, add appropriate text to the site, and then format the text you added. You'll view the code, upload the modified pages to the remote site, and then preview the remote site.

1. Open the SushiYaYa site you created in Tutorial 2, Case 4, and then open the index.htm page.
2. Export the styles from the home page to an external style sheet named "sushiyaya_styles.css" stored in a new folder named "Stylesheets" in the local root folder for the site.
3. Delete the styles from the home page, attach the external style sheet to the page, and then save and close the page and the style sheet.
4. Open each page in the site, delete the styles from the page, attach the style sheet to the page, and then save and close the page.

Explore

5. Open the index.htm page and review the styles that Dreamweaver created. Make a list of additional styles you need to create. (*Hint.* Look at the styles that were needed for the Catalyst site and for the sites in the other Case Problems.)
6. Create the rest of the styles that you will need for the site based on the list you created in Step 5. Remember to save the style sheet.

Explore

7. Create the navigation system for the home page. Remember to create links to all the other pages in the SushiYaYa site.

Explore

8. Copy the links from the home page to the other pages.
9. Preview the site in a browser, testing the links to be sure they work.
10. Copy the text in the **SushiYa-YaContent.doc** document located in the **Tutorial.03\Cases** folder included with your Data Files throughout the pages in the site as appropriate.

Explore

11. Apply the styles you created to the text you added to the pages, creating any additional styles as needed. Save and close the pages.
12. Upload the SushiYaYa site to your remote server, and then test the remote site in a browser.

Quick Check Answers

Session 3.1

1. You can type in the Document window, or you can copy and paste text from another document.
2. False; you should proofread a page for incorrectly used words that are spelled correctly.
3. Property inspector
4. hyperlinks or links
5. a relative link
6. Some Text
7. anchor

Session 3.2

1. a rule that defines the appearance of an element in a Web page by redefining an existing HTML tag or by creating a custom style
2. True
3. custom style class
4. True; in an external style sheet
5. by giving you more control over the appearance of a Web page because it controls the way elements appear in the end-user's browser rather than allowing the browser to interpret the tag
6. when they are creating a style that will apply to only a few items, or a style that will be an exception to the norm
7. a period

Session 3.3

1. .css
2. True, but you must first export the styles to an external style sheet.
3. to help keep them uncluttered and streamlined
4. because the older formatting might override the CSS style you apply or it might combine with the CSS style, causing the text to display differently than you had intended
5. False
6. Any element to which the style is applied is updated automatically to reflect the changes.
7. because the styles are embedded in the head of the Web page
8. False

Dreamweaver DRM 167

Tutorial 4

Objectives

Session 4.1
- Review graphic formats and compression
- Add graphics to a Web page
- Format and edit graphics
- Create graphic hyperlinks and an image map
- Create a rollover

Session 4.2
- Create tables and enter table content
- Select tables and table elements
- Format and resize tables
- Format, resize, add, and delete cells, rows, and columns
- Explore the HTML code of tables

Session 4.3
- Create tables in Layout mode
- Use invisible graphics as spacers
- Select tables and table elements in Layout mode
- Format and resize tables in Layout mode
- Format, resize, add, and delete cells, rows, and columns in Layout mode

Organizing Page Content and Layout

Working with Graphics, Rollovers, and Tables

Case

Catalyst

Now that the content has been placed in the site, it is time to add graphics to the pages. Sara Lynn, the president of Catalyst, hired an artist to design a new graphic logo for Catalyst. She wants you to add this new logo to each page in the Catalyst site and to link it to the site's home page. To match the style of the new logo, she also had the artist create graphics to replace the text links that make up the navigation system on each page. In addition, Brian Lee, public relations and marketing director at Catalyst, has asked you to add tables to the Tour Dates page containing the tour date information for various regions of the country as well as add a map containing links to the tables. He also wants you to create a table in the Catalogue page to hold the graphics and song lists in place. In addition, after meeting with Sara, Brian decided to add a page to the Web site to promote new releases.

To accomplish this, you will first add the new Catalyst logo to all of the pages in the site, and then format it. Then you will add a map of the United States in the Tour Dates page and make each region of the map a link to a table listing the tour dates for that region. Next you will replace the text links with the new graphics. Then you will add tables in the Tour Dates page, listing the tour dates for each region in the country. Finally, you will create a new page for the site describing one of the label's bands; you'll use a table to hold the content of the new page, and then create a link from the home page to the new promotional page.

Student Data Files

▼**Tutorial.04 folder**

▽ Tutorial folder
    CatalystLogo.gif
    CatalystLogoRollover.gif
    SurfaceSuctionCDcover.jpg
    USmap.gif

▽ Review folder
    DizziedConnectionsCDcover300.jpg
    LifeInMinorChordsCDcover300.jpg
    SlothChildCDcover300.jpg
    SurfaceSuctionCDcover300.jpg

▽ Cases folder
    BookCoverPunch.jpg
    BookCoverPunchSmall.jpg
    HrochLogo.gif
    MuseumLogo.gif
    MuseumLogoRollover.gif
    NORMlogo.gif
    NORMlogoRollover.gif
    SushiYaYaLogo.gif
    SushiYaYaLogoRollover.gif
    TikkaRollTuna.gif

Session 4.1

Understanding Graphics and Compression

Graphics can make a site more interesting and provide valuable information. For example, maps and graphs can summarize information more succinctly and intuitively than a written description. As a society, we are accustomed to distilling information from images. Therefore, the graphics you add to a Web site should enhance the feel you are trying to create and provide users with visual clues about the page content and/or the site's intended message. Most importantly, the graphics you add to a Web site should reinforce the goals of the Web site. When choosing graphics for a Web site, consider what each graphic will add to the page. Will it supply information or reinforce the page content? Will it aid the user in navigating through the Web site? Will it help the page to maintain the look of the site? If the graphic does not add anything to the page, it should not be used.

For the Catalyst site, you will add a graphic logo to each page. The logo will increase the brand recognition of Catalyst, which is a major goal of the site. Because the logo was designed with the site metaphor in mind, it will enhance the intended look and feel of the site. You will also add graphics of the CD cover art to the Catalogue page to help promote the bands and to sell products, two additional goals of the site. Like the logo, these graphics have a look that is appealing to the target audience; they will further extend the site metaphor and add to the cohesive look of the site. Other graphics will be added as needed to carry the look and feel of the site throughout the pages.

Because graphics files are usually large, the graphics you add to a Web site are stored in compressed file formats. **Compression** shrinks the graphic's file size by using different types of encoding to remove redundant or less important information. The smaller the graphic's file size, the faster the graphic will load in a browser. When considering what file size a graphic should be, you must consider the total file size of all the graphics in the Web page and the connection speed that the target audience will have. If you are going to include only one graphic in a page, the file size of that graphic can be larger. If you are going to include several graphics in a page, the size of each graphic will contribute to the amount of time it takes a user's browser to download the page. In this case, you might want to make the file size of each graphic smaller. In addition, if the target audience is using dial-up service to connect to the Internet, it will take them longer to download graphic-intensive pages, so you might consider keeping the graphics to a minimum or choosing graphics with small file sizes. Finally, you should consider the importance of the graphic when looking at file size. A user will be more willing to wait for a page to download if the page is interesting and provides content that the user is looking for. Figure 4-1 lists the approximate times it takes to download files of various sizes over a standard 56-Kbps (kilobits per second) dial-up connection, a DSL connection, and a cable modem connection.

Figure 4-1   Approximate download times for files of different sizes

Connection Type (speed in Kilobytes per second)	Size of Page (in Kilobytes)				
	10 KB	50 KB	100 KB	200 KB	400 KB
	Very Small Download	Small Download	Medium Download	Large Download	Very Large Download
Dial-up 56 Kbps (approx. 5 KBps)	2 seconds	10 seconds	20 seconds	40 seconds	80 seconds
Home DSL 640 Kbps (approx. 80 KBps)	< 1 second	< 1 second	1.25 seconds	2.5 seconds	5 seconds
Cable Modem 1.5 Mbps (approx. 190 KBps)	< 1 second	< 1 second	< 1 second	1 second	2.1 seconds

Current versions of Internet Explorer and Netscape Navigator can universally display three file formats for graphics: GIF, JPEG, and PNG. All three formats compress graphic files, but in different ways. If you want to use graphic images that are in another format, you will need to use a graphics processing program such as Adobe Photoshop, Adobe ImageReady, or Macromedia Fireworks to convert them to GIF, JPEG, or PNG.

Using GIF

GIF (Graphics Interchange Format) was invented by the CompuServe Company to provide its customers with a means to exchange graphics files online. Unisys, which now owns the patent on the type of compression used in GIFs, requires that software producing GIFs license the GIF patent. However, graphics compressed as GIFs can be used free of charge. Files saved as GIF images have the file extension *.gif*. The GIF format is usually used on images that have large areas of flat, or nongradient, color. **Nongradient** refers to color that is one shade and does not vary with subtle darkening or lightening. Many line-drawn graphics and non-photographic images use GIF. GIF supports a palette of up to 256 colors, one of which may be used for single-color transparency. GIF transparency is usually used to create a clear background for graphics. For example, if you want an image to appear on a Web site without its background, you can make the background transparent so that the color of the Web page or the background image behind it is visible. In GIF format, greater compression (and therefore smaller file size) is achieved by further limiting the graphic's color palette. This means that the fewer colors used in a GIF image, the smaller the file size. You need to find a balance between how colorful an image you want to use and how fast the target audience can load the image.

The new Catalyst logo that will appear in each page of the Web site is shown in Figure 4-2. Brian has compressed the new logo using GIF because it is comprised of flat colors and has a transparent background. The transparent background enables the logo to be laid over the background of the Web pages seamlessly. The logo file size is 3.8 K.

Catalyst logo as a GIF image — **Figure 4-2**

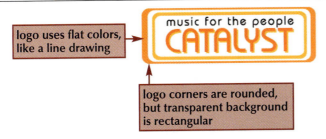

Using JPEG

A committee from the Joint Photographic Experts Group created the **JPEG** format to digitize photographic images. Files saved as JPEG images have the file extension *.jpg*. The JPEG format is usually used on photographic images and on graphics that have many gradient colors. The JPEG format can support millions of colors but does not support transparency.

JPEG is a **lossy** compression format, which means that it discards (or loses) information to compress an image. Because it was designed for photographic images, JPEG discards the information that is less perceptible to the human eye, such as the fine details in the background of a photograph. However, as an image is compressed further, additional information is discarded and, as the blurry spots increase in size, the image becomes less and less sharp. So, as with a GIF image, you must make a tradeoff between the image quality and the file size (or download time).

The CD covers for use in the Bands page will be JPEG images because each CD cover contains photographic images, which will be more effectively compressed using this format. Figure 4-3 shows the surface suction: black lab CD cover as a JPEG image.

Figure 4-3 ▶ **CD cover as a JPEG image**

surface suction CD cover is 50 K

photographic elements and layers of varying color make this graphic perfect for JPEG compression

Using PNG

PNG (Portable Network Graphics), a newer graphic compression format, was created by a group of designers who were frustrated by the limitations of existing compression formats. PNG files use the file extension *.png*. PNG supports up to 48-bit true color or 16-bit grayscale. It uses **lossless** compression, so no information is discarded when the file is compressed. It also supports **variable transparency**, the ability to make the background of the image transparent at different amounts; for example, a background can fade (using gradient shades of color) from a dark color to transparent. Generally, PNG compresses files 5 percent to 25 percent better than GIF. For transmission of photographic style images, JPEG is still a better choice because the file size of a photographic style image compressed with JPEG is usually smaller than the file size of a photographic style image compressed with PNG. The biggest drawback of the PNG format is that variable transparency usually does not display correctly in Internet Explorer. If your images use transparency, PNG may not be the most effective choice.

Figure 4-4 shows a graphic from the Dizzied Connections CD cover saved as a PNG. The graphic has gradient colors fading to transparency; therefore, the image is a perfect example of variable transparency.

Figure 4-4 ▶ **CD cover graphic as a PNG image**

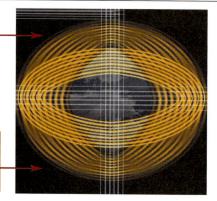

graphic on Dizzied Connections CD cover saved as a PNG

black background behind the graphic illuminates the image's variable transparency

Adding Graphics to Web Pages

Graphics are an integral part of Web pages. When you made the site plan, you decided on the overall look you wanted to achieve. Before you add the graphics to a site, you need to make sure that each graphic is saved at the proper size for insertion into the pages. You should not adjust the size a graphic after it has been added to a Web page, because the graphic is included in the page at its original size and then resized on the user's computer. This can make the Web page load much slower. In addition to being sized prior to insertion into the page, each graphic should be compressed to the smallest possible file size you can achieve without losing image quality. Be sure to retain the original uncompressed graphics in addition to the compressed Web versions because you may need to return to the original version to create another variation of the graphic in the future. Once a graphic has been compressed, it cannot return to its original resolution. It is also a good idea to use descriptive names that have meaning when you are creating graphic files. Logical naming structures will save you time in later identifying the files. Once you have the final version of all your graphics, you can add them to the pages in your Web site.

Reference Window

Adding a Graphic to a Web Page

- Click the Image button in the Images list in the Common category on the Insert bar.
- Navigate to the file you want to insert in the Select Image Source dialog box, select the file, and then click the OK button.

or

- Click the Assets tab in the Files panel group.
- Click the Images button on the Assets panel toolbar to display the list of images stored in the site.
- Click the file in the list of images that you want to insert, click the Insert button in the Assets panel, and then drag the image from the top of the Assets panel to its position in the page (*or* drag the filename from the list in the Assets panel to its position in the page).

There are two ways to add graphics to a Web site using Dreamweaver: you can use the Insert bar or the Assets panel. The first time you place a graphic in the site, you use the Insert bar to place the graphic in the page. Once a graphic is stored in the local root folder, it appears in the Assets panel and then you can use either method to insert that graphic into the pages.

When you add a graphic to a Web site, you should store it in the Graphics folder within the site's local root folder so that Dreamweaver always knows where to locate the image. You need to include only one copy of each graphic in the Graphics folder, even when you plan to use the same image in several pages.

When you place a graphic in a page, what you are really doing is placing an image tag, <img>, in the page. The image tag tells the page to display the graphic, which you placed in the Graphics folder, at that spot in the Web page. When the same graphic appears multiple times in a site, Dreamweaver will retrieve the graphic from the Graphics folder and display it in the various pages. This is helpful because, if you decide to change the graphics in a site, you can simply replace the old graphic with a new one, and each page that displayed the old graphic will then display the new one.

Using the Insert Bar to Add Graphics

The new Catalyst logo is a GIF graphic that will be included in the upper-left corner of every page in the site. You will use the Insert bar to add the image to the home page and the Label page. When you insert a graphic, you move the insertion point to the location where you want the image to appear in the page and then use the Image button located in the Common category on the Insert bar to place the image. If the image is not already stored within the site, Dreamweaver will copy the file to the Graphics folder within the local root folder. This ensures that the correct image is always available to Dreamweaver.

Brian asks you to add the redesigned Catalyst logo to the site. You'll start with the home page.

To add a graphic to a page using the Insert bar:

1. Open the **NewCatalyst** site that you modified in the Tutorial 3 Review Assignments, and then open the **index.htm** page in the Document window in Design view. The home page opens with the insertion point in the upper-left corner.

2. Delete the styles from the page, and then attach the **catalyst_styles.css** style sheet to the page.

3. Collapse any open panel groups, and then expand the **Files** panel group.

4. Click the **Images** list arrow in the **Common** category on the Insert bar, and then click the **Image** button. The Select Image Source dialog box opens.

5. Navigate to the **Tutorial\Tutorial.04** folder included with your Data Files, and then click the **CatalystLogo.gif** graphic file. The Image Preview box displays the graphic image and lists its specifications.

6. Click the **OK** button. A copy of the image is saved in the Graphics folder in the site's local root folder, and the image appears in the page.

7. Click the **Plus (+)** button next to the Graphics folder in the Files panel to view the contents of the folder. See Figure 4-5.

Figure 4-5   Catalyst logo in the home page

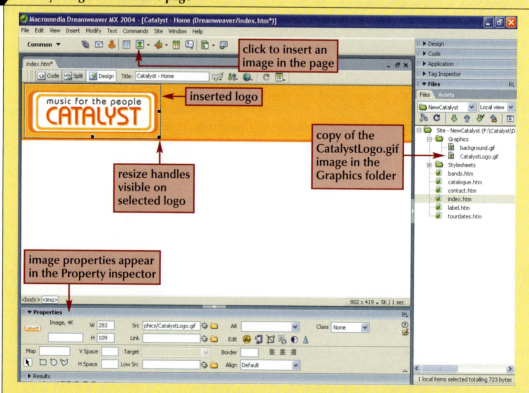

Trouble? If the Image Tag Accessibility Attributes dialog box opens, the Accessibility dialog boxes are activated on your computer. Click the Cancel button to close the dialog box. To avoid seeing this and similar dialog boxes as you complete the steps in these tutorials, click Edit on the menu bar, click Preferences to open the Preferences dialog box, click Accessibility in the Category list, uncheck all of the check boxes indented in the Show Attributes When Inserting list, and then click the OK button.

The Catalyst logo is surrounded by a black box with squares in the corners and on the sides because the graphic is selected. The squares are **resize handles**. If you drag a resize handle it will resize the selected object, which you do not want to do. To select an object such as a graphic, you can click it. When you click another area of the page, the graphic is deselected.

8. Click anywhere inside the Document window but outside the logo to deselect the logo.
9. Save and close the home page.

You'll repeat this process to insert the logo in the Label page, except that you'll use the GIF image you already saved in the Graphics folder.

To add a graphic from the Graphics folder using the Insert bar:

1. Open the **label.htm** page in the Document window.
2. Click the **Image** button in the **Images** list in the **Common** category on the Insert bar. The Select Image Source dialog box opens.
3. Navigate to the **Graphics** folder in the site's local root folder, click **CatalystLogo.gif**, and then click the **OK** button. The Catalyst logo appears in the upper-left corner of the Label page and the text moves down in the page. You will adjust the position of the text later.
4. Save and close the Label page.

Another way to add graphics to Web pages is to use the Assets panel.

Using the Assets Panel to Insert Graphics

In Dreamweaver, **assets** are the images, colors, URLs, Flash, Shockwave, movies, scripts, templates, and library items that you use throughout a site. The Assets panel is used to manage these assets. It helps you keep track of the assets in the site by listing them all in one place. Once a graphic has been stored in the site's local root folder, you can use the Assets panel to place the graphic in other pages. When you display images in the Assets panel, the graphic image appears in the upper pane and the graphic's filename, type, size, and location appear in the lower pane.

You'll open the Assets panel.

To open the Assets panel:

1. Click the **Assets** tab in the Files panel group. The Assets panel opens.
2. Click the **Images** button on the Assets panel toolbar, if necessary, and then click the **Site** option button at the top of the Assets panel, if necessary. The images in the site are listed in the Assets panel.

3. Click **CatalystLogo.gif** in the Images list in the Assets panel. The selected image appears in the top pane of the Assets panel. See Figure 4-6.

Figure 4-6 **Images in the Assets panel**

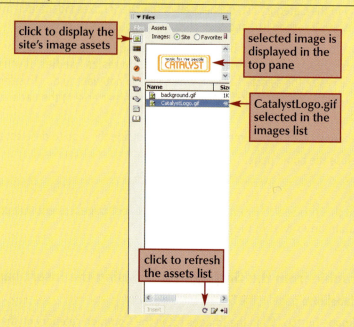

Trouble? If you don't see the CatalystLogo.gif file in the Assets panel, click the Refresh button at the bottom of the Assets panel. If you see additional files in the list, right-click any of the files, and then click Recreate Site List on the context menu.

You'll use the Assets panel to place the Catalyst logo in the remaining pages of the Catalyst site.

To insert a graphic using the Assets panel:

1. Click the **Files** tab in the Files panel group to display the Files panel, and then double-click **bands.htm** to open the page in the Document window. The insertion point is positioned in the upper-left corner of the Bands page.

2. Click the **Assets** tab in the Files panel group to open the Assets panel, click **CatalystLogo.gif** in the Images list, if necessary, and then click the **Insert** button at the bottom of the Assets panel. The logo is inserted in the Bands page and the text moves down.

3. Save and close the Bands page.

4. Switch to the **Files** panel, and then open the **catalogue.htm** page in the Document window.

5. Switch to the **Assets** panel, and then drag the **CatalystLogo.gif** image from the top pane in the Assets panel to the upper-left corner of the Catalogue page in the Document window.

6. Save and close the Catalogue page.

7. Insert the Catalyst logo in the Contact and Tour Dates pages from the Assets panel, using either method, and then save and close each page.

You can change some of the formatting attributes of inserted graphics.

Formatting Graphics Using CSS Styles and the Property Inspector

Some elements of style can be added to the Web site by formatting graphics. You format graphics either by creating a CSS style and applying it to the graphic or by selecting the graphic and setting the attributes in the Property inspector. If you plan to add the same attributes to multiple graphics in the Web site, it is a good idea to create a CSS style that contains the desired attributes to ensure you use the same formatting on all the graphics. It also enables you to easily change and update the formatting for all the graphics in the site. You create and apply CSS styles to graphics in the same way that you create and apply CSS styles to text. In addition, all of the same categories of attributes are available. CSS styles are commonly used to add borders to graphics; define the border style, width, and color; add margins or padding to graphics; and align or position graphics. If you define an attribute in the style that is not applicable to a graphic element, such as a font group, then that attribute will not affect the display of the graphic element to which it is applied. You can also redefine the image tag, <img>, if you have style elements that you want to apply to all the images in a site.

Brian wants you to create a CSS style for the Catalyst logo that sets the border to 0 pixels and adds an invisible margin of 5 pixels to the left and right of the graphic.

To create and apply a CSS style to a graphic:

1. Switch to the **Files** panel, open the **index.htm** page in the Document window, and then expand the **CSS Styles** panel, if necessary.

2. Click the **New CSS Style** button in the CSS Styles panel, and then create a custom class style with the name **.logostyle** placed in the **catalyst_styles.css** style sheet.

3. In the CSS Style Definition dialog box, click **Box** in the Category list, click the **Same for All** check box in the Margin section to remove the check mark, and then type **5** in the Right and Left text boxes.

4. Click **Border** in the Category list, click the **Same for All** check box to insert a check mark in the Width section, if necessary, type **0** in the Top row, and then click the **OK** button.

5. Click the **Catalyst logo** to select it in the page, click the **Class** list arrow in the Property inspector, and then click **logostyle**. The style is applied and the graphic moves 5 pixels to the right. See Figure 4-7.

Figure 4-7 Logo on home page formatted with CSS style

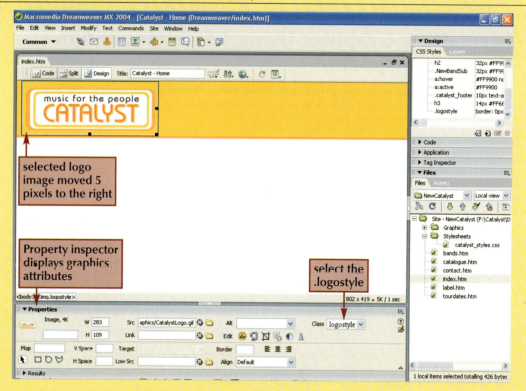

6. Save and close the page, and then save and close the style sheet.
7. Open each page in the site (**bands.htm**, **catalogue.htm**, **contact.htm**, **label.htm**, and **tourdates.htm**), and then repeat Steps 5 and 6 to apply the new CSS style to the logo in rest of the pages.

If you are formatting only one graphic, you can either create a CSS style or you can set the attributes for that graphic in the Property inspector. When a graphic is selected in the Document window, the Property inspector displays a small picture of the graphic and the graphic's attributes. Graphic attributes listed in the Property inspector include:

- **Image.** A descriptive name of the image. The image name is used in some advanced forms of programming to allow you to tell Dreamweaver or the browser what to do with the image. The name does not have to be the same as the filename, but it should enable you to identify the image. The image name must begin with a letter or an underscore, the rest of the name can contain letters and numbers, but it cannot contain any spaces or symbols. You cannot name an image with a CSS style. You must name the image in the Property inspector or by typing the information directly into the code.
- **W (Width)** and **H (Height).** The horizontal and vertical dimensions of the graphic in pixels. You can resize the image by changing the values or dragging a resize handle on the image in the Document window. Although you can resize a graphic in Dreamweaver, if you do, the Web site will load more slowly because Dreamweaver must transmit the original graphic to the end user's computer and then resize the image on the client computer. Also, resizing an image larger than its original size will degrade the image quality. Instead, you should use an image processing program to resize a graphic, and then insert it at the size you want to display it, or you should resample the graphic after you adjust the width or height. You will learn about resampling in the Editing Graphics from Within Dreamweaver section.

- **Reset image size.** Once you have changed the width or height of an image, the Resize Image Size button appears between the W and H text boxes. Clicking the button will restore the selected image to its original width and height.
- **Src (Image Source File).** The file path (which includes the filename) of the graphic. It will either be a relative or an absolute path, depending on what you selected when you inserted the graphic. Most often a relative path is used because, if you change the site's URL or move the root directory of the site, a relative path will still work. You can swap an image by replacing the source file with the path to the new image, clicking the Browse for File button and navigating to the new image, or by dragging the Point to File button to the new file. You can also double-click the image in the Document window and enter the new path information in the Select Image Source dialog box.
- **Alt (Alternate).** Text that appears in place of the graphic when the page is viewed with a browser that displays only text or when a browser is set to only download images manually. In some browsers, the Alt text also appears in a tooltip when the pointer is positioned over the graphic. You should add an Alt message that describes the image to all graphics. This is extremely helpful for individuals who have visual disabilities and rely on screen readers to verbally communicate the graphic information. You cannot set the Alt description of an image with a CSS style. You must do this in the Property inspector or by typing the information directly into the code.
- **Class.** A list of the CSS styles that you have created. Selecting a graphic and then selecting a style from the list will apply that style to the graphic. If the attributes defined in the style are text attributes, you will not see any change in the graphic's display.
- **V Space** and **H Space.** The blank space, in pixels, that appears vertically along the top and bottom of the image or horizontally along the left and right sides of the image.
- **Low Src (Low Resolution Image Source File).** The path (including the filename) to a low-resolution image that displays while the high-resolution image is downloading. This enables clients with slow connections to see something while they wait for the high-resolution image to load. It is not necessary to use a low-resolution image.
- **Border.** A rectangular group of lines that surrounds a graphic. The width of the lines is measured in pixels. A border of 0 pixels (the default) is equivalent to no visible border. If there is no value in the Border text box, it will default to the user's browser setting. For most browsers, this is equivalent to 0. If the image is linked, then the border is the link color you specified in the page properties; otherwise, the border is the text color of the paragraph around the image.
- **Align.** The possibilities for alignment of the graphic with text that is next to it on the page. Default uses the browser's default setting for alignment; this is usually baseline. Baseline and Bottom align the bottom of the graphic to the baseline of the text. (The **baseline** is the imaginary line on which the text is sitting.) Top aligns the top of the graphic to the top of the tallest item, whether an image or text, in the same line. Middle aligns the middle of the graphic to the baseline of the text. TextTop aligns the top of the graphic to the top of the tallest character in the text line. Absolute Middle aligns the middle of the graphic to the middle of the text line. Absolute Bottom aligns the bottom of the graphic to the bottom of the lowest character in the text line, for example, with the bottom of a lowercase g. Left aligns the left edge of the graphic at the left margin and wraps text around its right side. Right aligns the right edge of the graphic at the right margin and wraps text around its left side.

The Property inspector can be expanded to show all the available graphic attributes, or collapsed to show only the most common ones.

You'll enter alternate text in the Property inspector for the Catalyst logo.

To add Alt text to a graphic:

1. Open the **index.htm** page in a Document window, and then click the **Expander arrow** button on the Property inspector to display all the attributes, if necessary.
2. Click the **Catalyst logo**. The logo is selected, and resize handles appear around the selected image.
3. Click in the **Alt** text box in the Property inspector, type **Catalyst company logo, link to home page**, and then press the **Tab** key. The Alt text is entered for the logo.
4. Save the page, and then preview the page in a browser.
5. Place the pointer over the Catalyst logo, but do not click. The Alt text description appears in the browser window. See Figure 4-8.

Figure 4-8   Alt text description for logo previewed in browser

6. Read the Alt text description, and then close the browser window and the page.
7. Repeat Steps 1 through 6 for the rest of the pages in the site: **bands.htm**, **catalogue.htm**, **contact.htm**, **label.htm**, and **tourdates.htm**.

You can also edit graphics in Dreamweaver.

Editing Graphics from Within Dreamweaver

You can change the appearance of a graphic by editing it. Unlike formatting, which changes the way the graphic is displayed by defining values for attributes such as borders, alignment, and spacing, editing a graphic is the process of changing and manipulating the actual image. Because it is often necessary to adjust graphics while you are working on a Web page, Dreamweaver includes some basic graphics editing components, such as crop, resample, brightness and contrast, and sharpen. You can use these editing components even if a graphics editing program is not installed on your computer.

- **Crop.** An image editing process that reduces the area of a graphic by deleting unwanted outer areas. For example, you might want to **crop** the surrounding area and other people from a photograph of your family at an amusement park, so that the image is framed to emphasize your family. When you click the Crop button, a dark filter with a clear center appears over the graphic. You select the area of the graphic that will remain in the page by dragging the resize handles of the inner clear area. You can crop only rectangular areas. Clicking the Crop button a second time removes any areas of the graphic that are covered by the dark filter.

- **Resample.** An image editing process that adds or subtracts pixels from a graphic that has been resized. Remember, when you resize a graphic, the graphic's file size does not change. **Resampling** the graphic reduces the file size and improves the image quality at the new size and shape. Only bitmap graphics (JPEGs and GIFs) can be resampled. Because resampling changes the file size of the actual graphic, it can create some problems. For example, if you used the same graphic in more than one location in a site, every instance of the graphic will have the new, smaller file size. Instances of the graphic that have not been resized smaller will probably display poorly because the smaller file size reduces the quality at the larger width and height.
- **Brightness and Contrast.** An image editing process that adjusts the brightness and contrast of the pixels in a graphic. Adjusting the Brightness and Contrast sliders in the Brightness/Contrast dialog box enables you to lighten a graphic that is too dark or darken a graphic that is too light.
- **Sharpen.** An image editing process that increases contrast of a graphic's edges to improve definition. You can adjust the sharpness of a blurry image to make it clearer.

When you edit a graphic, the actual graphic is altered and your edits cannot be undone. It is a good idea to keep a copy of the original graphic outside the local root folder so that you can reinsert the original graphic in the page if you dislike the edited version. You have all the original graphics used in the Catalyst site included with your Data Files.

Brian wants you to open the Catalogue page, insert the SurfaceSuctionCDcover.jpg graphic, and then edit the graphic.

To edit a graphic:

1. Open the **catalogue.htm** page in the Document window, and then click to the left of the SurfaceSuction: Black Lab subheading to position the insertion point to the left of the subheading (you may need to scroll to see the subheading), press the **Shift+Enter** keys, and then press the **Up Arrow** key to move the insertion point to the blank line.

2. Click the **Image** button in the **Images** list in the **Common** category on the Insert bar, navigate to the **Tutorial.04\Tutorial** folder included with your Data Files, click the **SurfaceSuctionCDcover.jpg** graphic, and then click the **OK** button. The graphic is inserted in the page above the Surface Suction: Black Lab subheading. The file size of the graphic appears to the right of the graphic's picture in the Property inspector.

3. Resize the graphic by dragging the lower-right resize handle until **200** appears in both the W and H text boxes in the Property inspector. The graphic's file size hasn't changed. The Reset Image Size button appears between the W and H text boxes so you can return the image to its original settings. See Figure 4-9.

| Figure 4-9 | **Resized graphic** |

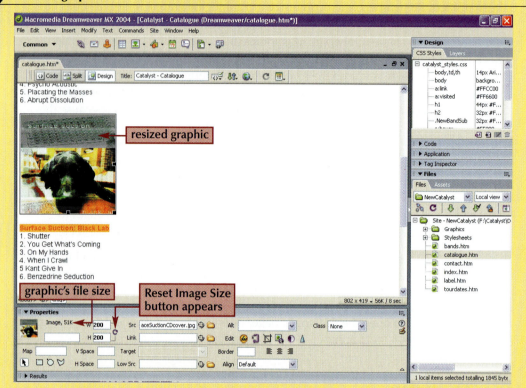

▶ 4. Click the **Reset Image Size** button in the Property inspector. The graphic returns to its original size.

▶ 5. Double-click the graphic. The Select Image Source dialog box opens and the image width, height, and file size appear below the graphic in the Image Preview box.

▶ 6. Click the **Cancel** button to close the Select Image Source dialog box, type **300** in the W and H text boxes in the Property inspector, and then double-click the graphic. The graphic's original width, height, and file size are still displayed at the bottom of the Image Preview box, because visually resizing an image does not change the graphic's dimensions or file size in the Graphics folder. (Remember that if you include a visually resized graphic in a page, the original graphic will be loaded in the user's browser and then resized on the client computer, which slows down the Web page.)

▶ 7. Click the **Cancel** button in the Select Image Source dialog box, click the **Resample** button in the Property inspector, and then click the **OK** button in the dialog box that warns that the resampling action will permanently alter the graphic. The graphic's new file size appears in the Property inspector.

▶ 8. Double-click the graphic. The new width, height, and file size appear below the Image Preview box. Resampling a graphic reduces the file size of the actual graphic in the Graphics folder. See Figure 4-10.

Figure 4-10

Resampled graphic

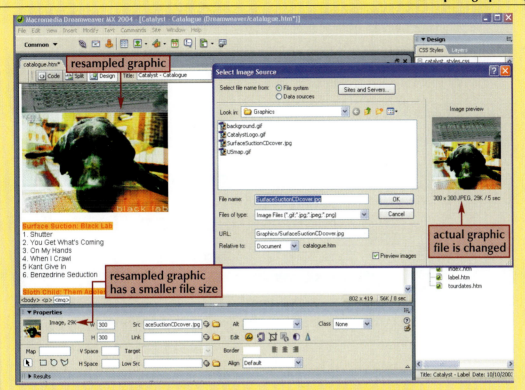

9. Click the **Cancel** button to close the dialog box, click the **Crop** button in the Property inspector, and then click the **OK** button in the dialog box that warns that the cropping action will permanently alter the graphic. A filter appears around the edges of the graphic and resize handles appear around the clear inner square.

10. Drag the resize handles so that only the dog's face remains in the clear inner area. See Figure 4-11.

Figure 4-11

Cropping a graphic

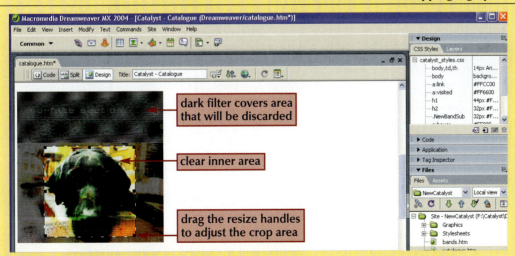

11. Press the **Enter** key. The graphic is cropped, and the new width, height, and file size appear in the Property inspector.

12. Click the **Brightness and Contrast** button in the Property inspector, and then click the **OK** button in the dialog box that warns that the action will permanently alter the graphic. The Brightness/Contrast dialog box opens.

13. Drag the **Brightness** slider to the right until 50 appears in the text box, and then drag the **Contrast** slider to the left until –40 appears in the text box. The graphic is lighter, and the contrast between colors is decreased. See Figure 4-12.

| Figure 4-12 | Brightness/Contrast dialog box |

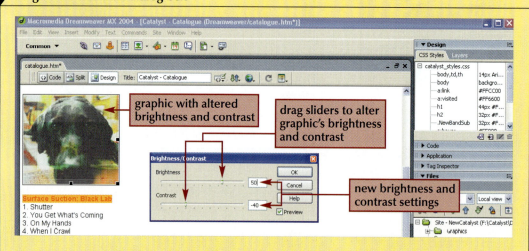

14. Click the **OK** button to close the Brightness/Contrast dialog box and accept the changes.

15. Click the **Sharpen** button in the Property inspector, and then click the **OK** button in the dialog box that warns that the action will permanently alter the graphic.

16. Drag the **Sharpen** slider to the right until 10 appears in the text box. See Figure 4-13.

| Figure 4-13 | Sharpen dialog box |

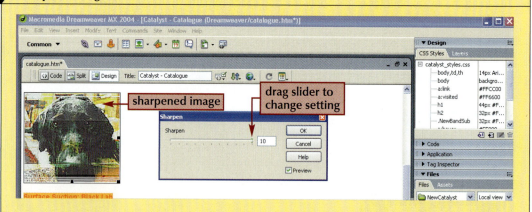

17. Click the **OK** button to close the dialog box and accept the changes, and then save and close the page.

Dreamweaver also includes tools that enable you to more easily work with graphics editing programs. The Optimize in Fireworks button enables designers who have Macromedia Fireworks installed on their machines to open Fireworks from within Dreamweaver, export a selected image to Fireworks, edit the image's optimization settings, and import the updated image back into Dreamweaver. The Edit button enables designers to start an image editing program they specify in the External Editor preferences and to open a selected image in that program for editing. After saving the edited graphic and returning to Dreamweaver, all the changes will be saved and the updated image is displayed in the page.

Another common use of graphics is as hyperlinks.

Creating Graphic Hyperlinks

As you have seen, graphics are not simply visual enhancements on a Web site; frequently, they are linked to other pages and sites. You can create a link for an entire image, or you can divide the image into smaller sections and create a link for each of those sections. Graphic links can be created in the same ways that text links are created. In the Property inspector, you type the path and filename in the Link text box, click the Browse for File button and navigate to the location of the link, or drag the Point to File button to the page to which you want to link in the Files panel.

Linking an Image

Creating a graphic hyperlink is similar to creating a text hyperlink. You select the graphic in the Document window, and then use the Browse to File button or the Point to File button in the Property inspector to browse to the page to which you want to link. Once you have created a link to a page, you can select it as the link for a selected graphic using the Links list box in the Property inspector. When a graphic is linked, the border appears as a rectangle around the graphic in the color you set for links in the page properties (unless the border is 0 pixels).

You will create a graphic link to the home page using the Catalyst logo. You won't see a rectangle around the graphic, because you set the border of the Catalyst logo to 0 in the .logostyle style. Using a logo as a link to the home page of a site is a common convention, and the Catalyst target audience should be familiar with this practice. You'll start by creating the link in the Label page, and then you'll repeat the process to create the link in all the other pages in the site except the home page. Because creating the link does not affect the appearance of the logo graphic, you should not create a link from the logo on the home page to itself.

To create a graphic hyperlink:

1. Open the **label.htm** page in the Document window.
2. Click the **Catalyst logo** to select it.
3. Click the **Browse for File** button next to the Link text box in the Property inspector, and then double-click the **index.htm** page in the Select File dialog box. The link information appears in the Link text box in the Property inspector
4. Save and close the page.
5. Open each of the following pages, and repeat Steps 2 through 4 to create a graphic hyperlink: **bands.htm**, **catalogue.htm**, **contact.htm**, and **tourdates.htm**.

In addition to creating a link from an entire image, you can create multiple links from different areas of an image.

Creating an Image Map

An **image map** is a graphic that is divided into invisible regions, or hotspots. A **hotspot** is an area of an image that you can click to cause an action, such as loading another Web page, to occur. Image maps are useful when you want to link parts of an image to different pieces of information. In a music site, for example, a map could be divided into touring regions and each region would be a hotspot. When the user clicks a particular region, the tour dates for that region would appear on the screen.

| Reference Window | **Creating an Image Map** |

- Select the image.
- Type a name in the Map text box in the Property inspector.
- For each hotspot, click a hotspot tool in the Property inspector, and then drag over the image to create the hotspot.
- Type alternate text in the Alt text box in the Property inspector for each hotspot.

You can create three types of hotspots: rectangular, oval, and polygonal. When an image is selected, you click the appropriate hotspot tool on the Property inspector, and then drag over the image to create a rectangular or oval hotspot, or click at various points to create a polygonal hotspot. Once hotspots have been created in the image, you create separate links for each hotspot.

You can move or resize a hotspot using the Pointer Hotspot Tool. If the hotspot is a polygon, you can move the individual points as well. When a hotspot is selected, the Property inspector displays the hotspot and pointer tools and the hotspot attributes, which include:

- **Link.** The Web page or file that opens when the hotspot is clicked. You can type a URL or path and filename into the Link text box, or use the Browse for File button to navigate to the page to which you want to link.
- **Target.** The frame or window in which the linked Web page will open. This option is available only after you specify a link for the hotspot.
- **Alt (Alternative).** The alternate text description for each link.
- **Map.** A descriptive name of the image map. The Map text box is displayed when a hotspot is selected. You do not have to name image maps; however, some advanced coding requires that objects be named so they may be referenced. If you do not name the image map after you create the first hotspot, Dreamweaver will assign the name *Map* to the first image map, *Map2* to the second image map, and so forth. Map names must begin with a letter or underscore, and can contain letters and numbers, but not spaces or symbols.

Brian asks you to delete the empty lines between the Catalyst logo and the site navigation text links in all the pages, add a map graphic to the Tour Dates page, and then use the graphic to create an image map.

To delete blank lines in Web pages:

▶ 1. Open the **tourdates.htm** page in the Document window, position the insertion point before the navigation links, and then click the **Show Codes and Design Views** button [Split] on the Document toolbar. See Figure 4-14.

Deleting lines from the Tour Dates page — **Figure 4-14**

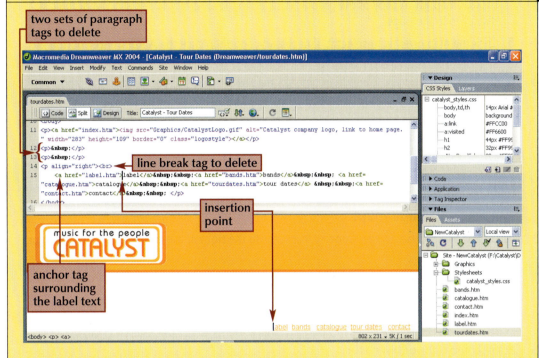

You'll delete the line break tags from the Code pane.

2. In the Code pane, select the line break tag <br> that precedes the anchor tag in which the insertion point is currently positioned, and then delete it from the code.

3. Locate the paragraph tag with the align attribute in it (do not delete this tag), select the two sets of paragraph tags directly above it, and then delete those tags from the page.

4. Click in the Design pane to view the changes, click the **Show Design View** button on the Document toolbar, and then save and close the page.

5. Repeat Steps 1 through 4 for the following pages: **bands.htm**, **catalogue.htm**, **contact.htm**, and **label.htm**.

Next, you'll add the map graphic to the Tour Dates page.

To insert a graphic in the Tour Dates page:

1. Open the **tourdates.htm** page in the Document window, move the insertion point after the link text, and then press the **Enter** key.

   Trouble? If the insertion point remains at the right of the screen, then you need to set the alignment for that line. click the Align Right button in the Property inspector to position the insertion point at the left of the screen.

2. Type **TOUR DATES**, apply the **Heading1** style to the text using the Format list in the Property inspector, and then press the **Enter** key twice to move the insertion point down two lines.

3. Click the **Image** button in the **Images** list in the **Common** category on the Insert bar. The Select Image Source dialog box opens.

4. Navigate to the **Tutorial.04\Tutorial** folder included with your Data Files, and then double-click **USmap.gif**. A copy of the graphic is saved in the Graphics folder and the graphic is displayed in the page.

5. Click the map graphic to select it, if necessary, and then click the **Align Center** button in the Property inspector. The map is centered on the page.

6. Click in the **Alt** text box, and then type **US map with links to tour dates by region**.

Next, you'll add hotspots to the map, which turns the graphic into an image map. You want to create a hotspot for the West Coast, Central, and East Coast regions on the map. You'll use a polygon hotspot so you can outline the irregular shape of each region.

To create an image map:

1. Click in the text box in the Property inspector to the right of the map image, and then type **USmapIM**.

2. Click the **Polygon Hotspot Tool** button in the Property inspector.

3. Click the upper-left corner of the West Coast region. The first point of the hotspot is added to the page. See Figure 4-15.

Figure 4-15   **First polygon hotspot inserted**

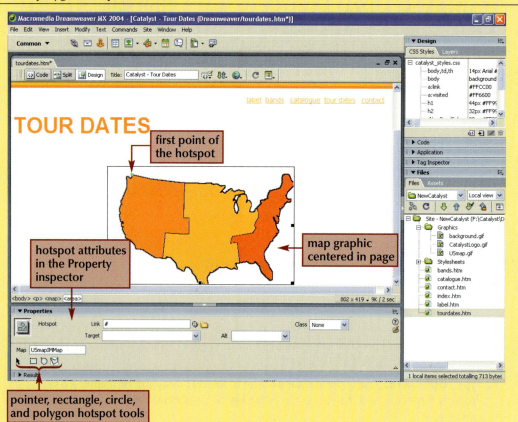

4. Continue to click around the perimeter of the West Coast region to add the hotspot border. See Figure 4-16.

Completed West Coast hotspot | **Figure 4-16**

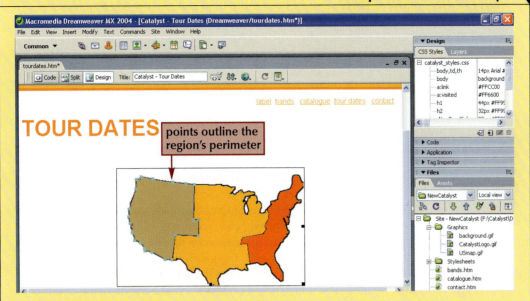

If any parts of the hotspot are not aligned correctly to the region's perimeter, you can use the Pointer Hotspot Tool to drag the appropriate points to realign the hotspot.

5. Click the **Pointer Hotspot Tool** button in the Property inspector, and then drag a point on the hotspot to adjust its position, if necessary.

6. Click in the **Alt** text box in the Property inspector, and then type **Link to West Coast tour dates**.

7. Click anywhere outside the hotspot but inside the graphic border to deselect the hotspot.

8. Repeat Steps 2 through 7 to create the hotspots for the Central and East Coast regions of the map. Use the name of each region in the Alt text for the corresponding hotspot. Make sure you click the **Pointer Hotspot Tool** button in the Property inspector before you click to deselect the hotspot.

   Notice that Dreamweaver added a Map name in the Map text box in the Property inspector by appending "Map" to the image name you typed in the Image box to the right of the map thumbnail in the Property inspector.

9. Save and close the page.

In the Review Assignments, you will link the regional hotspots to the text they reference.

Creating Rollovers

A **rollover** is an image that changes when the pointer moves across it. In actuality, a rollover enables two seemingly stacked graphics—the original graphic and the rollover graphic—to swap places during a specified browser action, such as a mouseover, and then to swap back during another specified browser action, such as when the pointer is moved off the images. The two graphics must be the same size.

Inserting Rollovers

You can use the Rollover Image button in the Images list in the Common category on the Insert bar to insert rollover buttons that change when the user points to them and that link the user to another page when the button is clicked. When you use the Rollover Image button to create rollovers, Dreamweaver does more than just create code to make the images swap. Once you fill in the requested information in the Insert Rollover Image dialog box, Dreamweaver creates all the code to make four separate things happen:

1. The graphics preload when the Web page is loaded so that they are in place when the browser action (such as a mouseover) occurs.
2. The graphics swap places when the mouse pointer is placed over the graphic.
3. The graphics swap places again when the mouse pointer is moved off of the graphic.
4. If a URL is specified in the When Clicked, Go To URL text box of the Insert Rollover Image dialog box, the user is hyperlinked to the new page when the mouse is clicked.

Technically, a rollover is a JavaScript behavior. **JavaScript** is a scripting language that works with HTML. A JavaScript behavior is a set of JavaScript instructions that tell the browser to do specified things. In earlier versions of Dreamweaver, you had to create three separate JavaScript behaviors to create a rollover. Now, you simply click the Rollover Image button and enter the image name, the original image source file, the rollover image source file, and a URL, if appropriate; Dreamweaver adds the JavaScripts for you.

The image name is the name that will appear in the Property inspector when one of the rollover graphics is highlighted. The image name does not replace the filename of either graphic you designate. The image name should begin with a letter or an underscore and should not have any spaces or special characters. You should use a descriptive name that includes the word "rollover" so you can easily see that a graphic has rollover behaviors attached to it. Unless the word "rollover" appears in the image name, you cannot tell that a graphic has rollover behaviors attached to it without looking at the code or previewing the page in a browser.

Reference Window	**Inserting a Rollover**

- Click the Rollover Image button in the Images list in the Common category on the Insert bar to open the Insert Rollover Image dialog box.
- Type a name for the rollover image in the Image Name text box.
- Click the Original Image Browse button, navigate to the file you want to insert as the original image, and then click the OK button.
- Click the Rollover Image Browse button, navigate to the file you want to insert as the rollover image, and then click the OK button.
- Click the Preload Rollover Image check box to check it.
- Type alternate text for the image in the Alternate Text text box.
- Click the When Clicked, Go To URL Browse button, navigate to the file to which you want to link, and then click the OK button.
- Click the OK button in the Insert Rollover Image dialog box.

You'll create a rollover for the Catalyst logo in the Bands page. Then, you'll replace the existing logo in each page of the Web site with the new rollover.

To insert a rollover:

1. Open the **bands.htm** page in the Document window, click the **Catalyst logo** to select it, and then press the **Delete** key. The logo image is deleted from the Bands page, and the text moves up in the page. (The link text may not be visible because it is the same color as the top stripe in the background.)

2. Click the **Image** list arrow in the **Common** category on the Insert bar, and then click the **Rollover Image** button. The Insert Rollover Image dialog box opens.

3. Type **LogoRollover** in the Image Name text box. Remember, graphic names cannot include any spaces. Whenever you see the name in the Property inspector, you'll be reminded that the image has rollover behaviors.

4. Click the **Browse** button beside the Original Image text box, navigate to the **Graphics** folder in the local root folder of the NewCatalyst site, if necessary, and then double-click **CatalystLogo.gif**. The path to the graphic appears in the Original Image text box.

5. Click the **Browse** button beside the Rollover Image text box, navigate to the **Tutorial.04\Tutorial** folder included with your Data Files, and then double-click **CatalystLogoRollover.gif**. The path to the graphic appears in the Rollover Image text box and a copy of the CatalystLogoRollover.gif graphic is saved in the Graphics folder in the local root folder of the site.

6. Click the **Preload Rollover Image** check box to insert a check mark, if necessary. Both graphics will load with the Web page.

7. Click in the **Alternate Text** text box, and then type **Catalyst company logo, link to home page**.

8. Click the **Browse** button beside the When Clicked, Go To URL text box, and then double-click the **index.htm** page in the local root folder of the NewCatalyst site.

9. Click the **OK** button in the Insert Rollover Image dialog box. The rollover image is added to the page.

10. Press the **Right Arrow** key to position the insertion point to the right of the logo, and then click the **rollover** to select the logo rollover. No information in the Property inspector identifies this graphic as a rollover except its name, which appears to the right of the image icon in the upper-left corner. See Figure 4-17.

Figure 4-17 Rollover in the Bands page

Next, you'll test the rollover by viewing the page in a browser, pointing to the logo, and trying the link.

11. Save the page, preview the page in a browser, and then point to the **Catalyst logo**. The rollover image appears in the browser. See Figure 4-18.

Figure 4-18   **Rollover previewed in a browser**

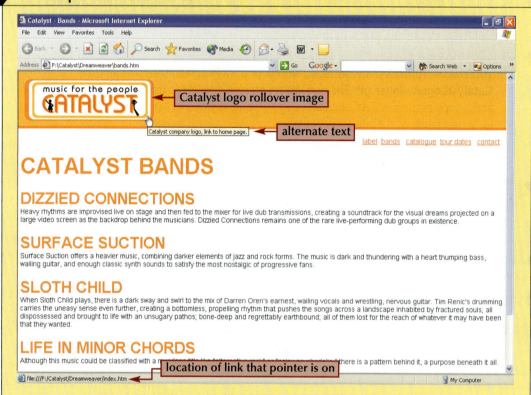

12. Click the **Catalyst logo** to open the home page, and then close the browser window.

You want the same logo rollover to appear in all the other pages of the Catalyst site. Rather than inserting the rollover in each page, you can copy it from the Bands page, and then paste it in the other pages.

To copy and paste a rollover:

1. Click the **Catalyst logo** in the Bands page to select it.
2. Click **Edit** on the menu bar, and then click **Copy HTML**.
3. Close the Bands page.
4. Open the **catalogue.htm** page in the Document window.
5. Select the **Catalyst logo**, and then press the **Delete** key. The logo is deleted from the page.
6. Click **Edit** on the menu bar, and then click **Paste HTML**. The logo rollover is inserted in the page.

   Because the new logo looks exactly the same as the graphic you just deleted, you can check to make sure it is the rollover graphic.

7. Click the **Catalyst logo** to select it, and then verify that the name in the upper-left corner of the Property inspector is "LogoRollover."

8. Save and close the page.
9. Open each of the following pages in the site, and then repeat Steps 5 through 8: **contact.htm**, **index.htm**, **label.htm**, and **tourdates.htm**.

You might want to modify a rollover.

Editing a Rollover

You can edit a rollover by changing the original graphic, changing the rollover graphic, or by editing the code of the rollover. There are several reasons that you might want to edit a rollover. For example, you may need to replace a graphic with an updated design, or you may decide to open the linked page in a new browser window. Dreamweaver does not have a special panel for modifying a rollover. However, you can edit a rollover graphic in three ways:

- Delete the original graphic and insert a new rollover using the Rollover Image button. This will delete all the code as well as the graphic and you can create a new rollover from scratch.
- Replace the original graphic or the rollover graphic with a new one. When you replace a graphic, the attached code remains. You can replace the original graphic by selecting the graphic and then selecting a new source file in the Property inspector. You can replace the rollover graphic by selecting the graphic, opening the Behaviors panel (in the Design panel group), double-clicking onMouseOver in the behavior list, and then selecting a new source file for the rollover graphic.
- Edit the code for the rollover graphic in Code view if you know JavaScript, or edit the behaviors in the Behaviors panel.

For now, you'll leave the original and rollover images.

Session 4.1 Quick Check

Review

1. What are the three types of file formats that browsers can display?
2. What is the best file format to use for photographs?
3. Why would you use the Assets panel?
4. What is an image map?
5. What is a hotspot?
6. What is a rollover?

Session 4.2

Creating Tables

In the early days of the Web, text and images were aligned to the left of the page. Designers soon discovered that they could use tables to provide a vertical and horizontal structure for the content of a Web page. This provided more flexibility in arranging the content and elements in the Web page. Today, tables are used in Web pages to simplify the presentation of data as well as to increase layout options, both of which aid in Web page design.

Tables are grid structures that are divided into rows and columns. **Rows** cross the table horizontally, whereas **columns** cross the table vertically. The container created by the intersection of a row and a column is called a **cell**. The four lines that mark the edges of a cell are called **borders**. Borders can be invisible or visible lines of a width you select. When the borders of the cells of a table are set to 0, the borders still exist but are invisible. The use of tables with invisible borders to place text and images on a Web page presented designers with a whole new world of choices for laying out Web page content.

Reference Window	**Inserting a Table**

- Click the Table button in the Common category on the Insert bar.
- Type the number of rows in the Rows text box.
- Type the number of columns in the Columns text box.
- Type a percentage value in the Table Width text box, click the Table Width list arrow, and then click Percent.
- Type a border width in the Border Thickness text box (type 0 if you do not want the table structure to appear on the Web page).
- Click the OK button.

Inserting a Table

You can quickly insert a table in a Web page. Simply move the insertion point to the location in the Web page where you want the table to appear, click the Table button in the Layout category or the Common category on the Insert bar, and then set the parameters for the table. Dreamweaver then inserts the HTML code for the table. The table parameters you can specify are:

- **Rows.** The number of rows for the table. You can also add rows to the table later.
- **Columns.** The number of columns for the table. You can also add columns to the table later.
- **Table Width.** The horizontal dimension of the table specified either in pixels or as a percentage of the width of the browser window. Specifying the table width in pixels creates a table that has a somewhat fixed width—the table will still expand to fit the content, if necessary, but it will not change size when the browser window is resized. Specifying the table width as a percentage creates a table that will adjust in size as the Web page is resized in the browser window. Initially, the table cells all have equal widths; however, you can adjust the height and width of cells, rows, and columns. Be aware that changing the width of a cell changes the width of all the cells in the column, and changing the height of a cell changes the height of all the cells in the row.
- **Border Thickness.** The size (in pixels) of the table border. A border of 0 creates an invisible table. When no value is specified, most browsers display the table as if the thickness were set to 1. It is a good idea to specify a border thickness to ensure that the table is displayed correctly. By default, the borders of an invisible table are visible within Dreamweaver so you can see the table structure, making the table easier to work with. You must preview the page in a browser to see what the table content will look like without borders.
- **Cell Padding.** The amount of empty space, measured in pixels, maintained between the border of a cell and the cell's content. When no cell padding is specified, most browsers display the table as if the cell padding were set to 1. In most cases, this is fine; however, it is a good idea to specify a cell padding to ensure that the table is always displayed correctly.

- **Cell Spacing.** The width of the cell walls measured in pixels. If you set the border to 0, then the table still will be invisible no matter what you set the cell spacing to. When no cell spacing is specified, most browsers display the table as if the cell spacing were set to 2. In most cases, this is fine; however, it is a good idea to specify a cell spacing to ensure that the table is always displayed correctly.
- **Header.** The row and columns of a table that contain heading information (also called header cells). There are four possible header options: None specifies no heading cells, Left makes the first column of cells heading cells, Top makes the first row of cells heading cells, and Both makes both the first row and the first column of cells heading cells. Designating heading cells enables visitors who use screen readers to more easily make sense of the table information.
- **Caption.** A table title that is displayed outside of the table. It is not necessary to type a caption, but a caption can aid visitors who are using assistive devices.
- **Align Caption.** Designates the alignment of the caption in relation to the table.
- **Summary.** A description of the table. Assistive devices read the summary, but the text is not displayed in the page.

You'll create a table to hold the West Coast region tour dates in the Tour Dates page. The table will have 3 columns, 14 rows, and no borders.

To insert a table:

1. If you took a break after the last session, make sure the **NewCatalyst** Web site is open.
2. Open the **tourdates.htm** page in the Document window, click to the right of the U.S. map, and then press the **Enter** key to move the insertion point below the map.
3. Click the **Table** button in the **Common** category on the Insert bar. The Table dialog box opens.

   You'll set the table parameters.
4. Type **14** in the Rows text box, press the **Tab** key, and then type **3** in the Columns text box, if necessary.
5. Press the **Tab** key, type **75** in the Table Width text box, click the **Table Width** list arrow, and then click **Percent**, if necessary.
6. Press the **Tab** key, and then type **0** in the Border Thickness text box.
7. Press the **Tab** key, and then type **1** in the Cell Padding text box.
8. Press the **Tab** key, and then type **2** in the Cell Spacing text box.
9. Click **Top** in the Header area.
10. Press the **Tab** key four times, and then type **Catalyst bands, west coast tour dates** in the Summary text box. See Figure 4-19.

Figure 4-19 | **Completed Table dialog box**

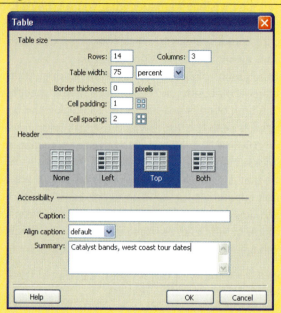

▶ **11.** Click the **OK** button. The table appears in the Document window and is selected. See Figure 4-20. You may need to scroll down to see the entire table.

Figure 4-20 | **Selected table in Tour Dates page**

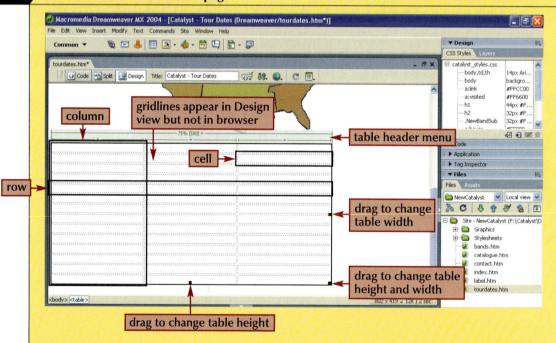

▶ **12.** Save the page.

When you create a table, Dreamweaver inserts a nonbreaking space in each cell. Some browsers collapse cells that are empty, thereby destroying the table structure. The nonbreaking space is invisible, but it keeps the cells from collapsing. To view a nonbreaking space, you must be in Code view or Split view.

You will view the nonbreaking space in the first cell of the table in the Tour Dates page.

To view a nonbreaking space:

1. Click in the upper-left cell of the table in the Tour Dates page to place the insertion point in the cell.
2. Click the **Show Code and Design Views** button [Split] on the Document toolbar. Notice the nonbreaking space ( ) to the right of the insertion point in the Code pane.
3. Click the **Show Design View** button [Design] on the Document toolbar.

Next, you will add content to the cells in the table you just created.

Adding Content to Cells

To add text to a cell, all you need to do is click in the cell and type. Pressing the Enter key adds another paragraph within the cell. You can also copy data between cells using the standard Copy and Paste commands. When you type or paste text into a cell, the text wraps within the cell to fit the width you defined. If you check the No Wrap check box in the Property inspector, the cell will expand to fit the text in a browser; however, the text will still wrap when you view the page in Dreamweaver.

There are several keyboard commands that will help you move through your table. To move to the next adjacent cell, press the Tab key. Pressing the Tab key in the last cell of the table adds a new row to the table. Pressing the Shift+Tab keys moves the insertion point to the previous cell. You also can use the arrow keys to move the insertion point to an adjacent cell.

In addition to text, you can insert graphics into table cells using the Image button in the Images list in the Common category on the Insert bar. When a graphic is inserted into a cell, the cell's column width and row height expand as needed to accommodate the graphic.

Brian has supplied the West Coast tour schedule for you to enter in the table in the Tour Dates page.

Like Word

To add text to a table:

1. With the insertion point in the first cell in the table, type **West Coast Tour Dates**, and then press the **Tab** key. The text appears in the first cell and the insertion point moves to the second column of the first row.
2. Press the **Left Arrow** key and then press the **Down Arrow** key. The insertion point moves to the cell in the first column and the second row.
3. Type the following information into the table, pressing the **Tab** key to move to the next cell (do not press the Enter key while typing text in a cell; the text will wrap by itself). Figure 4-21 shows most of the table in Design view; you need to scroll to see all the rows.

Date	Location / Venue	Band
1/4 to 1/6	Seattle, WA / Graceland	Life in Minor Chords, Dizzied Connections
1/11 to 1/13	San Francisco, CA / Bottom of the Hill	Dizzied Connections
1/18 to 1/20	Monterey, CA / The Long Bar	Life in Minor Chords, Dizzied Connections
2/8 to 2/10	Silverlake, CA / Spaceland	Surface Suction
2/15 to 2/17	Arcata, CA / Depot	Dizzied Connections

2/22 to 2/24	San Diego, CA / Casbah	Surface Suction
3/8 to 3/10	Portland, OR / Blackbird	Life in Minor Chords, Dizzied Connections
3/15 to 3/17	Monterey, CA / The Long Bar	Surface Suction
3/22 to 3/24	Los Angeles, CA / Spaceland	Dizzied Connections
4/5 to 4/7	San Francisco, CA / The Dance Hall	Surface Suction
4/12 to 4/14	Seattle, WA / Graceland	Dizzied Connections
4/19 to 4/21	Phoenix, AZ / Modified	Life in Minor Chords, Dizzied Connections

Figure 4-21   Table with content

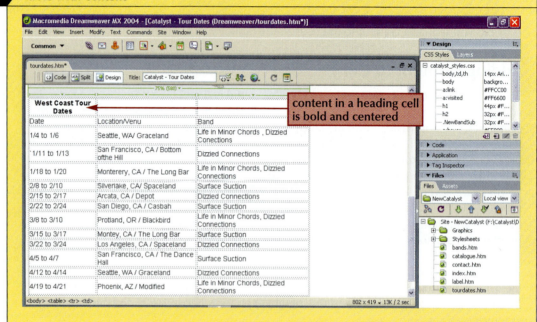

Trouble? If you don't have enough rows for all the entries, press the Tab key in the last cell of the table. If you have a blank row at the end of the table, you pressed the Tab key after the final entry. You'll learn how to delete this extra row shortly.

4. Save the page.

All the formatting options available for text in a Web page can also be applied to text in a table. Text formatting attributes are available in the Property inspector when you select a cell, a row, or a column. You can also create CSS styles for table text.

Selecting Tables and Table Elements

You will want to modify a table and its elements to fit the needs of a particular Web page layout or specific content. To work with a table or table element, you need to select it. You can select a table cell, a row, a column, or the table itself. Anytime the table or a table element is selected, the table header menu appears at the top of the table. You can switch to Expanded Table view in the Layout category on the Insert bar. Expanded Table view increases the width of the cell walls to enable you to more easily select various table elements.

Selecting a Table

When you want to change attributes that affect the entire table, the whole table must be selected. When the entire table is selected, a bold black line surrounds the table and resize handles appear on the left side, in the lower-right corner, and at the bottom of the table. The attributes in the Property inspector also change to reflect the entire table.

You'll use two methods to deselect and then select the table in the Tour Dates page.

To select an entire table:

1. Switch to the **Layout** category on the Insert bar. Notice that the table is currently displayed in Standard mode.
2. Click outside the table to deselect the table.
3. Right-click the table, point to **Table** on the context menu, and then click **Select Table**. The table is selected, and the table properties appear in the Property inspector. See Figure 4-22.

Table selected in the Tour Dates page — Figure 4-22

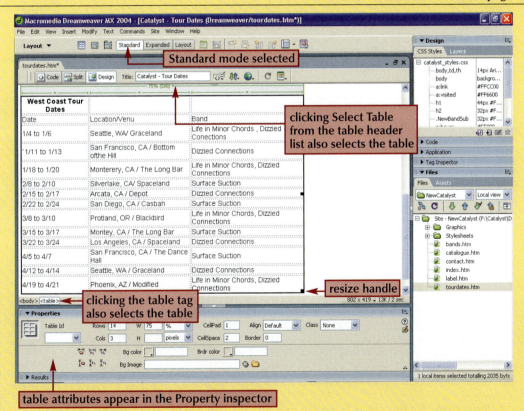

4. Click anywhere in the Document window outside the table to deselect it.
5. Position the pointer over the upper-left corner of the table so that the pointer changes to ↖, and then click. The entire table is selected.

Selecting a Table Cell

When you want to adjust the attributes of a single cell, you must select that cell. To select the entire cell, you press the Ctrl key and then click inside the cell. The cell borders are bold black when it is selected. If the cell contains any content, the content is selected as well. Clicking in a cell does not select the cell, but it does display the cell properties in the Property inspector. The process is the same to select a group of cells except that you press and hold the Ctrl key while you click in each cell. You can also drag across all the cells you want to select. The borders of all the selected cells are bold black, and any content within the selected cells is also selected.

You'll select a single cell and a group of cells in the table in the Tour Dates page.

To select cells:

1. Press and hold the **Ctrl** key, click the cell at the upper-left corner of the table, and then release the **Ctrl** key. The cell is selected. See Figure 4-23.

Figure 4-23   **Cell selected in the table**

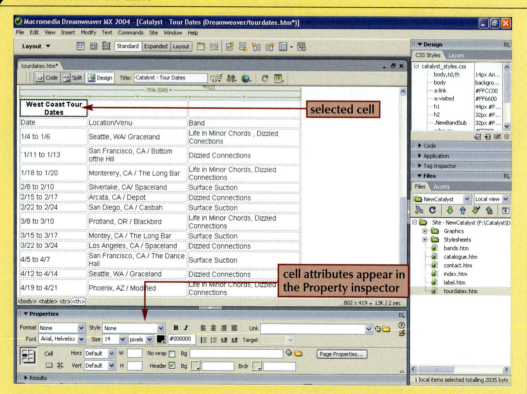

2. Drag across the three cells in the top row until they have bold black borders. The three cells are selected.
3. Click outside the table to deselect the cells.

Selecting Columns and Rows

You can use the mouse to select one or more columns or rows. To select a column, click the list arrow in the header menu above the top border of the column you want to select, and then click Select Column. To select a row, click to the left of the row you want to select. If you want to select multiple columns or rows, you drag across additional columns or rows. The borders of all the cells in the selected column or row are bold. You can also tell that a column or row is selected because the word *Column* or *Row* appears in the Property inspector alongside an icon showing a highlighted column or row in a table. Selecting all the cells in a row or column is the same as selecting the row or column.

You'll select the third column in the table in the Tour Dates page, and then you'll select the second row of cells.

To select a row and a column of cells:

1. Click in the table, click the list arrow above the top border of the third column of the table, and then click **Select Column**. The third column of the table is selected. See Figure 4-24.

Column selected in the table   **Figure 4-24**

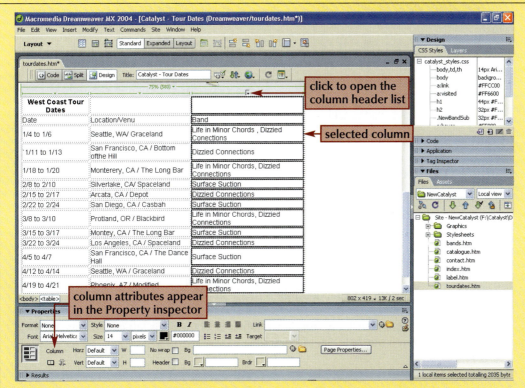

2. Point outside the left border of the second row of the table. The pointer changes to .
3. Click the mouse button. The second row of the table is selected. See Figure 4-25.

| Figure 4-25 | Row selected in the table |

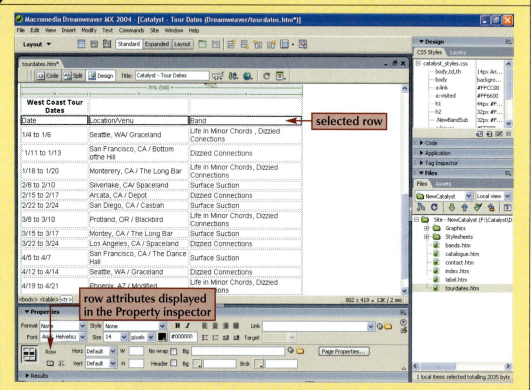

4. Click anywhere outside the table to deselect the row.

Using Expanded Tables Mode

If you are having difficulty selecting a table element, you can use Expanded Tables mode. Expanded Tables mode temporarily adds cell padding and spacing to all the tables in the page so that you can more easily select table elements and more precisely position the pointer inside cells. When you are in Expanded Tables mode, tables may not be positioned precisely in the page because of the additional cell padding and spacing. Make sure that you return to Standard mode before you check the final page layout. You select tables and table elements in Expanded Tables mode in the same way you do in Standard mode.

You'll switch to Expanded Tables mode, and then select various table elements. When you are finished, you'll return to Standard mode.

To select table elements in Expanded Tables mode:

1. Click the **Expanded Tables Mode** button in the **Layout** category on the Insert bar, and then click the **OK** button in the Getting Started in Expanded Tables Mode dialog box, if necessary. The page changes to Expanded Tables mode.

2. Click the left corner of the table. The table is selected and takes up more space in the page. See Figure 4-26.

Tutorial 4 Organizing Page Content and Layout | Dreamweaver

Table selected in Expanded Tables mode | Figure 4-26

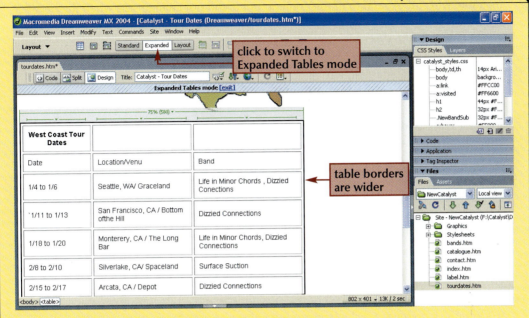

3. Click the list arrow above the first column, and then click **Select Column** to select the column.
4. Click outside of the table to deselect it, and then select the third row of the column. Notice that it is easier to select table elements when the borders are wider.
5. Click the **Standard Mode** button in the **Layout** category on the Insert bar to return to Standard mode.

Next, you'll work with the entire table.

Working with the Entire Table

Once a table is selected you can change the attributes of the table, resize the table, move the table, or delete the table.

Modifying Table Attributes

Sometimes it is necessary to change the attributes of a table. You can change the attributes for an existing table in the Property inspector, you can create a CSS style with the attributes that you want to use for the table, or you can create a CSS style to modify the <table> tag if you want to change the attributes for all the tables in the site. When the entire table is selected, the Property inspector includes the attributes from the Table dialog box: rows, columns, width, border, cell padding, and cell spacing, as well as additional formatting attributes. The additional attributes available in the Property inspector include:

- **Table ID.** A unique descriptive name for the table. The table name helps you to distinguish between tables when you have more than one table in a Web page. Also, some programming languages use the name to refer to the table. The Table ID must begin with a letter or underscore and can contain letters and numbers, but not spaces or symbols.
- **H (Height).** The vertical dimension of the table in pixels or a percentage of the height of the browser window. Most of the time it is not necessary to specify a table height. If no value is entered in the Height text box, the cells remain at their default height.

Specifying the table height in pixels creates a table that has a somewhat fixed height: the table will still expand to fit the content, but it will not change size when the browser window is resized. Specifying the table height as a percentage creates a table that will adjust in size as the Web page is resized in the browser window.

- **Align.** The alignment of the table within the Web page. Table alignment can be the browser's default alignment, left, right, or center.
- **Clear Row Heights** and **Clear Column Widths.** Buttons that remove all row height and column width settings from the table.
- **Convert Table Widths to Pixels** and **Convert Table Heights to Pixels.** Buttons that change the table width or table height from a percentage to its current width or height in pixels.
- **Convert Table Widths to Percent** and **Convert Table Heights to Percent.** Buttons that change the current table width or height from pixels to a percentage of the browser window.
- **Bg Color (Background Color).** The background color for the entire table. You specify a color by typing its hexadecimal color code in the Bg Color text box or by selecting the color with the color picker. If a background color is not specified, the Web page background is seen through the table.
- **Brdr Color (Border Color).** The border color for the entire table. You can specify a color in the same manner as for the background color using the Brdr Color text box or the color picker. (Note that some versions of Netscape Navigator do not display border color correctly.)
- **Bg Image (Background Image).** The background image for the table. You can type the file path and filename in the Bg Image text box, or use the Browse for File button or Point to File button to select a graphic file to use as the background image. (When you set a background image for the table, Netscape Navigator will tile the image in each cell of the table as if you had set the image as the background in each individual cell. Internet Explorer will display the image across all of the cells.)

Because there are differences in the way that browsers handle tables (such as the differences in the way browsers display border color and background image), it is very important to preview Web pages that use tables in all the different browsers that you intend to support. If you find problems in the way a browser displays the tables you have created, you can look at sites such as www.blooberry.com as well as support sites from browser manufacturers like www.microsoft.com and www.home.netscape.com to research issues and fixes for specific browsers and browser versions.

You'll name the table in the Tour Dates page and align the table to the center of the page.

To change table attributes:

1. Select the table in the Tour Dates page.
2. Type **WestCoastTourDates** in the Table Id text box in the Property inspector.
3. Click the **Align** list arrow in the Property inspector, and then click **Center**. The table is centered on the page.
4. Double-click in the **CellPad** text box, type **0**, double-click in the **CellSpace** text box, type **0**, and then press the **Enter** key. The cell padding and cell spacing tighten up. See Figure 4-27.

Table with modified attributes

Figure 4-27

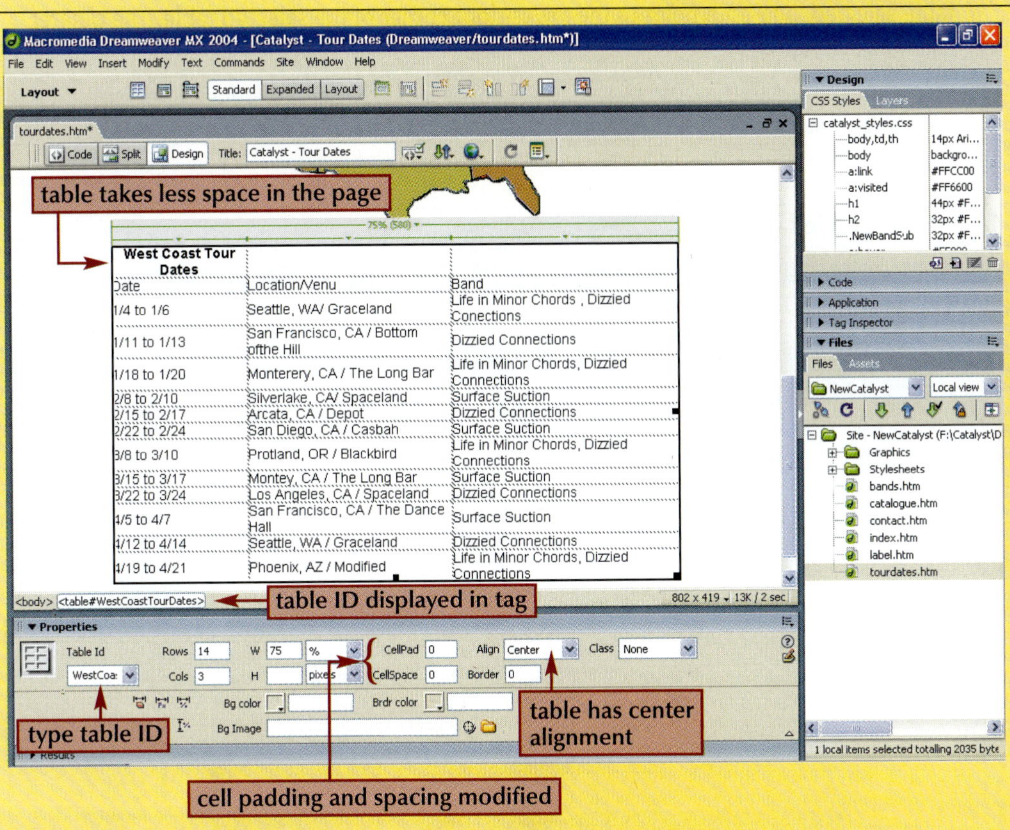

[Screenshot of Dreamweaver MX 2004 showing the tourdates.htm page with the West Coast Tour Dates table, with annotations:]
- table takes less space in the page
- table ID displayed in tag
- type table ID
- cell padding and spacing modified
- table has center alignment

5. Save the page.

Next, you'll change the table's size and location.

Resizing and Moving a Table

Sometimes you know how you want a table to look on a page, but you don't know the exact dimensions to create that look. When a table is selected, you can adjust the size (height and width) and position manually from within the Document window. To resize the table, you drag the lower-right corner of the table until the table is the size you want. A dotted border appears as you drag, indicating the new dimensions the table will have when you release the mouse button. When you resize a table manually, Dreamweaver inserts the new width and height values, which you can see in the Property inspector. The values are calculated in the unit of measure (percentage or pixels) that you specified previously for the attribute. If no height value was specified previously, the new value will be in pixels. You can move a table on the page by cutting and pasting the table or by dragging the table to the new location.

You will adjust the size and location of the table in the Tour Dates page.

To resize and move a table:

1. If the rulers are not visible, click **View** on the menu bar, point to **Rulers**, and then click **Show**.

2. Click **View** on the menu bar, point to **Rulers**, and then click **Pixels**, if necessary.

3. Click a **resize handle** on the table to make the Document window active and keep the table selected, and then point to the lower-right corner of the selected table. The pointer changes to ↘.

4. Press and hold the left mouse button, drag down and to the right about 200 pixels, but do not release the mouse button. A dotted border shows the new dimensions of the table. See Figure 4-28.

| Figure 4-28 | Table being resized |

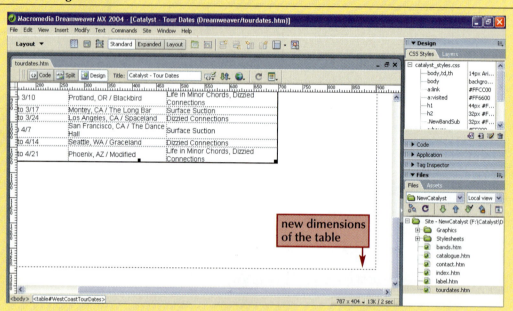

new dimensions of the table

Trouble? If the exact numbers on your screen are different than those shown (in other words, if the table is in a different position relative to the measurements on the rulers), then your screen size is different than the one shown in the figure. Continue with Step 5.

5. Release the mouse button. The height and width values change in the Property inspector, reflecting the larger table size. The table doesn't need to be this large, so you'll try a smaller size.

6. Drag the lower-right corner of the table up and to the left about 300 pixels to reduce the table size. The new height and width values appear in the Property inspector, reflecting the smaller table size.

   The text is difficult to read in the smaller table, so you'll return to the original table size by resetting the values in the Property inspector.

7. Double-click in the **W** text box in the Property inspector, type **75**, double-click in the **H** text box, press the **Delete** key to delete the value in the Height text box, and then press the **Enter** key. The table returns to its original size.

   Next, you'll move the table to another location.

8. Click **View** on the menu bar, point to **Rulers**, and then click **Show** to hide the rulers.

9. Position the pointer in the upper-left corner of the selected table so that the pointer changes to ⊞.

10. Press and hold the left mouse button, and then drag the table above the map. The table moves to the new location.

   Trouble? If there is no blank line between the page heading and the map, release the mouse button when the indicator line is to the left of the map.

> 11. Drag the table to its original position below the map, and then save the page.
>
> **Trouble?** If the window won't scroll when you try to reposition the table, move the pointer near the vertical scroll bar as you drag.

Deleting a Table

While creating a Web page, you may need to delete a table completely. To delete a table, simply select the table and then press the Delete key. The table as well as any content in the table is deleted from the page.

Working with Table Cells

You can customize tables by modifying individual cells or groups of cells. When a cell or a group of cells is selected, you can change its attributes in the Property inspector, including modifying the formatting attributes of the cell content and changing the cell properties.

Modifying Cell Formatting and Layout

Cells have a different set of attributes than tables. Once a cell has been selected, you can change the attributes, and the attributes of any content within the cell, in the Property inspector. Cell attributes include text formatting, because within a table, content can be contained only in cells.

You can format the content of an entire table by selecting all the cells in the table and then changing the text formatting attributes. Text formatting attributes are not available when you select the table itself because the HTML code for text formatting is in the tags for the individual cells and rows, not in the code for the table itself. This setup allows for formatting variations within cells and makes tables more flexible.

In addition to the familiar text formatting attributes, you can use the following options in the Property inspector to change the cell's layout attributes:

- **Merges Selected Cells Using Spans.** Joins all selected cells into one cell. This button is active only if more than one cell is selected.
- **Splits Cell into Rows or Columns.** Divides a single cell into multiple rows or columns. This button is active only when a single cell is selected.
- **Horz (Horizontal).** The horizontal alignment options for the cell's content. Content can be aligned to the browser's default setting, left, right, or center.
- **Vert (Vertical).** The vertical alignment options for the cell's content. Content can be aligned to the browser's default setting, top, middle, bottom, or baseline.
- **No Wrap.** Enables or disables word wrapping. Word wrapping enables a cell to expand horizontally and vertically to accommodate added content. If the No Wrap check box is checked, the cell will expand only horizontally to accommodate the added content.
- **Header.** Formats the selected cell or rows as a table header. By default, the content of header cells is bold and centered; however, you can redefine the header cell tag with CSS styles to create a custom look.
- **Bg (Background Image).** The background image for a cell, column, or row. You can type the file path and filename of the background image or browse to select the background image. If no image is specified, the Web page background is seen through the cell. The background image for a cell takes precedence over the background color for the cell. Also, the background image for a cell takes precedence over a background image or color for the table.

DRM 206 Dreamweaver Tutorial 4 Organizing Page Content and Layout

- **Bg (Background Color).** The background color for the selected cells. You can specify a color by typing its hexadecimal color code in the Bg text box or by selecting the color with the color picker. If no color is specified, the Web page background is seen through the cell. The background color for a cell takes precedence over the background image or color for the table.
- **Brdr (Border Color).** The color of the cell border. You can type a hexadecimal color code in the Brdr text box or select a color with the color picker. If the cell borders for the table are set to 0, the border is not seen.

When a single cell is selected, the word *Cell* and an icon of a table with a selected cell appear in the lower-left corner of the Property inspector. You can then verify that you have selected the correct element before you begin to adjust the attributes.

You'll merge the cells in the top row of the table, and then make the new cell a header cell.

To adjust cells:

1. Select the three cells in the top row of the table in the Tour Dates page.
2. Click the **Merges Selected Cells Using Spans** button in the Property inspector. The three cells are combined into one, and the text moves to the center of the table because this is a header cell. See Figure 4-29.

Figure 4-29 | **Cells merged as header cell**

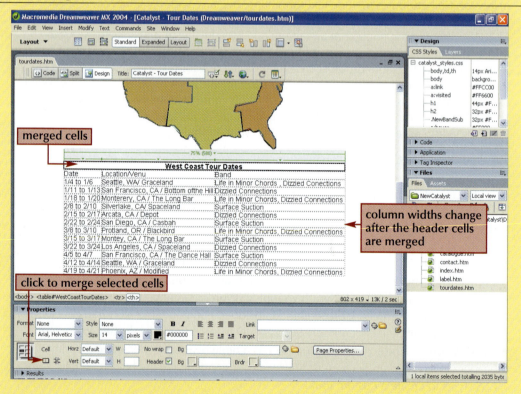

3. Save the page.

Next, you'll adjust the height and width of cells.

Adjusting the Row Span and Column Span of Cells

You can adjust the row span and the column span of individual cells of a table. **Row span** is the height of the cell measured in rows. **Column span** is the width of the cell measured in columns. You can change the row and column spans by increments of one. For example, increasing a cell's row span makes the selected cell span the height of two rows of the table. If you increase the row span of a cell twice, the cell becomes three rows high. Decreasing the row span removes one increment. If a cell is only one row high, decreasing the row span does not work. Adjusting column span works the same way. Increasing the column span of a cell makes the selected cell span the width of two columns of the table. If you increase the column span of a cell twice, it becomes three columns wide. Decreasing the column span removes one increment. If a cell is only one column wide, decreasing the column span does not work.

You'll adjust the row span and the column span of cells in the table in the Tour Dates page.

To adjust row span and column span of cells:

1. Right-click the cell in the first column and the second row of the table, point to **Table** on the context menu, and then click **Increase Row Span**. The cell's height spans two table rows. (Actually the cell merges with the one below it and the content of both cells is combined.)

2. Right-click the cell in the first column and the second row of the table, point to **Table** on the context menu, and then click **Increase Column Span**. The cell's width spans two table columns. Because the merged cell was the height of two cells in the adjoining column before you executed the command, the three cells merged and all of the cell content was combined. See Figure 4-30.

Cell after increasing row and column spans **Figure 4-30**

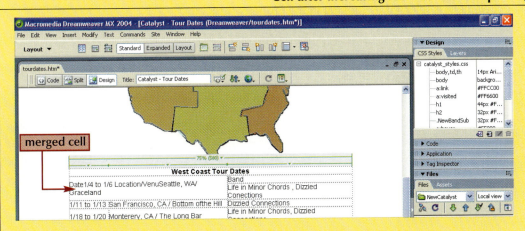

The cell doesn't need to have a different height or width, so you'll decrease the row span and the column span.

3. Right-click the cell in the first column and the second row of the table, point to **Table** on the context menu, and then click **Decrease Row Span**.

4. Right-click the cell in the first column and the second row of the table, point to **Table** on the context menu, and then click **Decrease Column Span**. The cell's height and width return to their original settings, but all the text is still in one cell.

5. Right-click the cell in the first column and the third row of the table, point to **Table**, and then click **Decrease Column Span**. The cell's height and width return to their original settings.

6. Select **1/4 to 1/6** in the cell in the first column and the second row, press the **Ctrl+X** keys to cut the selected text, click in the first cell in the third row in the table, and then press the **Ctrl+V** keys to paste the cut text.

7. Cut **Location / Venue** from the first cell in the second row, and paste the cut text into the cell in the second column and second row of the table.

8. Cut **Seattle, WA / Graceland** from the first cell in the second row, and paste the cut text into the cell in the second column and third row of the table. The text is in the correct cells again.

9. Save the page.

You can also modify entire rows and columns in a table, not just individual cells.

Working with Rows and Columns

Table rows and columns provide the vertical and horizontal structure for the content of the table as well as for the content of some Web pages. When a row or column is selected, you can change its attributes, and resize, add, or delete the entire row or column. Selecting all the cells in a row or column is the same as selecting the row or column.

Modifying Rows and Columns

The attribute options available for rows and columns are the same as those for cells. When you modify attributes while a row or column is selected, the changes apply to all of the cells in the selected row or column. Before you change attributes, verify that the correct element is selected by looking in the Property inspector.

You want to change the second row of the table to a header row.

To change row attributes:

1. Select the second row of the table.

2. Click the **Header** check box in the Property inspector to check it. The content of each cell in the row is centered and in boldface.

3. Save the page.

Next, you'll resize the columns.

Resizing Columns and Rows

When a table is created, columns are all of equal width and rows are all the default height. You can adjust the width of a selected column by typing a new value in the W (Width) text box or by dragging a column's left or right border to the desired position. When you adjust a column width manually, Dreamweaver calculates the width you selected. You can adjust the height of a selected row by typing a new height value into the H (Height) text box or by dragging the row's top or bottom border to the desired position. When you adjust a row height manually, Dreamweaver calculates the height you selected.

You may need to resize the columns in the table to better fit the content.

To resize columns:

1. Position the pointer on the right border of the first column. The pointer changes to ┿.
2. Drag the border so that the content in the first column appears on only one line, if necessary. See Figure 4-31.

Resizing a table column — Figure 4-31

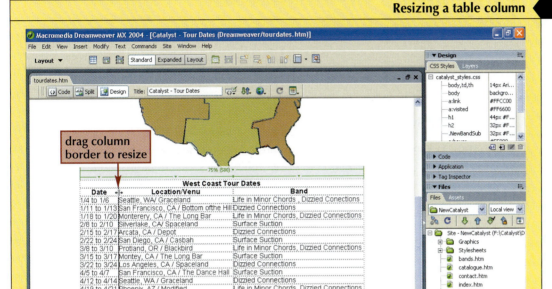

3. Point to the right border of the second column, and then drag the border so that the content in the cell in the third row from the bottom fills one line, if necessary.
4. Save the page.

Next, you'll delete a row in the table.

Adding and Deleting Columns and Rows

As you work, you might find you need more or fewer columns and rows in a table. To insert a column, you select a cell or a column and use the Insert Column command. A new column of the same width as the selected cell or column is inserted to the left of the selection. To insert a row, you select a cell or a row and use the Insert Row command. The new row is added above the selected cell or row. You can also add a new row at the end of the table by clicking in the last cell of the table and pressing the Tab key. You can add multiple columns or rows by using the Insert Rows or Columns command; when you click this command, a dialog box opens and you set the number of columns or rows you want to insert and where you want to insert them relative to the selection.

If you need to remove extra columns or rows, you can select the column or row and then use the Delete Column or Delete Row command. Be aware that all the content in that column or row is also deleted. Once a column or row is selected, you can also press the Delete key to remove the selected column or row and all of its content.

Brian tells you that the shows in Phoenix on 4/19 to 4/21 have been postponed. He asks you to delete the row with that information from the table.

To delete a row:

1. Select the last row of the table.
2. Right-click the selected row, point to **Table** on the context menu, and then click **Delete Row**. The row and all its content are removed from the table.
3. If necessary, delete any extra blank rows from the table.
4. Save the page.

The table still needs additional formatting.

Using Preset Table Designs

Because some commonly used table designs are cumbersome to create, Dreamweaver added the Format Table dialog box. The Format Table dialog box contains a number of preset table designs, as well as options to further customize the preset designs. Applying the customized designs to tables saves you the time of having to change all the attributes yourself. The features in the Format Table dialog box include:

- **Preset table design list.** A list of available preset table designs. When you click a design, the sample table on the right shows the attributes associated with that design. The text in the sample table enables you to preview any text formatting options, but the text will not be included in the table.
- **Row Colors.** The colors and alternating pattern to apply to rows. You can enter the hexadecimal color code or use the color picker to choose two colors for the rows in a table. The first color will appear first in the color rotation; the second color will appear second. The Alternate list box enables you to choose the frequency with which the chosen colors are used in the table.
- **Top Row.** Customization options for formatting the cells in the top row of the table. Attributes include align, text style, background color, and text color.
- **Left Col (Left Column).** Customization options for formatting the cells in the left column of the table. Attributes include alignment and text styles.
- **Table.** Customizations that apply to the entire table. You can change the border size in the Border text box.
- **Apply All Attributes to TD Tags Instead of TR Tags.** If you leave this check box unchecked (the default), the attributes are applied to the row tags for the table. If the check box is checked, the attributes are applied to cell tags. (Cells are distinguished in HTML with the TD tag; rows are distinguished with the TR tag. Table tags will be discussed in depth in the next section.)

For better readability, Brian wants you to add alternating colors to the table rows. Rather than changing the row colors manually, you'll use the Format Table dialog box.

To use the format table feature:

1. Click anywhere in the table, click **Commands** on the menu bar, and then click **Format Table**. The Format Table dialog box opens.
2. Click **AltRows:Blue&Yellow** in the preset table designs list.

3. In the Row Colors section, replace the hexadecimal color code in the First text box with **#FF6600**, replace the color code in the Second text box with **#FF9900**, and then press the **Tab** key. The colors you selected are shown in the table preview.

4. Click the **Alternate** list arrow, and then click **Every Other Row**, if necessary.

5. Click the **Align** list arrow in the Left Col section, and then click **Center**.

   You do not need to choose any options in the Top Row section, as you have already applied the Heading 1 style to the top row in the table. If you do not change the Top Row or Left Column attributes in the Format Table dialog box, they will not change in the table.

6. Double-click in the **Border** text box, and then type **0**.

7. Click the **Apply All Attributes to TD Tags Instead of TR Tags** check box to check it. See Figure 4-32.

Figure 4-32 Completed Format Table dialog box

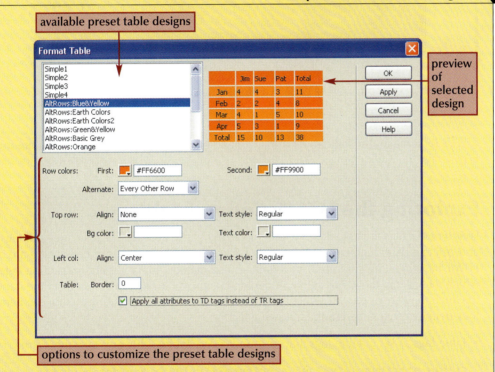

8. Click the **OK** button. The colors are applied to every other row of the table and the content of each cell is centered in the cell. See Figure 4-33.

Figure 4-33   **Table with new format attributes applied**

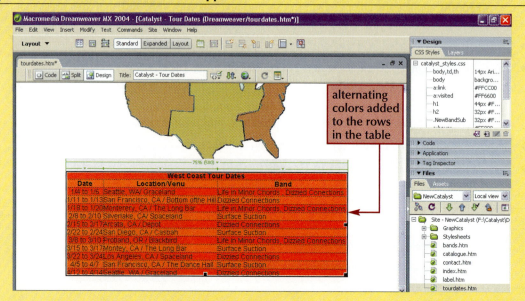

9. Save the page, preview the page in a browser, and then close the page.

This look makes the table more attractive and easier to read. Next, you'll explore the HTML tags that define tables.

Exploring the HTML Code of Tables

Four types of tags are associated with tables: table tags, table row tags, header cell tags, and cell tags. Although Dreamweaver allows you to select columns of cells, there are no HTML tags to define columns. All of the tags associated with tables are **bracketing tags**, which means that they consist of an opening tag and a closing tag that bracket the content to which they are applied. All the tags can contain a number of parameters for the items they define, as explained in the following list:

- **Table tags.** A set of table tags that surrounds every table. Table tags take the form:

```
<table attribute1="value" attribute2="value">tags defining table rows and cells</table>
```

If you apply attributes to the entire table (when the table is selected), the parameters for those attributes appear in the opening table tag.

- **Table Row tags.** A set of row tags surrounds every row. An opening table row tag always appears after the opening table tag, because every table must have at least one row. Table row tags take the form:

  `<tr>all the tags for the cells in the row</tr>`

  If you apply attributes to a row of cells, the parameters for those attributes usually appear in the tags for the cells, not in the tag for the row.
- **Cell tags.** A set of cell tags surrounds every cell (except those cells you designate as header cells). Cell tags are nested inside the row tags. Every table must have at least one cell. Cell tags take the form:

  `<td attribute1="value" attribute2="value">text in the cell</td>`

  Every cell in the table has its own set of cell tags (unless it is a header cell), and any attributes applied to the cell are contained in the opening cell tag. Attributes that you apply to columns appear in the cell tags for each cell in the column. If you check the Apply All Attributes to TD Tags Instead of TR Tags check box in the Format Table dialog box, then the row attributes you apply will appear in the cell tags as well.
- **Header Cell tags.** A set of header cell tags surrounds every cell that you designate as a header cell by checking the Header Cell check box in the Property inspector while the cell is selected. Like regular cell tags, header cell tags are nested between the row tags. Header cell tags take the form:

  `<th attribute1="value" attribute2="value">text in the cell</th>`

  Every header cell in the table has its own set of header cell tags, and any attributes applied to the cell are contained in the opening tag.

A table may seem complex; however, all table code can be broken down into the four types of tags described above.

Figure 4-34 shows the table in the Tour Dates page in Code view.

Figure 4-34 Table tags in Code view

- opening table tag with table attributes → line 44
- table row tags for the first row → lines 45, 47
- opening table heading cell in the first row → line 46
- three table heading cells in the second row → lines 49–51
- three regular cells in the third row → lines 54–56
- closing table tag → line 108

```html
<table width="75%" border="0" align="center" cellpadding="0" cellspacing="0" id="West Coast Tour Dates" summary="Catalyst bands, west coast tour dates">
  <tr>
    <th colspan="3" bgcolor="#FF6600" scope="col">West Coast Tour Dates </th>
  </tr>
  <tr>
    <th align="center" bgcolor="#FF9900">Date</th>
    <th bgcolor="#FF9900">Location/Venu</th>
    <th bgcolor="#FF9900">Band</th>
  </tr>
  <tr>
    <td align="center" bgcolor="#FF6600">1/4 to 1/6 </td>
    <td bgcolor="#FF6600">Seattle, WA/ Graceland </td>
    <td bgcolor="#FF6600">Life in Minor Chords , Dizzied Conections </td>
  </tr>
  <tr>
    <td align="center" bgcolor="#FF9900">1/11 to 1/13 </td>
    <td bgcolor="#FF9900">San Francisco, CA / Bottom ofthe Hill </td>
    <td bgcolor="#FF9900">Dizzied Connections </td>
  </tr>
  <tr>
    <td align="center" bgcolor="#FF6600">1/18 to 1/20 </td>
    <td bgcolor="#FF6600">Monterery, CA / The Long Bar </td>
    <td bgcolor="#FF6600">Life in Minor Chords, Dizzied Connections </td>
  </tr>
  <tr>
    <td align="center" bgcolor="#FF9900">2/8 to 2/10 </td>
    <td bgcolor="#FF9900">Silverlake, CA/ Spaceland </td>
    <td bgcolor="#FF9900">Surface Suction </td>
  </tr>
  <tr>
    <td align="center" bgcolor="#FF6600">2/15 to 2/17 </td>
    <td bgcolor="#FF6600">Arcata, CA / Depot </td>
    <td bgcolor="#FF6600">Dizzied Connections </td>
  </tr>
  <tr>
    <td align="center" bgcolor="#FF9900">2/22 to 2/24 </td>
    <td bgcolor="#FF9900">San Diego, CA / Casbah </td>
    <td bgcolor="#FF9900">Surface Suction </td>
  </tr>
  <tr>
    <td align="center" bgcolor="#FF6600">3/8 to 3/10 </td>
    <td bgcolor="#FF6600">Protland, OR / Blackbird </td>
    <td bgcolor="#FF6600">Life in Minor Chords, Dizzied Connections </td>
  </tr>
  <tr>
    <td align="center" bgcolor="#FF9900">3/15 to 3/17 </td>
    <td bgcolor="#FF9900">Montey, CA / The Long Bar </td>
    <td bgcolor="#FF9900">Surface Suction </td>
  </tr>
  <tr>
    <td align="center" bgcolor="#FF6600">3/22 to 3/24 </td>
    <td bgcolor="#FF6600">Los Angeles, CA / Spaceland </td>
    <td bgcolor="#FF6600">Dizzied Connections </td>
  </tr>
  <tr>
    <td align="center" bgcolor="#FF9900">4/5 to 4/7 </td>
    <td bgcolor="#FF9900">San Francisco, CA / The Dance Hall </td>
    <td bgcolor="#FF9900">Surface Suction </td>
  </tr>
  <tr>
    <td align="center" bgcolor="#FF6600">4/12 to 4/14 </td>
    <td bgcolor="#FF6600">Seattle, WA / Graceland</td>
    <td bgcolor="#FF6600">Dizzied Connections </td>
  </tr>
</table>
```

Handwritten annotation: Columns defined by cells (TD) — keep same number

Redefining Table Tags Using CSS Styles

One hallmark of good Web design is to create all the tables in a site with a consistent look. It's also a good idea to keep the fonts and font styles within the table consistent with the font choices you made for the rest of the site. One way to do this is to use CSS styles.

Reference Window: Redefining Table Tags Using CSS Styles

- Click the New CSS Style button in the CSS Styles panel.
- Click the Tag option button.
- Click the Tag list arrow, and then select the table tag you want to modify.
- Click the appropriate option button to define the style in a style sheet file or in this document only.
- Set the appropriate options in the CSS Style Definition dialog box, and then click the OK button.

You specified the page font when you set page properties, and Dreamweaver modified the body tag, the table row tag, and the table heading tag to include font group, font size, and font color attributes. The table text is already formatted because the tags were already modified. You can also create styles that will specify background, positioning, and border elements in tables.

In this session, you've created a table, added content, and formatted it in Standard mode and in Extended Table mode. In the next session, you'll work with a layout table in Layout mode.

Session 4.2 Quick Check (Review)

1. What is a table cell?
2. True or False? Table borders can be invisible.
3. Explain the difference between cell padding and cell spacing.
4. Explain what pressing the Tab key does when you are entering data into a table.
5. Describe what happens when you merge two cells.
6. What is the opening HTML tag for a table row?
7. What is the opening HTML tag for a table cell?

Session 4.3

Planning a Table in Layout Mode

Tables are frequently used by designers to provide structure for the layout of Web pages. For example, you can use the rough sketches of a Web site as a blueprint to create a table that fills a Web page and that has a cell across the top to hold the company logo, a cell for the navigation system, a cell for the content, and so forth. Creating tables for the layout of a Web page in Standard mode can get tricky because it is sometimes necessary to merge and split cells many times to achieve the desired design.

To make it easier to create tables that will be used for Web page layout, Dreamweaver provides a special setting called Layout mode, which enables you to draw tables and table cells directly onto an empty Web page. Drawing individual cells is the most common way of working in Layout mode. When you draw a cell on the page, Dreamweaver adds a table that fills the page and additional cells that hold your cell in position. The cells you draw are transparent with blue outlines; the cells Dreamweaver creates are translucent gray with white outlines. When you add additional cells, Dreamweaver modifies the cells it created to hold all your cells in place. This method is far more convenient than creating a table in Standard mode and then merging and splitting the cells yourself.

In addition to drawing cells, you can also draw tables in Layout mode. If you draw a table in an empty page, it is positioned in the upper-left corner of the page. Once you have a table, you can draw cells in the table and Dreamweaver will create additional cells to hold yours in place. Additional layout tables created outside the original table will be flush with the lower-left corner of the top table. You cannot leave space between layout tables because they provide structure for the page, and leaving spaces between tables makes their position less stable.

If you need to add additional rows and columns that do not align with the structure of the rows and columns you already created, you can draw another table inside an existing table or you can draw a table that surrounds an existing layout table to create a **nested table**. The inside table is the nested table. You cannot draw a nested table inside a cell that you created, only inside a cell that Dreamweaver created to hold your cells in place.

Once you have created tables in Layout mode, you can add, resize, and adjust the elements on the page. You cannot create a table in Layout mode if the Web page already contains any content. However, you can adjust and resize existing tables even after content has been added to the page. You can switch back and forth between Standard mode and Layout mode when you are working on tables. Any table selected in Standard mode is considered a regular table and any table selected in Layout mode is considered a layout table. This is true regardless of the view in which the table was created.

It is a good idea to sketch the tables for the layout of a Web page before you start to create them. Just like planning the Web site, planning the placement of the cells and tables on the page will help you avoid reworking the page elements, thus saving you time and frustration in the end. Planning the page layout enables you to determine where to place the cells and tables on the page so that the information can be conveyed effectively.

Brian wants you to add a new page titled "What's Hot" to the NewCatalyst site. There will be a link from the home page of the site that, when clicked, will load the What's Hot page in a new browser window. The What's Hot page will be used to promote new CD releases. It will use tables for structure. It will not have a navigation structure because it is a pop-up promotion instead of another regular page in the site. Figure 4-35 shows a sketch of the layout for the new page.

Figure 4-35

Sketch of layout for new What's Hot page

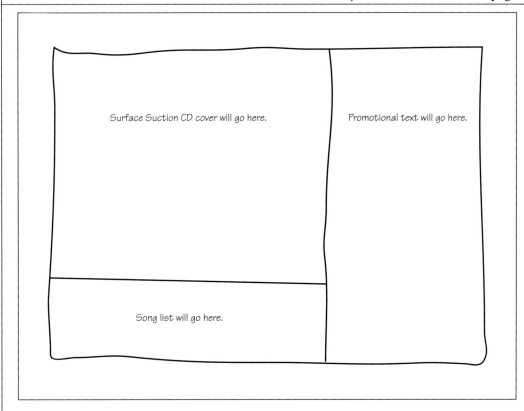

You'll start by creating the What's Hot page, adding a page heading, and attaching the external style sheet to the page.

To create the page and attach the style sheet:

1. If you took a break after the previous session, make sure that the **NewCatalyst** site is open.
2. Click **HTML** in the Create New list on the Start page. A new page opens in the Document window.

   Trouble? If the Start page is not displayed, you can use the menus to create a new page. Click File on the menu bar, click New to open the New Document dialog box, click Basic Page in the Category list on the General tab, click HTML in the Basic Page list, and then click the Create button. The new page opens in the Document window. Continue with Step 3.
3. Type **Catalyst - What's Hot** in the Title text box on the Document toolbar, and then press the **Enter** key.
4. Click **File** menu on the menu bar, click **Save As** to open the Save As dialog box, type **whatshot.htm** in the File Name text box, and then click the **Save** button. The whatshot.htm page is saved to the local root folder of the site and is visible in the Files panel.
5. Expand the **CSS Styles** panel, if necessary, and then click the **Attach Style Sheet** button in the CSS Styles panel. The Attach External Style Sheet dialog box opens.

6. Click the **Browse** button, navigate to the **Stylesheets** folder in the local root folder of your NewCatalyst site, and then double-click the **catalyst_styles.css** external style sheet.
7. Click the **OK** button in the Attach External Style Sheet dialog box, and then save the page.

Next, you'll create a layout table for the What's Hot page in Layout mode.

Creating a Table in Layout Mode

Once you are in Layout mode, you can create a table either by drawing a cell and having Dreamweaver create a table around it or by drawing a table and populating it with cells.

Reference Window

Creating a Table in Layout Mode

- Click the Layout button in the Layout category on the Insert bar.
- Click the Draw Layout Cell button in the Layout category on the Insert bar, and then drag on the page to draw a table cell.
- Click the Draw Layout Table button in the Layout category on the Insert bar, and then drag on the page to draw a table.

You'll start by switching to Layout mode.

To switch to Layout mode:

1. Switch to the **Layout** category on the Insert bar, if necessary. The Standard button is selected because you are in Standard mode.
2. Click the **Layout** button. A light blue bar with the words *Layout mode [exit]* appears at the top of the Document window, indicating that the Document window is now in Layout mode.

   Trouble? If the Getting Started in Layout Mode dialog box opens, click the OK button.
3. Click **View** on the menu bar, point to **Rulers**, and then click **Show**, if necessary, to display the rulers.

Next, you will draw a cell.

Drawing Cells in Layout Mode

You can use the Draw Layout Cell button in the Layout category on the Insert bar to create a table or to add cells to an existing table (even if you drew the table in Standard mode). A cell cannot exist outside a table. If you draw a cell before you have drawn a table or if you draw a cell outside a table, Dreamweaver will create a table around the cell to fill the Document window. The number and placement of cells that Dreamweaver creates to fill this table depend on the size of the Document window. The cells that you create have a white background, whereas the additional cells that Dreamweaver creates for maintaining the structure are gray. Cells cannot overlap.

While you are drawing a cell, the measurements of the cell, in pixels, are visible on the right side of the status bar. You can use these measurements or the rulers at the top and left of the Document window to help you draw accurately sized cells.

You'll draw a cell in Layout mode in the What's Hot page. This cell will be the cell in which you will place the CD cover graphic.

To draw a cell in Layout mode:

1. Click the **Draw Layout Cell** button in the **Layout** category on the Insert bar. The pointer changes to +.

2. Click in the upper-left corner of the What's Hot page, and then drag down diagonally to draw a square cell approximately 230 pixels by 230 pixels, but do not release the mouse button. You can use the rulers to help you measure or you can use the pixel measurements in the status bar at the bottom of the Document window as your guides. See Figure 4-36.

Drawing a table cell in Layout mode — Figure 4-36

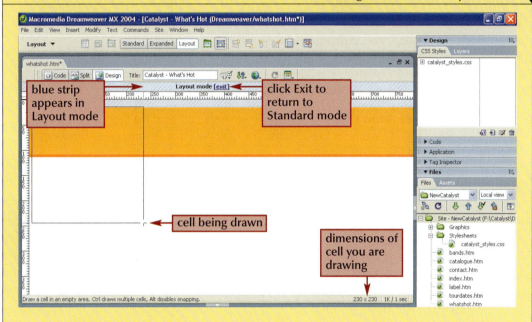

Trouble? If the ruler units are not in pixels, click View on the menu bar, point to Rulers, and then click Pixels.

3. Release the mouse button. The transparent cell you drew and any gray structure cells that Dreamweaver drew appear in a table that fills the Document window. See Figure 4-37.

Figure 4-37   Cell drawn in Layout mode

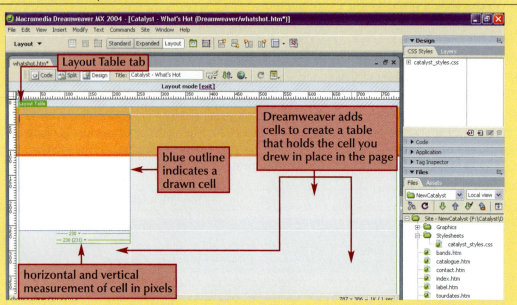

   4. Click the **Collapse arrow** button in the lower-right corner of the Property inspector to collapse the Property inspector to two rows. The gray cells that Dreamweaver drew expand to fill the resized Document window.

   5. Click the **Expander arrow** button in the Property inspector to expand the Property inspector to its full size. The gray cells return to their original size.

   6. Save the page.

Next, you'll add a second table in Layout mode.

Drawing a Table in Layout Mode

You can use the Draw Layout Table button to draw a table in the same way that you drew a cell. Once you have drawn the table, you will have to add cells. You can add more than one table to a page; you can even add a nested table within a table by simply drawing it there. Nested tables are beneficial because each table retains its own attributes. However, some older browsers have difficulty displaying nested tables properly, so consider your target audience before you create a complex table structure for a page layout.

Brian asks you to create an additional table in the What's Hot page to hold the promotional text.

To create a table in Layout mode:

   1. Click the **Layout Table** button in the **Layout** category on the Insert bar.

   2. To the right of the existing cell (and inside the existing table), drag to draw a table that is approximately 230 pixels by 230 pixels. The green outline indicates a table in Layout mode. See Figure 4-38.

Nested table in Layout mode **Figure 4-38**

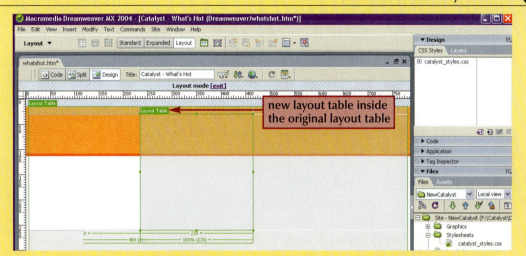

3. Click the **Draw Layout Cell** button in the **Layout** category on the Insert bar, and then draw one cell in the new table. The cell should be the same size as the table. The cell you create has a blue outline. See Figure 4-39.

Nested table and cell in Layout mode **Figure 4-39**

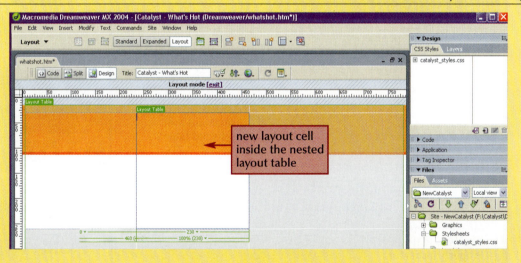

4. Save the page.

You need to be able to select layout tables and cells.

Selecting Tables and Cells in Layout Mode

Once you have created a table, you can work with it in Layout mode in much the same way you work with tables in Standard mode. Just like Standard mode, before you can move, size, and format tables or cells, they must be selected.

Selecting Tables in Layout Mode

You select tables in Layout mode by clicking anywhere in them. You can also click the Layout Table tab at the upper-left corner of the table. To select a table that is completely filled with a cell, you must click the Layout Table tab. After you select a table, the table border changes from a dotted green line to a solid green line and green resize handles surround the table. Also, an image of a table and the words *Layout Table* appear in the upper-left corner of the Property inspector to indicate that a table in Layout mode is selected. You need to select a table to make any other changes to it.

You'll select the tables in the What's Hot page in Layout mode.

To select a table in Layout mode:

1. Click anywhere in the outer table. The resize handles appear and the outer table is selected.
2. Click the **Layout Table** tab at the top of the nested table. The resize handles appear and the nested table is selected, as indicated in the Property inspector. See Figure 4-40.

Figure 4-40 Selected nested table in Layout mode

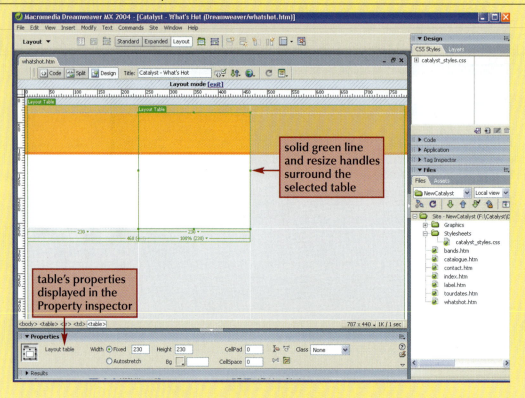

You can also select cells in Layout mode.

Selecting Cells in Layout Mode

When the pointer is positioned over the border of an unselected cell that you created, the border changes from a dotted blue line to a solid red line. You select a cell in Layout mode by clicking the cell's border. When a cell is selected, the perimeter changes to a solid blue line and resize handles appear. Also, an image of a cell and the words *Layout*

Cell appear in the Property inspector. Cells in Layout mode can be **active**—ready to accept input—but not selected. When a cell in Layout mode is active, the cell border is a solid blue line and the insertion point blinks inside the cell, but no resize handles appear.

You will select a cell on the layout table in the What's Hot page.

To select a cell in Layout mode:

1. Point to the perimeter of the left cell. The cell perimeter turns red.
2. Click the red cell perimeter. The cell is selected and the perimeter changes to a solid blue line with resize handles visible. See Figure 4-41.

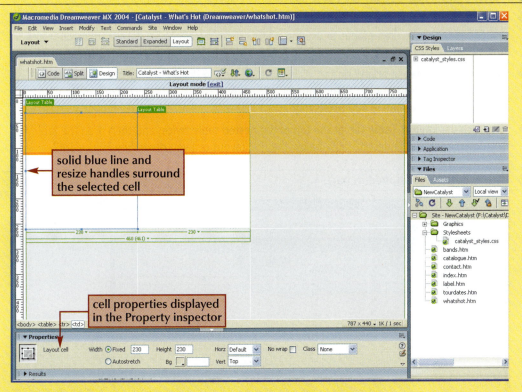

Selected cell in Layout mode — Figure 4-41

3. Select the right cell, position the pointer inside the cell, and then click. The resize handles disappear and the cell is active, but not selected.

Once a table cell is selected, you can work with it.

Working with Tables in Layout Mode

Once a table or cell in Layout mode is selected, you can change its attributes, resize it, move it, or delete it.

Resizing Tables in Layout Mode

Once a table has been selected in Layout mode, you can drag the table's resize handles to change its size. Nested tables can be moved freely within the outer table. A nested table cannot overlap a cell that you drew in Layout mode, but it can overlap the gray cells that Dreamweaver drew to hold the cells that you created in place. Tables in Layout mode can also be resized by changing the attributes in the Property inspector while the table is selected.

You'll resize the tables in the What's Hot page.

To move and resize a table in Layout mode:

1. Click the upper-left **Layout Table** tab twice to select the outer table.

2. Drag the right **resize handle** to the right until the width of the table is approximately 815 pixels wide. (Remember to use the rulers.) It will be necessary for you to scroll to see the entire page.

3. Click the **Collapse arrow** button ▼ Properties in the Property inspector title bar to collapse the Property inspector entirely, and then drag the bottom **resize handle** until the table is approximately 500 pixels high.

4. Click the **Layout Table** tab at the top of the nested table twice, and then drag the table tab down to move the nested table below the first layout cell you drew. See Figure 4-42.

Figure 4-42   Layout table repositioned in page

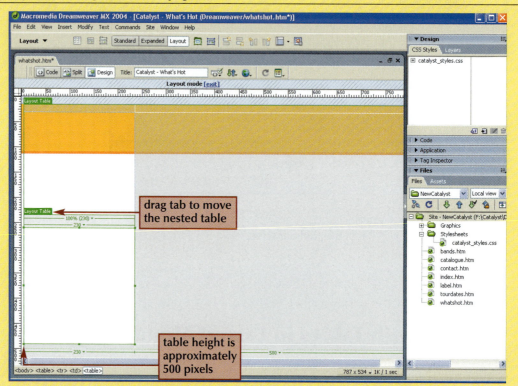

5. Scroll to the bottom of the Document window, click the bottom (green) border of the outer table, and then drag the bottom **resize handle** of the outer table up so that the bottom of the outer table is flush with the bottom of the table you just moved.

6. Drag the **Layout Table** tab of the nested table back to its original position, and then drag the bottom **resize handle** of the nested table down to meet the bottom of the outer table (so that the nested table is approximately 500 pixels high). See Figure 4-43.

Resized tables in Layout mode   Figure 4-43

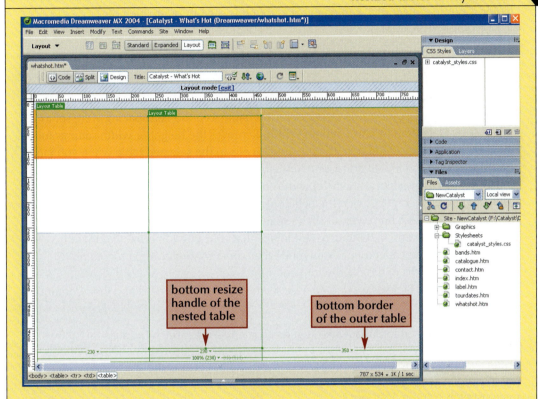

7. Save the page.

You can also add formatting to layout tables.

Modifying Table Attributes in Layout Mode

You can customize tables either by changing their attributes in the Property inspector or by adding CSS styles to the table. The attributes are visible in the Property inspector when a table is selected in Layout mode. You can verify that the table is selected by checking the image and label in the upper-left corner of the Property inspector. The attributes in the Property inspector for tables selected in Layout mode are similar to those for tables selected in Standard mode except for the Autostretch option, Border, and Border Color. Table attributes in Layout mode include:

- **Width.** The horizontal dimension of the table. There are two types of widths in Layout mode: fixed and autostretch. Fixed width is a numeric value, specified in pixels, that does not change when you add content to the cell, and it applies to the entire table. You can enter a fixed width in the Property inspector. Autostretch sets the width of one column to resize automatically with the width of the browser window. Only one column in each table can be set to autostretch. To create a table that autostretches, you select the Autostretch option in the Property inspector and then designate which column you want to autostretch. The default option is fixed width, which you establish when you drag to create the table.

- **Height.** The vertical dimension of the table in pixels. Dreamweaver calculates the height when you draw the table and displays it in the Height box. You can modify this by typing a new value in the Height text box.
- **Bg (Background Color).** The background color for the table. You enter the hexadecimal color code into the Bg text box or use the color picker to select a color. If a background color is not specified, the Web page background is seen through the table.
- **Cell Padding.** The amount of empty space, measured in pixels, maintained between the border of a cell and the cell's content. When you don't specify cell padding, most browsers display the table as if the cell padding were set to 1.
- **Cell Spacing.** The width of the invisible cell walls, measured in pixels. If the border is set to 0, then the table structure will be invisible despite thick walls. When you don't specify cell spacing, most browsers display the table as if the cell spacing were set to 2.
- **Clear Row Height** and **Clear Column Width.** Removes the height or width settings for all the cells in a selected table. If there are no cells in the selected table when you clear row heights, the table will collapse completely.
- **Make Widths Consistent.** Resets the widths of the fixed width cells in the selected table to match the cell content when the cell content is wider than the fixed width.
- **Remove All Spacers.** Removes all of the spacer images from the selected layout table. A **spacer image** is a one-pixel transparent image that is inserted into the fixed-width columns in a table created in Layout mode that contains an autostretch column to maintain the widths of the fixed-width columns.
- **Remove Nesting.** Deletes a selected nested table and adds the cells and their content to the parent table.

Tables that are used for layout are often designated as autostretch because this allows the content of the Web page to adjust to the size of the user's browser window. When you format a table as autostretch, you are asked if you want to create and use a spacer image. The spacer image maintains a minimum width for the fixed-width columns in a table with an autostretch column. Without spacer images, the fixed-width columns in a table with an autostretch column might disappear in the Design window. The first time you choose autostretch as an option in a Web site, a dialog box opens asking if you want Dreamweaver to create a spacer image file, if you want to use an existing graphic file for your spacer image, or if you don't want to use spacer images in autostretch tables. Usually, you would choose to have Dreamweaver create a spacer image. When prompted, you should store the spacer image Dreamweaver creates in the Graphics folder for your site.

When a column in a table is set to autostretch in Layout mode, a double set of wavy lines appears at the top of the column. When a column in a table has a fixed width, in Layout mode the numeric value of the width appears at the top of the column in the Document window. The sum of the values of the column widths of the table equals the width of the table.

Brian asks you to set the attributes for the outer table in the What's Hot page. You will change the table to an autostretch table so that the contents of the table can scale in the user's browser window. When you select the autostretch option, you will enable Dreamweaver to create a spacer image and then place it in the Graphics folder in the site's local root folder. You will also change the height of the table to accommodate the graphic and text that you will place in the table.

To set table attributes in Layout mode:

1. Scroll to the top of the Document window, if necessary, and then click the **Layout Table** tab of the outer table twice to select the outer table and expand the Property inspector.

2. Click the **Autostretch** option button in the Property inspector to set the width of the selected table to autostretch. Because you have not yet set autostretch options for this site, the Choose Spacer Image dialog box opens.

   Trouble? If the Choose Spacer Image dialog box does not open, continue with Step 4.

3. Click the **Create a Spacer Image File** option button, if necessary, click the **OK** button, navigate to the **Graphics** folder within the local root folder of your NewCatalyst site, and then click the **Save** button. Once the spacer image is set, Dreamweaver will continue to use that spacer image for all the layout tables in the site; you specify the image only once.

4. Double-click in the **Height** text box, type **650**, and then press the **Enter** key.

5. Save the page.

You can also delete tables in Layout mode.

Deleting a Layout Table

You may need to delete a table in Layout mode. To delete a table, you need to select the table and press the Delete key, just as you would delete a table in Standard mode. If you want to delete a nested table, including the cells and content in the nested table, you select the nested table and press the Delete key. If you want to delete a nested table, but add the cells and content from the nested table to the outer table, you first select the nested table and then click the Remove Nesting button in the Property inspector.

You'll delete the nested table from the What's Hot page, but you'll add the cells and content to the outer table.

To delete a nested table in Layout mode:

1. Select the nested table in the What's Hot page.
2. Click the **Remove Nesting** button in the Property inspector. The nested table structure is deleted from the page, and the cell is added to the outside table. See Figure 4-44.

Nested table deleted in Layout mode — Figure 4-44

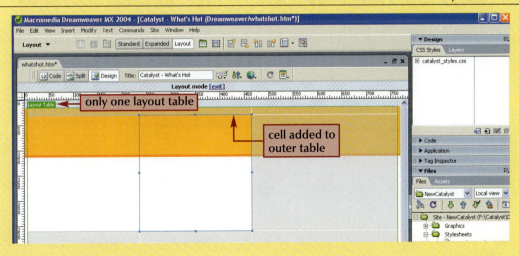

3. Save the page.

Next, you'll work with cells in Layout mode.

Working with Cells in Layout Mode

Working with cells in Layout mode is similar to working with cells in Standard mode. Once a cell is selected, the cell can be moved, sized, formatted, or deleted.

Moving and Resizing Cells in Layout Mode

When a cell is selected in Layout mode, you can move it by clicking the blue border between the resize handles and dragging the cell to the desired location. When the cell is placed in a new location within a table in Layout mode, Dreamweaver creates all the additional cells necessary to hold the selected cell in place. To resize a cell, you drag a blue resize handle to the desired dimensions, or you select the cell and specify the desired dimensions in the Property inspector.

You'll move and resize the cells in the table in the What's Hot page.

To resize and move cells in Layout mode:

1. Select the left cell and drag the top resize handle to the top of the table, if necessary, and then drag the bottom resize handle until the cell is approximately **425** pixels in height.

2. Select the right cell in the table and drag the top resize handle to the top of the table, if necessary, and then drag the bottom resize handle until the cell is approximately **220** pixels in height.

3. Click the left edge of the right cell between the blue resize handles and drag the cell below the left cell.

4. Select the bottom cell, and then drag the resize handle at the bottom of the selected cell down to the bottom of the table, if necessary.

5. Select the top cell and drag the right resize handle to the right until the cell is approximately **425** pixels in width.

6. Click the **Draw Layout Cell** button in the **Layout** category on the Insert bar, and then draw a third cell to the right of the upper-left cell that fills the gray space on the right side of the table.

7. Collapse the Property inspector so that you can get a better look at the table. See Figure 4-45.

New cell added to the table in Layout mode

Figure 4-45

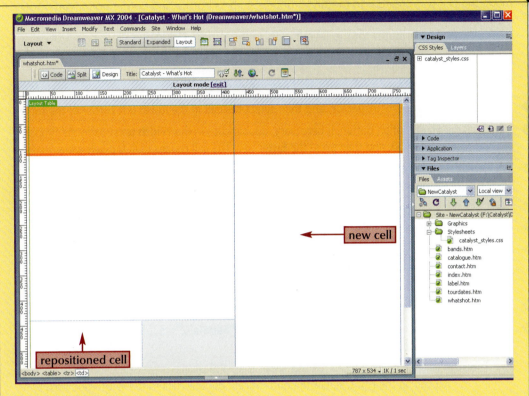

8. Save the page.

You can also modify cell attributes in Layout mode.

Modifying Cell Attributes in Layout Mode

When a cell is selected in Layout mode, the formatting attributes for the cell that are associated with the Layout mode are visible in the Property inspector. Once a cell has been selected, you can change the attributes of that cell in the Property inspector, or you can add CSS styles to the cell. Make sure you select the cell to change its attributes. If the cell is only active (ready to accept input), the attributes associated with text appear in the Property inspector instead of the cell attributes. Cell attributes in Layout mode include:

- **Width.** The horizontal dimension of the cell. In Layout mode, a cell, like a table, can be fixed width or autostretch width.
- **Height.** The vertical dimension of the cell in pixels. You can change the value in the Height text box. If you do not change it, the cell remains the height that it was drawn.
- **Bg (Background Color).** The background color for the cell. You can enter the hexadecimal color code in the Bg text box or use the color picker to select a color. If a background color is not specified, the Web page background is seen through the table.
- **Horz (Horizontal).** The horizontal alignment of the cell's content. Content can be aligned to the browser's default setting, left, right, or center.
- **Vert (Vertical).** The vertical alignment of the content of the cell. Content can be aligned to the browser's default setting, top, middle, bottom, or baseline.
- **No Wrap.** Enables or disables word wrap within the cell.

You can switch back and forth between Standard mode and Layout mode when you are working with cells. Any cell selected in Standard mode is considered a regular cell and any cell selected in Layout mode is considered a layout cell. This is true regardless of which mode the cell was created. To modify attributes such as border and border color, you must be in Standard mode. To modify attributes such as autostretch, you must be in Layout mode. You'll set the attributes for the layout cells in the What's Hot page.

To set the attributes of cells in Layout mode:

1. Expand the Property inspector, and then select the cell in the lower-left corner of the table.
2. Click the **Fixed** option button, if necessary, double-click in the **Width** text box in the Property inspector, type **400**, and then press the **Enter** key. The cell resizes to 400 pixels wide.
3. Select the cell again, if necessary, click the **Horz** list arrow, and then click **Center** to change the horizontal alignment to center.
4. Click the **Vert** list arrow, and then click **Top** to change the vertical alignment to top.
5. Select the cell in the upper-left corner of the table.
6. Click the **Fixed** option button in the Property inspector, if necessary, double-click in the **Width** text box, type **400**, press the **Tab** key to move to the Height text box, type **400**, and then press the **Enter** key.
7. Change the horizontal alignment to **Left**, and change the vertical alignment to **Bottom**.
8. Select the right cell, and then drag the left **resize handle** to the left until the cell is flush with the other cells in the table.

   Trouble? If the lower-left cell resized wider than 400 pixels, preventing you from widening the tall cell on the right, select the bottom cell, double-click in the Width text box, type 400, press the Enter key, and then try Step 8 again.

9. Click the **Autostretch** option button in the Property inspector, and then change the horizontal alignment to **Center** and the vertical alignment to **Middle**. See Figure 4-46.

Figure 4-46   Modified cells in Layout mode

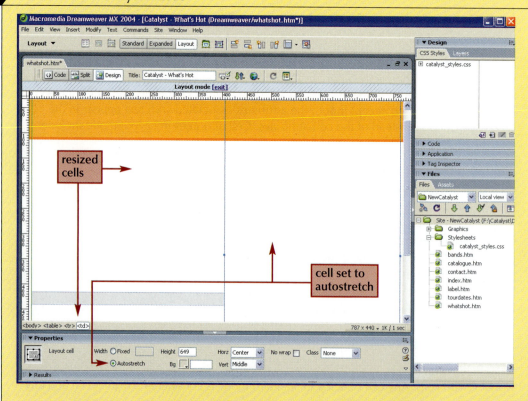

10. Click **View** on the main menu bar, point to **Rulers**, and then click **Show** to hide the rulers.
11. Save the page.

Now you are ready to add content to the cells you drew in Layout mode.

Adding Content to Cells in Layout Mode

You can add content to cells in either Layout mode or Standard mode. Adding content to a cell in Layout mode is just like adding content to a cell in Standard mode. Just click in the cell and start typing. To add a graphic to a cell in Layout mode, click in the cell and use the Image button in the Images list in the Common category on the Insert bar to select the desired graphic.

Brian wants you to place a graphic of a CD cover in the upper-left cell and a song list in the lower-left cell. You will type the promotional text in the right cell of the table.

To add content to cells in Layout mode:

1. Click in the upper-left cell of the table. The insertion point blinks at the lower-left corner of the cell.
2. Click the **Image** button in the **Images** list in the **Common** category on the Insert bar, and then insert the **SurfaceSuctionCDcover.jpg** graphic located in the **Tutorial.04\Tutorial** folder included with your Data Files. A dialog box opens with the message that the file already exists in the Graphics folder and asks whether you want to overwrite the file.
3. Click the **Yes** button to replace the copy of the graphic that you edited earlier. The new copy is saved in the Graphics folder in the local root folder of the NewCatalyst site.

   The new graphic will also be visible in the Catalogue page.
4. Open the **catalogue.htm** page in the Document window, and then scroll if necessary to see the graphic. The graphic was updated in the Catalogue page. Although the graphic was resized smaller in the Catalogue page, the file size is the same as the graphic in the Graphics folder because you replaced the graphic that you edited with a copy of the original graphic.
5. Select the **Surface Suction: Black Lab CD title** and **song list**, click **Edit** on the menu bar, click **Copy HTML**, and then close the page.
6. Click in the lower-left cell of the table in the What's Hot page, press the **Enter** key, click **Edit** on the menu bar, and then click **Paste HTML**.
7. Click in the cell on the right side of the table, and then type **Black Lab: The latest release from Surface Suction**.
8. Select the text you just typed, click the **Format** list arrow in the Property inspector, and then click **Heading1**.
9. Press the **Right Arrow** key, press the **Enter** key to skip a line, and then type **Available at record stores in your area**.
10. Select the text you just typed, click the **Style** list arrow in the Property inspector, and then click **NewBandSub**.
11. Save the page, and then preview the page in a browser. See Figure 4-47.

| Figure 4-46 | What's Hot page previewed in browser |

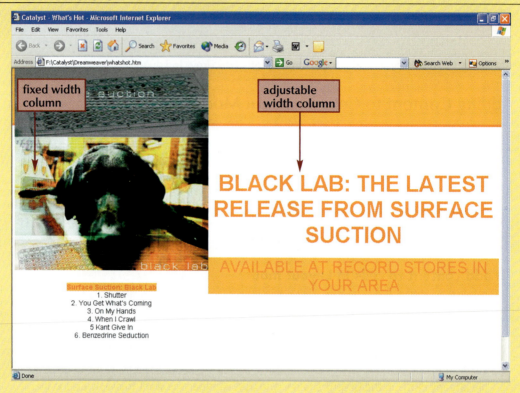

12. Drag the lower-right corner of the browser window to resize the window larger and then smaller so that the text on the right rewraps as you resize the window. The right column has an adjustable width, whereas the left column has a fixed width.

    Trouble? If your browser window is maximized, click the Restore button in the browser window title bar, and then try Step 12 again.

13. Close the browser window, and then close the page.

Finally, you will add a text hyperlink to the home page that opens the What's Hot page in a new window. You can specify where a linked Web page will open by defining a target for the linked page. A **target** is the page or browser window in which a linked Web page will open.

To add a targeted link to the What's Hot page:

1. Open the **index.htm** page in the Document window.
2. Click **Exit** in the blue bar at the top of the Document window to return to Standard mode.
3. Place the pointer to the right of the logo, press the **Enter** key seven times, and then type **What's Hot at Catalyst**.
4. Click the **New CSS Style** button in the CSS Styles panel and create a new style named **WithLines** in the **catalyst_styles.css** style sheet.

5. Click **Text** in the Category list, if necessary, select **18** pixels in the Size list, click **Block** in the Category list, select **Center** in the Text Align list, select **Block** in the Display list, click **Border** in the Category list, uncheck the **Same for All** check boxes, select **Solid** in the Top and Bottom lists in the Style column, select **Medium** in the Top and Bottom lists in the Width column, type **#FF9900** in the Top and Bottom text boxes in the Color column, and then click the **OK** button.

6. Select the text you just typed, and click **WithLines** in the Styles list in the Property inspector.

7. Drag the **Point to File** button beside the Link text box in the Property inspector to **whatshot.htm** in the Files panel to create a link.

8. Click the **Target** list arrow in the Property inspector, click **_blank**, and then click in the Document window to deselect the text. The linked page will open in a new browser window when the link is clicked. See Figure 4-48.

Figure 4-48   Targeted link created for the What's Hot page

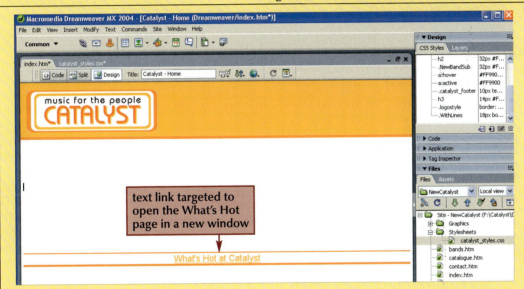

Trouble? If the Target list box is inactive, click anywhere in the Document window to deselect the link text, and then select the line again.

9. Save the page, and then save and close the style sheet.

10. Preview the page in a browser, and then click the **What's Hot** link. A new browser window opens displaying the What's Hot page.

11. Close the browser windows, close the home page, and then collapse the Design panel group.

Now you will upload the site to the remote server.

Updating the Web Site on the Remote Server

As a final review of the changes you made to the Catalyst site, you'll update the files on the remote server and review the pages over the Internet. You need to upload every page of the site (bands.htm, catalogue.htm, contact.htm, index.htm, label.htm, tourdates.htm, and whatshot.htm) because you have made changes to every page. When you upload the pages, you will also need to include the dependent files so that the new graphics and new CSS styles are uploaded to the remote server. Then you'll preview the site on the Web.

To upload a site to the remote server:

1. Click the **Connects to Remote Host** button on the Files panel toolbar to connect to the remote host.
2. Click the **View** list arrow on the Files panel toolbar, and then click **Local View**.
3. Select **bands.htm**, **catalogue.htm**, **contact.htm**, **index.htm**, **label.htm**, **tourdates.htm**, and the **whatshot.htm** files in the Local file list, and then click the **Put File(s)** button on the Files panel toolbar.
4. Click the **Yes** button when asked if you want to include dependent files, because you have not yet uploaded the new dependent files for the site.
5. Click the **View** list arrow on the Files panel toolbar, and then click **Remote View**.
6. Double-click the **Graphics** folder in the Remote file list in the Files panel. Copies of the new graphic files (CatalystLogoRollover.gif, spacer.gif, SurfaceSuctionCDcover.jpg, and USmap.gif) are uploaded to the remote site.
7. Click the **Disconnects from Remote Host** button on the Files panel toolbar, click the **View** list arrow on the Files panel toolbar, and then click **Local View**.
8. Close the NewCatalyst site.

Next, you'll preview the updated site in a browser. The site will include all of the new styles and text that you added to your local version.

To preview the updated site in a browser:

1. Open your browser, type the URL of your remote site in the Address bar on the browser toolbar, and then press the **Enter** key. The home page opens in the browser window.
2. Type **/label.htm** and then press the **Enter** key to make sure that the label page was successfully uploaded.

   Trouble? If the new CSS styles that you created do not appear in your browser window, click the Refresh button on the browser window toolbar.

3. Move the pointer over the **Catalyst logo** in the Label page to see the rollover graphic, and then click the **logo** to return to the home page.
4. Click the **Back** button on the browser toolbar to return to the Label page, click the **bands** link to make sure that the page was successfully uploaded, and then move the pointer over the **Catalyst logo**.
5. Click the **catalogue** link to make sure that the page was successfully uploaded, and then move the pointer over the **Catalyst logo**.
6. Click the **tour dates** link to make sure that the page was successfully uploaded, and then move the pointer over the **Catalyst logo**.
7. Click the **contact** link to make sure that the page was successfully uploaded, and then move the pointer over the **Catalyst logo**.
8. Click the **What's Hot at Catalyst** link to make sure that the page was successfully uploaded, and then examine the What's Hot page.
9. Close the browser windows.

In this session, you created and added content using layout tables.

Review

Session 4.3 Quick Check

1. What is a nested table?
2. Why is it a good idea to plan the page layout when you are using tables?
3. True or False? A cell cannot exist outside a table.
4. What does Dreamweaver do automatically if you draw a cell in Layout mode before you draw a table?
5. Can you resize a cell by dragging its resize handles when it is active in Layout mode?
6. What is a spacer image?

Review

Tutorial Summary

In this tutorial, you learned about the different types of graphics you can use in a Web site. You added the Catalyst logo to each page and formatted the logo. You created a link to the logo graphic, you created an image map, and you inserted a rollover object for the Catalyst logo. You inserted tables in Standard mode, and then selected, modified, moved, resized, and deleted a table and table elements. You explored the HTML tags associated with tables. You worked in Layout mode, drawing layout cells and layout tables, and then selecting, sizing, moving, and modifying them. You also added content to the layout table. Finally, you updated the files on the Web and previewed the remote Web site.

Key Terms

active	GIF (Graphics Interchange Format)	PNG (Portable Network Graphics)
asset		resample
baseline	hotspot	resize handles
border	image map	rollover
bracketing tag	JavaScript	row
cell	JPEG	row span
column	lossless	spacer image
column span	lossy	table
compression	nested table	target
crop	nongradient	variable transparency

Practice

Practice the skills you learned in the tutorial.

Review Assignments

Data Files needed for the Review Assignments: DizziedConnectionsCDcover300.jpg, SurfaceSuctionCDcover300.jpg, SlothChildCDcover300.jpg, LifeInMinorChordsCDcover300.jpg

Brian asks you to create a variety of tables in the other pages of the Catalyst site to insert content and organize the layout. You'll create tables in Standard mode for Central tour dates and East Coast tour dates in the Tour Dates page. Then, you'll hyperlink the hotspots on the map to the appropriate tables. For the Catalogue page, you'll delete the resized graphic from the page, create a table in Standard mode, insert graphics of the CD covers as well as text of the CD titles and song lists, and then you will edit the graphics.

1. Open the NewCatalyst Web site that you modified in this tutorial, and then open the tourdates.htm page in the Document window.
2. Select the cells in the West Cost Tour Dates table and click the Align Center button on the Property inspector to align all the text in the table to the center of the cells.

3. Click below the West Coast Tour Dates table in the Tour Dates page, and then click the Table button in the Common category on the Insert bar. Create a table in Standard mode with 3 columns and 13 rows, table width 75 percent, 0 border thickness, 0 cell padding, and 0 cell spacing. Click Top in the Header area, if necessary, and then type "Catalyst bands, central U.S. tour dates" in the Summary text box.
4. Enter "CentralUSTourDates" in the Table Id text box in the Property inspector.
5. Merge the top row of cells in the table.
6. Select the top two rows of the table, and then check the Header check box make them header cells.
7. Type "Central U.S. Tour Dates" in the top row.
8. Click the Align list arrow in the Property inspector, and then click Center to align the table to the center. (*Hint:* If you have trouble selecting the table, switch to Extended Tables mode while you are working with the tables.)
9. Adjust the widths of the columns so they are the same as the column widths in the West Coast table.
10. Type the information from the following table into the three columns in the Central U.S. Tour Dates table.

Date	Location / Venue	Band
1/4 to 1/6	Cleveland, OH / Grog Shop	Surface Suction
1/11 to 1/13	Chicago, IL / Abbey Pub	Surface Suction
2/8 to 2/10	Minneapolis, MN / 9th Street Entry	Surface Suction
2/15 to 2/17	Iowa City, IA / Gabe's Oasis	Surface Suction
2/22 to 2/24	Lawrence, KS / Bottleneck	Surface Suction
3/15 to 3/17	Denton, TX / Rubber Gloves	Surface Suction
3/22 to 3/24	Austin, TX / Emo's	Surface Suction
4/12 to 4/14	Houston, TX / Sidecar Pub	Surface Suction

11. Click Commands on the menu bar, and then click Format Table to open the Format Table dialog box. To format the table, click AltRows:Blue&Yellow, type "#FF6600" into the First text box, type "#FF9900" into the Second text box, select Every Other Row from the Alternate list, select Center in both Align list boxes, type "0" in the Border text box, check the Apply All Attributes to TD Tags Instead of TR Tags check box, and then click the OK button.
12. Select the empty cells and delete them.
13. Repeat Steps 3 through 12 to create a third table, typing "Catalyst bands, east coast tour dates" in the Summary text box, typing "EastCoastTourDates" in the Table Id text box, typing "East Coast Tour Dates" in the top row, and using the following information.

Date	Location / Venue	Band
1/4 to 1/6	Atlanta, GA / Echo Lounge	Sloth Child
1/11 to 1/13	Carbord, NC / Room Four	Sloth Child
2/8 to 2/10	Baltimore, MD / Ottobar	Sloth Child
2/15 to 2/17	Washington, DC / Black Cat	Sloth Child
2/22 to 2/24	Philadelphia, PA / Unitarian Church	Sloth Child
3/15 to 3/17	Cambridge, MA / Middle East	Sloth Child
3/22 to 3/24	New York, NY / Bowery Ballroom	Sloth Child
4/13 to 4/14	New York, NY / Knitting Factory	Sloth Child

14. Select all the cells in the Central U.S. Tour Dates and East Coast Tour Dates tables, and then click the Align Center button in the Property inspector to align all of the text in the table to the center of the cells.
15. Create a named anchor for the West Coast Tour Dates table. Select the text in the first row of the first table, and then click the Named Anchor button in the Common category on the Insert bar. In the Named Anchor dialog box, type "westcoast" in the

Anchor Name text box, and then click the OK button. A box with an anchor appears to the right of the selected text.

16. Repeat Step 15 to create a named anchor for the Central U.S. Tour Dates table named "central" and for the East Coast Tour Dates table named "eastcoast."
17. Add a link from each hotspot to a named anchor. Click the hotspot at the left of the U.S. map, and then type "#westcoast" in the Link text box in the Property inspector; click the hotspot in the center of the U.S. map, and then type "#central" in the Link text box in the Property inspector; and click the hotspot at the right of the U.S. map, and then type "#eastcoast" in the Link text box in the Property inspector.
18. Save the page, and then test the links to the anchors by previewing the page in a browser and clicking each hotspot on the map. (*Hint*: If each table does not move to the top of the window when you click the appropriate hotspot in the browser window, you may not have enough blank lines at the end of your Web page. Open the page in the Document window and add extra lines to the end of the page by pressing the Enter key.) Close the page when you are finished.
19. Open the catalogue.htm page in the Document window, insert a table below the CDS heading that has 4 rows, 2 columns, 75% table width, 0 border thickness, 4 cell padding, 0 cell spacing, and no header cells. Select the table, and then select Center from the Align list in the Property inspector.
20. Select "Dizzied Connection: Spinning Life" and the song list below it, cut the selected text, and then paste the text into the first cell in the second row of the table.
21. Delete the Surface Suction CD cover from the page, select "Surface Suction: Black Lab" and the song list below it, cut the selected text, and then paste the text into the second cell in the second row of the table. (*Hint:* If you have difficulty selecting the right column, click the Extended Table mode button in the Layout category on the Insert bar.)
22. Select "Sloth Child: Them Apples" and the song list below it, cut the selected text, and then paste the text into the first cell in the fourth row of the table.
23. Select "life in minor chords: i believe in ferries" and the song list below it, cut the selected text, and then paste the text into the second cell in the fourth row of the table.
24. Insert the following images located in the **Tutorial.04\Review** folder included with your Data Files in the specified location in the table:
DizziedConnectionsCDcover300.jpg in the first cell in the first row,
SurfaceSuctionCDcover300.jpg in the second cell in the first row,
SlothChildCDcover300.jpg in the first cell in the third row, and
LifeInMinorChordsCDcover300.jpg in the second cell in the third row.
25. Select each cell with text, and then select Center in the Horz list and Top in the Vert list. (*Hint:* If you do not see all the cell formatting options, click the Expander arrow button in the Property inspector.)
26. Select the Dizzied Connections CD cover and increase its sharpness by 1. Select the Life in Minor Chords CD cover, and then decrease its brightness by 10 and increase its contrast by 20.
27. Select each row with graphics in it, and then select Center in the Horz list and Bottom in the Vert list in the Property inspector.
28. Select the table and make sure the width is 75% by checking the W text box in the Property inspector, and changing it if necessary. (Sometimes the width will change when you add graphics.)
29. Save the page, preview the page in a browser, scroll to the bottom of the page to see if the paragraph below the VINYL heading appears inside the orange bar, and then close the browser window. If necessary, click below the table, scroll down so you can see the entire orange bar, and then press the Delete key as many times as necessary to move up the paragraph so that it is all inside the orange bar when previewed in the browser.

30. Copy the copyright line from the Catalogue page, paste the text at the bottom of the the home page, the Contact page, and the Tour Dates page, apply the catalyst_footer style, and then save and close each page.
31. Connect to your remote server, upload the site, and then preview the site over the Web.

Case Problem 1

Data File needed for this Case Problem: HrochLogo.gif

Hroch University Anthropology Department As you continue working on Dr. Matt Hart's Web site, you'll add the Hroch University logo to every page of the site and create a hyperlink from the logo to Dr. Hart's home page. Then, you'll create a table to contain the information in each area of research and put placeholder text in the tables while the research is being completed.

1. Open the Hart site you modified in Tutorial 3, Case 1, open the index.htm page in the Document window, and place the insertion point in the upper-left corner of the page, if necessary.
2. Using the Image button in the Images list in the Common category on the Insert bar, insert the logo graphic **HrochLogo.gif** located in the **Tutorial.04\Cases** folder included with your Data Files.
3. Delete spaces after the logo graphic as needed so that the links are in their original positions, and then save and close the page.
4. For the rest of the pages in the site, repeat Step 2 to insert the logo, create a hyperlink from the logo to the home page, repeat Step 3 to delete extra spaces after the logo, and then save and close the page: contact.htm, cultural_cross_pollination.htm, linguistic_differences.htm, prof_hart.htm, and rituals_and_practices.htm.
5. Open the linguistic_differences.htm page, click to the right of the Linguistic Differences heading, and then press the Enter key to position the insertion point below the heading.
6. Use the Table button in the Common category on the Insert bar to insert a table that has 3 rows, 1 column, 100% table width, 0 border thickness, 0 cell padding, 0 cell spacing, no header cells, and no summary, caption, or table ID because the table is being used for layout rather than to display information.
7. Select the table, or Table ID click Left in the Align list in the Property inspector, select the top cell, and type "#910C26" in the second Bg (Background Color) text box.
8. Copy the Linguistic Differences heading and paste the text into the top cell of the table. (*Hint:* You may need to reapply the Heading 1 tag from the Format list in the Property inspector.)
9. Delete the old heading text and any extra spaces, click in the second cell and type "Research in process, check back soon.", and then press the Enter key twice to add blank lines.
10. Click in the bottom cell, click the Copyright button in the Characters list in the Text category on the Insert bar, press the Right Arrow key, press the spacebar, and then type "Copyright Dr. Matthew Hart, Hroch University Anthropology Dept., 2006." Select the text and click Center in the Horz list in the Property inspector.
11. Copy the table, save and close the page, open the cultural_cross_pollination.htm page, select the current heading, paste the table in the Cultural Cross-pollination page in place of the current heading, replace the text in the top cell with "Cultural Cross-pollination," and then save and close the page.

Explore

12. Open the rituals_and_practices.htm page, select the current heading, paste the table in the Rituals and Practices page in place of the current heading, replace the text in the top cell with "Rituals and Practices," and then save the page.
13. Preview the site in a browser, and then close the browser window and the page.
14. Upload the site to your remote server, and then preview the site over the Web, checking the links and pages to ensure the upload was successful.

Case Problem 2

Data Files needed for this Case Problem: MuseumLogo.gif, MuseumLogoRollover.gif

Apply

Add a logo rollover and move the navigation links into a table you create in a Web site for an art museum.

Museum of Western Art C. J. Strittmatter asks you to use the new graphics that the art department has provided to create a rollover image out of the new Museum of Western Art logo, and then to replace the text logo in each page of the site with the new logo rollover, which will link to the home page. In addition, you will add a table in the home page and move the navigation links into the table. Then, you'll copy the new navigation table to the other pages of the site.

1. Open the Museum site you modified in Tutorial 3, Case 2, and then open the index.htm page in the Document window.
2. Select the text logo at the top of the page, and then delete the text.
3. Click the Rollover Image button in the Images list in the Common category on the Insert bar. In the Insert Rollover Image dialog box, type "MuseumLogoRollover" in the Image Name text box. Click the Original Image Browse button and double-click **MuseumLogo.gif** located in the **Tutorial.04\Cases** folder included with your Data Files. Click the Rollover Image Browse button and double-click **MuseumLogoRollover.gif** located in the **Tutorial.04\Cases** folder included with your Data Files. Type "Museum of Western Art Logo with link to the home page" in the Alternate Text text box, click the Browse button next to the When Clicked, Go To URL text box, browse to and double-click the index.htm page, and then click the OK button.
4. Save the page, preview the page in a browser, place the pointer over the rollover image to see the image change and view the tooltip, and then close the browser window.

Explore

5. Select the rollover image and then copy it using the Copy HTML command on the Edit menu. Replace the text logo in the art.htm, artists.htm, location.htm, and museum.htm pages with the new logo rollover image using the Paste HTML command on the Edit menu.
6. Save each page, preview the pages in a browser, testing the new logo in each page, and then close the browser window and each page.
7. Open the index.htm page in the Document window, position the insertion point to the right of the navigation text and insert a table with 4 rows, 1 column, 100 pixels table width, 1 pixel border thickness, 0 cell spacing, 0 cell padding, no header cells, no caption and "Site navigation." as the summary.

Explore

8. Select the table, if necessary, and click Right in the Align list in the Property inspector (the table will move to the right of the Welcome text), type "#006666" in the Bg Color text box and "#ECB888" in the Brdr Color text box.
9. Using the Copy HTML and Paste HTML commands, copy the Museum text link into the first cell, copy the Art text link into the second cell, copy the Artists text link into the third cell, and then copy the Location text link into the fourth cell. Then delete the original text links from the page and delete any extra lines between the table and the horizontal line.

10. Edit the .menustyle style in the CSS Styles panel. Select Center in the Text Align list in the Block category to align the text to the center of the cells.
11. Edit the h2 style in the CSS Styles panel. In the Type category, set the size to 42 pixels, and then click Normal in the Weight list. In the Block category, click Right in the Text Align list. The heading text moves to the right of the table.
12. Position the insertion point before the heading text, and then insert line breaks as needed to move the text to below the table.
13. Save and close the style sheet, save the home page, preview it in a browser, and then close the browser window.

Explore

14. Select the table, use the Copy HTML and Paste HTML commands to copy and paste the table into the art.htm, artists.htm, location.htm, and museum.htm pages to the right of the navigation text. Delete the old navigation text and any extra spaces from each page, position the insertion point before the heading text, and then insert line breaks as needed to move the text to below the table. Save each page.
15. Preview the site in a browser, and then close the browser window and any open pages.
16. Upload the site to your remote server, and then preview the site over the Web, checking the links and pages to ensure the upload was successful.

Challenge

Add a rollover logo graphic and insert page content into tables you create in a Web site for an independent publisher of fringe writing.

Case Problem 3

Data Files needed for this Case Problem: NORMlogo.gif, NORMlogoRollover.gif, BookCoverPunchSmall.jpg, BookCoverPunch.jpg

NORM Mark Chapman asks you to add a new logo graphic to the NORM site and to create a rollover image out of it, linking users back to the home page. You'll create a two-cell table in the home page, and add the book list to one cell and a new book cover graphic in the other cell of the table.

1. Open the NORM site you modified in Tutorial 3, Case 3, and then open the index.htm page in the Document window.
2. Select the text logo at the top of the home page, and then delete the text.
3. Use the Rollover Image button in the Images list in the Common category on the Insert bar to insert a new logo with a rollover. Name the image "NORMlogoRollover," use the **NORMlogo.gif** located in the **Tutorial.04\Cases** folder included with your Data Files for the original image, use the **NORMlogoRollover.gif** located in the **Tutorial.04\Cases** folder included with your Data Files for the rollover image, type "NORM logo with link to home page" in the Alternate Text text box, and browse to the index.htm page in the When Clicked, Go To URL text box.
4. Save the page, and then preview the page in a browser.

Explore

5. Copy the logo to the books.htm, company.htm, contact.htm, and links.htm pages to replace the text logos on those pages. (*Hint*: Use the Copy HTML and Paste HTML commands on the Edit menu.) Save the pages as you go and preview the site when you are finished to ensure that the rollover images are working.
6. Open the index.htm page, position the insertion point directly before the NORM BOOK LIST heading, and insert a table with 1 row, 2 columns, 100% table width, 0 border thickness, 0 cell spacing, 0 cell padding, no header cells, and no summary, caption, or table ID because the table is being used for layout rather than to display information.

Explore

7. Select the NORM BOOK LIST heading and the following list of books and authors, drag the selected text into the left cell of the table, and then delete any blank lines from the page.

8. Drag the right border of the first cell to the left until it is directly beside the longest line of content in the cell, position the insertion point in the right cell and type "Featured Book," and then select the text and apply the .norm_sub_headings CSS style.
9. Select the left cell, click Top from the Vert list in the Property inspector, select the right cell, and then click Top in the Vert list in the Property inspector.
10. Place the insertion point after the text in the right cell, press the Shift+Enter keys to create a new line, and then insert in the cell the **BookCoverPunchSmall.jpg** located in the **Tutorial.04\Cases** folder included with your Data Files. Save and close the page.
11. Create a new page. Type "NORM - Featured Book" in the Title text box on the Document toolbar, expand the CSS Styles panel, and attach the page to the norm_styles.css style sheet. Save the page as featuredbook.htm in the site's local root folder.
12. Click the Layout Mode button in the Layout category on the Insert bar.
13. Click the Draw Layout Cell button and, in the left corner of the page just below the white horizontal line, draw a cell that is 250 pixels wide by 350 pixels high. Insert the **BookCoverPunch.jpg** located in the **Tutorial.04\Cases** folder included with your Data Files in the cell and resize the cell so that the cell is the same size as the graphic. (*Hint:* You'll need to switch to the Common category on the Insert bar to insert the image.)
14. Click the Draw Layout Cell button and draw a second layout cell directly below the first one. The second cell will have the same width as the first cell and should be 85 pixels high. (*Hint*: If you can't draw the second cell 85 pixels high, then you need to increase the size of the outer table so that it is at least 435 pixels high.)
15. Draw a third cell to the right of the first cell (also just below the white horizontal line). The third cell should be the combined height of the first two cells you drew and 525 pixels wide.
16. Select the table, and then click the Autostretch option button in the Property inspector. If the Choose Spacer Image dialog box opens, click the Create a Spacer Image File option button, and then browse to the Graphics folder in the local root folder for the NORM site.

Explore

17. Position the insertion point in the lower-left cell, and then type "Punch by Kelly Moore," select "Punch" and then apply the .norm_book_titles CSS style.
18. Position the insertion point in the right cell and type: "A wacky, eccentric collection of female voices searching for meaning in a world gone awry. Punch is a hilarious romp." - Melissa Thurman, Voice.
19. Select the cell and then click Middle in the Vert list in the Property inspector.
20. Select the graphic, and then increase its sharpness by 2 and increase its brightness by 22. Save and close the page.
21. Open the index.htm page, link the book cover graphic to the Featured Book page and target the page to open in a new browser window (_blank), and then link the text "Featured Book" to the Featured Book page. Target both links to open in another browser window.
22. Select the graphic, and then click the Align Center button in the Property inspector.
23. Save the page, and preview the site in a browser window.
24. Upload the site to your remote server, and then preview the site over the Web.

DRM 242 | Dreamweaver | Tutorial 4 Organizing Page Content and Layout

Create

Add a rollover graphic and create tables in Layout mode to enter content for a new page in a Web site for a newly opening sushi restaurant.

Explore

Explore

Explore

Explore

Case Problem 4

Data Files needed for this Case Problem: SushiYaYaLogo.gif, SushiYaYaLogoRollover.gif, TikkaRollTuna.gif

Sushi Ya-Ya Mary O'Brien asks you to add graphics and tables to the Sushi Ya-Ya site. You'll add the new Sushi Ya-Ya logo, with a rollover and a hyperlink to the home page, to every page of the site. Then, you'll create a Specials button in the home page. Finally, you'll create a new Specials page. You will create tables in Layout mode to structure the new page.

1. Open the SushiYaYa site you modified in Tutorial 3, Case 4, and then open the index.htm page in the Document window.
2. Select the text logo if there is one, and delete the text.
3. Add a graphic logo (either the one provided by the design team or one that you created yourself) to the top of each page in the site by using the Rollover Image button in the Images list in the Common category on the Insert bar to insert the logo into the home page, and then copying the logo and the functionality to the other pages of the site (use the Copy HTML and Paste HTML commands to copy the logo and functionality). Use the **SushiYaYaLogo.gif** located in the **Tutorial.04\Cases** folder included with your Data Files as the original image, and the **SushiYaYaLogoRollover.gif** located in the **Tutorial.04\Cases** folder included with your Data Files as the rollover image (or use your own graphics). Add alternate text and a link to the home page.
4. Create a new page in the Sushi YaYa site with the page title "Sushi Ya-Ya - Specials" saved as specials.htm in the site's local root folder, attach the page to the external stylesheet, and then save the page.
5. Design a layout for the Specials page. The special is the Tikka roll. The page will contain a graphic of the roll (use the **TikkaRollTuna.gif** located in the **Tutorial.04\Cases** folder included with your Data Files, or create your own graphic), the name of the special ("Tikka Roll"), a description of the special ("The Tikka Roll combines spicy tuna and rice wrapped in a seaweed roll."), and the price ("$3.00").
6. Once you have decided in a layout for the page, create a table in Layout mode to hold the content, and then place the content into the page. Edit the graphic, if necessary, to fit the page layout.
7. Create a specials link in the home page of the Sushi Ya-Ya site. You can use the graphic you used in the Specials page as well as text. You might want to create a table to hold the link in place on the page and you might want to create a style for the graphic that creates borders in a desired color to frame the graphic. Target the link to open the Specials page in a new browser window.
8. Save your changes, and then preview the site in a browser.
9. Upload the site to your remote server, and then preview the site over the Web, checking all the links and the added page.

Quick Check Answers

Session 4.1

1. GIF, JPEG, and PNG
2. JPEG
3. You can use the Assets panel to manage the assets of your site.
4. An image map is a graphic that is divided into hotspots.
5. A hotspot is an area of an image map that you can click to cause an action to occur.
6. A rollover is an image that changes when the pointer moves across it.

Session 4.2

1. A table cell is the intersection of a row and a column in the table.
2. True
3. Cell padding is the amount of empty space maintained between the border of a cell and the cell's content. Cell spacing is the width of the cell walls.
4. Pressing the Tab key moves the insertion point to the next cell to the right or, if the insertion point is in the last cell in a row, to the first cell in the next row. If the insertion point is in the last cell in the table, pressing the Tab key inserts a new row and moves the insertion point to the first cell in the new row.
5. When you merge two cells, the content is merged into one cell and the new cell is the width and the height of the two original cells put together.
6. <tr>
7. <td>

Session 4.3

1. A nested table is a table inside another table.
2. It is a good idea to plan the layout of Web pages when you are using tables because it helps avoid reworking the page elements once you have placed them on the page.
3. True
4. Dreamweaver inserts the rest of the cells and a table to hold the cell you drew.
5. No. When a cell is active it is ready to accept input. A cell must be selected and the resize handles visible in order to resize it by dragging the resize handles.
6. A spacer image is a one-pixel transparent image that is inserted into the fixed-width columns in a table that contains an autostretch column.

Dreamweaver DRM 245

Tutorial 5

Objectives

Session 5.1
- Insert a navigation bar
- Copy a navigation bar to other pages
- Modify a navigation bar

Session 5.2
- Understand frames and framesets
- Create a Web page with frames
- Adjust frame properties and attributes

Session 5.3
- Add content to frames
- Create hyperlinks with targets
- Explore the HTML behind frames, framesets, and targets
- Troubleshoot common problems with frames

Adding Shared Site Elements

Creating a Navigation Bar and Using Frames

Case

Catalyst

As you add pages to a Web site, you include more and more content that needs to be organized in a way that is easy for the user to navigate and understand, and, at the same time, catches the user's eye. You have organized some of the content in the Catalyst site using tables. Now you'll add pages that are organized with frames and that use the navigation bar object.

Brian Lee, public relations and marketing director at Catalyst, has reviewed your work on the new Catalyst site. He's impressed with your work so far, and he wants you to make a few more changes. He has decided to replace the text navigation system with a navigation bar using a series of rollover elements for the navigation links. Each rollover element includes a series of graphics. A different graphic will be used as the link for the four states of each element: Up, Over, Down, and Over While Down. The different graphics will provide the user with additional information, such as which page of the site is currently open. Also, the look of the graphic elements will add to the look and feel of the site.

In addition, Brian wants you to create a Web page for the band Life in Minor Chords. He plans to use this page to promote the band (thus fulfilling another of the site goals). You'll add links to the new page from the band's name in the Bands page and from the CD cover graphic in the Catalogue page. You will use frames when you design the new page.

Student Data Files

▼**Tutorial.05 folder**

▽ **Tutorial folder**

bands.gif	contactOver.gif	LIMCmainframetext.doc
bands.htm	contactOWD.gif	LIMCmembers.gif
bandsDown.gif	label.gif	LIMCmembersOVER.gif
bandsOver.gif	labelDown.gif	LIMCphotos.gif
bandsOWD.gif	labelOver.gif	LIMCphotosOVER.gif
catalogue.gif	labelOWD.gif	LIMCtours.gif
catalogueDown.gif	LifeBanner.jpg	LIMCtoursOVER.gif
catalogueOver.gif	LIMCcds.gif	tourdates.gif
catalogueOWD.gif	LIMCcdsOVER.gif	tourdatesDown.gif
contact.gif	LIMChistory.gif	tourdatesOver.gif
contactDown.gif	LIMChistoryOVER.gif	tourdatesOWD.gif

▽ **FrameTest folder**
   ▽ **Dreamweaver folder**
      LIMCContent1.htm
      LIMCContent2.htm
      LIMCContent3.htm
      LIMCContent4.htm
      LIMCFrameSet.htm
      LIMCLogoFrame.htm
      LIMCNavBarFrame.htm
▽ **Graphics folder**
   background.gif
   bands.gif
   bandsDown.gif
   bandsOver.gif
   bandsOWD.gif
   catalogue.gif
   catalogueDown.gif
   catalogueOver.gif
   catalogueOWD.gif
   CatalystLogo.gif
   CatalystLogoRollover.gif
   contact.gif
   contactDown.gif
   contactOver.gif
   contactOWD.gif
   label.gif
   labelDown.gif
   labelOver.gif
   labelOWD.gif
   spacer.gif
   tourdates.gif
   tourdatesDown.gif
   tourdatesOver.gif
   tourdatesOWD.gif

▽ **Stylesheets folder**
   catalyst_styles.css
▽ **Review folder**
   DCbanner.jpg
   DCbottombanner.jpg
   DCcdsOver.jpg
   DCcdsUp.jpg
   DChistoryOver.jpg
   DChistoryUp.jpg
   DCmembersOver.jpg
   DCmembersUp.jpg
   DCphotosOver.jpg
   DCphotosUp.jpg
   DCtoursOver.jpg
   DCtoursUP.jpg
▽ **Cases folder**
   AmongTheLedHorses.htm
   AmongTheLedHorsesBig.jpg
   AmongTheLedHorsesSmall.jpg
   featured_author_bio.htm
   featured_excerpt.htm
   HcontactinformationDown.gif
   HcontactinformationUp.gif
   HculturalcrosspollinationDown.gif
   HculturalcrosspollinationUp.gif
   HlinguisticdifferencesDown.gif
   HlinguisticdifferencesUp.gif
   HprofessorhartDown.gif
   HprofessorhartUp.gif
   HritualsandpracticesDown.gif
   HritualsandpracticesUp.gif
   LoveCallBig.jpg
   LoveCallSmall.jpg
   LucklessHunterBig.jpg

LucklessHunterSmall.jpg
PunchAuthorBioOver.gif
PunchAuthorBioUp.gif
PunchExcerptOver.gif
PunchExcerptUp.gif
PunchPressOver.gif
PunchPressUp.gif
RiderlessHorseBig.jpg
RiderlessHorseSmall.jpg
SushiCaliforniaRoll.gif
SushiCompanyOver.gif
SushiCompanyUp.gif
SushiContactOver.gif
SushiContactUp.gif
SushiDescriptions.doc
SushiMenuOver.gif
SushiMenuUp.gif
SushiSalmon.gif
SushiTunaHandRoll.gif
TheLoveCall.htm
TheLucklessHunter.htm
TheRiderlessHorse.htm

Session 5.1

Creating a Navigation Bar Object

There are many ways to add navigation to a Web site. As you learn more advanced Web design techniques, the number of options available to you increases. You have used text hyperlinks to enable the user to move between Web pages in the Catalyst site. You have defined CSS styles to customize the look of the various states of the hyperlink tags. You have also created a rollover button for the Catalyst site logo. Now you will replace the customized text links with a navigation bar.

In general practice, any navigation or menu system that is placed in a Web page can be referred to as a navigation bar. In Dreamweaver, however, the **navigation bar** is a specific item, which consists of a series of rollover graphics that change state when specific browser actions occur, such as when the user places the pointer over a graphic. The rollover graphics are held in place in the Web page by a container, such as a table. Each rollover is called an **element** and can have up to four states. The **Up state** refers to the element before the user clicks it. The **Over state** refers to the element when the pointer is positioned over the Up graphic. The **Down state** refers to the element after it has been clicked. The **Over While Down state** refers to the element when the pointer is placed over the Down graphic. You create a navigation bar by clicking the Navigation Bar button in the Images list in the Common category on the Insert bar and filling in the requested information. Dreamweaver will then create all the components of the navigation bar and insert them for you. In this tutorial, the term *navigation bar* refers to the specific Dreamweaver navigation bar object.

Creating a Navigation Bar

Reference Window

- Click the Navigation Bar button in the Images list in the Common category on the Insert bar.
- Type a name for the first element in the navigation bar in the Element Name text box.
- Click the Browse button next to each Image text box to navigate to the image you want to display for that element.
- Type alternate text in the Alternate Text text box.
- Click the When Clicked, Go To URL Browse button, and then navigate to the file to which you want to link the element.
- Click the Target list arrow, and then select the target window for the link.
- Click the Preload Images check box to check it.
- If this element represents the current page, click the Show "Down Image" Initially check box to check it; otherwise, leave it unchecked.
- Click the Insert list arrow, and then select the orientation of the navigation bar.
- Click the Use Tables check box to check it.
- Click the Add Item button above the Nav Bar Elements list to add another element to the bar, and then enter the information for that element. Repeat for each element you want to add to the navigation bar.
- Click the OK button.

As with any complex process, understanding the components used in the navigation bar will help you understand what it does. The navigation bar uses hyperlinks, rollovers, and tables; therefore, what you have learned about these items will enable you to better understand how the navigation bar works. When you use the navigation bar, several things happen:

- As with a rollover, the graphics in a navigation bar preload when the Web page is loaded, if the preload option is selected, so that they are in place when the browser action occurs.
- A series of navigation bar elements is defined. (Each element is similar to a rollover button with a set of up to four state images.)
- The navigation bar is placed within a table in the Web page if the Use Table check box is checked; otherwise, the elements are placed directly in the Web page. It is best to place the navigation bar in a table because it keeps the elements in their proper positions in the page.
- If you set a URL for each element, then the user will jump to the new page when they click an element, just like when they click a text link.

You will open a sample of the Bands page in the Catalyst site with a navigation bar inserted in the page so you can explore the elements of the navigation bar from within a Web page. (You will not be able to jump to the other pages of the site.)

To examine a navigation bar in a Web page:

1. Start your browser.
2. Click **File** on the menu bar, and then click **Open**.
3. Click the **Browse** button, navigate to the **Tutorial.05\Tutorial** folder included with your Data Files, double-click **bands.htm**, and then click the **OK** button. The Bands page with a navigation bar opens in the browser window. See Figure 5-1.

Figure 5-1   Navigation bar with the bands element in the Down state

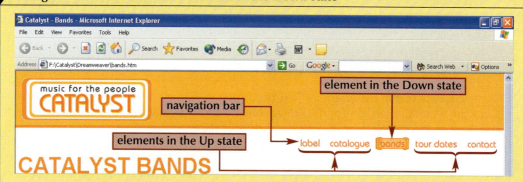

Graphics have been created for each link in the navigation bar. The bands element is in the Down state because the Bands page is currently visible in the browser. The other elements—label, catalogue, tour dates, and contact—are in the Up state.

4. Move the pointer over the **bands** element, but do not click. The element changes to the Over While Down state to indicate that the link cannot be clicked because you are currently on that page. See Figure 5-2.

Figure 5-2   Navigation bar with the bands element in the Over While Down state

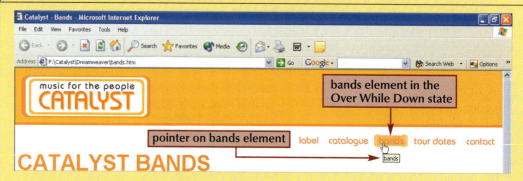

5. Move the pointer over the **label** element. The element changes to the Over state. See Figure 5-3.

Figure 5-3

6. Close the browser window.

You will insert a navigation bar in the pages of the Catalyst site.

Inserting a Navigation Bar

Before you create a navigation bar, you need graphics to use for each state of the elements. The graphics must be saved in one of the Web-safe formats (GIF, JPEG, or PNG) to be used in a Web page. You can create graphics in a graphics processing program, such as Adobe Photoshop, Macromedia Fireworks, or Adobe Illustrator. When you add an image to the navigation bar, you should place a copy of it in the Graphics folder within the site's local root folder, just as you have done when adding other graphics to the site. To create a navigation bar, you'll enter the following information:

- **Nav Bar Elements.** A list of elements included in the navigation bar. Once you have created elements, you can add, delete, or reorder the elements in the list.
- **Element Name.** The name of each element you add to the navigation bar. When you rename an element, its name will change in the Nav Bar Elements list. Element names must start with a letter or an underscore, and they can contain only letters and numbers (no spaces or symbols).
- **Up Image.** The graphic that will be used when the element is in the Up state. You can type the path to the image or browse to select the image. You must include a graphic for the Up image for the navigation bar to work. The other states are optional.
- **Over Image.** The graphic that will be used when the element is in the optional Over state. You can type the path to the image or browse to select the image.
- **Down Image.** The graphic that will be used when the element is in the optional Down state. You can type the path to the image or browse to select the image.
- **Over While Down Image.** The graphic that appears when the element is in the optional Over While Down state. This optional graphic can provide users a visual cue that the button cannot be clicked again from that particular part of the Web site. For example, if the navigation bar includes an Over While Down image that grays out the bands element in the Bands page of the Catalyst site, the image will be gray when a user points to the bands element on the navigation bar—indicating that the Bands page is displayed and that link cannot be clicked. You can type the path to the image or browse to select the image.
- **Alternate Text.** Text that appears in place of the image in browsers that display only text. This is the text that a screen reader will read or that will appear in tooltips.

- **When Clicked, Go To URL.** The URL or file path to which you want the element to hyperlink, along with the window or frame in which you want the new URL to appear (frames will be explored later in this tutorial). The Main Window option opens the new Web page in the existing browser window.
- **Options.** Options that affect the entire navigation bar, not each individual element. The Preload Images option enables the browser to download all the graphics used in the navigation bar when the page is loaded. If you don't preload images, users might experience a delay before the Over image appears when they move the mouse over a button. The Show "Down Image" Initially option enables Dreamweaver to display the Down state of an element (rather than the default Up state) when the page is loaded. (The Up state of the element is displayed by default when a page is loaded.) This feature is used to show a user which page of the Web site is displayed. For example, you'll show the Down state of the label element in the navigation bar in the Label page of the Catalyst site; when the Label page is loaded in the browser, the user knows it is open because the label element in the navigation bar is in the Down state.
- **Insert.** The option to insert elements either horizontally to create a horizontal navigation bar or vertically to create a vertical navigation bar. This option applies to the entire navigation bar. Once you have created a horizontal or vertical navigation bar, you cannot change this setting. If you want to switch the orientation of the navigation bar, you must delete the existing navigation bar and create a new one.
- **Use Tables.** The option to use tables to keep the navigation bar elements in place. This option applies to the entire navigation bar. It is a good idea to create navigation bars with tables.

Brian asks you to upgrade the navigation system for the Catalyst site by deleting the current text links and creating a navigation bar in each page of the site. When you create the new navigation bar in the first page, you will include a graphic for each state of each element. You should include a copy of each graphic in the Graphics folder within the site's local root folder. When you create the navigation bar in the other pages of the Web site, you should browse to the graphics in the Graphics folder rather than include additional copies of the same graphics for each page. Reusing graphics keeps the Web site lean. Also, if you decide later to change the look of the navigation bar, you have to replace only one set of images instead of a set for each page.

You'll start by creating the navigation bar in the Label page. You'll open the page, turn on the rulers so that you can better see where the navigation bar and heading text are placed in the page, and then delete the current text links.

To turn on the rulers and delete text links:

1. Open the **NewCatalyst** Web site that you modified in the Tutorial 4 Review Assignments, and then open the **label.htm** page in the Document window.
2. Click the **Show Design View** button [Design] on the Document toolbar, if necessary.
3. Click **View** on the menu bar, point to **Rulers**, and then click **Show** to display the rulers in the Document window, if necessary.
4. Drag to select the link text for the current navigation system, and then press the **Delete** key. The text links disappear from the page.

Next, you'll create a graphic-based navigation bar. For each element, you'll include an Up image, an Over image, a Down image, and an Over While Down image. Brian has supplied the graphics you should use for each element in the four states. You want the images to preload and you want the element that represents the current page to show the Down image initially. To match the design plan, you'll make the navigation bar horizontal and use tables.

To create a navigation bar:

1. Click the **Images** list arrow in the Common category on the Insert bar, and then click the **Navigation Bar** button. The Insert Navigation Bar dialog box opens. See Figure 5-4.

Figure 5-4 Insert Navigation Bar dialog box

2. Type **Label** in the Element Name text box.
3. Click the **Up Image Browse** button to open the Select Image Source dialog box, navigate to the **Tutorial.05\Tutorial** folder included with your Data Files, and then double-click **label.gif**. A copy of the label.gif graphic is placed in the site's Graphics folder and the file path appears in the Up Image text box.

   You'll repeat this process to insert the images for the Over, Down, and Over While Down states.
4. Click the **Over Image Browse** button, and then double-click **labelOver.gif** located in the **Tutorial.05\Tutorial** folder included with your Data Files.
5. Click the **Down Image Browse** button, and then double-click **labelDown.gif** located in the **Tutorial.05\Tutorial** folder included with your Data Files.
6. Click the **Over While Down Image Browse** button, and then double-click **labelOWD.gif** located in the **Tutorial.05\Tutorial** folder included with your Data Files.

7. Click in the **Alternate Text** text box, and then type **label**.
8. Click the **When Clicked, Go To URL Browse** button, and then double-click **label.htm** in the local root folder of your NewCatalyst Web site.
9. If necessary, click the **Target** list arrow (next to the word "in"), and then click **Main Window**.
10. Click the **Preload Images** check box to check it, if necessary. Now all of the graphics in the navigation bar will preload.

    You want to show the Down image initially for the bands link to give a visual cue to the user that this is the currently displayed page of the Catalyst site.

11. Click the **Show "Down Image" Initially** check box to check it. An asterisk appears next to the element name in the Nav Bar Elements list to indicate that the Down image (rather than the Up image) will be displayed initially in the page.
12. If necessary, click the **Insert** list arrow, and then click **Horizontally**. The navigation bar will display horizontally.
13. Click the **Use Tables** check box to check it, if necessary. The navigation bar will be inserted as a table. You've entered all the information for the first element. See Figure 5-5.

Figure 5-5 | **Completed label element information**

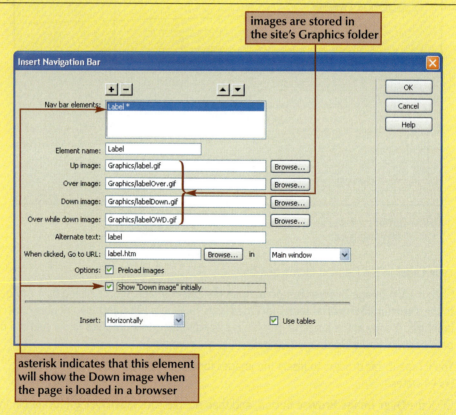

You'll repeat the same process to add the elements for the other pages in the Catalyst site.

To add elements to a navigation bar:

1. Click the **Add Item** button [+] above the Nav Bar Elements list in the Insert Navigation Bar dialog box. The text boxes and options are cleared so you can add the next element; and the next element name, currently unnamed1, is added to the Nav Bar Elements list.

2. Type **Bands** in the Element Name text box.

3. Browse to the **Tutorial.05\Tutorial** folder included with your Data Files to insert the following graphics for each state.

Element	Graphic
Up Image	bands.gif
Over Image	bandsOver.gif
Down Image	bandsDown.gif
Over While Down Image	bandsOWD.gif

4. Type **bands** in the Alternate Text text box.

5. Click the **When Clicked, Go To URL Browse** button, and then double-click **bands.htm** in the local root folder of your NewCatalyst Web site.

6. If necessary, click the **Target** list arrow, and then click **Main Window**.

7. Verify that the **Show "Down Image" Initially** check box is unchecked.

   You do not need to change the Preload Images, Insert, or Use Tables attributes, because you already set them when you set the attributes for the first element and these options affect the entire navigation bar. You'll follow the same procedure to create the elements for the Catalogue, Tour Dates, and Contact pages.

8. Repeat Steps 1 through 7 for the **catalogue** element, the **tour dates** element, and the **contact** element, using the following files located in the **Tutorial.05\Tutorial** folder included with your Data Files for the graphics. For the tour dates element, use "TourDates" (no space) as the element name.

Element	Catalogue	Tour Dates	Contact
Up Image	catalogue.gif	tourdates.gif	contact.gif
Over Image	catalogueOver.gif	tourdatesOver.gif	contactOver.gif
Down Image	catalogueDown.gif	tourdatesDown.gif	contactDown.gif
Over While Down Image	catalogueOWD.gif	tourdatesOWD.gif	contactOWD.gif
Alternate Text	catalogue	tour dates	contact
URL	catalogue.htm	tourdates.htm	contact.htm

9. Click the **OK** button. The navigation bar is inserted in the Label page in a table, and the table is selected. See Figure 5-6. The label link is in the Down state to indicate that you are viewing the Label page.

Figure 5-6 | **Label page with unformatted navigation bar**

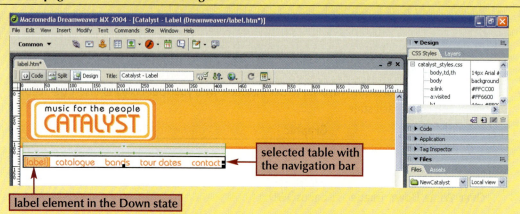

Trouble? If you find the page heading is displayed in two lines, you need to add a paragraph return after the navigation bar table. Click to the right of the navigation bar table, and then press the Enter key.

You want the navigation bar to be aligned along the right edge of the page. You'll make this change, and then test the navigation bar in a browser.

To format and test a navigation bar:

1. Select the table that contains the navigation bar, if necessary, click the **Align** list arrow in the Property inspector, and then click **Right**. The navigation bar moves to the right side of the page and the table is still selected.

   Trouble? If you have trouble selecting the table, switch to Expanded Tables mode, select the table, and then switch back to Standard mode.

2. Click outside the table to deselect it. See Figure 5-7.

Figure 5-7 | **Label page with the formatted navigation bar**

3. Save the page, and then preview it in a browser.
4. In the browser window, move the pointer over the **label** link to see how the link changes.
5. Move the pointer over the rest of the links to see how they change.

6. Click the **tour dates** link, and watch as the image briefly changes after the link is clicked and before the Tour Dates page opens.

7. Close the browser window, and then close the page.

You need to add a navigation bar to each of the other pages in the Catalyst site. You do not want to add more copies of the navigation bar graphics to the Web site, because this will increase the size of the site unnecessarily. Instead, you'll browse to the Graphics folder located within the site's local root folder and use the graphics that you placed there. Once you have added the navigation bar to each page, you'll adjust the location of the navigation bar and heading text so that they are in the same location in each page.

To create a navigation bar in the Bands page:

1. Open the **bands.htm** page in the Document window, and then delete the text links at the top of the page.

2. Click the **Navigation Bar** button in the Images list in the Common category on the Insert bar.

3. Create the following elements, using the graphics files located in the **Graphics** folder within the local root folder of your NewCatalyst site.

Element	Label	Bands	Catalogue	Tour Dates	Contact
Element Name	Label	Bands	Catalogue	TourDates	Contact
Up Image	label.gif	bands.gif	catalogue.gif	tourdates.gif	contact.gif
Over Image	labelOver.gif	bandsOver.gif	catalogueOver.gif	tourdatesOver.gif	contactOver.gif
Down Image	labelDown.gif	bandsDown.gif	catalogueDown.gif	tourdatesDown.gif	contactDown.gif
Over While Down Image	labelOWD.gif	bandsOWD.gif	catalogueOWD.gif	tourdatesOWD.gif	contactOWD.giv
Alternate Text	label	bands	catalogue	tour dates	contact
URL	label.htm	bands.htm	catalogue.htm	tourdates.htm	contact.htm
Show "Down Image" Initially	unchecked	checked	unchecked	unchecked	unchecked

4. Make sure the **Preload Images** check box is checked, **Horizontally** is selected in the Insert list, and the **Use Tables** check box is checked.

5. Click the **OK** button. The navigation bar appears in the Bands page with the bands element showing the Down state.

6. Right align the navigation bar and make sure that it is located one line below the top border of the page with the heading text just below it.

7. Save the page, preview the page in a browser, test the links, and then close the browser window.

You will copy the navigation bar to the rest of the pages in the site.

Copying a Navigation Bar

You could continue to create the navigation bar for each page manually, but a faster method is to copy an existing navigation bar and then modify the appropriate elements for that page. When you copy the navigation bar to a new page, Dreamweaver cannot automatically determine which element should be displayed in the Down state so you must change these elements yourself. Once you have copied the navigation bar to a new page, you will open the Modify Navigation Bar dialog box and manually change the navigation bar to display the element that represents the current page in the Down state.

To copy a navigation bar to another page:

1. Select the navigation bar table in the Bands page, click **Edit** on the menu bar, click **Copy HTML**, and then close the page.

2. Open the **catalogue.htm** page, select the link text, press the **Delete** key, click **Edit** on the menu bar, and then click **Paste HTML**. The navigation bar table is pasted in the Catalogue page.

3. If necessary, right-align the navigation bar and make sure that it is located one line below the top border of the page with the heading text just below it.

   Next, you will modify the navigation bar by changing the bands element to show the Up state initially and changing the catalogue element (the element that represents the current page) to show the Down state initially.

4. Click **Modify** on the menu bar, and then click **Navigation Bar**. The Modify Navigation Bar dialog box opens.

5. Click **Bands*** in the Nav Bar Elements list, and then click the **Show "Down Image" Initially** check box to uncheck it.

6. Click **Catalogue** (the element for the current page) in the Nav Bar Elements list, and then click the **Show "Down Image" Initially** check box to check it. See Figure 5-8.

Figure 5-8   Modify Navigation Bar dialog box

asterisk indicates that the Catalogue element will show the Down image when the page is loaded in a browser

7. Click the **OK** button, save the page, preview the page in a browser, test the navigation bar, and then close the browser window and the page.

8. Repeat Steps 2 through 7 for the **contact.htm** and **tourdates.htm** pages, changing the element that represents the current page to show the Down image initially.

9. Open the **index.htm** page, click to the right of the logo image, click **Edit** on the menu bar, and then click **Paste HTML**. The navigation bar is pasted in the page.

   When you modify the navigation bar in the home page, you will not designate an element to show the Down image initially, because no element in the navigation bar represents the home page.

10. Click **Modify** on the menu bar, click **Navigation Bar**, click **Bands*** in the Nav Bar Elements list, click the **Show "Down Image" Initially** check box to uncheck it, and then click the **OK** button.

11. Save the page, preview the page in a browser, test the navigation bar, and then close the browser window.

Next, you will learn to make additional modifications to the navigation bar.

Modifying the Navigation Bar

As a Web site grows and changes, you will undoubtedly need to modify the navigation bar. You might need to add new elements, delete current elements, reorder existing elements, change the graphics associated with the various states of the elements, and update the URLs to which elements are hyperlinked. Remember, you cannot change the horizontal or vertical orientation of a navigation bar once it has been created. To change the orientation of the navigation bar, you must delete the current navigation bar and create a new one.

Modifying a Navigation Bar | Reference Window

- Click Modify on the menu bar, and then click Navigation Bar to open the Modify Navigation Bar dialog box.
- Click the element you want to modify in the Nav Bar Elements list.
- Change the options as needed.
- Click the OK button.

Brian has decided that placing the catalogue element of the navigation bar before the bands element will be more effective in achieving the site goal of promoting CDs. He asks you to modify the navigation bar in the Catalyst site so that the catalogue element appears before the bands element.

To modify a navigation bar:

1. Click **Modify** on the menu bar, and then click **Navigation Bar**. The Modify Navigation Bar dialog box opens.

2. Click **Catalogue** in the Nav Bar Elements list box to select it.

3. Click the **Up Arrow** button above the Nav Bar Elements list one time so that the element is second in the list. See Figure 5-9.

Figure 5-9 | Elements reordered in the Modify Navigation Bar dialog box

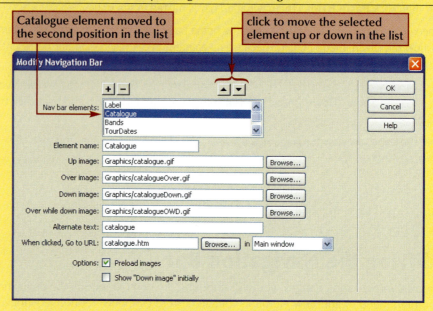

4. Click the **OK** button. The elements are reordered in the navigation bar.
5. Click outside the navigation bar to deselect it. See Figure 5-10.

Figure 5-10 | Home page with reordered navigation bar elements

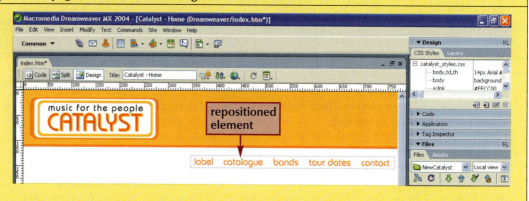

6. Save and close the page.
7. Repeat Steps 1 through 6 for the **bands.htm**, **catalogue.htm**, **contact.htm**, **label.htm**, and **tourdates.htm** pages.
8. Starting with the home page, preview all the pages of the site in a browser.

So far, you have created and modified the navigation bar in each page of the Catalyst site. In the next session, you will create frames and framesets.

Session 5.1 Quick Check

1. What is a navigation bar?
2. Up to how many states can each element in a navigation bar have?
3. In which state is a navigation bar element when the pointer is positioned over the element before the graphic has been clicked?
4. True or False? You do not need to add graphics that you use in navigation bar elements to the Graphics folder in the site's local root folder.
5. True or False? When you copy a navigation bar from one page to another, Dreamweaver automatically adjusts the elements so that the element for the link to the page in which you are pasting shows the Down state.
6. What property of a navigation bar cannot be changed once the navigation bar has been created?

Session 5.2

Understanding Frames and Framesets

Frames divide one Web page into multiple HTML documents. Each frame contains a single HTML document with its own content and, if necessary, its own scroll bars. For example, you will create a new page in the Catalyst site for the band Life in Minor Chords. The new page will have three frames. The top frame will contain an HTML document with the band logo, a frame at the left of the page will contain an HTML document with the navigation bar for the page, and a frame at the right of the page will contain one of the many HTML documents with content. When a user selects a different link, the HTML document with the requested information will display in the content frame in the page; the other two frames in the page will remain the same.

A Web page with frames is held together by a frameset. A **frameset** is a separate HTML document that defines the structure and properties of a Web page with frames. The frameset page is not displayed in the browser; its only function is to store the information about how the frames will display in the Web page and to provide the browser with that information when the page is loaded. Every frame must be contained in a frameset. When you create frames in Dreamweaver, code to display NoFrames content is automatically added to the code of the frameset page. **NoFrames content** is the content shown by browsers that cannot display frames to provide information for users who cannot view the frames. You will learn more about NoFrames content when you add content to the frames.

The biggest benefit of frames is that they can be used to keep some parts of a Web page static while other parts of the page are updated. For example, frames can keep the portions of Web pages that remain consistent throughout a site (such as logos and navigation bars) separate from the portions of the Web pages that change (such as the content). This is done so that users do not wait for the logo and the navigation bar to reload every time they click a new link. This makes the users' experience more pleasant because pages load faster.

When used correctly, frames can add a lot to a site. However, there are some drawbacks with using frames. Frames are not supported in browsers earlier than Netscape Navigator 2.0 and Internet Explorer 3.0 (however, very few people are using these browsers). Also, frames run more slowly in Internet Explorer prior to version 5.5 because older versions open an additional, invisible browser window for each frame in the page. These additional invisible browser windows take processing power and make things slower, eliminating the benefit of using the frames. If you are supporting very old browsers, you should not use frames. Secondly, using frames in a page makes it difficult for users to bookmark specific content because bookmarks mark the initial state of the frameset. If the user has clicked a navigation element or link and the content of the page has changed, the changes are usually not reflected when the bookmark is loaded. This can irritate users who want to come back to a particular place in a site. Along the same lines, the URL no longer constitutes a complete specification of the information shown in the browser window because the URL marks the initial state of the frameset. You can only create a link to the site as it is initially displayed in the browser. This reduces the usefulness of shortcuts and hyperlinks because you cannot link to specific information, only to the general site. Finally, using frames in a site can make it difficult for search engines to list the site.

Over the years, frames have gotten a bad reputation, primarily because many sites make poor use of them. The two most common mistakes are using too many frames in a page and miscoding frames so that information is loaded into pages incorrectly. Using too many frames in a page fragments the page and makes it difficult to read. When frames were first introduced, many designers went overboard, placing so many frames into their pages that users found the sites confusing and hard to follow. When you add frames to a site, ask yourself why you are adding the frames and what they will add to the site. Add frames only when they will contribute to the overall site design. When you create a frameset and frames, it is important to code them correctly. Some common mistakes include targeting a link to open in the wrong frame and miscoding so that multiple instances of the same frame open within one Web page. You will learn the correct way to create frames in this session.

Even if you decide not to use frames in your sites, it is a good idea to develop an understanding of the way they work because as a professional designer you will run into frames from time to time.

Before you start using frames, you will explore a Web page that uses frames from within your browser. The sample Web page is the page that was used during planning stages to develop the Life in Minor Chords frame layout. The borders of the frames have been made visible so that you can see where the frames are located, and one of the sample links is targeted to open in the wrong frame so that you can experience the effects of mistargeting a link (one of the most common mistakes designers make when working with frames). Experiencing the effects of a mistargeted link will help you recognize the mistake if it occurs when you create your own frames. The sample Web page contains text placeholders where the finalized artwork, navigation bar, and content will be. Designers often use text placeholders to help with the layout of Web pages while finalized art and content are being created. In the final version of the page, the Life in Minor Chords logo art will be substituted for the text in the top frame, a navigation bar will be created for the left frame, finalized content will be added to content frames, and the frame borders will be invisible.

To explore a Web page that uses frames in a browser:

1. Start your browser.

2. Click **File** on the menu bar, click **Open**, click the **Browse** button, navigate to the **Tutorial.05\Tutorial\FrameTest\Dreamweaver** folder included with your Data Files, double-click **LIMCFrameSet.htm**, and then click the **OK** button. The sample page with frames loads in the browser window. See Figure 5-11.

Sample Web page with frames

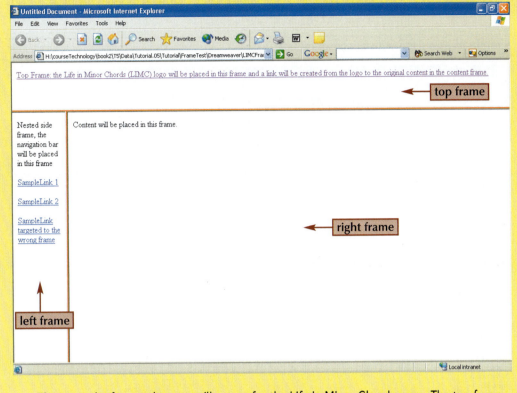

Figure 5-11

These are the frames that you will create for the Life in Minor Chords page. The top frame is where the logo will be placed, the left frame will contain the navigation bar, and the right frame will display the changing page content.

3. Read all the text in the page, and then click the **SampleLink 1** link. The content in the main content frame (the right frame) changes. See Figure 5-12.

Content changed in the right frame

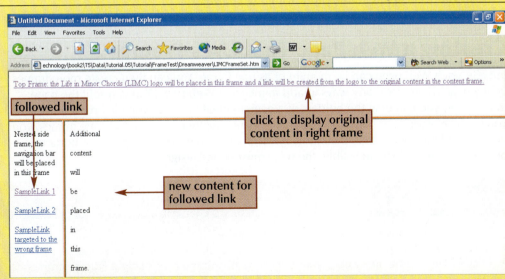

Figure 5-12

4. Click the **Top Frame** link in the top frame. The text that was originally in the content frame reappears.

5. Click the **SampleLink targeted to the wrong frame** link in the left frame. The new content replaces the navigation text, making it impossible to navigate through the page, which is a very common mistake. See Figure 5-13.

Figure 5-13 | **Sample frames page with mistargeted link**

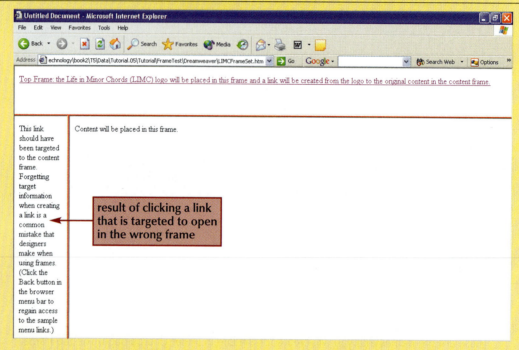

6. Click the **Back** button on the browser window toolbar to return to the navigation links in the left frame.
7. Close the browser window.

Next, you will explore frames from within Dreamweaver.

Creating a Web Page That Uses Frames

Initially, each Web page can be thought of as one frame. You can then create more frames in any page. There are many ways to add frames to a Web page. You can split the page into frames, you can drag the borders of a page to create frames, you can insert frames, or you can use predefined framesets. No matter which method you use to create frames, you need to set Dreamweaver so that frame borders are visible. To view the frame borders once you have made them visible, the page must be in Design view.

Reference Window | **Creating a Web Page with Frames**

- Open the page in which you want to create frames.
- Click View on the menu bar, point to Visual Aids, and then click Frame Borders.
- Click Modify on the menu bar, point to Frameset, and then click a Split Frame command.

or

- Drag a frame border.

or

- Click a Frames button in the Frames category on the Insert bar to insert a predefined frameset.

You'll display the frame borders for the home page.

To view frame borders in Dreamweaver:

1. If you took a break after the last session, make sure the **NewCatalyst** site is open.
2. Open the **index.htm** page in the Document window.
3. Click **View** on the menu bar, point to **Visual Aids**, and then click **Frame Borders**. A gray frame border surrounds the entire page. See Figure 5-14.

Home page with a frame border 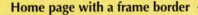 Figure 5-14

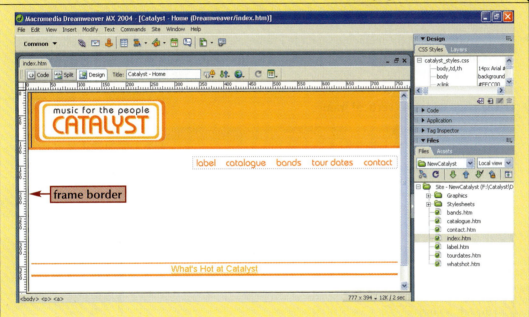

A border surrounds each frame in the page. In this case, there is only one frame border because you haven't yet created any frames. To select a frame, you click within that frame in the Document window. When you are working with frames, each time you close a page and reopen it, you will need to redisplay the frame borders.

Next, you'll use the different methods to create frames in the home page.

Creating Frames by Splitting a Web Page

You can create frames in a Web page by splitting the page. When you split a page, the Document window divides into two frames—either vertically (left and right) or horizontally (top and bottom). The Web page properties and any content move into the specified frame (left, right, top, or bottom). You can continue to split the page by selecting a frame and splitting it until you have achieved the desired number of frames. The four ways to split a page are:

- **Split Frame Left.** Splits the page vertically into two frames, and moves the Web page properties and any content into the left frame.
- **Split Frame Right.** Splits the page vertically into two frames, and moves the Web page properties and any content into the right frame.

- **Split Frame Up.** Splits the page horizontally into two frames, and moves the Web page properties and any content into the top frame.
- **Split Frame Down.** Splits the page horizontally into two frames, and moves the Web page properties and any content into the bottom frame.

If you decide you don't want a frame you just added, you can use the Undo command on the Edit menu to remove the frame.

You'll create frames in the home page so that you can become familiar with the way creating frames affects the content of Web pages. First, you will create frames by splitting the Web page.

To split a Web page into frames:

1. Click **Modify** on the menu bar, point to **Frameset**, and then click **Split Frame Left**. The home page splits into two vertical frames with the content in the left frame and nothing in the right frame. The left frame also has its own scroll bar. See Figure 5-15.

Figure 5-15   **Home page with two vertical frames**

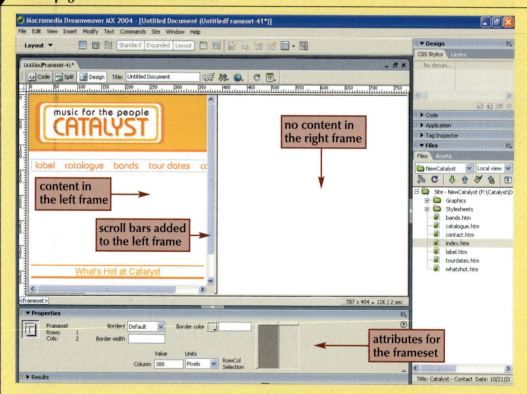

2. Click in the left frame to make it active, click **Modify** on the menu bar, point to **Frameset**, and then click **Split Frame Up**. The left frame splits into two horizontal frames with the content in the upper frame. See Figure 5-16.

Figure 5-16 Home page split into three frames

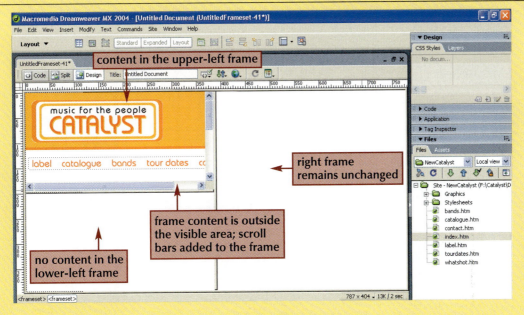

3. Click **Edit** on the menu bar, and then click **Undo Insert Frame**. The page returns to two vertical frames.
4. Click **Edit** on the menu bar, and then click **Undo Insert Frame**. The page returns to one frame.

You'll try another method to create frames.

Creating Frames by Dragging Borders

When frame borders are visible, you can create frames in a page by dragging the frame borders at the perimeter of the Web page up, down, left, or right. If a Web page already has frames, you can create additional frames by dragging the borders of the outside frames away from the edges of the page. Dragging the frame borders that do not touch the edge of the Web page will resize the frames. Be careful; the frame (and any content it contains) is deleted if you drag the frame border back to the Web page perimeter.

You'll create frames by dragging the borders of a Web page.

To create frames by dragging borders:

1. Position the pointer over the **left page border** (all the way on the left side of the screen). The pointer changes to ↔.
2. Drag the **border** to the right approximately one-third of the way to the center of the page to create two vertical frames. Use the rulers to help you, if necessary. The Web page content and settings (such as the page background) are in the larger right frame. See Figure 5-17.

| Figure 5-17 | Home page with uneven vertical frames |

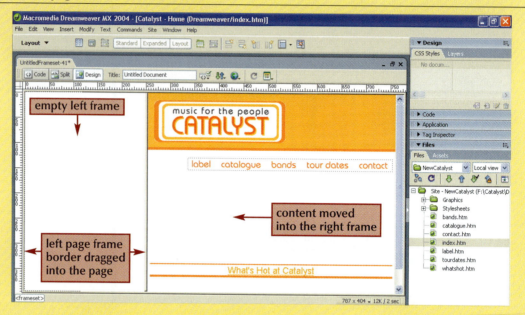

3. Position the pointer over the **top page border** so the pointer changes to ↕, and then drag the **border** down approximately one-third of the way toward the center of the page to create horizontal frames. The content moves into the lower-right frame. See Figure 5-18.

| Figure 5-18 | Home page with four frames |

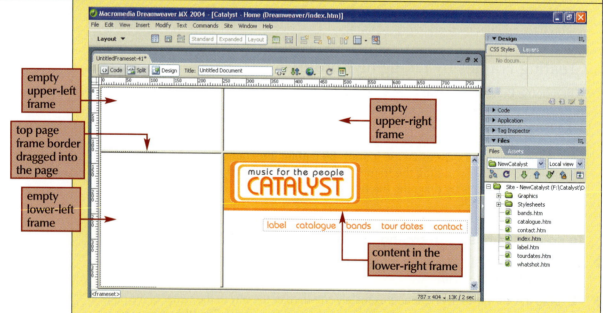

4. Press the **Ctrl+Z** keys to undo the horizontal frames.

   You'll use the mouse to remove the left frame.

5. Use the ↔ pointer to drag the **horizontal frame border** left to the edge of the Document window. The empty left frame disappears.

Trouble? If the page content is deleted, then you dragged the frame border to the right. Click Edit on the menu bar, and then click Undo Delete Frame to reverse the deletion. Then repeat Step 5, being careful to drag the frame border to the left.

6. Close the home page.

Another way to add frames to a page is with predefined framesets.

Using a Predefined Frameset

You can select from several predefined framesets to add frames to Web pages. These framesets create commonly used frame layouts. Using them can save you the time of creating each frame yourself. In addition to creating simple left, right, top, and bottom frames, there are also predefined framesets for more complex layouts that split a page into three or four frames of different sizes. Some of these more complex predefined framesets include nested framesets. A **nested frameset** is a frameset that is inside another frameset. The frameset that holds the nested frameset is called the **parent frameset**.

Once you have inserted a predefined frameset, you can resize the frames by dragging any frame border inside the Web page. Remember, dragging a frame border from the perimeter of the Web page will add frames.

You will create a new section of the Web site devoted to the Life in Minor Chords band. This section will have its own look that will distinguish it from the rest of the site, because it will function as the Life in Minor Chords Web site and should create a specific look that will be identified with the band. Brian asks you to use frames for this part of the site.

You'll create a new folder called "LifeInMinorChords" so that all the pages and assets associated with this unique section of the Web site are in one place. This will keep the Web site organized. You will name the new page "limc_content1.htm" because, when you add frames to the page, this will become the default content for the main frame.

To create a new folder and a new page:

1. Click **HTML** in the Create New section on the Start page. Dreamweaver creates a new page. You'll save the page in a new folder in the local root folder of the site.

2. Click **File** on the menu bar, click **Save As**, and then navigate to the local root folder of the NewCatalyst site.

3. Click the **Create New Folder** button in the Save As dialog box, and then name the new folder **LifeInMinorChords**. You'll save the new page in this folder.

4. Type **limc_content1.htm** in the File Name text box, and then click the **Save** button. The new page is saved in the LifeInMinorChords folder.

5. Select the text in the Title text box on the Document toolbar, type **Life in Minor Chords - content 1 frame**, and then press the **Enter** key. You are adding page titles to help you identify the individual frames; users will see only the title of the frameset in the browser window title bar.

6. Type **Content 1 frame** in the Document window to help identify the page. See Figure 5-19.

Figure 5-19 New limc_content1.htm page

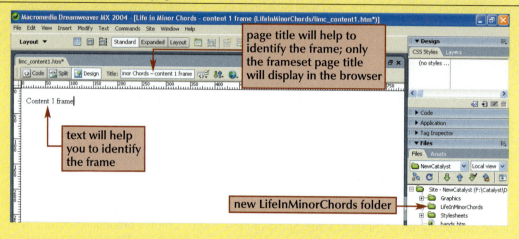

7. Save the limc_content1.htm page.

Once the page is created, you can add the predefined frameset.

To add a predefined frameset:

1. Click the **Frames** button list arrow in the Layout category on the Insert bar. Buttons for the 13 predefined framesets are displayed in the list.
2. Click the **Top and Nested Left Frames** button. The page is split into three frames and the content of the page is displayed in the lower-right frame. See Figure 5-20.

Figure 5-20 Page with top and nested left frames

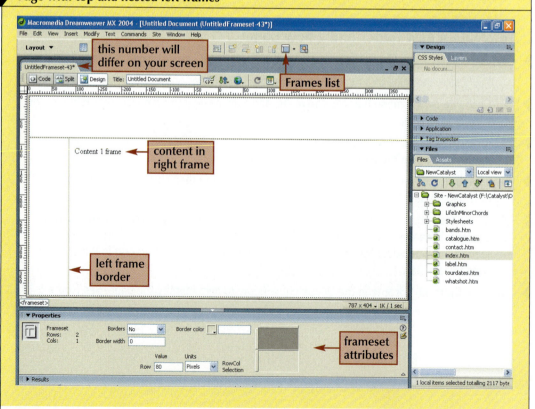

Selecting and Saving Frames

Once you have created frames in a Web page, you must save them before you begin working on the page. Each frame contains a separate HTML document, so you will select and save the document in each frame individually. To select the HTML document in a frame, you place the pointer in that frame in the Document window. You select a frame when you want to add content to the HTML document in that frame or when you want to save the HTML document that is in that frame. Once you have selected the frame, you can save it.

Saving a Frame

Reference Window

- Select the frame in the Document window or in the Frames panel.
- Click File on the menu bar, and then click Save Frame.
- Type a filename in the File Name text box.
- Click the Save button.

You will save the top and left frames that you created for the Life in Minor Chords page. You will add a page title and identifying text when you save each frame. (You saved the HTML document in the right frame when you created the page, so you do not need to save it again.)

To save frames:

1. Click in the **top frame** to make that frame active, and then type **LIMC - top frame**.
2. Type **Life in Minor Chords top frame** in the Title text box on the Document toolbar, and then press the **Enter** key.
3. Click **File** on the menu bar, and then click **Save Frame**. The Save As dialog box opens.
4. Navigate to the local root folder of the NewCatalyst site and double-click the **LifeInMinorChords** folder to open it, if necessary. Type **limc_top_frame.htm** in the File Name text box, and then click the **Save** button. The new HTML document appears in the LifeInMinorChords folder in the Files panel and the filename appears in the Document window title bar. See Figure 5-21.

Modified top frame   Figure 5-21

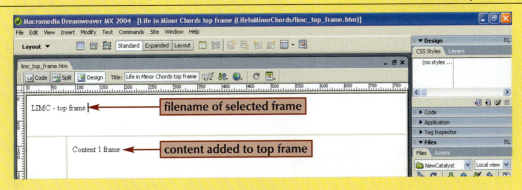

You'll repeat this process to save the left frame.

5. Click in the **left frame** in the Document window to make that frame active, type **LIMC - left frame**, type **Life in Minor Chords - left frame** in the Title text box on the Document toolbar, and then press the **Enter** key.
6. Click **File** on the menu bar, click **Save Frame**, and then save the frame in the **LifeInMinorChords** folder with the filename **limc_left_frame.htm**.

Selecting and Saving the Frameset

Once you have saved the HTML document in each frame of the page, you must save the frameset. The frameset is a separate page that contains all the information about how the frames will display in the Web page and what HTML documents will initially be loaded into each frame. (When you adjust the size of a frame, the attributes of a frame, or the attributes of the frameset, that information is stored in the frameset page.) In addition, the frameset page title is displayed in the browser window title bar whenever any of the frames included in the frameset are displayed.

You select the frameset from the Document window by selecting the outer border of the page. (The frame borders must be visible to select the frameset in the Document window.) When the frameset is selected, a dotted line is visible inside the border of one frame or all the frames in the Document window and the frameset properties are visible in the Property inspector.

Reference Window | Saving a Frameset

- Select the frameset in the Document window or in the Frames panel.
- Click File on the menu bar, and then click Save Frameset.
- Type a filename in the File Name text box, and then click the Save button.

You'll select the frameset you created for the LIMC page and save it.

To select and save the frameset:

1. Make sure the frame borders are visible, and then click the **border** that surrounds the entire page in the Document window. The frameset is selected. See Figure 5-22.

Figure 5-22 | **Selected frameset**

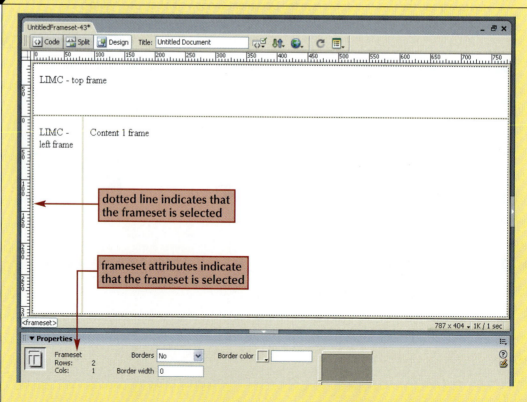

2. Type **Catalyst - Life in Minor Chords** in the Title text box on the Document toolbar, and then press the **Enter** key.

3. Click **File** on the menu bar, and click **Save Frameset**. The Save As dialog box opens.

4. Save the frameset in the **LifeInMinorChords** folder with the filename **limc_frameset.htm**. The frameset filename will appear in the browser window title bar. These tutorials use the word *frameset* in the filename to avoid confusion, but it is not usually considered good practice in Web site design because it is meaningless to the user.

5. Preview in a browser the four pages that you created and stored in the LifeInMinorChords folder, and then close the pages.

Once you have saved the frames and the frameset, you can save any changes you make to the frames or frameset by clicking the Save All command on the File menu. This will resave any frame that has been changed.

If you want to work on or view the Web page that contains the frames, you open the frameset page because it contains all the instructions for creating the frames. You can also open each frame individually in the Document window by selecting the desired page in the Files panel.

Next you will explore the frameset and the individual HTML documents that are in each frame.

Adjusting Page Properties for Frames

Once you have saved all the frames and the frameset for a Web page, you can adjust page properties and attributes for each HTML document. Because each frame contains a separate HTML document, you must set page properties and attributes for each frame separately, or you can create an external style sheet with styles that set the desired attributes and then connect each HTML document to the external style sheet. As with other elements, you adjust the attributes of any page content by selecting the content and adjusting the attributes in the Property inspector, or creating additional styles in the style sheet and applying those styles to the content.

You will open the limc_top_frame.htm page. This is the HTML document that is displayed in the top frame of the limc_frameset. You will set the page properties, and then you will export the styles to an external style sheet, delete the styles from the page, attach the page to the external style sheet, and attach the other pages to the style sheet. Finally, you will open the limc_frameset page, select the HTML documents that are displayed in the other frames, and then attach the style sheet to those HTML documents as well.

To set page properties for the top frame:

1. Open the **limc_top_frame.htm** page in the Document window. The HTML document that is displayed in the top frame of the limc_frameset page is open in the Document window.

2. Click the **Page Properties** button in the Property inspector. The Page Properties dialog box opens.

3. Click **Arial, Helvetica, sans-serif** in the Page Font list, select **14 pixels** from the Size list, type **#666666** in the Text Color text box, type **#A1CEF4** in the Background Color text box, and then type **0** in the margin text boxes.

4. Click **Links** in the Category list, type **#FFFFFF** in the Link Color, Rollover Links, and Active Links text boxes, type **#CCCCCC** in the Visited Links text box, and then click **Always Underline** in the Underline Style list, if necessary.

5. Click the **OK** button, and then save the page. See Figure 5-23.

Figure 5-23 | Page properties set for the top frame page

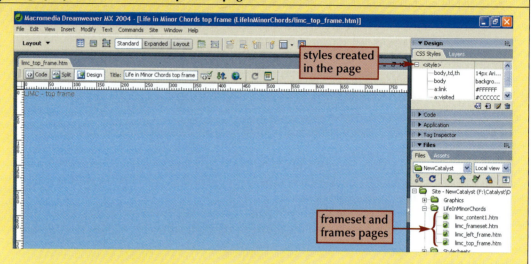

Next, you will export the styles to an external style sheet.

To export page properties to an external style sheet:

1. Click **File** on the menu bar, point to **Export**, and then click **CSS Styles**. The Export Styles As CSS File dialog box opens.

2. Navigate to the **Stylesheets** folder in the site's local root folder, type **limc_styles.css** in the File Name text box, and then click the **Save** button. The new style sheet is created and saved in the Stylesheets folder.

   Because you exported the styles to an external style sheet, you'll delete the styles from the page.

3. Select **<style>** in the CSS Styles panel, and then click the **Delete CSS Style** button. The styles are deleted from the page and the page no longer displays the formatting.

You'll attach the external style sheet to each of the pages in the frameset.

To attach an external style sheet to pages in a frameset:

1. Click the **Attach Style Sheet** button in the CSS Styles panel. The Attach External Style Sheet dialog box opens.

2. Click the **Browse** button beside the File/URL text box. The Select Style Sheet File dialog box opens.

3. Double-click **limc_styles.css** in the **Stylesheets** folder, and then click the **OK** button in the Attach External Style sheet dialog box. The style sheet is attached to the page and the page elements are again formatted.

4. Save the page.

   Now, you'll attach the style sheet to the other documents that are displayed in the limc_frameset.

5. Close the limc_top_frame.htm page, and then open the **limc_frameset.htm** page. Notice that the HTML document that is displayed in the top frame is formatted with the styles you just created. See Figure 5-24.

External style sheet attached to top frame of frameset **Figure 5-24**

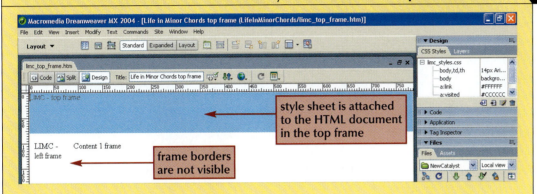

6. Click **View** on the menu bar, point to **Visual Aids**, and then click **Frame Borders**. The frame borders are visible. See Figure 5-25.

Frame borders displayed in frameset **Figure 5-25**

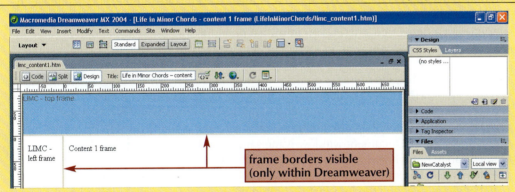

7. Click in the **lower-left frame** in the Document window to select it, click the **Attach Style Sheet** button in the CSS Styles panel, and then attach the **limc_styles.css** style sheet to the page.

8. Click in the **lower-right frame** in the Document window to select it, click the **Attach Style Sheet** button in the CSS Styles panel, and then attach the **limc_styles.css** style sheet to the page.

9. Click the **gray border** around the page to select the frameset, click **File** on the menu bar, and then click **Save All** to save the changes you made to all the frames. See Figure 5-26.

Figure 5-26 **Formatted frameset**

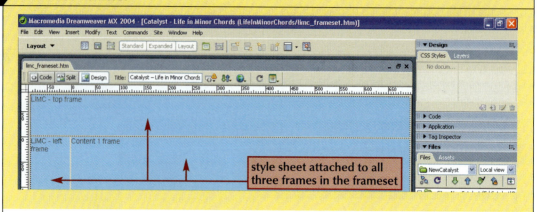

Next, you will use the Frames panel to adjust the frame and frameset attributes.

Adjusting Frame and Frameset Attributes

You set and adjust attributes for each frameset and frame individually. This enables you to customize the way each frame is displayed in the browser. For example, you can make the borders of one frame visible and make the borders of other frames invisible. To adjust the attributes of a frame or frameset, you must first open the frameset page and then select the frame or frameset you want to modify in the Frames panel. The Frames panel enables you to select and adjust the frame and frameset information that is contained in the frameset page. Remember, the frameset contains all the instructions for creating the frames, and the individual HTML pages contain the content that is displayed in the frames. When you select a frame in the Document window, you are actually selecting the HTML document contained in that frame (because the frameset page is not actually displayed). Selecting the frameset in the Document window is the same as selecting the frameset from the Frames panel, but it only provides you with access to the main frameset information (not the elements in the frameset page). When you select a frame or frameset from the Frames panel, you are selecting the information within the frameset page that pertains to the selected item.

You will open the Frames panel and select the frames and framesets in the limc_frameset.htm page.

To select frames and framesets in the Frames panel:

1. Click **Window** on the menu bar, and then click **Frames**. The Frames panel opens below the Files panel group.
2. Click in the **top frame** in the Frames panel. The top frame is selected in the Document window, and its attributes are visible in the Property inspector. See Figure 5-27.

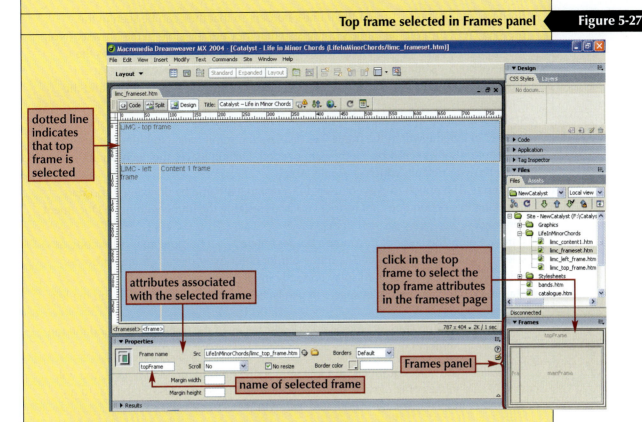

Figure 5-27 Top frame selected in Frames panel

3. Click the **top frame** in the Document window. The attributes for the HTML document displayed in the top frame are visible in the Property inspector.
4. Click the **left frame** in the Frames panel. The leftFrame element is selected within the frameset, and the leftFrame attributes are visible in the Property inspector.
5. Click the **outermost border** in the Frames panel. The limc_frameset is selected and the frameset attributes are visible in the Property inspector.

You will explore frame attributes, and then set the attributes for the frames you have created.

Adjusting Frame Attributes

You adjust the attributes of frames by selecting the frame in the Frames panel and changing its attributes in the Property inspector. Frame attributes include:

- **Frame Name.** A descriptive name you give the frame. The frame name will appear in the Property inspector when the frame is selected, and the name will appear in the Frames panel. The name will also be used for hyperlink targets, so the name must begin with a letter and cannot include spaces or special characters. Also, the frameset uses these names as a reference to know where to load the file.
- **Src (Source).** The filename of the page that will appear in the frame. If you have already saved the frame, the filename you assigned will appear in this text box.

- **Borders.** The option to turn on the frame's borders so that they can be seen in the browser (Yes), turn off the frame's borders so that they are invisible in the browser (No), or default to the frameset settings (Default). The frame border setting overrides the frameset border setting. However, the border can be turned off only if all adjacent frames borders are also set to No, or if all adjacent frames are set to Default and the frameset is set to No.
- **Scroll.** The option to display scroll bars when there is not enough room to display the content of a frame within the frame. Yes displays the scroll bars. No hides the scroll bars. Auto displays scroll bars if they are needed. Default leaves the decision up to the user's browser default, which is usually Auto.
- **No Resize.** The option to prevent users from resizing a frame by dragging its borders. Checking this option does not restrict you from resizing the frame within the Document window.
- **Border Color.** The color of the frame's border entered as a hexadecimal color code or selected with the color picker. The frame border color overrides any frameset border color. This attribute does not display correctly in all browsers.
- **Margin Width.** The amount of space, in pixels, between the frame content and the left and right borders.
- **Margin Height.** The amount of space, in pixels, between the frame content and the top and bottom borders.

You will set the frame attributes for the frames in the limc_frameset.htm page. You will customize the frame name of each frame, and then set the borders to 0, scroll bar to no, resize option to no, and margin width and height to 0.

To set the frame attributes:

1. Select the **top frame** in the Frames panel.
2. Type **LIMCtop** in the Frame name text box in the Property inspector, press the **Enter** key, and then verify that **limc_top_frame.htm** appears in the Src text box. The top frame in the Frames panel is named **LIMCtop**.
3. Click the **Borders** list arrow and click **No**, and then click the **Scroll** list arrow and click **No**, if necessary.
4. Click the **No Resize** check box to check it, if necessary.
5. Type **0** in the Margin Width text box, and then type **0** in the Margin Height text box. See Figure 5-28.

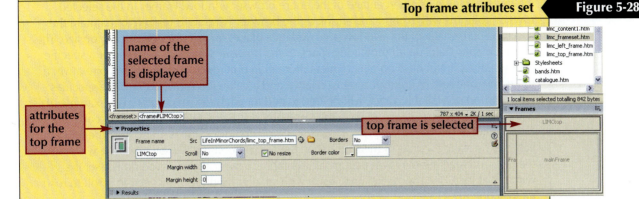

Figure 5-28 Top frame attributes set

6. Click the **left frame** in the Frames panel.
7. Type **LIMCleft** in the Frame name text box in the Property inspector, press the **Enter** key, and then verify that **limc_left_frame.htm** appears in the Src text box.
8. If necessary, click **No** in the Borders list, click **No** in the Scroll list, click the **No Resize** check box to check it, type **0** in the Margin Width text box, and then type **0** in the Margin Height text box.
9. Select the **right frame** (main frame) in the Frames panel.
10. Type **LIMCcontent** in the Frame name text box in the Property inspector, press the **Enter** key, and then verify that **limc_content1.htm** appears in the Src text box.
11. If necessary, click **No** in the Borders list, click **Auto** in the Scroll list, click the **No Resize** check box to check it, type **0** in the Margin Width text box, and then type **0** in the Margin Height text box.
12. Click **File** on the menu bar, and then click **Save All**.

Next, you will adjust the attributes of the frameset.

Adjusting Frameset Attributes

Frameset attributes are adjusted in the same way that frame attributes are adjusted: by selecting the frameset in the Frames panel and changing its attributes in the Property inspector. When you use nested framesets (such as the lower frame of the LIMC page, which is divided into a nested left frame and right frame), Dreamweaver inserts additional framesets within the code of the main frameset page to designate the nested frames. In addition to selecting and setting the attributes of the main frameset for the page, you can select and set attributes for the nested framesets. You select a nested frameset by selecting the raised border that surrounds the nested frameset in the Frames panel. (In this case, a raised border surrounds the left and right frame because the lower frame has been split into a nested frameset.)

Frameset attributes include two of the same attributes available for frames: borders and border color. You can also set the border width and the frame size in the frameset attributes. Border width, measured in pixels, affects all the borders within the frameset. The frame size is set separately for each frame within the frameset. You can set the frame size of frames by clicking the buttons at the top or the left of the RowCol Selection box, typing a value for the selected row or column in the Value text box, and selecting a unit of measure for the selected row or column in the Units list. Frames that are in the selected row or column will resize to the entered values. The unit of measure for rows and columns can be pixels, percent, or relative. Pixels sizes the row or column to the specified pixel value. Percent sizes the row or column as a percentage of the entire browser window. Frames in the selected rows or columns will expand and shrink as the browser window is resized to maintain the specified percentage of the window area. Relative places an asterisk in the code for size. The asterisk means "take up all remaining space in the browser window." If you enter a specific relative value, it will have no effect unless more than one row or column is set to relative. If more than one row or column is set to relative and a value is specified, the value specifies what portion of available space will be designated for each row or column. For example, if two rows are set to relative and have the same numeric value (1, 2, 3, etc.), then each will occupy half of the available space. However, if one column value is 1 and the other column value is 2 (totaling 3 units of measure), then the second column will be twice the width of the first, and together they will occupy all available browser space. If you do not set the width of at least one row to Relative, users with smaller monitors may need to scroll to read all the content.

You'll set the frameset attributes for the new page.

To set frameset attributes:

1. Click the **outermost border** of the frameset in the Frames panel. The Property inspector shows the frameset attributes.

2. If necessary, in the Property inspector, click the **Borders** list arrow, click **No**, and then type **0** in the Border Width text box.

3. In the Property inspector, click the **top box** in the RowCol Selection box, type **130** in the Value text box, and then, if necessary, click the **Units** list arrow and click **Pixels**.

4. In the Property inspector, click the **bottom box** in the RowCol Selection box, and then, if necessary, type **1** in the Value text box, click the **Units** list arrow, and click **Relative**.

   Next, you will set the attributes for the nested frameset.

5. Click the **nested frameset border** in the Frames panel. The nested frameset includes the lower-left and lower-right frames. See Figure 5-29.

Figure 5-29   **Nested frameset selected**

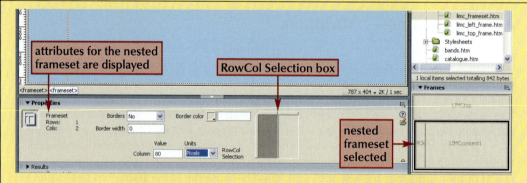

6. If necessary, in the Property inspector, click the **Borders** list arrow, click **No**, and then type **0** in the Border Width text box.

7. In the Property inspector, click the **left column** in the RowCol Selection box, type **100** in the Value text box, click the **Units** list arrow, and then click **Pixels**.

8. In the Property inspector, click the **right column** in the RowCol Selection box, and then, if necessary, type **1** in the Value text box, click the **Unit** list arrow, and click **Relative**.

9. Click **File** on the menu bar, and then click **Save All**. The changes you made are saved.

10. Preview the page in a browser. See Figure 5-30.

Frameset page previewed in a browser | Figure 5-30

In this session, you've created a new Web page with frames for the Life in Minor Chords band, set the properties for the HTML documents that are displayed in the frames, set attributes for the frames, and set attributes for the framesets. In the next session, you'll add content to the frames.

Session 5.2 Quick Check | Review

1. What are frames?
2. When a Web page contains frames, what can each frame contain?
3. What is a frameset?
4. Why does Dreamweaver create NoFrames content when you create frames?
5. True or False? The only way to create frames on a page in Dreamweaver is to use one of the preset frames by clicking a button in the Frames list in the Layout category on the Insert bar.
6. What is a nested frameset?
7. Why do you need to save a frameset?

Session 5.3

Inserting Frames and NoFrames Content

You need to add content to the frames that you created for the Life in Minor Chords page. You also need to add NoFrames content for browsers that cannot display frames.

Adding Content to Frames

There are several ways to place content in a frame. You can open the frameset page, select the HTML document in a frame, and create the content in the frame using the same techniques that you would use to insert content into a Web page that does not contain frames. You can open the HTML document in the Document window and create the content in the regular way. (When you open the frameset, the content will be displayed.) You can also select a Web page you have already created as the Source in the Property inspector when the frame properties are selected. The existing Web page will open in the selected frame by default whenever the frameset page is opened. If the frameset is open, you must resave each frame every time that you make a change within that frame. Remember, you can use the Save All command on the File menu to save all the open frames and the frameset in one step.

Brian asks you to add the content to the frames of the Life in Minor Chords page. You'll insert a graphic of the Life in Minor Chords logo with background artwork taken from the band's latest CD in the top frame of the new Web page. Then you'll insert and format text in the main frame of the Web page.

To insert a graphic into a frame:

1. If you took a break after the previous session, make sure the **NewCatalyst** site is open, the **limc_frameset.htm** page is open, and the frame borders are displayed.
2. Click in the **top frame** in the Document window. You will insert the graphic into this frame.
3. Delete the text in the frame, click the **Images** list arrow in the Common category on the Insert bar, and then click the **Image** button. The Select Image Source dialog box opens.
4. Navigate to the **Tutorial.05\Tutorial** folder included with your Data Files, and then double-click **LifeBanner.jpg**. The image is added in the top frame of the page. See Figure 5-31.

| Figure 5-31 | Frameset page with inserted graphic |

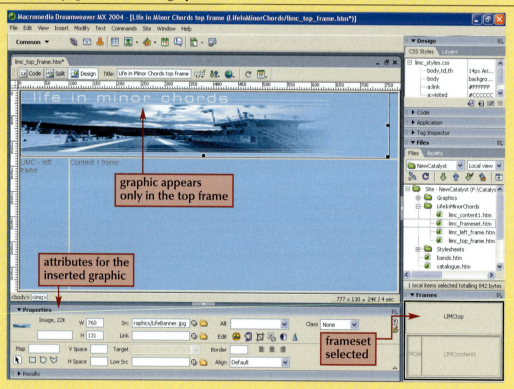

5. Click **File** on the menu bar, click **Save Frame**, and then close the page.

Next, you'll open the HTML document that is displayed in the right frame of the frameset page in the Document window and add the text content to the document. Then you will format the text. Brian has supplied the text in a Word document, so you can copy and paste the content rather than retyping it. You also want to format the text you add to the frame.

To paste text into a document:

1. Open the **LIMCmainframetext.doc** document located in the **Tutorial\Tutorial.05** folder included with your Data Files in Word or another word processing program, copy the entire document, and then close the document and word processing program.

2. Open the **limc_content1.htm** page, select the text in the Document window, click **Edit** on the menu bar, and then click **Paste Text** to paste the text you copied. The copied content appears in the Document window.

3. Click the **New CSS Style** button in the CSS Styles panel, and create a CSS style for the heading text named **.limc_heading**. In the Type category, type **28** in the Size text box, click **pixels** in the Size list if necessary, click **Lowercase** in the Case list, type **#FFFFFF** in the Color text box, then click the **OK** button to create the style.

4. Select the heading text, click the **Style** list arrow in the Property inspector, and then click **.limc_heading**. The style is applied to the heading.

5. Select the last two paragraphs of the body text (beginning with "'Sure we sold out...'" and ending with "'...makes us authentic.'"), and then click the **Text Indent** button in the Property inspector. The text in the limc_content1.htm page is formatted.

6. Save and close the page, and then save and close the limc_styles.css style sheet.

7. Open the **limc_frameset.htm** page. The new content is displayed in the right frame. See Figure 5-32.

Frameset page with content **Figure 5-32**

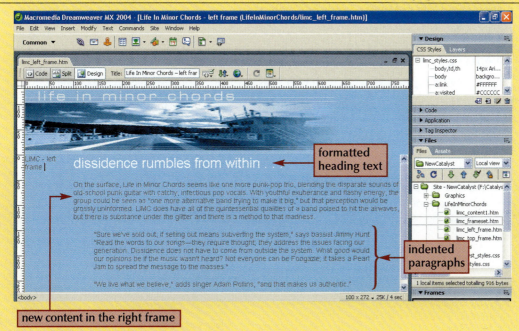

8. Preview the page in a browser.

Next, you will add NoFrames content to the page.

Adding NoFrames Content

The NoFrames code is automatically added to the HTML code for the frameset page when you create frames in Dreamweaver. You can add NoFrames content just as you would add content to any other frame or Web page. The content you add will be displayed in place of the regular Web page when a user's browser does not support frames. (Frames are not supported in browsers earlier than Netscape 2.0 and Internet Explorer 3.0, or in some devices, such as PDAs, that support limited Web browsing.) The NoFrames content should be simple text that explains that the page users are attempting to view has frames and cannot be seen by their browser. The text should also provide a brief explanation of the purpose of the page, links to alternate pages where users can locate information, or contact information so users have another way to get the information they were trying to obtain from the Web page.

Reference Window

Adding NoFrames Content

- Open the frameset page in the Document window.
- Click Modify on the menu bar, point to Frameset, then click Edit NoFrames Content.
- Type the content you want to appear in browsers that cannot display frames.
- Add a link to the home page.
- Click File on the menu bar, and then click Save All.

You'll add content to the NoFrames code for the LIMC frameset page. The content will be text that provides users with a link to the main Catalyst site so they can get more information about Life in Minor Chords or Catalyst.

To add NoFrames content to a frameset page:

1. Click **Modify** on the menu bar, point to **Frameset**, and then click **Edit NoFrames Content**.

2. Type **This Web page uses frames. Click here for more information about the band Life in Minor Chords or about the Catalyst label.**

   You'll link the word *here* to the home page of the Catalyst site.

3. Select the word *here*.

4. Click the **Browse for File** button in the Property inspector, navigate to the site's local root folder, and then double-click **index.htm**. The path to the home page appears in the Link text box. See Figure 5-33.

Figure 5-33 NoFrames content added

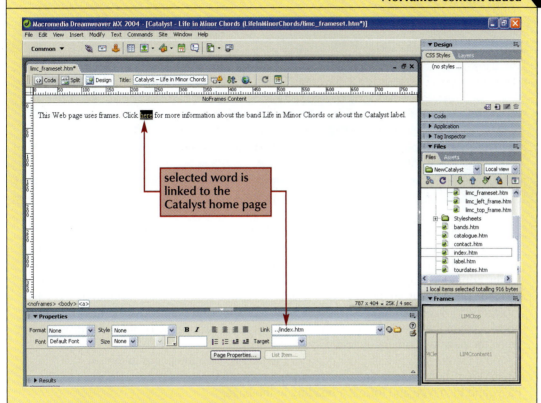

You will switch back to the frameset page.

5. Click **Modify** on the menu bar, point to **Frameset**, and then click **Edit NoFrames Content** to toggle back to the frameset page.

6. Click **File** on the menu bar, click **Save All**, and then close the page. The frameset page is saved with the NoFrames content.

You can use hyperlinks with frames.

Using Hyperlinks with Frames

When you click a hyperlink in a Web page, the linked page usually replaces the current page in the browser window. In a frames page, where more than one HTML page composes one Web page, you don't always want the linked page to replace the HTML page in the same frame. For example, consider the common practice of creating a navigation bar in a frame at the left or top of a page. When a user clicks an element in the navigation bar, the linked page opens in the main frame of the Web page (rather than replacing the navigation bar). You can change where a Web page will open by modifying the target for the linked page. In addition to specifying a browser window in which a linked Web page will open, a target can also specify the frame in which the linked page will open. Figure 5-34 lists the target options.

Figure 5-34 Target options

Target Option	Description
_blank	Opens the link in a new browser window and leaves the current window open.
_parent	Opens the link in the parent frameset if you are using nested framesets. (Remember, the parent frameset is the frame that holds the nested frameset.)
_self	Opens the new page in the same frame as the link. If there are no frames, self replaces the old page with the new page. This is the default target.
_top	Replaces all the frames and the content of the current Web page with the content of the new page.
named frames	Opens the new page in the frame you select. The names you gave each frame appear at the end of the Target list.

Brian wants you to create targeted hyperlinks for the frames you created for the Life in Minor Chords page. You'll create a navigation bar in the nested left frame and then target the links to the LIMCcontent frame. Brian has another team member creating the content for the additional pages, so you need to create placeholder pages for that content. Also, you'll create a link from the LIMCbanner.gif to the limc_content1.htm page and target the link to the LIMCcontent frame. This will provide the illusion that the user is linking to the home page of the LIMC site when the logo is clicked, because the content that displayed when the page was originally loaded will reappear.

You'll create each placeholder page for the targets, save the pages in the LifeInMinorChords folder, enter a page title, attach the limc_styles.css style sheet to the page, and then type and format a heading in the page.

To create placeholder pages:

1. Click **HTML** in the Create New section in the Start page. A new HTML page opens.
2. Save the page in the **LifeInMinorChords** folder in the site's local root folder with the filename **limc_content_history.htm**.
3. Type **LIMC - History** in the Title text box on the Document toolbar, and then press the **Enter** key.
4. Click the **Attach Style Sheet** button in the CSS Styles panel, and then attach the **limc_styles.css** style sheet to the page.
5. Type **LIMC History** in the page, select the text you typed, click the **Style** list arrow in the Property inspector, and then click **limc_heading**. The style is applied to the heading text. See Figure 5-35.

Tutorial 5 Adding Shared Site Elements | Dreamweaver **DRM 285**

Life in Minor Chords History page Figure 5-35

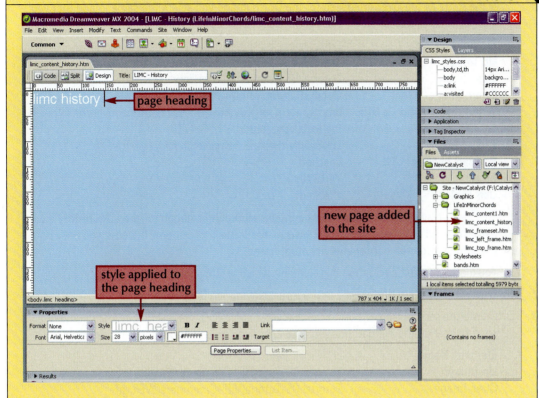

6. Save and close the page.

   You'll repeat this process for each placeholder HTML document you need to create.

7. Repeat Steps 1 through 6 to create the following the pages.

Filename	Title	Page heading
limc_content_members.htm	LIMC - Members	LIMC Members
limc_content_cds.htm	LIMC - CDs	LIMC CDs
limc_content_tours.htm	LIMC - Tours	LIMC Tours
limc_content_photos.htm	LIMC - Photos	LIMC Photos

Next, you'll insert the navigation bar in the nested left frame of the limc_frameset.htm page. Each element in the navigation bar will display graphics. For each element, you'll specify the linked page and the target frame. (You will add alternate text for each element in the Review Assignments.)

To create a navigation bar with targeted links:

1. Open the **limc_frameset.htm** page in the Document window, click **View** on the menu bar, point to **Visual Aids**, and then click **Frame Borders** to make the frame border visible.

2. Click in the **lower-left frame** to make it active, select the text in the frame, and then press the **Delete** key. The lower-left frame is active and empty.

3. Click the **Images** list arrow in the Common category on the Insert bar, and then click the **Navigation Bar** button. The Insert Navigation Bar dialog box opens.

▸ **4.** Create the first element using the following name and images. (Note that the Down image is the same as the Over image, so for the Down image you select the same image that you stored in the Graphics folder when you specified the Over image.)

Element Name	LIMChistory
Up Image	Tutorial.05\Tutorial\LIMChistory.gif
Over Image	Tutorial.05\Tutorial\LIMChistoryOVER.gif
Down Image	Catalyst\Graphics\LIMChistoryOVER.gif
When Clicked, Go To URL	limc_content_history.htm (in the LifeInMinorChords folder in the local root folder)
Target in	LIMCcontent (this is the name of the target frame)
Preload Images	checked
Insert	Vertically
Use Tables	checked

The Insert Navigation Bar dialog box contains all the information for the LIMChistory element. You did not check the Show Down Image Initially check box, because you are using the same navigation bar for every content frame.

You'll add the next navigation bar element, which is LIMCmembers.

▸ **5.** Click the **Add Item** button [+] in the Insert Navigation Bar dialog box.

▸ **6.** Create the second element using the following name and images. Remember you do not need to change the Preload Images, Insert, or Use Tables options for each element.

Element Name	LIMCmembers
Up Image	Tutorial.05\Tutorial\LIMCmembers.gif
Over Image	Tutorial.05\Tutorial\LIMCmembersOVER.gif
Down Image	Catalyst\Graphics\LIMCmembersOVER.gif
When Clicked, Go To URL	limc_content_members.htm (in the LifeInMinorChords folder in the local root folder)
Target in	LIMCcontent

▸ **7.** Click the **Add Item** button [+] in the Insert Navigation Bar dialog box, and then create the third element using the following name and images.

Element Name	LIMCcds
Up Image	Tutorial.05\Tutorial\LIMCcds.gif
Over Image	Tutorial.05\Tutorial\LIMCcdsOVER.gif
Down Image	Catalyst\Graphics\LIMCcdsOVER.gif
When Clicked, Go To URL	limc_content_cds.htm (in the LifeInMinorChords folder in the local root folder)
Target in	LIMCcontent

▸ **8.** Click the **Add Item** button [+] in the Insert Navigation Bar dialog box, and then create the fourth element using the following name and images.

Element Name	LIMCtours
Up Image	Tutorial.05\Tutorial\LIMCtours.gif
Over Image	Tutorial.05\Tutorial\LIMCtoursOVER.gif
Down Image	Catalyst\Graphics\LIMCtoursOVER.gif
When Clicked, Go To URL	limc_content_tours.htm (in the LifeInMinorChords folder in the local root folder)
Target in	LIMCcontent

9. Click the **Add Item** button ⊕ in the Insert Navigation Bar dialog box, and then create the fifth element using the following name and images.

Element Name	LIMCphotos
Up Image	Tutorial.05\Tutorial\LIMCphotos.gif
Over Image	Tutorial.05\Tutorial\LIMCphotosOVER.gif
Down Image	Catalyst\Graphics\LIMCphotosOVER.gif
When Clicked, Go To URL	limc_content_photos.htm (in the LifeInMinorChords folder in the local root folder)
Target in	LIMCcontent

   All the elements for the navigation bar are created with the appropriate names, graphics, linked pages, and target frames.

10. Click the **OK** button in the Insert Navigation Bar dialog box. The navigation bar appears in the nested left frame. See Figure 5-36.

Navigation bar in the nested lower-left frame Figure 5-36

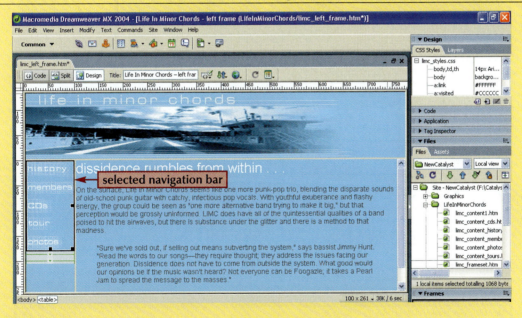

11. Click **File** on the menu bar, click **Save All**, and then preview the page in a browser.

Next, you'll use the Property inspector to create the targeted link from the logo in the top frame to the HTML document that was originally displayed in the LIMCcontent frame. You'll target the link to open in the LIMCcontent frame.

To create a targeted link using the Property inspector:

1. Click the **graphic** in the top frame to select it, click the **Browse for File** button 📁 next to the Link text box in the Property inspector, and then double-click the **limc_content1.htm** page in the **LifeInMinorChords** folder in the site's local root folder.

2. Click the **Target** list arrow in the Property inspector, and then click **LIMCcontent**. See Figure 5-37.

| Figure 5-37 | Target information for the top frame |

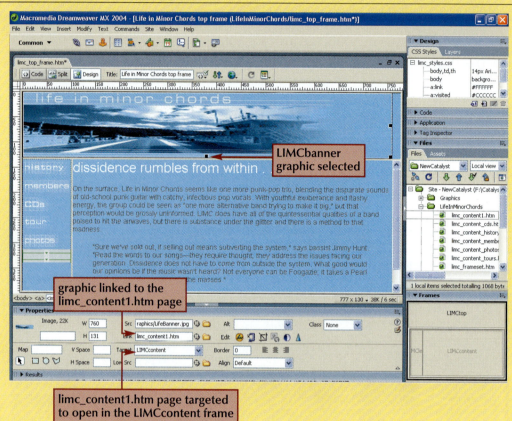

3. Click **File** on the menu bar, and then click **Save All**.
4. Preview the page in a browser, click each link in the navigation bar in the left frame, and then click the graphic link in the top frame. See Figure 5-38.

| Figure 5-38 | Completed limc_frameset.htm page previewed in browser |

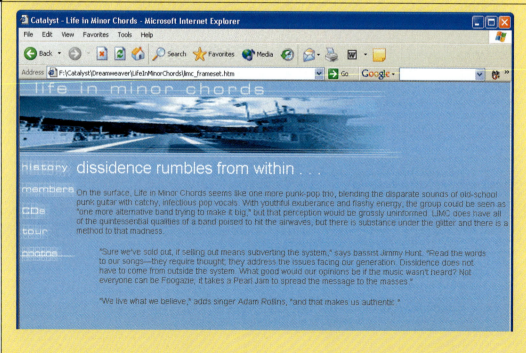

> 5. Close the browser window, and then close the page.

Next, you'll add links from the Bands page and the Catalogue page to the limc_frameset.htm page. You'll target the links to open in a new browser window so that the limc_frameset page does not replace the Catalyst page. This enables the user to easily return to the main portion of the Catalyst site.

> **To create additional targeted links using the Property inspector:**
>
> 1. Open the **bands.htm** page in the Document window, and then select the **Life In Minor Chords** subheading text.
> 2. Click the **Browse for File** button in the Property inspector, and then double-click **limc_frameset.htm** in the **LifeInMinorChords** folder in the site's local root folder.
> 3. Click the **Target** list arrow in the Property inspector, and then click **_blank** to open the link in a new browser window.
> 4. Save the page, preview the page in a browser, and then click the **LIFE IN MINOR CHORDS** link. The Life in Minor Chords page opens in a new browser window.
> 5. Close both browser windows, and then close the page.
> 6. Open the **catalogue.htm** page, select the **Life in Minor Chords CD cover** graphic, and then link the CD cover to the **limc_frameset.htm** page targeted to open in a new browser window.
> 7. Save the page, preview the page in a browser, and then click the **Life in Minor Chords CD cover** graphic. The linked page opens in a new browser window.
> 8. Close both browser windows, and then close the page.

You'll look at the tags used with frameset pages.

Reviewing HTML Associated with Frames and Targets

When you use frames in a Web page, all the frame tags associated with the Web page are in the frameset page. Additional content pages are simply regular Web pages that are targeted to open in one of the frames. The following three tags, described below and shown in Figure 5-39, are associated with frameset pages:

- **Frameset tags.** A set of frameset tags surround the frameset and, if nested frames are used, additional sets of frameset tags surround the nested frames within the parent frameset. The opening frameset tag contains the values for the frameset attributes.
- **Frame tag.** A frame tag is inserted between the opening and closing frameset tags for each frame in the frameset. There is no closing frame tag. It is one of the few HTML tags that is not in a pair. The frame tag contains the values for the frame attributes.
- **Noframes tags.** The noframes tags are inserted after the closing frameset tag. They surround content that is seen by browsers that do not support frames.

Figure 5-39 HTML frame tags

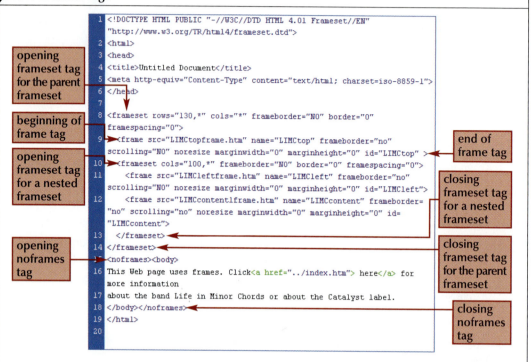

When you set a target for a hyperlink, the target information is added to the HTML code for the hyperlink in the following format:

```
<a href="theURL" target="value">Linked text or graphic</a>
```

where the target value options are the same options listed in the Target list in the Property inspector: _blank, _parent, _self, _top, and named frames.

Next, you will examine the code of the limc_frameset page and review the frameset, frame, and noframes tags—as well as the hyperlink tags with target information inserted into them.

To examine HTML code in the frameset page:

1. Open the **limc_frameset.htm** page in the Document window, and then select the frameset in the Frames panel.

2. Click the **Show Code View** button on the Document toolbar. The code for the limc_frameset.htm page appears in the Document window. The parent frameset tags and everything between them are highlighted. See Figure 5-40.

Figure 5-40

Code for the limc_frameset.htm page

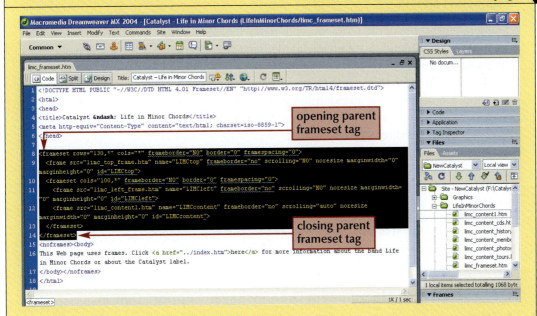

Trouble? If your screen does not match the screen shown in Figure 5-40, click the Show Design View button on the Document toolbar, select the outermost frame in the Frames panel again, and then repeat Step 2.

▸ 3. Locate the opening frameset tag and examine the frameset attributes and their values.

▸ 4. Right-click the opening frameset tag, click **Reference** on the context menu, and then read the reference information in the Reference panel of the Code panel group.

▸ 5. Locate the closing frameset tag.

▸ 6. Find the nested frameset, and then locate the first frame in the nested frameset.

▸ 7. Examine the frame attributes in the first frame.

▸ 8. Right-click the frame tag, click **Reference** on the context menu, and then read the reference information in the Reference panel of the Code panel group.

▸ 9. Click the **Show Design View** button on the Document toolbar, and then close the page.

▸ 10. Collapse the Frames panel group and the Code panel group, and then expand the Files panel group.

You can use the Dreamweaver Support Center to troubleshoot common frame problems.

Finding Solutions to Common Frame Problems

The Macromedia Dreamweaver Support Center (*http://www.macromedia.com/support/dreamweaver*) contains a wealth of information pertaining to frames. It can be a great resource when you need to find solutions for common frames problems. From the Support Center, you can also access Macromedia Exchange for Dreamweaver, which contains a number of Dreamweaver add-ons that other developers have written and decided to share. You can download and install these add-on tools to your copy of Dreamweaver free of charge. Two of the most popular frame solutions on Macromedia Exchange for Dreamweaver are:

- **FrameJammer.** One of the problems with pages that use frames is that the individual frames can be loaded independently of the frameset. For example, a search engine might follow the links in your navigation frame and index the individual content pages. Clicking one of these links would then load the content page without its surrounding frameset. FrameJammer is an extension you can download that will insert code into any Web page that uses frames to ensure that your page is always shown in its frameset, even if a user links directly to the frame.
- **Frame Buster.** Some Web sites keep one of their frames open while they display your pages, and some Web pages even surround a page from your Web site with their navigation systems and logo. Frame Buster is an extension you can download that will insert code into your Web pages to prevent them from being loaded within a frameset.

Brian asks you to log on to the Macromedia Dreamweaver Support Center and research possible problems with frames pages.

To do research on Macromedia Dreamweaver Support Center:

1. Start your browser, type **www.macromedia.com/support/dreamweaver** into the Address text box, and then press the **Enter** key. The Macromedia Dreamweaver Support Center page opens. See Figure 5-41.

Figure 5-41   Macromedia Dreamweaver Support Center page

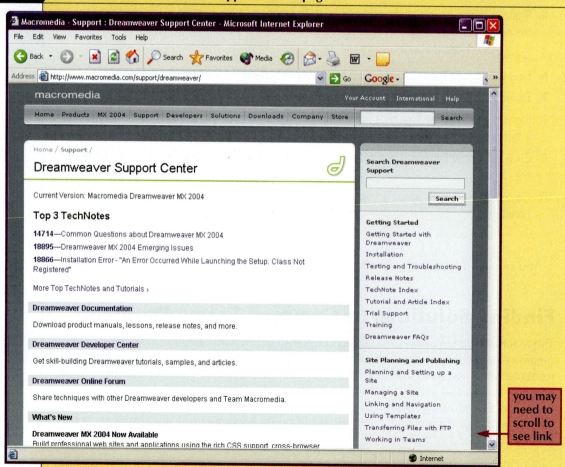

you may need to scroll to see link

2. Click the **Using Frames** link in the Creating and Designing Pages category in the right column in the page (you may need to scroll). A list of tutorials, articles, and technical notes appears.

3. Click a link for a document that interests you, and read it. When you're finished, click the **Back** button on the browser toolbar twice to return to the Macromedia Dreamweaver Support Center.

4. Click the **Dreamweaver Exchange** link in the Downloads category at the bottom of the right column in the page. The Dreamweaver Exchange page opens.

5. Click the **Exchange Help** link at the bottom of the right column on the page to view the Macromedia Exchange Help page, click the **What is an extension?** link in the About Extensions category, read about Dreamweaver extensions, and then close the page.

6. Click the **Search Exchanges** link at the top of the page to open the Exchange Search page, type **frame** in the upper-left text box, select **Dreamweaver Exchange** from the list box, and then click the **Search** button. A list of extensions related to frames appears. See Figure 5-42.

Figure 5-42 — Search results for frame extensions

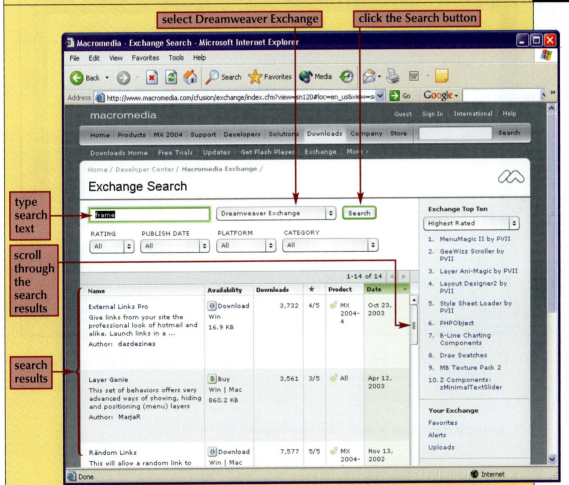

Trouble? If your search results differ from the list shown in Figure 5-42, extensions might have been added, removed, or updated since this book was published.

7. Click the **FrameJammer** link, and then read about the extension.

8. Click the **Developers** button on the navigation bar to open the Developer Center page, and then click the **Dreamweaver** link in the Product Developer Centers category to open the Dreamweaver Developer Center page.

9. Click the **Dreamweaver Online Forum** link to open the Dreamweaver Forums page, and then click the **Dreamweaver General Discussion** link.

10. Type **frames** in the Search Category text box, and then click the **Search!** button. A list of topics related to the keyword "frames" is loaded. See Figure 5-43.

Figure 5-43   Search results for frame discussion topics

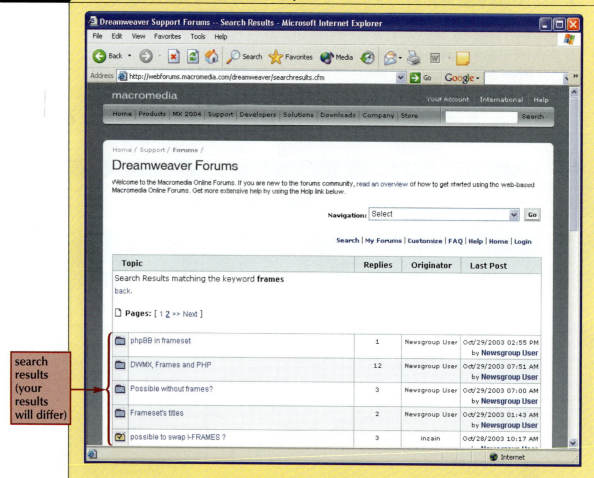

search results (your results will differ)

11. Click the link for the top folder to display the discussion related to that topic, read the information, and then close any open browser windows.

Before you end your work session, you'll update the remote site.

Updating the Web Site on the Remote Server

As a final review of the changes you made to the Catalyst site, you'll update the files on the remote server and review the pages over the Internet. You need to upload every page in the site because you have made changes on all of them. This includes the bands.htm page, the catalogue.htm page, the contact.htm page, the index.htm page, the label.htm page, the tourdates.htm page, and the whatshot.htm page, as well as all the pages in the LifeInMinorChords folder (limc_frameset.htm, LIMCcds.htm, LIMCcontent1frame.htm, LIMChistory.htm, limc_left_frame.htm, LIMCmembers.htm, LIMCphotos.htm, limc_top_frame.htm, and LIMCtours.htm). When you upload the pages, you will include dependent files so that the new graphics and new CSS styles are uploaded to the remote server. Then you'll preview the Catalyst site on the Web.

To upload a site to the remote server:

1. Click the **Connects to Remote Host** button on the Files panel toolbar.
2. Click the **View** list arrow on the Files panel toolbar, and then click **Local View**.
3. Select the **LifeInMinorChords** folder, the **Graphics** folder, and the **bands.htm**, **catalogue.htm**, **contact.htm**, **index.htm**, **label.htm**, **tourdates.htm**, and **whatshot.htm** files in the Local View list, and then click the **Put File(s)** button on the Files panel toolbar.

   Trouble? If you can't select only the files you want, click the Minus (–) button next to the LifeInMinorChords folder to collapse the file list in the folder, press and hold the Ctrl key, and then click the folders and files you want to upload.

4. Click the **Yes** button when asked if you want to include dependent files, because you have not selected the new dependent files for the site yet.
5. Click the **Disconnects from Remote Host** button on the Files panel toolbar, click the **View** list arrow on the Files panel toolbar, and then click **Local View**.

Next, you'll preview the updated site in a browser. The site will include all the new styles and text that you added to local version of the site.

To preview the updated site in a browser:

1. Start your browser, type the URL of your remote site in the Address bar on the browser toolbar, and then press the **Enter** key. The home page opens; you'll explore the remote site.
2. Click the **catalogue** link, click the **Life in Minor Chords CD cover** to open the Life in Minor Chords page in a new browser window, and then close the new browser window that opened.
3. Click the **bands** link in the Catalogue page, and then click the **LIFE IN MINOR CHORDS** subheading to open the Life in Minor Chords page in a new browser window.
4. In the Life in Minor Chords page, click the **history**, **members**, **CDs**, **tour**, and **photos** links to make sure that each link is appropriately targeted and that all of the HTML documents were uploaded.
5. Click the **graphic** at the top of the Life in Minor Chords page to redisplay the original information that appeared on the page when it was opened, and then close the Life in Minor Chords browser window.
6. On the home page, click the **label** link, click the **tour dates** link, click the **contact** link, and then click the **Catalyst** logo to return to the home page.
7. Click the **What's Hot at Catalyst** link.
8. Close both browser windows.

In this session, you added content to the frames you created, reviewed the HTML associated with frames and targets, and did research about frames on the Macromedia Dreamweaver Support Center.

Review

Session 5.3 Quick Check

1. Name two ways to insert content into a frame.
2. True or False? You can add NoFrames content to a frameset page.
3. What is typically added as NoFrames content for a frameset?
4. Why is it common practice to place a navigation bar in a frame?
5. True or False? A link cannot be targeted to open in a different frame on the page.
6. What are three HTML tags associated with frameset pages?

Review

Tutorial Summary

In this tutorial, you worked on shared site elements. You inserted a navigation bar into the Catalyst site, copied the navigation bar to all the pages in the Web site, and then modified the navigation bar. Then you learned about frames and framesets. You used several techniques to create frames. You saved the frames page, and then set page properties and attributes for frames and framesets. Next, you added content to the HTML documents in the frames, and then you created hyperlinks and targeted the links to specific frames. You explored the HTML behind frames and targets, and finally reviewed problems that are common in pages that use frames.

Key Terms

Down state	navigation bar	Over While Down state
element	nested frameset	parent frameset
frame	NoFrames content	Up state
frameset	Over state	

Practice

Practice the skills you learned in the tutorial.

Review Assignments

Data Files needed for the Review Assignments: DCbanner.jpg, DCbottombanner.jpg, DCcdsUp.jpg, DCcdsOver.jpg, DChistoryUp.jpg, DChistoryOver.jpg, DCmembersUp.jpg, DCmembersOver.jpg, DCphotosUp.jpg, DCphotosOver.jpg, DCtoursUp.jpg, DCtoursOver.jpg

Brian asks you to create a Web page for Dizzied Connections similar to the one you created for Life in Minor Chords. You will create a page with a navigation bar and frames. The Dizzied Connections page uses colors and a style similar to the Catalyst site, so you will attach the catalyst_styles.css style sheet to all the HTML documents to format the page. Because you do not want the background image from the Catalyst site to appear in each frame of the Dizzied Connections page, you will create an additional custom style called .dc_body and set the background color to #FFFFFF and the background image to none, then apply the style to the body tag in each document. When the page is complete, you'll link the new page to the band name in the Bands page. Once all of the changes are complete, you'll upload the Catalyst site to the Web server.

1. Open the NewCatalyst site that you modified in this tutorial, right-click the local root folder for your NewCatalyst site in the Files panel, click New Folder on the context menu, and then name the new folder "DizziedConnections."
2. Right-click the new folder in the Files panel, click New File on the context menu to create a new page in the DizziedConnections folder, and then name the page "dc_content.htm."
3. Open the dc_content.htm page in the Document window, click in the page in the Document window, and then click the Top and Bottom Frames button in the Frames list in the Layout category on the Insert bar to insert frames into the page.
4. Click in the top frame, click File on the menu bar, click Save Frame to open the Save As dialog box, navigate to the DizziedConnections folder in the local root folder of the NewCatalyst site, and then save the HTML document as "dc_top_frame.htm."
5. Click in the bottom frame, click File on the menu bar, click Save Frame to open the Save As dialog box, navigate to the DizziedConnections folder in the local root folder of the NewCatalyst site, and then save the frame as "dc_bottom_frame.htm."
6. Select the frameset, change the title to "Catalyst - Dizzied Connections," click File on the menu bar, click Save Frameset, and then save the frameset in the DizziedConnections folder as "dc_frameset.htm."
7. Click in the top frame, click the Attach Style Sheet button in the CSS Styles panel, and then attach the catalyst_styles.css style sheet. Attach the catalyst_styles.css style sheet to the documents in the middle and bottom frames.
8. Click in the top frame, change the title to "DC - top frame," click the New CSS Style button in the CSS Styles panel, click the Class style type, name the style ".dc_body," and define the style in the catalyst_styles.css style sheet. Click Background in the Category list, type "#FFFFFF" in the Background Color text box, click None in the Background Image list, and then click the OK button.
9. Click in the top frame if necessary, click the <body> tag on the status bar to select it, and then click .dc_body in the Style list in the Property inspector. The top frame displays a white background.
10. Click the Image button in the Images list in the Common category on the Insert bar, and then insert the **DCbanner.jpg** graphic located in the **Tutorial.05\Review** folder included with your Data Files. Notice that the graphic is 5 pixels from the left border; you'll change this to 0.
11. Expand the Tag Inspector panel group, select the .dc_body style in the CSS Styles panel, click the Show List View button in the CSS Properties panel if necessary, scroll to the margin-left attribute, click in the value side of the margin-left attribute, type "0," and then press the Enter key.
12. Collapse the Tag Inspector panel group, and then save and close the catalyst_styles.css style sheet.
13. Select the graphic, create a hyperlink to the dc_content.htm page, and then target the link to the main frame by selecting mainFrame from the Target list in the Property inspector. Save all the frames and the frameset.
14. Click in the middle frame, change the title to "DC - content," click the <body> tag to select it, then click dc_body in the Style list in the Property inspector to apply the style to the body tag. The tag in the status bar changes to <body.dc body> and the background changes to white.
15. Type "dizzied connections. . ." in the middle frame, select the text you just typed, and then apply the Heading 2 from the Format list in the Property inspector.

16. Click in the bottom frame, and then change the title to "DC - bottom frame."
17. Create a new Class style named ."dc_bottomframe" and defined in the catalyst_styles.css style sheet. In the Background category, insert the **DCbottombanner.jpg** graphic located in the **Tutorial.05\Review** folder included with your Data Files as the Background Image, click Left in the Horizontal Position list, and then click Top in the Vertical Position list.
18. Click in the bottom frame, select the body tag in the status bar, and then click dc_bottomframe in the Style list in the Property inspector to apply the style to the body tag in the document in the bottom frame. The background graphic is displayed.
19. Save all the frames and the frameset, and then close the page and the style sheet.
20. Create a new HTML page, save the new page as **dc_cds.htm** in the DizziedConnections folder in the site's local root folder. Attach the catalyst_styles.css style sheet to the page, apply the dc_body style to the body tag in the page, change the page title to "DC - CDs," type "Dizzied Connections - CDs . . ." in the page, apply the Heading 2 tag, and then save and close the page.
21. Repeat Step 20 to create the following pages: dc_history.htm, dc_members.htm, dc_photos.htm, and dc_tours.htm pages. Make sure you change the page title for each page and type appropriate heading text on each page (for example, for the dc_history page, type "Dizzied Connections - History . . .").
22. Open the dc_frameset.htm page, click at the top of the bottom frame, and then click the Navigation Bar button in the Images list in the Common category on the Insert bar to insert a navigation bar. (*Hint:* View the frame borders if necessary.)
23. Create the first element in the navigation bar using the following name and images. (*Hint:* The Down image is the same as the Up image, so for the Down image you select the same image that you stored in the Graphics folder when you specified the Up image.)

Element Name	DCcds
Up Image	Tutorial.05\Review\DCcdsUp.jpg
Over Image	Tutorial.05\Review\DCcdsOver.jpg
Down Image	Catalyst\Dreamweaver\Graphics\DCcdsUp.jpg
Alternate Text	Dizzied Connections CDs
When Clicked, Go To URL	DCcds.htm (in the DizziedConnections folder in the local root folder)
Target in	mainFrame
Preload Images	checked
Insert	Horizontally
Use Tables	checked

24. Click the Add Item button in the Insert Navigation Bar dialog box to add a new element to the navigation bar, using the following name and images.

Element Name	DChistory
Up Image	Tutorial.05\Review\DChistoryUp.jpg
Over Image	Tutorial.05\Review\DChistoryOver.jpg
Down Image	Catalyst\Dreamweaver\Graphics\DChistoryUp.jpg
Alternate Text	Dizzied Connections History
When Clicked, Go To URL	DChistory.htm (in the DizziedConnections folder in the local root folder)
Target in	mainFrame

25. Add a third element to the navigation bar using the following name and images.

Element Name	DCmembers
Up Image	Tutorial.05\Review\DCmembersUp.jpg
Over Image	Tutorial.05\Review\DCmembersOver.jpg
Down Image	Catalyst\Dreamweaver\Graphics\DCmembersUp.jpg
Alternate Text	Dizzied Connections Members
When Clicked, Go To URL	DCmembers.htm (in the DizziedConnections folder in the local root folder)
Target in	mainFrame

26. Add a fourth element to the navigation bar using the following name and images.

Element Name	DCphotos
Up Image	Tutorial.05\Review\DCphotosUp.jpg
Over Image	Tutorial.05\Review\DCphotosOver.jpg
Down Image	Catalyst\Dreamweaver\Graphics\DCphotosUp.jpg
Alternate Text	Dizzied Connections Photos
When Clicked, Go To URL	DCphotos.htm (in the DizziedConnections folder in the local root folder)
Target in	mainFrame

27. Add a fifth element to the navigation bar using the following name and images.

Element Name	DCtours
Up Image	Tutorial.05\Review\DCtoursUp.jpg
Over Image	Tutorial.05\Review\DCtoursOver.jpg
Down Image	Catalyst\Dreamweaver\Graphics\DCtoursUp.jpg
Alternate Text	Dizzied Connections Tours
When Clicked, Go To URL	DCtours.htm (in the DizziedConnections folder in the local root folder)
Target in	mainFrame

28. Click the OK button, click the Save All command on the File menu, preview the dc_frameset page in a browser, and then close the page.

29. Open the limc_left_frame.htm page in the Document window, click Modify on the menu bar, and then click Navigation Bar. To add alternate text for each element, click the element in the Nav Bar Element list, click in the Alternate Text text box, and then type "Life in Minor Chords - " followed by the name of the element; for example, for the LIMChistory element, type "Life in Minor Chords - History." Click the OK button, and then save and close the page.

30. Open the catalogue.htm page, select the Dizzied Connections CD cover graphic, and create a link to the dc_frameset.htm page, targeting the link to open in a new browser window (_blank), and then save and close the page.

31. Open the bands.htm page, select the Dizzied Connections subheading, and create a link to the dc_frameset.htm page, targeting the link to open in a new browser window, and then save the page.

32. Preview the site in a browser, test the new links, and then close the browser windows and the page.

33. Upload the site to your remote server, and then preview the site over the Web.

DRM 300 | Dreamweaver | Tutorial 5 Adding Shared Site Elements

Apply

Create a navigation bar for a Web site about small rural communities of northern Vietnam.

Case Problem 1

Data Files needed for this Case Problem: HprofessorhartUp.gif, HprofessorhartDown.gif, HlinguisticdifferencesUp.gif, HlinguisticdifferencesDown.gif, HculturalcrosspollinationUp.gif, HculturalcrosspollinationDown.gif, HritualsandpracticesUp.gif, HritualsandpracticesDown.gif, HcontactinformationUp.gif, HcontactinformationDown.gif

Hroch University Anthropology Department Professor Hart wants you to create a navigation bar for the site. An artist has already created the graphic elements that you will need. You will create the navigation bar in the home page of the site; then you will copy it to the other pages of the site: the prof_hart.htm page, the linguistic_differences.htm page, the cultural_cross_pollination.htm page, the rituals_and_practices.htm page, and the contact.htm page. You will then modify the navigation bar in these pages so the element that represents the selected page appears in the Down state when the page is loaded into a browser window.

1. Open the Hart site that you modified in Tutorial 4, Case 1, open the index.htm page in the Document window, delete the text links, and then place the insertion point below the red stripes.
2. Click the Navigation Bar button in the Images list in the Common category on the Insert bar. The Insert Navigation Bar dialog box opens.

Explore

3. Create the first element using the following name and images. The Down image is the same as the Over image, so for the Down image you select the same image that you stored in the Graphics folder for the Over image. (*Hint:* To save time, you can copy the text from the Over Image text box and paste it into the Down Image text box.)

Element Name	Hprofessorhart
Up Image	Tutorial.05\Cases\HprofessorhartUp.gif
Over Image	Tutorial.05\Cases\HprofessorhartDown.gif
Down Image	Hart\Dreamweaver\Graphics\HprofessorhartDown.gif
When Clicked, Go To URL	prof_hart.htm
Target in	Main Window
Preload Images	checked
Insert	Horizontally
Use Tables	checked

4. Add a second element to the navigation bar using the following name and images.

Element Name	Hlinguisticdifferences
Up Image	Tutorial.05\Cases\HlinguisticdifferencesUp.gif
Over Image	Tutorial.05\Cases\HlinguisticdifferencesDown.gif
Down Image	Hart\Dreamweaver\Graphics\HlinguisticdifferencesDown.gif
When Clicked, Go To URL	linguistic_differences.htm
Target in	Main Window

5. Add the third element using the following name and images.

Element Name	Hculturalcrosspollination
Up Image	Tutorial.05\Cases\HculturalcrosspollinationUp.gif
Over Image	Tutorial.05\Cases\HculturalcrosspollinationDown.gif
Down Image	Hart\Dreamweaver\Graphics\HculturalcrosspollinationDown.gif
When Clicked, Go To URL	cultural_cross_pollination.htm
Target in	Main Window

6. Add the fourth element using the following name and images.

Element Name	Hritualsandpractices
Up Image	Tutorial.05\Cases\HritualsandpracticesUp.gif
Over Image	Tutorial.05\Cases\HritualsandpracticesDown.gif
Down Image	Hart\Dreamweaver\Graphics\HritualsandpracticesDown.gif
When Clicked, Go To URL	rituals_and_practices.htm
Target in	Main Window

7. Add the fifth element using the following name and images.

Element Name	Hcontactinformation
Up Image	Tutorial.05\Cases\HcontactinformationUp.gif
Over Image	Tutorial.05\Cases\HcontactinformationDown.gif
Down Image	Hart\Dreamweaver\Graphics\HcontactinformationDown.gif
When Clicked, Go To URL	contact.htm
Target in	Main Window

Explore

8. Add appropriate Alternate Text to each element, and then click the OK button.
9. Save the page, and then preview the page in a browser.
10. Select the entire navigation bar, including the table, in the Document window, copy the navigation bar using the Copy HTML command on the Edit menu, and then save and close the page. (*Hint:* You can switch to Extended Tables mode, if necessary.)
11. Open the prof_hart.htm page, select the link text, delete it, paste the navigation bar into the page using the Paste HTML command on the Edit menu, and then save the page.

Explore

12. Delete any extra spaces that were added above or below the navigation bar, click the Navigation Bar command on the Modify menu, select the Hprofessorhart element, check the Show Down Image Initially check box, and then click the OK button. The navigation bar is modified to show the Down image of the Hprofessorhart element.
13. Save and close the page.
14. Repeat Steps 11 through 13 for the linguistic_differences.htm page, the cultural_cross_pollination.htm page, the rituals_and_practices.htm page, and the contact.htm page using the element that corresponds to the page as the Down image.
15. Preview the pages in a browser, clicking each link to test it, and then close the browser window.
16. Upload the site to your remote server, and then preview the site over the Web.

Case Problem 2

Challenge

Create a frames page with small graphics of paintings that link to larger graphics in a Web site for an art museum.

Data Files needed for this Case Problem: LoveCallSmall.jpg, AmongTheLedHorsesSmall.jpg, LucklessHunterSmall.jpg, RiderlessHorseSmall.jpg, AmongTheLedHorses.htm, TheRiderlessHorse.htm, TheLoveCall.htm, TheLucklessHunter.htm, AmongTheLedHorsesBig.jpg, RiderlessHorseBig.jpg, LoveCallBig.jpg, LucklessHunterBig.jpg

Museum of Western Art C. J. Strittmatter asks you to create a page for the artist Fredric Remington. The page will contain small graphics of some of the artist's more famous paintings. When the user clicks a painting, the page will display a larger version of the painting as well as a detailed description. You'll use frames for the new page and link the page to the artist's name in the artist page. Another designer has created content pages that you'll add to the site to complete the Fredric Remington page.

1. Open the Museum site that you modified in Tutorial 4, Case 2, and create a new folder named "Remington" in the site's local root folder.
2. Create a new page in the Remington folder with the filename "remington_content.htm," and then open the page.
3. Attach the museum_styles.css style sheet to the page, change the page title to "Museum of Western Art - Remington Content frame," and then save and close the page.
4. Repeat Steps 2 and 3 to create and format a new page named "remington_top.htm."

Explore
5. Open the remington_content.htm page in the Document window, add a top frame to the page by clicking the Top Frame button in the Frames list in the Layout category on the Insert bar, save the frameset in the Remington folder with the name "remington_frameset.htm."
6. View the frame borders in the Document window, if necessary.

Explore
7. Select the topFrame in the Frames panel, and then link the Src text box in the Property inspector to the remington_top.htm page in the Remington folder to load that page in the top frame when the page is displayed in a browser.
8. Select the frameset in the Frames panel, change the page title to "Museum of Western Art - Remington," and then save the frameset.

Explore
9. Select the mainframe (the bottom frame) in the Frames panel. The Src text box in the Property inspector displays the remington_content.htm page, which is the page that will load in the bottom frame when the page is displayed in the browser.
10. Click in the bottom frame and type "Click any of the Fredric Remington paintings to view a larger version and a detailed description."
11. Click in the top frame, type "The Art of Fredric Remington," and then apply the Heading 1 style to the text.
12. Press the Right Arrow key, press the Enter key, and then create a table in the top frame with 1 row, 4 columns, a cell padding of 5, no header cells, no caption, and no summary. Select the table, and then center-align it.
13. Insert the graphic file **LoveCallSmall.jpg** located in the **Tutorial.05\Cases** folder included with your Data Files in the first cell in the table. Drag the right border of the cell until it is snug against the graphic (there is a cell padding of 5 pixels so the border will remain 5 pixels from the edge of the graphic). Select the graphic and align the graphic to Middle in the Property inspector.
14. Insert the graphic file **AmongTheLedHorsesSmall.jpg** located in the **Tutorial.05\Cases** folder included with your Data Files in the second cell in the table. Resize the cell horizontally until it is snug against the graphic. Then select the graphic and align the graphic to Middle in the Property inspector.
15. Insert the graphic file **LucklessHunterSmall.jpg** located in the **Tutorial.05\Cases** folder included with your Data Files in the third cell in the table. Resize the cell horizontally until it is snug against the graphic. Then select the graphic and align the graphic to Middle in the Property inspector.
16. Insert the graphic file **RiderlessHorseSmall.jpg** located in the **Tutorial.05\Cases** folder included with your Data Files in the fourth cell in the table. Then select the graphic and align the graphic to Middle in the Property inspector. Save all the frames and the frameset.

Explore
17. Drag the lower border of the frame down to resize the frame until you can see the entire table and the page heading in the top frame. The bottom frame may almost disappear from view if the Document window is small.

Explore

18. Copy the following pages from the **Tutorial.05\Cases** folder included with your Data Files and paste them in the Remington folder: **AmongTheLedHorses.htm**, **TheRiderlessHorse.htm**, **TheLoveCall.htm**, and **TheLucklessHunter.htm**. To copy each page, display the site list in the Files panel, navigate to the **Tutorial.05\Cases** folder included with your Data Files, right-click the file you want to copy, point to Edit, click Copy on the context menu, navigate back to the Museum site local root folder, right-click the Remington folder in the Files panel, and then click Paste on the context menu.
19. Open the AmongTheLedHorses.htm page in the Document window, click in the left column of the table, and insert the **AmongTheLedHorsesBig.jpg** graphic located in the **Tutorial.05\Cases** folder included with your Data Files in the cell, and then save and close the page.
20. Repeat Step 19 for the TheRiderlessHorse.htm page, the TheLoveCall.htm page, and the TheLucklessHunter.htm page using the corresponding big graphic for each page (**RiderlessHorseBig.jpg**, **LoveCallBig.jpg**, and **LucklessHunterBig.jpg**).

Explore

21. Select the small **LoveCall.jpg** graphic in the first cell of the table in the top frame of the remington_frameset.htm page and link it to the TheLoveCall.htm page. Target the link to open in the bottom frame of the page by selecting mainFrame from the Target list in the Property inspector.
22. Repeat Step 21 for the AmongTheLedHorses, LucklessHunter, and RiderlessHorses graphics.
23. Create a Class style named ".image_border" and define it in the museum_styles.css style sheet. Click Border in the Category list, check the Same for All check boxes, if necessary, click Solid in the Top text box in the first row of the Style column, click Thin in the Top text box in the Width column, type "#ECB888" in the Top text box of the Color column, and then click the OK button.
24. Select each image, click the Class list arrow in the Property inspector, and then click image_border to apply the style to each of the following graphics: **LoveCallSmall.jpg**, **AmongTheLedHorsesSmall.jpg**, **LucklessHunterSmall.jpg**, and **RiderlessHorseSmall.jpg**. Click the Save All command on the File menu, and then close the page.
25. Open the artists.htm page, select the Fredric Remington heading text, and link the text to the remington_frameset.htm page. Target the link to open in a new browser window, and then save the page.
26. Preview the page in a browser, click the Fredric Remington link, click the links in the Remington page to test them, and then close the browser windows and the page.
27. Upload the site to your remote server, and then preview the site over the Web.

Challenge

Create a navigation bar and add frames to the Featured Books page in a Web site for an independent publisher of fringe writing.

Case Problem 3

Data Files needed for this Case Problem: PunchAuthorBioUp.gif, PunchAuthorBioOver.gif, PunchExcerptUp.gif, PunchExcerptOver.gif, PunchPressUp.gif, PunchPressOver.gif

NORM The Featured Books page has generated so much response that Mark Chapman wants to improve the page by adding more information. You'll add frames to the existing Featured Books page and expand it to include an author bio, an excerpt from the book, and a navigation bar.

1. Open the NORM site you modified in Tutorial 4, Case 3, and then open the featured_books.htm page.
2. Click the Left Arrow key to move the pointer to the left of the table, and then insert frames into the page by clicking the Top and Nested Left Frames button in the Frames list in the Layout category on the Insert bar. A top frame and a nested left frame are added to the page and the content moves to the lower-right frame.

3. Click in the top frame, change the page title to "Featured - top," and then attach the norm_styles.css style sheet to the HTML document.
4. Create a new Class style named ".feature_body" and defined in the norm_styles.css style sheet; in the Background category, type "#003366" in the Background Color text box and click None in the Background Image list. Select the body tag in the status bar and apply the new style.
5. Save the frame as "featured_top.htm" in the site's local root folder, and then save and close the style sheet.
6. Click in the left frame, change the page title to "Featured - left," attach the norm_styles.css style sheet, and then apply the .featured_body style to the body tag. Save the frame as "featured_left.htm" in the site's local root folder.
7. Select the frameset in the Frames panel, and then, in the Property inspector, click Yes in the Borders list, set the Border Width to 1, set the Border Color to #FFFFFF, and change the Title to "Featured book - frameset." Repeat for the nested frameset.

Explore
8. Select the right frame in the Frames panel, and then, in the Property inspector, click Auto in the Scroll list to enable the frame to display its own scroll bar when the frame content extends beyond the borders.

Explore
9. Click in the right frame, switch to Code view, locate the opening body tag (<body>), place the pointer after the word body and before the closing bracket, press the spacebar, and then type "class="featured_body"." (Hint: The entire tag will read: <body class="featured_body">.) Switch to Design view. The new body style is visible in the frame.
10. Use the Save All command on the File menu to save the frameset in the site's local root folder with the filename "featured_frameset.htm."

Explore
11. Copy the featured_author_bio.htm page and the featured_excerpt.htm page located in the **Tutorial.05\Cases** folder included with your Data Files, and paste them in the root folder of the NORM site. To copy each page, display the site list in the Files panel, navigate to the **Tutorial.05\Cases** folder included with your Data Files, select both files you want to copy, right-click the selected files, point to Edit, click Copy on the context menu, navigate back to the NORM site local root folder, right-click in the Files panel, and then click Paste on the context menu.

Explore
12. Insert a vertical navigation bar in the left frame.

Explore
13. Create the first element in the navigation bar using the following name and images. The Down image is the same as the Up image, so for the Down image you select the same image that you stored in the Graphics folder for the Up image. (*Hint:* To save time, you can copy the text from the Over Image text box and paste it into the Down Image text box.)

Element Name	AuthorBio
Up Image	Tutorial.05\Cases\PunchAuthorBioUp.gif
Over Image	Tutorial.05\Cases\PunchAuthorBioOver.gif
Down Image	NORM\Dreamweaver\Graphics\PunchAuthorBioUp.gif
When Clicked, Go To URL	featured_author_bio.htm
Target in	mainFrame
Preload Images	checked
Use Tables	checked

Explore
14. Create the second element in the navigation bar using the following name and images.

Element name	Excerpt
Up Image	Tutorial.05\Cases\PunchExcerptUp.gif
Over Image	Tutorial.05\Cases\PunchExcerptOver.gif

Down Image	NORM\Dreamweaver\Graphics\PunchExcerptUp.gif
When Clicked, Go To URL	featured_excerpt.htm
Target in	mainFrame

15. Create the third element in the navigation bar using the following name and images.

Element Name	Press
Up Image	Tutorial.05\Cases\PunchPressUp.gif
Over Image	Tutorial.05\Cases\PunchPressOver.gif
Down Image	NORM\Dreamweaver\Graphics\PunchPressUp.gif
When Clicked, Go To URL	featuredbooks.htm (this is the page that was originally in the frame)
Target in	mainFrame

Explore
Explore

16. Add appropriate Alternate Text for each element, and then click the OK button.
17. Adjust the width of the left frame so that the entire image is visible. (*Hint:* Drag the right border of the frame.)
18. Create a new Class style named ".featured_heading" and defined in the norm_styles.css style sheet. In the Type category, set the size to 50 pixels, set the color to #CCCC33, and then click the OK button.
19. Type "PUNCH by Kelly Moore" in the top frame, select the text, and then apply the featured_heading style.
20. Save all the frames and the frameset, close all open pages, and then open and preview the featured_frameset.htm page in a browser, testing the links and reading all the text, and then close the browser window and the page.
21. Open the index.htm page, select the Featured Books text, and then, in the Property inspector, change the link to the featured_frameset.htm and verify that the link is still targeted to _blank so that the page opens in a new browser window.
22. Select the featured book graphic and change the link to featured_frameset.htm; verify that the link is still targeted to _blank.
23. Save the page, preview the page in a browser, click the Featured Book links to test them, and then close the browser windows and the page.
24. Upload the site to your remote server, and then preview the site over the Web.

Case Problem 4

Create

Create a navigation bar and a frames page showing different types of sushi in a Web site for a newly opening sushi restaurant.

Data Files needed for this Case Problem: SushiCompanyUp.gif, SushiCompanyOver.gif, SushiMenuUp.gif, SushiMenuOver.gif, SushiContactUp.gif, SushiContactOver.gif, SushiCaliforniaRoll.gif, SushiTunaHandRoll.gif, SushiSalmon.gif, SushiDescriptions.doc

Sushi Ya-Ya Mary O'Brien asks you to create a navigation bar for the Sushi Ya-Ya site, and then to create a new page in the site. The new page will provide pictures of some common types of sushi. When a user clicks each picture, information about the sushi type shown in the picture will be displayed. You'll use frames for this page.

1. Open the SushiYaYa site that you modified in Tutorial 4, Case 4, and then open the index.htm page.
2. Delete the link text, place the pointer to the left of the logo, and then create a table with 2 columns, 1 row, and 5 pixels of cell padding.
3. Drag the SushiYaYa logo into the left column, and then adjust the width of the column so that it is snug against the outer border of the graphic.

Explore

4. Click in the right column of the table and insert a horizontal navigation bar with the following elements (as well as elements needed to reflect any additional pages in your SushiYaYa site): company, menu, and contact. Use the **SushiCompanyUp.gif**,

SushiCompanyOver.gif, **SushiMenuUp.gif**, **SushiMenuOver.gif**, **SushiContactUp.gif**, and **SushiContactOver.gif** images located in the **Tutorial.05\Cases** folder included with your Data Files to create the elements in your navigation bar, or create your own graphics. Use the Over image as the Down image. Add appropriate alternate text, and link each element to its corresponding page. (If your site does not include pages that correspond to the navigation bar elements, rename existing pages or create new ones now.)

5. Select the navigation bar table and right-align it, resize the outer table wider, if necessary, to accommodate the graphics, and delete any spaces that were introduced into the page by the creation of the table. This will delete the horizontal blue line from the page.
6. Select the outer table and apply the logo style. The horizontal blue line reappears. Save the page.
7. Copy the entire top table including the logo and navigation bar to the company.htm page, the menu.htm page, and the contact.htm page (as well as to any other pages in your SushiYaYa site). Modify the table in each page so that the navigation bar element that represents the selected page is in the Down state when the page is displayed in a browser window. Save and close any open pages.

Explore

8. Create a new page, add top and bottom frames to the page so that the page contains three frames, change the title of each frame and the frameset, and then save everything with an appropriate name. (*Hint:* The frameset name should be "sushi_descriptions_frameset.htm".)
9. Attach the HTML document in each frame to the style sheet.
10. Click in the top frame and type "Sushi Descriptions," select the text, and then apply the headings style.
11. Create a table with 3 columns and 1 row in the middle frame. Set the borders of the table to 1 and the border color to black, then place the **SushiCaliforniaRoll.gif** graphic in the first column, the **SushiTunaHandRoll.gif** in the second column, and the **SushiSalmon.gif** graphic in the third column. (The graphic files are located in the **Tutorial.05\Cases** folder included with your Data Files.)
12. Adjust the column widths so that the columns are flush against the sides of the graphics, center-align the table, select the frameset in the Frames panel, select the middle column in the RowCol Selection box in the Property inspector, type "90" in the Row Value text box, and then select pixels for the Row Units.
13. Click in the bottom frame, type "Click on the sushi picture to view the name and description," and then press the Enter key.
14. Save all the frames and the frameset.
15. Create three new pages named "tuna_hand_roll.htm," "california_roll.htm," and "salmon.htm" and save them in the site's local root folder. For each page, enter an appropriate page title, and then attach the style sheet.
16. Open the **SushiDescriptions.doc** document located in the **Tutorial.05\Cases** folder included with your Data Files in Word or another word processing program, copy the name and description of each type of sushi into its respective page, click at the end of the description you pasted, press the Enter key, format the text using CSS styles, and then save the page.
17. Click each sushi graphic, create a link to the appropriate description page, and then target the link to the bottom frame. Save all the frames and the frameset.
18. Open the menu.htm page, and then type "Sushi Descriptions" below the horizontal line. (If you do not have a menu page, create one now.)
19. Select the text, apply the subheadings style, and then create a link to the sushi_descriptions_frameset.htm page and target the link to open in a new browser window.

20. Save the page, preview the page in a browser, testing the new link and the links on the Sushi Descriptions page, and then close the browser windows and the page.
21. Upload the site to your remote server, and then preview the site over the Web.

Review

Quick Check Answers

Session 5.1

1. a specific item that consists of a series of rollover graphics that change state when specific browser actions occur, such as when the user places the pointer over a graphic
2. four
3. Over state
4. False
5. False
6. the vertical or horizontal orientation of the navigation bar

Session 5.2

1. Frames divide a Web page into multiple documents.
2. a single HTML document with its own content and scroll bars
3. a separate HTML document that defines the structure and properties of a Web page with frames
4. NoFrames content is added to the frameset so that you can provide information for browsers that cannot view frames.
5. False
6. a frame that is inside another frame
7. because the frameset is a separate page that contains all of the information about how the frames will display in the Web page and which HTML document initially will be loaded into each frame

Session 5.3

1. You can open the frameset page, select the HTML document in a frame, and create the content in the frame using the same techniques that you would use to insert content into a Web page that is not part of a frameset. You can open the HTML document in the Document window and create the content in the regular way. You can select a Web page you have already created as the Source in the Property inspector when the frame properties are selected so that page will open in the selected frame whenever the frames page is opened.
2. True
3. Typical content is text that explains that the page users are attempting to view uses frames and cannot be seen by their browser. The text should include a brief explanation of the purpose of the page, links to alternate pages where users can locate information, or contact information.
4. so that the linked page opens in the main frame of the Web page rather than replacing the navigation bar, and the navigation bar remains on the user's screen
5. False
6. frameset tags, frame tags, and noframes tags

Dreamweaver DRM 309

Tutorial 6

Objectives

Session 6.1
- Insert a layer into a Web page
- Select, resize, and move a layer
- Add content to a layer

Session 6.2
- Adjust layer stacking order
- Adjust layer attributes
- Align layers
- Nest layers

Session 6.3
- Add behaviors to a page
- Create an e-mail link
- Edit and delete behaviors

More behaviors + JavaScript

Creating Dynamic Pages

Inserting Layers and Adding Behaviors

Case

Catalyst

Sara Lynn, president of Catalyst, has reviewed the new Catalyst site. Sara likes the general look of the pages, but she wants to add a small information box about the Dizzied Connections band to the home page. Brian Lee, public relations and marketing director, decides to use layers to create a more interesting display of the information. Sara also wants a page for Sloth Child with a link from the home page to that page. Brian suggests making the Sloth Child page a dynamic page, so that the user can point to or click items on the page to cause the page to change in the user's browser. Sara thinks this is a good idea and gives Brian the go-ahead. You'll modify the home page to add the layer and create the Sloth Child page.

Student Data Files

▼**Tutorial.06 folder**

▽ **Tutorial folder**
SlothChildLayer2.jpg
SlothChildLayer3.jpg
SlothChildLayer4.jpg
SlothChildWebPageImage.jpg
SurfaceSuctionCDcover200.jpg

▽ **Review folder**
(no starting Data Files)

▽ **Cases folder**
AFigureOfTheNight.jpg
AQuietDayInUtica.jpg
BookCoverBasketSm.gif
BookCoverQueenSm.gif
BookCoverStopGapSm.gif
BuffaloRunners.jpg
CowpunchingSometimes.jpg
DeerInForest.jpg
HartCourseList.gif
HrochNewCourse.gif
IndiansHuntingBuffalo.jpg
TheBucker.jpg

TheCowPuncher.jpg
WasabiChili.jpg
WasabiCold.gif
WasabiHotWings.jpg
WasabiLowRiseJeans.jpg
WasabiLukeWarm.gif
WasabiOnFire.gif
WasabiOriginal.gif
WasabiPicture.gif
WasabiPictureSmall.gif
WasabiToasty.gif
WasabiWasabi.gif

Session 6.1

Using Layers

A **layer** is a transparent container you place in a Web page to hold different types of content. Like tables and frames, layers can be used to lay out a Web page, dividing it into segments that can hold specific text, graphics, and other elements. You can insert more than one layer in a page, and you can draw nested layers. In addition, layers have benefits and potentials beyond the other layout options. Layers can be dragged and positioned anywhere on the screen with great accuracy and reliability, and they stay exactly where you place them relative to the top and left margins of the page regardless of how a user resizes the browser window. This is called **absolute positioning**. Although this could be accomplished with some of the earlier layout techniques you used, creating interesting layouts is far less complicated and more accurate when done with layers. Unlike tables and frames, layers can be stacked one on top of another, so that content overlaps. They can also be animated, made visible or invisible, and the order of stacked (overlapping) layers can be changed. Furthermore, you can use CSS styles to customize the display attributes of a layer.

Layers are part of CSS styles and are used in conjunction with dynamic HTML. **Dynamic HTML** is a combination of HTML enhancements and a scripting language that work together to add animation, interactive elements, and dynamic updating to Web pages. For example, you can place content in layers, use dynamic HTML to hide a layer, and then have it become visible in response to something the user does (mouseover, mouse click, and so forth).

A drawback of using layers is that all browsers do not display layers correctly or in the same way. Browsers prior to Internet Explorer 4.0 and Netscape Navigator 4.0 do not correctly display layer properties, such as absolute positioning, so users with older browsers may not see the page as you intended. Internet Explorer and Netscape Navigator implement dynamic HTML differently, so some discrepancy exists in how the layers display. Therefore, even users of current browsers may not see the page exactly as you designed.

Brian wants you to add a new section to the home page of the Catalyst site. The new section will contain two text links and a graphic link to the What's Hot page. This content is designed to promote the new release that appears in the What's Hot page. He wants you to use a layer to place the new content, because the new content needs to maintain a consistent position in the page.

Inserting Layers

To insert a layer in a page, you click the Draw Layer button in the Layout category on the Insert bar, and then draw the layer in the page in Design view. The borders of each layer that you draw in a page are visible in the Dreamweaver environment to make them easier to work with. However, the layer borders do not appear in the browser window.

You will insert a layer in the home page of the Catalyst site. The layer will contain a link to the What's Hot page.

To insert a layer:

1. Open the **NewCatalyst** site you modified in the Tutorial 5 Review Assignments, and then open the **index.htm** page.

2. If the rulers are not visible, click **View** on the menu bar, point to **Rulers**, and then click **Show**.

3. If the units on the ruler are not pixels, click **View** on the menu bar, point to **Rulers**, and then click **Pixels**.

4. Click the **Draw Layer** button in the **Layout** category on the Insert bar. The pointer changes to +.

5. Position the pointer approximately 50 pixels below the navigation bar in the home page, and then drag to draw a layer approximately the width of the navigation bar and 100 pixels high. The rectangular layer appears below the navigation bar when you release the mouse button. See Figure 6-1.

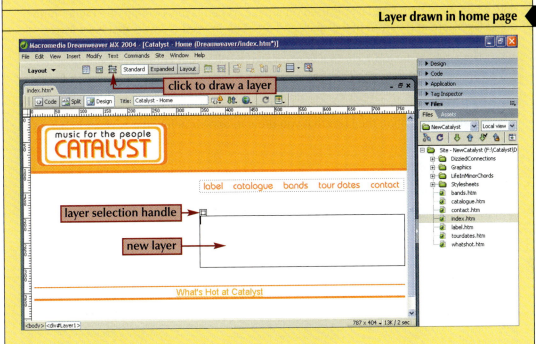

Figure 6-1 Layer drawn in home page

You will resize and reposition the layer in the next section.

6. Click in a blank area of the Document window, and then save the page.

Once you have inserted a layer, you can move and resize it.

Selecting, Resizing, and Moving a Layer

As with other container objects, such as tables, a layer can be active or selected. When a layer is active, the layer border is visible and the layer selection handle appears in the upper-left corner of the layer. To make a layer active, you click in the layer. You must select a layer before you can reposition or resize it. When a layer is selected, resize handles appear all around the layer and the layer selection handle appears in the upper-left corner. To select a layer in the Document window, you click the edge of the layer when the layer border is visible, or you click the layer selection handle if the layer is active. You can also select a layer by clicking its name in the Layers panel, which is located in the Design panel group. If the page contains multiple layers on top of one another, the selected layer always temporarily becomes the top layer so that you can work with its contents. You can select more than one layer at a time by pressing and holding the Shift key while you click the layers.

After you insert a layer, you may need to resize it. To resize a layer, you drag any of the resize handles until the layer is the desired size. If you know the exact size you want to make the layer, you can enter the new height and width values in the Property inspector.

At times, you might want to reorder or move layers. Layers are positioned in a page using x, y, and z coordinates, much like graphs. The x and y coordinates correspond to the layer's Left and Top positions, respectively. Left and Top refer to the distance from the left and the top of the page; if the layer is nested inside another layer, Left and Top refer to the distance from the left and the top of the parent layer. When you view a layer in a browser window, the layer remains in the exact same place, even when the browser window is resized. The z coordinate—sometimes called the **z-index number**—determines the layer's stacking order; that is, the order in which the layer is stacked in the user's browser window when more than one layer is used on a page. When layers overlap, the higher numbered layers are at the front of the stack and are seen in front of layers that have lower numbers. If a top layer has transparent areas, layers stacked below it are visible in those areas. The areas of the top layer that contain text, background color, or images obscure any layers stacked below it. You can move a layer by dragging the layer or layer selection handle to the desired location, or by entering new Left, Top, and z-index numbers in the Property inspector.

You want to reposition the layer that you drew to appear below the navigation bar, over to the right.

To select, resize, and move a layer:

1. Place the pointer over the border of the layer. The layer border becomes red when the pointer is positioned over it. See Figure 6-2.

Figure 6-2   **Drawn layer**

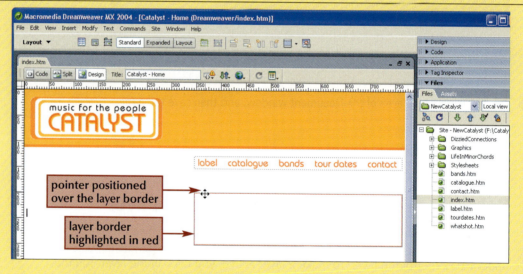

2. Click the red **layer border**. The layer is selected; resize handles appear around the layer and the layer selection handle appears. Note the values in the W (width) and H (height) text boxes in the Property inspector. See Figure 6-3.

Selected layer ◄ **Figure 6-3**

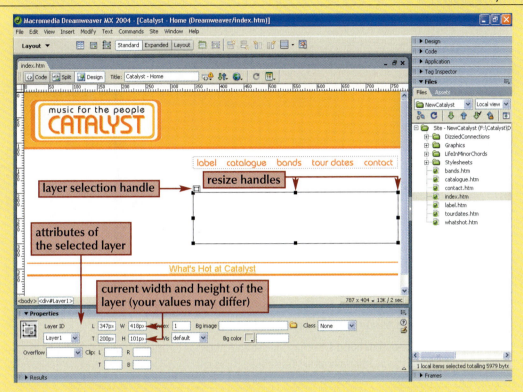

3. Drag the right resize handle approximately 250 pixels to the left, as shown in Figure 6-4. The W value in the Property inspector changes as you drag the layer border.

Resizing a layer ◄ **Figure 6-4**

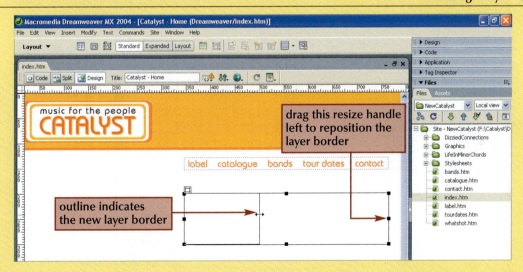

4. Release the mouse button. The right border of the layer is adjusted. See Figure 6-5.

Figure 6-5 | **Resized layer**

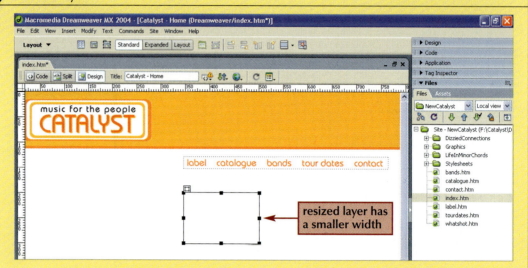

5. Position the pointer over the layer selection handle so that the pointer changes to ✥.

   You will drag the layer to a new position. The value in the L (Left) text box in the Property inspector changes as you drag the layer.

6. Drag the layer selection handle to the right so that the right edge of the layer is aligned with the right edge of the navigation bar above it, as shown in Figure 6-6.

Figure 6-6 | **Repositioning a layer**

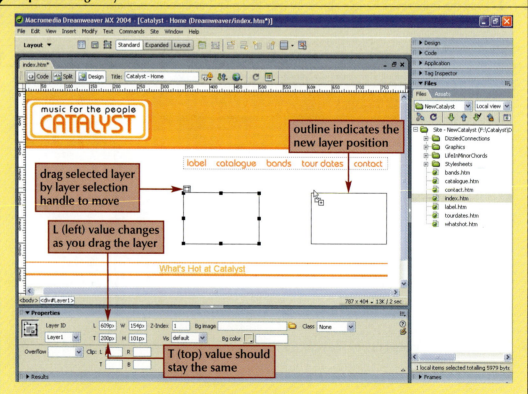

7. Release the mouse button. The layer is repositioned.
8. Click anywhere in the Document window to deselect the layer, and then save the page.

Now that you've inserted a layer, you need to add content to it.

Adding Content to a Layer

A layer can contain almost any type of content, including text, graphics, forms, multimedia content, tables, and other layers. Layers cannot contain frames, but you can place a layer within a frame. You add content to a layer using the same methods you use to insert content directly into a Web page. You can also move existing content from the page to a layer by dragging it. Similar to layout cells, layers need to be active to accept content. To enter text into a layer, for example, you need to first click inside the layer to make it active.

Brian wants to add text and the Surface Suction CD cover graphic in the layer in the home page. This new content will draw attention to the What's Hot page. He also wants a user to be able to click anywhere in the layer to open the What's Hot page in a new browser window. You'll add content to the layer you created in the home page, and then create hyperlinks to the What's Hot page.

To add content to a layer:

1. Click in the layer to make it active.
2. Select the **What's Hot at Catalyst** text in the home page, drag the selected text into the layer, and then press the **Right Arrow** key to deselect the text. See Figure 6-7.

Figure 6-7 Layer with text content

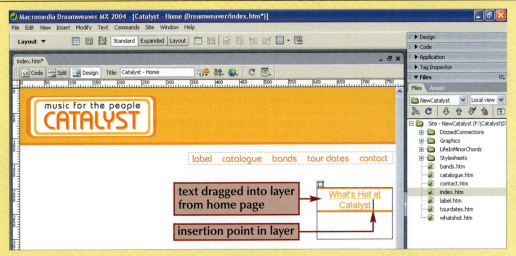

3. Press the **Enter** key to move the insertion point down one line in the layer. You'll insert the CD cover graphic on this line.
4. Click the **Image** button in the **Images** list in the **Common** category on the Insert bar, navigate to the **Tutorial.06\Tutorial** folder included with your Data Files, and then double-click **SurfaceSuctionCDcover200.jpg**. The Surface Suction CD cover is added to the layer, and the layer expands to accommodate the new content. The width of the text content remains unchanged. See Figure 6-8.

Figure 6-8 Layer with text and image content

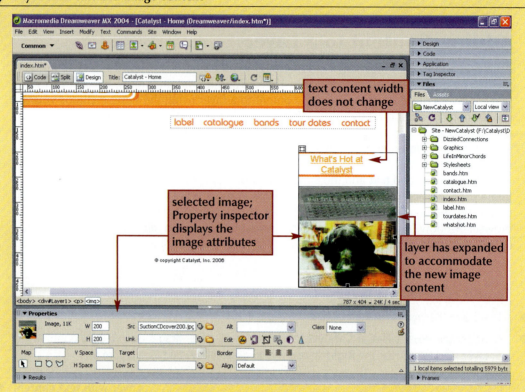

> **Trouble?** If the footer changes format and has lines above and below it, then it picked up the WithLines styles from the What's Hot at Catalyst text. Select the footer text, click the Format list arrow in the Property inspector, click catalyst_footer, click the CD cover image in the layer, and then continue with Step 5.

▶ 5. Press the **Right Arrow** key to deselect the graphic, press the **Enter** key to move the insertion point down one line in the layer, and then type **What's Hot** below the graphic.

▶ 6. Click outside the layer to deselect it, and then press the **Enter** key eight times to move the copyright line below the layer.

Because the right border of the layer expanded automatically, the width value in the Property inspector still reflects the old width of the layer. This is why the top What's Hot text does not extend all the way to the right border of the expanded layer. You will update the layer width, format the text you typed in the layer, and then create links from the text and the graphic in the layer to the What's Hot page.

To update the layer width, format layer text, and create links from a layer:

▶ 1. Click the **layer border**, and then click the **layer selection handle** to select the layer. The layer width is updated in the Property inspector and the top What's Hot text extends to the right edge of the layer. See Figure 6-9.

Link width updated in Property inspector Figure 6-9

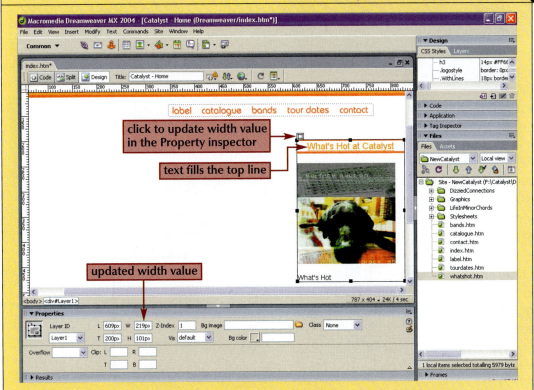

Trouble? If the layer doesn't resize, click a right resize handle to extend the layer width.

You'll format the text at the bottom of the layer, and then link the formatted text to the What's Hot page.

2. Select the **What's Hot** text at the bottom of the layer, click the **Style** list arrow in the Property inspector, and then click **WithLines**. The selected text is reformatted to match the text at the top of the layer.

3. Create a link from the formatted text to the **whatshot.htm** page, click the **Target** list arrow, and then click **_blank**. When a user clicks the link, the What's Hot page will open in a new browser window. You do not need to create the link for the text at the top of the layer because it is already linked.

   You'll center the graphic in the layer, and then link the graphic to the What's Hot page.

4. Click the graphic to select it, and click the **Align Center** button in the Property inspector to align the graphic to the center of the layer.

5. Create a link from the selected graphic to the **whatshot.htm** page, click the **Target** list arrow, and then click **_blank**. See Figure 6-10.

Figure 6-10   **Attributes for the selected graphic in the layer**

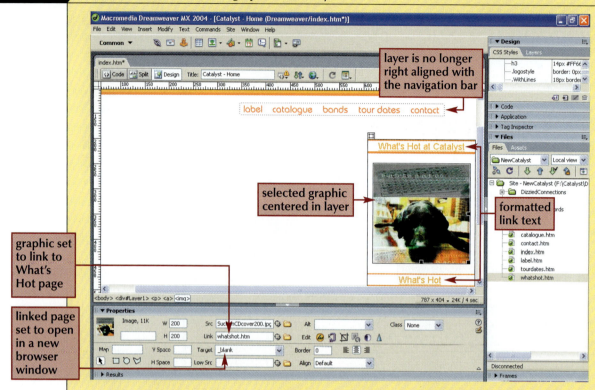

All three items in the layer are linked to the What's Hot page; when a user clicks any of the links, the What's Hot page will open in a new browser window. You'll right align the layer with the navigation bar.

6. Click the **layer selection handle**, and then press the **Left Arrow** key until the right border of the layer is positioned at 755 pixels. Use the rulers to help you measure the position. If the Document window is opened to 787 x 404, the right border of the layer is aligned with the right border of the navigation bar.

7. Click outside the layer to deselect it, and then save the page.

The content in the layer is complete. You'll preview the page with the layer in a browser to test the links.

To preview a page containing a layer:

1. Preview the home page in a browser. The position of the layer is absolute; therefore, it will remain in the same location regardless of the size of the browser window. The position of the navigation bar is relative; therefore, it will always align to the right of the window, regardless of the window size. See Figure 6-11.

Figure 6-11

Home page previewed in browser window before window is maximized

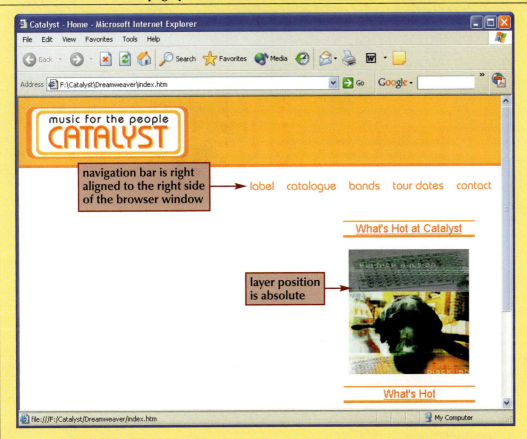

2. Click the **Maximize** button on the browser window title bar. The window increases in size. The layer remains in the same location, and the navigation bar shifts to remain right aligned in the window. The layer remains stationary even when the window changes size. See Figure 6-12.

Figure 6-12 Home page previewed in maximized browser window

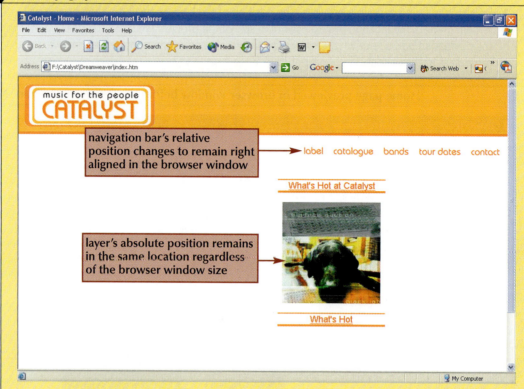

Trouble? If the browser window did not change size, then your window was already maximized. Click the Restore button on the browser window title bar, view the positions of the layer and the navigation bar, and then repeat Step 2.

3. Click the top **What's Hot** link. The What's Hot page opens in a new browser window.
4. Close the What's Hot window, and then click the **graphic**. The What's Hot page again opens in a new browser window.
5. Close the What's Hot window, and then click the bottom **What's Hot** link to reopen the What's Hot page.
6. Close both browser windows.

You can also adjust the attributes of a layer.

Adjusting Layer Attributes

Sometimes it is necessary to change the attributes of a layer. You can change the attributes for an existing layer in the Property inspector, or you can create a CSS style with the desired layer attribute values and attach that style to one or more layers that you want to have the same attributes. To adjust the attributes in the Property inspector, the layer must be selected. When the layer is selected, the Property inspector includes the following attributes:

- **Layer ID.** A unique name for that layer. The layer ID name cannot contain any spaces or symbols, because it will be used in HTML code to refer to the layer. If you don't specify a name, Dreamweaver assigns the name Layer1 to the first layer you draw, Layer2 to the second, and so on.

- **L (Left)** and **T (Top).** The horizontal (L) and vertical (T) positions of a layer measured in pixels from the left margin and the top margin. If a layer is nested within another layer, the values reference the distance from the left and top edge of the parent layer instead of the page margin. As you have already seen, these numbers adjust automatically to reflect the layer's position in the page when you drag the layer.
- **W (Width)** and **H (Height).** The horizontal (W) and vertical (H) dimensions of a layer. You can drag the layer to the desired width and height, or you can type the desired values into the W and H text boxes. If you delete the width, the layer will scale with the browser window.
- **Z-Index.** A number that indicates the layer's stacking order. Layers with higher numbers are stacked in front of layers with lower numbers.
- **Vis (Visibility).** A list of the layer's visibility options indicating whether the layer is visible when the Web page is loaded. If a layer is hidden when the page is loaded, different actions by the user can make it visible. The Default option uses the browser's default visibility. The Inherit option sets the same visibility property as the parent layer of a nested layer. Inherit is the default visibility option for most browsers. The Visible option displays the layer contents when the page is loaded. The Hidden option hides the layer content when the page is loaded.
- **Bg Image (Background Image).** The background image for a layer. You can type the path or browse to select the background image file. If no image is specified, the Web page background is seen through the layer.
- **Bg Color (Background Color).** The background color for the layer. You can type the hexadecimal color code in the Bg Color text box or select a color with the color picker. If no color is specified, the layer is transparent and the Web page background is seen through the layer.
- **Class.** A list of styles you created. You can select a style from the list to apply that style to the layer.
- **Overflow.** A list of options for how a layer will appear in a browser window if its content exceeds its specified size. The Visible option expands the layer to display the overflow content. The Hidden option maintains the layer's size and prevents the overflow text from being displayed in the browser. The Scroll option adds scroll bars to the layer in the browser (whether they are needed or not) in Internet Explorer, and behaves as the Auto option in Netscape Navigator. The Auto option displays scroll bars for the layer in the browser only if the content overflows. Overflow options are not supported in all browsers.
- **Clip.** The portion of a layer that will be visible in a browser. If you specify Clip values, only the portion of the layer in the Clip area appears in the browser. Clip does not work correctly in all browsers.

You need to name the layer you created in the home page. Because the content of the layer you created might overflow the layer boundaries, you also need to adjust the Overflow attribute.

To adjust layer attributes in the Property inspector:

1. Click the **layer border**, and then click the **layer selection handle** to select the layer.
2. Double-click the **Layer ID** text box in the Property inspector, and then type **WhatsHot** (do not type an apostrophe before the s).
3. Click the **Overflow** list arrow in the Property inspector, and then click **Visible**. The layer will expand to display any overflow content.
4. Save the page.

Next, you'll create a CSS style to add a colored medium-width double line around the layer. Because these attributes will be saved in a style, you can quickly apply them to other layers you create in the Catalyst site.

To create a CSS style for a layer:

1. Click the **New CSS Style** button in the CSS Styles panel, name the new style **whats_hot_layer**, and then define the style in the **catalyst_styles.css** style sheet.
2. Click **Border** in the Category list, click **Double** in the Top list in the Style column, click **Medium** in the Top list in the Width column, and then type **#FF9900** in the Top text box in the Color column.
3. Make sure that the **Same for All** check boxes are checked, and then click the **OK** button.
4. Select the **WhatsHot** layer, click the **Class** list arrow in the Property inspector, and then click the **whats_hot_layer** style to apply the style to the layer. See Figure 6-13.

Figure 6-13   Layer with CSS style applied in Dreamweaver

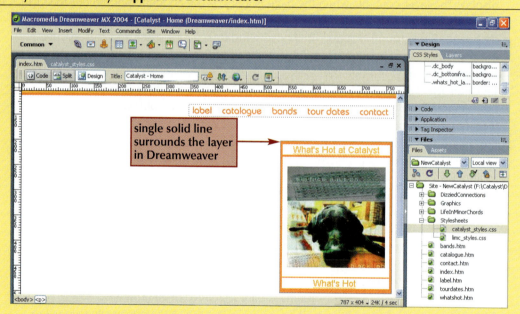

You must view the page in a browser to see the double-line border that you used in the whats_hot_layer style. Within Dreamweaver, the borders of the layer are outlined by a single line.

5. Save the page, save and close the style sheet, and then preview the home page in a browser. The double lines around the layer are visible. See Figure 6-14.

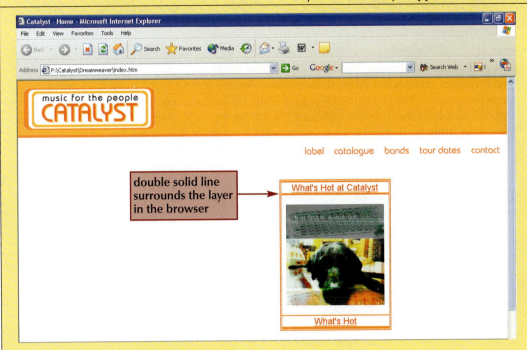

Figure 6-14

Layer with CSS style applied in browser

double solid line surrounds the layer in the browser

6. Close the browser window.

You'll review the HTML code used with layers.

Examining the Code for Layers

Layers are actually div tags that use CSS styles to define the positions of the content elements within the opening and closing div tags. Remember that a div tag is just a generic block-level HTML tag. It can be used for many things, and you have examined it in earlier tutorials. When you create a layer in Dreamweaver, a CSS style that defines the type of positioning, the layer's left and top coordinates, the layer's width and height, the overflow value, and the z-index number is placed **inline** (in the actual code for the tag). The style is defined inline because, often, layer positioning is unique to that particular layer and it is not useful to clutter a style sheet (or the head portion of the page) with a bunch of styles that will be used only one time. When you view the code for the WhatsHot layer in the home page, you will see that the code is:

```
<div id="WhatsHot" style="position:absolute; left:535px; top:200px;
width:219px; height:101px; z-index:1; overflow: visible;"
class="whats_hot_layer">

    <p><a href="whatshot.htm" target="_blank" class="WithLines">What's
    Hot at Catalyst </a></p>
    <p align="center"><a href="whatshot.htm" target="_blank"><img
    src="Graphics/SurfaceSuctionCDcover200.jpg" width="200"
    height="200" border="0"></a></p>
    <p class="WithLines"><a href="whatshot.htm" target="_blank">What's
    Hot</a> </p>

</div>
```

The style (style="position:absolute; left:535px; top:200px; width:219px; height:101px; z-index:1; overflow: visible;") is placed as an attribute in the opening div tag; *style* is the attribute name and everything to the right of the equal sign and in quotation marks is the value. Notice that the tag also references the external whats_hot_layer style that you created. The layer content appears between the opening and closing div tags. When you drag a layer to a new position or when you change the attributes in the Property inspector, Dreamweaver updates the inline style. Inline styles are not displayed in the CSS Styles panel; however, if you select the layer (or the div tag in Code view), the attributes of the style are visible in the Relevant CSS panel in the Tag Inspector panel group. You can change layer style attributes there in the same way you adjust other style attributes.

It is sometimes useful to create external styles to define the layer positioning, for instance, if you plan to use the same positioning for multiple layers. If you create a site that enables users to choose from a variety of looks for the display of the pages (depending on which style sheet is attached to the page), creating external styles for the layers will enable you to change the location of the layers in each style sheet to accommodate the corresponding look. There are many other reasons as well. When you drag a layer whose positioning is defined externally to a new position in the page, the style is updated with the new positioning coordinates in the same way an inline style would be. This can cause problems if you have attached more than one layer to the style and want to reposition only one layer. As you can see, there are drawbacks and benefits for both methods of layer positioning. However, because Dreamweaver automatically places layer positioning styles in line, we'll use that method in these tutorials. As a side note, there is a layer tag (<layer></layer>) in HTML, but that tag is supported only by older versions of Netscape Navigator and is not generally used.

You'll examine the HTML code for the WhatsHot layer in the home page.

To examine the HTML code for a layer:

1. Select the **WhatsHot** layer in the home page, and then click the **Show Code and Design Views** button ![Split] on the Document toolbar. The home page is in Split view with the layer and the layer code selected.

2. Drag the bottom border of the top pane (and scroll if necessary) until all the layer code is visible, and then identify the inline style. See Figure 6-15.

Figure 6-15   **Layer in Split view**

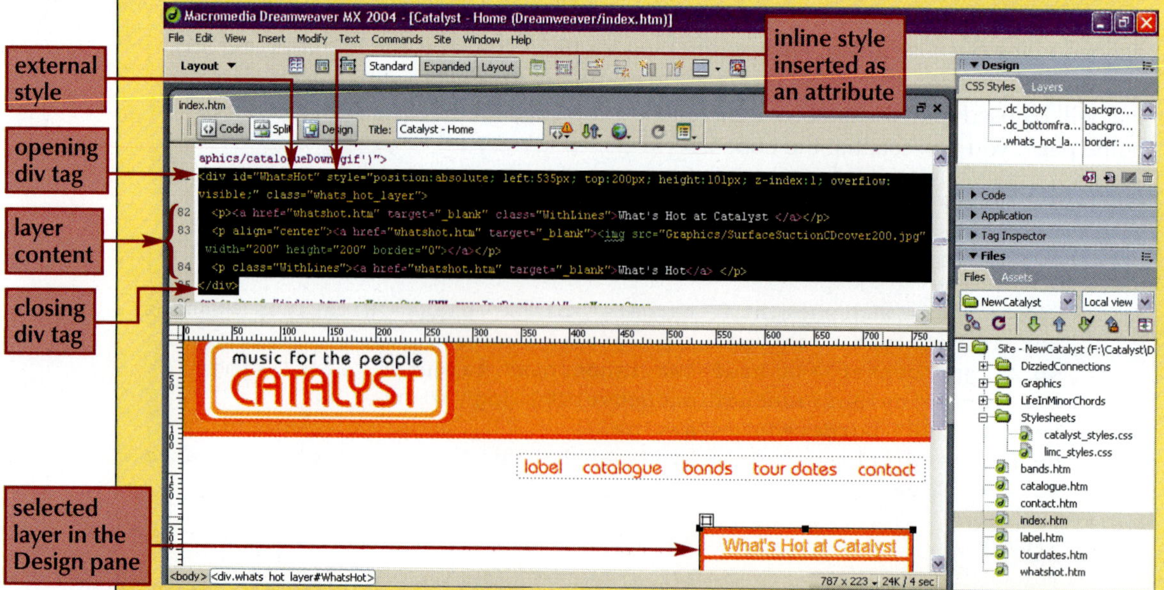

3. In the Design pane, drag the selected layer to the left. The left and top values change in the code as well as the Property inspector.

4. Click **Edit** on the menu bar, and then click **Undo Move Layer**. The layer returns to its former position.

5. Locate the content of the WhatsHot layer in the Code pane (refer to Figure 6-15). The WithLines style is attached to the text in the layer.

6. Locate the three <a> tags that link the top text, the graphic, and the bottom text to the whatshot.htm page.

7. Locate the <img> tag.

8. Click the **Show Design View** button [Design] on the Document toolbar.

So far, you have created a single layer on a page, inserted content in the layer, adjusted the layer attributes, and examined the code for layers. In the next session, you will create multiple layers, including a nested layer, and you will adjust the stacking order of the layers.

Session 6.1 Quick Check

1. What is a layer?
2. What is dynamic HTML?
3. Are layers part of CSS styles?
4. Describe two ways to select a layer.
5. What is the *z*-index number?
6. Describe the Visibility attribute of layers.

Session 6.2

Modifying Layers

Designing Web pages using layers gives you more control over the placement of the content in your pages. Once you have added a layer to a page, you will most likely need to modify the layer. You can change the stacking order of layers, you can align layers to each other or to an invisible grid, and you can nest one layer inside another layer.

Adjusting Layer Stacking Order

One benefit of using layers in a Web page is that layers can be stacked or overlapped. Think of each layer as a clear acetate sheet, such as those used for overhead projectors. You can stack one layer on top of another and you will be able to see the bottom layer through any transparent portions of the top layer. If the top layer does not have any transparent portions, the bottom layer will be hidden from view. Stacking enables you to create more sophisticated and interesting layout designs. Also, because layers can be animated, stacking enables you to create interesting user interactions. For example, you could stack two layers that contained text, so that the text in the back layer is hidden by the front layer, and then animate the layers so that the stacking order of the layers is switched when the user clicks a button. This would bring the back layer to the front so that you can see the text in it.

Each new layer is assigned a *z*-index number in the order in which it is created—the first layer you create is 1, the second is 2, and so on. When layers appear on the screen, layers with higher *z*-index numbers appear in front of the layers with lower *z*-index numbers. You can change the stacking order of layers by changing the *z*-index number. For example, a layer with the *z*-index number of 2 appears behind a layer with a *z*-index number of 3. If you change the first layer to a z-index number of 4, then it will appear in front of the second layer when the layers are stacked. You change the z-index numbers of layers in the Property inspector.

Another way to change the stacking order of layers is to use the Layers panel. Layers first appear in the Layers panel in the order in which they are created. You change the stacking order by dragging a layer to a new position in the list. When you reposition a layer in the Layers panel, the z-index numbers are automatically updated to correspond to the layers' new stacking order.

Brian wants to add a Dizzied Connections section to the home page. You will add a second layer to the home page, and then you will adjust the stacking order.

To create a new layer:

1. If you took a break after the last session, make sure the **NewCatalyst** site is open, and the **index.htm** page is open.

2. Draw a new layer in the home page approximately 250 pixels wide and 100 pixels high, starting 50 pixels below the navigation bar, and aligned with the left edge of the navigation bar. The new layer should overlap the WhatsHot layer that you drew in the last session. See Figure 6-16.

Figure 6-16   Second layer drawn in the home page

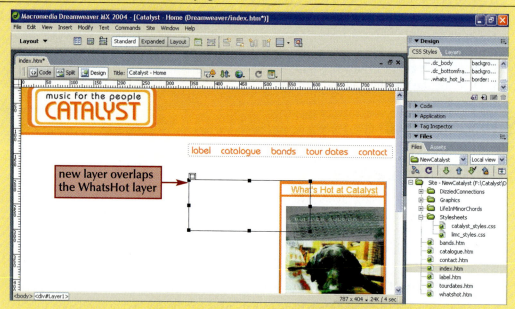

Trouble? If you cannot draw the new layer in front of the WhatsHot layer, the Prevent Overlaps check box in the Layers panel is probably checked. Expand the Design panel group, click the Layer tab to display the Layers panel, click the Prevent Overlaps check box in the Layers panel to uncheck it, click the layer selection handle to select the layer you just drew, press the Delete key, and then repeat Step 2.

Trouble? If the layer is not positioned or sized correctly, you need to move or resize it. Click the layer selection handle to select the layer, and then drag the layer to the correct position or drag a resize handle to resize it.

3. Click in the new layer to make it active, type **Dizzied Connections**, press the **Enter** key, and then type **Information about the band will be here soon.** (including the period).

4. Select **Dizzied Connections**, click the **Format** list arrow in the Property inspector, click **Heading 2**, and then deselect the text. Both lines of text overlap the first layer. See Figure 6-17.

Figure 6-17 Formatted text in the second layer

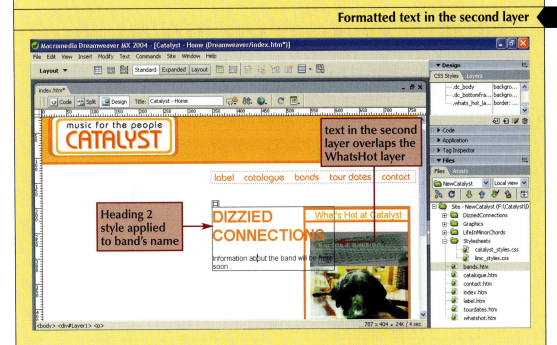

You'll expand the Layers panel, name the new layer in the Property inspector, and then look at the stacking order in the Layers panel. Dreamweaver gives a generic name to each new layer—the first unnamed layer is Layer1, the second is Layer2, and so forth. Because the first layer you created has a layer name, the new layer is named Layer1.

To adjust the layer stacking order in the Layers panel:

1. Click the **Layers** tab in the Design panel group. The Layers panel expands. See Figure 6-18.

Figure 6-18 Layers panel

You will name the new layer.

2. Click the new layer's border to select it, double-click the **Layer ID** text box in the Property inspector to select the text, type **DizziedConnections**, and then press the **Enter** key. The layer name changes in the Layers panel.

   The DizziedConnections layer has a z-index of 2, which means that it is in front of the WhatsHot layer, which has a z-index of 1. This is evident in the Document window.

3. Click **DizziedConnections** in the Layers panel, and then drag it down below the **WhatsHot** layer, as shown in Figure 6-19.

Figure 6-19   Changing the layers' stacking order in the Layers panel

4. Release the mouse button when the indicator line is below the WhatsHot layer. The WhatsHot layer is stacked in front of the DizziedConnections layer in the Document window, obscuring the text in the DizziedConnections layer. See Figure 6-20.

Figure 6-20   Layer stacking order changed

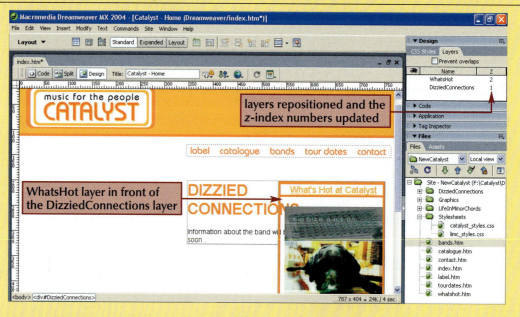

5. Save the page, and then preview it in a browser. Some of the text in the DizziedConnections layer is hidden.

6. Close the browser window.

You'll reposition the DizziedConnections layer in the Document window so that the content in both layers is visible. The DizziedConnections layer is stacked behind the WhatsHot layer. When you select the back layer or make the back layer active, the back layer temporarily moves to the front so that you can modify it. The z-index number in the Property inspector and in the Layers panel remains unchanged.

To work with a layer stacked behind another layer:

1. Click in the **DizziedConnections** layer in the Document window to make it active, and then click the **layer selection handle** to select the layer. The DizziedConnections layer moves to the front. Although the DizziedConnections layer appears in front of the WhatsHot layer in the Document window, the z-index number in the Property inspector and in the Layers panel remains 1.

2. Click in a blank area outside the DizziedConnections layer in the Document window. The layer again appears behind the WhatsHot layer.

3. Select the **DizziedConnections** layer, and then drag it approximately **50** pixels to the left so that the text is no longer obscured by the WhatsHot layer. See Figure 6-21.

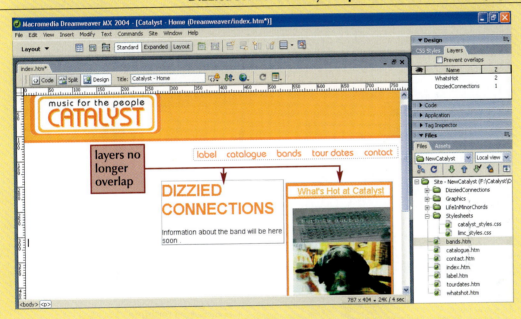

Figure 6-21 DizziedConnections layer repositioned on the home page

4. Click in a blank area of the Document window, and then save the page.

Once you have more than one layer in a page, you can align them.

Aligning Layers

As you know, you can drag layers around the page to reposition them, using the rulers as a guide. In some pages, you might want to align the elements so that the page looks tidy. You can align layers to the left, right, top, or bottom of another layer. To align layers, you select one layer, press and hold the Shift key, and then click any other layers you want to align. The last layer that you select will remain stationary and the other layers will align to it. The Left Align command aligns the left borders of selected layers to the horizontal position of the left border of the last layer you select. The Right Align command aligns the right borders of selected layers to the horizontal position of the right border of the last layer you select. The Top Align command aligns the top borders of the selected layers to the vertical position of the top border of the last layer you select. Finally, the Bottom Align command aligns the bottom borders of the selected layers to the vertical position of the bottom border of the last layer you select.

Brian asks you to align the tops of the two layers in the home page.

To align layers using the Align commands:

1. Select the **DizziedConections** layer, press and hold the **Shift** key, click the **WhatsHot** layer, and then release the **Shift** key. The two layers are selected. The Property inspector indicates that multiple layers are selected. The resize handles for the WhatsHot layer are black, which indicates that this is the layer that will remain stationary and any other selected layers will align with it.

2. Click **Modify** on the menu bar, point to **Align**, and then click **Top**. The selected layers align their tops at the horizontal position of the top of the WhatsHot layer. See Figure 6-22.

Figure 6-22   Layers top aligned

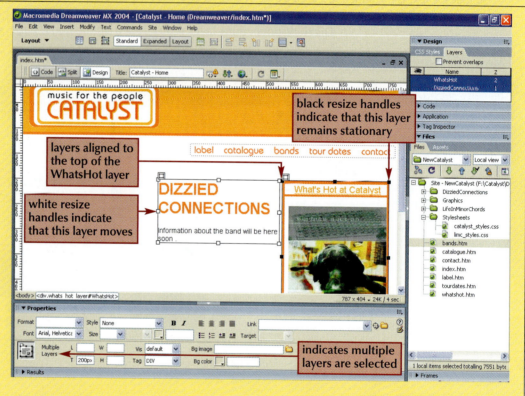

3. Save the page.

Next, you will position the layers in the page using the grid.

Positioning Layers and Other Elements Using the Grid

In addition to the Align commands, you can also use the grid to help you adjust the position of layers and other elements in a Web page. The **grid** is a series of parallel horizontal and vertical lines that overlap to create equal-sized squares in the background of the Document window. The grid provides a guide for positioning or resizing layers or other elements. The default is for the grid to be hidden, but you can display it. If you want to change the size of the grid squares so that you can align elements more precisely, you can adjust the grid's line spacing in the Grid Settings dialog box. You can also use the Grid Settings dialog box to change the appearance of the grid.

You will use the grid to position the elements in the home page.

To align elements using the grid:

1. With both layers still selected, click **View** on the menu bar, point to **Grid**, and then click **Show Grid**. Grid lines appear in the background of the Document window creating 50 pixel squares.

2. Press the **Arrow** keys to nudge the layers to align the left edge of the DizziedConnections layer with a grid line and the base of the word "Dizzied" with a grid line. The two layers move together because they are both selected. You can also drag the layers with the mouse pointer. See Figure 6-23.

Figure 6-23 Layer aligned to grid

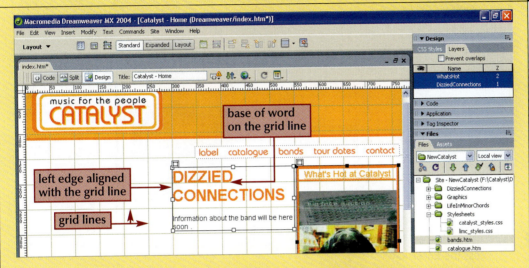

3. Click **View** on the menu bar, point to **Grid**, and then click **Show Grid** to hide the grid lines.
4. Click in the Document window outside the selected layers to deselect them, and then save the page.

It can be convenient to have two or more layers move together. Next, you will learn how to use nesting to group layers.

Creating Nested Layers

A **nested layer** is a layer contained within an outer (parent) layer similar to nested tables and nested frames. With layers, however, nesting does not refer to the layers' physical positions, but to the underlying code. This means that the nested layer does not have to touch its parent layer on-screen to be nested. Nesting is used to group layers. When layers are nested, if you move the parent layer, the nested layer will move with it. This is because the position of the nested layer is relative to the left and top borders of the parent layer rather than the left and top borders of the page. A nested layer also shares other attributes with its parent layer.

To nest a layer, you draw the parent layer in the Document window, and then you draw the layer you want to nest. You can draw the nested layer anywhere in the page. To nest the layers, press and hold the Ctrl key, and then, in the Layers panel, drag the layer you want to nest over the parent layer. The nested layer is indented under the parent layer in the Layers panel. To un-nest a nested layer, you drag the nested layer to an empty spot in the Layers panel.

Brian asks you to create a new layer that will contain information about Sloth Child. You'll nest this layer with the DizziedConnections layer.

To create a nested layer:

1. Draw a **100-pixel** square layer below the DizziedConnections layer in the home page. See Figure 6-24.

Figure 6-24 | Third layer drawn in home page

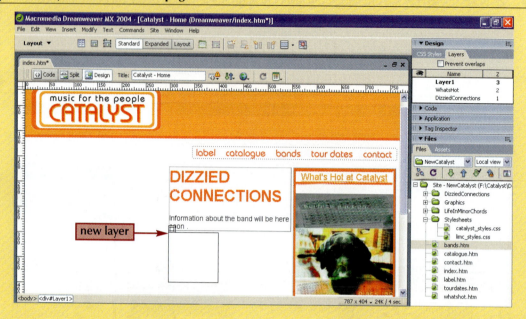

2. Click in the new layer to make it active, if necessary, type **Sloth Child** in the layer, and then press the **Enter** key.

3. Click the **layer selection handle** on the new layer to select it, double-click in the **Layer ID** text box in the Property inspector, type **SlothChild**, and then press the **Enter** key.

4. Press and hold the **Ctrl** key, and then, in the Layers panel, drag the **SlothChild** layer over the DizziedConnections layer, and then release the **Ctrl** key and the mouse button. See Figure 6-25.

Figure 6-25 | Nested SlothChild layer repositioned

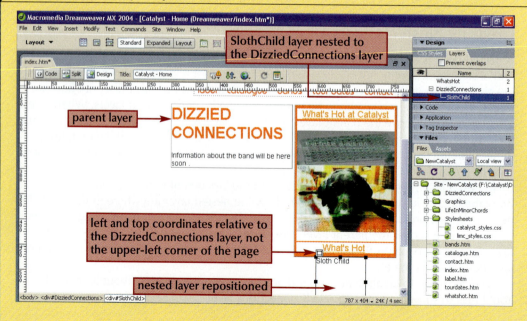

The SlothChild layer is indented under the DizziedConnections layer in the Layers panel. The SlothChild layer shifts to the bottom of the page in the Document window because its position is now relative to the top and left of the DizziedConnections layer and not the top and left of the page.

▶ 5. Save the page.

Netscape Navigator 4 can have difficulty displaying layers properly when the user resizes the browser window. You'll fix this problem on the home page.

Using the Netscape Resize Fix

Although Netscape Navigator has been capable of displaying layers since version 4, if someone using Netscape Navigator 4 resizes the browser window when viewing a page with layers, the layers tend to move around, scale improperly, or disappear completely. Dreamweaver provides a built-in fix that by default is added automatically to pages that use layers. The **Netscape Resize Fix** is JavaScript code that forces the page to reload every time the browser window is resized, thus eliminating the problems. The Netscape Resize Fix option is available in the Layers category in the Preferences dialog box. You should make sure the Netscape Resize Fix is turned on before adding layers to your pages.

Adding the Netscape Resize Fix to a Web Site

Reference Window

- Click Edit on the menu bar, and then click Preferences.
- Click Layers in the Category list.
- Click the Netscape 4 Compatibility check box to check it.
- Click the OK button.

The Netscape Resize Fix should have been added to your pages by default. You'll verify this in the Preferences dialog box.

To turn on the Netscape Resize Fix:

▶ 1. Click **Edit** on the menu bar, and then click **Preferences**. The Preferences dialog box opens.

▶ 2. Click **Layers** in the Category list.

▶ 3. Click the **Netscape 4 Compatibility** check box to check it, if necessary. See Figure 6-26.

Figure 6-26   **Layers category in Preferences dialog box**

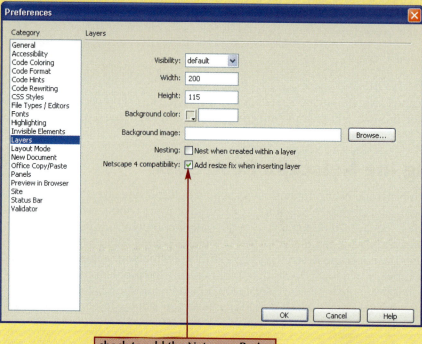

check to add the Netscape Resize Fix to all pages that use layers

4. Click the **OK** button.

Because very old browsers cannot display layers properly, there are times that you might decide to create a version of your Web site that uses tables instead of layers. You'll convert the layers in the home page to tables.

Converting Layers to Tables

Layers are great tools for creating Web page layout, but they do have drawbacks. Only version 4 and later of both Netscape Navigator and Internet Explorer support layers effectively. So, if your target audience includes users of very old browsers, they will not be able to view the pages properly. One solution is to use layers to create the site you want, and then to create another version of the site in which the pages use tables rather than layers. You can then add code to the page that automatically routes anyone using an older browser to the non-layer version of the site.

Reference Window | **Converting Layers to a Table**

- Click Modify on the menu bar, point to Convert, and then click Layers to Table.
- Click the Most Accurate option button.
- Click the Use Transparent GIFs check box to check it.
- Make sure no other check boxes are checked.
- Click the OK button.

Rather than having to manually create both the layer version and the table version of the same site, you can use the Layers to Table command to convert the layers in the page to a table. This command will not work on a Web page with layers that are nested or overlapped, because cells in tables cannot overlap. If you plan to convert layers to tables, you can check the Prevent Overlap check box in the Layers panel to automatically prevent layers from overlapping.

When a table is created from layers, Dreamweaver maintains the original layout of the page by creating empty cells around the layers to hold that content in place, much like a table in Layout view. This can result in entire columns and rows being empty. In order to maintain the width of any empty columns, Dreamweaver creates a file named transparent.gif, which is (as the name implies) a transparent, one-pixel GIF file, and places this file in a blank row at the bottom of the table. The row is only one pixel high, the height of the GIF file. Dreamweaver scales the width of the transparent GIF as necessary to maintain the width of each column.

Because of the way Dreamweaver interprets the position of the layers, the various elements may be moved around in the page so that the resulting layout does not reflect your original plan. Therefore, you need to examine the resulting table and overall page layout and make any necessary adjustments.

Similarly, you can use the Tables to Layers command to convert existing tables to layers. This is useful if you created a page using tables and you want to take advantage of some of the layers features that are not available with tables.

Although the target audience of the Catalyst site does not necessarily include users with very old browsers, Brian wants to create both a layer version and a non-layer version of the site. If the non-layer pages are close to the original layout, you will use them to create an alternate site for users with very old browsers. If the conversion causes too many problems, you will abandon the idea. You'll convert the layers in the home page into a table to test the feasibility of creating an alternate non-layer site.

To convert layers into tables:

1. Drag the **SlothChild** layer in the Layers panel up to the top of the list to un-nest the layer. The DizziedConnections layer moves back up to the top of the page.

2. Save the page.

3. Click **Modify** on the menu bar, point to **Convert**, and then click **Layers to Table**. The Convert Layers to Table dialog box opens.

4. Make sure the **Most Accurate** option button is selected, click the **Use Transparent GIFs** check box to check it, if necessary, and then make sure the rest of the check boxes in the dialog box are not checked. See Figure 6-27.

Figure 6-27   Convert Layers to Table dialog box

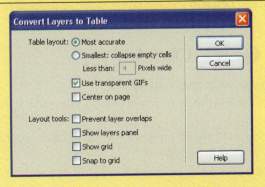

5. Click the **OK** button. The dialog box closes and the layers are converted to a table.
6. Scroll down the Document window and compare your screen to Figure 6-28. The Catalyst logo and the navigation bar appear below the table at the bottom of the page, which will need to be fixed.

Figure 6-28   **Table created from layers**

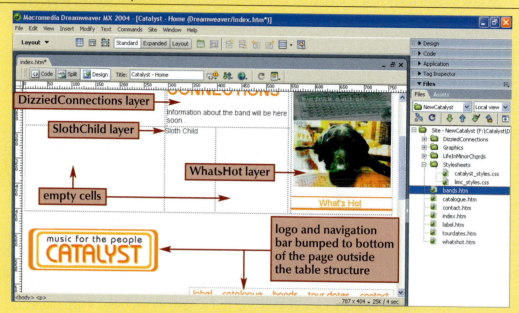

Because you want to keep the home page in its original state with the layers intact, you need to save the test page with a new name.

7. Click **File** on the menu bar, click **Save As**, navigate to the site's local root folder, if necessary, type **homepagewithtables.htm** in the File Name text box, and then click the **Save** button. The new page is added to the Files panel. The transparent.gif file also appears in the list.
8. Close the new page.

For now, Brian does not want you to fix the layout of or create any links to the version of the home page without layers. Later, he will use that page to determine the difficulty of creating a version of the site without layers.

So far, you have created nested and un-nested layers in a page, changed the stacking order of layers, aligned layers, and converted layers to a table for older browsers. In the next session, you will add behaviors to the layers to allow users to interact with them.

Review

Session 6.2 Quick Check

1. True or False? Layers can be overlapped.
2. Do layers with higher z-index numbers appear in front of or behind layers with lower z-index numbers?
3. When you align layers, to which layer will the other layers align?
4. In Dreamweaver, what is the grid?
5. Does a nested layer need to be positioned inside of its parent layer?
6. What is the Netscape Resize Fix?

Session 6.3

Understanding Behaviors

In Dreamweaver, a **behavior** is code added to a Web page that enables users to interact with various elements in the Web page, to alter the Web page in different ways, or to cause tasks to be performed. For example, in a Web page with two layers, you could stack the two layers and then create a behavior that switches the stacking order of the layers when the user clicks a button. The word *behavior* is a Macromedia convention for describing interactive functions in multimedia programs that are managed by the program and accessed through an authoring interface, in this case the Behaviors panel.

A behavior is like a mathematical equation that consists of three elements: *object + event = action*. An **object** is the element in the Web page to which the behavior is attached, such as a graphic or a layer. An event has two components: the user event and the event handler. The **user event** is what the user does to trigger the action. Common user events are moving the pointer over an object (mouseover), clicking an object, and so forth. The **event handler** is the code used to refer to the event. For example, the code used to refer to a mouseover is onMouseOver. The **action** is what you want to happen when the event is performed on the object.

Dreamweaver provides three ways to insert behavior functionality into Web pages: the preset behavior tools, the Behaviors panel, and custom scripting. Figure 6-29 explains each method.

Methods of inserting behaviors in Dreamweaver — Figure 6-29

Tool	Description	You...	Dreamweaver...
Preset behavior tools	You use buttons located throughout Dreamweaver to perform common tasks.	Enter requested information, for example, which graphic you want to use, in the dialog box, if necessary.	Writes the behavior and inserts it for you automatically.
Behaviors panel	You choose the event handler and action for a behavior from a prewritten list.	Select the elements of the behavior from drop-down lists.	Writes the code and inserts it into the page.
Custom scripting	You write your own code (usually JavaScript) in the Document window in Code view or by using the Script button in the HTML category on the Insert bar.	Write the code and insert in the page; your code then appears as a custom script in the Behaviors panel.	

Using a preset behavior tool is the easiest way to insert behaviors into Web pages. Preset behavior tools are buttons that perform common tasks for you and insert the behaviors into a page automatically. They are located throughout Dreamweaver. You have already used many of the preset behavior tools, including the Rollover button and the Navigation Bar button. When you use the Rollover button, Dreamweaver inserts a swap image behavior and a preload behavior as you insert the rollover images. The swap image behavior consists of the action (the images being swapped) triggered by a user event (the user rolling the mouse to place the pointer over the image). The image is the object. The preload behavior consists of the action (the image being downloaded) triggered by a user event (the user loading the Web page into a browser window). The Web page is the object. When you select an object in the Document window and open the Behaviors panel, the behaviors that Dreamweaver inserted for you appear in the list.

> **Reference Window**
>
> ### Adding the Show-Hide Layers Prewritten Behavior
>
> - Select the layer image or hotspot to which you want to add the behavior.
> - Open the Behaviors panel.
> - Click the Add Behavior button in the Behaviors panel, point to Show Events For, and then click the desired browser choices.
> - Click the Add Behavior button in the Behaviors panel, then click Show-Hide Layers.
> - Click each layer that you want to react to the user event, and then click the Show button to show the layer or click the Hide button to hide the layer.
> - Click the OK button.

You can use the Behaviors panel to create more customized behaviors. When you use the Behaviors panel to create behaviors, you select an object and then you select from lists of prewritten actions and event handlers, which Dreamweaver combines to create the behavior. Dreamweaver will allow you to choose only actions that work with the object you have selected, and it will allow you to choose only event handlers that go with the action you selected. For example, if you select text as the object, you cannot select swap image as the action. You can also limit the behavior list options by browser version or browser brand and version. In general, the more complex behaviors require version 4.0 and later browsers, whereas simpler behaviors work with 3.0 browsers. If your target audience includes users of browsers older than 3.0, you may need to create an alternate site that does not use behaviors. Some discrepancy exists in the way that different browsers interpret JavaScript, so you need to test pages that use behaviors extensively in all the browsers you intend to support. In addition, some users turn off JavaScript in their browsers so that pop-up ads on Web sites will not be able to run. This means that some users with newer browsers will still not be able to access Web sites that use behaviors. Therefore, even if your target audience does not include users of older browsers, you should consider providing links to alternate pages or an alternate site for anyone whose browser has difficulty running JavaScript.

You can add the advanced functionality of behaviors to a Web page yourself by writing your own code (usually JavaScript) in the Insert Script panel or in the Document window in Code view. When you write the code yourself, the code you create is not actually considered a behavior because it is not added to the reusable prewritten choice lists that Dreamweaver provides in the Behaviors panel. Instead, code you write is considered a custom script, and will appear in the Behaviors panel when you select the object to which it is attached.

Adding Behaviors Using the Behaviors Panel

The Behaviors panel is like a sophisticated menu for ordering behaviors. First, you choose an object in the page, and then you select a target browser brand and version. The Behaviors panel will display only actions that are compatible with the selected object and browser. You then choose an action from the list in the Behaviors panel. You can select only the actions that are available for use with the object you selected; actions that are not available for use with the selected object are dimmed. If you don't choose any object, the actions listed are available for the page itself. Once you have selected an action, Dreamweaver provides a list of possible events—with the most common event associated with that action selected by default. You choose an event from that list. Based on your selections, Dreamweaver creates the behavior and inserts the code.

Sara and Brian like the way the Life in Minor Chords page looks in the site, and they want you to create a page for Sloth Child. You'll make this an interactive page that uses layers and behaviors to show or hide the various layers, depending on what the user points to. You'll start by creating the new page.

To create a new page:

1. If you took a break after the previous session, make sure the **NewCatalyst** site is open, and the Design panel group is collapsed.

2. Create a new folder named **SlothChild** within the site's local root folder, create a new page, and then save the new page in the SlothChild folder with the filename **sloth_child.htm**.

3. Open the **sloth_child.htm** page, if necessary, change the page title to **Catalyst - Sloth Child**, and then modify the page properties as follows (you will not create an external style sheet because the Sloth Child styles will be used only within this page):

Property	Attribute
Page font	**Arial, Helvetica, sans-serif**
Size	**14 pixels**
Text color	**#FFFFFF**
Background color	**#000000**
Margins	**0**
Color for all links	**#FFFFFF**
Link underline style	**Always Underline**

4. Save the page.

You'll add four layers to the new sloth_child.htm page. For each layer, you'll set the properties, insert an image, and then adjust the layer position in the page.

To add layers to a page:

1. Draw a layer in the middle of the Document window, approximately **300** pixels wide and **150** pixels high. See Figure 6-30.

First layer drawn in the Sloth Child page Figure 6-30

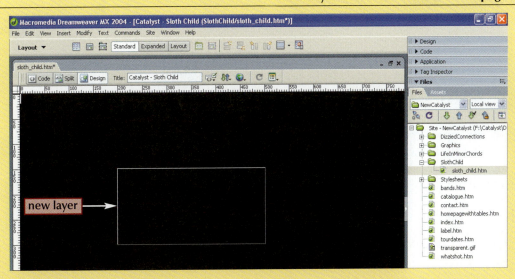

2. Select the layer, and then, in the Property inspector, type **background** in the Layer ID text box, click the **Vis** list arrow, and then click **Visible**.

3. Click in the layer, click the **Images** button in the **Image** list in the **Common** category on the Insert bar, browse to the **Tutorial.06\Tutorial** folder included with your Data Files, and then double-click **SlothChildWebPageImage.jpg**. The layer expands to accommodate the inserted figure, which includes the words *sloth child* in the upper-left corner and a photo and the words *try an apple* in the lower-right corner.

4. Scroll to the upper-left corner of the Document window, click the **layer selection handle** to select the layer instead of the graphic, and then drag the **layer selection handle** to the upper-left corner of the page. See Figure 6-31.

| Figure 6-31 | Graphic added to the background layer |

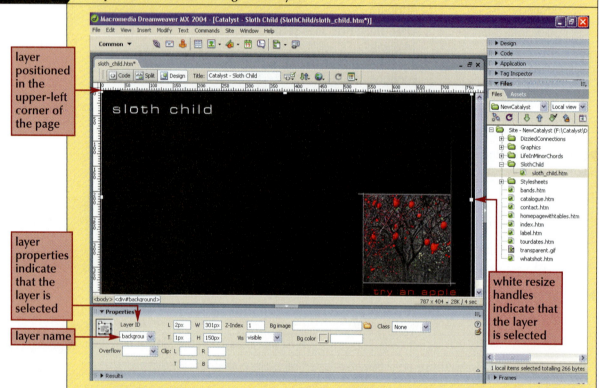

Trouble? If you have difficulty positioning the layer at the upper-left corner of the page, press the Arrow keys to nudge the selected layer into position.

Next, you'll draw hotspots on the graphic in the background layer.

5. Click in the layer to select the graphic. The graphic is selected when "Image" appears in the upper-left corner of the Property inspector, the <img> tag is selected in the status bar, and black resize handles appear around the graphic. See Figure 6-32.

Figure 6-32

Selected graphic in background layer

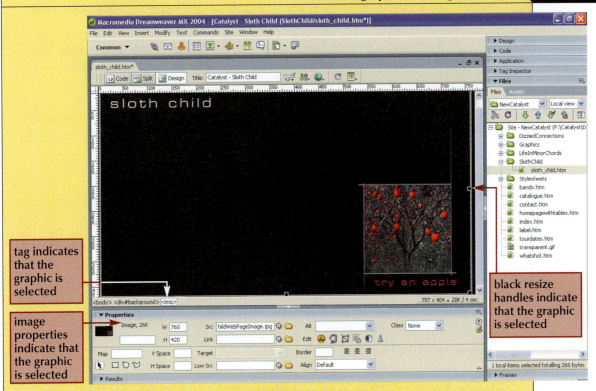

- tag indicates that the graphic is selected
- image properties indicate that the graphic is selected
- black resize handles indicate that the graphic is selected

6. Click the **Oval Hotspot Tool** button in the Property inspector, and draw a hotspot over the rightmost apple, about one-third of the way down the photo.

7. Draw a second oval hotspot over the centermost apple on the apple tree, and then draw a third oval hotspot over the apple at the upper-middle of the tree. See Figure 6-33.

Figure 6-33

Hotspots added to the graphic in the background layer

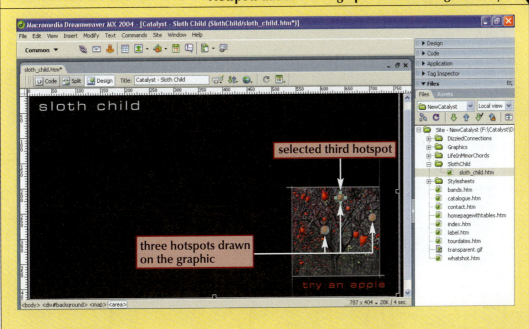

- selected third hotspot
- three hotspots drawn on the graphic

Trouble? If the hotspots on your graphic are in the wrong position, click the Pointer Hotspot Tool button in the Property inspector, and then drag each hotspot to the position that matches the hotspot placement shown in Figure 6-33.

8. Click the **Rectangular Hotspot Tool** button in the Property inspector, and draw a fourth hotspot over the Sloth Child band name in the upper-left corner of the layer.

You will draw four additional layers in the Sloth Child page, and modify the attributes of the layers so that they are hidden. You will later attach behaviors to make the layers visible when a user event occurs.

To draw layers and modify their attributes:

1. Expand the **Layers panel** in the CSS Design panel group, if necessary.
2. Draw a second layer on top of the background layer that is about **25** pixels below the band name, approximately **100** pixels high, and the same width as the band name.
3. Select the new layer, and then, in the Property inspector, change the layer ID to **SCLayer2**, click the **Vis** list arrow, and click **Hidden**.
4. Click in the **SCLayer2** layer to make it active, and then insert the **SlothChildLayer2.jpg** graphic located in the **Tutorial.06\Tutorial** folder included with your Data Files. The layer expands to accommodate the inserted graphic.

Trouble? If you can't see the new layer in the Document window, you clicked outside the layer and the Hidden attribute became effective. Click SCLayer2 in the Layers panel to select the layer and make its borders visible in the Document window.

5. Create a link from the graphic in the SCLayer2 layer to the **bands.htm** page. See Figure 6-34.

Figure 6-34 | SCLayer2 layer added to the Sloth Child page

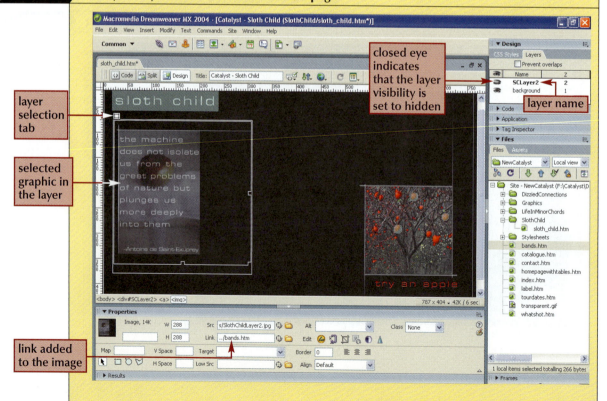

6. Click in the background layer outside SCLayer2. The SCLayer2 layer disappears because its visibility is set to Hidden.

7. Draw a third layer to the right of the band name and inside the background layer that is approximately **250** pixels wide and **100** pixels high, select the layer, change the layer ID to **SCLayer3**, click the **Vis** list arrow, click **Hidden**, insert the **SlothChildLayer3.jpg** graphic located in the **Tutorial.06\Tutorial** folder included with your Data Files, and then create a link from the graphic in the SCLayer3 layer to the **index.htm** page.

8. Reposition the layer, if necessary, so that no part of the image overlaps the band name or the apple tree photograph. See Figure 6-35.

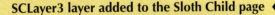 SCLayer3 layer added to the Sloth Child page Figure 6-35

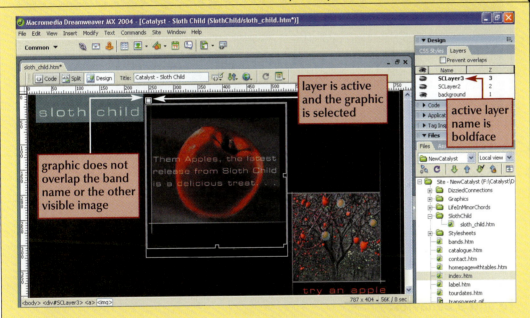

9. Click in the background layer outside the two hidden layers, draw a fourth layer to the left of the apple tree image that is approximately **250** pixels wide and **100** pixels high, change the layer ID to **SCLayer4**, click the **Vis** list arrow, click **Hidden**, insert the **SlothChildLayer4.jpg** graphic located in the **Tutorial.06\Tutorial** folder included with your Data Files, and then create a link from the graphic in the SCLayer4 layer to the **catalogue.htm** page.

10. Reposition the SCLayer4 layer, if necessary, so that the left border of the layer starts about **225** pixels from the left margin, the image does not overlap the apple tree photograph, and the bottom of the image (not necessarily the bottom of the SCLayer4 layer) aligns with the bottom of the apple tree photograph. See Figure 6-36.

| Figure 6-36 | SCLayer4 layer added to the Sloth Child page |

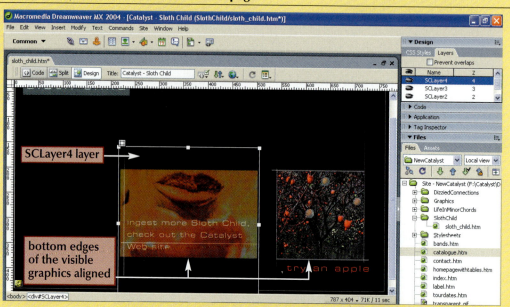

11. Click in a blank area of the Document window. Only the first layer that you drew is visible.
12. Save the page.

Next, you'll add behaviors to the hotspots in the SCLayer2 layer so that when a user points to a hotspot, the appropriate hidden layer will become visible in the page in the browser window.

To add a behavior:

1. Expand the **Tag Inspector** panel group, and then click the **Behaviors** tab. The Behaviors panel is displayed. See Figure 6-37.

| Figure 6-37 | Behaviors panel displayed |

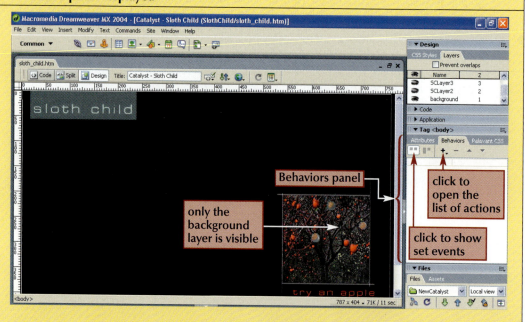

2. In the Document window, click the hotspot over the rightmost apple. The selected hotspot is the object to which you want to apply the behavior.

3. Click the **Add Behavior** button 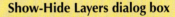 in the Behaviors panel, point to **Show Events For**, and then click **3.0 and Later Browsers**.

4. Click the **Add Behavior** button in the Behaviors panel, and then click **Show-Hide Layers** (the action). The Show-Hide Layers dialog box opens.

   You want the first hidden layer, SCLayer2, to become visible when the user event occurs, and you do not want either of the other two layers to be visible when this happens. You set the layer visibility in the Show-Hide Layers dialog box.

5. Click **layer "SCLayer2"** in the Named Layers list, and then click the **Show** button.

   If either of the other two layers whose Visibility attribute is set to Hidden are visible when the user event occurs, you want them to be hidden.

6. Click **layer "SCLayer3"** in the Named Layers list, click the **Hide** button, click **layer "SCLayer4"** in the Named Layers list, and then click the **Hide** button. You do not need to make a selection for the background layer because it never changes; that is, it is always visible. See Figure 6-38.

Figure 6-38 Show-Hide Layers dialog box

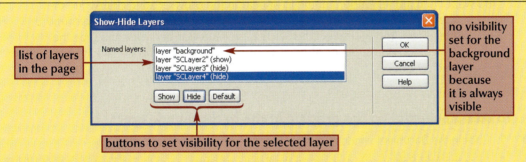

7. Click the **OK** button. The dialog box closes and the first behavior is added to the list in the Behaviors panel. The event handler "onMouseOver" is associated automatically with this behavior because it is the most frequently chosen event handler for this action. See Figure 6-39.

Figure 6-39 Behavior added to the selected hotspot

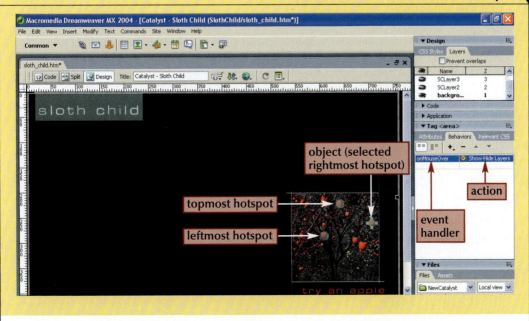

You'll repeat the same process to add the Show-Hide behavior to the other apple hotspots. Each hot spot will show a different layer and make the remaining layers hide.

To add behaviors to the other hotspots:

1. Select the hotspot over the leftmost apple. No behaviors are listed in the Behaviors panel because the Behaviors panel displays only behaviors attached to the selected object; you have not yet created a behavior for the selected hotspot.
2. Click the **Add Behavior** button ➕ in the Behaviors panel, and then click **Show-Hide Layers**. The Show-Hide Layers dialog box opens.
3. Show the **SCLayer3** layer, hide the **SCLayer2** and **SCLayer4** layers, and then click the **OK** button.
4. Select the topmost hotspot, click the **Add Behavior** button ➕ in the Behaviors panel, and then click **Show-Hide Layers**.
5. Hide the **SCLayer2** and **SCLayer3** layers, show the **SCLayer4** layer, and then click the **OK** button.

You want the band and album name to appear in the browser status bar when the mouse pointer is positioned over any part of the background image. The background graphic is the object. You will select the Set Text of Status Bar behavior and type the desired message. OnMouseOver is the default event handler for this behavior, so you do not need to select one.

To add a behavior to the graphic in the background layer:

1. Click in the Document window to select the image in the background layer.
2. Click the **Add Behavior** button ➕ in the Behaviors panel, point to **Set Text**, and then click **Set Text of Status Bar**. The Set Text of Status Bar dialog box opens.
3. Type **sloth child: try an apple**, and then click the **OK** button. The behavior is added to the graphic in the background layer.
4. Save the page.

You must preview a page that includes behaviors in a browser to test whether the behaviors work. You'll preview the Sloth Child page in your browser, and then test behaviors you added to the hotspots and the graphic in the background layer.

To test behaviors in a browser:

1. Preview the Sloth Child page in a browser, and then maximize the browser window, if necessary.
2. Position the pointer anywhere in the window except on one of the hotspots in the apple photograph. The pointer changes to 🖑 and the status bar shows the band and album name (sloth child: try an apple).

3. Position the pointer over the rightmost hotspot on the apple photograph. The image in the SCLayer2 layer appears, and the status bar shows the file path. See Figure 6-40. The layer will remain visible until the pointer moves over another hotspot.

Hidden layer previewed in a browser   **Figure 6-40**

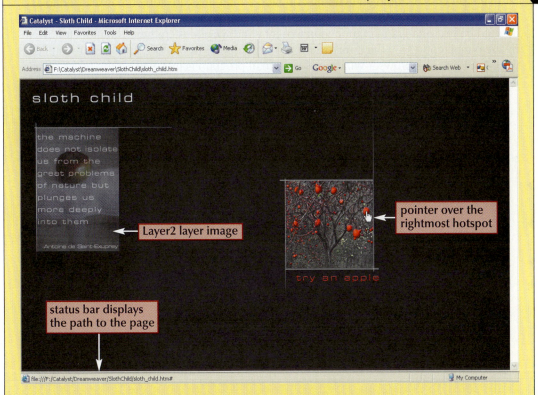

4. Position the pointer over the visible layer and read the text in the layer. The pointer changed to , because the graphic in the layer is linked to the Bands page.
5. Click the visible layer. The Bands page is displayed in the browser window.
6. Click the **Back** button on the browser toolbar to return to the Sloth Child page.
7. Position the pointer over the centermost hotspot on the apple photograph. The image in the SCLayer2 layer is hidden and the image in the SCLayer3 layer appears.
8. Read the text in the visible layer, and then position the pointer over the topmost hotspot on the apple photograph. The image in the Layer4 layer appears and the image in the SCLayer3 layer is hidden.
9. Close the browser window.

You can also add e-mail links to hotspots.

Adding an E-mail Link to a Page

An **e-mail link** is a link in a browser window that a user can click to start his or her default e-mail program, and open a blank message window with the e-mail address specified in the e-mail link already entered in the To field. The process of adding an e-mail link is similar to the process of adding a hyperlink. In fact, e-mail links are sometimes referred to as e-mail URLs. To create an e-mail link, you select the object (in this case, the hotspot, but it could be text or a graphic) in the Document window, and then, type "mailto:" followed by the e-mail address in the Link text box in the Property inspector. A user can then click the e-mail link in a browser window. If no e-mail program is installed on the user's computer, the e-mail link will not work.

You'll create an e-mail link from the band name to a general information e-mail address at Catalyst.

To add the e-mail link to a hotspot:

1. Click the rectangular hotspot over the band name. The Property inspector changes to show that a hotspot is selected.

2. Double-click the **Link** text box in the Property inspector, type **mailto:info@catalystnoise.com** (make sure that there are no spaces), and then press the **Enter** key.

3. Save the page, and then preview the page in a browser.

4. Click the **Sloth Child logo** to test the e-mail link, and then close the browser window and the message window.

   Trouble? If clicking the link does not open a message window in an e-mail program, your computer may not have a default e-mail program installed and configured. Close the browser window and continue with the tutorial.

Next, you'll add a custom script to the page.

Adding a Custom Script to a Page

When you used the Rollover Image button and the Navigation Bar button in the Common category on the Insert bar, you used the preset behavior tools to insert behaviors. In the Sloth Child page, you added behaviors to the hotspots using the Behaviors panel. Now you will add a custom script written by another programmer to the Sloth Child page. If you know JavaScript you can write your own scripts. You can also find scripts other people have written and posted for public use. However, you'll often need to fine-tune scripts that you use in Web pages, so it is a good idea to learn at least enough JavaScript so you can debug a page. Some good basic JavaScript resources include *www.docjs.com*, *www.javascript.com*, and *javascript.internet.com*. The script you are adding will cause the browser window containing the Sloth Child page to adjust itself, upon opening, to a particular size. The user can still resize the window once it is open.

Tutorial 6 Creating Dynamic Pages | Dreamweaver | DRM 349

To add a custom script to a page:

1. Click the **Script** button  in the **Script** list in **HTML** category on the Insert bar. The Script dialog box opens. You will enter the custom script.
2. Click the **Language** list arrow, and then click **JavaScript**, if necessary.
3. Click in the **Content** text box, type **function NuResizer(theW,theH){** and then press the **Enter** key, type **if(document.all || document.layers){** and then press the **Enter** key, type **window.resizeTo(theW,theH);** and then press the **Enter** key, type **}**, press the **Enter** key, and then type **}**. See Figure 6-41.

Figure 6-41   Script dialog box

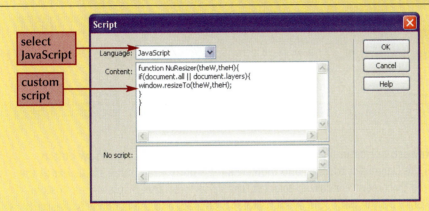

4. Click the **OK** button. This script creates the custom action of forcing the Sloth Child browser window to resize once the page is loaded. (The Sloth child page is the object.)

   Trouble? If a dialog box opens, indicating that you won't see this element unless Invisible Elements are displayed, click the OK button and then click View on the menu bar, click Visual Aids, and then click Invisible Elements if necessary to check the option.

   Now you will add the event handler to the opening body tag for the page.

5. Click the **Show Code View** button on the Document toolbar. The Document window switches to Code view and the code inserting the script you just wrote is highlighted. See Figure 6-42.

Figure 6-42   Sloth Child page in Code view

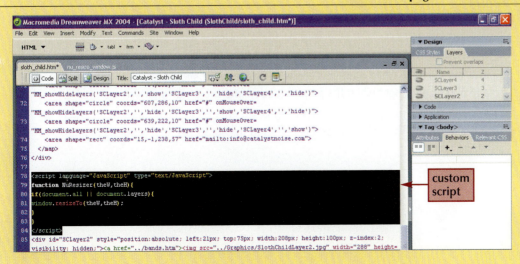

Trouble? If the script was inserted on a different line in your page, the script will work correctly. Continue with Step 6.

6. Scroll up a few lines and click before the closing bracket of the opening body tag.

7. Press the **spacebar**, and then type **onLoad="NuResizer(800,600)"** in the Code pane. The word *NuResizer* references the script you just wrote. The (800, 600) are attributes that tell the script the actual width and height at which to open the window. The word *onLoad* is the event handler associated with the event of the Sloth Child window opening. See Figure 6-43.

Figure 6-43 Event handler added to the opening body tag

opening body tag with the event handler added

8. Click the **Refresh** button in the Behaviors panel, click the **Show Design View** button on the Document toolbar, and then click the **<body>** tag in the status bar at the bottom of the Document window to select it. The Behaviors panel displays your custom script. The object is the page, the event handler is onLoad, and the action is NuResizer() with width and height attributes of 800, 600. Notice that your action is listed in the Behaviors panel.

Trouble? If the custom script is not listed in the Behaviors panel, click in the upper-left corner of the Document window, press the Up Arrow key, press the Left Arrow key, and then click the body tag in the status bar again.

9. Save the page.

Now that you are finished adding scripts and behaviors to the page, you need to test the behaviors again. It is important to continue testing all the scripts each time you add a new one to the page because new behaviors can affect the behaviors that are already in the page.

To test behaviors:

1. Preview the Sloth Child page in a browser. The browser should resize to 800 pixels width and 600 pixels height when the page is loaded into the window (or onLoad).

2. Position the pointer anywhere in the window except on the band name or on one of the apple hotspots. The pointer changes to 👆 and the status bar shows the band and album name.

3. Position the pointer over the rightmost hotspot on the apple tree photograph. The image in the SCLayer2 layer appears, and the status bar changes to reflect the file path. See Figure 6-44.

Figure 6-44

Sloth Child page in the resized browser window

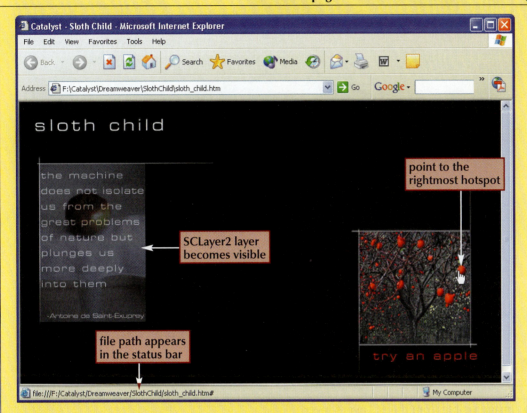

4. Click the graphic in the layer. The Bands page opens, but the browser window does not change size.
5. Click the **Back** button on the browser toolbar. The Sloth Child page is reloaded and the SCLayer2 layer is hidden.
6. Point to the leftmost hotspot on the apple tree photograph. The image in the SCLayer3 layer appears. See Figure 6-45.

DRM 352 | Dreamweaver | Tutorial 6 Creating Dynamic Pages

Figure 6-45   **Image visible from the SCLayer3 layer**

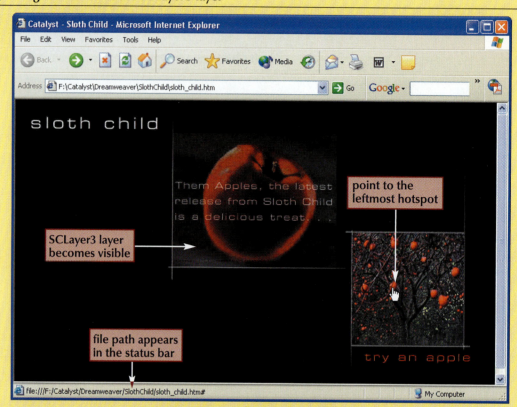

7. Point to the topmost hotspot on the apple tree photograph. The image in the SCLayer4 layer appears and the image in the SCLayer3 layer is hidden. See Figure 6-46.

Figure 6-46   **Image visible from the SCLayer4 layer**

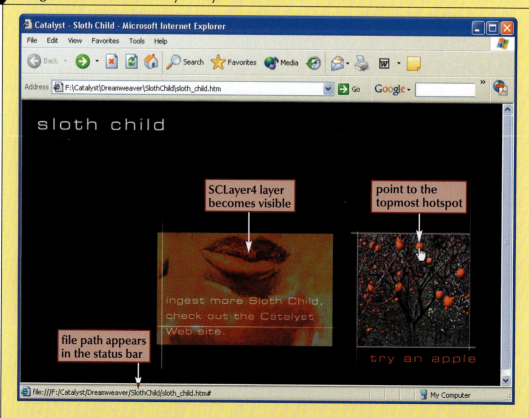

8. Click the graphic in the layer to open the Catalogue page in the browser window, and then click the **Back** button on the browser toolbar to reload the Sloth Child page with no layers visible.

9. Click the band name hotspot. Your default e-mail program starts and a new message window opens with "info@catalystnoise.com" in the To field.

   Trouble? If a new e-mail message window does not open, then your e-mail program may not be configured. Close any dialog boxes and windows that open and continue with Step 10.

10. Close the message window, if necessary, and then close the browser window.

You can also edit and delete behaviors. You want to see if a different event handler would be a better choice for the apple hotspots. You decide to delete the behavior that displays a message in the status bar because you don't want the pointer to look like it is positioned over a link when it isn't.

Editing and Deleting Behaviors

Once a behavior has been created, you can change the event handler associated with the behavior or you can delete the behavior. If you want to change the action, you need to delete the old behavior, select the object, and then attach the new behavior. You can do this in the Behaviors panel.

You will edit one of the behaviors associated with the rightmost hotspot on the apple tree photograph. You will also delete the behavior that displays text in the status bar.

To edit behaviors:

1. Select the rightmost hotspot on the apple tree photograph. The behavior is listed and selected in the Behaviors panel.

2. Click the behavior in the Behaviors panel, and then click the **Events** list arrow. The events that are supported by 3.0 and later browsers and the Show-Hide Layers action are listed—onClick, onMouseOut, and onMouseOver.

3. Click **onClick**. The behavior's event is changed so that the action will occur when the user clicks this hotspot.

4. Click anywhere in the Document window to select the image in the background layer. The action "Set Text of Status Bar" appears in the Behaviors panel.

5. Click the behavior in the Behaviors panel, if necessary, to select it, and then click the **Remove Event** button in the Behaviors panel to delete the selected behavior.

6. Save the page, preview the page in a browser, and position the pointer anywhere in the window except over a hotspot. The status bar no longer displays "sloth child: try an apple."

7. Click the rightmost hotspot on the apple tree photograph. The image in the SCLayer2 layer appears, and a blue border is visible around the background image. See Figure 6-47.

Figure 6-47   **Edited behavior for the SCLayer2 layer**

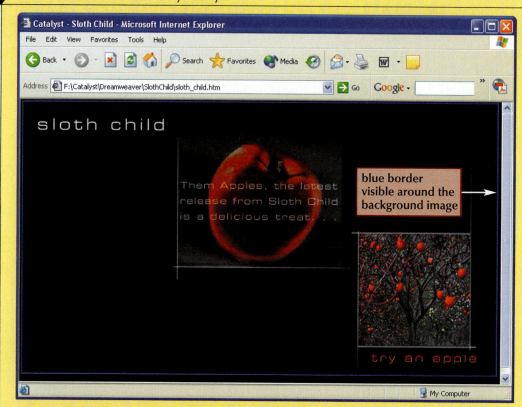

Small changes in code sometimes affect the page display so it is important to check modified pages in a browser window. You decide it is better if the user simply points at the apple hotspots and to remove the blue border around the background image.

▶ 8. Close the browser window, click the rightmost hotspot on the apple tree photograph, click the behavior in the Behaviors panel to select it, click the **Events** list arrow, and then click **onMouseOver**. The event is changed back to mouseover.

▶ 9. Click the background graphic to select it, and then type **0** in the Border text box in the Property inspector.

▶ 10. Save the page, preview the page in a browser, test the mouseovers and links, and then close the browser window and the page.

The Sloth Child page is complete. You will add a link to this page in the Review Assignments.

Updating the Web Site on the Remote Server

As a final review of the changes you made to the Catalyst site, you'll update the files on your remote server and review the pages over the Internet. You will upload the pages and files of the site that have changed or been added. This includes the Graphics folder, the SlothChild folder, the homepagewithtables.htm page, the index.htm page, and the transparent.gif file. Then you'll preview the site on the Web.

To upload a site to the remote server:

1. Collapse the Design panel group and the Tag Inspector panel group, and then click the **Connects to Remote Host** button on the Files panel toolbar.
2. If necessary, click the **View** list arrow on the Files panel toolbar, and then click **Local View**.
3. Select the **SlothChild** folder, the **homepagewithtables.htm** page, the **index.htm** page, and the **transparent.gif** file in the Local View list, and then click the **Put File(s)** button on the Files panel toolbar.

   Trouble? If you can't select only the files you want, click the Minus (–) button next to the SlothChild folder to collapse the file list in the folder, press and hold the Ctrl key, and then click the folders and files you want to upload.
4. Click the **Yes** button when asked if you want to include dependent files because you have not selected the new dependent file for the site yet.
5. Click the **Disconnects from Remote Host** button on the Files panel toolbar, click the **View** list arrow on the Files panel toolbar, and then click **Local View**.

Next, you'll preview the updated site in a browser. The site will include all the new features and pages you added to the local version.

To preview the updated site in a browser:

1. Open your browser, type the URL of your remote site in the Address bar on the browser toolbar, and then press the **Enter** key.
2. Click the top **What's Hot** link to open the What's Hot page in a new browser window, and then close the new browser window that opened.
3. Repeat Step 2 for the graphic in the WhatsHot layer and for the bottom **What's Hot** link.
4. Click in the **Address** text box in the browser window, press the **Right Arrow** key to position the insertion point at the end of the current URL, type **/SlothChild/sloth_child.htm**, and then press the **Enter** key. The Sloth Child page opens in the same browser window.
5. Point to each of the three hotspots on the apple photograph to test the behaviors.
6. Click the band name to open a new e-mail message window, and then close the message window.

   Trouble? If a new e-mail message window does not open, then your e-mail program may not be configured. Close any dialog boxes and windows that open and continue with Step 7.
7. Close the browser window.

Sara and Brian are pleased with the Catalyst site. It has a nice look and useful functionality.

Review

Session 6.3 Quick Check

1. What is a behavior?
2. What is an event?
3. What is an action?
4. Are all behaviors selected and assigned in the Behaviors panel?
5. True or False? You cannot change the action associated with a behavior.
6. What is a custom script?

Review

Tutorial Summary

In this tutorial, you inserted layers into a Web page. You selected, moved, resized, and added content to a layer. You also adjusted the layer's attributes. You adjusted the stacking order of layers. You aligned layers, created nested layers, and applied Dreamweaver's built-in Netscape Resize Fix to Web pages that contain layers. You also converted layers to tables and reviewed the HTML involved with layers. Finally, you added behaviors to a Web page, and then you edited and deleted behaviors.

Key Terms

absolute positioning	event handler	Netscape Resize Fix
action	grid	object
behavior	inline	user event
dynamic HTML	layer	z-index number
e-mail link	nested layer	

Practice

Practice the skills you learned in the tutorial.

Review Assignments

There are no Data Files needed for the Review Assignments.

Brian asks you to complete the home page for the new Catalyst site. You'll move, resize, and align the layers that you have already created and fill them with content. Then you will create new layers and fill them with content. Finally, you will create links from the content to the other pages of the site.

1. Open the NewCatalyst Web site that you modified in this tutorial, open the index.htm page in the Document window, expand the Layers panel, and then select the DizziedConnections layer.
2. Move the DizziedConnections layer so that the left border is approximately 10 pixels from the left page border. (*Hint:* Show the rulers if you need help measuring distance.)
3. Hold down the Shift key and select the WhatsHot layer to select both layers.
4. Click Modify on the menu bar, point to Align, and then click Top to align the top border of the two layers. Because the WhatsHot layer was selected last, the DizziedConnections layer aligns to it.
5. Drag the right resize handle of the DizziedConnections layer to the right, leaving approximately 10 pixels between it and the left border of the WhatsHot layer.
6. Click after "Dizzied Connections," press the spacebar, and then type "Heads West."
7. Select the text "Information about the band will be here soon." and then type "The boys have packed up their toys and are heading to the West Coast to play for a while. Check out the tour dates to see if they'll be stopping by your hometown."

8. Select "Dizzied Connections Heads West," create a link from the selected text to the dc_frameset.htm page in the DizziedConnections folder, click the Target list arrow in the Property inspector, and then click _blank.
9. Select the words "tour dates" and create a link to the tourdates.htm page.
10. Select the h2 style in the CSS Styles panel, click the Edit Style button, click Normal in the Weight list, type 28 in the Size text box, and then click the OK button. The heading text in the DizziedConnections layer changes size and weight to match the edited h2 style.
11. If the DizziedConnections layer is longer than the text inside of it, select the layer, and then drag the bottom resize handle up to resize the layer to a smaller size. If the layer will not resize, click in the blank line at the bottom of the layer, and then press the Backspace key as many times as necessary to move the insertion point so that it is positioned immediately after the end of the last sentence, and then resize the layer.
12. Use the Align command to align the SlothChild and DizziedConnections layers to the left border of the DizziedConnections layer. (*Hint*: Select the SlothChild layer first. If the Dizzied Connections layer moves, you selected it first; click Edit on the menu bar, click Undo Align, and then try again.)
13. Select only the SlothChild layer, and then press the Arrow keys to nudge the layer until the top border of the layer is about 20 pixels from the bottom border of the DizziedConnections layer.
14. Select the words "Sloth Child," apply the Heading 2 tag from the Format list in the Property inspector, link the selected text to the sloth_child.htm file in the SlothChild folder, and then click _blank in the Target list.
15. Select the layer and drag the right resize handle until the words "Sloth Child" fit on one line. (*Hint:* The layer will be approximately 200 pixels in width.)
16. Click below the Sloth Child heading, and then type "The new release is shaking things up. Check out the catalogue to see what the buzz is all about."
17. Select the word "catalogue" and link it to the catalogue.htm page.
18. Draw another layer approximately 15 pixels to the right of the SlothChild layer. Make the layer the same height as the SlothChild layer, and extend the layer to the right until its right border aligns with the right border of the DizziedConnections layer above it.
19. Click in the new layer, name the layer "LIMC," type "Life in Minor Chords" in the new layer, press the Enter key, select the text you typed, and then apply the Heading 2 style from the Format list in the Property inspector. Adjust the width of the layer if necessary to fit the heading on one line.
20. Move the insertion point below the Life in Minor Chords heading, and then type "If you are an LIMC fan, keep checking their Web site over the next few weeks! The new look is in place and we are adding more every day."
21. Drag the bottom border of the layer up so it just fits to the text.
22. Select the heading text, link it to the limc_frameset.htm page in the LifeInMinorChords folder, and then click _blank in the Target list.
23. Align the top border of the LIMC layer to the top border of the SlothChild layer.
24. Select the DizziedConnections, SlothChild, LIMC, and WhatsHot layers, and then press the Up Arrow key to nudge them up to approximately 20 pixels below the navigation bar, if necessary.
25. Save the page, save and close the catalyst_styles.css page, preview the page in a browser, test the new links, close the browser window, and then close the page.
26. Upload the changed pages to your remote server, and then preview the site over the Web.

Case Problem 1

Apply

Create a new page with layers for a Web site about small rural communities of northern Vietnam.

Data Files needed for this Case Problem: HartCourseList.gif, HrochNewCourse.gif

Hroch University Anthropology Department Professor Hart is going to be teaching several new courses this semester. He wants you to create a new page for the site with descriptions of these classes. To do this, you will use layers in the new page. You will also create a layer beside the logo in the home page with a link to the new page.

1. Open the Hart site that you modified in Tutorial 5, Case 1 and, in the Files panel, copy the linguistic_differences.htm page, and then paste a copy of the page in the site's local root folder.
2. Rename the copied page "new_courses.htm," open the new page in the Document window, update the links, and then change the page title to "Hroch University Anthropology Dept. - Prof. Hart - New Courses."
3. Draw a layer approximately 500 pixels wide and 25 pixels high at the bottom of the page, and then enter "Footer" as the layer ID.
4. Copy the footer information from the table, paste it into the Footer layer, drag the resize handles so that the layer is the width of the footer, and then position the layer at the bottom of the page approximately 200 pixels below the table.
5. Select the entire Linguistic Differences table and delete it from the page, and then delete the navigation bar from the page. Everything below the logo and above the Footer layer is removed from the page.
6. Draw a layer approximately 150 pixels square at the left of the window, approximately 20 pixels below the lowest horizontal line and 10 pixels from the edge of the window, and then enter "CourseList" as the layer ID.
7. Insert the **HartCourseList.gif** graphic located in the **Tutorial.06\Cases** folder included with your Data Files in the CourseList layer, and then drag the borders of the layer to fit snugly against the borders of the graphic.
8. Draw a third layer about 20 pixels to the right of the CourseList layer that is approximately 400 pixels wide and the same height as the CourseList layer, enter "OpeningText" as the layer ID, and then type the following text into the layer: "Professor Hart has developed two exciting courses based on the findings of his most recent trip to study the people of Northern Vietnam. To view a course description, select the course that interests you. (These courses are available only to graduate students or by permission of the instructor.)"
9. Align the top of the OpeningText layer with the top of the CourseList layer.

Explore

10. Hide the OpeningText layer from view by clicking in the column with the eye icon beside the layer name in the Layers panel until the closed eye icon appears.
11. Draw a fourth layer to the right of the CourseList layer, approximately the same size and in the same position as the OpeningText layer. (It is fine to overlap the hidden OpeningText layer.) Enter "LinguisticDifferences" as the layer ID, and then type the following text in the layer:
"Anthropological study of cultural patterning in linguistic variations among the people of Northern Vietnam; survey of historical and theoretical development of linguistic evolution in the area; case studies based on Dr. Hart's most recent field work; emphasis on ethnography of speaking and verbal art. Graduate standing or consent of instructor required."

Explore

12. Align the LinguisticDifferences layer with the top and left border of the OpeningText layer. (*Hint*: Because the OpeningText layer is invisible, select the layers in the Layers panel. The hidden layer will become visible while it is selected and will return to its hidden state when it is not selected.)

Explore

13. Hide the LinguisticDifferences layer by clicking in the column with the eye icon beside the layer name in the Layers panel until the closed eye icon appears.
14. Repeat Steps 11 through 13, but this time enter "Rituals" as the layer ID, and then type the following text in the layer:
"How the minority cultures of Northern Vietnam conceptualize the biophysical environment through religious beliefs and ritualistic practices; how images of the environment influence activities and how they are incorporated into tribal life."

Explore

15. Click the closed eye icon next to the OpeningText layer in the Layers panel to make the OpeningText layer visible.
16. Select the CourseList graphic, click the Rectangular Hotspot Tool in the Property inspector, draw a hotspot over the top course in the list, and then draw another rectangular hotspot over the second course in the list.
17. Expand the Tag Inspector panel group, and then click the Behaviors panel to open it. (You may see a behavior in the list, depending on where the insertion point is in the page.)
18. Select the top hotspot, click the Add Behavior button in the Behaviors panel, click Show-Hide Layers, and then set the layers visibility to show the Footer, CourseList, and LinguisticDifferences layers and to hide OpeningText and layer Rituals layers.
19. Select the bottom hotspot, click the Add Behavior button in the Behaviors panel, click Show-Hide Layers, and then set the layers visibility to show the Footer, CourseList, and Rituals layers and to hide the LinguisticDifferences and OpeningText layers.
20. Select the Footer layer, and then move the layer until the top of the layer is positioned at approximately 250 pixels. (*Hint:* You can press the Up Arrow key to shift the vertical position without affecting its horizontal position.)
21. Click the Script button in the Script list in the HTML category on the Insert bar, click JavaScript in the Language list if necessary, type the following into the Content text box, and then click the OK button to add a custom script to the page that will resize the page when it loads in a browser window:
    function NuResizer(theW,theH){
    if(document.all || document.layers){
    window.resizeTo(theW,theH);
    }
    }
22. Switch to Code view, click in the opening body tag after the word "body," press the spacebar, type "onLoad="NuResizer(650,475)"", and then switch to Design view.
23. Save the page, preview the page in a browser to confirm that the browser window opens to 650 x 475 pixels, test each of the hotspots, and then close the browser window and the page.
24. Open the index.htm page, draw a layer 100 pixels wide and 75 pixels high in the colored banner at the top of the home page positioned above the Contact Information link in the navigation bar.
25. Insert the **HrochNewCourse.gif** graphic located in the **Tutorial.06\Cases** folder included with your Data Files into the layer, resize the layer so that it fits snugly around the graphic, and then use the Arrow keys to nudge the layer so the graphic is completely within the colored bar.
26. Select the graphic, create a link to the new_courses.htm page, and then target the link to open the page in a new browser window.
27. Save the page, preview the page in a browser window, test the New Courses link, and then close the browser windows and the page.
28. Upload the site to the remote server, and then preview the site over the Web.

Apply

Add layers with graphics and behaviors to display related information when a user mouses over the painting in a Web site for an art museum.

Explore

Case Problem 2

Data Files needed for this Case Problem: AQuietDayInUtica.jpg, BuffaloRunners.jpg, CowpunchingSometimes.jpg, IndiansHuntingBuffalo.jpg, AFigureOfTheNight.jpg, TheBucker.jpg, TheCowPuncher.jpg, DeerInForest.jpg

Museum of Western Art C. J. Strittmatter asks you to add the art to the Art page of the museum's Web site. Because the museum has so many paintings, C.J. has decided to feature a few paintings at a time from the collection. You'll use layers to add paintings to the page. You'll create an additional layer for painting information, attach the Set Layer Text behavior to each painting graphic, and then set the text in the new painting information layer. You'll use onMouseOver as the event handler, which will cause the painting information layer to update with information associated with the painting that the user mouses over.

1. Open the Museum site that you modified in Tutorial 5, Case 2, and then open the art.htm page.
2. Open the index.htm page, use the Copy HTML command on the Edit menu to copy the "WELCOME" text, and then close the page.
3. Place the insertion point to the left of the menu bar table in the Art page, click to the right of the menu bar table, press the Enter key, use the Paste HTML command on the Edit menu to paste the text you copied, right align it, select the text you pasted, and then type "ART."
4. Show the rulers and the grid if they are not already visible in the Document window.
5. Draw a layer approximately 150 pixels wide and 100 pixels high, and then drag the layer approximately 10 pixels from the left border of the page and approximately 20 pixels below the bottom of the menu table (located at the right of the page). (*Hint:* Use the grid to help you position the layer.)
6. Insert the **AQuietDayInUtica.jpg** graphic located in the **Tutorial.06\Cases** folder included with your Data Files into the layer, drag the borders of the layer so that the layer fits snugly around the graphic, and then enter "UticaPic" as the layer ID.
7. Select the graphic, and then apply the image_border style from the Class list in the Property inspector.
8. Repeat Steps 5 through 7 to add seven more layers. Draw each layer approximately 20 pixels to the right of the previous layer until there are four layers across; then draw the other four layers in a second row approximately 20 pixels below the bottom border of the top row of layers. Use the following list to add graphics to the layers and to name the layers. To add the layers, draw the first layer (to hold the BuffaloRunners.jpg graphic), insert the graphic, name the layer, and then draw the next layer.

Graphic	Layer ID
BuffaloRunners.jpg	BuffaloPic
CowpunchingSometimes.jpg	CowPic
IndiansHuntingBuffalo.jpg	IndianPic
AFigureOfTheNight.jpg	FigurePic
TheBucker.jpg	BuckerPic
TheCowPuncher.jpg	PuncherPic
DeerInForest.jpg	DeerPic

9. Select all the graphics in the top row, click Modify on the menu bar, point to Align, click Top to fine-tune the horizontal alignment of the graphics, and then do the same for the graphics in the second row.
10. Select the two graphics in the first column, use the Align command to align their left borders to fine-tune the alignment of the graphics in the first column, and then do the same for the graphics in the other three columns.

11. Draw a new layer centered above the four columns of paintings and with the top border of the new layer aligned with the top border of the table that holds the menu bar. Make the layer approximately 200 pixels wide and 50 pixels high. (*Hint:* Once the layer is drawn, the center resize handles should be visually aligned with the center space between the four columns of paintings.)
12. Name the new layer "PaintingID," and then apply the .image_border style from the Class list in the Property inspector.
13. Place the insertion point inside the PaintingID layer, and then type "Point to each painting to view additional information." Select the text and apply the menustyle style. (The text you typed will be displayed in the layer until the user mouses over a painting.)
14. Select the **AQuietDayInUtica.jpg** graphic, click the Add Behavior button in the Behaviors panel, point to the Show Events list, click IE 4.0, click the Add Behavior button, point to Set Text, and then click Set Text of Layer.

Explore

15. In the Set Text of Layer dialog box, click layer "PaintingID" in the Layer list, and then type the following HTML code in the New HTML text box that tells the browser how to display the text as well as the text to display. (*Hint:* You can press the Enter key at the end of each line to keep the lines organized as they are here, or you can type all of the text on one line; either way the text will display correctly.)
    <span class="menustyle">
    A Quiet Day in Utica
    Charles M. Russell
    1907
    Oil on canvas
    </span>
16. Click the OK button, and then save the page and preview the page in a browser. The text you typed directly into the PaintingID layer is displayed when the page is initially loaded. Point to the UticaPic layer; the image changes to the text you typed in Step 15. Notice that the code you typed is not displayed. Close the browser window. (*Hint:* If you made a mistake when you typed the text in Step 15, click the graphic to display the behavior in the Behaviors panel, double-click the Set Layer Text action to open the Set Layer Text dialog box with the text you typed displayed, correct the text, press the OK button, and then save and preview the page in a browser again.)
17. Repeat Steps 14 through 16 to add the Set Layer Text behavior to each painting, using the following text for each painting:

Graphic	Layer	Text
BuffaloRunners.jpg	PaintingID	<span class="menustyle"> Buffalo Runners-Big Horn Basin Frederic Remington 1909 Oil on canvas </span>
CowpunchingSometimes.jpg	PaintingID	<span class="menustyle"> Cow Punching Sometimes Spells Trouble Charles M. Russell 1889 Oil on canvas </span>

	IndiansHuntingBuffalo.jpg	PaintingID	\<span class="menustyle"\> Indians Hunting Buffalo\<br\> (Wild Men's Meat; Buffalo Hunt)\<br\> Charles M. Russell\<br\> 1894\<br\> Oil on canvas\<br\> \</span\>
	AFigureOfTheNight.jpg	PaintingID	\<span class="menustyle"\> A Figure of the Night\<br\> (The Sentinel)\<br\> Frederic Remington\<br\> 1908\<br\> Oil on canvas\<br\> \</span\>
	TheBucker.jpg	PaintingID	\<span class="menustyle"\> The Bucker\<br\> Charles M. Russell\<br\> 1904\<br\> Pencil, watercolor, and gouache on paper\<br\> \</span\>
	TheCowPuncher.jpg	PaintingID	\<span class="menustyle"\> The Cow Puncher\<br\> Frederic Remington\<br\> 1901 \<br\> Oil (black and white) on canvas\<br\> \</span\>
	DeerInForest.jpg	PaintingID	\<span class="menustyle"\> Deer in Forest\<br\> (White Tailed Deer)\<br\> Charles M. Russell\<br\> 1917\<br\> Oil on canvas\<br\> \</span\>

18. Save the page, preview the page in a browser, test the behaviors by moving the mouse pointer across each row of paintings, and then close the browser window and the page.
19. Upload the site to the remote server, and then preview the site over the Web.

Apply

Add layers with graphics and behaviors to display related information when a user mouses over a book cover in a Web site for an independent publisher of fringe writing.

Case Problem 3

Data Files needed for this Case Problem: BookCoverQueenSm.jpg, BookCoverBasketSm.gif, BookCoverStopGapSm.jpg

NORM Mark Chapman asks you to add book covers to the Books page in the NORM site using layers. He also wants you to add behaviors to create some interactivity in the site. You'll add behaviors so that when a user points to a book cover, information about the book will appear at the bottom of the screen.

1. Open the NORM site that you modified in Tutorial 5, Case 3 and then open the books.htm page.
2. Replace the "COMING SOON" text with "NORM Books." The text is displayed in all uppercase because of the attributes of the applied style.

3. Draw a 150-pixel square layer at the left of the page 10 pixels below the text you just typed, enter "PunchCover" as the layer ID, insert the **BookCoverPunchSmall.jpg** graphic located in the **Graphics** folder in the site's local root folder into the layer, type "1" in the Border text box in the Property inspector, and then resize the layer so it fits snugly around the graphic.
4. Draw another layer to the right of the PunchCover layer approximately the same size as the first layer, enter "QueenCover" as the layer ID, insert the **BookCoverQueenSm.jpg** graphic located in the **Tutorial.06\Cases** folder included with your Data Files, type "1" in the Border text box in the Property inspector, and then resize the layer to fit snugly around the graphic.
5. Repeat Step 4 for the **BookCoverBasketSm.gif** and the **BookCoverStopGapSm.jpg** graphics located in the **Tutorial.06\Cases** folder included with your Data Files, entering "BasketCover" and "StopGapCover" for the layer IDs, respectively.
6. Adjust the horizontal spacing of the layers to add 15 pixels between each layer, and then align the tops of the layers.
7. Draw a new layer approximately 25 pixels below the book covers that extends from the middle of the first book cover to the middle of the fourth book cover and is approximately 100 pixels high, and then enter "PunchText" as the layer ID.
8. Type the following text into the layer:
"Punch by Kelly Moore
Punch is a wacky, eclectic collection of monologues that give voice to the psyche of the modern woman with stories that range from heroic to tragic to just plain goofy."
9. Apply the norm_book_titles style to the book title, and then hide the layer in the Layers panel.
10. Repeat Steps 7 through 9 for each of the remaining book titles, using the following layer names and text:

Layer Name	Layer Text
QueenText	Queen of Chimeras by Sajanya BaRae
	Queen of Chimeras is the story of Sheila Helt, a woman who is part misfit and part mystic. It is a story for every woman who has dared to follow her own path and stumbled a bit along the way.
BasketText	Basket Dropping 101 by Tika
	A story for those who are strong at heart, this book is an edgy, graphic, and perversely hilarious account of life through the eyes of a young woman struggling to find dignity in poverty and to create her place in the world.
StopGapText	Stop Gap by Kim Flores
	Stop Gap is an investigation of the effects of the new global economy on the exploited workers in Third World countries. Kim Flores uses her background in economics, sociology, and international business to shed light on the complex problems associated with globalization, and to suggest practical, real-world solutions.

11. Select all of the text layers in the Layers panel and align them to the top and to the left.
12. Select the graphic in the PunchCover layer, expand the Behaviors panel, and then add the Show-Hide Layers behavior.
13. In the Show-Hide Layers dialog box, show the PunchText layer, hide the QueenText, BasketText, and StopGapText layers (do not set the BookCover layers to Show or Hide because they never change), click the OK button, and then change the event handler to onMouseOver in the Behaviors panel, if necessary.
14. Repeat Step 13 for the graphics in the QueenCover, BasketCover, and StopGapCover layers using the corresponding text layer as the layer to show each time.

DRM 364 Dreamweaver | Tutorial 6 Creating Dynamic Pages

15. Position the insertion point in the Document window to the right of the text "NORM BOOKS" and type "(Place your mouse over a book cover to view a description.)" Select the text you just typed and remove the CSS style applied to it by selecting the text and clicking None in the Style list in the Property inspector.
16. Save the page, preview the page in a browser window, move the mouse over each book cover to show the hidden layers, and then close the browser window and close the page.
17. Upload the site to the remote server, and then preview the site over the Web.

Create

Add a new page that uses layers with graphics and behaviors to display the spiciness of selected food items in a Web site for a newly opening sushi restaurant.

Case Problem 4

Data Files needed for this Case Problem: WasabiChili.jpg, WasabiHotWings.jpg, WasabiLowRiseJeans.jpg, WasabiPicture.gif, WasabiOriginal.gif, WasabiCold.gif, WasabiLukeWarm.gif, WasabiToasty.gif, WasabiOnFire.gif, WasabiWasabi.gif, WasabiPictureSmall.gif

Sushi Ya-Ya Mary O'Brien asks you to create a How Hot Is Wasabi page for the Sushi Ya-Ya site. The page will use layers and behaviors to create an interactive thermometer that will "measure" the hotness of different objects. You will place graphics of a pepper, a plate of hot wings, low-rise jeans, and wasabi in layers at the bottom of the page. You will place a graphic of a thermometer in a layer above them. You will include alternate thermometer graphics in hidden layers. The alternate graphics will show the thermometer with the temperature at various levels. You will then use the Show-Hide behavior to show various hotness levels when each graphic is selected. Finally, you will create a link from the home page to the How Hot Is Wasabi page.

1. Open the SushiYaYa site you modified in Tutorial 5, Case 4, copy the menu.htm page, paste a copy of the page in the local root folder of the site, and then rename the copied page "wasabi.htm."
2. Open the wasabi.htm page, and then delete the Sushi Descriptions text, the coming soon text, and the navigation bar.
3. Type "How Hot Is Wasabi?" below the horizontal line and apply the page heading style that you created to the text.
4. Draw a layer 20 pixels from the left border of the page and 10 pixels below the heading text, enter "ChiliPic" as the layer ID, insert the **WasabiChili.jpg** graphic located in the **Tutorial.06\Cases** folder included with your Data Files, and then apply the imageborders style to the graphic.
5. Draw a layer 20 pixels below the ChiliPic layer, enter "HotWingsPic" as the layer ID, insert the **WasabiHotWings.jpg** graphic located in the **Tutorial.06\Cases** folder included with your Data Files, and then apply the imageborders style to the graphic.
6. Draw a layer at the right of the page, across from the ChiliPic layer and starting at approximately 500 pixels, enter "JeansPic" as the layer ID, insert the **WasabiLowRiseJeans.jpg** graphic located in the **Tutorial.06\Cases** folder included with your Data Files, and then apply the imageborder style to the graphic.
7. Draw a layer 20 pixels below the JeansPic layer, enter "WasabiPic" as the layer ID, insert the **WasabiPicture.gif** graphic located in the **Tutorial.06\Cases** folder included with your Data Files, and then apply the imageborders style to the graphic.
8. Align the top border of the top row of graphics, and then align the top border of the bottom row of graphics.
9. Draw a layer in the center of the page, enter "ThermoOriginal" as the layer ID, and then insert the **WasabiOriginal.gif** graphic located in the **Tutorial.06\Cases** folder included with your Data Files.

10. Draw another layer in the center of the page, enter "ThermoCold" as the layer ID, insert the **WasabiCold.gif** graphic located in the **Tutorial.06\Cases** folder included with your Data Files, and then hide the layer.
11. Repeat Step 10 to create layers with each of the following graphics:

Graphic	Layer Name
WasabiLukeWarm.gif	ThermoLukeWarm
WasabiToasty.gif	ThermoToasty
WasabiOnFire.gif	ThermoOnFire1
WasabiWasabi.gif	ThermoWasabi

12. Select the ThermoOriginal, ThermoCold, ThermoLukeWarm, ThermoToasty, ThermoOnFire1, and ThermoWasabi layers in the Layers panel, and then align them Top and Left.
13. While all the Thermo graphics are still selected, reposition them in the page, if necessary, so that they are centered between the other graphics.

Explore
14. Select the ThermoOriginal layer in the Layers panel, click the closed eye icon to open it, click the z-index number, and then type 5, if necessary. The ThermoOriginal layer moves to the number 5 position in the stacking order.
15. Select the graphic in ChiliPic layer, add the Show-Hide Layers behavior, and then show the ThermoOnFire1 layer, hide the ThermoToasty, ThermoLukeWarm, ThermoCold, and ThermoWasabi layers, and do nothing to the ThermoOriginal, ChiliPic, HotWingsPic, JeansPic, and WasabiPic layers.

Explore
16. In the Behaviors panel, select the event, click the list arrow, point to Show Events For, click IE 4.0, click the list arrow again, and then click (onClick) in the list.
17. Select the graphic in the HotWingsPic layer, add Show-Hide Layers behavior, and then show the ThermoToasty layer, hide the ThermoOnFire1, ThermoLukeWarm, ThermoCold, and ThermoWasabi layers, and do nothing to the ThermoOriginal, ChiliPic, HotWingsPic, JeansPic, and WasabiPic layers.

Explore
18. In the Behaviors panel, select the event, click the list arrow, and then click (onClick) in the list.
19. Select the graphic in the JeansPic layer, add the Show-Hide Layers behavior, and then show the ThermoCold layer, hide the ThermoOnFire1, ThermoToasty, ThermoLukeWarm, and ThermoWasabi layers, and do nothing to the ThermoOriginal, ChiliPic, HotWingsPic, JeansPic, and WasabiPic layers.
20. In the Behaviors panel, select the event, click the list arrow, and then click (onClick) in the list.
21. Select the WasabiPic layer, add the Show-Hide Layers behavior, and then show the ThermoWasabi layer, hide the ThermoOnFire1, ThermoToasty, ThermoLukeWarm, and ThermoCold layers, and do nothing to the ThermoOriginal, ChiliPic, HotWingsPic, JeansPic, and WasabiPic layers.

Explore
22. In the Behaviors panel, select the event, click the list arrow, and then click (onClick) in the list.
23. Save the page, preview the page in a browser window, click each graphic, and then close the browser window.
24. Open the index.htm page, click in the cell that contains the heading text, and then split the cell into two columns. (*Hint:* Right-click the cell, point to Table, and then click Split Cell.) Select the heading text and move it to the center cell.
25. Click in the new left cell, insert the **WasabiPictureSmall.gif** graphic located in the **Tutorial.06\Cases** folder included with your Data Files, apply the imageborder style, and then deselect the graphic. In the Property inspector, click Center in the Horz list, click Top in the Vert list, and then press the Enter key.

26. Type "How Hot Is Wasabi???", apply the subheadings style, place the pointer before "Wasabi???," and then press the Shift+Enter keys to create a line break.
27. Select the Wasabi graphic, create a link to the wasabi.htm page, and then target the link to open in another window. Select the text, link it to the wasabi.htm page, and target the link to open in a new browser window. Move the right border of the first cell to the left, and the left border of the last cell to the right until all of the heading text appears on one line.
28. Save the page, preview the page in a browser, click the Wasabi graphic and text, and then close the browser windows.
29. Upload the site to the remote server, preview the site over the Web, and test all the new links.

Review

Quick Check Answers

Session 6.1

1. a transparent container you place in a Web page to hold different types of content
2. a combination of HTML enhancements and a scripting language that work together to add animation, interactive elements, and dynamic updating to Web pages
3. Yes; layers are actually div tags that use CSS styles to define the positions of the content elements within the opening and closing div tags.
4. click the edge of the layer or click the layer selection handle if the layer is active
5. It determines the order in which the layer is stacked in the user's browser window when more than one layer is used on a page; higher numbered layers are at the front of the stack and are seen in front of layers with lower numbers.
6. The Visibility attribute indicates whether the layer is visible when the Web page is loaded; if a layer is hidden when the page is loaded, actions taken by the user can make it visible.

Session 6.2

1. True
2. in front of
3. the last layer selected, as indicated by black selection handles
4. a series of parallel horizontal and vertical lines that overlap to create equal squares in the background of the Document window to provide a guide for positioning or resizing layers or other elements
5. No; in fact, it does not need to even be touching its parent layer.
6. JavaScript code that forces the page to reload every time the browser window is resized to avoid the layers moving around, scaling improperly, or disappearing completely

Session 6.3

1. code that is added to a Web page that enables users to interact with various elements in the Web page, to alter the Web page in different ways, or to cause tasks to be performed
2. An event is comprised of a user event and an event handler. The user event is what the user does to trigger the action; the event handler is the code used to refer to the event.
3. what happens when an event is performed on an object
4. No; preset behaviors are available in different areas of the Dreamweaver environment, such as the rollover behavior; you can also write code for new behaviors.
5. False
6. code you write (usually in JavaScript) in Code view or by using the Script button in the HTML category on the Insert bar

New Perspectives on
Macromedia® Dreamweaver® MX 2004

Tutorial 7   DRM 371
Adding Rich Media to a Web Site
Inserting Flash, Shockwave, Sound, and Video Elements

Tutorial 8   DRM 421
Creating Reusable Assets and Forms
Creating Meta Tags, Library Items, Templates, and Forms

Tutorial 9   DRM 481
Adding Database Functionality
Collecting and Viewing Form Data in a Database

Additional Cases ADD 543
Building a Web Site with a Form
Coffee Lounge
Building a Web Site with Database Functionality
Tweetie

Appendix A   DRM 549
Introduction to Fireworks MX 2004

Appendix B   DRM 585
Guide to Using Dreamweaver on the Macintosh

Task Reference REF 589

New Perspectives Series

Read This Before You Begin: Tutorials 7–9

To the Student

Data Files

To complete Tutorials 7–9 of this text, you will need the starting student Data Files. Your instructor will either provide you with these Data Files or ask you to obtain them yourself.

Tutorials 7–9 require the folders shown to complete the Tutorials, Review Assignments, and Case Problems. You will need to copy these folders from a file server, a standalone computer, or the Web to the drive and folder where you will be storing your Data Files. Your instructor will tell you which computer, drive letter, and folder(s) contain the files you need. You can also download the files by going to www.course.com; see the inside back or front cover for more information on downloading the files, or ask your instructor or technical support person for assistance.

▼ **Dreamweaver MX 2004**
  Tutorial.07
  Tutorial.08
  Tutorial.09

To the Instructor

The Data Files are available on the Instructor Resources CD for this title. Follow the instructions in the Help file on the CD to install the programs to your network or standalone computer. See the "To the Student" section above for information on how to set up the Data Files that accompany this text.

You are granted a license to copy the Data Files to any computer or computer network used by students who have purchased this book.

System Requirements

If you are going to work through this book using your own computer, you need:

- **System Requirements** This text assumes a default installation of Macromedia Dreamweaver MX 2004. A text editor and a Web browser (preferably Internet Explorer or Netscape Navigator, versions 4.0 or higher) must be installed on your computer. If you are using a nonstandard browser, it must support frames and HTML 6.0 or higher. The screenshots in this book were taken using a computer running Windows XP Professional and, when showing a browser, Internet Explorer 6. If you are using a different operation system or a different browser, your screen might differ from the figures shown in the book.

  Macromedia recommends the following Windows system configuration: 600 MHz Intel Pentium III processor or equivalent; Windows 98 SE (4.10.2222 A), Windows 2000, or Windows XP; 128 MB RAM (256 MB recommended); and 275 MB available disk space. Dreamweaver MX 2004 does not support monitor resolutions below 1024 x 768 pixels.

- **FTP Trouble?** With some Windows servers, the Dreamweaver built-in FTP client does not work properly and may give continuous or intermittent errors. If FTP/connection errors occur, first double-check all the remote and testing server configuration settings. Next, review the following support documents on the Macromedia Web site: http://www.macromedia.com/support/dreamweaver/ts/documents/emerging_issues.htm
http://www.macromedia.com/support/dreamweaver/ts/documents/troubleshooting_ftp.htm

  If you cannot resolve the problem, you may need to utilize a separate FTP program (see www.ipswitch.com).

- **Server Requirements** Tutorial 9 requires you to create or upload a database to a server. This text was written to and tested on both a Linux server and Windows server. The recommended server configurations are listed below.

  For a Linux server:
  - Apache 1.3.26 or above
  - PHP 4.3.2 or above
  - MySQL 3.23 or above
  - Any current distribution of Linux

  For a Windows server:
  - Windows 2000 IIS 5.0 or above
  - Running .net 1.1 framework
  - The IIS User must have write permissions for the database directory

- **Data Files** You will not be able to complete the tutorials or exercises in this book using your own computer until you have the necessary starting Data Files.

www.course.com/NewPerspectives

Dreamweaver | DRM 371

Tutorial 7

Objectives

Session 7.1
- Learn about adding media to a Web site
- Insert a Flash movie into a Web page and adjust its attributes
- Insert Flash text into a Web page
- Review Flash button styles

Session 7.2
- Insert a Shockwave movie into a Web page and adjust its attributes
- Embed a sound-only Flash movie in a Web page
- Start a Flash movie with a button
- Create a link to an MP3 sound file

Session 7.3
- Download the RealMedia Suite Extension for Dreamweaver
- Insert a RealVideo video clip into a Web page and adjust its attributes
- Download the RealPlayer for Internet Explorer
- Update the code for the RealMedia video clip

Adding Rich Media to a Web Site

Inserting Flash, Shockwave, Sound, and Video Elements

Case

Catalyst

Sara has gotten great response to the Sloth Child page. She has received several complimentary e-mail messages and heard positive comments from quite a few fans at local shows. Now she wants to incorporate rich media elements into the site in hopes that the other pages in the site generate the same kind of buzz.

You will replace the current What's Hot section in the home page with a Flash movie that links to the What's Hot page. The Flash movie will draw attention to the new Catalyst products. Some other team members are creating a Shockwave game, which will be added to the Bands page. Brian wants you to add a Shockwave promo for the game in the spot that the game will eventually occupy. Also, you'll add some audio samples and video clips to the Catalogue page so that users can get a chance to hear and see the bands.

Student Data Files

▼Tutorial.07 folder

▽ Tutorial folder
    FlashSoundButton.gif
    GamePromo.drc
    MP3SoundButton.gif
    spin.mp3
    spinmovie.swf
    sunshine.mp3
    sunshine.swf
    sunshineVideo.rm
    WhatsHot.swf

▽ Review folder
    limcVideo.rm
    sunshine_autostart.swf

▽ Cases folder
    HartBreathySample.rm
    HartHarshSample.rm
    HartHarshwhSample.mp3
    HartModalSample.mp3
    museumtour.dcr
    MuseumTour.doc
    normform.dcr
    sushigame.dcr
    wasabisound_autoplay.swf

Adding Media to a Web Site

Media refers to any special configurable object you add to a Web page that needs a player or an application that is not part of the browser, such as plug-ins, ActiveX controls, or helper applications, to display within a browser. The terms *player* and *plug-in* are used in this tutorial to refer generally to the above technologies. Some of the most useful media used in Web pages are Flash, Shockwave, sound, and video.

No matter what media you add to a site, it is important to make sure that you have a purpose for including that element. The animation, game, audio, or movie must enhance the site, contribute to the user experience, and reinforce the site goals. Furthermore, be discriminating when adding media to a Web site. You do not want to overwhelm the user with too much glitz on pages. When trying to decide what to add to pages, ask yourself whether the proposed element will enhance the user's ability to grasp the site goals or distract them from focusing on the message. If the element will distract the user, discard it. When you follow these guidelines to determine what media to include in a site, you may find yourself cutting some of the coolest elements that you have created. Even the most innovative or creative element should be cut if it does not reinforce the site goals and enhance the user's experience.

You should also consider the technological limitations of the target audience when adding media to a site. Review your research to ensure that the target audience can easily access media elements that communicate necessary information. For example, if you plan to communicate vital information in audio files, make sure that most users will have access to computers with sound capabilities. Most media require some sort of plug-in to run on the client computer. Some plug-ins are included with the latest browsers, whereas others must be downloaded separately by the end user. Before incorporating media into Web pages, learn what plug-ins users will need to view each element, determine the likelihood that users will have the needed plug-ins, and assess how difficult it will be for users to get a needed plug-in. (The plug-in requirements for Flash, Shockwave, sound, and video will be discussed as each element is reviewed.) Be aware that media elements often use considerable bandwidth. Evaluate the connection speed and the computer speed for your target audience to determine if the client computer can display the media element effectively without prolonged delays. If users have to wait too long to view a page, they will often lose interest and move to another site. Users will usually wait longer for an item they perceive to be important than for an item they perceive to be unimportant. If you are asking users to wait for your site to load, make sure that the wait is worth their time.

In addition to these general concerns, you should explore the most common use of each media type (for example, Flash is frequently used to create animations and so forth) and consider both the pros and the cons associated with each type of media element. In this tutorial, you learn about Flash, Shockwave, sound, and video, and then add each type of element to the Catalyst site.

Understanding Macromedia Flash

Macromedia **Flash**™ was one of the first widely used animation programs that used vector-based graphics. Because vector-based graphics can scale and compress to a very small file size without losing quality, Flash has become one of the premier solutions for creating and delivering interactive animations for display on the Web. Over time, Flash development has continued. The latest version of Flash also contains video handling capabilities, is better at compressing bitmap-based animation, has more developed coding capabilities, and includes excellent audio capabilities. Flash is a good choice for lightweight interactive components (such as an address book or an animated menu system), Web applications, slide show-type presentations, vector-based animation, some bitmap-based animation, some video that has additional animation or text laid over it, and sound.

Flash is both the name of the software you use to create animations and the name commonly used to refer to the completed animation files. Flash files are also called Flash movies. The two types of Flash files that you will see most frequently are:

- **.fla.** The source files used by the Flash program when you are creating Flash movies. The .fla file is the file you edit when you want to make changes to a Flash movie. These authoring files can be opened only in the Flash program. Files must be exported from Flash as .swf files to be viewed on the Web.
- **.swf.** Compressed Flash files that are viewable in a browser and can be previewed in Dreamweaver. You'll use .swf Flash files in the Catalyst site.

Like every program, there are both positive and negative aspects of using Flash. Figure 7-1 lists these benefits and drawbacks.

Figure 7-1 Pros and cons of using Flash

Pros	Cons
As of December 2003, 98% of users have the Flash Player plug-in (it has a 97% browser penetration). The Flash Player plug-in is included with the latest versions of Internet Explorer and Netscape Navigator.	The playback speed of a Flash movie depends on the client computer because Flash renders the movies on the client computer.
A Flash movie will look the same in all browsers and across platforms.	There are limitations to the amount of interactivity and control you can achieve with Flash.
Flash compresses movies to a reasonable size.	Although there is a 97% browser penetration for Flash, not all users have the latest version; therefore, problems sometimes arise in playback due to version differences. (You can overcome this by making the movie check to see which version the user has and then downloading the current version automatically if necessary, but you must know Flash to do this.)
You can use any fonts within a Flash movie because Flash is not dependent on the fonts on users' computers.	
Some alternative and portable devices, such as some PDAs, wireless handsets, and interactive television systems, can play Flash movies.	

You can find additional information and statistics about the pros and cons of using Flash on the Macromedia site at *www.macromedia.com/software/flashplayer*. The Macromedia Flash Player Statistics section provides current statistical data regarding Flash Player browser penetration (and version penetration), a current market breakdown that includes Flash Player and competing technologies, user profiles, and a list of partnering companies that include the Flash Player.

Before you add a Flash movie to the Catalyst site, Brian asks you to research the integration of Flash elements into a Web site. You will go to the Macromedia site and review the current Flash information and statistics.

To research Flash on the Macromedia site:

1. Start your browser, type **www.macromedia.com/software/flashplayer** into the Address bar, and then press the **Enter** key. The Macromedia Flash Player home page opens.

   Trouble? If the Macromedia Flash Player home page does not open, type www.macromedia.com in the Address bar, press the Enter key to open the Macromedia home page, click the Flash MX 2004 link to open the Macromedia Flash home page, click the Macromedia Flash Player link to open the Macromedia Flash Player home page, and then continue with Step 2.

2. Click the **Flash Player Statistics** link to view the current statistical breakdown of market penetration for each of the most popular media players. See Figure 7-2.

Figure 7-2   **Flash Player statistics**

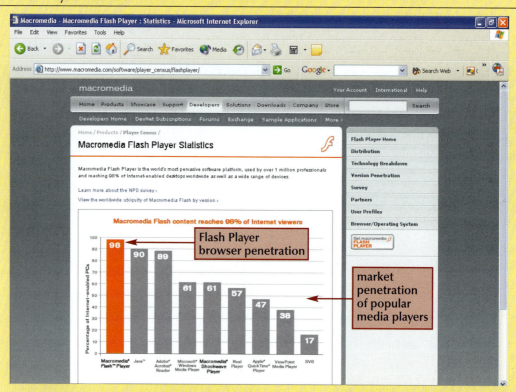

   Trouble? If the data you see differs from Figure 7-2, Macromedia has updated the data since this tutorial was published. Continue with Step 3.

3. Once you have reviewed the information, click the **Version Penetration** link. The version penetration statistics for Flash Player appear in the browser window.

4. Click the **Distribution** link to see an overview of the penetration statistics. See Figure 7-3.

Figure 7-3

Flash Player penetration

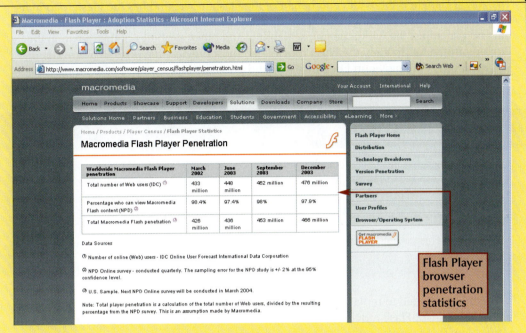

Flash Player browser penetration statistics

Trouble? If the data you see differs from Figure 7-3, Macromedia has updated the data since this tutorial was published. Continue with Step 5.

5. Close the browser window.

The statistics show that the Flash Player has a larger share of the market than any of the competing technologies. It is included with most current browsers. Because of this, it is highly likely that most end users will be able to view the Flash components that you add to any Web site. This is one reason that Flash is one of the most widely used media on the Web.

Adding Flash Movies to Web Pages

You will add a Flash movie to the home page of the Catalyst site. Adding a Flash movie to a Web page is simple. You use the Flash button in the Media list in the Common category on the Insert bar to insert a movie into a page. When you insert a movie, Dreamweaver places the code for the movie into the page. Dreamweaver will ask whether you want to include a copy of the element in the site's local root folder. You should place a copy of the element in the local root folder so that all the materials for the site are in one place. Also, remember, any links to elements outside the local root folder will be incorrect once the site is uploaded to the remote server. If you are using only a few media elements in a site, you can place the files in the Graphics folder. However, if you plan to use many media elements in a site, it is a good idea to create a new folder for each type of element so that the site remains organized and files are easy to find. You'll create a new Media folder to store the Flash, Shockwave, sound, and video files Brian wants you to add to the Catalyst site.

Once a Flash movie has been added to a page, a gray rectangle appears in the page. The gray rectangle is the width and height of the Flash movie and has the Flash logo in its center. The width and height of the Flash movie is determined when the movie is created, but you can adjust the width, height, scalability, and other attributes of the movie in the Property inspector. To view the Flash movie, you must preview the page in a browser or you must select the movie in Dreamweaver and press the Play button in the Property inspector.

Reference Window | Adding a Flash Movie to a Web Page

- Click the location in the page where you want to add the Flash movie.
- Click the Flash button in the Media list in the Common category on the Insert bar.
- Navigate to the Flash movie file, and then double-click the file.
- Click the Yes button, navigate to the folder in which you want to save the file, and then click the Save button.
- Select the Flash movie, and then adjust Flash movie attributes as needed in the Property inspector.

Brian has decided to replace the WhatsHot layer in the home page of the Catalyst site with a What's Hot Flash movie. Another member of the design team created the movie in Flash. Now Brian wants you to delete the old elements from the page and insert the new Flash movie. You will also create a new Media folder in the site to store all the different media files that you will add to the Catalyst site.

To add a Flash movie to a Web page:

1. Open the **NewCatalyst** Web site you modified in the Tutorial 6 Review Assignments, and then open the **index.htm** page in the Document window.

2. Delete the text and graphic in the WhatsHot layer in the home page. The borders of the layer are formatted to display an orange line. That formatting will remain.

   Trouble? If elements are still visible at the top of the layer, you need to delete them. Press the Backspace key.

3. Click in the **WhatsHot** layer, and then click the **Flash** button in the **Media** list in the **Common** category on the Insert bar. The Select File dialog box opens.

4. Double-click the **WhatsHot.swf** file located in the **Tutorial.07\Tutorial** folder included with your Data Files. A dialog box opens, asking if you would like to place a copy of the file in the root folder.

5. Click the **Yes** button. The Copy File As dialog box opens.

6. Browse to the local root folder of your NewCatalyst site, click the **Create New Folder** button to create a new folder in the local root folder, type **Media** as the folder name, and then press the **Enter** key.

7. Double-click the **Media** folder to open it, and then click the **Save** button to place a copy of the WhatsHot.swf file in the folder. A gray rectangle, the dimensions of the Flash movie, appears in the WhatsHot layer in the Document window. See Figure 7-4.

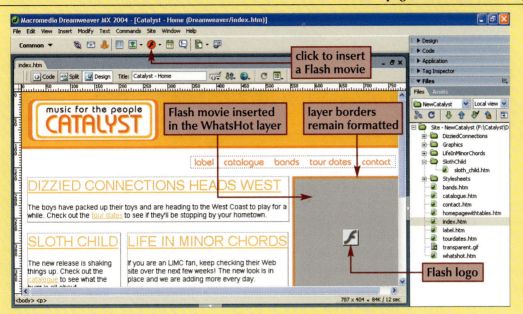

Figure 7-4 Home page with Flash movie

8. Select the **Flash** movie, and then click the **Play** button in the Property inspector. The Flash movie plays in the Document window and the Play button changes to a Stop button. See Figure 7-5.

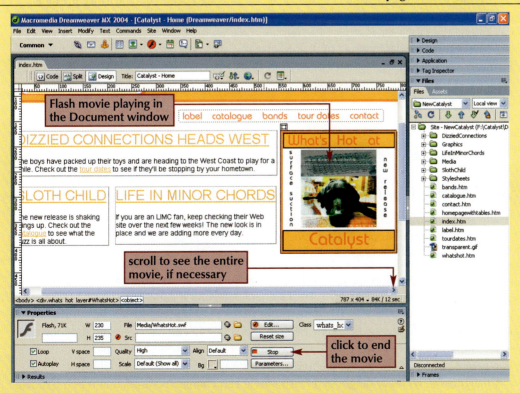

Figure 7-5 Home page with Flash movie

9. Watch the movie, and then click the **Stop** button when you are finished.
10. Save the page, preview the page in a browser, and then view the Flash movie. The movie will start automatically when the page is loaded in the browser. See Figure 7-6.

Figure 7-6   **Flash movie previewed in browser**

Trouble? If you do not have the latest version of the Macromedia Flash Player plug-in, a Warning dialog box opens when you try to preview the page in a browser. Click the Yes button to update the version. Once the new Flash Player is downloaded, the movie will start playing automatically.

Trouble? If the page continues to load for an extended period of time (twice the time it would usually take you to load it), you need to download the most recent version of the Flash Player from the Macromedia Web site. Type www.macromedia.com/downloads in the Address bar in your browser, press the Enter key, click the Flash Player link, click the Install Now button, and then click the Yes button in the Security Warning dialog box. Close the browser window, and then preview the page in a browser.

11. Close the browser window.

The movie looks good in the site. Next, you will adjust some attributes of the Flash movie.

Adjusting Attributes of a Flash Movie

Many attributes of Flash movies can be adjusted within Dreamweaver. Like other elements, you adjust the attributes of a Flash movie in the Property inspector when the movie object is selected. The Flash attributes include:

- **Name.** Identifies the movie for scripting. A movie name can contain letters and numbers. It cannot contain spaces or special characters, and it cannot start with a number.
- **W (Width) and H (Height).** The dimensions of the Flash movie, which are set when the movie is created and measured by default in pixels. You can also measure the movie in picas (pc), points (pt), inches (in), millimeters (mm), centimeters (cm), and percentage of a parent object (%) by typing the unit abbreviation after the number in the W text box. Changing the width or height of a Flash movie can change the aspect ratio of the movie. It can cause the movie to play more slowly because every frame of the movie must be rendered and changed on the client computer, and it can cause the movie to look distorted, especially if the movie contains a lot of text.

- **File.** The path to the Flash movie file (.swf).
- **Src (Source File).** The path to the Flash source file (.fla) for the .swf movie file in a Web page; available only if Flash is installed on your local computer.
- **Edit.** Launches Macromedia Flash MX 2004 and opens the .fla file specified in the Src text box so you can edit the Flash movie. When you save the .fla file, Flash re-exports the .swf movie file with the changes. If Flash is not installed on your local computer, the Edit button is disabled.
- **Reset Size.** Returns the movie to its original size if you have altered the size of the Flash movie.
- **Class.** A list of CSS styles that you can apply to the object.
- **Loop.** When checked, the movie plays continuously as long as the page is loaded in the browser; when unchecked, adds code that plays the movie only once.
- **Autoplay.** When checked, the movie plays automatically when the page is loaded in a browser window.
- **V Space (Vertical Space) and H Space (Horizontal Space).** The number of pixels of white space to be inserted above and below the movie or to the left and right of the movie. If left blank, no code is specified and the browser adds 0 pixels of white space around the movie.
- **Quality.** Controls the anti-aliasing (smoothing of diagonal or jagged lines) when the movie is played; options include Low, Auto Low, Auto High, and High. Movies with High anti-aliasing look best but require more processing speed to render correctly on the screen. Low emphasizes speed over appearance. Auto Low emphasizes speed, but also improves appearance when the speed is acceptable. Auto High emphasizes both appearance and speed, but will sacrifice appearance for speed if necessary. High emphasizes appearance over speed.
- **Scale.** Controls how the Flash movie displays in the dimensions set in the W and H text boxes. Default (Show All) displays the movie at the greatest size possible within the designated space while still maintaining aspect ratio and showing all the content; the background color may appear on two sides of the movie. No Borders fits the movie into the designated space so that no borders show and the movie maintains the original aspect ratio (a portion of the movie may not be seen). Exact Fit scales the movie to the exact dimensions set in W and H, regardless of the aspect ratio of the movie. The entire movie is seen, but it may be distorted to fit in the space.
- **Align.** Sets the alignment of the movie in the page. The alignment options are the same as for an image: Default, Baseline, Top, Middle, Bottom, Text Top, Absolute Middle, Absolute Bottom, Left, and Right.
- **Bg (Background Color).** Specifies a color for the background of the movie area. This color also appears in the page if the movie is not playing, such as while the page is loading.
- **Play.** Starts the movie in the Dreamweaver environment. The movie plays in the Document window and a Stop button, which ends the movie, replaces the Play button.
- **Parameters.** Opens a dialog box for entering parameters that are passed to a movie if the movie was designed to receive them. Parameters entered in the Parameters dialog box are placed in the appropriate places in the code for the page.

Brian asks you to name the Flash movie, check the Loop and Autoplay check boxes, if necessary, and then save the page.

To adjust the attributes of a Flash movie:

1. Click the Flash movie to select it, and then type **WhatsHot** in the Flash text box in the upper-left corner of the Property inspector. This renames the Flash movie.
2. Click the **Loop** and **Autoplay** check boxes, if necessary, to insert check marks. This ensures that the movie plays continuously and starts as soon as the page is loaded in a browser window.
3. Click the **Play** button in the Property inspector. The WhatsHot Flash movie plays in the Document window. The movie restarts from the beginning once it has reached the end. This continues until you click the Stop button.
4. Click the **Stop** button in the Property inspector. The movie ends and the Play button reappears.
5. Save and close the page.

You can also use Flash to add text to Web pages.

Adding Flash Text to Web Pages

You can use a Flash movie to add text that uses designer fonts in a Web page. Because Flash movies are self-contained and do not require fonts to be installed on the client computer, they are a good vehicle for adding custom fonts to Web pages. For example, you might use a Flash movie to add page headings that use the logo font to the pages of the Catalyst site.

The downside to using Flash text is that the text is no longer attached to the style sheet. Therefore, if you change the styles for a site, you must modify each Flash text movie separately. You edit a Flash text movie by double-clicking the Flash text and changing attributes in the Insert Flash Text dialog box. This can be a big job if you are working on a large site that contains many Flash text movies; therefore, it is a good idea to use Flash text sparingly. Also, Flash text sometimes appears poorly rendered in the Dreamweaver environment. You need to preview the page to see the text as it will appear in a browser.

Reference Window | Adding Flash Text in a Web Page

- Click in the page where you want to add the Flash text.
- Click the Flash Text button in the Media list in the Common category on the Insert bar.
- Select the font, size, and color, and then type the text for the Flash text.
- Click the Browse button, navigate to the folder in which you want to save the Flash text, and then click the Save button.
- Click the OK button.

You can create a Flash text movie from within Dreamweaver even if you do not have Flash installed on your computer. Just click the Flash Text button in the Media list in the Common category on the Insert bar to create a small Flash movie that contains text and a link.

You set the attributes for the text in the Insert Flash Text dialog box, including:

- **Font.** All the TrueType fonts loaded on your computer. A font must be on your local system in order for you to use that font.
- **Size.** The size of text in points.
- **Bold and Italicize.** Style attributes for text.
- **Alignment.** Text alignment options: left, center, or right.
- **Color.** The text color; type a hexadecimal color code or use the color picker to select a color.
- **Rollover Color.** The text color that appears when the mouse is positioned over linked text in a browser; type a hexadecimal color code or use the color picker to select a color.
- **Text.** The text you want in the Flash text movie.
- **Show Font.** The option to display the font style in the Text field in the Insert Flash Text dialog box.
- **Link.** A link between the Flash text and another page in the current Web site or in another Web site. Use an absolute link; relative links do not necessarily work with Flash movies and may cause problems with the Flash text feature. To link text to another page in the site, you must use the absolute path (beginning with *http://*) the page will have when it is uploaded to the remote server in order for the link to work in the remote site. (The absolute path for the link may prevent the link from working when you view the page locally.) You can avoid problems by not creating links to other pages in a site from Flash text.
- **Target.** The target for the linked page: _blank, _parent, _self, or _top.
- **Bg (Background) Color.** The color that displays behind the text; type a hexadecimal color code or use the color picker to select a color.
- **Save As.** The option to browse to the save location, name the file, and save the file. When you use the Flash text object to create custom text elements for Web pages, Dreamweaver saves the files as .swf files. You should place the files in the folder with your other Flash elements.

Brian thinks that all of the main page headings in the Catalyst site would look better in the Bauhaus Md BT font (the Catalyst logo font). It is your job to replace the existing page headings with customized Flash text headings. You need to make the change in the Bands page, the Catalogue page, the Contact page, the Label page, and the Tour Dates page.

To add Flash text to Web pages:

1. Open the **bands.htm** page in the Document window, select the **CATALYST BANDS** heading, and then press the **Delete** key. The text is deleted from the page.
2. Click the **Flash Text** button in the **Media** list in the **Common** category on the Insert bar. The Insert Flash Text dialog box opens.
3. Click **Bauhaus Md BT** in the Font list, type **55** in the Size text box, type **#FF9900** in the Color text box, and then type **CATALYST BANDS** in the Text text box.

   Trouble? If you do not have the Bauhaus Md BT font, use Arial or choose a font that is similar to the font in the Catalyst logo. It may be necessary to select a different size as well.

4. Click the **Browse** button next to the Save As text box. The Select File dialog box opens.
5. Navigate to the **Media** folder in the site's local root folder, type **HeadingBands.swf** in the File Name text box, and then click the **Save** button. The Select File dialog box closes and Media/HeadingBands.swf appears in the Save As text box. See Figure 7-7.

Figure 7-7 — Insert Flash Text dialog box

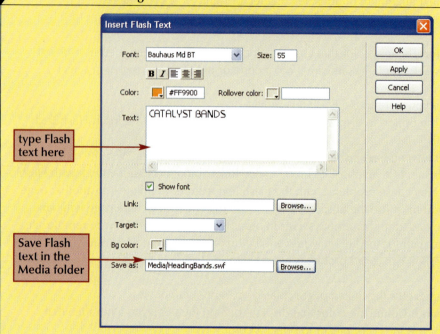

- type Flash text here
- Save Flash text in the Media folder

6. Click the **OK** button. The Flash text appears in the Bands page. Sometimes the text has some artifacts (it is a bit jagged) when it is displayed in the Document window. The artifacts will not appear in the browser. See Figure 7-8.

Figure 7-8 — Bands page with Flash text

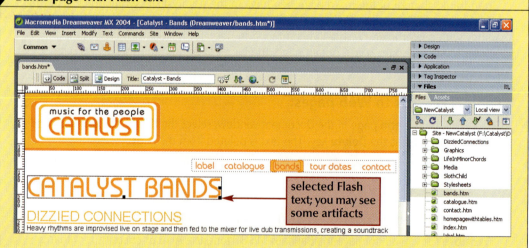

- selected Flash text; you may see some artifacts

7. Save the page, and preview the page in a browser. Notice that the text no longer has any artifacts (it is smooth). See Figure 7-9.

Figure 7-9
Flash text in a browser

8. Close the browser window, and then close the page.
9. Repeat Steps 1 through 8 to add Flash text with the page name in the following pages: **catalogue.htm**, **contact.htm**, **label.htm**, and **tourdates.htm**.

Another way to use Flash in a Web page is to add Flash buttons.

Using Flash Buttons

Dreamweaver includes a set of predesigned, customizable Flash buttons that you can use in Web pages to add motion and excitement. You add Flash buttons to a site with the Flash Button button located in the Media list in the Common category on the Insert bar. In the Insert Flash Button dialog box, you can select a button style from the Style list. After you select a style, you can view the various states of the button in the Sample box. Move the pointer over a button in the Sample box to view the Over state and click the button in the Sample box to view the Down state. Once you have selected a button style, you can add text to the button, select a font and font size, add a link, select a target, and add a background color for the button. The Sample box will not show changes to text, but the changes will appear in the Document window once you have added the button to the page. You can also download additional Flash button styles from the Macromedia Web site by clicking the Get More Styles button in the Insert Flash Button dialog box.

There are a few downsides to adding Flash buttons to a Web site. Buttons enable the user to navigate through the site; however, users who do not have the Flash Player will not be able to navigate through the pages of the site. Also, Flash buttons are templates, which means that the same buttons will appear in many sites. If you choose to use a Flash button, your site will look more generic and less like an original, professionally designed site.

Brian asks you to review the available Flash button styles and see whether any are suitable for the Catalyst site.

To review Flash button styles:

1. Open the **index.htm** page in a Document window, and then click the **Flash Button** button in the **Media** list in the **Common** category on the Insert bar. The Insert Flash Button dialog box opens with the first button style selected. See Figure 7-10.

Figure 7-10   **Insert Flash Button dialog box**

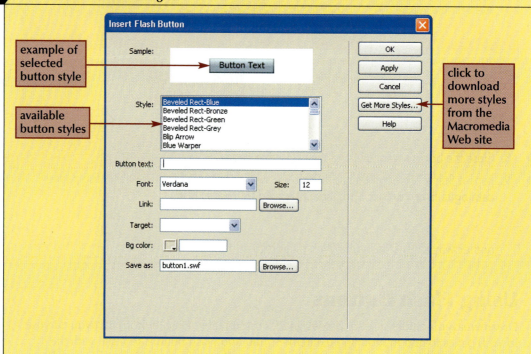

2. Click the second button style in the Style list, and then view the button in the Sample box.
3. Move the pointer over the button in the Sample box, and then click the button. The button changes states.
4. Review the remaining styles in the list.
5. Click the **Cancel** button to close the dialog box without adding a Flash button.
6. Close the page.

None of the button styles seem appropriate for the Catalyst site. To keep the site unique, you won't add any Flash buttons to the text.

So far, you learned about the different media you can add to a site. Then, you added a Flash movie and Flash text to the Catalyst site and reviewed the available Flash buttons. In the next session, you'll add a Shockwave movie and sound to the Catalyst site.

Session 7.1 Quick Check

1. What is media?
2. What will a user need in order to view media in a browser?
3. What is the file extension for Flash movies that you place in Web pages?
4. True or False? The Flash Player is included with the latest versions of Internet Explorer and Netscape Navigator.
5. True or False? You can create Flash text in Dreamweaver only if you have the Flash program installed on your computer.
6. True or False? You can create customizable Flash buttons in Dreamweaver.

Session 7.2

Understanding Macromedia Shockwave

Shockwave® is the Macromedia solution for delivering interactive multimedia on the Web. You use Shockwave for more complex interactive media components, such as games, interactive 3D, database-driven multimedia, multi-user applications, and educational materials.

Unlike Flash files, which are created in the Flash program, Shockwave files are created in Macromedia Director®. **Director** is a program that is used to create comprehensive multimedia solutions deployable across multiple media, including CD-ROM, DVD, Web, Kiosk, and so forth. Most interactive CDs are produced in Director.

Several file extensions are associated with Director, including:

- **.dcr (Shockwave).** A compressed file that is viewable in a browser and can be previewed in Dreamweaver. You'll use .dcr files in the Catalyst site for Shockwave movies.
- **.dir.** The source files used by Director when you are creating movies. These authoring files can be opened in Director. Unlike Flash authoring files, .dir files can be called by Director projectors for playback. (**Director projectors** are standalone executable files that do not need any software or plug-ins to run on the client computer.) Files that are going to be viewed on the Web are usually exported from Director as .dcr files.
- **.dxr.** Director files that are locked for distribution. **Locked** files cannot be opened in the authoring environment. Usually, .dxr files are used with Director projectors to deliver material via CD.
- **.cst.** Files that contain additional information used in a .dir or .dxr file.
- **.cxt.** .cst files that are locked for distribution.

Although Flash and Shockwave files are often used in similar ways, there are some marked differences between them. Because Director movies are prerendered, Shockwave files are less dependent on the processing speed of the user's computer for playback speed than Flash files, which are rendered on the client computer. For this same reason, the file size of a Flash movie with vector graphics is usually smaller than the file size of a Director movie with the same content. Shockwave movies tend to process complex coding faster than Flash movies. Shockwave movies can display a wider range of media formats; for example, all Flash video is converted to the Sorenson Spark codec (.flv video files) format, whereas Shockwave can display video in a wide range of native formats. Finally, the Shockwave Player must be installed on the client computer for Shockwave movies to be displayed. Unlike the Flash Player plug-in, the Shockwave Player is not generally distributed with current browsers and must be downloaded separately by end users.

Some positive and negative aspects of using Shockwave are listed in Figure 7-11.

Figure 7-11   **Pros and cons of using Shockwave**

Pros	Cons
Shockwave files are less dependent on the processing speed of the end user's computer for playback speed.	As of December 2003, only 61% of users have the Shockwave Player plug-in (Shockwave has a 61% browser penetration). The Shockwave Player plug-in is not included with the latest versions of Internet Explorer and Netscape Navigator, and must be downloaded by the end user.
Shockwave movies tend to process complex code faster than Flash movies.	Shockwave file size may be larger than Flash files because the files are prerendered.
Shockwave movies can display a wide range of media formats.	
Shockwave movies will look the same across browsers and across platforms.	
You can use any fonts you want within a Shockwave movie because Shockwave is not dependent on the fonts on the client computer.	

You can find additional information and statistics about Shockwave on the Macromedia site at *www.macromedia.com/software/player_census/shockwaveplayer*. The Macromedia Web site also provides a Flash and Director comparison at *www.macromedia.com/software/director/resources/integration* and a Shockwave/Flash movie comparison at *www.macromedia.com/software/director/resources/integration/flash*.

Brian asks you to research the integration of Shockwave elements in the Catalyst site. You will go to the Macromedia site and review the current Shockwave information and statistics. Then you will review the Shockwave/Flash comparisons.

To research Shockwave:

▶ 1. Open a browser window, type **www.macromedia.com/software/shockwaveplayer** in the Address bar, and then press the **Enter** key. The Macromedia Shockwave Player home page opens in the browser window. See Figure 7-12.

Trouble? If the Macromedia Shockwave Player home page does not open, type www.macromedia.com in the Address bar, press the Enter key to open the Macromedia home page, click the Director MX 2004 link to open the Macromedia Director home page, click the Shockwave Player link to open the Macromedia Shockwave Player home page, and then continue with Step 2.

Tutorial 7 Adding Rich Media to a Web Site | Dreamweaver | DRM 387

Macromedia Shockwave Player home page | Figure 7-12

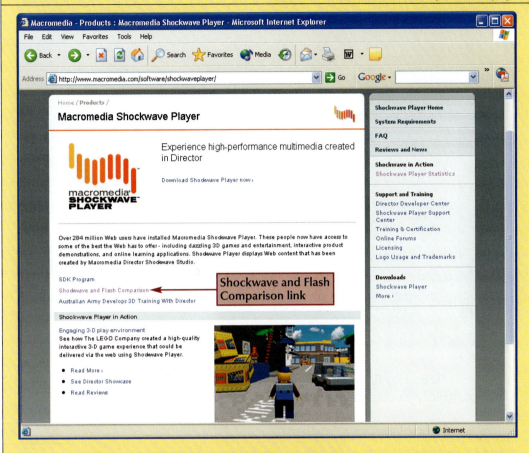

2. Click the **Shockwave and Macromedia Flash Comparison** link to view the Macromedia Flash and Director Resource Center page.

3. Click the **Quick Comparison Chart** link in the Flash and Director Comparison list, read the information, and then click the **Back** button on the browser toolbar to return to the list of links.

4. Repeat Step 3 for all the links in the list.

5. Click the **Shockwave Player Statistics** link located on the right of the page, read the adoption statistics, and then click the **Penetration** link to view browser penetration statistics. See Figure 7-13.

| Figure 7-13 | **Shockwave Player penetration** |

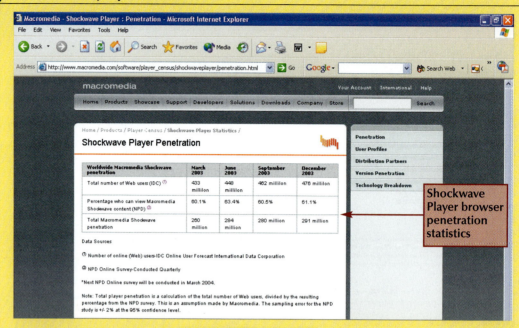

Trouble? If the data you see differs from Figure 7-13, Macromedia has updated the data since this tutorial was published. Continue with Step 6.

6. Click the **Technology Breakdown** link to view the technology breakdown statistics for the various multimedia plug-ins. See Figure 7-14.

| Figure 7-14 | **Shockwave Player technology breakdown** |

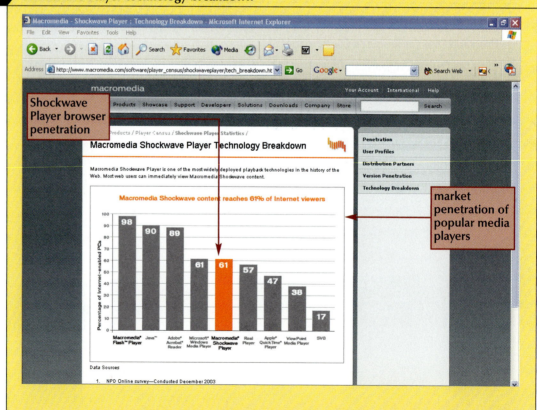

> **Trouble?** If the data you see differs from Figure 7-14, Macromedia has updated the data since this tutorial was published. Continue with Step 7.
>
> 7. Close the browser window.

Now that you have a better understanding of when to use Flash and when to use Director/Shockwave, you will add a Shockwave movie to the Catalyst site.

Adding Shockwave Movies to Web Pages

Adding a Shockwave movie to a Web page is very similar to adding a Flash movie to a Web page. You use the Shockwave button in the Media list in the Common category on the Insert bar to insert a Shockwave movie into a page. When you insert a movie, Dreamweaver places the code for the movie into the page. When you add a Shockwave movie that is located outside of the site's local root folder to a page, Dreamweaver will ask whether you want to include a copy of the file in the root folder. You should place a copy of the file in the Media folder in the root folder for your site so that all the materials for the site are located in one place.

Once the Shockwave movie has been added to a page, a small gray rectangle with the Shockwave logo appears in the page. The gray rectangle is 32 × 32 pixels, regardless of the size at which the Shockwave movie was created. (This occurs because a bug in the Shockwave button prevents the program from seeing the correct dimensions of the movie.) You must enter the correct width and height for the movie in the Property inspector to see the movie in a browser or to play the movie from within Dreamweaver. In addition, the Play button in the Property inspector may not start the movie; you may need to preview the page in a browser to see the movie.

Reference Window — Adding a Shockwave Movie to a Web Page

- Click in the layer in the page where you want to add the Shockwave movie.
- Click the Shockwave button in the Media list in the Common category on the Insert bar.
- Navigate to the Shockwave movie file, and then double-click the file.
- Click the Yes button, navigate to the folder in which you want to save the file, and then click the Save button.
- Adjust Shockwave movie attributes in the Property inspector as needed.

Brian has decided to add an interactive game to the Bands page. The new game will be a Shockwave movie. The game is still in production, but the game group has provided an animated promo for the game in the Shockwave format. Although the preview is animation without interactivity and could be delivered as a Flash movie, the team wants to deliver the preview as a Shockwave movie so it can test for problems that might arise. It is a good idea to use the intended final technology when making placeholder objects because it enables you to test the technology in advance. You will add the Shockwave movie game placeholder to the Bands page.

Before you can add the Shockwave movie to the page, you need to create two new layers in the page and add the page content to the layers. You will use the layers to position the text around the Shockwave movie.

To add layers in a Web page:

1. If you took a break after the previous session, make sure the **NewCatalyst** site is open.
2. Open the **bands.htm** page in the Document window, click the **Draw Layer** button in the **Layout** category on the Insert bar, and then draw a layer in the blank area to the right of the page heading.
3. Select the layer, if necessary, and then type **DizziedConnections** in the Layer ID text box in the Property inspector to name the layer.
4. Select the **Dizzied Connections** paragraphs, including the heading and text, and then drag the text into the layer. See Figure 7-15.

Figure 7-15   Bands page with the DizziedConnections layer

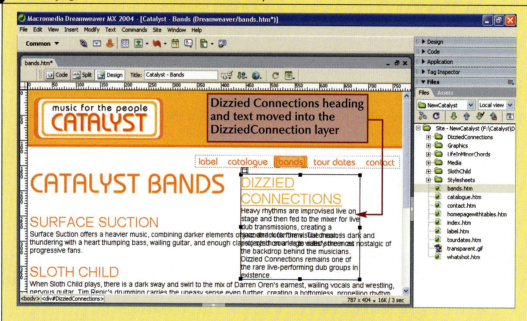

5. Click the **Draw Layer** button in the **Layout** category on the Insert bar, draw a layer over the page heading, name the layer **RemainingText**, and then drag the remaining text (but do not include the page heading, navigation bar, logo, or footer) into the second layer.
6. Click **View** on the menu bar, point to **Rulers**, and then click **Show** to display the rulers, and then click **View** on the menu bar, point to **Rulers**, and then click **Pixels**, if necessary, to change the measurement.
7. Select the **RemainingText** layer, and then drag it down so that the top of the layer is positioned vertically at the 500-pixel mark in the page.

    Trouble? If the layer overlaps the footer (the copyright notice), you need to fix the footer placement. You'll do this after you work with the DizziedConnections layer.

8. Select the **DizziedConnections** layer, drag the layer **25** pixels below the page heading and **10** pixels from the left border, and then resize the layer to the same width as the page heading and the same height as the layer text. See Figure 7-16.

Bands page with the repositioned DizziedConnections layer — Figure 7-16

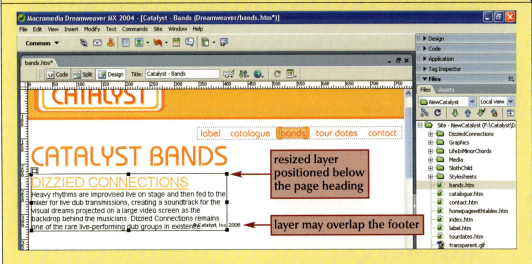

Trouble? If the footer is visible behind the text, you need to reposition it. Click in the page below the page heading, and then press the Enter key until the footer appears below the DizziedConnections layer.

9. Select the **RemainingText** layer, move the layer **25 pixels** below the DizziedConnections layer, and then align the RemainingText layer to the left border of the DizziedConnections layer.

10. If necessary, click the **Restore** button on the Document window title bar and set the Window Size to **760 × 420**.

11. Select the **RemainingText** layer, and then drag its right border until it is aligned with the end of the last word in the navigation bar. See Figure 7-17.

RemainingText layer positioned in the Bands page — Figure 7-17

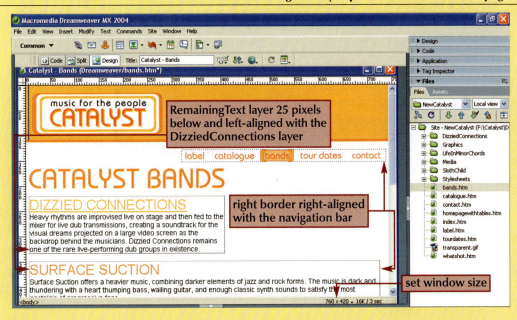

Trouble? If the footer is visible behind the text, you need to reposition it. Click in the page below the page heading, and then press the Enter key until the footer appears below the RemainingText layer.

12. If necessary, click the **Maximize** button on the Document window title bar to maximize the Document window.

Next, you will add a new layer next to the page heading, and you will insert the Shockwave movie into the layer.

To insert a Shockwave movie into a new layer:

1. Draw a small layer in the blank area to the right of the page heading, and then name the new layer **GamePromo**. The layer appears in the Bands page.

2. Position the GamePromo layer **15** pixels below the navigation bar and **20** pixels from the right edge of the page heading.

3. Click in the **GamePromo** layer, and then click the **Shockwave** button in the **Media** list in the **Common** category on the Insert bar. The Select File dialog box opens.

4. Double-click the **GamePromo.dcr** file located in the **Tutorial.07\Tutorial** folder included with your Data Files, click the **Yes** button in the message text box, and then place a copy of the file in the **Media** folder. The GamePromo.dcr Shockwave movie is inserted into the layer and a small gray rectangle with the Shockwave logo in the center is visible in the layer. See Figure 7-18.

Figure 7-18 Shockwave movie added to the Bands page

Trouble? If the size of your GamePromo layer differs from the one shown in Figure 7-18, you will adjust its size later.

The Shockwave movie is not embedded at the proper size and will not play. You must change the width and height of the movie to its original creation size to view the movie.

Adjusting Attributes of a Shockwave Movie

Shockwave movies have some of the same attributes as Flash movies. You can adjust the attributes in the Property inspector when the Shockwave movie is selected. Shockwave attributes include: Name, W, H, File, Play, Parameters, V Space, H Space, Align, and Bg. For descriptions of these attributes, refer to the "Adjusting Flash Attributes" section.

You'll change the width and height of the Shockwave movie so that it will display in the browser.

To adjust Shockwave attributes:

1. Select the Shockwave movie, if necessary.
2. In the Property inspector, type **240** in the W text box, type **240** in the H text box, and then press the **Enter** key. The gray square increases in size.
3. Move the GamePromo layer so that its right border is aligned with the right border of the RemainingText layer. See Figure 7-19.

Figure 7-19   Edited Shockwave movie

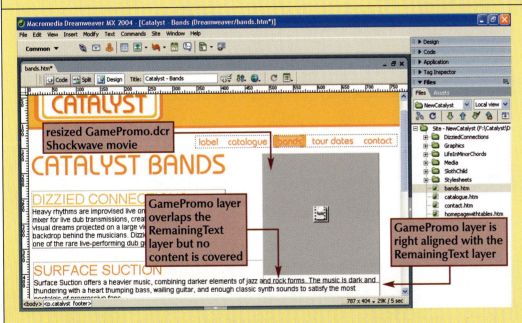

Trouble? If the Shockwave movie obscures any of the text in the other layers, you need to reposition the layers. Move the layers down until all the text is visible.

4. Save the page, and then preview the page in a browser. See Figure 7-20.

Figure 7-20   **Bands page with Shockwave movie previewed in browser**

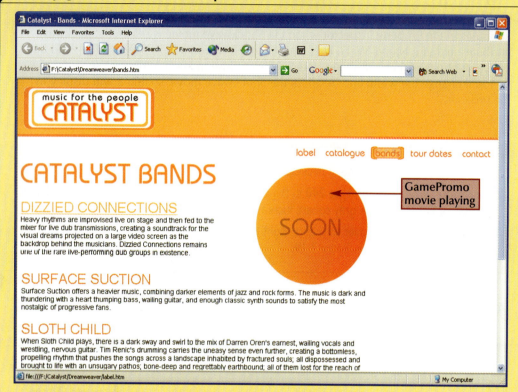

Trouble? If a dialog box opens or an icon appears, asking you to install the latest version of the Shockwave Player, click the Yes button to install the player. You cannot view the Shockwave movie without the latest version of the player.

Trouble? If the movie displays poorly (the words are split between lines and so forth), you are probably viewing the Shockwave movie in the wrong font. You are probably logged in to your computer as a restricted user and do not have access to some system folders that are necessary to view the movie in the correct font. This is one of the potential drawbacks of using media elements in a Web site. Continue with Step 5.

5. Close the browser window, and then close the page.

You have inserted Flash and Shockwave movies in the Catalyst site. Next, you'll add sound to select pages.

Understanding Sound

As you create more advanced Web sites, you may want to include sound on some of the pages. Sound can add richness and depth to Web sites when used wisely. Remember, the sound that you add to a site should reinforce the site goals and enhance the user's experience. Some common uses of sound on the Web are music, narration, and sounds paired with user actions, such as sound that plays when the pointer is positioned over a button or other element.

When deciding whether to add sound to a site, you must first consider whether the target audience even has sound playback hardware and capabilities. If they do, then think about issues such as user connection speed and computer speed. You must also determine whether sound is appropriate to the site goals and whether it will truly add value to the site for the end users.

Designers add sound to a site in two ways. Sound may be embedded directly in a page, or sound may be included as a link. With most sound formats, sound streams to the end user's computer. **Streaming** means that sound can begin to play after only a small portion downloads and will continue to play while the rest of the file is downloading. Streaming is especially helpful to users with slow connections because they can begin to hear the sound without waiting for large files to download completely.

When sound is embedded directly in a page, the sound files begin to download to the client computer as soon as the page is loaded. Embedded sound files can either start automatically or be set up to start when the user clicks a start button. Either way, the embedded file begins to download as soon as the page loads, allowing relatively quick automatic playback or preloading so that it starts as soon as the user clicks the start button. However, beginning to download many files that a user might not even play wastes the user's time and consumes unnecessary bandwidth.

Many music sites, which often include a lot of sound files, use links to the sound files. When a page is linked to sound files, the file does not download to the client computer until the user clicks the link. The user then decides which sound files are worth downloading and may have to wait for a partial download of the files before playback begins. However, the wait time after making a choice can become frustrating, especially on slower connections.

Sound files are created or recorded with programs outside of Dreamweaver, such as SoundForge, Audition, or ProTools. You can add sound files to Web pages, and in some cases preview them, within Dreamweaver.

Many formats can be used to store and play sound on a computer. Sound files can be fairly large and, like graphics, must be compressed to be delivered over the Web. Remember that compression is the process of eliminating redundant and less important details from a file in order to shrink its size. The different types of compression used for sound are often called **sound formats**. Each sound format uses a different CODEC as the sound is compressed for delivery and decompressed for playback. **CODEC**, short for COmpressor/DECompressor, is the software that converts sound to digital code, shrinks the code to the smallest possible size for faster transmission, and later expands the code for playback on the client computer. There are several different popular CODECs used for sound on the Web, including MP3, RealMedia, QuickTime®, and Windows Media®. In the past, each format was better for some types of sound and worse for others. Today, all the formats provide high-quality sound for nearly any application.

For a client computer to play sound, most sound formats require the end user to download some type of plug-in or player. Plug-ins and players are additional software that knows how to interpret the sound format and convert the code back to sound. When a user installs plug-in or player software, it often includes both browser integration (sound that plays from within the browser) as well as a standalone player with its own interface and controls. Most users have several players installed on their systems, and most players work with a wide range of sound formats. For example, the QuickTime Player will work with QuickTime formats as well as with RealMedia and Windows Media formats.

With care, you can make sure that sound will work for the majority of the target users. However, making sound work the same on all end users' systems is complex and sometimes impossible. The inability to control a user's experience with sound is one of the challenges to adding sound to a Web page. The difficulties depend on the user's installed players and hardware configuration. For example, a single user might have the RealMedia, QuickTime, and Windows Media players installed on his or her system. When the user visits a site that includes a RealMedia Audio clip, any of the installed players might handle the sound. And, depending on configuration, the sound might just play or a separate player window with sound controls (and ads) might pop up, which often is not desirable. Also, depending on configuration, the sound can either start automatically or require the user to push the Play button on the launched player. For another user who has the same players installed, a different player may respond to the RealMedia Audio clip and that user may have a completely different experience.

One way to alleviate this confusion, and to ensure the same sound experience for all site visitors, is to use the Flash format to add sound to Web pages. Many professional sites further ease the potential problems by including a choice between two or more sound formats containing the exact same content. This gives the user more control and increases the potential for trouble-free sound playback.

Embedding a Sound-only Flash Movie

Although Flash is more often thought of as a way to add animation to Web sites, it is also a very consistent and reliable method for adding sound to Web pages. Because the Flash Player is widely installed and does not open a separate application when used to play sound, Flash will deliver sound without disrupting the aesthetic of Web pages. When you use Flash to add sound to a page, you are simply adding a Flash movie that does not contain any images. Therefore, you use the same process as you would use to add a regular Flash movie to a page. Because this Flash movie has no visual content and will be used only for sound, it is generally created at a size of 1 × 1 pixel and with the same background color as the page.

There are two types of sound-only Flash movies: those that prevent automatic play, and those that play automatically when the page loads. (When creating a sound-only Flash movie, adding a stop action to the first frame will prevent automatic play, whereas omitting this action will allow automatic play.) Flash movies that play automatically are used to add background sound to pages. For example, a Web page that loads music when the home page loads in the browser might use a sound-only Flash movie that plays automatically. Sound-only Flash movies that do not play automatically are often used to provide sounds that the user can activate with the click of a button. For example, when you include more than one sound-only Flash movie in a page, you can create a Play button for each movie that the user can click to play a particular movie. The Control Shockwave or Flash behavior can be attached to a button to make it control sound-only Flash movies. In addition to creating a Play button, you can use different attributes in the Behavior dialog box when you attach the Control Shockwave or Flash behavior to make other sound control buttons, such as rewind and so forth.

Reference Window | Adding a Sound-only Flash Movie to a Web Page

- Click in the layer in the page where you want to add the Flash movie.
- Click the Flash button in the Media list in the Common category on the Insert bar.
- Navigate to the Flash movie file, and then double-click the file.
- Click the Yes button, navigate to the folder in which you want to save the file, and then click the Save button.
- Adjust Flash movie attributes in the Property inspector as needed.

Sara wants to add audio files for some of the songs in the Catalogue page, and Brian has asked you to make these additions. You will add a sound-only Flash movie to the page that does not play automatically. Then you will add a button to the page and attach a behavior to the button that will cause the sound to play when clicked.

To add sound to a page using Flash:

1. Open the **catalogue.htm** page in the Document window, click to the right of the song title "Sunshine" in the Sloth Child song list, and then press the **Enter** key. You'll add the sound-only Flash movie in this new line.

2. Click the **Flash** button in the **Media** list in the **Common** category on the Insert bar. The Select File dialog box opens.

3. Double-click the **sunshine.swf** movie located in the **Tutorial.07\Tutorial** folder included with your Data Files, and then place a copy of the Flash movie in the **Media** folder. A very small (1 pixel) box appears below the "Sunshine" song title. If you cannot see the Flash movie, you can select the line in which it was inserted to select the movie and view its attributes in the Property inspector. (Remember that the Flash movie will not be visible in the browser.) See Figure 7-21.

Sound-only Flash movie in the Catalogue page

Figure 7-21

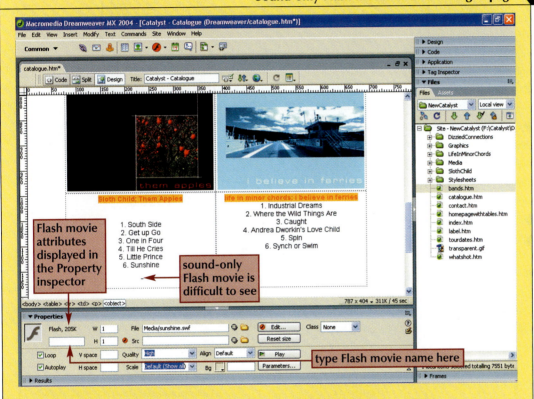

4. Select the **sunshine.swf** movie, if necessary, type **SunshineFlash** in the Flash text box in the upper-left corner of the Property inspector, and then press the **Enter** key to rename the Flash movie.

Next, you will add a button to the page. Then you will add a Control Shockwave or Flash behavior to the button, enabling the button to start the sound-only Flash movie in the page.

To start a Flash movie with a button:

1. Click to the right of the "Sunshine" song title, and then click the **Image** button in the **Images** list in the **Common** tab on the Insert bar.

2. Double-click the **FlashSoundButton.gif** located in the **Tutorial.07\Tutorial** folder included with your Data Files to insert the image and place a copy of the image in the Graphics folder.

3. Select the **FlashSoundButton** image, if necessary, click the **Align** list arrow in the Property inspector, and then click **Top**.

4. Expand the **Behaviors** panel, click the **Add Behavior** button  in the Behaviors panel, and then click **Control Shockwave or Flash**. The Control Shockwave or Flash dialog box opens. See Figure 7-22.

Figure 7-22   Control Shockwave or Flash dialog box

5. Click the **Movie** list arrow, click **movie "SunshineFlash,"** click the **Play** option button, if necessary, and then click the **OK** button. The behavior is added to the button.

6. If necessary, click the **Events** list arrow in the Behaviors panel, and then click **(onClick)**. The image will play when clicked by the user.

   Trouble? If you don't see the onClick option in the Events list, you need to show events for 4.0 and later browsers. Click the Add Behavior button in the Behaviors panel, point to Show Events For, click 4.0 and Later Browsers, and then repeat Step 6.

7. Save the page, and then preview the page in a browser.

8. Click the **Flash sound** image to play the sound-only Flash movie. See Figure 7-23.

Figure 7-23   Sound-only Flash movie in the Catalogue page previewed in a browser

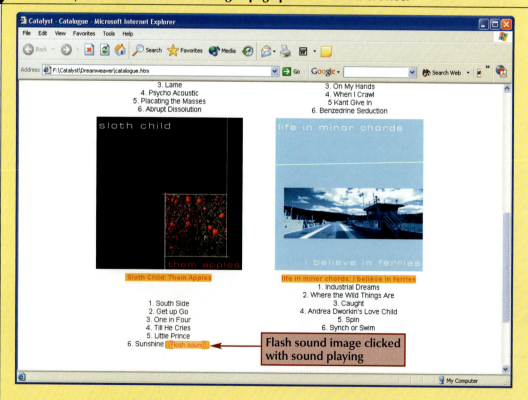

9. Close the browser window.

You can adjust the attributes of a sound-only Flash movie.

Adjusting Attributes of a Sound-only Flash Movie

Once you have added a Flash movie to a Web page, you may need to set some of the attributes in the Property inspector. Most of these settings are irrelevant to sound-only Flash movies; they affect only visual aspects of the movie. The only attributes that you set when working with a sound-only Flash movie are the Loop and Autoplay check boxes. When using a movie that is designed to prevent automatic play, checking the Loop and Autoplay check boxes will have no effect, but they will function as usual with a movie that is designed to allow automatic play when the page loads.

You do not need to set any attributes for the SunshineFlash movie you added to the Catalogue page.

Embedding Other Sound Formats

Embedding other types of sound files (MP3, RealMedia, and so forth) is a bit more difficult than embedding a sound-only Flash movie because Dreamweaver does not have a custom control for embedding the other types of files. You can use the generic Plugin button in the Media list in the Common category on the Insert bar, but you must type many parameters to make the sound work, or you must download an extension from the Macromedia Exchange. Once you have downloaded an extension, embedding other types of sound files follows the same basic process as embedding a sound-only Flash movie. You will learn more about downloading extensions in the next session when you download the RealMedia extension to embed video in a page.

Creating a Link to an MP3 Sound File

MP3 is a very commonly used sound format that can contain very high-quality sound with a surprisingly small file size. This is perfect for sending sound over the Web, especially when the end user has a slow connection. It is such a popular format that most computers come preconfigured with a player that will play MP3 files, avoiding the need to download any additional software. MP3 files are a good choice when you want to link to a sound file instead of embedding the file in a page because it is very likely that the sound will play as expected even though there are many different players that might handle MP3 on an end user's computer. Using a link, instead of embedding, will ensure that whatever player handles MP3 will not display its own sound control interface in the Web page, potentially interfering with your design.

Brian wants to provide users with a choice of sound formats. You have already added sound to the page by embedding a sound-only Flash movie in the page; now you will create a link to an MP3 file that contains the same sound content as the Flash file. When the user clicks the link, the sound file will begin to download and will be played back by whatever player is configured to handle MP3s on the end user's computer.

To add a link to an MP3 file to a Web page:

1. Click to the right of the Flash sound image in the Catalogue page, and then press the **Shift+Enter** keys to move the insertion point to the next line.

2. Click the **Image** button in the **Images** list in the **Common** category on the Insert bar, and then double-click the **MP3SoundButton.gif** file located in the **Tutorial.07\Tutorial** folder included with your Data Files. The MP3SoundButton image is inserted into the page.

3. Click to the left of the MP3SoundButton image, and then press the **Ctrl+Shift+Spacebar** keys to add nonbreaking spaces until the image is aligned with the FlashSoundButton.gif image above it.

4. Select the **MP3SoundButton** image, click the **Browse for File** button next to the Link text box in the Property inspector, double-click the **sunshine.mp3** file located in the **Tutorial.07\Tutorial** folder included with your Data Files, and then place a copy of the sunshine.mp3 file in the **Media** folder in the site's local root folder. See Figure 7-24.

Figure 7-24	MP3 sound button added to the Catalogue page

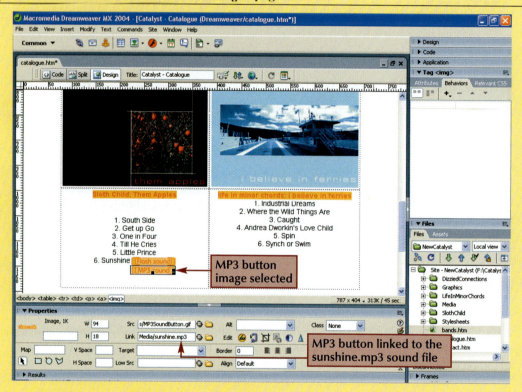

5. Save the page, and then preview the page in a browser.
6. Click the **MP3 sound** button. Sound will play and, depending on which player is playing the sound, a number of things could happen: a player could appear in the browser, a player could appear outside the browser, or the sound might simply begin to play without any player opening. See Figure 7-25.

Tutorial 7 Adding Rich Media to a Web Site | Dreamweaver | DRM 401

Windows Media Player opened in browser | Figure 7-25

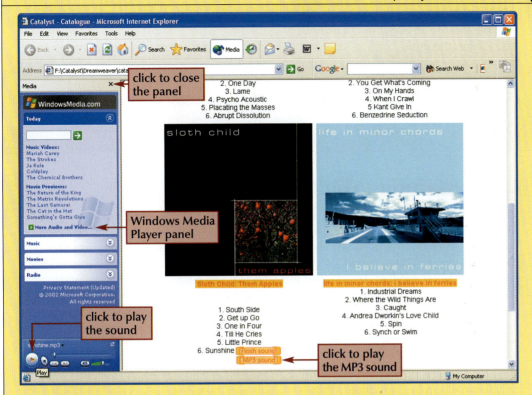

Trouble? If no sound plays and a player opens, you may need to click the Play button in the player to start the sound.

Trouble? If a Media Bar Settings dialog box opens, asking whether Internet Explorer should play this link in its own window so it will be easier to see and hear, you need to determine which player you want to use. Click the Yes button (only if you do not have another media player installed) to install the latest version of Windows Media Player, and open a side panel with the player in your browser. Click the No button if you have another player you prefer to use. The other player then opens to play the audio clip.

7. Close the browser window, close the player and panel, if necessary, and then close the page.

You can also create links to other sound files.

Creating Links to Other Sound Files

You can create a link to any of the commonly used sound file formats, including MP3, RealMedia, QuickTime, and Windows Media. (Generally, it is not a good idea to link directly to sound-only Flash movies; they should only be embedded in a page so they play reliably.) You link to the other types of sound files in the same way that you link to an MP3 file. Simply add a button to the page, create a link to the sound file, and include a copy of the sound file in the Media folder in the root folder of the site. In addition, one file format will basically work as well as another, and the CODECs needed to play each format are included in all the popular media players.

In this session, you added a Shockwave movie to the Catalyst site, and you embedded and linked sound files. In the next session, you will add video to the site.

DRM 402 | Dreamweaver | Tutorial 7 Adding Rich Media to a Web Site

Review

Session 7.2 Quick Check

1. What program is used to create Shockwave movies?
2. What is the Shockwave file extension?
3. Define streaming.
4. What are two ways to include sound in a page?
5. List four popular sound formats.
6. What is the one sound format to which you should not link directly?

Session 7.3

Understanding Digital Video

Video can add excitement to a Web page and greatly enhance the experience of site visitors. However, even with compression, video files are relatively large and may be slow to download, especially for users who have dial-up connections. Because video includes moving images and often sound, it requires more focused attention from site visitors. This can be both good and bad. The positive aspect is that video can really reinforce what you are trying to say. Users tend to pay attention, so it is a good way to drive home an important message. The negative aspect is that it is easy to overload users with too much motion in the page. When users are barraged with too much motion or too many messages, the video becomes a distraction and can detract from the effectiveness of the Web site rather than reinforce it. The steeper user requirements (more time to download and more focused attention from the user) associated with video mean that video should be included in a site only when it is truly appropriate for the site goals and the target audience.

When deciding whether to use video in a site, consider that when site visitors must wait for something large to download, their expectations are raised. Or, put another way, site visitors will wait for downloads only when they perceive that the content is something worth waiting for.

Video files, like sound files, must be compressed to make them small enough to deliver over the Web. Several major factors affect the file size of a digital video clip, including frame size, playback quality, and sound parameters. Some common video frame sizes used on the Web are 320 × 240 pixels and 240 × 180 pixels—the smaller frame size creates a smaller video file. Playback quality for digital video is often adjusted to match the target connection speed and is usually measured in the amount of data that needs to be downloaded per second. For example, 31 Kbps (kilobits per second) might be used with a video clip intended for standard modems, whereas 400 Kbps might be used to provide higher-quality video to users with high-speed connections. Video quality affects the amount of detail and motion in the video image. Higher-quality video contains cleaner, more detailed images and smoother movement than lower-quality video. Sound parameters in digital video include the choice of stereo or mono and the resolution or clarity of the sound. Stereo and high resolution occupy more file space than mono and lower resolution.

To ensure continuous playback of a video clip, it must be **buffered**, which means that the first five or 10 seconds of the clip are downloaded before it begins to play. After the clip begins to play, as long as the current download is at or past the current clip playback location, the playback will continue without interruption. A user who has a fast, consistent connection is more likely to be able to download enough of the clip each second to view a continuous playback. If the download does not keep up with the playback (that is, if the next piece of needed file hasn't completed downloading yet), then the video playback will be interrupted. The user may see any of a number of things: the video may stop until the download catches up, the video may become jittery and chunks of it may not play, and sometimes a warning appears telling the user that the download is being interrupted. Any of these things can be very annoying and cause the user to leave the page before he or she has viewed the entire video clip.

Web sites that include digital video use several different solutions to minimize playback interruptions and maximize the viewing experience of the user. These solutions include multiple clip options, multiple formats, and specialized video servers. By offering the same digital video clip in multiple file sizes, a site can satisfy a wide range of visitors. Sites taking this approach often offer each clip in low, medium, and high resolution. They may sometimes instead offer dial-up and broadband sizes, which means that they have used the compression parameters discussed earlier to offer the same clip in lower-quality/smaller-frame size for visitors using slower dial-up connections and in higher-quality/larger-frame size for visitors using faster broadband connections. Some sites also offer different format options, knowing that some users prefer the QuickTime format and player, whereas others might choose RealMedia or Windows Media. In addition, bigger-budget Web sites might use a specialized video server to monitor a user's connection and adjust the video quality to compensate for slowdowns, increasing the likelihood that the user can view the video clip without interruption. Another benefit provided by a video server is the ability to allow thousands of users to view the same clip simultaneously, which is impossible when including video on a standard Web server.

Video files are created or recorded with programs outside of Dreamweaver, such as Avid and Premier, but can be added to Web pages in Dreamweaver.

Reviewing Video File Formats

Digital video can have many different formats. Most of the popular sound formats can also be used for video, including RealMedia, QuickTime, and Windows Media. As with audio formats, earlier versions of these video formats were preferred for different uses. Although there are still differences, all three of these formats provide excellent video performance with a wide range of materials. Today, most Web sites that include video offer the user a choice of formats.

On the Web, these formats are identified by their file extensions. Some of the most common extensions are:

- **.mov.** A QuickTime movie that can contain sound, video, and animation tracks. QuickTime is a very popular cross-platform format from Apple used for both Web and CD-ROM video.
- **.rm.** A RealMedia movie, which is another popular format for Web and intranet streaming video. When you add RealMedia to a site, you add an .rm file to the page and Dreamweaver creates an .rpm file for you.
- **.rpm.** A metafile that contains the location of the RealMedia file to be played. When using RealMedia, links should always go to a metafile, which points to the RealMedia file.
- **.smil.** A Synchronized Multimedia Integration Language (SMIL) file used with RealMedia to create time-based multimedia presentations that can include audio, video, graphics, animation, and text.
- **.wmv.** A Windows Media File, which is a format for Web- and CD-based digital video made popular by Microsoft.
- **.avi.** An earlier Microsoft format designation that has largely been replaced by the newer Windows Media format (.wmv).
- **.mpg.** A format created by the Motion Picture Experts Group that is generally used for CDs, DVDs, and multimedia pieces rather than for Web distribution.

Most of the popular players will play back both sound and video. The makers of the RealMedia, QuickTime, and Window Media formats each provide a free player that can be downloaded. And, as with sound, the players include both standalone player functionality as well as browser integration, which allows the browser to play video embedded directly in a Web page.

Adding Video to a Web Page

There are several steps involved in adding video to a Web page. First, you must download an extension that enables you to insert video into Web pages from the Macromedia Exchange. Next, you use the extension tools to insert video into a Web page. Then, you download a player into your browser. Finally, you view the page in a browser.

Dreamweaver does not come with an object designed to embed video the way the Flash object is customized to embed a Flash movie. It does come with a generic Plug-in object that can be used to add a variety of media to your pages. However, because the Plug-in object is fairly generic, you must type quite a bit of code to make any video solution work. Another option is to download an extension from the Macromedia Exchange. Video extensions add tools to Dreamweaver that are designed specifically to embed the video format you have chosen into a Web page. Also, if you do not already have a player installed to view the video in your browser, you will need to download one.

In this session you will use the RealMedia format for video. (You could also choose QuickTime or Windows Media.) No matter which format you use, you will follow the same general process to add video to a Web page:

- Visit the Macromedia Exchange for Dreamweaver site and locate the appropriate extension(s) that will add tools to Dreamweaver that enable you to insert video (in the chosen format) into Web pages.
- Download and install the selected extension.
- Use the extension to add a video clip to a Web page in Dreamweaver.
- Adjust the attributes for the video clip in the Property inspector.
- Save the Web page.
- Visit the format maker's Web site to learn about the format (in this case, the RealMedia site).
- Download the appropriate player from the maker's site and install it, if necessary.
- Preview the Web page that includes a video clip.

Now that you understand what is involved in adding video to a Web page, you will start the process by downloading the RealMedia extension for Dreamweaver.

Downloading the RealMedia Suite Extension for Dreamweaver

Before you can add video to a Web site using the RealMedia format, you need to download the RealMedia Suite extension for Dreamweaver from the Macromedia Exchange Web site. You must be connected to the Internet to download the extension. If you are not connected to the Internet, see your instructor on how to proceed. You must log in to the site to download the extension. If you have never created a login for the Macromedia Exchange, you must do that before you can begin the download steps.

To download the RealMedia Suite Extension:

1. If you took a break after the previous session, make sure the **NewCatalyst** site is open.
2. Click **Help** on the menu bar, and then click **Dreamweaver Support Center**. A browser window opens to the Macromedia Dreamweaver Support Center.

   Trouble? If the page does not open, you are not connected to the Internet. You must be connected to the Internet to download extensions.

3. Scroll down and click the **Dreamweaver Exchange** link located at the right of the page. The Dreamweaver Exchange page opens in the browser.
4. Click the **Search Exchanges** link located in the upper-right corner of the page. The Exchange Search page opens.
5. Type **RealMedia** in the Search text box, click **Dreamweaver Exchange** in the exchange list, and then click the **Search** button to begin your search. A list of all the RealMedia extensions found on the Exchange site appears in the page. See Figure 7-26.

Figure 7-26   Exchange Search page

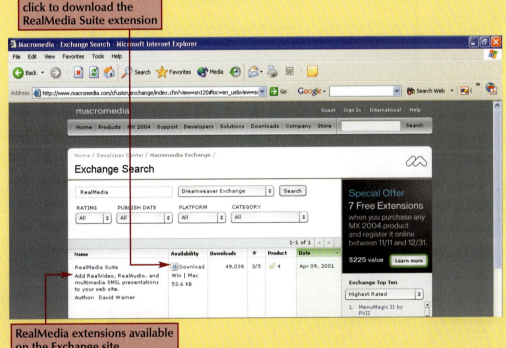

click to download the RealMedia Suite extension

RealMedia extensions available on the Exchange site

Trouble? If your list differs from the one shown in Figure 7-26, the Exchange has been updated since this tutorial was published and your list shows all the current RealMedia extensions.

6. Click the **Download** button beside the RealMedia Suite extension. The Extension Download License page of the Macromedia Exchange site opens in a browser.

   Trouble? If you cannot download the extension, then you are not logged in and the Sign In page opens in the browser window. Log in, and then continue with Step 7. If you do not have a login ID, click the No, I will create one now link, create a login, and then continue with Step 7.

7. Click the **Accept** button to download the extension. The extension starts to download and the File Download dialog box opens.

▶ 8. Click the **Open** button to open the extension. The Macromedia Extension Manager dialog box opens and displays the Macromedia Extension Disclaimer.

▶ 9. Click the **Accept** button to accept the terms of the disclaimer. The extension installs into the Macromedia Extension Manager, and a dialog box opens indicating that the extension has been installed successfully.

▶ 10. Click the **OK** button. The RealMedia Suite extension is listed in the Macromedia Extension Manager window. See Figure 7-27.

Figure 7-27 | **Macromedia Extension Manager window**

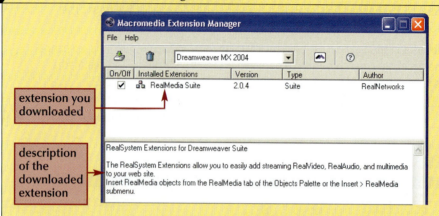

▶ 11. Click the **Close** button ✖ in the title bar of the Macromedia Extension Manager window to close it, and then close the browser window.

▶ 12. Exit and restart **Dreamweaver**, and then open the **index.htm** page of the NewCatalyst site in the Document window. The downloaded extension becomes active and a RealAudio category is added to the Insert bar. See Figure 7-28.

Figure 7-28 | **Insert bar with the RealMedia extension**

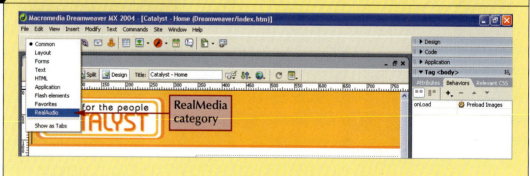

Once you have added RealMedia to Dreamweaver, you can add video clips to Web pages.

Adding a RealMedia Video Clip to a Web Page

Now that the RealMedia tools are installed in Dreamweaver, adding a RealMedia video clip is simple. The Sloth Child band is in the process of shooting a video for its new single, "Sunshine." Sara wants to promote the upcoming video on the Catalyst site.

Reference Window

Adding a RealVideo Clip to a Web Page

- Click in the page where you want to add the video.
- Click the Insert RealVideo button in the RealAudio category on the Insert bar.
- Navigate to the video file, and then double-click the file.
- Click the Yes button, navigate to the folder in which you want to save the file, and then click the Save button.
- Adjust RealMedia video clip attributes in the Property inspector as needed.

You will add a RealMedia video clip with a promo for the upcoming video below the SlothChild layer in the home page. The video contains audio. The audio does not loop, so it will play only once in the browser.

To add video to a Web page:

1. Draw a small layer 10 pixels below the SlothChild layer in the home page, select the layer, and then type **Video** in the Layer ID text box in the Property inspector to name the layer.

2. Click in the **Video** layer, and then click the **RealVideo** button in the **RealAudio** category on the Insert bar. The Select File dialog box opens.

3. Double-click the **sunshineVideo.rm** file located in the **Tutorial.07\Tutorial** folder included with your Data Files, click the **Yes** button, and then place a copy of the video clip in the **Media** folder. A black square the size of the video clip with the RealMedia logo appears in the layer. See Figure 7-29.

RealMedia video clip added to the home page — Figure 7-29

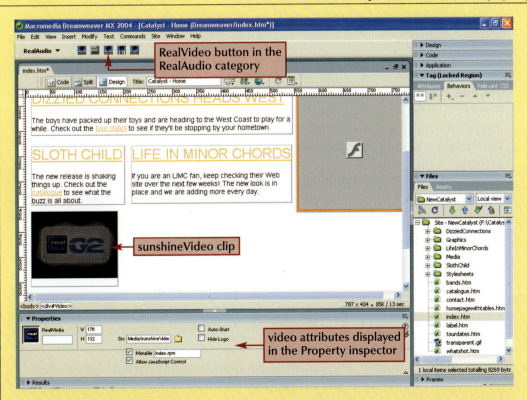

Trouble? If an error message dialog box opens, click the OK button (you may need to do this twice). The error message is most likely because you do not have the latest version of the RealPlayer installed. You will install this later.

4. Select the **Video** layer, and then align it to the left border of the SlothChild layer.
5. Save the page.

Next, you will adjust the attributes of the video clip.

Adjusting the Attributes of a Video Clip

No matter which video format you use, you can adjust the attributes associated with the video clip in the Property inspector when you select the clip. Some attributes are commonly available within all the formats, whereas others are specific to a particular format.

The attributes that are commonly available in all the formats are:

- **Name.** The name for the inserted object, which can be used for identification and to refer to the object in scripts you write to control the clip.
- **W and H.** The width and the height of the video clip. These dimensions are usually set automatically when you insert the video clip and should be the actual size of the clip. Setting this value for a size other than that of the clip is not recommended because it may degrade video performance. If you want to change the size of a video clip, the clip should usually be remade at the desired size.
- **Src.** The filename of the video clip that you selected when you inserted the RealMedia object. You can select a different video clip to display.
- **Auto-Start.** The option to play the video clip just after the page loads. Users with slower connections may see a short delay before the clip begins to play.

In addition to these common attributes, each format also offers some unique attributes that are not available in the other formats. These attributes are also located in the Property inspector. The unique attributes of the RealMedia format are:

- **Hide Logo.** The option to hide the RealMedia logo. This setting does not have any effect on some systems.
- **Metafile.** The name of a file that was automatically created when you inserted the RealMedia object. This simple text file has an .rpm extension and contains the name and possible location of the .rm file to be played. The metafile controls should remain in their default settings unless you are an advanced user, otherwise the video may not play properly.
- **Allow JavaScript Control.** The option to include JavaScripts that will control the RealMedia object. If you do not include JavaScripts that will control the RealMedia object, then this setting has no effect.

You will name the movie clip that you added to the home page and set the movie to start automatically when the page is downloaded. Then you will preview the page. If you do not have a player, you must install a player before you can view the video.

To adjust the attributes of a RealMedia video clip:

1. Select the **sunshineVideo.rm** video clip.
2. In the Property inspector, type **SunshineVideo** in the RealMedia text box, and then click the **Auto-Start** check box to insert a check mark.
3. Save the page, and then preview the page in a browser. The home page opens in a browser and the video (with audio) plays if you have a player installed in your browser that plays the RealMedia format. See Figure 7-30.

Figure 7-30 Home page with the video clip previewed in a browser

sunshineVideo playing in the page (with audio)

Trouble? If the RealMedia logo or an X appears where the video should be, wait a few moments to see if the video is downloading. The logo appears while the video is downloading to the client computer unless the Hide logo option is selected. If the video does not load, you need to download a player to view the video. Complete the next section, "Downloading the RealPlayer for Internet Explorer," and then repeat Step 3.

The next section provides steps for downloading the RealPlayer® for Internet Explorer. If you have the player, read but do not complete the steps in this section.

Downloading the RealPlayer for Internet Explorer

To view video added to a Web site, you must install a player in your browser that will enable you to view the video. Installing a player on your computer does not enable other users to view the video on their computers. The player must be installed on the client computer for that user to see the video. This is one of the downsides to using video in a Web site as well as one of the reasons to consider the browser penetration of a technology before deciding to use the media in Web pages. The higher browser penetration a media has, the more likely it is that end users will already have the player. Some users who don't have a player will not take the time to download the player and will simply skip that portion of the site.

Because you are using RealMedia for the video, you will download and install the RealPlayer for your browser. The following steps are for installing the RealPlayer in Internet Explorer. If you are using another browser, you will need to download and install the RealPlayer designed for that browser. Remember, most of the new players will play any of the popular video formats, so there is a good chance that other users will not have the exact same viewing experience.

To install the RealPlayer in Internet Explorer:

1. Type **www.real.com** in the Address bar in your browser, and then press the **Enter** key. The Real.com page opens.

   Trouble? Check with your instructor or technical support person before downloading and installing the RealPlayer to ensure you have the appropriate access and permissions.

2. Click the **Download RealPlayer** link, and then click the **Download Free RealPlayer** link (not the free trial of the RealPlayer for which you must eventually pay). The Download Manager opens.

   Trouble? If you don't see the Download RealPlayer link or the Download Free RealPlayer link, then the Web site might have been updated since this tutorial was published. Look for and then click the link to download the free RealPlayer.

3. Click the **Yes** button in the Download Manager. The RealPlayer begins to download. See Figure 7-31.

Figure 7-31   Download Manager

shows the progress of the download

advertising content will change

   Trouble? If the RealPlayer Update dialog box opens, you already have the RealPlayer installed on your computer. The RealPlayer Update dialog box updates the player as needed, and then the RealPlayer Install Wizard opens. Continue with Step 5.

4. Click the **Yes** button to begin downloading the RealPlayer. When the download is complete, the RealPlayer Install Wizard opens. See Figure 7-32.

Figure 7-32 Install Wizard

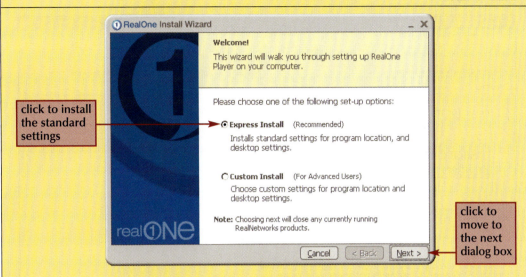

▶ **5.** Click the **Express Install** option button, if necessary, and then click the **Next** button to advance to the next page.

▶ **6.** Click the **Accept** button. The Install Wizard installs the files.

   Trouble? If a dialog box opens, informing you that the RealPlayer is already installed, click the OK button to reinstall the player.

▶ **7.** Click the **Finish** button. The installation is complete, the RealPlayer Install Wizard closes, and the RealPlayer dialog box opens with a welcome page visible.

▶ **8.** Click the **Next** button to move to the next page. The RealPlayer connects to the Internet.

▶ **9.** Click the **Continue** button to add the RealPlayer toolbar to Internet Explorer. A Product Registration opens and prompts you to enter information.

▶ **10.** Fill out the form, and then click the **Create** button. A confirmation page opens.

▶ **11.** Click the **Basic Setup** button, and then click the **Continue** button. The RealPlayer launches.

▶ **12.** Close all of the open browser windows, close the RealPlayer, and then preview the home page in a browser to view the video. See Figure 7-33.

Figure 7-33   **Home page with video previewed in browser**

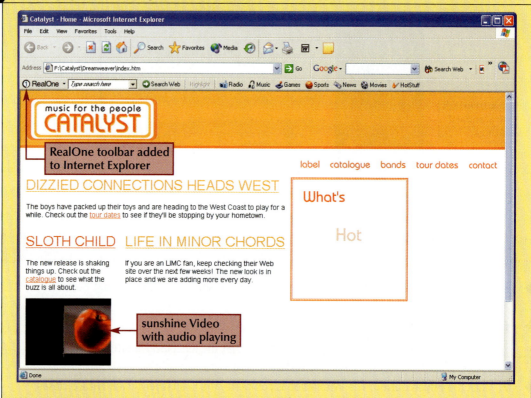

13. Close the browser window.

Adjusting a RealMedia Video Clip to Display over the Internet

When you add a RealMedia video clip to a page, an additional file is added to the Web site. This file is a .rpm file, which contains instructions for the movie. When you look in the Files panel, you see that the new file has the name of the Web page to which the movie was added followed by the file extension .rpm. For example, there is an index.rpm file below the index.htm file in the Files panel for your Catalyst site.

    Before you can view RealMedia movies over the Web, you must adjust the code in the .rpm files. A bug in the current version of the extension you downloaded prevents the movie from playing once you upload the site to the Web. To adjust the code, you need to open the .rpm file in either Notepad (which is included with Windows) or Textpad; it will not open from within Dreamweaver. You then replace the URL of the movie with an absolute link to the movie on your remote Web server, and then save the file. You must do this for each RealMedia movie you add to a page. Once you make this change, movies will no longer play when you preview them from your local computer because the absolute path specifies the location of the movie on your remote server. If you do not know the absolute link information for your remote server, ask your instructor or technical support person.

    You'll update the code for the movie you added to the home page.

To change the .rpm file:

1. Click the **Start** button, point to **All Programs** on the Start menu, point to **Accessories**, and then click **Notepad** in the Accessories menu. Notepad opens.
2. Click **File** on the menu bar, click **Open**, click **All Files** in the Files of Type list; navigate to the site's local root folder, click the **index.rpm** file, and then click the **Open** button. The movie file opens in the Notepad window.
3. Delete **file:** and type the absolute path to the movie on your remote server (the path will start with **http://www** and end with **/Media/sunshineVideo.rm**).
4. Click **File** on the menu bar, and then click **Save**. The absolute path you added to the movie file is saved in the file.
5. Click the **Close** button ❌ on the Notepad window title bar. Notepad closes.

You have fixed the bug that prevents the movie file from playing in the browser. Remember that the movie will not play from within Dreamweaver now. Next, you will upload the site to your remote server and view the movie.

Updating the Web Site on the Remote Server

As a final test of the media elements you've added to the Catalyst site, you'll view the pages over the Web. You'll upload the pages you changed and the Media folder to your remote server, and then view the site over the Web.

To upload a site to the remote server:

1. Click the **Connects to Remote Host** button on the Files panel toolbar.
2. Click the **View** list arrow on the Files panel toolbar, and then click **Local View**.
3. Click the **index.htm**, **index.rpm**, **bands.htm**, and **catalogue.htm** files and the **Media** folder in Local view to select them, and then click the **Put File(s)** button ⬆ on the Files panel toolbar.
4. Click the **Yes** button when asked if you want to include dependent files because you have not selected the new dependent files for the site yet.

   A dialog box opens with the message that the requested file is not found.
5. Click the **OK** button.
6. Click the **Disconnects from Remote Host** button on the Files panel toolbar.
7. Click the **View** list arrow on the Files panel toolbar, and then click **Local View**. The Files panel returns to the Local view.

Next, you'll view the updated remote site in a browser. The remote site will include all of the new elements that you added to your local version of the site.

To view the updated remote site in a browser:

1. Open a browser, type the URL for your remote site in the Address text box on the browser toolbar, and then press the **Enter** key.
2. Explore the home page on the remote site from within the browser.

> **Trouble?** If you cannot view the video from your remote server, you need to manually adjust the index.rpm file. Once you make the change, you can no longer view the video locally. See your instructor for the steps to modify the index.rpm file.
>
> 3. Click the **bands** link to open the Bands page, and then watch the Shockwave movie.
> 4. Click the **catalogue** link to open the Catalogue page, and then scroll to the bottom of the Catalogue page.
> 5. Click the **Flash sound** button, and listen to the sound clip.
> 6. Click the **MP3 sound** button, and listen to the sound clip.
> 7. Close the browser window.

In this session, you downloaded an extension from the Macromedia Exchange that enabled you to insert video into Web pages. You used the extension tools to insert video into a page. You downloaded the RealOne Player into your browser and viewed the video in a browser. Then you uploaded the site to your remote server and viewed the pages over the Web.

Session 7.3 Quick Check

1. List three things that might affect the file size of a video clip.
2. What is the RealMedia file extension?
3. Why must a video clip be buffered?
4. Name three commonly used video file formats.
5. True or False? Most of the popular sound formats can also be used for video.
6. True or False? Installing a video player on your computer enables all other users to view the video on their computers.

Tutorial Summary

In this tutorial, you explored the benefits and drawbacks of adding media to a site. You added a Flash movie, Flash text, and a Shockwave movie to a Web page. Then, you added sound to a Web page. You used a Flash movie to add the sound and added a button to play the sound. You also added an MP3 file to the Web page and added a button to play the sound. Next, you explored adding video to a site. You downloaded the RealMedia extension from the Macromedia Exchange, you embedded a video clip in a page, and you updated the absolute link to the movie in the .rpm file. You downloaded the RealPlayer, and then you viewed the video over the Web.

Key Terms

buffer	Flash	Shockwave
CODEC	locked file	sound formats
Director	media	streaming
Director projector	MP3	

Practice

Practice the skills you learned in the tutorial.

Review Assignments

Data Files needed for the Review Assignments: sunshine_autostart.swf, limcVideo.rm

Brian asks you to add some additional media elements to the Catalyst site. First, you'll change the text on the What's Hot page to Flash text so that it can be displayed in the logo font. You'll also add a sound-only Flash movie that is set to play automatically to the Sloth Child page. The movie will add sound to the background of the page. The Life in Minor Chords band is going to be releasing a video of some live performances that were filmed during its most recent tour. The band has created a short promo video to create some buzz. You will embed the video promo in the tour section of the LIMC page.

1. Open the NewCatalyst site that you modified in this tutorial, and then open the whatshot.htm page in the Document window.
2. Select the "BLACK LAB: THE LATEST RELEASE FROM SURFACE SUCTION" text in the upper-right corner of the What's Hot page, and then press the Delete key.
3. Click the Flash Text button in the Media list in the Common category on the Insert bar to open the Insert Flash Text dialog box, click Bauhaus Md BT (or Arial or a font of your choice that resembles the Catalyst logo font) in the Font list, type "55" in the Size text box, click the Align Center button, type "#FF9900" in the Color text box, and type the following in the Text text box:

    Black Lab:
    the latest
    release
    from
    Surface Suction

4. Click the Browse button next to the Save As text box, navigate to the Media folder, name the file "WhatsHotText1.swf," and then click the Save button.
5. Click the OK button to close the Insert Flash Text dialog box, view the text in the What's Hot page, and then save and close the page.
6. Open the sloth_child.htm page located in the SlothChild folder in the local root folder, and then draw a small layer beside the Sloth Child logo.
7. Click inside the layer, click the Flash button in the Media list in the Common category on the Insert bar, double-click the **sunshine_autostart.swf** file located in the **Tutorial.07\Review** folder included with your Data Files, and then place a copy of the file in the Media folder in the site's local root folder.
8. Select the Flash movie, and then check the Autoplay and Loop check boxes in the Property inspector, if necessary.
9. Save the page, and then preview the page in a browser. The sound will begin to play when the page is loaded. Close the page.
10. Open the limc_content_tours.htm page located in the LifeInMinorChords folder in the site's local root folder, and then draw a layer below the page heading.
11. Click in the layer, click the RealVideo button in the RealAudio category on the Insert bar, double-click the **limcVideo.rm** file located in the **Tutorial.07\Review** folder included with your Data Files, and then place a copy of the file in the Media folder in the site's local root folder.
12. Select the layer, and then resize the borders of the layer so that they fit snugly against the borders of the movie.
13. Move the layer so that its top border is 50 pixels below the page heading and its left border is aligned with the end of the page heading text.

14. Select the video clip, and then in the Property inspector, check the Auto-Start check box and type "limcVideo" in the RealMedia text box.
15. Save and close the page, open the limc_frameset.htm page in the Document window, preview the page in your browser, click the tour link to view the video, and then close the page. (*Hint:* The video has audio in it.)
16. Start Notepad, open the limcVideo.rpm file in Notepad, delete "file:.." from the line, type the absolute path, save the file, and then close the Notepad window.
17. Upload the site to your remote server, and then preview the site over the Web.

Apply

Add audio and video clips to demonstrate linguistic differences in a Web site about small rural communities of northern Vietnam.

Case Problem 1

Data Files needed for this Case Problem: **HartHarshSample.rm, HartHarshwhSample.mp3, HartModalSample.mp3**

Hroch University Anthropology Department Professor Hart has put together two MP3 audio clips and one video clip that demonstrate some of the linguistic differences he found in northern Vietnam. He asks you to place each example in the Linguistic Differences page.

1. Open the Hart site that you modified in Tutorial 6, Case 1, and then open the linguistic_differences.htm page in the Document window.
2. Delete the text in the second row of the table, and then type "Research in process; in the meantime, click on the video and audio files to preview some interesting findings." in the row.
3. Press the Enter key to create another line in the table row, and then click the RealVideo button in RealAudio category on the Insert bar.
4. Double-click the **HartHarshSample.rm** file located in the **Tutorial.07\Cases** folder included with your Data Files, create a new folder named "Media" in the site's local root folder, and then place a copy of the HartHarshSample.rm file in the Media folder.
5. Select the video file, and then check the Auto-Start check box in the Property inspector.
6. Insert 14 nonbreaking spaces in the page to the right of the video. (*Hint:* Press the Ctrl+Shift+Spacebar keys to insert a nonbreaking space.)
7. Type "audio 1," insert another 14 nonbreaking spaces in the page, and then type "audio 2."

Explore

8. Select the audio 1 text, click the Browse for File button next to the Link text box in the Property inspector, double-click the **HartHarshwhSample.mp3** file located in the **Tutorial.07\Cases** folder included with your Data Files, and then place a copy of the MP3 file in the Media folder.

Explore

9. Select the audio 2 text, click the Browse for File button next to the Link text box in the Property inspector, double-click the **HartModalSample.mp3** file located in the **Tutorial.07\Cases** folder included with your Data Files, and then place a copy of the MP3 file in the Media folder.
10. Save the page, preview the page in a browser, and then close the browser window and the page.
11. Upload the site to your remote server, and then preview the site over the Web.

Tutorial 7 Adding Rich Media to a Web Site | Dreamweaver **DRM 417**

Challenge

Add a promotional Shockwave movie and a Flash button to play the movie in a Web site for an art museum.

Case Problem 2

Data Files needed for this Case Problem: MuseumTour.doc, museumtour.dcr

Museum of Western Art The Museum of Western Art is sponsoring a regional tour of some of their more popular paintings. C. J. Strittmatter asks you to create a new page to promote the tour. The page will eventually include an interactive educational Shockwave movie that provides information about the paintings and promotes the tour. The team that is creating that movie has made a promotional Shockwave movie to include in the page until the interactive educational movie is complete. You'll add the promotional Shockwave movie to the page. Then you'll add a Flash button to the home page of the site, and link the button to the new page.

1. Open the Museum site you modified in Tutorial 6, Case 2.
2. In the Files panel, copy the location.htm page, and then paste a copy of the Location page in the site's local root folder.
3. Rename the Copy of Location page to "tour.htm," and then open the tour.htm page in the Document window.
4. Delete the navigation bar and all the text below the page heading from the page. The page is empty except for the logo, the horizontal rule, and the heading.
5. Change the page title to "Museum of Western Art - Tour."
6. Change the page heading to "THE TOUR," copy the text from the **MuseumTour.doc** located in the **Tutorial.07\Cases** folder included with your Data Files, and then paste the text in the new Tour page below the page heading.
7. Click to the left of the page heading, and then click the Shockwave button in the Media list in the Common category on the Insert bar.
8. Double-click the **museumtour.dcr** file located in the **Tutorial.07\Cases** folder included with your Data Files, create a new folder named "Media" in the site's local root folder, and then place a copy of the museumtour.dcr file in the Media folder.
9. Select the Shockwave movie, and then, in the Property inspector, type "323" in the W text box, type "240" in the H text box, click Top in the Align list, type "#006666" in the Bg text box, and then press the Enter key.
10. Save the page, preview the page in a browser, and then close the browser window and the page.
11. Open the index.htm page in the Document window, and then draw a small layer at the right of the logo and above the horizontal rule.

Explore
12. Click in the new layer, and then click the Flash Button button in the Media list in the Common category on the Insert bar. The Insert Flash Button dialog box opens.
13. Click Simple Tab in the Style list, type "Regional Tour" in the Button Text text box, click Times New Roman in the Font list, and then type "15" in the Size text box.

Explore
14. Click the Browse button next to the Link text box to open the Select File dialog box, browse to the site's local root folder, and then double-click the tour.htm page.

Explore
15. Click _blank in the Target list, click the color picker, and then drag the eyedropper to the background of the Tour page to select the background color of the page as the background color for the Flash button.

Explore
16. Click the Browse button next to the Save As text box to open the Select File dialog box, browse to the site's local root folder, type "TourButton.swf" in the File Name text box, click the Save button in the Select File dialog box, verify the file path in the Save As text box, and then click the OK button. The Flash button is added to the Tour page.
17. Select the layer and adjust the borders of the layer so that they fit snugly against the edges of the Flash button.

DRM 418 | Dreamweaver | Tutorial 7 Adding Rich Media to a Web Site

18. Move the layer so that the button is right aligned to the 750 pixel marker and its bottom edge touches the top of the horizontal rule. (*Hint:* Show the Rulers, if necessary.)
19. Save the page, preview the page in a browser, test the button, and then close the browser windows and the page.
20. Upload the site to your remote server, and preview the site over the Web.

Apply

Create an order form with a Shockwave movie in a Web site for an independent publisher of fringe writing.

Case Problem 3

Data File needed for this Case Problem: normform.dcr

NORM Norm Blinkered wants to increase catalogue orders for his publishing company. Mark Chapman has already created a Shockwave movie that contains a catalogue order form. You will create a new page for the site, and then place the Shockwave movie into the new page. Then you will add a Flash button to the top of the home page. The Flash button will link to the new page and target the page to open in a new browser window.

1. Open the NORM site you modified in Tutorial 6, Case 3.
2. In the Files panel, copy and paste one of the existing pages to add a new page to the site, rename the new page "catalogue_order.htm," and then open the catalogue_order.htm page in the Document window.
3. Delete everything below the navigation bar from the page, and then enter "NORM - Catalogue Order" as the page title.
4. Click in the upper-left corner of the page below the navigation bar.
5. Click the Shockwave button in the Media list in the Common category on the Insert bar, double-click the **normform.dcr** file located in the **Tutorial.07\Cases** folder included with your Data Files, create a new folder in the site's local root folder named "Media," and then place a copy of the normform.dcr file in the Media folder.
6. Select the Shockwave movie and, in the Property inspector, type "500" in the W text box, type "330" in the H text box, press the Enter key, and then save and close the page.
7. Open the index.htm page in the Document window, and then draw a layer at the right of the page above the horizontal rule.
8. Click in the new layer, and then click the Flash Button button in the Media list in the Common category on the Insert bar.

Explore

9. Click Translucent Tab in the Style list, type "NORM CATALOGUE" in the Button Text text box, click Verdana in the Font list, type "10" in the Size text box, click the Browse button next to the Link text box and double-click the catalogue_order.htm page in the site's local root folder, click _blank in the Target list, type "#003366" in the Bg Color text box, type "CatalogueOrderButton.swf" in the Save As text box, and then click the OK button.
10. Select the layer, and then move the layer so that the bottom of the button is touching the horizontal rule and the right border is positioned at 700 pixels. (*Hint:* Show the Rulers, if necessary.)
11. Save the page, preview the page in a browser, test the button, and then close the browser windows and the page.
12. Upload the site to your remote server, and then preview the site over the Web.

Create

Add a Shockwave movie and a sound clip to a Web site for a newly opening sushi restaurant.

Case Problem 4

Data Files needed for this Case Problem: sushigame.dcr, wasabisound_autoplay.swf

Sushi Ya-Ya Mary O'Brien has decided to add a Sushi-Shell Game to the Specials page. The game will be a Shockwave movie that e-mails the user a coupon for a free piece of the sushi special if the user finds the wasabi hidden under the sushi. Mary also wants you to add a sound clip to the Wasabi page. The sound file is a sound-only Flash movie that will play automatically when the page is loaded.

1. Open the SushiYaYa site you modified in Tutorial 6, Case 4.
2. Open the specials.htm page in the Document window, and then draw a layer below the table.
3. Click in the layer, and then click the Shockwave button in the Media list in the Common category on the Insert bar.
4. Double-click the **sushigame.dcr** file located in the **Tutorial.07\Cases** folder included with your Data Files, create a new folder in the site's local root folder named "Media," and then place a copy of the sushigame.dcr file in the folder.
5. Select the Shockwave movie and, in the Property inspector, type "500" in the W text box, and then type "330" in the H text box.
6. Save the page, preview the page in a browser, test the game, and then close the browser window.

Explore

7. Adjust the layer so that the game is placed in an aesthetically pleasing place in the page.
8. Save the page, preview the page in a browser, and then close the browser window and the page.
9. Open the wasabi.htm page in the Document window, place the pointer to the right of the page heading, and then click the Flash button in the Media list in the Common category on the Insert bar.
10. Double-click the **wasabisound_autoplay.swf** file located in the **Tutorial.07\Cases** folder included with your Data Files, and then place a copy of the wasabisound_autoplay.swf file in the Media folder.
11. Select the Flash movie, check the Autoplay check box in the Property inspector, if necessary, and then uncheck the Loop check box, if necessary.

Explore

12. Click the Play button to preview the sound.
13. Save the page, preview the page in a browser, and then close the browser window and the page.
14. Upload the site to your remote server, and then preview the site over the Web.

Review

Quick Check Answers

Session 7.1

1. any special configurable objects that you might add to the pages of your site, which need a player or application that is not part of the browser—such as plug-ins, ActiveX controls, or helper applications—to display within a browser
2. some type of plug-in or player
3. .swf
4. True
5. False
6. True

Session 7.2

1. Director
2. .dcr
3. Sound can begin to play after only a small portion downloads and will continue to play while the rest of the file continues to download.
4. Embed the sound in the page or link to the sound file. When sound is embedded directly in a page, the sound files in the page begin to download to the client computer as soon as the page is loaded. When you link to sound files, the file does not download to the client computer until the link is clicked.
5. RealMedia, MP3, QuickTime, and Windows Media
6. sound-only Flash movies; you should only embed sound-only Flash movies in a page.

Session 7.3

1. frame size, playback quality, and sound parameters
2. .rm
3. To ensure continuous playback of a video clip, it must be buffered, which means that the first 5 or 10 seconds of the clip are downloaded before it begins to play.
4. RealMedia, QuickTime, and Windows Media
5. True
6. False

Dreamweaver | DRM 421
Tutorial 8

Objectives

Session 8.1
- Explore the head content of a page
- Add keywords to a page
- Add a meta description to a page
- Explore libraries and create a library item
- Add a library item to Web pages

Session 8.2
- Create a template
- Create Web pages from a template
- Edit a template
- Create a nested template

Session 8.3
- Add a form to a Web page
- Set form attributes
- Add form objects to a form
- Add the Validate Form behavior to a form

Creating Reusable Assets and Forms

Creating Meta Tags, Library Items, Templates, and Forms

Case

Catalyst

Brian Lee, public relations and marketing director at Catalyst, has been reviewing the Catalyst site and has some additions and changes he wants made. He wants you to add keywords and a meta description to each page, which will be useful when he lists the pages with search engines after the site is launched. He has also decided that you should convert some of the commonly used site elements, such as the footer, into library items. In addition, he wants you to create templates for the site to make it simpler to add new pages and update the look and feel of all the existing pages. Finally, he has decided to gather some additional information about the users of the Catalyst site, and asks you add a form to the Contact page that users can fill out and submit.

Student Data Files

▼ **Tutorial.08 folder**

▽ **Tutorial folder**
form_test.htm

▽ **Review folder**
(no starting Data Files)

▽ **Cases folder**
form_test.htm
sushi_menu.htm

Session 8.1

Reviewing Head Content

All Web pages contain head content. Remember that head content refers to anything that is placed within the <head> tags of Web pages. Users usually cannot see elements that are placed in the head of a page when the page is viewed in a browser. Head content typically either adds functionality to a page when viewed in a browser or provides information about the page for search engines. Browsers use head content to work with a page. For example, you placed <title> tags in the head of each page to display a page title in the title bar of a browser window. Two commonly used tags that add functionality to a page are:

- **Base.** Inserts a base tag into the head. The base tag is used to enter the desired base URL for the page's document relative links.
- **Link.** Inserts a link tag into the head. The link tag is used most often to link an external style sheet to a page.

Link and Base buttons appear in the Head category on the Insert bar.
  Search engines use head content to learn about a page by looking for information in some of the meta tags included in the head of Web pages. A **meta tag** is a tag in the head content that holds information about the page, gives information to the Web server, or adds functionality to the page. For example, the description of pages that many search engines display when a user performs a search is pulled from the description meta tag in the head of the pages. In addition to the page description, you use meta tags to add information such as keywords, author names, a copyright statement, and so forth to the code of a Web page. The exact purpose of each meta tag is defined by its attributes. You can use more than one meta tag in a page. The most important meta tags are:

- **Meta.** Inserts a generic meta tag into the head and enables you to set attributes, values, and content for the meta tag.
- **Keywords.** Inserts a meta tag with the attribute name="keywords" into the head, which enables you to enter keywords for the page. The keywords meta tag is one of the most frequently used meta tags.
- **Description.** Inserts a meta tag with the attribute name="description" into the head, which enables you to enter a description for the page. The description meta tag is one of the most frequently used meta tags.
- **Refresh.** Inserts a meta tag with the attribute http-equiv="refresh" into the head, which enables you to enter amount of delay, in seconds, before the page is refreshed and choose whether to refresh the current page or open a new URL. Refreshing to a new URL is often used when a site has moved, redirecting users who visit the old URL to the new location.

The Head list in the HTML category on the Insert bar provides buttons for inserting these commonly used meta tags. You'll add keywords and a meta description to the head content of Web pages in the Catalyst site.

Optimizing Web Pages for Search Engine Placement

Optimizing the pages in a Web site for search engine placement is an important part of designing a Web site because search engines enable people to find the site. Optimizing a page means doing everything you can to the page to ensure that it is ranked highly in target search engines. Be aware that each search engine has a different set of formulas that determine page placement. These placement formulas change frequently and are a closely guarded secret to prevent designers from using this information to manipulate page placement. Optimizing Web pages does not automatically get them placed in search engines, but it will help a site receive higher listings when it is listed. Having a Web site not listed appropriately with search engines is like having a business located in an unmarked building with no published address: There is no way for people to know about the amazing things inside.

There are hundreds of search engines, but the top 10 to 12 major engines direct 90% of traffic. Some longer-standing top search engines are Google, Yahoo!, and AltaVista. Unfortunately, the major search engines change frequently. The major engines also feed information to many smaller engines. You should concentrate on getting a site placed in the top 10 to 12 major engines to get the most listings for the site. To list a site with search engines, you can go to the Web site for each search engine and follow the guidelines to list pages of the site in that engine, or you can pay a service to list the site for you. In addition, some search engines send out **robots**, software that searches the Web and sends information back to the engine, to compile information that is used to list pages in the search engines. However, robots are unpredictable. In order to maintain a favorable listing position (a listing within the first page of results), you must list the pages yourself or pay a service to list them for you. Finally, you should relist the pages in the site with each engine to maintain a favorable position. Some engines allow you to relist pages monthly, whereas others prefer that you relist only a few times a year. Guidelines for relisting pages can be found with the listing information on the Web site for each major search engine.

There are many things you can do to optimize your pages for search engine placement. The two most basic things you should do to every Web page are to add keywords and a meta description to the head of the pages. In this session, you will begin to optimize the pages in the Catalyst site for search engine placement by adding keywords and a meta description to each page.

Adding and Editing Keywords

Keywords are one of the elements many search engines use to index Web pages. A **keyword** is a descriptive word or phrase that is placed in the meta tag with the attribute name="keywords". You add one keywords meta tag to the head of each page and then list all the keywords for the site in that tag. The keywords you choose should be the words you think most people will type into search engines to look for that site or the words you want people to find the site under. Remember to include the name of the company and products or services in the list. It can also be helpful to include common misspellings of the company or product name. For example, good keywords for the Catalyst site would be *Catalyst Records*, the band names, and the album titles.

Keywords can be individual words or short phrases fewer than six words. (Some search engines may penalize you for adding longer phrases by decreasing your ranking order or by dropping the site from its index.) When you use phrases, generally each word is indexed separately and together. For example, if you use the phrase "indie music" for the Catalyst site, the word *indie* and the word *music* will both be indexed as well as the phrase "indie music."

You can use as many keywords as you would like; however, the first 10 words are the most important because many search engines use only the first 10 words in the keywords list to index a site. Additionally, search engines often give higher placement to sites that use the keywords within the page content, so make sure that the Web site contains the keywords many times. For example, because the Catalyst site uses the words *indie* and *music* many times within the text of the pages, the pages of the Catalyst site may be ranked higher in value under these keywords than the pages of a site that uses these keywords but does not use the words in its page content. Another example is if you use the word *hippopotamus* in the keywords list for the Catalyst pages. The pages in the Catalyst site may receive a lower ranking under that keyword because the word *hippopotamus* never appears in the page content of the Catalyst site. Conversely, using the keywords excessively in the page content of a site may lead to penalties, including decreased ranking of the site or complete removal of the site from the index because many search engines see this as an attempt at spamming or artificially attempting to inflate the site's listing position.

Adding Keywords and Examining the Code

Although you can type the keywords meta tag directly in Code view, it is simpler to use a dialog box to add keywords to a page and let Dreamweaver create the code. You add keywords to a page with the Keywords button in the Head list in the HTML category on the Insert bar. When entering keywords, you should use all lowercase letters because in most search engines, lowercase letters represent both uppercase and lowercase letters, whereas uppercase letters makes an item case specific. You should also separate each word or phrase with a comma. When you add keywords to a page, the following code is inserted into the head of the page:

```
<meta name="keywords" content="keyword1, keyword2, keyword3">
```

Meta tags are unpaired tags. This means that each tag stands alone and not as part of a set of opening and closing tags. Like all tags, the meta tag starts with an opening bracket followed by the name of the tag, meta. The tag name is followed by a series of tag attributes and values. The first attribute in the keywords meta tag is *name* and its value is the type of meta tag, *"keywords"*. The second attribute is *content* and its value is the content of the tag, or the list of keywords. The tag ends with a closing bracket.

Brian asks you to insert the list of keywords into the home page of the Catalyst site. Then you'll examine the code in Code view.

To add keywords to a page:

1. Open the **NewCatalyst** site that you modified in the Tutorial 7 Review Assignments, and then open the **index.htm** page in the Document window.

2. Click the **Keywords** button in the **Head** list in the **HTML** category on the Insert bar. The Keywords dialog box opens so you can type the words you want. Remember to use all lowercase letters and to separate each word or phrase with a comma.

3. Type **catalyst records, indie music, sloth child, dizzied connections, life in minor chords, surface suction, spinning life, black lab, them apples, i believe in ferries, independent scene, denton music, underground sound** in the Keywords text box. See Figure 8-1.

Figure 8-1 Keywords dialog box

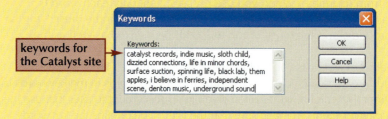

keywords for the Catalyst site

4. Click the **OK** button, and then save the page. The keywords meta tag is added to the head of the page. Its exact location within the head content may vary depending on where the insertion point was located in the page when you clicked the Keywords button.

5. Click the **<head>** tag in the status bar at the bottom of the Document window to select it.

6. Click the **Show Code View** button on the Document toolbar to switch to Code view, and then scroll, if necessary, to view the keywords meta tag in the Document window. The tag is located somewhere in the head section of the page.

7. Click in the keywords meta tag. The <meta> tag is selected in the status bar and the list of keywords appears in the Property inspector. See Figure 8-2.

Keywords meta tag in Code view — Figure 8-2

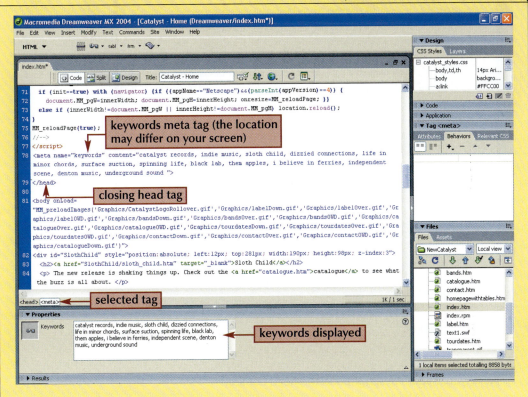

Next, you will edit the keywords.

Editing Keywords

Sometimes you'll want to add another keyword to the list, delete a keyword from the list, or correct the spelling of a keyword in the list. You can do any of these by editing the list of keywords that has already been added to a page. To edit the keywords, you open the page in Code view and then either edit the list directly in Code view or select the keywords meta tag and edit the list in the Property inspector.

Sara's research shows that Catalyst is frequently misspelled as *Catalist*. You'll add this misspelling to the list of keywords in the home page.

To edit the list of keywords:

1. Click after the last word in the Keywords text box in the Property inspector, type **,** (a comma), press the **spacebar**, and then type **catalist**. The new keyword is added in the Property inspector, but the code will not be refreshed in the Document window until you click outside the tag.

2. Click outside the tag, and then click the tag again to view the change in both the code and the Property inspector. See Figure 8-3.

Figure 8-3   **Edited keywords list**

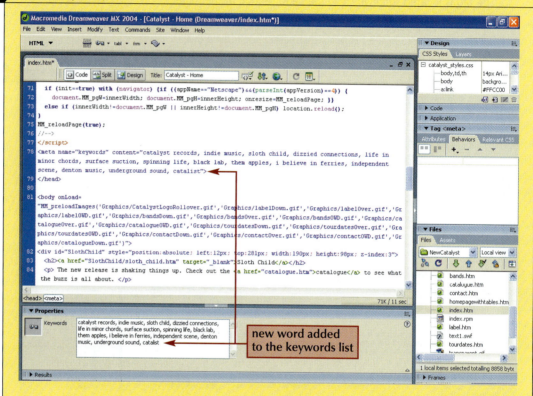

3. Save the page.

Next, you'll add a description to the head content.

Adding and Editing a Meta Description

Many search engines also use the meta description to index Web pages. A **meta description** is a short summary of the Web page that is placed in the meta tag with the attribute *name="description"*. The description should contain a concise summary of the site's content and goals. For example, the Catalyst site description will be "Catalyst is an indie label that has tapped into a vein of post-discord punk music. Our mission is to expose the world to exceptional indie music. Catalyst promotes bands that we believe will change and infuse the planet with original good music." Some search engines also display the first part of the description in the search results page when a user looks up a word or phrase. Therefore, it is a good idea to use the first line or two of the description as a short caption for the site. Think of it as a newspaper headline, summarizing the highlights of the page content. Some engines also penalize a page with very long descriptions, so you should make your description fairly short—no more than six average lines of text.

Adding a Meta Description and Viewing the Code

You add the meta description to a page with the Description button in the Head list in the HTML category on the Insert bar. The description should use standard capitalization, spelling, grammar, and punctuation for ease of user reading. Users quickly scan search results looking for a particular topic or site and may skip over difficult-to-read descriptions. The description meta tag is similar to the keywords meta tag.

```
<meta name="description" content="The description text goes here.">
```

The tag begins with an opening bracket followed by the name of the tag, *meta*. The *name* attribute has the value of *"description"* to specify that this tag provides a summary of the Web site. The value of the *content* attribute is the description text. The tag ends with a closing bracket.

Brian has written a meta description for the Catalyst site that he wants you to add to the home page.

To add a meta description to a page:

1. Click at the end of the keywords meta tag (to the right of "...catalist">"), and then press the **Enter** key. The insertion point is positioned where you'll add the meta description—below the keywords.

2. Click the **Description** button in the **Head** list in the **HTML** category on the Insert bar. The Description dialog box opens.

3. Type **Catalyst is an indie label that has tapped into a vein of post-discord punk music. Our mission is to expose the world to exceptional indie music. Catalyst promotes bands that we believe will change and infuse the planet with original good music.** in the Description text box. See Figure 8-4.

Figure 8-4 Description dialog box

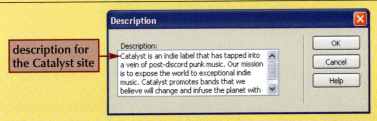

description for the Catalyst site

4. Click the **OK** button. The description appears below the keywords in the Document window.

5. Click the **Refresh** button in the Property inspector, and then click in the meta description tag in the Document window. The description appears in the Property inspector. See Figure 8-5.

Figure 8-5 | **Description meta tag in Code view**

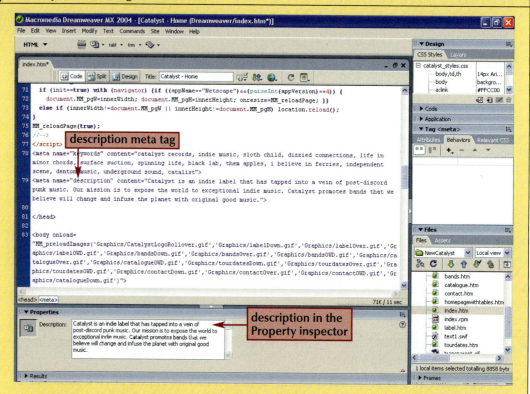

Trouble? If you cannot find the description, click the Refresh button on the Document toolbar to update the screen to show the changes, and then look for the description in Code view.

6. Save the page.

You can edit a meta description.

Editing a Meta Description

Periodically you may want to update a meta description to reflect changes in the Web site or the company and its products. You can edit a meta description in the same ways that you edit keywords. Click in the description in the Document window in Code view, and then change the description in either the Property inspector or the Document window.

Keywords and descriptions should be added to all the pages of a Web site. You will add them to the remaining pages of the Catalyst site in the Review Assignments.

Understanding Library Items

Sometimes you need to add an element to many pages in a site. As a site-centric design tool, Dreamweaver has features, such as library items, to help you automate site design and decrease redundant work. A **library item** is a page element (a piece of a Web page) saved as an .lbi file that can be inserted in more than one page of a site. It is useful to create library items for elements that you intend to reuse or update frequently, such as footers or an upcoming events list that will be displayed in several pages of a site. Using a library item will not only save time, but also ensure consistency of that element throughout the site. You can have any number of library items in a site, but making an element a library item is helpful only if you are going to reuse the element a number of times.

A library item can include most elements in the body of a Web page, including bits of code, text, images, tables, forms, formatting, and so forth. You can even include a navigation bar in a library item, but you cannot use the Show "Down State" Initially feature effectively because every page in which the library item is included would show the Down state for the same button. Library items can only be elements found in the body of a Web page. You cannot create a library item for head content.

When you include a library item in a Web page, the regular HTML code for the element is inserted into the page along with a hidden link to the library item. When you edit a library item, Dreamweaver updates each page in which the library item is used and changes the code in each page. For example, you'll create a library item for the footer in the Catalyst Web pages that includes the footer text, formatting, and a link. By making the footer a library item and then inserting the library item in the pages of the site, you can easily change the footer as needed. If, for instance, the footer link changes, you simply change the link once in the library item and Dreamweaver changes the link in every page in which the footer library item is used. This can save a great amount of time in a large site.

Library items are stored in the Dreamweaver library for the site. A **library** is a collection of library items that are located in the Library folder in the site's local root folder. Every site created in Dreamweaver that has library items will have a Library folder. You can view the library in the Assets panel when you click the Library button. The library and library items are Dreamweaver authoring tools. This means that unlike other items that you have added to pages, CSS styles for example, libraries and library items do not exist outside Dreamweaver. When you make a change in a library item, Dreamweaver updates each page in which the library item is used and changes the code in each page. When you upload the site to a remote server, you do not need to upload the Library folder because all the code for each library item has been added to the individual pages in which an instance of that item is found.

The downside to using library items is that you cannot change an individual instance of the item without disconnecting that instance from the library item. For example, if you decide that the footer should be bold in one page of the Catalyst site, you cannot change the instance of the library item only in that page. Instead, you must delete the library item from that page and create a unique footer. You could also change the library item, which would change the look of the footer on every page in the site. This all-or-nothing aspect of library items can be somewhat limiting.

Creating and Using a Library Item

You can create as many library items as you need for a site. To create a library item, you simply create the element in a page, select the element, and then drag the selected element to the library in the Assets panel. It is important to select all the text, the formatting elements, and anything else you want to include in the library item. For example, if you want to include a blank line above and below the footer in the library item, you must select the line break above and below the footer when you create the library item. It is important to pay attention to what you are selecting because everything you select will be included in the library item. It is sometimes useful to switch to Split view so that you can see the tags that are included in the library item as well as viewing the item in the page. Once all the elements are included in the library item, you then name the new library item and it will be added to the library. It is a good idea to choose a descriptive name that will help you identify the content of the library item. As with other filenames, use only alphanumeric characters, do not use spaces or special characters, and do not start the name with a number. Every library item is saved as an .lbi file.

Because library items can contain only elements found in the body of a Web page, a library item will display CSS styles only if a style sheet that has a style definition that is referenced in the library item code is attached to the page in which it is inserted. Recall that the CSS style sheet code is inserted either in the head of the page or in an external style sheet. When you create a library item from a page that uses CSS styles, the library item will include the code that references the CSS style. As long as the pages in which the library item is inserted are attached to a style sheet that has a style definition for the referenced style, the library item will look the same in the new pages. A library item can be inserted into pages that are attached to different style sheets. Each style sheet can define the style in a different way so that the same library item can look different in different pages.

Reference Window | Creating a Library Item

- Create the page element you want as the library item, if necessary.
- Drag the selected page element to the library in the Assets panel.
- Type a name for the new library item, and then press the Enter key.

or

- Click the New Library Item button in the library in the Assets panel.
- Type a name for the new library item, and then press the Enter key.
- Click the Edit button in the library in the Assets panel.
- Create the page element you want as the new library item, and then save and close the library item.

Brian has noticed that the footer text is inconsistent within the Catalyst site. To ensure consistency, you will create a library item that contains footer information, and then use it to replace the existing footers.

To create a library item:

1. Click the **Show Design View** button [Design] on the Document toolbar, scroll to the bottom of the page, and then select the footer and the blank line above the footer.

2. Collapse any open panels except the Files panel group, click the **Assets** tab in the Files panel group, and then click the **Library** button in the Assets panel. The library is displayed in the Assets panel.

3. Drag the selected footer and blank line to the library. A dialog box opens, warning you that the selection may not look the same when placed in other documents because the style sheet information is not copied with it.

   Trouble? If the dialog box does not open, then the message was disabled for your installation of Dreamweaver. Continue with Step 5.

4. Click the **OK** button. An untitled library item is added to the library. See Figure 8-6.

Figure 8-6 Library displayed in the Assets panel

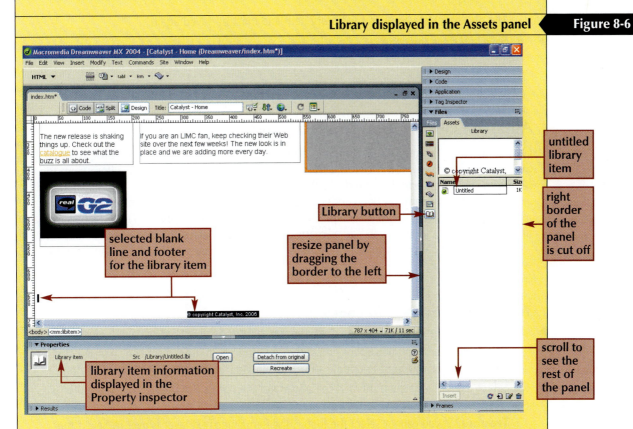

5. Type **catalyst_footer**, and then press the **Enter** key to name the library item. The Update Library Items dialog box opens, so you can update the library item you just created in the What's Hot page.

6. Click the **Update** button.

7. Click in the Document window, and then press the **Right Arrow** key to deselect the footer. The footer is highlighted in yellow, indicating that it is a library item. See Figure 8-7.

Figure 8-7 Library item created from footer

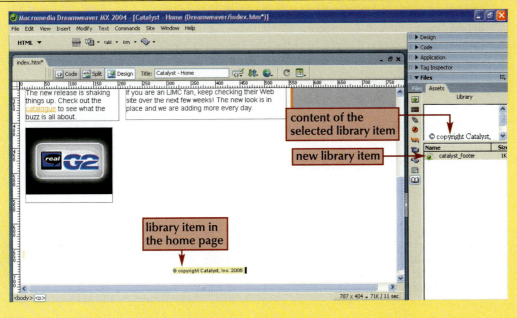

The page contains a link to the library item and must be saved again.

8. Save and close the page.

Now you will add the library item to the other pages of the Catalyst site.

Adding a Library Item to Web Pages

Once you create a library item, you can add it to any page in the Web site. Simply open the page to which you want to add a library item, and then drag the library item from the library in the Assets panel to the desired location in the page.

Once the library item has been added to a page, you can move it within the page by selecting it and dragging it to the new location. You can add the same library item to a page as many times as you want, and you can add as many different library items to a page as you need.

You'll add the catalyst_footer library item to the other pages of the site, and then you will view the code.

To add a library item to pages:

1. Display the Files panel, and then open the **bands.htm** page in the Document window.

   Trouble? If a dialog box opens, indicating that the library item has been changed and asking whether you want to update all the documents in your site, click the OK button.

2. Select the footer at the bottom of the page, and then press the **Delete** key. The footer is removed from the page.

   Trouble? If you cannot select the footer, the RemainingText layer is over it. Select the layer and drag the bottom selection handle until the bottom border of the layer is just below the text in the layer. The footer is now positioned below the layer. Select the footer and press the Delete key.

3. Display the library in the Assets panel.

4. Drag the **catalyst_footer** library item to the bottom of the Bands page below the RemainingText layer. The catalyst_footer library item is inserted into the Bands page.

5. Press the **Right Arrow** key to deselect the footer. The footer is highlighted in pale yellow.

6. Save and close the page.

   You need to add the footer to the rest of the pages in the site.

7. Repeat Steps 1 through 6 to add the footer library item to each of the following pages: **catalogue.htm**, **contact.htm**, **label.htm**, and **tourdates.htm**. (The Tour Dates page is long; to ensure that the anchors in the page work properly, place the footer within the yellow strip where it will be visible rather than at the bottom of the page.)

Next, you will open the Bands page and view the code for the catalyst_footer library item.

Examining the Code for a Library Item

The code for the page elements is added to the page along with a hidden link to the library item.

```
<!-- #BeginLibraryItem "/Library/catalyst_footer.lbi"-->
<p align="center"> </p>
<p class="catalyst_footer"> &copy; copyright
 Catalyst, Inc. 2004</a></p>
<!-- #EndLibraryItem -->
```

The library item starts with a comment tag. **Comment tags** are unpaired tags that are used to add notes that do not appear in the page or affect the way the HTML is rendered, to the code. For example, you might use a comment tag to add a note that helps you remember the use or purpose of a section of code. Comment tags are used to denote library items because comment tags will not cause problems even when the page is edited in another program. The comment tag begins with an opening bracket followed by an exclamation point and two dashes, <!--, and ends with two dashes followed by a closing bracket, -->. Everything that appears between the dashes is considered a comment and will be ignored by the browser. Every library item begins with a comment tag that tells Dreamweaver that a library item has started, <!--#BeginLibraryItem, includes a path to that library item, "/Library/catalyst_footer.lbi", followed by two dashes and the closing bracket of the comment tag. All code for the page element in the library item follows the comment tag. Each library item ends with a second comment tag that tells Dreamweaver the library item is ending, <!--#EndLibraryItem-->.

To view the library item code:

1. Open the **bands.htm** page in the Document window, select the footer, and then click the **Show Code and Design Views** button [Split] on the Document toolbar. The code for the catalyst_footer library item is selected in the Code pane. See Figure 8-8.

Figure 8-8 catalyst_footer library item in Split view

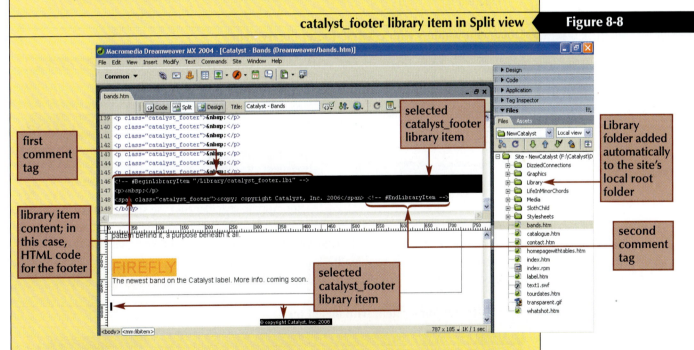

Trouble? If you do not see paragraph tags at the beginning and end of the footer library item code, you probably did not select both the line above the footer and the footer when you created the library item. Insert an additional line above the footer whenever you insert the catalyst_footer library item in a page to separate the footer from the page content.

2. Identify the first comment tag, the library item path, the page element code, and the second comment tag.

3. Click the **Show Design View** button [Design] on the Document toolbar.

If you discover you need to make a change to a library item, you can edit it.

Editing a Library Item

One of the most useful aspects of a library item is that you can update every instance of the item by editing the library item itself. This is much faster, not to mention possibly more accurate, than having to edit the same element in many pages. To edit a library item, you simply open the library item and make the changes. You open a library item either by double-clicking the library item in the library or by selecting an instance of the library item in a page and clicking the Open button in the Property inspector. Once you have completed the changes, you save the library item in the same way that you would a regular HTML page. Dreamweaver presents a list of all the pages in which that library item has been used and asks if you would like to update the files. When you choose to update the files, Dreamweaver makes the changes to the library item in each page that was listed. After the pages are updated, a log may open, showing the history of the changes made to the pages.

Brian has decided that it would be beneficial to make the footer an e-mail link so users can quickly contact the company.

To edit a library item:

1. Select the **catalyst_footer** library item in the page, and then click the **Open** button in the Property inspector. The catalyst_footer libarary item opens in the Document window. See Figure 8-9.

Figure 8-9   Document window with catalyst_footer library item

Remember, the text does not have the appropriate style because the style sheet is not attached to the actual library item. When you view the library item from within the pages in the site it will again display the appropriate style. Next, you'll add the e-mail link to the text.

2. Select the footer text, type **mailto:info@catalystnoise.com** in the Link text box in the Property inspector, press the **Enter** key, and then deselect the text. See Figure 8-10.

Figure 8-10   catalyst_footer library item with linked text

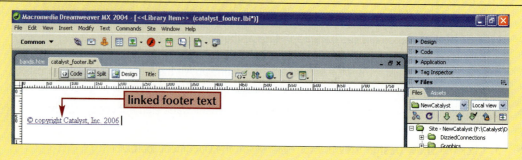

You'll also change the format of the footer text to ensure that the CSS style will be inserted in the paragraph tag, which is a block-level tag. Only block-level tags can be centered.

3. Select the footer text, click the Format list arrow in the Property inspector, and then click Paragraph.
4. Save the catalyst_footer library item. The Update Library Items dialog box opens, listing all the pages that contain that library item. See Figure 8-11.

Update Library Items dialog box — **Figure 8-11**

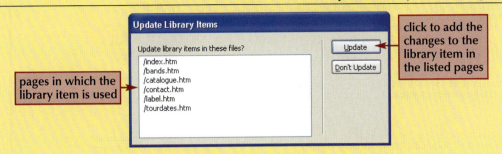

5. Click the **Update** button to update the library item in the listed pages. Dreamweaver updates all the pages that contain the library item and the Update Pages dialog box opens, showing a log of the updates. See Figure 8-12.

Update Pages dialog box — **Figure 8-12**

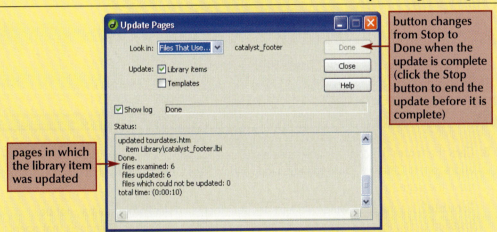

6. Click the **Close** button to close the dialog box, and then close the catalyst_footer library item.
7. Scroll to the bottom of the Bands page. Notice that the footer is a link and is displayed with the appropriate CSS styles.
8. Save the page, and then preview the page in a browser. See Figure 8-13.

Figure 8-13   **Bands page with e-mail link footer previewed in a browser**

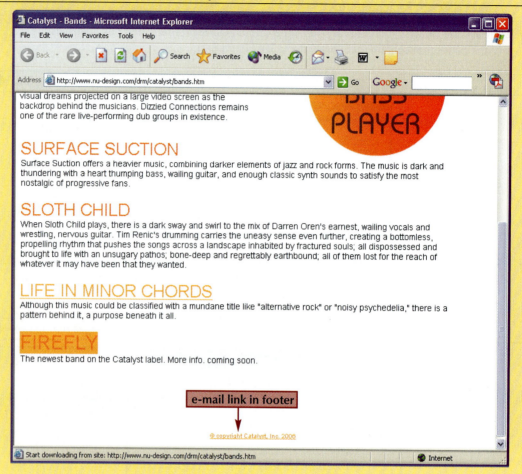

8. Click the **footer** link to test the e-mail link (a message window opens with the e-mail addressed to Catalyst), close the message window, close the browser window, and then close the page.

   Trouble? If a message window does not open, then an e-mail program may not be installed or configured on your computer. Close any dialog boxes and windows that open, and then continue with Step 9.

9. Open each page in the site, preview the page, test the footer, close the message window, and then close the browser window and the page.

If you don't need a specific library item, you can delete it.

Deleting a Library Item

You can delete a library item from Web pages or from the library. If a library item is no longer appropriate to include in a specific page, you can quickly delete it from the page by selecting the library item in the page and then pressing the Delete key. That instance of the library item is deleted from the page, but the library item remains available in the library. If a library item is no longer appropriate to include anywhere in a site, you can delete it from the library by selecting the library item in the library and dragging it to the Delete button 🗑 in the Assets panel. If you delete a library item from the site while it is being used in the pages of the site, the content of the library item will remain in each page in which it was placed, but the items will no longer be library items. It is a good idea to delete unused library items from the library so that your site remains uncluttered and well organized.

In this session, you added the keywords and description meta tags to the head content of pages and you added a library item to the Catalyst site. In the next session, you will create templates for the Web site.

Session 8.1 Quick Check

1. What are meta tags?
2. List two frequently used meta tags.
3. Why are keywords important?
4. Where are library items stored?
5. What type of tag begins and ends the code for a library item?
6. What is one of the most useful aspects of a library item?

Review

Session 8.2

Understanding Templates

Professional designers sometimes plan and design Web sites based on templates. A **template** is a special page that enables the designer to separate the look and layout of the page from the content by "locking" the page layout. The designer designates what is locked in a page by creating editable regions and noneditable regions. **Editable regions** are areas that can be changed in the pages created from a template. **Noneditable regions** are areas that can be changed in the template, but cannot be changed in the pages created from a template. You use a template to create multiple Web pages that share the same layout, use the same attached style sheet, and contain the same content, which is placed in the noneditable regions of the template. For example, you can create a template from which to create new pages added to the Catalyst site. The template should include all the elements that are used in every page—such as the Catalyst logo, the navigation bar, and the footer—in noneditable regions. The style sheet should also be attached to the template, so that the pages created from the template will have the appropriate style sheet attached. The template should include editable regions for elements that vary from page to page, such as the page heading and content sections of the pages.

Creating a template for a Web site requires more planning and forethought than creating individual pages. You need to thoroughly plan the layout of the pages before creating the site to ensure that you have set up the appropriate editable regions—the only regions that can contain unique page content. For example, you need to include an editable region for the page heading in the template for the Catalyst site because a unique page heading appears in the same location in every page. You also need to include an editable region for page content because each page displays unique content below the page heading. Although it is important to include editable regions for each general area of the page, it is also important not to create too many specific editable regions, which would limit the flexibility of the pages. For example, you do not want to set up separate editable regions for subheadings because subheadings are not used in every page. Adding a separate editable region for a subheading would add a separate subheading region to every page created from the template. Instead, you will include subheadings in pages that require them in the editable region that you set up for content. It is tempting to shortcut the planning phase when designing sites with simple pages that are not template-based. When you begin to design large, professional, template-based sites, the pages are more interconnected and the design requires a great deal of forethought.

Templates are an amazing tool because, like style sheets, they reduce much of the redundant work that goes into creating and maintaining a Web site. You do the work once to set up the page layout, including CSS styles, a navigation bar, and a footer, in a template. You or others can use that template to quickly create any number of pages with that same layout. Anyone can then add content to the pages without affecting the layout or design. If you later decide to modify the layout, you need to make the changes only in one place—the template. Any pages created from a template are connected to that template. If you modify a template, all the pages connected to that template are updated to reflect the changes. This saves you time and ensures consistency across the pages.

The drawback to using templates is that they can limit your flexibility to vary the content of pages created from the template. For example, to a large extent head content is locked in pages created from templates, so you cannot add many common elements that add code to the head of a page to the template-based pages. Also, you cannot add content outside the established editable regions.

There is usually only one main template used in a site, but you can use more than one main template if you have distinctly different styles of pages in one site. For example, if Brian decided that each band under the Catalyst label was going to have its own Web page in the Catalyst site and that these band pages were going to have a completely different look and feel than the other pages of the site, you could create a separate template for those pages. Using more than two main templates in one site is generally not a good idea because the site can get cumbersome and confusing. In addition, it is easy to forget to make changes that affect the whole site to every template.

You will create a template for the Catalyst site.

Creating a Template

Templates can be created from a new blank page or an existing page in a site. To create a template from a new blank page, either click the New command on the File menu, click Template Page in the Category list, click HTML Template in the Template Page list, and then click the Create button, *or* click the Templates button in the Assets panel, and then click the New Template button. To create a template from an existing page, open the page on which you want to base the template, click the Make Template button in the Templates list in the Common category on the Insert bar, and then name and save the template. As with other filenames, use only alphanumeric characters, do not use spaces or special characters, and do not start the name with a number. If you create more than one main template in a site, choose a name that will help you to identify the template. The template file is saved with a .dwt extension in a Templates folder in the site's local root folder. If the Templates folder does not already exist, Dreamweaver creates one. You can view all the templates for a site in the Assets panel when the Templates button is selected.

When you create a template from a blank page, you must add all the elements that you want to include in pages made from the template to the template page. In the Catalyst site, for example, you must attach the CSS style sheet to the template and create any new CSS styles you plan to use in the subsequent pages, you must add the Catalyst logo at the top of the template page to have the logo appear in the new pages, and you must add the keywords and meta description that will be used in the pages. When you create a template from an existing page, all of these shared elements are already in the page. The page from which you created the template is unaffected and is not attached to the template.

Although you can save a template from one site to another site and use that template to create pages in the other site, it is not a good idea to do so. Copying a template from one site to another causes all of the relative links in the template (including links to graphics and other materials used in the template) to become absolute links. To use the template in the new site, you must change the links to relative links and copy the materials used in the template to the new site's local root directory. Furthermore, choosing a template from another site when you create a new Web page causes these same problems, and it does not move a copy of the template to the new site. Also, if you choose a template from another site and you leave the Update Page When Template Changes check box checked (which is its default state), then the links will be in a locked area of the template and you cannot change them. Thus, you will not be able to view the template content when you post the new page to the Web. Because of these problems, it is a good idea to create a new template for each site.

Reference Window

Creating a Template

- Open an existing page, and then click the Make Template button in the Templates list in the Common category on the Insert bar (*or* to create a template from a blank page: open the Assets panel, click the Templates button, and then click the New Template button *or* click File on the menu bar, click New, click Template Page in the Category list, click HTML Template in the Template Page list, and then click the Create button).
- Type a name for the template, and then save the template.
- If you created a new template from the Assets panel, select the template in the Assets panel, and then click the Edit Template button.
- Add editable regions to the template using the buttons in the Templates category on the Insert bar.
- Save the template.

You'll create a template for the Catalyst site based on the existing Label page. You'll use the Label page because it has the most basic layout of all the existing pages—it doesn't contain any special media elements—and will be the easiest page to modify. Brian is developing a series of new pages with information about indie music and the current underground music scene in the United States. The template will be used to create these new pages in the site. Eventually, the existing pages in the Catalyst site will be converted to the template so that the look of the entire site can be managed and updated more easily.

To create a template from an existing page:

1. If you took a break after the previous session, make sure the **NewCatalyst** site is open.
2. Open the **label.htm** page in the Document window, and then click the **Make Template** button in the **Templates** list in the **Common** category on the Insert bar. The Save As Template dialog box opens.
3. If necessary, click the **Site** list arrow, and then click **NewCatalyst**. This selects the site in which you will save the template.
4. Type **catalyst_main** in the Save As text box, and then click the **Save** button. Click **Yes** if a dialog box opens, asking you to update links. Dreamweaver creates a copy of the page with the name catalyst_main.dwt, creates a Templates folder in the site's local root folder, and then saves the template in that folder. See Figure 8-14.

Figure 8-14 New template page

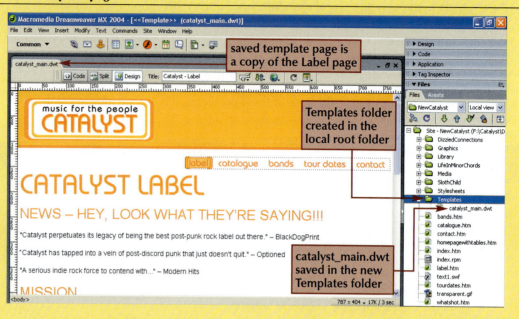

You'll delete the page-specific content from the template as you add editable regions to the page.

Adding Regions to a Template

When you create a template, the entire document is locked. In other words, the page is one big noneditable region and only the template itself can be edited. You must add at least one editable region to the template to be able to change page content and other elements in the pages created from the template. Anything outside an editable region can be altered only within the template.

You can add several types of regions to a template:

- **Editable Region.** An area in a template-based page that can be edited. Any area can be defined as an editable region. You can designate either an entire table or a single table cell as editable; however, you cannot designate multiple cells as one editable region. Also, layers and layer content are separate elements. Designating a layer as editable enables you to move the layer. Designating the area inside the layer as editable enables you to change the layer content.
- **Optional Region.** A noneditable region for which you set conditions for displaying the content in that region in template-based pages. You set parameters for displaying the optional region content when you create the template. The regions are displayed in the pages created from the template only if those conditions or parameters are met.
- **Repeating Region.** A region that can be duplicated within the pages made from the template, enabling the region to expand without altering the page design. For example, you can designate a table row as a repeating region, and then you can repeat the table row in the template-based pages to create expanding lists and so forth. The repeating region is used so frequently with tables that Dreamweaver has a special Repeating Table button in addition to the Repeating Region button in the Templates category on the Insert bar.

- **Editable Optional Region.** An optional region that is editable.
- **Editable Tag Attribute.** A tag attribute that you unlock in a template so that the attribute can be edited in the pages created from the template. For example, you can "lock" which graphic appears in the template-based pages and then create an editable tag attribute that enables the person editing these pages to set the graphic's alignment.

You'll create editable regions in the catalyst_main template.

With the exception of the title and a few other page-specific elements, the head content is locked in the pages created from a template. This means that you cannot add navigation bars and many other common elements that place code into the head of the page to template-based pages. Many elements that add code to the head of a page must be added either directly in the template or, sometimes, in a library item that is placed in an editable region.

Regions added to templates are invisible elements. When you show Invisible Elements, a border appears around the regions in both the template and the template-based pages and a tab appears at the top of each region in the Document window. Although the border and tab help you to quickly identify each region, they also interfere slightly with the way the layout appears in the Document window. To see a page as it will appear in browsers, you must hide the Invisible Elements or preview the page in a browser.

You will show the Invisible Elements, if necessary, and then add editable regions to the template in the Catalyst site. You'll begin by creating an editable region named "PageHeading" at the top of the template. You want to make the page heading an editable region so that you can change the heading for each new page created from the template.

To add an editable region to a template:

1. If necessary, click **View** on the menu bar, point to **Visual Aids**, and then click **Invisible Elements** to check it. You will be able to see any Invisible Elements you add in the page.
2. Select the **Catalyst Label** Flash text. The page heading is selected.
3. Click the **Editable Region** button in the **Templates** list in the **Common** category on the Insert bar. The New Editable Region dialog box opens.
4. Type **PageHeading** in the Name text box, and then click the **OK** button. The new editable region is added to the template, a blue border surrounds the page heading text, and a tab appears over the text. See Figure 8-15.

Editable region added to the template page   Figure 8-15

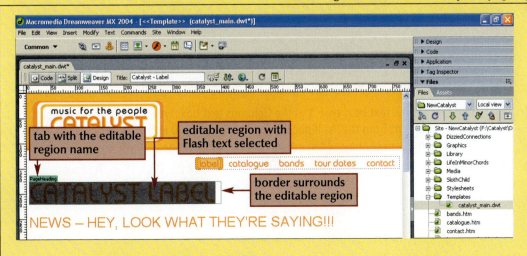

Trouble? If the tab is not visible in the Document window, then Invisible Elements are hidden in the Document window. Click View on the menu bar, point to Visual Aids, and then click Invisible Elements.

You'll change the page heading from the page-specific content to generic placeholder text. You need to create a new Flash text file with the placeholder text, otherwise the Flash text in the Label page will change as well because the same Flash text file will be used in both pages.

▶ 5. Double-click the **Flash text** to open the Insert Flash Text dialog box.

▶ 6. Type **NEW PAGE HEADING** in the Text text box to replace the CATALYST LABEL text. This is the generic placeholder text.

▶ 7. Type **../Media/HeadingTemplate.swf** in the Save As text box, and then click the **OK** button. The placeholder text is saved in the Media folder and appears in the template.

Next, you'll create a repeating region with a table. You will use the Repeating Table button and the table will be added to the repeating region for you. The Repeating Table button also adds an editable area in the table so that you can add content to the table in pages that are created from the template. Remember that repeating regions can be editable or noneditable. If you plan to add content in the repeating region within the pages created from the template, you must add an editable region within the repeating region.

You'll delete the body text from the template and add a repeating table with an editable region named "Content." You'll use this repeating table to enter the general content for each page that is created from the template.

To create a repeating table:

▶ 1. Delete all the text below the page heading and above the footer in the template.

▶ 2. Click the **Repeating Table** button in the **Templates** list in the **Common** category on the Insert bar. The Insert Repeating Table dialog box opens. See Figure 8-16.

Figure 8-16   Insert Repeating Table dialog box

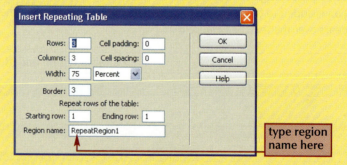

▶ 3. Type **1** in the Rows text box, type **1** in the Columns text box, type **100** in the Width text box, select **Percent** from the list if necessary, and then type **0** in the Border text box. This will create a borderless one-cell table the full width of the page.

▶ 4. Type **Content** in the Region Name text box, and then click the **OK** button. A repeating table named "Content" with an unnamed editable region is placed in the page below the page heading.

5. Click in a blank area of the page to deselect the table. See Figure 8-17.

Repeating table with an editable region

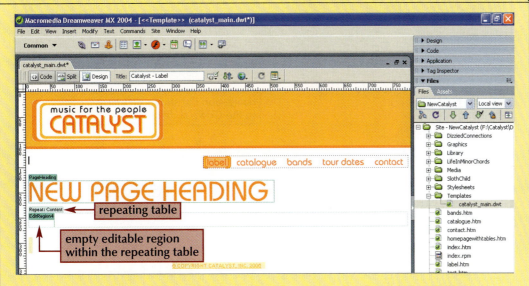

Figure 8-17

6. Click in the editable region in the repeating table, and then type **Add content here.** (including the period). This placeholder text will act as a reminder to enter appropriate content in the template-based pages.

Finally, you will modify the navigation bar so that no images appear in the Down state when the page is loaded. This is necessary because you will not be able to modify the navigation bar in the pages created from the template. If the navigation bar was not altered, all the pages created from the template would display the label button in the Down state initially.

To modify the navigation bar:

1. Click **Modify** on the menu bar, and then click **Navigation Bar**. The Modify Navigation Bar dialog box opens.
2. If necessary, click **Label *** in the Nav Bar Elements list.
3. Click the **Show "Down Image" Initially** check box to uncheck it, and then click the **OK** button.
4. Save the template, and then preview the template in a browser. See Figure 8-18.

   Trouble? If you are previewing the template in Netscape Navigator and a dialog box opens indicating that Netscape does not know how to handle this type of file, click the Cancel button in the dialog box, and then continue with Step 5.

Figure 8-18 Template page previewed in a browser

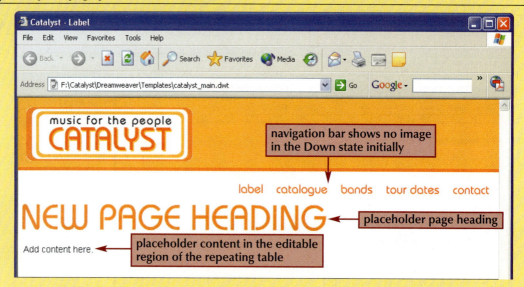

> **Trouble?** If a dialog box opens, stating that you have placed the PageHeading inside a paragraph tag or block tag and that users of the template will not be able to create paragraphs in this region, click the OK button. If additional dialog boxes open, click the OK button to close each additional dialog box. The PageHeading region is inside <h1> tags (which are block tags); any text entered in the field will have the h1 style, which is good, in this case, because the heading text had the h1 style applied to it. Because the heading is now Flash text, the tags do not affect it. This dialog box may open whenever you save the page; if it does, click the OK button each time.

5. Close the browser window, and then close the page.

After you create a template, you should test it by creating a page from the template.

Creating Web Pages from a Template

There are two ways to create a Web page from a template. You can create a new page based on the template and then add the appropriate content to the editable regions, or you can apply the template to an existing page that already contains content.

Creating a New Template-Based Page

Creating a new page from a template is similar to creating a new blank page using the New command on the File menu. However, you click the Templates tab in the New Document dialog box, select the current site, and then select the template you want to use to create the page. Once the page is created, you add content to the editable regions and then save the page as usual.

Tutorial 8 Creating Reusable Assets and Forms | Dreamweaver | DRM 445

Reference Window

Creating a Template-Based Page

- Click File on the menu bar, and then click New.
- Click the Templates tab in the New Document dialog box.
- Select the current site, and then select the template from which you want to create the page.
- Click the Create button.
- Enter the appropriate content into the editable regions of the page, and then save the page.

Brian wants to see a sample page from the new template before more pages are added to the Catalyst site. You will create a new page from the catalyst_main template, and then add a new page heading and some content to the test page.

To create a new Web page from a template:

1. Click **File** on the menu bar, and then click **New**. The New Document dialog box opens.

   Trouble? If the New From Template dialog box opens, the Templates tab is already selected. Continue with Step 3.

2. Click the **Templates** tab. The Templates tab is selected and the dialog box changes to New From Template. See Figure 8-19.

Figure 8-19   New From Template dialog box

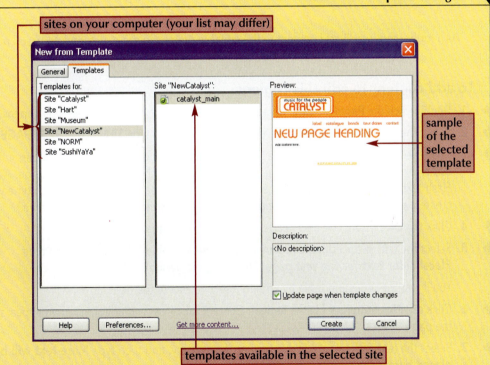

3. Click **Site "NewCatalyst"** in the Templates For list, if necessary, and then click **catalyst_main** in the Site "NewCatalyst" list (the list of templates in the selected site).
4. Verify that the **Update Page When Template Changes** check box is checked.
5. Click the **Create** button. The new page opens in a Document window. See Figure 8-20.

Figure 8-20   New page created from the catalyst_main template

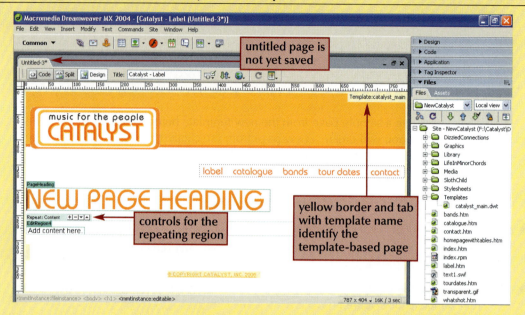

6. Save the page as **template_test.htm** in the site's local root folder.

As a further test, you'll add content to the editable regions in the new template-based page.

To add content to editable regions:

1. Double-click the **PageHeading** editable region. The Insert Flash Text dialog box opens.
2. Select the text in the Text text box, if necessary, and then type **TEMPLATE TEST PAGE**.
3. Click the **Browse** button beside the Save As text box, navigate to the **Media** folder, if necessary, type **HeadingTest** in the File Name text box, and then click the **Save** button. A new Flash text file is created for the page heading of the test page. (Remember, each time you create a page from the template, you must save the Flash text with a new filename.)
4. Click the **OK** button. The new heading appears in the PageHeading region.
5. Select the text in the editable region in the repeating table Content, and then type **Placeholder text for the test page.** (including the period).

You'll test the repeating table by adding a second row to the table.

6. Click the **Plus** button in the Repeat: Content tab. A second editable region appears in the page.
7. Select the text in the new editable region, if necessary, and then type **More text will be placed here.** (including the period).
8. Select **Label** in the Title text box on the Document toolbar, type **Test**, and then press the **Enter** key to change the page title. See Figure 8-21.

Test page with new content ◀ **Figure 8-21**

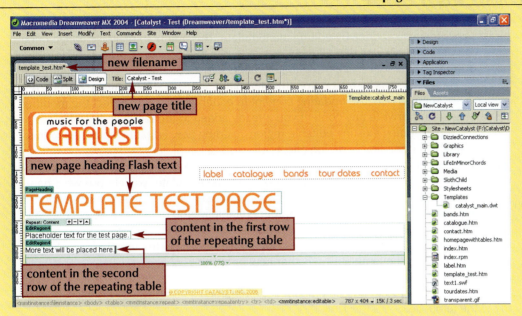

9. Save the page, and then preview the page in a browser. See Figure 8-22.

Test page previewed in a browser ◀ **Figure 8-22**

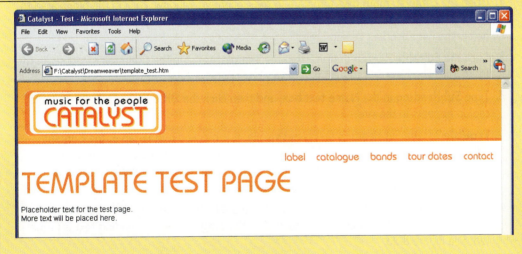

10. Close the browser window, and then close the page.

If you already have a page with content, you can apply a template to it.

Applying a Template to an Existing Web Page

You can apply a template to an existing Web page by opening the page in the Document window, selecting the template in the Assets panel, and then clicking the Apply button. When you apply a template to an existing page, the page uses the layout of the template page and a dialog box opens so you can designate into which regions the existing content will be placed. This can get a bit confusing at times, especially with complex pages that contain a lot of content. It is usually easier to create a new template-based page and move the content from the existing page into the new page.

Editing a Template

One of the most powerful aspects of using templates is that you can adjust all the template-based pages in a site at once by editing the template. This ability to make a change once saves you time and ensures that all the pages maintain a consistent design, similar to the benefits of using CSS styles. Adjusting the elements in the editable regions of a template will affect only new pages created from that template. Pages that have already been created are not affected because updating content in editable regions to reflect the modified template would overwrite any content you already added to the template-based pages. However, repositioning existing editable regions, adding new editable regions, or adjusting anything in a noneditable region affects all existing template-based pages as well as any new pages created from the template. You can also delete the various regions from the template. When you delete an editable region from the template, you choose what happens to the content in that region in the existing template-based pages. You can either move any content from that region to another editable region or you can delete the content in that region from the page. You can add, edit, or delete content from the noneditable regions. Any changes made to the noneditable regions in the template affect all pages created from the template—whether new or existing.

Brian has noticed that every page in the Catalyst site has a subheading below the page heading. He wants you to add an editable region named "SubHeading" for the subheading to the template.

To edit a template:

1. Open the **catalyst_main.dwt** template in the Document window, click in the blank area to the right of the PageHeading region, and then press the **Enter** key. A new line is created below the PageHeading region.

2. Click the **Editable Region** button in the **Templates** list in the **Common** category on the Insert bar. The New Editable Region dialog box opens.

3. Type **SubHeading** in the Name text box, and then click the **OK** button. The new editable region appears in the site.

   Trouble? If the SubHeading text is not visible, it is blocked by the tab of the Content repeating table and you need to hide the invisible elements. Click View on the menu bar, point to Visual Aids, and then click Invisible Elements to hide the tab and view the text, complete Step 4, and then show the Invisible Elements.

4. Click in the **SubHeading** placeholder text in the SubHeading region, click the **Format** list arrow in the Property inspector, and then click **Heading 2**. The SubHeading text is formatted. See Figure 8-23.

Edited template page — **Figure 8-23**

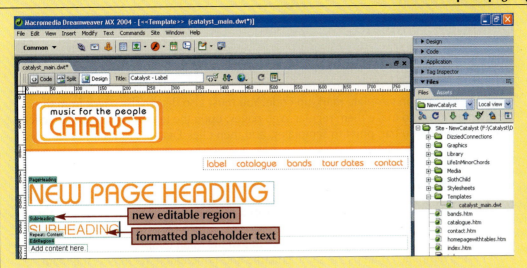

5. Save the template. The Update Template Files dialog box opens, asking if you want to update the pages created from the template to reflect the changes in the template. You want this change to appear in the existing template-based pages—in this case, the template_test.htm page.

   Trouble? If a dialog box opens, stating that the PageHeading region is in a paragraph or block tag, click the OK button. This dialog box may open whenever you save the page; if it does, click the OK button each time.

6. Click the **Update** button to update the page, and then click the **Close** button when the update is complete.

7. Close the catalyst_main template, and then open the **template_test.htm** page. The subheading has been added to this page, which you earlier created from the template.

8. Select the placeholder text in the SubHeading region, and then type **template test subheading**.

9. Save the page, and then preview the page in a browser. See Figure 8-24.

Edited template page previewed in a browser — **Figure 8-24**

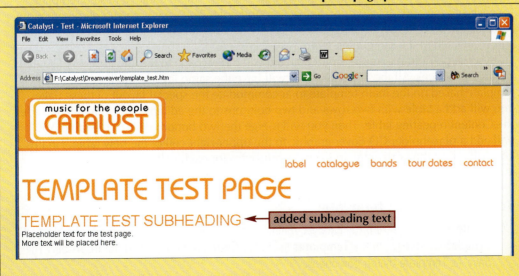

10. Close the browser window, and then close the page.

You can delete templates.

Deleting a Template

If a template is no longer relevant for a site, you can delete the entire template. You delete an entire template from a site by selecting the template in the Assets panel and clicking the Delete button 🗑. When you delete a template, the pages that were created from that template still contain template mark-up code. You must also detach the pages from the attached template to make them regular Web pages; open the template-based page, click Modify on the menu bar, point to Templates, and then click Detach From Template.

Creating Nested Templates

You can create nested templates for a site. **Nested templates** are templates created from the main template so that you can create a more defined structure for some pages of a site. Each nested template inherits all the features of the main template. In other words, each nested template contains the same editable and noneditable regions as the main template and is linked to the main template. You can add additional editable regions to the nested template, but only within the editable regions that exist in the main template. When you make a change to the main template, it affects all the nested templates as well as any pages created from the main template and the nested templates. When you make a change to a nested template, it affects only the pages created from that nested template.

Nested templates enable you to maintain even greater control over the look of the pages in a site because you further limit the choices people have when they input content into those pages. For example, because many of the pages in the Catalyst site have subheadings below the page heading followed by a paragraph of text and another subheading, you could create a nested template with an editable region for a subheading followed by an editable region for text within the editable region that is designated for content in the main template.

Nested templates are also useful when you have more than one major style of page in a Web site. For example, consider a site with both informational pages and product pages. If informational pages have one style and the product pages have the same basic page properties (CSS styles, navigation bar, and so forth) but a somewhat different style, you can create a main template for the site and a nested template for each type of page. Another example is a site with the same basic layout for all pages, but that uses a different background color for each major section of the site. You might create a nested template for each section and change only the background color. You save time and eliminate work because the basic layout for each type of page is already designed and all your pages are still connected to the same main template.

At some point in the future, Brian plans to add a new page to the site for every CD that Catalyst produces. All the new CD pages will have the same layout. You'll create a nested template based on the main template to accommodate the special layout of these pages. You will add a table with two rows and two columns to the editable region located inside the Content repeating table. Then you will merge the two bottom cells of the table. You will add a placeholder CD cover graphic to the upper-right cell of the new table. Finally, you will adjust the horizontal and vertical attributes for each cell.

To create a nested template:

1. Create a new page from the catalyst_main.dwt template, and then click the **Make Nested Template** button 📄 in the **Templates** list in the **Common** category on the Insert bar. The Save As Template dialog box opens.

Trouble? If a dialog box opens, stating that the PageHeading region is in a paragraph or block tag, click the OK button. This dialog box may open whenever you save the page; if it does, click the OK button each time.

2. Type **catalyst_cd** in the Save As text box, and then click the **Save** button to save the nested template.

3. Delete all the text in the EditRegion within the Repeat:Content region, click the **Table** button in the **Common** category on the Insert bar, and then create a table with 2 rows, 2 columns, 100% width, 0 border thickness, no cell padding, and no cell spacing. The new table appears in the nested template.

4. Merge the bottom cells, top-align both cells in the top row, and then left-align the upper-right cell.

5. Type **Add content here.** in the upper-left cell.

6. Click in the upper-right cell, and then insert the **DizziedConnectionCDcover300.jpg** graphic located in the **Graphics** folder in the site's local root folder.

7. Type **Add additional content here.** in the bottom cell. See Figure 8-25.

Figure 8-25   Nested template page

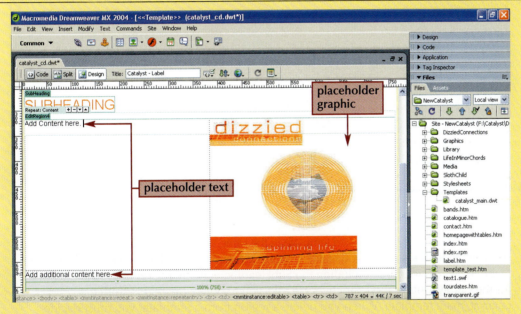

8. Save the nested template, and then click the **Yes** button in the dialog box that opens to update all the documents in your local site that use the template. The Update Pages dialog box opens.

Trouble? If a dialog box opens, stating that the PageHeading region is in a paragraph or block tag, click the OK button. This dialog box may open whenever you save the page; if it does, click the OK button each time.

9. Click the **Close** button once the pages are done updating. The nested template appears in the Templates folder in the Files panel.

Trouble? If you don't see catalyst_cd.dwt in the Templates folder, you may need to refresh the Files panel. Click the Refresh button on the Files panel toolbar to display the new template in the Templates folder.

10. Preview the catalyst_cd template in a browser. See Figure 8-26.

Trouble? If you are previewing the template in Netscape Navigator and a dialog box opens indicating that Netscape does not know how to handle this type of file, click the Cancel button in the dialog box, and then continue with Step 11.

Figure 8-26 | Nested template previewed in a browser

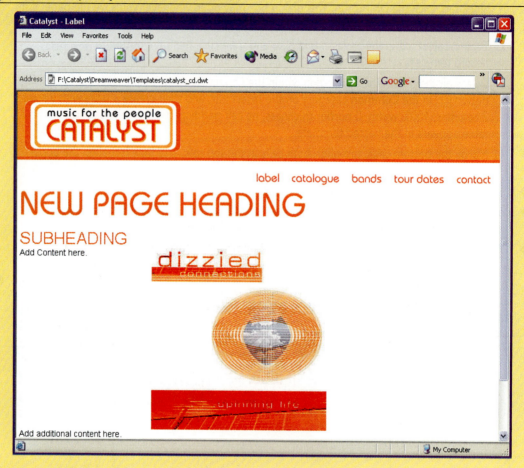

▶ 11. Close the browser window, and then close the nested template.

You create pages from a nested template in the same way that you create pages from the main template. The changes you make to the main template flow through to nested templates.

Brian has decided that including the SubHeading editable region in the main template for the Catalyst site is too restrictive. He asks you to delete the region from the catalyst_main template. When you delete a region from a template, you must decide where to move the text that was located in that region in the existing template-based pages. You can choose to move the content either to another editable region that is in the page or nowhere, which then deletes the content from the pages.

To delete a region in a template:

▶ 1. Open the **catalyst_main.dwt** template in the Document window, select the **SubHeading** editable region, and then press the **Delete** key. The region is removed from the template.

▶ 2. Save the template. The Update Template Files dialog box opens.

Trouble? If a dialog box opens, stating that the PageHeading region is in a paragraph or block tag, click the OK button. This dialog box may open whenever you save the page; if it does, click the OK button each time.

▶ 3. Click the **Update** button to update the nested template and the page you created from the template. The Inconsistent Region Names dialog box opens. See Figure 8-27.

Figure 8-27 Inconsistent Region Names dialog box

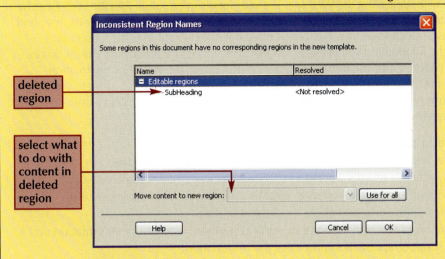

deleted region

select what to do with content in deleted region

▶ 4. Click **SubHeading** (the region that was deleted from the template) in the Name list, click the **Move Content to New Region** list arrow, click **Nowhere**, and then click the **OK** button. The text that was in the SubHeading region is cleared from the nested template and the template-based page.
▶ 5. Click the **Close** button in the Update Pages dialog box, and then close the template.
▶ 6. Open the **catalyst_cd.dwt** nested template in the Document window, verify that the SubHeading region was deleted from the nested template, and then close the nested template.
▶ 7. Open the **template_test.htm** page in the Document window, verify that the text from the SubHeading region was deleted, and then close the page.

In this session, you created a template, added editable regions to the page, and then created a new page based on the template. You also created a nested template and edited the main template. In the next session, you'll add a form to the Contact page.

Session 8.2 Quick Check

Review

1. Does creating a template-based site require more or less planning than creating a regular Web site? Explain your answer.
2. What are noneditable regions?
3. How does editing a template affect pages that were created from that template?
4. What is a nested template?
5. True or False? Nested templates inherit all the characteristics of the main template.
6. What happens when you delete an editable region from the main template?

Session 8.3

Understanding Forms

Forms have become an important element in Web design because they provide a way to interact with users. A **form** is a means of collecting information from users. You can use forms to gather information about the user, create a user log in, gather user feedback, and so forth.

Forms encourage user interaction because they enable the user to enter and send information over the Web without leaving the Web site. The user inputs information into the Web page by typing requested data into designated fields or clicking check boxes, option buttons, lists, and so forth to make selections. Once the form is filled out, the user submits the information, which sends the information somewhere, usually to the server, for processing. Forms do not process information. Once the form information is processed, the server (or information-processing destination) sends requested information back to the user, such as search information, or performs tasks based on the collected information, such as logging in a user.

Several steps must occur for a form to work:

- The designer creates a form in a Web page.
- The designer installs a script or application in the designated information-processing destination, which is usually a server, to process the form information. (Most forms cannot work without server-side scripts or applications that process the information.)
- The user fills out the form and clicks the Submit button.
- The information-processing destination, such as a server, receives the information and a server-side script or application processes the information.
- The server or information-processing destination sends requested information back to the user or performs an action based on the form's information.

You will create a form in the Contact page to enable users to communicate with Catalyst and enable Catalyst to gather information about the users of the Catalyst site.

Creating a Form

You can create a form in any Web page. Before you create a form, you should plan what information you want to collect, how the form should be designed to best collect that information, and in which page to create the form. For example, Sara wants to collect information from users to determine which bands they are listening to and what types of music they like, as well as their mailing address and e-mail information. The form will be in the Contact page.

Reference Window	**Creating a Form**

- Add the script that will process the form data to the server or information-processing destination.
- Open the page in which you want a form, position the insertion point at the location you want to insert the form, and then click the Form button in the Forms category on the Insert bar.
- Set the form attributes, including Form Name, Action, Method, Enctype, and Target.
- Add form objects and explanations for each form object to the form, and then set the attributes for each form object, including a name.
- Add a Submit button to the form.
- Add the Verification behavior to the form.
- Test the form in a browser.

The general process for creating a form is to add a form to a Web page, set form attributes, add form objects, and then validate form data.

Adding a Form to a Web Page

The first step in creating a form is to add the form to a page. Basically, adding a form to a Web page places a container in the page for the form content that you will add. You should try to add the form at the page location where you want the form to appear, but you can reposition the form later if you change your mind. When you add a form to a Web page, Dreamweaver inserts <form> </form> tags in the code for the page and a red dotted line appears in the Document window in Design view. The red line designates the form area in Dreamweaver and is invisible in the browser window.

You'll add a form at the bottom of the Contact page.

To add a form to a Web page:

1. If you took a break after the previous session, make sure the **NewCatalyst site** is open.

2. Open the **contact.htm** page in the Document window, click in the blank line below the Directions content, and then press the **Control+Enter** keys. You'll insert the form on this new line.

3. Click the **Form** button in the **Forms** category on the Insert bar. A red dotted line appears in the Contact page below the content. See Figure 8-28.

Figure 8-28

Form added to the Contact page

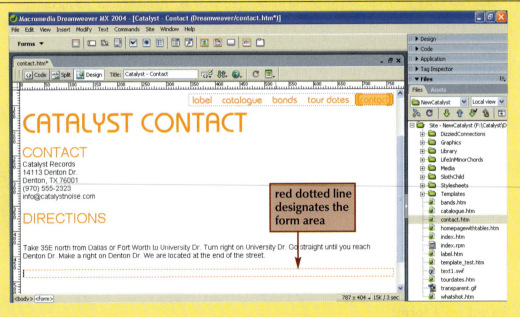

4. Save the page.

Next, you'll set the form attributes.

Setting Form Attributes

Once you have added a form to a page, you can adjust the form attributes in the Property inspector when the form is selected. To select the form, click the red dotted line that designates the form area. You must set all of the form attributes except the Target attribute, which is optional. Form attributes include:

- **Form Name.** A unique name for the form. The form name enables the form to be referenced or controlled with a scripting language. If you do not name the form, Dreamweaver will generate a unique name for it. The form name can include alphanumeric characters, but cannot begin with a number or include spaces or special characters.

- **Action.** The path to the location of the script you will use to process the form data. You must install the script or create the page in the desired location prior to setting the Action. You can also type "mailto:" followed by an e-mail address in the Action text box to send the form information to a specified e-mail address (the mailto: link will work only if the user is on a computer configured to send e-mail), or you can type the name of a JavaScript function in the Action text box if you are using a JavaScript to process the form.
- **Method.** The way form data will be sent to the location specified in the Action text box. POST embeds form data in an HTTP request. When you use the POST method, the form data is not visible. POST is the preferred method for most forms. GET appends the form data to the end of the path specified in the Action text box. When you use the GET method, form data is limited to 8,192 characters of information and is visible because it is added to the end of the URL. GET is frequently used for search engine requests. Default uses the browser default of the user's browser to send form data. The script or application you use to process form data may affect the method that you will need to use to send the form data.
- **Target.** The target destination for any response from the form. For example, if the script attached to the form sends a response to the user, such as "Thank you for filling out the form. We have received your information.", that response will appear in the target destination. Target options are the usual _blank, _parent, _self, and _top.
- **Enctype (Encoding Type).** The Multipurpose Internet Mail Extensions encoding type (MIME type) for the form data. The MIME type is a file identification based on the MIME encoding system, which is the standard for identifying content on the Internet. Most forms use the application/x-www-form-urlencoded MIME type. The multipart/form-data MIME type is used for uploading files, such as when you use a file-upload field in a form.

You'll set each of these attributes for the form in the Contact page. You'll use "ContactForm" as the form name. The action will eventually point to a script placed on the server to process the form data. The programming team is writing the script, but is waiting for information from the ISP. In the meantime, they have created a Web page with a script that will enable you to test the form by displaying the data that the form will send to the server when the Submit button is clicked. For now, you will place a copy of the test script Web page in the local root folder of the Catalyst site and set the action to form_test.htm. GET is the method for data delivery. The enctype is application/x-www-form-urlencoded. The target is _blank.

To set up a form:

1. Copy the **form_test.htm** file located in the **Tutorial.08\Tutorial** folder included with your Data Files, and then paste it in the site's local root folder.
2. Click the red dotted line to select the form. You'll set the form attributes in the Property inspector.
3. Type **ContactForm** in the Form Name text box.
4. Type **form_test.htm** in the Action text box.
5. Click the **Method** list arrow, and then click **GET**.
6. Click the **Enctype** list arrow, and then click **application/x-www-form-urlencoded**.
7. Click the **Target** list arrow, and then click **_blank**. See Figure 8-29.

Figure 8-29 Form attributes added to the form

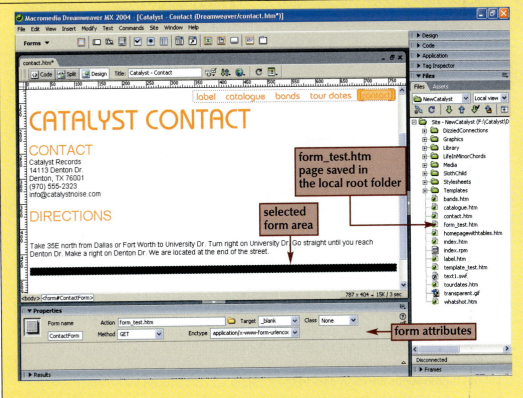

8. Save the page.

Next, you will add form objects to the form.

Adding Form Objects

You must add form objects to a form to make it useful. **Form objects** are generally the mechanisms that enable users to interact with a form. Each form object has a specific function:

- **Text Fields and Text Areas.** A text box into which a user can type input in a form. Text fields are usually used for short-answer input. Text areas are usually used for long-answer input. Text fields are displayed as a single-line box, whereas text areas are displayed as a multiple-line box. Both can accept either single or multiple lines of input. The input can be displayed as typed or as a series of dots or asterisks to protect private information. For example, a password is usually displayed as a series of asterisks when typed into a browser window.
- **Hidden Fields.** Fields used to include information in a form that will be sent along with the form data to the server or designated processing location and which the user cannot see. For example, if a site has more than one form, you can use a hidden field to send the name of the form with the collected form data.
- **Checkbox.** A predefined toggle selection object in a form. Each checkbox can be toggled "on (checked)" or "off (unchecked)." A checkbox is toggled on or off independently, enabling the user to check as many items in a series of checkboxes as is appropriate. For example, you might use a series of checkboxes to have a user select all the types of music he or she listens to.

- **Radio Button and Radio Group.** A group of selection objects that work together in a form. The user can select only one radio button from a radio button group. Unlike a checkbox, which can be toggled on and off independently, a selected radio button can be deselected only when the user selects another radio button within the radio button group. The Radio Button object adds a single radio button at a time, whereas the Radio Group object inserts an entire radio button group.
- **List/Menu.** A list of preset input choices in a form. List presents a list of possible input choices in a designated area, providing a scroll bar, if necessary, that enables users to navigate through the list. The user can select multiple items in a list. Menu presents the user with a list of choices in a drop-down menu. The user can select only one item from a menu.
- **Jump Menu.** A special menu that contains a list of active links to other pages, graphics, or any type of file that can be opened in a browser. When a user selects an item from the jump menu, the new page or document opens. Unlike other form objects, the jump menu can be used within or outside a form because it includes form tags and a Submit button.
- **Image Field.** A graphic used as a Submit or Reset button in a form. You can also use graphics as buttons that perform other tasks by adding behaviors.
- **File Field.** A file upload field in the form that enables the user to upload a file from the client computer to the server. The file field contains a Browse button and a text box. The user can select the file using the Browse button or by typing the file path into the text box. You must use the POST method to send files from the browser to the server, and your Web server must be set up to handle this type of file upload.
- **Button.** A button in the form that performs the behavior you specify. The button can be designated as a Submit button or a Reset button, or it can have no designation at all. A Submit button sends the form data to the location you designated for processing. A Reset button clears any content from the form so that the user can start over. You can also add behaviors to the button, enabling it to perform other functions.

You'll use text fields, checkboxes, radio buttons, a list, a Submit button, and a Reset button in the Contact page form.

You set the attributes for a form object in the Property inspector when that object is selected in the form. Each type of object has its own unique set of attributes. However, every object has a name attribute. It is important to name every form object because the scripting language uses this name to identify the form object. If you do not name an object, Dreamweaver will name it for you, using the object type and a number as its name. It is better to name form objects yourself because the field name will be paired with the data from that field when it is sent to the processing destination. When you view the data collected from forms, you use the field name to identify the information beside it. If the name does not identify the field, you may have trouble understanding the information you collect. For example, you'll name the text field where users input their last name "LastName" so that when you view the data you see LastName beside the data captured in the last name field. Without this descriptive name, you might have trouble distinguishing the user's first name from the user's last name.

Creating the Form Structure

You want to add form objects to a form in logical groupings. For example, all similar or related information should be placed together so users can enter that data, such as all their personal information, at the same time. You should also include a label with brief instructions or a description of the information being requested for each object so users know what to do.

The requested information should be organized clearly within the form. You can use line breaks, paragraph breaks, tables, and so forth within forms to lay out the form objects. However, a table is usually the simplest way to keep forms fairly clean. For example, you could insert a two-column table in a form that includes a separate row for each form object. Then you can right-justify the form labels in the left column and left-justify the corresponding form objects in the right column. This will create a form that is well organized and easy to follow. It will also create a form that is fairly stable across browsers. Different versions of browsers sometimes display form objects in slightly different ways. Putting form objects in a table helps to keep them in the same place in a page regardless of how a user's browser displays the form. However, the form layout may still vary slightly in different browsers.

You'll use a two-column table without a border to organize the form in the Contact page.

To add a table to the form:

1. Click in the form area, and then click the **Table** button in the **Common** category on the Insert bar. The Insert Table dialog box opens.

2. Create a table with 9 rows, 2 columns, 100% width, 0 border thickness, 10 cell padding, and no cell spacing.

3. Align the left column to the **Right** and the **Top**.

4. Align the right column to the **Left** and the **Top**.

5. Merge the cells in the top row.

    You'll add the form heading to this merged row.

6. Type **Catalyst – Contact Form** in the top row, **Center** the form heading text, apply the **Heading 2** style to the heading text, and then deselect the text. See Figure 8-30.

Contact form with inserted table Figure 8-30

With the table structure in place, you can begin adding form objects to the form. You will start by inserting text fields into the form.

Inserting Text Fields and Areas into a Form

Text fields and areas are used to gather information that a user types. Most commonly, they are used for collecting name, address, and e-mail address information. You can set a number of attributes to control how each text field or area appears and functions in the form. In addition to Name, attributes include:

- **Char Width (Character Width).** The maximum number of characters that can be displayed. When the character width value is smaller than the maximum characters value, the text field or area will not display all the input without scrolling.
- **Max Chars (Maximum Characters)/Num Lines (Number of Lines).** The maximum number of characters that the user can input into a single-line text field or the height of a multiple-line text area. You can use Max Chars to limit a user's response. For example, you can limit the number of characters in a text field used to input ZIP code information to five characters.
- **Type.** The designated appearance. Single line creates a text field that is one line in height. Multi Line creates a text area that is more than one line in height and has scroll bars. Password displays the data as dots or asterisks to protect the data.
- **Init Val (Initial Value).** Text that is displayed until the user types new input.

You'll add single-line text fields for collecting the user's first name, last name, and e-mail address. Then you'll add a multi-line text area for collecting user comments.

To add text fields to a form:

1. Click in the upper-left cell of the table below the form heading, type **First Name:** to enter the label for the first text field, and then press the **Tab** key to move the insertion point to the next cell.
2. Click the **Text Field** button [I] in the **Forms** category on the Insert bar. A text field is inserted in the cell. You'll set its attributes in the Property inspector.
3. Type **FirstName** in the TextField text box, type **50** in the Char Width text box, type **100** in the Max Chars text box, and then click the **Single Line** option button, if necessary. See Figure 8-31.

Figure 8-31

Text field added to the form

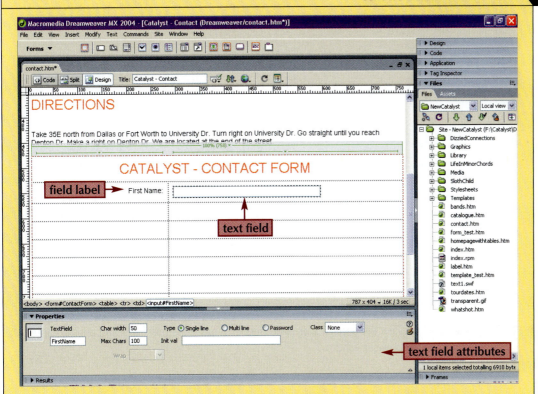

Next, you'll add the LastName label and text field to the third row of the table.

4. Click in the left column of the third row of the table, type **Last Name:** to enter the label, and then press the **Tab** key to move the insertion point to the next cell.

5. Click the **Text Field** button in the **Forms** category on the Insert bar to insert another text field, type **LastName** in the TextField text box, type **50** in the Char Width text box, type **100** in the Max Chars text box, and then click the **Single Line** option button, if necessary.

   You'll add the EmailAddress label and text field to the fourth row of the table.

6. Click in the left column of the fourth row, type **E-mail Address:** to enter the label, and then press the **Tab** key to move the insertion point to the next cell.

7. Click the **Text Field** button in the **Forms** category on the Insert bar to insert another text field, type **EmailAddress** in the TextField text box, type **50** in the Char Width text box, type **100** in the Max Chars text box, and then click the **Single Line** option button, if necessary.

   You'll add the Comments label and text area to the fifth row of the table.

8. Click in the left column of the fifth row, type **Comments:** to enter the label, and then press the **Tab** key to move the insertion point to the next cell.

9. Click the **Textarea** button in the **Forms** category on the Insert bar. A text area is added to the cell.

10. Type **Comments** in the TextField text box, type **44** in the Char Width text box, type **10** in the Num Lines text box, and then click the **Multi Line** option button, if necessary. See Figure 8-32.

Figure 8-32   **Form with text fields**

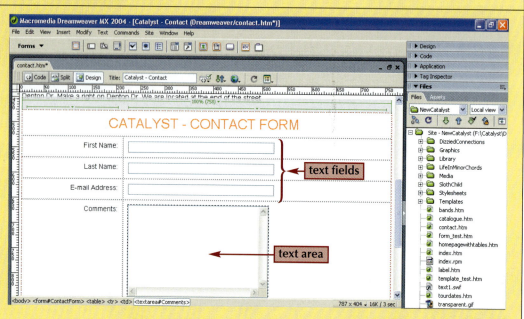

▶ **11.** Save the page, preview the page in a browser (the form has three text fields and one text area), and then close the browser window.

Next, you will add a series of checkboxes to the form.

Inserting Checkboxes into a Form

Checkboxes have only two attributes in addition to Name. Because some forms use many checkboxes, it is often convenient to use a code, instead of a name, in the script to process them. The other attributes are Checked Value and Initial State. Checked Value is where you can assign a value or a numeric code for a checkbox. The Checked Value is sent to the processing location along with the name when the checkbox is checked. Nothing is sent to the processing location if the checkbox is unchecked. Initial State sets whether the checkbox starts out checked or unchecked when a user first views a form.

Sara wants to find out what styles of music users like. You will insert a series of checkboxes into the form to enable users to select the types of music they enjoy. You will not include a checked value for these checkboxes.

To add checkboxes to a form:

▶ **1.** Click in the left column of the sixth row, type **Check all of the musical styles that interest you.** (including the period), and then press the **Tab** key to move the insertion point to the next cell.

▶ **2.** Click the **Checkbox** button ☑ in the **Forms** category on the Insert bar to insert a checkbox in the cell.

▶ **3.** In the Property inspector, type **Punk** in the CheckBox Name text box, and then click the **Unchecked** option button, if necessary.

▶ **4.** Click to the right of the checkbox, type **Punk**, and then press the **Shift+Enter** keys to create a new line in the cell.

5. Repeat Steps 2 through 4 to create the following checkboxes: **Alternative**, **Trance**, and **Jazz**. See Figure 8-33.

Form with checkboxes

Figure 8-33

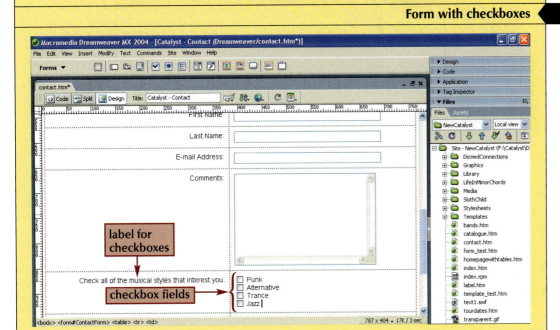

6. Save the page.

Next, you'll add radio buttons to the form.

Adding Radio Buttons to a Form

Radio buttons are a group of selection objects that work together in a form. Users can select only one radio button from a radio button group. You can insert a group of radio buttons into your form using the Radio Group button. When you click the Radio Group button, a dialog box opens so you can name the radio group, label each radio button with the text you want to appear beside it in the form, and enter a value for the Checked Value of each button. Unlike checkboxes, the label information for a selected radio button does not appear when the information is sent to the processing location. You must enter a unique value for each radio button to distinguish which radio button was selected. When you click the OK button, the radio group is added to the form. When you select a radio button in a form, the name of the radio group to which the button belongs appears in the Radio Button text box, its value appears in the Checked Value text box, and you can choose Checked or Unchecked as the initial state for the button.

Brian has decided to start a newsletter and he wants to give users the option to join the newsletter mailing list. You'll add a radio group with two radio buttons to the form to collect this information.

To add a group of radio buttons to a form:

1. Click in the left column of the seventh row, type **Would you like to receive a monthly newsletter with updates about the Catalyst bands?**, and then press the **Tab** key to move the insertion point to the next cell.

2. Click the **Radio Group** button in the **Forms** category on the Insert bar. The Radio Group dialog box opens. See Figure 8-34.

Figure 8-34 | Radio Group dialog box

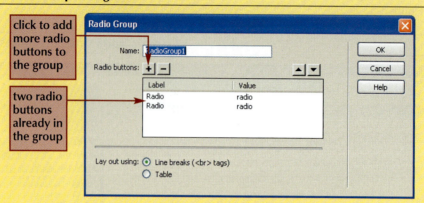

▶ 3. Type **Newsletter** in the Name text box, click **Radio** in the first row of the Label column, type **Yes**, click **Radio** in the first row of the Value column, and then type **Yes**.

▶ 4. Click **Radio** in the second row of the Label column, type **No**, click **Radio** in the second row of the Value column, and then type **No**.

▶ 5. In the Lay Out Using section, click the **Line Breaks** option button, if necessary.

▶ 6. Click the **OK** button. The Yes and No radio buttons are added to the form.

You want the Yes radio button to be selected initially, so you'll change its initial state.

▶ 7. Select the **Yes** radio button in the Document window, and then click the **Checked** option button in the Initial State section in the Property inspector. See Figure 8-35.

Figure 8-35 | Form with radio group

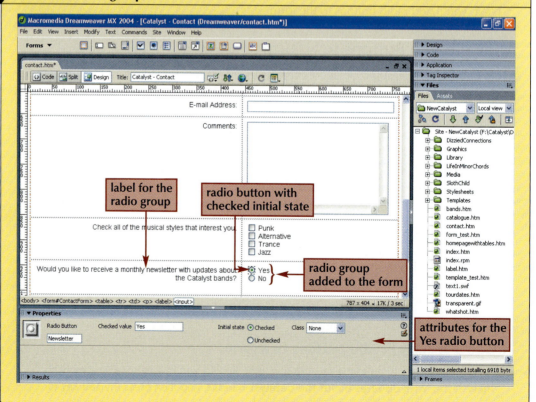

▶ 8. Save the page.

Next, you'll add a list to the form.

Adding Lists to a Form

Lists are another way to enable users to choose several items from a group. There are a few attribute choices associated with lists. Height enables you to set how many rows are visible in the list box. You can add as many items to the list as you want. If the list includes more items than are visible in the list box, scroll bars enable the users to view all of the selections. The Selections check box enables you to set whether users can select only one item in the list (unchecked) or more than one item in the list (checked). The List Values button opens the dialog box in which you type the items that will appear in a list or edit existing items in a list. You can also associate a value with each item, which can be used by a script to identify the list item. The Initially Selected list enables you to select one or more items from the list to appear selected in the list. This option is often used to create a default selection, such as selecting Dallas from a list of cities because Catalyst is based near Dallas and it is assumed that more users will be from that area. If you prefer the list to appear as a menu, click the Menu option button in the Type section.

Sara wants to know which bands users listen to. You will add a list field to the form that includes all the Catalyst bands. The Catalyst bands list will be three rows high, each band will be a list item, and users will be able to select multiple bands from the list.

To add a list to a form:

1. Click in the left column of the eighth row, type **Select all of the bands that you enjoy from the list.** (including the period), and then press the **Tab** key to move the insertion point to the next cell.

2. Click the **List/Menu** button in the **Forms** category on the Insert bar to insert a list in the cell. A small list box appears in the form.

3. In the Property inspector, type **BandsList** in the List/Menu text box, click the **List** option button in the Type section, type **3** in the Height text box, check the **Allow Multiple** check box in the Selections section, if necessary, and then click the **List Values** button. The List Values dialog box opens. See Figure 8-36.

Figure 8-36 List Values dialog box

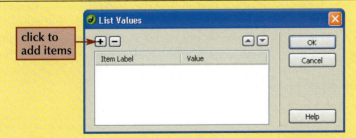

4. Click in the first row under Item Label column, and then type **sloth child**.
5. Click the **Add Item** button to add another item, and then type **dizzied connections**.
6. Repeat Step 5 to add **Life in Minor Chords** and **surface suction** to the list.
7. Click the **OK** button. The items appear in the list. See Figure 8-37.

Figure 8-37   **Completed list/menu box**

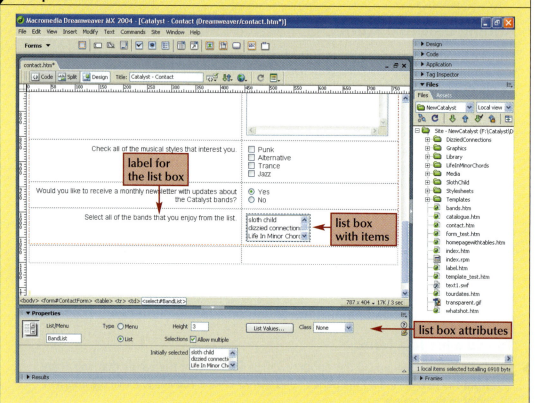

Finally, you will add a Reset button and a Submit button to the form.

Adding Buttons to a Form

You must add a Submit button to a form to enable users to send the form data to the location where it will be processed. It is a good idea to add a Reset button as well so that users can clear any data they input into the form with one click and start over if necessary. When you click the Button button in the Forms category on the Insert bar, it defaults to the Submit Form action, which creates a Submit button. You can also choose the Reset Form action to create a Reset button, or you can choose None and then add other behaviors to the button. In addition to an action, you should type a name and a label for the button. The label will appear as text on the button, and the name is used to reference the button in the code.

You'll add a Submit button and a Reset button to the form.

To add a Submit button and a Reset button to a form:

1. Click in the left column of the last row, and then click the **Button** button in the **Forms** category on the Insert bar. A Submit button appears in the form. See Figure 8-38.

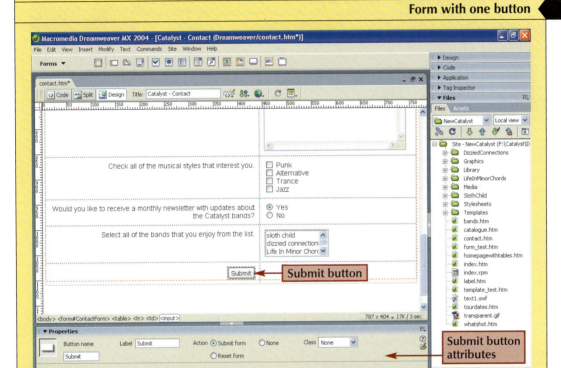

Figure 8-38

Form with one button

Trouble? If your button does not say Submit, you need to adjust the button attributes. You'll do this in the following steps; continue with Step 2.

2. If necessary, in the Property inspector, click the **Submit Form** option button in the Action group, type **Submit** in the Button Name text box, and then type **Submit** in the Label text box.

3. In the Document window, click in the blank space to the right of the Submit button, and then click the **Button** button in the **Forms** category on the Insert bar to insert another button.

4. In the Property inspector, click the **Reset Form** option button in the Action group, type **Reset** in the Button Name text box, and then type **Reset** in the Label text box, if necessary. The Reset button is added to the form. See Figure 8-39.

Figure 8-39   **Form with two buttons**

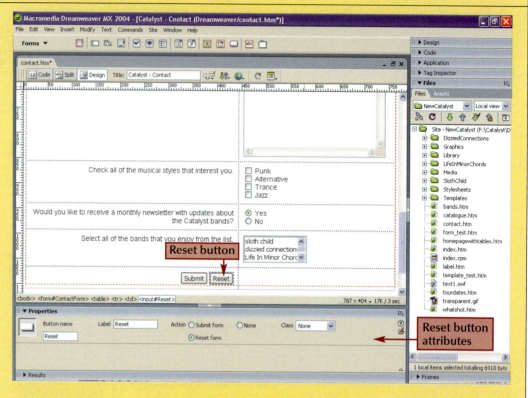

5. Save the page.

Next, you will add the Validate Form behavior to the form.

Validating Form Data

The **Validate Form behavior** enables you to create requirements/limits that check the form data before the form is submitted. When you click Validate Form in the Behavior list, a dialog box opens so you can select each form object and then set limits/requirements. When the user clicks the Submit button, the data is checked to make sure the data meets the limits/requirements that were set for each object in the Validate Form behavior. If information is missing or is not within the set limits, a dialog box opens asking the user to change incorrect information or add missing information and then click the Submit button again.

The Validate Form dialog box displays all of the form objects in the Named Fields list box. You select a field from the list and then set the requirements/limits for that field. You first set whether the selected field is required or optional by checking or unchecking the Required check box in the Value section. The user must enter information into a required field in order to submit the form. If the field is optional, the form will be submitted even if the user does not enter information in that field. You can also set a variety of limits for the data the user enters into the selected field in the Accept section of the dialog box. Accept limits include:

- **Anything.** Allows the user to enter anything into the selected field.
- **Number.** Allows the user to enter only numeric values into the selected field. This limit is often used in fields that are used to input phone numbers or ZIP codes.
- **Email Address.** Allows the user to enter only information that follows the format of an e-mail address (for example, something@something.atopleveldomain). This limit does

not ensure that the user has inserted a valid e-mail address, only that the submitted address is in the correct format.
- **Number From.** Enables you to set a range of acceptable numeric values for the field. The first text box is the lowest acceptable numeric value for the field, and the second text box is the highest acceptable numeric value for the field. For example, you might use this limit when you ask a question such as "How old is your teenager?" The lowest value would be 13 and the highest value would be 19. If a user inputs a number below 13 or above 19, the Validate Form behavior would inform the user that the data was outside the acceptable range and then ask the user to input an acceptable value and resubmit the form.

You'll add the Validate Form behavior to the form. You'll make the FirstName, LastName, and EmailAddress fields required fields and set the Email Address limit for the EmailAddress field to ensure that all submitted addresses are in the correct format.

To add the Validate Form behavior to a form:

1. Select the form, click the **Add Behavior** button in the Behaviors panel, and then click **Validate Form**. The Validate Form dialog box opens. See Figure 8-40.

Figure 8-40 Validate Form dialog box

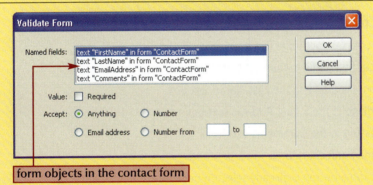

form objects in the contact form

2. Select **text "FirstName" in form "ContactForm"** in the Named Fields list, if necessary, and then check the **Required** check box to make the field a required field. The text "(R)" appears after the field name to indicate that the field is required.
3. Select **text "LastName" in form "ContactForm"** in the Named Fields list, and then check the **Required** check box to make the field a required field.
4. Select **text "EmailAddress" in form "ContactForm"** in the Named Fields list, and then check the **Required** check box.
5. Click the **Email Address** option button in the Accept group to set a limit requiring the data to follow the standard e-mail format.
6. Click the **OK** button.
7. Look at the Behavior list in the Behaviors panel to verify that the Validate Form behavior has been added to the list.
8. Click the **Events** list arrow in the Behaviors panel, and then click **OnSubmit**, if necessary. This will cause the behavior to run when the Submit button is clicked.
9. Save the page.

Finally, you will test the form.

Testing a Form

You should test a form to ensure that it displays properly in a browser and to ensure that the form functionality is working. You should view the form locally to verify that the form objects are laid out properly, and then you should upload the site and test the functionality of the form over the Web. It is sometimes possible to test the functionality of a form locally, but often, when the form-processing script resides on a Web server, the script will not work properly until the site is posted to the remote server. When you test a form, you should input data in each field to verify that it is functioning and then submit the form to verify that the processing script is working properly and that any requested information is returned to the end user. If the form returns an error, you should check the form attributes to make sure that the action, method, and enctype are correct. If you are still having problems, you must check the script to make sure that it is in the correct location and that it has been configured correctly. In this case, the script is located in a Web page and is set up to test the form. When you click the Submit button, the script will display the information that would be sent to the server if the script were located there.

You will test the form in the Contact page. Because the script is in a Web page, you can test the form locally. The process for testing the form is the same as it would be if you were testing the form over the Web.

To test a form:

1. Preview the Contact page in a browser.
2. Type your first name in the First Name text box.
3. Type your last name in the Last Name text box.
4. Type **potato** in the E-mail Address text box.
5. Type **testing** in the Comments text area.
6. Check the **Punk** check box.

   The Yes radio button is already selected because its initial state is set to checked.

7. Click **sloth child** in the bands list. See Figure 8-41.

Contact page with the completed form | **Figure 8-41**

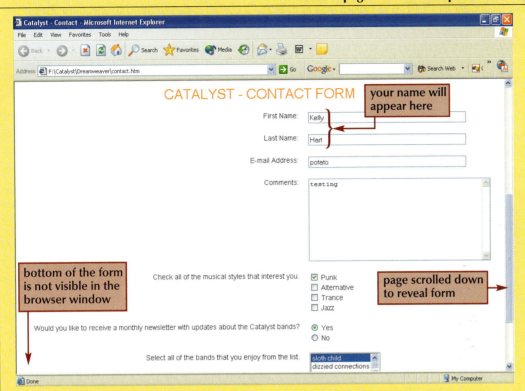

8. Click the **Submit** button. A dialog box opens, explaining that the E-mail Address text box must contain an e-mail address. This means that the Validate Form behavior determined that "potato" is not in the correct format for an e-mail address.

9. Click the **OK** button, type your e-mail address in the E-mail Address text box, and then click the **Submit** button. The test script opens another browser window with the form data that would be submitted to the server. See Figure 8-42.

Form data | **Figure 8-42**

Trouble? If you do not have an e-mail address, type "info@catalystnoise.com" in the E-mail Address text box.

Trouble? If you notice different symbols in the submitted form data (for example "@" may appear as "%40" and spaces may appear as "%20"), it is due to the URL encoding. This is not an error; continue with Step 10.

10. Close the browser window with the form data, click the **Reset** button in the form to clear the information from the form, and then close the browser window with the form and close the page.

The form in the Contact page is complete.

Updating the Web Site on the Remote Server

As your last task, you'll upload the site to the remote server and preview the site over the Web. This way you can see all the changes you made to the Catalyst site, including the library item footer and the form.

To upload a site to the remote server:

1. Click the **Connects to Remote Host** button on the Files panel toolbar.
2. Click the **View** list arrow on the Files panel toolbar, and then click **Local View**.
3. Select the **index.htm, bands.htm, catalogue.htm, form_test.htm, contact.htm, label.htm, tourdates.htm**, and **whatshot.htm** files in Local view, and then click the **Put File(s)** button on the Files panel toolbar.
4. Click the **Yes** button when asked if you want to include dependent files because you have not selected the new dependent files for the site yet.
5. Click the **Disconnects from Remote Host** button on the Files panel toolbar.
6. Click the **View** list arrow on the Files panel toolbar, and then click **Local View**. The Files panel returns to the local view.

Next, you'll preview the updated site in a browser. The site will include the new footer and the form that you added to the local version of the Catalyst site.

To preview the updated site in a browser:

1. Open a browser, type the URL of your remote site into the Address bar on the browser toolbar, and then press the **Enter** key.
2. Click the **bands** link to view the Bands page, and then click the **footer** link to test it.
3. Close the message window that opens.
4. Click the **contact** link to view the Contact page, and then enter information in the form to test it.
5. Submit the form.
6. Close any open browser windows.

In this tutorial, you added keywords and a meta description to the head content, created and used library items in pages, created and used templates, and added a form to the Catalyst site.

Review

Session 8.3 Quick Check

1. What is a form?
2. True or False? Forms process data.
3. What is a form object?
4. List three types of form objects.
5. Which behavior do you add to the form that enables you to create requirements/limits that check the form data before the form is submitted?
6. What is the final step in creating a form?

Review

Tutorial Summary

In this tutorial, you explored the head content for a page. You learned how to optimize a page for search engine placement, and then you added keywords and a meta description to the pages. You created a library item and added it to the pages. You created a template and then you created a new page based on the template. You also created a nested template. Finally, you created a form, added form attributes and form objects, and then validated the form data.

Key Terms

comment tag	library	noneditable region
editable region	library item	robot
form	meta description	template
form object	meta tag	Validate Form behavior
keyword	nested template	

Practice

Practice the skills you learned in the tutorial.

Review Assignments

There are no Data Files needed for the Review Assignments.

Brian asks you to add the list of keywords and the meta description to every page of the Catalyst site. You'll also add the keywords and description to the template so that future pages will have this head content. Then, you'll create a form in the tour section of the Life In Minor Chords page to enable users to be placed on a list to receive notice when the new tour video is released. You'll use the form_test.htm file already in the Catalyst site as the form action so that you can test the form.

1. Open the NewCatalyst site you modified in this tutorial, and then open the bands.htm page in the Document window.
2. Click the Keywords button in the Head list in the HTML category on the Insert bar, and then type "catalyst records, indie music, sloth child, dizzied connections, life in minor chords, surface suction, spinning life, black lab, them apples, i believe in ferries, independent scene, denton music, underground sound, catalist" into the Keywords text box. (*Hint:* Use all lowercase letters and separate each word or phrase with a comma.)

3. Select the entire list of keywords in the Keywords text box, copy the list, click the OK button to add the keywords to the page, and then save and close the page.
4. Open each of the following pages in the Document window, click the Keywords button in the Head list in the HTML category on the Insert bar, paste the list of keywords in the Keywords text box, click the OK button to add the list to the page, and then save and close the page: catalogue.htm, contact.htm, label.htm, tourdates.htm, whatshot.htm, and catalyst_main.dwt. (*Hint:* When you add the keywords to the template, update the pages made from the template.)
5. Open the bands.htm page in the Document window, click the Description button in the Head list in the HTML category on the Insert bar, and then type "Catalyst is an indie label that has tapped into a vein of post-discord punk music. Our mission is to expose the world to exceptional indie music. Catalyst promotes bands that we believe will change and infuse the planet with original good music." in the Description text box.
6. Select the text in the Description text box, copy it, click the OK button, and then save and close the page.
7. Open each of the following pages in the Document window, click the Description button in the Head list in the HTML category on the Insert bar, paste the description in the Description dialog box, click the OK button, and then save and close the page: catalogue.htm page, contact.htm, label.htm, tourdates.htm, whatshot.htm, and catalyst_main.dwt. (*Hint:* When you add the description to the template, update the pages made from the template.)
8. Open the limc_content_tours.htm page located in the LifeInMinorChords folder, click outside the layer in the page, and then press the Enter key until the pointer is positioned below the movie in the page.
9. Click the Form button in the Forms category on the Insert bar to add the form area to the page.
10. Type "LIMCvideoForm" in the Form Name text box, click the Browse For File button next to the Action text box, and then double-click the form_test.htm page in the site's local root folder.
11. Click GET in the Method list, click application/x-www-form-urlencoded in the Enctype list, and then click _blank in the Target list to set the form attributes.
12. Click in the form area, click the Table button in the Common category on the Insert bar, and then create a table with 5 rows, 2 columns, 100% table width, and 10 cell padding.
13. Align the left column of the table to the Right and Top, and then align the right column of the table to the Left and Top.
14. Click in the upper-left cell, type "first name:", press the Tab key to move the insertion point to the next cell, click the Text Field button in the Forms category on the Insert bar to add a text field into the form, and then type "first name" in the TextField text box in the Property inspector.
15. Click in the left cell of the second row, type "last name:", press the Tab key, click the Text Field button in the Forms category on the Insert bar, and then type "lastname" in the TextField text box in the Property inspector.
16. Click in the left cell of the third row, type "email address:", press the Tab key, click the Text Field button in the Forms category on the Insert bar, and then type "email" in the TextField text box in the Property inspector.

17. Click in the left cell of the fourth row, type "Notify me when the new video is released.", press the Tab key, click the Radio Group button in the Forms category on the Insert bar, type "notifyvideorelease" in the Name text box in the Radio Group dialog box, click the first row in the Label column and type "yes," click the first row in the Value column and type "Yes," click the second row in the Label column and type "no," click the second row in the Value column and type "No," and then click the OK button to insert the radio group.
18. Select the Yes radio button in the form, and then click the Checked option button in the Property inspector.
19. Press the Tab key twice to move to the lower-right cell, click the Button button in the Forms category on the Insert bar to insert a Submit button, and then click the Button button again to insert a second button.
20. Select the second button, click the Reset Form option button in the Property inspector, type "Reset" in the Button Name text box, and then type "Reset" in the Label text box, if necessary.
21. Click the Add Behavior button in the Behaviors panel, and then click Validate Form.
22. Click the text "FirstName" in the form "LIMCvideoForm" in the Named Fields list, and then check the Required check box.
23. Click the text "LastName" in the form "LIMCvideoForm" in the Named Fields list, and then check the Required check box.
24. Click the text "Email" in the form "LIMCvideoForm" in the Named Fields list, check the Required check box, click the Email Address radio button in the Accept group, and then click the OK button.
25. Save the page, preview the page in a browser, test the form, and then close the browser windows and the page.
26. Upload the site to your remote server, preview the site over the Web, and then test the form.

Apply

Add keywords, a meta description, and a footer library item to a Web site about small rural communities of northern Vietnam.

Case Problem 1

There are no Data Files needed for this Case Problem.

Hroch University Anthropology Department Professor Hart wants you to add keywords and a meta description to the pages of his site to help optimize the pages in his site for search engines. He also wants you to create a library item for the footer, and then add the library item to every page of the site.

1. Open the Hart site you modified in Tutorial 7, Case 1, and then open the index.htm page in the Document window.
2. Click the Keywords button in the Head list in the HTML category on the Insert bar, and then type "hroch university, social anthropology, northern vietnam, linguistic differences, cultural cross-pollination, rituals, matthew hart, anthropological research, hroch" in the Keywords text box.
3. Select the words in the Keywords text box, copy them, click the OK button, and then save and close the page.
4. Open each of the following pages in the Document window, click the Keywords button in the Head list in the HTML category on the Insert bar, paste the list of keywords into the Keywords text box, click the OK button, and then save and close the page: contact.htm, cultural_cross_pollination.htm, linguistic_differences.htm, new_courses.htm, prof_hart.htm, and rituals_and_practices.htm.

5. Open the index.htm page in the Document window, click the Description button in the Head list in the HTML category on the Insert bar, and then type "Research and study of the language and rituals of peoples of Northern Vietnam by Dr. Matthew Hart of Hroch University." in the Description text box.
6. Select the text in the Description text box, copy it, click the OK button, and then save and close the page.
7. Open each of the following pages in the Document window, click the Description button in the Head list in the HTML category on the Insert bar, paste the description into the Description text box, click the OK button, and then save and close the page: contact.htm, cultural_cross_pollination.htm, linguistic_differences.htm, new_courses.htm, prof_hart.htm, and rituals_and_practices.htm.
8. Open the linguistic_differences.htm page in the Document window, scroll to the bottom of the page, and then select the footer.

Explore
9. Click the Library button on the Assets panel toolbar, drag the footer to the panel, and then name the library item "footer."

Explore
10. Double-click the footer library item in the Assets panel to open it, select the text, and then click the Align Center button in the Property inspector.
11. Save and close the footer library item, and then save and close the page.
12. Open each of the following pages in the Document window, drag the footer library item from the Assets panel to the bottom of the page, and then save and close the page: contact.htm, cultural_cross_pollination.htm, index.htm, new_courses.htm, prof_hart.htm, and rituals_and_practices.htm. (*Hint:* If a page already has a footer, delete the existing footer before adding the footer library item to the page. In the new_courses.htm page, place the library item in the layer.)
13. Open the index.htm page, preview each page of the site in a browser, and then close the browser window and the page.
14. Upload the site to your remote server, and then preview the site over the Web.

Apply

Create a template and a footer library item for a Web site for an art museum.

Case Problem 2

There are no Data Files needed for this Case Problem.

Museum of Western Art C. J. Strittmatter has decided to make the Museum site a template-based site, which will make it faster to update the site. C.J. asks you to create a template for the site based on the Museum page and include a footer library item, which you need to create. There is no need to add the footer library item to the existing pages of the site because you will move the existing pages over to the template once it is approved.

1. Open the Museum site you modified in Tutorial 7, Case 2, and then open the museum.htm page in the Document window.
2. Click the Make Template button in the Templates list in the Common category on the Insert bar.
3. Type "museum_main" in the Save As text box, and then click the Save button. Click the Yes button to update links.
4. Select the page heading in the museum_main.dwt template, click the Editable Region button in the Templates list in the Common category on the Insert bar, and then name the region "PageHeading."
5. Select the page heading text, and then type "PAGE HEADING" as placeholder text.
6. Delete all the text below the page heading and navigation bar.
7. Click the Editable Region button in the Templates list in the Common category on the Insert bar, and then name the region "Content."

Explore

8. Move the insertion point to the line below the editable region, click the Copyright button in the Characters list in the Text category on the Insert bar to insert the © symbol, and then type "copyright Museum of Western Art, 2006."
9. Select the copyright text, and then click the Align Center button in the Property inspector.
10. Click the Library button on the Assets panel toolbar, drag the selected copyright text to the library in the Assets panel, and then name the new library item "footer."
11. Save and close the template.
12. Create a new page from the template.
13. Type "TEST PAGE" in the PageHeading editable region, type "Test Content" in the Content editable region, change the page title to "Museum of Western Art – Template Test," and then save the page as template_test.htm in the site's local root folder.
14. Preview the page in a browser, and then close the browser window and the page.
15. Upload the site to your remote server, and then preview the site over the Web.

Apply

Create a template for a Web site for an independent publisher of fringe writing.

Case Problem 3

There are no Data Files needed for this Case Problem.

NORM Mark Chapman asks you to create a template for the NORM site and then apply the template to the Contact page. Once this page is approved, the template will be applied to the other existing pages of the site.

1. Open the NORM site you modified in Tutorial 7, Case 3, and then open the contact.htm page in the Document window.
2. Click the Make Template button in the Templates list in the Common category on the Insert bar, type "norm_main" in the Save As text box, and then click the Save button. Click the Yes button to update links.
3. Select the page heading, click the Editable Region button in the Templates list in the Common category on the Insert bar, and then name the region "PageHeading."
4. Select the text in the PageHeading region, and then type "Page Heading" to insert placeholder text.
5. Delete the text below the PageHeading region, click the Editable Region button in the Templates list in the Common category on the Insert bar, and then name the Editable Region "PageContent."
6. Click to the right of the new editable region, and then press the Enter key to move to the next line.
7. Click the Copyright button in the Characters list in the Text category on the Insert bar, press the spacebar, type "copyright NORM, Inc. 2006.", center the text, and then save and close the page.
8. Open the contact.htm page, and then delete the navigation bar and the logo from the page because those elements already exist in the template.

Explore

9. Click the Templates button on the Assets panel toolbar, select norm_main in the templates list, and then click the Apply button at the bottom of the Assets panel. The Inconsistent Region Names dialog box opens.
10. Click the Document Body region in the Editable Regions list, and then click PageHeading in the Move Content to New Region list.
11. Click the Document Head region in the Editable Regions list, and then click Head in the Move Content to New Region list.
12. Click the OK button to connect the Contact page to the template; the page content moves into the PageHeading region.

Explore

13. Select the text below the page heading, drag it into the PageContent region, delete the placeholder text from the PageContent region, and then, if necessary, remove any extra spaces from the PageHeading region.
14. Save the page, preview the page in a browser, and then close the browser window and the page.
15. Upload the site to your remote server, and then preview the page over the Web.

Create

Create an online order form for a Web site for a newly opening sushi restaurant.

Case Problem 4

Data Files needed for this Case Problem: form_test.htm, sushi_menu.htm

Sushi Ya-Ya Mary O'Brien asks you to create an online order form for the Menu page of the Sushi Ya-Ya site. Because the server-side script is still being finalized, you'll add the form_test.htm page to the site so you can test the form.

1. Open the SushiYaYa site you modified in Tutorial 7, Case 4.
2. Copy the **form_test.htm** page located in the **Tutorial.08\Cases** folder included with your Data Files to the site's local root folder.
3. Open the menu.htm page in the Document window, delete the "Coming Soon!" text, and then insert a form into the page.
4. In the Property inspector, change the form's name to "Menu," set the Action to the form_test.htm page in the site's local root folder, set the Target to _blank, change the Method to GET, and then set the Enctype to application/x-www-form-urlencoded.
5. Type "Menu" in the form area, and then apply the SubHeadings style.
6. Copy the **sushi_menu.htm** page located in the **Tutorial.08\Cases** folder included with your Data Files to the site's local root folder, and then open the page in the Document window.

Explore

7. Copy the table from the Sushi Menu page into the form below the Menu text in the Menu page.
8. Apply applicable CSS styles to the table as needed.
9. Insert a text field in the cell in the first column of the second row.
10. In the Property inspector, name the text field "KappaRoll," set the character width to 6, and then set the maximum characters to 2.
11. Insert a text field in the cell in the first column of the next row, type the sushi name as the text field name, set the character width to 6, and then set the maximum characters to 2. (*Hint:* Do not include spaces in the field name.)
12. Repeat Step 11 to add text fields for the remaining sushi.
13. Insert a button in the lower-right cell, verify that "Submit" appears in the Button Name and Label text boxes, and then set the Action to Submit Form.
14. Insert a second button, change the Action to Reset Form, and then type "Reset" in the Button Name text box.
15. Add the Validate Form behavior from the Behavior list in the Behaviors panel to the form.

Explore

16. In the Validate Form dialog box, select the first item in the Named Fields list (text "KappaRoll" in form "Menu"), click the Number From option button in the Accept group, and then type "1" and "10" in the text boxes.

Explore

17. Select each of the remaining items in the Named Fields list, set a number from limit from 1 to 10, and then click the OK button.
18. Save the page, preview the page in a browser, test the form, and then close the browser window and the page.
19. Upload the site to your remote server, preview the site over the Web, and then test the form.

Review

Quick Check Answers

Session 8.1

1. Tags used in the head of a page to record information about the page or to give information to the server. The exact purpose of the meta tag is defined by its attributes.
2. keywords meta tag and description meta tag
3. Keywords are one of the elements many search engines use to index Web pages; the keywords you choose should be the words you feel most people will type into search engines to look for the site or the words you want people to find your site under.
4. in the library, which you can access from the Assets panel or in the Library folder in the root folder for the site
5. A comment tag is placed at the beginning and end of every library item.
6. You can update every instance of the item by editing the library item itself.

Session 8.2

1. More; when you begin to design large, professional, template-driven sites, the pages are more interconnected and the design requires a great deal more forethought than designing a regular Web site.
2. areas that can be changed in the template but cannot be changed in the template-based pages
3. When you edit a template, the changes are also made in all the pages that were created from that template.
4. a template that is created from the main template, which enables you to create a more defined structure for some pages of the site
5. True
6. The region is also deleted from the nested template, and you can select whether to move the content to another editable region on pages created from the template or nested template.

Session 8.3

1. A form is a means of collecting information from users. A user can input information into the Web page by typing into designated fields or clicking various elements to make selections. Once the form is filled out, the information is submitted to a server (or other information-processing location) for processing.
2. False
3. the mechanism that enables users to interact with a form
4. any three of the following: text fields (text areas), hidden fields, checkboxes, radio buttons (radio groups), menus/lists, jump menus, file fields, image fields, and buttons
5. Validate Form behavior
6. testing the form

Dreamweaver | **DRM 481**
Tutorial 9

Objectives

Session 9.1
- Learn about creating dynamic database content for Web pages
- Create database-driven pages using MySQL and PHP for a Linux server
- Create a database on a remote Linux server
- Connect a Web site to a database
- Add server behaviors to Web pages
- Create pages to view data in a database
- Create a Login page

Session 9.2
- Create database-driven pages using Access and ASP for a Windows server
- Upload a database to a remote Windows server
- Connect a Web site to a database
- Add server behaviors to Web pages
- Create pages to view data in a database
- Create a Login page

Adding Database Functionality

Collecting and Viewing Form Data in a Database

Case

Catalyst

Sara Lynn, president of Catalyst, believes it would be helpful to collect the data that is received from users who complete and submit the form in the Contact page. Brian Lee, public relations and marketing director, asks you to create a database to store the information collected from the form and connect the form in the Contact page to the database. He also wants you to create pages that enable you to view the data collected in the database. Finally, he asks you to create a Login page and connect the pages that display collected database information to the Login page so that users must have a valid login and password to view the data.

Student Data Files

▼**Tutorial.09 folder**

▽ Tutorial folder
    catalystdb.mdb
    catalystdb.sql

▽ Review folder
    (no starting Data Files)

▽ Cases folder
    hartdb.mdb
    hartdb.sql
    museumdb.mdb
    museumdb.sql
    normdb.mdb
    normdb.sql
    sushidb.mdb
    sushidb.sql

Session 9.1

Exploring Databases and Dynamic Page Content

One of the best ways to extend the functionality of a Web site is to connect the site to a database. A **database** is a collection of information that is arranged for ease and speed of search and retrieval and usually associated with a specific software package, such as MySQL or Microsoft Access. A database can be a simple list of people's names or it can collect large quantities of complex information, such as product inventory. A **database-driven Web site** is a Web site that uses a database to gather, display, or manipulate information. For example, e-commerce sites often use a database to store online orders and billing information, and weather sites often retrieve current weather conditions from a database and display it in a Web page. The Catalyst site will use a database to store the information collected from the form in the Contact page.

There are different ways to create database-driven Web sites; the method depends on the amount of data being served out, the number of users potentially accessing that information simultaneously, the budget available, and the technology already being used. Large companies, such as Amazon and Google, use expensive database software like Oracle or DB2 to serve out massive amounts of data to multiple users. If you plan to serve out massive amounts of information to thousands of users simultaneously and have access to a large budget, this is a great solution. However, if you are creating a medium or small database-driven site, other database software is more accessible.

The two database software packages that are most frequently used with medium and small Web sites are MySQL and Microsoft Access. MySQL is a free open-source database engine that was designed specifically for Web use. It is usually installed by default on Linux servers. MySQL can also be installed on Windows servers, but it requires a more complex procedure. Additional information about MySQL is available at *www.mysql.com*. Access is a database management program that is part of the Microsoft Office suite. Windows servers can serve out Access files by default if the permissions are set correctly for the database file.

In addition to selecting a database, you must also select the programming or scripting language that you will use to create server behaviors. **Server behaviors** are behaviors that run on the Web server before the Web page is sent to a user's browser and are written in PHP, ASP, JSP, or ColdFusion. You will use server behaviors to communicate with a database (send data and retrieve data) and to turn data into plain HTML that can be displayed in a browser as part of a Web page. All server behaviors use SQL when addressing databases. **SQL** (Structured Query Language) is a specialized language used for working with databases. When Web pages display data stored in a database, they are said to be **dynamically generated**. You will use server behaviors to process data from the form in the Contact page in the database, to create HTML that will display an overview of the data stored in the database in the database.php page, and to display the details of selected records in the database_details.php page. Using server behaviors to generate dynamic pages is much more efficient than updating content manually each time the information changes.

This tutorial provides two methods for creating the database-driven pages in the Catalyst site. If you are working with a Linux server, you will use a MySQL database and PHP to create the database-driven pages. If you are working with a Windows server, you will use an Access database and ASP to create the pages. Each method requires different steps and methodologies, both of which are provided in this tutorial.

Regardless of which method you use, the general process for creating the database-driven pages in the Catalyst site is:

- Adjust the form in the Content page
- Create the Web pages you will need
- Place or create the database on the remote server
- Add server behaviors to the form to connect the database
- Add server behaviors to view the data collected in the database from within the designated Web pages
- Format the Login page
- Set the database pages to display only when a user has logged in

If you are working on a Linux server with MySQL and PHP, continue with the next section. If you are working on a Windows server with Access and ASP, continue with Session 9.2. If you are unsure which type of server you are using, ask your instructor or technical support person for help.

Creating Database-Driven Pages Using MySQL and PHP

Adding database functionality to a Web site can be quite complex. Just as it is a good idea to make a plan prior to creating a Web site, it is also a good idea to plan the database-driven portion of the site in advance. Brian has created a site plan for the new portion of the Catalyst site.

Based on his plan, the Catalyst technical team will create the SQL for a database that stores the information collected from the form in the Contact page. You'll modify the form to work with the database. You'll create the pages that you will need for the new portion of the site: thankyou.htm, access_denied.htm, database.php, database_details.php, and login.php. You'll create the database on the remote server using the SQL provided by the technical team, and then you'll connect the site to the database. Next, you'll add server behaviors to the pages you created to enable the form data to be sent to and stored in the database and to enable the database.php and database_details.php pages to display the information stored in the database. Finally, you'll create a login.php page and add code to the backend pages that will prevent unauthorized users from viewing the content of those pages.

When the database-driven pages are complete, the survey information received from users who completed the form in the Contact pages will be stored in a database that only authorized users can access.

Creating Database-Driven Pages for a Linux Server

Reference Window

- Create the Web pages you need.
- Create a database on your remote server.
- Add server behaviors to connect the site to the database.
- Add server behaviors to send and store submitted data in the database and to view the data collected in the database from within designated Web pages.
- Create a Login page.
- Add code to the backend pages to prevent unauthorized users from viewing the content of those pages.

Modifying the Form

Before you create the database-driven pages of the Catalyst site, you'll modify the form in the Contact page to work with the database that you will place on your remote server. You will delete the list box with the band names from the form, and then create a series of checkboxes to collect this same information. You are replacing the list box to keep things simpler because it is requires more steps and custom scripts to process data from a list box for storage in a database.

To modify the form:

1. Open the **NewCatalyst** site you modified in the Tutorial 8 Review Assignments, and then open the **contact.htm** page in the Document window.

2. Select the list box in the right column near the bottom of the form, and then press the **Delete** key. The list box is removed from the page.

3. Click the **Checkbox** button in the **Forms** category on the Insert bar to insert the first checkbox, type **sloth_child** in the CheckBox Name text box, click to the right of the checkbox to deselect the checkbox, type **sloth child** beside the checkbox, and then press the **Shift+Enter** keys to move the insertion point down one line. You've entered the first checkbox and label in the form. See Figure 9-1.

Figure 9-1 Form in the Contact page

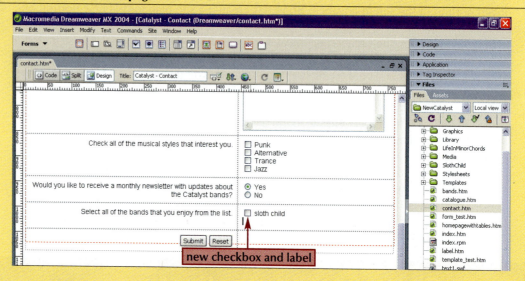

4. Repeat Step 3 to create checkboxes and labels for the following bands, replacing the spaces in the band names with underscores in the CheckBox Name text box: **dizzied connections**, **Life In Minor Chords**, and **surface suction**.

5. Select the sentence in the left column next to the new checkboxes, and then type **Check all of the bands that you enjoy.** (including the period). See Figure 9-2.

Modified form | Figure 9-2

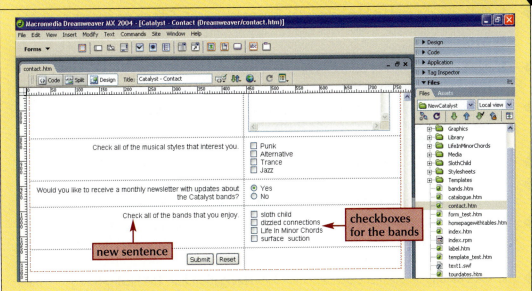

6. Save and close the page, and then upload the page to your remote server.

Next, you'll create the additional pages you need.

Creating New Pages

You need five pages for the database-driven portion of the site. You will create all of these pages now so that they will be available when you need them. According to the plan that Brian created for the database-driven portion of the Catalyst site, you will create the following pages:

- **thankyou.htm** - A page thanking the user for his or her submission that displays when the user submits the form in the Contact page.
- **access_denied.htm** - A page informing the user that the wrong user name or password has been entered that displays when a user attempts to log in on the Login page with incorrect information or if a user attempts to access a password-protected page without logging in. After a four-second delay, the user will be returned to the Login page.
- **database.php** - A page showing an overview of the data stored in the database. Once the Login page is created, users cannot access this page unless they log in.
- **database_details.php** - A page showing the details of a selected record that displays when a user clicks a record in the Database page. Once the Login page is created, users cannot access this page unless they log in.
- **login.php** - A page in which a user enters his or her user name and password and then clicks the Login button. If the information is correct, the Database page will display; if the information is incorrect, the Access Denied page will display.

Three of the pages you will create are PHP pages. You can create a PHP page by typing .php as the file extension when you name the page.

To create pages:

1. Right-click the **contact.htm** page in the Files panel, point to **Edit** on the context menu, and then click **Duplicate**. A new page named Copy of contact.htm appears at the bottom of the list in the Files panel.

2. Right-click the **Copy of contact.htm** page, point to **Edit** on the context menu, click **Rename**, type **thankyou.htm**, and then press the **Enter** key. The page is renamed.

3. Open the **thankyou.htm** page in the Document window, select **Contact** in the Title text box on the Document toolbar, type **Thank you**, and then press the **Enter** key. The new page title is displayed.

4. Double-click the page heading. The Insert Flash Text dialog box opens.

5. Select the text in the Text text box, type **CATALYST THANK YOU**, select the text in the Save As text box, type **Media/HeadingThankyou.swf**, and click the **OK** button.

6. Select all the content below the heading and above the footer, press the **Delete** key to remove it from the page, and then type **Thank you for submitting your information.** (including the period) in the line below the heading text.

7. Click **Modify** on the menu bar, and then click **Navigation Bar**. The Modify Navigation Bar dialog box opens.

8. Click **Contact** in the Nav Bar Elements list, click the **Show "Down Image" Initially** check box to uncheck it and remove the asterisk from Contact in the Nav Bar Elements list, click the **OK** button, and then click in the Contact page to deselect the navigation bar element. The Contact button is no longer displayed in the Down state. See Figure 9-3.

Figure 9-3   New thankyou.htm page

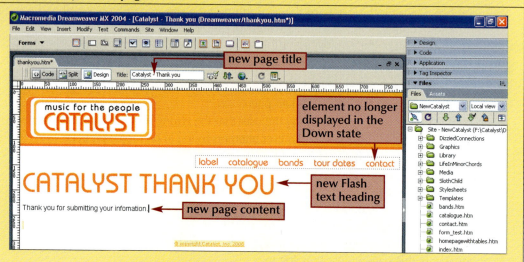

9. Save and close the page, and then upload the page to your remote server.

You'll use the same process to create the rest of the pages, except you will add content to the pages later (so you will not type any text in Step 6).

▶ **10.** Repeat Steps 1 through 9 to create the following pages, typing .php as the file extension for the last three pages in Step 2 and not typing any new page content in Step 6:

Filename	Page Title	Page Heading	Save Page Heading As
access_denied.htm	Catalyst - Access Denied	CATALYST ACCESS DENIED	Media/HeadingAccessDenied.swf
database.php	Catalyst - Database	CATALYST DATABASE	Media/HeadingDatabase.swf
database_details.php	Catalyst - Database Details	CATALYST DATABASE DETAILS	Media/HeadingDatabaseDetails.swf
login.php	Catalyst - login	CATALYST LOGIN	Media/HeadingLogin.swf

Now that you modified the form and created the new pages, you are ready to create the database on your remote server.

Creating a Database on a Remote Server

You must create the database on the remote server so it can send data to and receive data from Web pages or Web applications. For example, in the Catalyst site, the form in the Contact page will send data to the database that you create on the remote server.

If your instructor has already created the database on your remote server, you should read but not complete the next set of steps. In this case, you will be sharing the same database with your classmates, so you might see data that you did not add in the database or data you added might be removed. If you are creating the database on your remote server, you will need to contact your ISP (or your IT department) and have them create an empty MySQL database, name the empty database "catalystdb," and provide you with access information. Once the empty database is available on your remote server, you will use the administrative tools your host provides to:

- Log in to the database management interface (use the information and steps provided by your ISP or IT department)
- Run the statements that are provided as SQL in the catalystdb.sql file located in the Tutorial.09\Tutorial folder included with your Data Files. (The steps will vary depending on the system your ISP or IT department uses.) Running the statements will create the database that will be used in this tutorial by filling the empty database on the remote server with the structure and content that the Catalyst technical team provided.

The following are the steps the authors' ISP provided to log in to the empty database and run the catalystdb.sql file using phpMyAdmin as the database management interface. phpMyAdmin is the most frequently used database management interface for MySQL databases. Additional information about phpMyAdmin can be found at *www.phpmyadmin.net*. If your ISP or IT department uses a different interface or if the interface is configured differently, your steps will vary slightly; contact your ISP or IT department for the exact steps you should follow. If your instructor has already created the database for you, read the following steps and then continue working in the Connecting a Web Site to a Database section.

To log in to the database management interface and run the SQL file:

1. Open a browser window, type the URL provided by your ISP or IT department in the Address text box, and then press the **Enter** key. A page or dialog box opens in which you enter log in information.

2. Type the user name and password information provided by your ISP or IT department in the appropriate text boxes, and then click the **OK** button. The default page of the database management interface that your ISP or IT department uses appears in the browser window. Figure 9-4 shows the default page for the phpMyAdmin database management interface.

Figure 9-4 phpMyAdmin default page

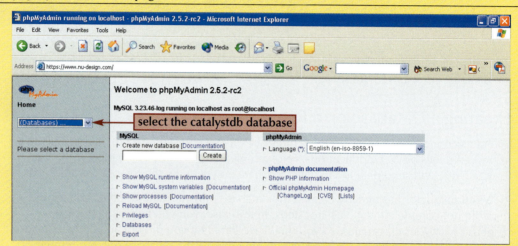

Trouble? If your screen does not match Figure 9-4, your ISP or IT department uses a different interface or has PHP MySQL configured differently. The same general steps should work; however, if you have difficulty, ask your instructor, technical support person, ISP, or IT department for instructions.

3. Click the **Databases** list arrow, and then click **catalystdb**, if necessary. The catalystdb detail page is displayed. See Figure 9-5.

Figure 9-5 catalystdb Detail page

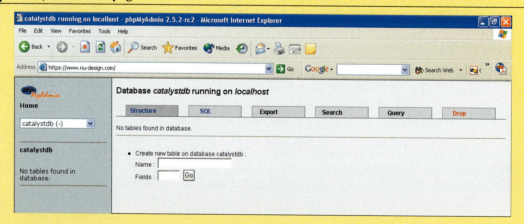

4. Click the **SQL** tab at the top of the page. The SQL page opens in the browser window.

5. Click the **Browse** button beside the Location of the Textfile text box to open the Choose File dialog box, navigate to the **Tutorial.09\Tutorial** folder included with your Data Files, click the **catalystdb.sql** file, and then click the **Open** button. The file path appears in the text box.

6. Click the **GO** button. The database management interface runs the SQL file, the database is created, and a list of the tables in the database appears at the left of the browser window below the database name. See Figure 9-6.

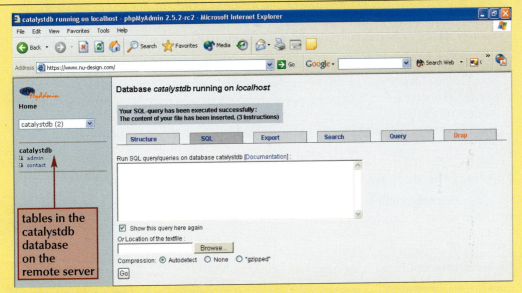

Figure 9-6 Database created on the remote server

7. Close the browser window.

Once the database is created on the remote server, you are ready to connect the Catalyst site to the database.

Connecting a Web Site to a Database

The database is created on the Web server, and now you are ready to connect the site to the database. When you open a Web page in the Document window that is not connected to the database, the Server Behaviors panel displays an interactive list of steps for setting up Dreamweaver to connect the site to the database. Clicking the linked text in each step opens the dialog boxes needed to complete that step. A check mark appears at the left of each step to indicate that all the necessary information has been entered and the step is completed.

The three main steps for connecting a Web page to the database are:

1. **Create a site for this file.** This step is checked because you have already set the local and remote information for the site when you created the site definition.
2. **Choose a document type.** In this step, you specify which document type you are using to create server behaviors. When you click the link text in Step 2, the Choose Document Type dialog box opens, and you can select ColdFusion, PHP, ASP JavaScript, ASP VBScript, or JSP as the document type. For the Catalyst site, you will use PHP.

3. **Set up the site's testing server.** In this step, you specify the testing server in the site definition. You cannot preview dynamic pages from within Dreamweaver until you specify a folder in which the dynamic pages can be processed. Dreamweaver uses this folder to generate dynamic content and connect to the database while you work. For the Catalyst site you will use the root folder you created on the remote server for your NewCatalyst site because the server usually runs an application server that can handle the dynamic pages. You can, however, specify a different location for the testing server as long as it can handle dynamic pages. When you set up the testing server for a professional site that is already live, you might designate a separate folder on another server where you can test the pages without affecting the live site. When you click the link text in Step 3, the Site Definition dialog box opens to the Testing Server category. The information for the remote server is displayed by default, but you may need to delete the first part of the file path in the URL Prefix text box.

Some of the files required for server-sided processing are located outside of the Web page. Therefore, whenever you upload pages to your remote or testing server, you must also upload dependent files.

You'll open the Contact page and complete Steps 2 and 3 in the Server Behaviors panel.

To select the document type and set the testing server:

1. Open the **contact.htm** page in the Document window, and then click the **document type** link in the Server Behaviors panel in the Application panel group. The Choose Document Type dialog box opens. See Figure 9-7.

Figure 9-7   **Choose Document Type dialog box**

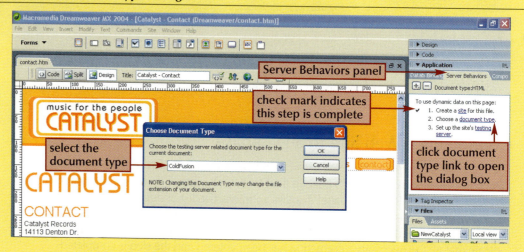

2. Click the list arrow, click **PHP**, and then click the **OK** button. The Update Files dialog box opens.

3. Click the **Update** button to update the links. The file extension for the Contact page changes to .php and a check mark appears in the Server Behaviors panel beside Step 2 to indicate that this step is complete. The Update Files dialog box opens, indicating that the contact.php page could not be updated.

4. Click the **OK** button. You'll update the link in the contact.php page yourself.

5. Click **Modify** on the menu bar, click **Navigation Bar**, click **Contact** in the Nav Bar Elements list, select **htm** in the When Clicked, Go To URL text box, type **php** to change the file extension, and then click the **OK** button.

6. Save the page, and then upload the page to your remote server, including the dependent files. (The contact.htm page remains in the site's root folder but is no longer used.)

Next, you'll complete Step 3.

7. Click the **testing server** link in Step 3 in the Server Behaviors panel. The Site Definition for NewCatalyst dialog box opens with the Advanced tab displayed and Testing Server selected in the Category list.

8. Click the **Server Model** list arrow, click **PHP MySQL**, click the **Access** list arrow, and then click **FTP**. Additional FTP options appear in the dialog box, displaying the information input in the Remote Info category.

9. Delete all the file path information in the URL Prefix text box, and then type the URL for your posted site. See Figure 9-8.

Figure 9-8   **Completed Testing Server information**

[Screenshot of Site Definition for NewCatalyst dialog box with Testing Server category selected and additional FTP access options shown (your information will differ).]

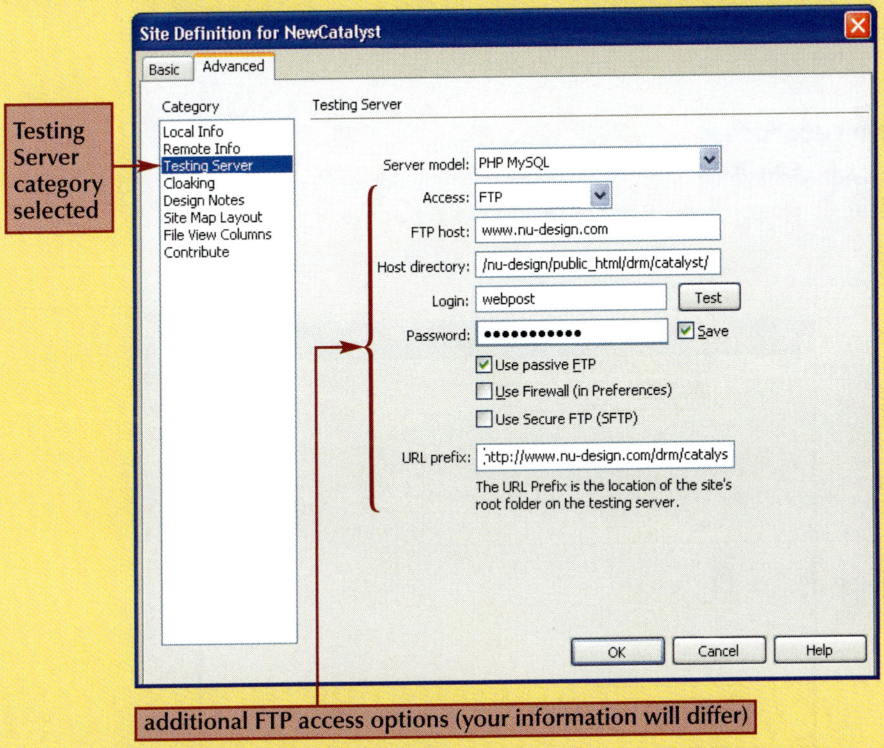

Trouble? If you do not know the URL for your remote site, ask your instructor, technical support person, or ISP for this information.

10. Click the **OK** button. The Testing Server information is set and a check mark appears beside Step 3 in the Server Behaviors panel.

Next, you'll add the server behaviors to the PHP page.

Adding Server Behaviors

Dreamweaver provides a list of prewritten server behaviors in the Server Behaviors panel once the page is connected to the database. You include these server behaviors in the page to extend the functionality of the page and to enable you to retrieve and display the data from the database.

You will include the following two server behaviors in the contact.php page:

- **Recordset.** The Recordset behavior enables you to specify which data you want to retrieve from the database and display in the Web page. A **recordset** is a temporary collection of data retrieved from a database and stored on the application server that generates the Web page when that page is loaded in a browser window. You specify the database and the records (or data) to include in the recordset when you set the parameters for the behavior. A recordset can include all the data in the database or a subset of the data. You must add the server-side behaviors that will create the recordset in which to store and retrieve data before you can use a database as a content source for a dynamic Web page. The server discards the recordset when it is no longer needed.

- **Insert Record.** The insert record behavior enables you to specify what will happen to the information collected from the Web page (in this case, when the form is submitted). You can specify in which database the data will be placed, where the data will be stored in the database, what columns of information will be included, and so forth. It also enables you to select the page that appears in the browser window once the form is submitted.

You'll create a recordset for the contact.php page.

To create a recordset:

1. Click the **Add Behavior** button at the top of the Server Behaviors panel, and then click **Recordset**. The Recordset dialog box opens. See Figure 9-9.

Figure 9-9   **Recordset dialog box**

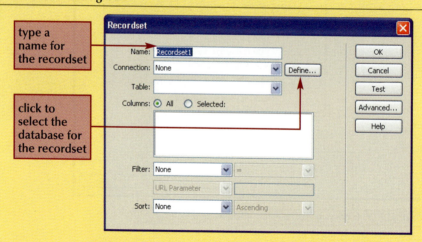

2. Click the **Define** button next to the Connection text box. The Connections for Site 'NewCatalyst' dialog box opens.

3. Click the **New** button. The MySQL Connection dialog box opens. See Figure 9-10.

Figure 9-10   **MySQL Connection dialog box**

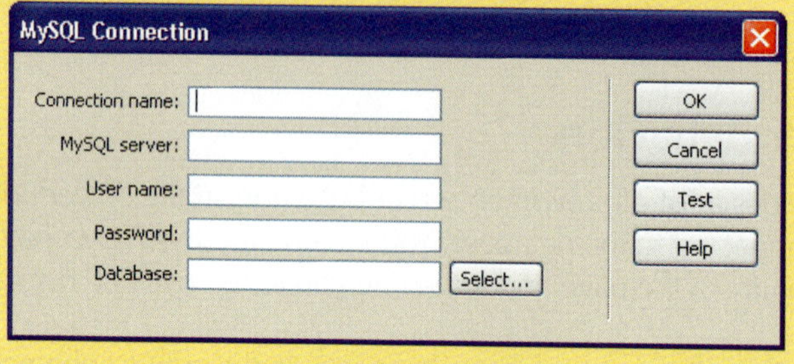

4. Type **CatalystDBconnection** in the Connection Name text box. This is an internal name that will be visible only when you are working in Dreamweaver.

5. Type **localhost** in the MySQL Server text box if your database server is the same as your Web server; otherwise, type the database server URL provided by your ISP when you requested access information.

   Trouble? If you are using a different testing server than the remote server, you will need different information for this text box. Ask your instructor or technical support person for help.

6. Type your user name in the User Name text box, and then type your password in the Password text box. You'll need to obtain this information from your instructor, technical support person, ISP, or IT department; these are unique for each connection.

7. Click the **Select** button next to the Database text box. Dreamweaver connects to the remote server, the Select Database dialog box opens, and the names of all the databases on the remote server to which you have access appear in the Select Database list.

8. Click **catalystdb** in the Select Database list to select it.

   Trouble? If an error message appears, Dreamweaver cannot connect to the database on the remote database server. Check the information you typed in the Testing Server category of the site definition and in the MySQL Connection dialog box, and then repeat Step 8. If you still have trouble, ask your instructor or technical support person for help.

9. Click the **OK** button in the Select Database dialog box, click the **OK** button in the MySQL Connection dialog box, and then click the **Done** button in the Connections for Site 'NewCatalyst' dialog box. The dialog boxes close.

10. Type **CatalystRecordset** in the Name text box in the Recordset dialog box.

11. Click the **Connection** list arrow, click **CatalystDBconnection**, click the **Table** list arrow, click **contact**, and then click the **OK** button. The Recordset behavior is added to the page and appears in the Server Behaviors panel. See Figure 9-11.

Recordset behavior added to the contact.php page

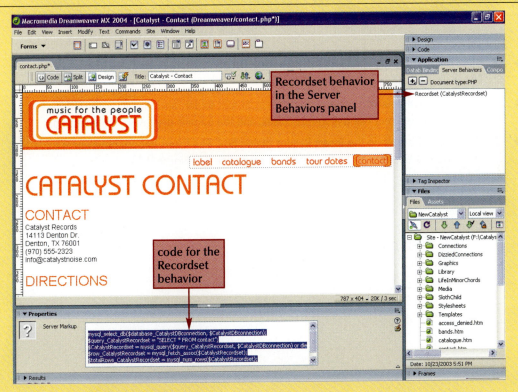

Next, you'll add the Insert Record behavior to the page.

To add the Insert Record behavior:

1. Click the **Add Behavior** button at the top of the Server Behaviors panel, and then click **Insert Record**. The Insert Record dialog box opens.

2. Click the **Submit Values From** list arrow and click **ContactForm**, if necessary, click the **Connection** list arrow and click **CatalystDBconnection**, and then click the **Insert Table** list arrow and click **contact**. The columns in the contact table are displayed in the Columns list. See Figure 9-12.

Figure 9-12   **Insert Record dialog box**

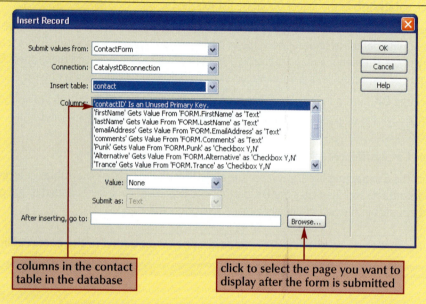

columns in the contact table in the database

click to select the page you want to display after the form is submitted

3. Click the **Browse** button next to the After Inserting, Go To text box. The Select a Redirect File dialog box opens.

4. Click the **thankyou.htm** page in the site's local root folder, and then click the **OK** button. The Select a Redirect File dialog box closes, and the page is displayed in the text box.

5. Click the **OK** button in the Insert Record dialog box. The Insert Record behavior is added to the page and appears in the Server Behaviors panel. See Figure 9-13.

Tutorial 9 Adding Database Functionality Dreamweaver DRM 495

Figure 9-13

Insert Record behavior added to the contact.php page

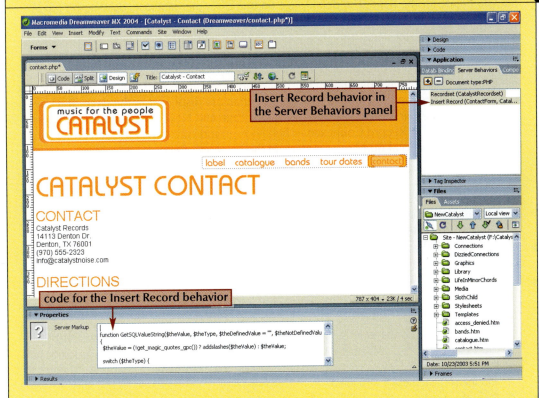

Before continuing, you'll test the Insert Record behavior you added to the contact.php page. You need to upload the page to the remote server, preview the page in a browser, and then complete and submit the form. The Thank You page should then display.

To test the Insert Record behavior:

1. Save the page, and then upload the page to the remote server. The Update Copy on Testing Server dialog box opens.

2. Click the **Yes** button to update the file on the testing server.

3. Preview the contact.php page in a browser, enter appropriate information in the form, and then click the **Submit** button to submit the form. The Thank You page displays in the browser window.

4. Close the browser window.

The page is connected to the database, and the behaviors have been added to the page. Next, you will create pages that enable you to view the data collected in the database.

Creating Backend Pages for Viewing Data in a Database

Pages that are intended for internal use are usually called backend pages. For the Catalyst site, the Database and Database Details pages are backend pages. You will set the database.php and database_details.php pages to display the data that you collect in the database. The Master/Detail Page Set button in the Application category on the Insert bar enables you to create a set of pages that present information in two levels of detail.

The master page (in this case, the database.php page) lists all the records in the recordset that you create for the page. The detail page (in this case, the database_details.php page) displays the detail of the selected record. You determine which fields of information are displayed in the master page and which fields of information are displayed in the detail page when you set the parameters for the pages. In addition to creating all the code needed to display the dynamic content in the pages, Dreamweaver also adds server behaviors to create a page navigation bar that enables you to move between the dynamic records if there are more records in the database than are displayed in the page. The navigation bar includes First Page, Last Page, Previous Page and Next Page buttons. The pages also include Display Record Count server behaviors to indicate which records are visible in the page and the total number of records in the database (Records *x* to *y* of *z*).

To create the master page:

1. Click **Recordset** in the Server Behaviors panel, right-click the selected behavior, and then click **Copy** on the context menu.
2. Open the **database_details.php** page, right-click in the Server Behaviors panel, and then click **Paste** on the context menu. The Recordset behavior is pasted in the Database Details page.
3. Place the insertion point in the heading line after the heading text, press the **Right Arrow** key to move the insertion point past the heading text, and then press the **Enter** key to move the insertion point to the next line.

   Trouble? If Dreamweaver locks up, then you've encountered a bug in Dreamweaver that causes the program to lock up if you place the insertion point in the line below the heading and then press the Enter key when using server behaviors. End the program, restart the computer, and then repeat Steps 1 through 3.

4. Open the **database.php** page in the Document window, right-click in the Server Behaviors panel, click **Paste** on the context menu to paste the Recordset behavior into the page, place the insertion point in the heading line, press the **Right Arrow** key to move the insertion point past the heading text, and then press the **Enter** key to move the insertion point to the next line.
5. Click the **Master Detail Page Set** button in the **Application** category on the Insert bar. The Insert Master-Detail Page Set dialog box opens. See Figure 9-14.

Figure 9-14   **Insert Master-Detail Page Set dialog box**

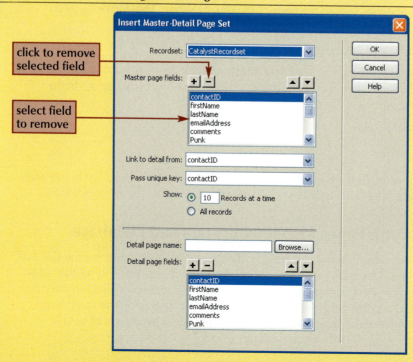

You will remove the fields from the Master Page Fields list that you do not want to display in the master page. You'll also change the field order so that the last name will appear in the first column.

6. Click **contactID** in the Master Page Fields list, if necessary, and then click the **Remove Item** button above the Master Page Fields list. The selected field name is removed from the list.

7. Repeat Step 6 to remove the following field names: **comments**, **Punk**, **Alternative**, **Trance**, **Jazz**, **sloth_child**, **dizzied_connections**, **Life_In_Minor_Chords**, and **surface_suction**. Only the names of fields that will be visible in the Database page appear in the Master Page Fields list.

8. Click **lastName** in the Master Page Fields list, and then click the **Move Item Up** button above the Master Page Fields list until the lastName field is at the top of the list. The fields will display in the page in the same order they appear in the list.

9. Click the **Link To Detail From** list arrow, and then click **lastName**. The data from the lastName field in the Database page is now linked to the record details, which will display in the Database Details page.

You'll set the record details to display in the database_details.php page. As with the master page, you'll delete unneeded fields and change the field order for the detail page.

To create the detail page:

1. Click the **Browse** button next to the Detail Page Name text box, click the **database_details.php** page in the Select File dialog box, and then click the **OK** button. The page name appears in the Detail Page Name text box.

2. Click **contactID** in the Detail Page Fields list, if necessary, and then click the **Remove Item** button. The field name is removed from the list and the field will not be displayed in the Database Details page.

3. Click the **Newsletter** field in the Detail Page Fields list, and then click the **Move Item Up** button until the field name is directly below the emailAddress field. See Figure 9-15.

Figure 9-15 Completed Insert Master-Detail Page Set dialog box

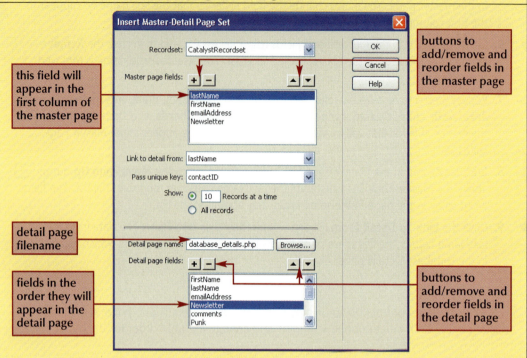

4. Click the **OK** button. The dialog box closes, and the master/detail pages are complete.

Dreamweaver adds elements to the pages that will enable you to view the data collected in the database as well as the details of selected records. Before continuing, you'll upload the pages to the remote server and preview the pages in the browser.

To view the Database Details page:

1. Save the Database page, and then upload the page to your remote server. Dreamweaver adds elements to the page that will enable you to view the data collected in the database. See Figure 9-16.

Database page Figure 9-16

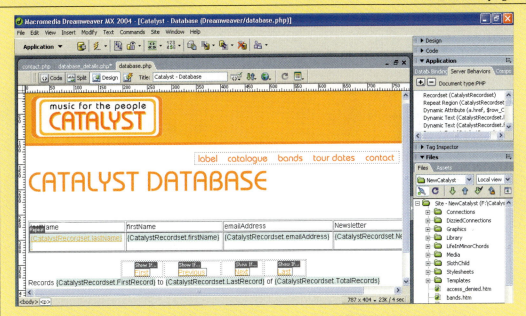

2. Click the **database_details.php** tab to view the Database Details page. Dreamweaver has also added elements to this page that will enable you to view the details of records selected in the Database page. See Figure 9-17.

Database Details page Figure 9-17

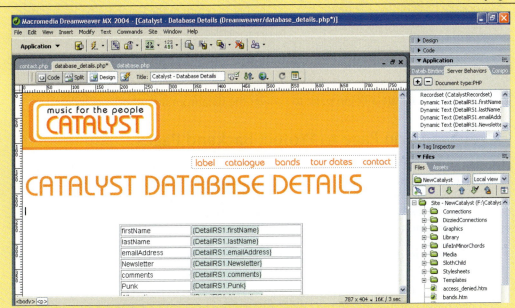

3. Save the page, and then upload the page to your remote server.
4. Click the **database.php** tab, and then preview the page in a browser, clicking the **No** button when Dreamweaver asks you to upload the changes to the testing server because you have already done that. The data that you collected from the form in the Contact page is displayed in the browser window. See Figure 9-18.

Figure 9-18   Database page previewed in a browser

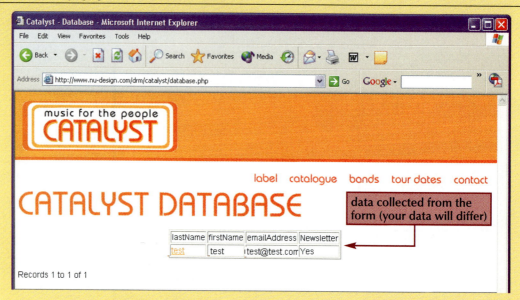

data collected from the form (your data will differ)

> **Trouble?** If you see more than the one record you entered into the contact form, then you're sharing the database with classmates and the database will include all the entries that have been submitted. In a professional environment, this would probably not be the case.

5. Click a link to view the details of a record. The details are displayed in the Database Details page.

6. Click the **Back** button ⬅ on the browser toolbar to return to the Database page, and then click another record if available.

7. Close the browser window, and then close all the pages.

Next, you will create a Login page to protect the data from unauthorized access.

Creating a Login Page to Protect Backend Pages

Data collected from a Web site and stored in a database is often displayed in Web pages. This convenience enables you to view the data from any computer that is connected to the Internet. However, most businesses do not want the general public to have access to this type of proprietary information. One way to restrict the access to Web pages is to require users to log in before they can view the pages. To add this functionality you must:

- **Create a table in the database that holds user names and passwords.** The team that created the SQL that you used to create the database included an administrative table with columns to collect user names and passwords. They also added one user name (catalyst) and one password (feelinit) in the table. You will use the user name and password included in the database to create and test the Login page.

- **Create a page that enables users to create accounts by entering a unique user name and password.** Because only one member of the Catalyst staff is in charge of monitoring and reporting the information collected in the database, you won't create this page now. The team member will use the supplied user name and password to log in to protected pages. Because you eventually want to enable other users to log in to the site, you will create additional pages that will enable users to create unique user names and passwords in the Review Assignments.

- **Create a page that enables users to log in to the site.** You have already created the Login page. Now you will create a form in the Login page that enables users to input their user name and password information. You will also add the Log In User server behavior to the page, which will check the database when a user submits the form to ensure that the user name and password are valid. If login is successful, the Database page will display in the user's browser window. If login is unsuccessful, the Access Denied page will display in the browser window.
- **Restrict access to the pages.** You add the Restrict Access To Page server behavior to the pages that you want to protect, in this case, the Database and Database Details pages. Once this behavior is added to the pages, users who are not logged in will be sent to the Access Denied page.

You'll create the form in the Login page, and then add the Log In User server behavior to the page.

To add content to the Login page:

1. Open the **login.php** page, place the insertion point in the heading line, press the **Right Arrow** key until the insertion point is positioned at the right of the heading text, and then press the **Enter** key. The insertion point moves to the next line.
2. Click the **Form** button in the **Forms** category on the Insert bar. The code for a form is inserted into the page.
3. Type **loginform** in the Form Name text box in the Property inspector. For this form, it is not necessary to enter information for the other attributes in the Property inspector because you will add behaviors to control the form.
4. Click inside of the form area (the dotted red lines), and then click the **Table** button in the **Common** category on the Insert bar. The Table dialog box opens.
5. Type **3** in the Rows text box, type **2** in the Columns text box, type **80** percent in the Table Width text boxes, type **2** in the Cell Padding text box, type **2** in the Cell Spacing text box, and then click the **OK** button. A table with three rows and two columns in inserted into the form.
6. Select the left column, click the **Horz** list arrow in the Property inspector and click **Right**, click the **Vert** list arrow in the Property inspector and click **Top**, select the right column, click the **Horz** list arrow in the Property inspector and click **Left**, and then click the **Vert** list arrow in the Property inspector and click **Top**.
7. Click in the first cell of the table, type **User name:** (including the colon), press the **Tab** key to move the insertion point to the upper-right cell, and then click the **Text Field** button in the **Forms** category on the Insert Bar to insert a text field.
8. Type **username** in the TextField text box, type **40** in the Char Width text box, and then type **20** in the Max Chars text box.
9. Click in the middle-left cell, type **Password:** (including the colon), and then press the **Tab** key to move the insertion point to the next cell.
10. Click the **Text Field** button in the **Forms** category on the Insert bar, type **password** in the TextField text box, type **40** in the Char Width text box, and then type **20** in the Max Chars text box.
11. Click in the bottom-right cell, click the **Button** button in the **Forms** category on the Insert bar, and then type **Login** in the Button Name and Label text boxes. See Figure 9-19.

Figure 9-19 Form in the Login page

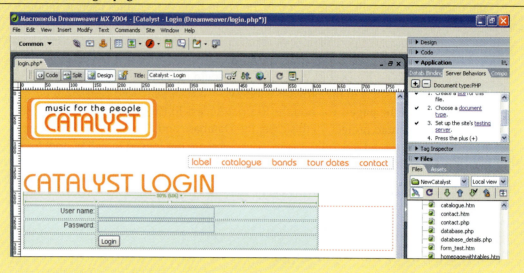

Next, you'll add the Log In User server behavior to the page, which will verify the submitted user name and password.

To add server behaviors to the Login page:

1. Select the **Login** button in the form, and then click **Log In User** in the **User Authentication** list in the **Application** category on the Insert bar. The Log In User dialog box opens.

2. Click **CatalystDBconnection** in the Validate Using Connection list, click **admin** in the Table list, if necessary, click **username** in the Username Column list, and then click **password** in the Password Column list.

3. Click the **Browse** button next to the If Login Succeeds, Go To text box, click the **database.php** page in the Select File dialog box, and then click the **OK** button. This sets the Database page to display in the browser window if the submitted user name and password are listed in the database.

4. Click the **Browse** button next to the If Login Fails, Go To text box, click the **access_denied.htm** page in the Select File dialog box, and then click the **OK** button. This sets the Access Denied page to display in the browser window if the submitted user name and password are not listed in the database. See Figure 9-20.

Log In User dialog box | Figure 9-20

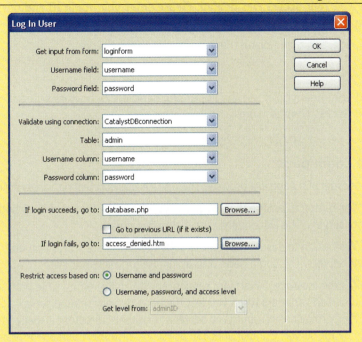

- 5. Click the **OK** button. The Log In User server behavior is added to the page.
- 6. Save the page, and then upload the page to your remote server.

You'll add a meta refresh tag to the Access Denied page, which tells the browser to automatically refresh the page (by reloading the current page or going to a different page) after a certain amount of time. You'll also add text to indicate that access was denied to that user.

To add a meta refresh tag and text to the Access Denied page:

- 1. Open the **access_denied.htm** page in the Document window.
- 2. Click the **Refresh** button 🗘 in the **Head** list in the **HTML** category on the Insert bar. The Refresh dialog box opens.
- 3. Type **4** in the Delay text box, and then type **login.php** in the Go To URL text box. See Figure 9-21.

Refresh dialog box | Figure 9-21

4. Click the **OK** button, place the insertion point after the heading text, press the **Enter** key, and then type **Your access was denied. Please enter your login ID and password again.** (including the period).

5. Save the page, and then upload the page to your remote server.

Before you continue, you'll test the Login page and the behaviors you added to the Database and Access Denied pages.

To test the Login page:

1. Preview the login.php page in a browser. The Update Copy on Testing Server dialog box opens.

2. Click the **Yes** button to ensure that the most recent copy of the page is on both the testing and remote servers. The Dependent Files dialog box opens.

3. Click the **Yes** button to ensure that all the dependent files are current on both the testing and remote servers. The Login page displays in the browser window.

   Trouble? If the message, "Warning: session_start():" followed by a file path and "failed: Permission denied" appears when you test the page on your remote server, you may need to adjust the permissions on your Web server's temporary directory (usually tmp) so that it is writable by the server. Contact your ISP or technical support person for assistance.

   You'll enter an invalid user name and password.

4. Type **test** in the User Name text box, type **test** in the Password text box, and then click the **Login** button. The login information is invalid, so the access_denied.htm page is displayed in the browser window. After four seconds, the Login page is redisplayed.

   Now, you'll enter a valid user name and password.

5. Type **catalyst** in the User Name text box, type **feelinit** in the Password text box, and then click the **Login** button. The Database page is displayed in the browser window.

6. Close the browser window, and then close the pages.

Finally, you will protect the Database and Database Details pages from unauthorized access by adding the Restrict Access server behavior to the pages.

To restrict access to pages:

1. Open the **database.php** page in the Document window.

2. Click the **Restrict Access To Page** button in the **User Authentication** list in the **Application** category on the Insert bar. The Restrict Access To Page dialog box opens.

3. Type **access_denied.htm** in the If Access Denied, Go To text box. See Figure 9-22.

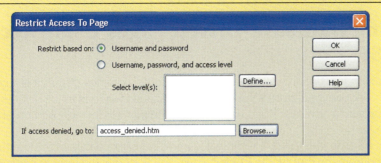

Figure 9-22

Restrict Access To Page dialog box

▶ 4. Click the **OK** button, save the page, and then upload the page to your remote server.
▶ 5. Open the **database_details.php** page in the Document window, and then repeat Steps 2 through 4.

Next, you'll test the behavior you added to the pages.

▶ 6. Preview the database.php page in a browser. Because you are not logged in, the Database page will not display in the browser window. Instead, the Access Denied page is displayed for four seconds, and then the Login page is displayed.

Trouble? If the Database page does display, you did not close the browser window after you logged in and you are still logged in. Close any open the browser windows and then repeat Step 6.

▶ 7. Close the browser window, and then close the pages.

In this session, you learned about creating database-driven Web sites working with a Linux server and a Windows server. Then, you created database-driven Web pages for the Catalyst site using MySQL and PHP for a Linux server. The database functionality will enable Sara and Brian to collect data about their customers' preferences. Analyzing this data will help them shape future marketing plans for Catalyst.

Session 9.1 Quick Check

1. What is a database?
2. What are two popular databases used by medium and small Web sites?
3. In addition to selecting a database you must also select a(n) _____ that you will use to create server behaviors.
4. What language do you use to create server behaviors when you use a MySQL database?
5. What is a server behavior?
6. Why do you need the Recordset behavior?
7. Why would you create a Login page?
8. What is the purpose of the meta refresh tag?

Session 9.2

Creating Database-Driven Pages Using Access and ASP

Adding database functionality to a Web site can be quite complex. Just as it is a good idea to make a plan prior to creating a Web site, it is also a good idea to plan the database-driven portion of the site in advance. Brian has created a site plan for the new portion of the Catalyst site.

Based on his plan, the Catalyst technical team will create a database to store the information collected from the form in the Contact page. You'll modify the form to work with the database. You'll create the pages that you will need for the new portion of the site: thankyou.htm, access_denied.htm, database.asp, database_details.asp, and login.asp. You'll upload the database file provided by the technical team to the remote server, and then you'll connect the site to the database. Next, you'll add server behaviors to the pages you created to enable the form data to be sent to and stored in the database and to enable the database.asp and database_details.asp pages to display the information stored in the database. Finally, you'll create a login.asp page and add code to the backend pages that will prevent unauthorized users from viewing the content of those pages.

When the database-driven pages are complete, the survey information received from users who completed the form in the Contact page will be stored in a database that only authorized users can access.

Reference Window — Creating Database-Driven Pages for a Windows Server

- Create the Web pages you need.
- Upload a database file in which to store data to your remote server.
- Add server behaviors to connect the site to the database.
- Add server behaviors to send and store submitted data in the database and to view the data collected in the database from within designated Web pages.
- Create a Login page.
- Add code to the backend pages to prevent unauthorized users from viewing the content of those pages.

Modifying the Form

Before you create the database-driven pages of the Catalyst site, you'll modify the form in the Contact page to work with the database that you will place on your remote server. You will delete the list box with the band names from the form, and then create a series of checkboxes to collect this same information. You are replacing the list box to keep things simpler because it requires more steps and custom scripts to process data from a list box for storage in a database.

To modify the form:

1. Open the **NewCatalyst** site you modified in the Tutorial 8 Review Assignments, and then open the **contact.htm** page in the Document window.

2. Select the list box in the right column near the bottom of the form, and then press the **Delete** key. The list box is removed from the page.

3. Click the **Checkbox** button in the **Forms** category on the Insert bar to insert the first checkbox, type **sloth_child** in the CheckBox Name text box, click to the right of the checkbox to deselect the checkbox, type **sloth child** beside the checkbox, and then press the **Shift+Enter** keys to move the insertion point down one line. You've entered the first checkbox and label in the form. See Figure 9-23.

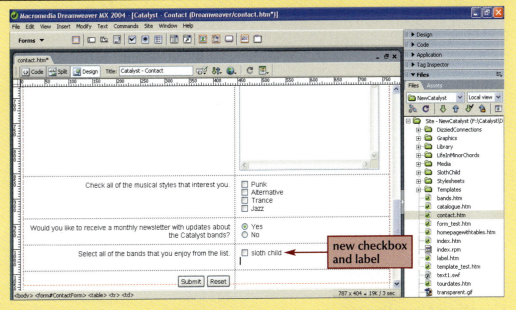

Figure 9-23 — Form in the Contact page

4. Repeat Step 3 to create checkboxes and labels for the following bands, replacing the spaces in the band names with underscores in the CheckBox Name text box: **dizzied connections**, **Life In Minor Chords**, and **surface suction**.

5. Select the sentence in the left column next to the new checkboxes, and then type **Check all of the bands that you enjoy.** (including the period). See Figure 9-24.

Figure 9-24 Modified form

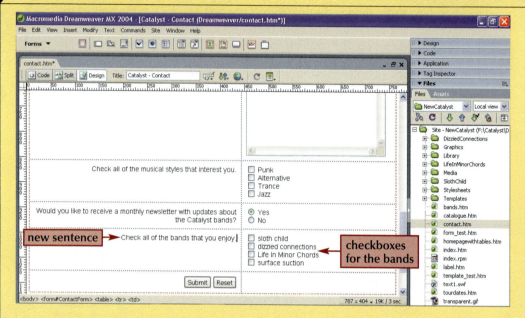

6. Save and close the page, and then upload the page to your remote server.

Next, you'll create the additional pages you need.

Creating New Pages

You need five pages for the database-driven portion of the site. You will create all these pages now so that they will be available when you need them. According to the plan that Brian created for the database-driven portion of the Catalyst site, you will create the following pages:

- **thankyou.htm** - A page thanking the user for his or her submission that displays when the user submits the form in the Contact page.
- **access_denied.htm** - A page informing the user that the wrong user name or password has been entered that displays when a user attempts to log in on the Login page with incorrect information or if a user attempts to access a password-protected page without logging in. After a four-second delay, the user will be returned to the Login page.
- **database.asp** - A page showing an overview of the data stored in the database. Once the Login page is created, users cannot access this page unless they log in.
- **database_details.asp** - A page showing the details of a selected record that displays when a user clicks a record in the Database page. Once the Login page is created, users cannot access this page unless they log in.
- **login.asp** - A page in which a user enters his or her user name and password and then clicks the Login button. If the information is correct, the Database page will display; if the information is incorrect, the Access Denied page will display.

Three of the pages you will create are ASP pages. You can create an ASP page by typing .asp as the file extension when you name the page.

To create pages:

1. Right-click the **contact.htm** page in the Files panel, point to **Edit** on the context menu, and then click **Duplicate**. A new page named Copy of contact.htm appears at the bottom of the list in the Files panel.

2. Right-click the **Copy of contact.htm** page, point to **Edit** on the context menu, click **Rename**, type **thankyou.htm**, and then press the **Enter** key. The page is renamed.

3. Open the **thankyou.htm** page in the Document window, select **Contact** in the Title text box on the Document toolbar, type **Thank you**, and then press the **Enter** key. The new page title is displayed.

4. Double-click the page heading. The Insert Flash Text dialog box opens.

5. Select the text in the Text text box, type **CATALYST THANK YOU**, select the text in the Save As text box, type **Media/HeadingThankyou.swf**, and then click the **OK** button.

6. Select all the content below the heading and above the footer, press the **Delete** key to remove it from the page, and then type **Thank you for submitting your information.** (including the period) in the line below the heading text.

7. Click **Modify** on the menu bar, and then click **Navigation Bar**. The Modify Navigation Bar dialog box opens.

8. Click **Contact** in the Nav Bar Elements list, click the **Show "Down Image" Initially** check box to uncheck it and remove the asterisk from Contact in the Nav Bar Elements list, click the **OK** button, and then click in the Contact page to deselect the navigation bar element. The Contact button is no longer displayed in the Down state. See Figure 9-25.

New thankyou.htm page

Figure 9-25

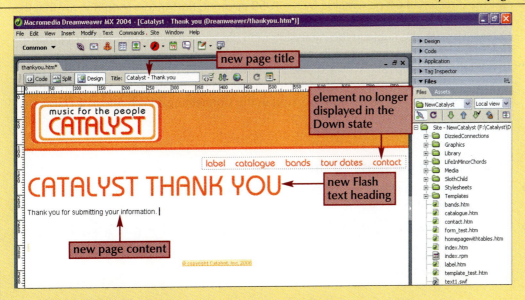

9. Save and close the page, and then upload the page to your remote server.

You'll use the same process to create the rest of the pages, except that you will add content to the pages later (so you will not type any text in Step 6).

10. Repeat Steps 1 through 9 to create the following pages, typing .asp as the file extension for the last three pages in Step 2 and not typing any new page content in Step 6:

Filename	Page Title	Page Heading	Save Page Heading As
access_denied.htm	Catalyst - Access Denied	CATALYST ACCESS DENIED	Media/HeadingAccessDenied.swf
database.asp	Catalyst - Database	CATALYST DATABASE	Media/HeadingDatabase.swf
database_details.asp	Catalyst - Database Details	CATALYST DATABASE DETAILS	Media/HeadingDatabaseDetails.swf
login.asp	Catalyst - Login	CATALYST LOGIN	Media/HeadingLogin.swf

Now that you have modified the form and created the new pages, you are ready to upload the database on your remote server.

Uploading a Database to a Remote Server

You must upload the database for the Catalyst site to your remote server so it can send data to and receive data from Web pages or Web applications. For example, in the Catalyst site, the form in the Contact page will send data to the database that you place on the remote server.

If your instructor has already uploaded the database to your remote server, you should read but not complete the next set of steps. In this case, you will be sharing the same database with your classmates, so you might see data that you did not add in the database or data you added might be removed. If you are uploading the database on your remote server, you will need to contact your ISP (or your IT department) and have them create a directory named "Database" on the remote server and provide you with the exact file path to the directory as well as the FTP host, host directory, login, and password you should use. The directory must be writable by the IUSR account. (Instructors should verify that the new directory is accessible to all of their students.) Once the database directory has been created, you can then upload the catalystdb.mdb file located in the Tutorial.09/Tutorial folder included with your Data Files to the Database directory on the remote server.

The following steps show how to use Dreamweaver to FTP the database file to your remote server. If your instructor has already uploaded the database for you, read the following steps and then continue working in the Connecting a Web Site to a Database section.

To upload the database to the remote server:

1. Click **Site** on the menu bar, and then click **Manage Sites**. The Manage Sites dialog box opens.
2. Click the **New** button, and then click **FTP & RDS Server**. The Configure Server dialog box opens. See Figure 9-26.

Configure Server dialog box ◂ **Figure 9-26**

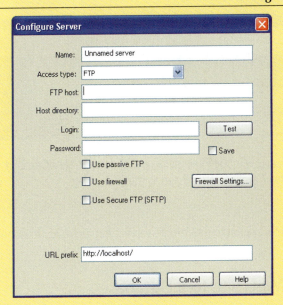

Trouble? If a dialog box opens to remind you that server connections allow you to work directly on the server but do not allow you to perform sitewide operations, click the OK button to close the dialog box. The Configure Server dialog box then opens. Continue with Step 3.

3. Type **RemoteCatalystFTP** in the Name text box, click **FTP** in the Access Type list, and then type the FTP host, host directory, login, and password that your ISP provided into the appropriate text boxes (make sure the host directory ends with /Database/).

4. Click the **Use Passive FTP** check box to insert a check mark, click the **OK** button in the Configure Server dialog box, and then click the **Done** button in the Manage Sites dialog box. The new FTP connection is open in the Files panel. See Figure 9-27.

FTP connection to remote server ◂ **Figure 9-27**

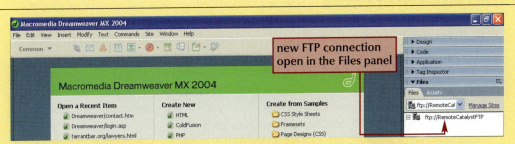

Trouble? If the FTP connection is not open in the Files panel, click the Site list arrow, click ftp://RemoteCatalystFTP, and then continue with Step 5.

5. Click the **Site** list arrow in the Files panel, navigate to the **Tutorial.09\Tutorial** folder included with your Data Files, right-click the **catalystdb.mdb** file, point to **Edit** on the context menu, and then click **Copy** to copy the file.

6. Click the **Site** list arrow in the Files panel, and then click **ftp://RemoteCatalystFTP**. The FTP connection is listed in the Files panel.

7. Right-click **ftp://RemoteCatalystFTP** in the file list, point to **Edit** on the context menu, and then click **Paste**. The catalyst.mdb database file is uploaded to the remote server and is listed in the Files panel. See Figure 9-28.

Figure 9-28   **Database copied to the remote server**

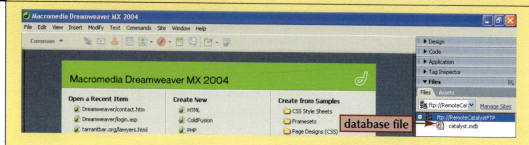

8. Click the **Site** list arrow in the Files panel, and then click **NewCatalyst**. The local root folder for your NewCatalyst site is listed in the Files panel.

Once the database is copied to the remote server, you are ready to connect the Catalyst site to the database.

Connecting a Web Site to a Database

The database is copied to your remote server, and now you are ready to connect the site to the database. When you open a Web page in the Document window that is not connected to the database, the Server Behaviors panel displays an interactive list of steps for setting up Dreamweaver to connect the site to the database. Clicking the linked text in each step opens the dialog boxes needed to complete that step. A check mark appears at the left of each step to indicate that all the necessary information has been entered and the step is completed.

The three main steps for connecting a page to the database are:

1. **Create a site for this file.** This step is checked because you have already set the local and remote information for the site when you created the site definition.
2. **Choose a document type.** In this step, you specify which document type you are using to create server behaviors. When you click the link text in Step 2, the Choose Document Type dialog box opens, and you can select ColdFusion, PHP, ASP JavaScript, ASP VBScript, or JSP as the document type. For the Catalyst site, you will use ASP JavaScript.
3. **Set up the site's testing server.** In this step, you specify the testing server in the site definition. You cannot preview dynamic pages from within Dreamweaver until you specify a folder in which the dynamic pages can be processed. Dreamweaver uses this folder to generate dynamic content and connect to the database while you work. For the Catalyst site, you will use the root folder you created on the remote server for your NewCatalyst site because the server usually runs an application server that can handle the dynamic pages. You can, however, specify a different location for the testing server as long as it can handle dynamic pages. When you set up the testing server for a professional site that is already live, you might designate a separate folder on another server where you can test the pages without affecting the live site. When you click the link text in Step 3, the Site Definition dialog box opens to the Testing Server category. The information for the remote server is displayed by default, but you may need to delete the first part of the file path in the URL Prefix text box.

Some of the files required for server-sided processing are located outside the Web page. Therefore, whenever you upload pages to your remote or testing server, you must also upload dependent files.

You'll open the Contact page and complete Steps 2 and 3 in the Server Behaviors panel.

To select the document type and set the testing server:

1. Open the **contact.htm** page in the Document window, and then click the **document type** link in the Server Behaviors panel in the Application panel group. The Choose Document Type dialog box opens. See Figure 9-29.

Figure 9-29   Choose Document Type dialog box

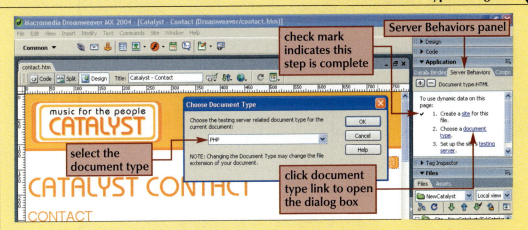

   Trouble? If the document type displayed in your list is different than the document type displayed in the figure, your default is set differently. You will select the document type in Step 2.

2. Click the list arrow, click **ASP JavaScript**, and then click the **OK** button. The Update Files dialog box opens.

3. Click the **Update** button to update the links. The page extension for the Contact page changes to .asp and a check mark appears in the Server Behaviors panel beside Step 2 to indicate this step is complete. The Update Files dialog box opens, indicating that the contact.asp page could not be updated.

   Trouble? When you save an .htm file as an .asp page, Dreamweaver does not insert code that may be necessary to identify the ASP scripting language at the top of the page. If you have an ASP JavaScript site, an .asp file requires the following code at the top of the page to work: <%@LANGUAGE="JAVASCRIPT" CODEPAGE="1252"%>. Without this code, the page may not function on the server, and Dreamweaver may not recognize or add server behaviors correctly. The solution is to manually add the missing code at the top of the file, close the file, and then reopen it in Dreamweaver.

4. Click the **OK** button. You'll update the link in the contact.asp page yourself.

5. Click **Modify** on the menu bar, click **Navigation Bar**, click **Contact** in the Nav Bar Elements list, select **htm** in the When Clicked, Go To URL text box, type **asp** to change the file extension, and then click the **OK** button.

6. Save the page, and then upload the page to your remote server including the dependent files. (The contact.htm page remains in the site's root folder but is no longer used.)

   Next, you'll complete Step 3.

7. Click the **testing server** link in Step 3 in the Server Behaviors panel. The Site Definition for NewCatalyst dialog box opens with the Advanced tab displayed and Testing Server selected in the Category list.

8. Click the **Server Model** list arrow, click **ASP JavaScript**, click the **Access** list arrow, and then click **FTP**. Additional FTP options appear in the dialog box, displaying the information input in the **Remote Info** category.

9. Delete all the file path information in the URL Prefix text box, and then type the URL for your posted site. See Figure 9-30.

Figure 9-30 | **Recordset dialog box**

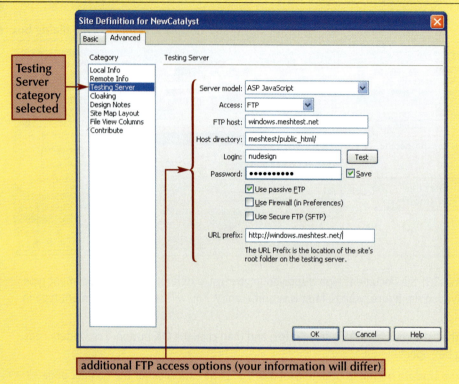

additional FTP access options (your information will differ)

Trouble? If you do not know the URL for your remote site, ask your instructor or technical support for help.

10. Click the **OK** button. The Testing Server information is set and a check mark appears beside Step 3 in the Server Behaviors panel.

Next, you'll add the server behaviors to the ASP page.

Add Server Behaviors

Dreamweaver provides a list of prewritten server behaviors in the Server Behaviors panel once the page is connected to the database. You include these server behaviors in the page to extend the functionality of the page and to enable you to retrieve and display the data from the database.

You will include the following two server behaviors in the contact.asp page.

- **Recordset.** The Recordset behavior enables you to specify which data you want to retrieve from the database and display in the Web page. A **recordset** is a temporary collection of data retrieved from a database and stored on the application server that generates the Web page when that page is loaded in a browser window. You specify the database and the records (or data) to include in the recordset when you set the parameters for the behavior. A recordset can include all the data in the database or a subset of the data. You must add the server-side behaviors that will create the recordset in which to store and retrieve data before you can use a database as a content source for a dynamic Web page. The server discards the recordset when it is no longer needed.

When you use ASP and an Access database, you must input a custom connection string that Dreamweaver inserts into the page's server behaviors to set up the recordset. A **connection string** is all the information that a Web application server needs to connect to a database. The connection string begins and ends with quotation marks; however, Dreamweaver automatically adds the quotation marks when it inserts the connection string into the code. The connection string has two parts:

- **Driver.** The Open Database Connectivity (ODBC) driver enables a database to connect to an application server.
- **DBQ.** The complete file path to the database. You'll need to obtain this information from your instructor, ISP, or IT department.
- **Insert Record.** The insert record behavior enables you to specify what will happen to the information collected from the Web page (in this case, when the form is submitted). You can specify in which database the data will be placed, where the data will be stored in the database, what columns of information will be included, and so forth. It also enables you to select the page that appears in the browser window once the form is submitted.

You'll create a recordset for the contact.asp page.

To create a recordset:

1. Click the **Add Behavior** button at the top of the Server Behaviors panel, and then click **Recordset**. The Recordset dialog box opens. See Figure 9-31.

Figure 9-31 Recordset dialog box

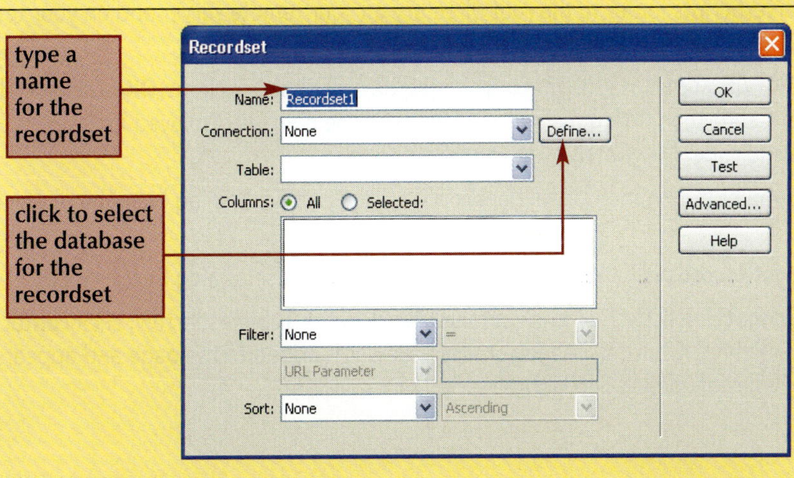

- type a name for the recordset
- click to select the database for the recordset

2. Click the **Define** button next to the Connection text box. The Connections for Site 'NewCatalyst' dialog box opens.
3. Click the **New** button, and then click **Custom Connection String**. The Custom Connection String dialog box opens. See Figure 9-32.

| Figure 9-32 | **Custom Connection String dialog box** |

4. Type **catalystdb** (the name of the database) in the Connection Name text box.

5. In the Connection String text box, type **Driver={Microsoft Access Driver (*.mdb)};DBQ=** and then type the exact path to your database. You did not type quotation marks around the connection string because Dreamweaver will add them automatically; if you type quotation marks, two sets of quotation marks will surround the connection string in the code and the connection string will not work.

6. Click the **Using Driver on Testing Server** option button, if necessary, and then click the **Test** button. A dialog box opens, stating that the connection was made successfully.

   Trouble? If error messages appear when you click the Test button, you probably mistyped the connection string. Click the OK button to close the message dialog box, delete the text in the Connection String text box, retype the information, and then repeat Step 6. If the test is still unsuccessful, verify the file path for your database with your instructor or technical support person and verify the information in the Testing Server category in the Site Definition dialog box. If you still are having trouble, use an outside FTP program to upload the _mmServerScripts folder to the root directory on your remote server and on your testing server if you are using a separate testing server.

7. Click the **OK** button to close the message dialog box, and then click the **OK** button to close the Custom Connection String dialog box. The database name is displayed in the Connections for Site 'NewCatalyst' dialog box.

8. Click the **Done** button in the Connections for Site 'NewCatalyst' dialog box. The dialog box closes.

9. Type **CatalystRecordset** in the Name text box of the Recordset dialog box.

10. Click the **Connection** list arrow, click **catalystdb**, click the **Table** list arrow, click **contact**, and then click the **OK** button. The Recordset behavior is added to the page and appears in the Server Behaviors panel. See Figure 9-33.

Recordset behavior added to the contact.asp page   Figure 9-33

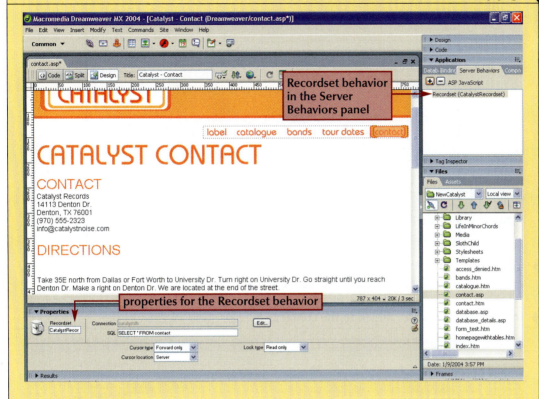

Next, you'll add the Insert Record behavior to the page.

To add the Insert Record behavior:

1. Click the **Add Behavior** button at the top of the Server Behaviors panel, and then click **Insert Record**. The Insert Record dialog box opens.

2. Click the **Connection** list arrow and click **catalystdb**, and then click the **Insert Into Table** list arrow and click **contact**.

3. Click the **Browse** button next to the After Inserting, Go To text box. The Select File dialog box opens.

4. Click **thankyou.htm** in the site's local root folder, and then click the **OK** button. The Select File dialog box closes, and the page is displayed in the text box.

5. Click the **Get Values From** list arrow, and then click **ContactForm**, if necessary. The contact form's elements are displayed in the Form Elements list and the column headings in the contact table are displayed in the Column list. See Figure 9-34.

| Figure 9-34 | **Insert Record dialog box** |

6. Click the **OK** button in the Insert Record dialog box. The Insert Record behavior is added to the page and appears in the Server Behaviors panel. See Figure 9-35.

| Figure 9-35 | **Insert Record behavior added to the contact.asp page** |

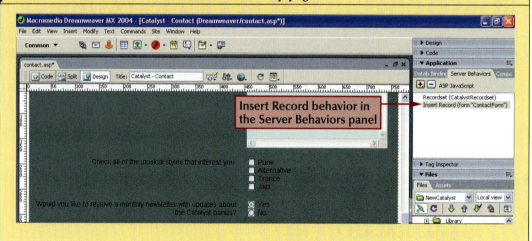

Before continuing, you'll test the Insert Record behavior you added to the contact.asp page. You need to upload the page to the remote server, preview the page in a browser, and then complete and submit the form. The Thank You page should then display.

To test the Insert Record behavior:

1. Save the page, and then upload the page to your remote server.
2. Preview the contact.asp page in a browser, enter appropriate information in the form, and then click the **Submit** button to submit the form. The Thank You page displays in the browser window.
3. Close the browser window.

The page is connected to the database, and the behaviors have been added to the page. Next, you will create pages that enable you to view the data collected in the database.

Creating Backend Pages for Viewing Data in a Database

Pages that are intended for internal use are usually called backend pages. For the Catalyst site, the Database and Database Details pages are backend pages. You will set the database.asp and database_details.asp pages to display the data that you collect in the database. The Master/Detail Page Set button in the Application category on the Insert bar enables you to create a set of pages that present information in two levels of detail. The master page (in this case, the database.asp page) lists all the records in the recordset that you create for the page. The detail page (in this case, the database_details.asp page) displays the detail of the selected record. You determine which fields of information are displayed in the master page and which fields of information are displayed in the detail page when you set the parameters for the pages. In addition to creating all the code necessary to display the dynamic content in the pages, Dreamweaver also adds server behaviors to create page navigation bar that enables you to move between the dynamic records if there are more records in the database than are displayed in the page. The navigation bar includes First Page, Last Page, Previous Page, and Next Page buttons. The pages also include Display Record Count server behaviors to indicate which records are visible in the page and the total number of records in the database (Records x to y of z).

To create the master page:

1. Click **Recordset** in the Server Behaviors panel, right-click the selected behavior, and then click **Copy** on the context menu.

2. Open the **database_details.asp** page in the Document window, right-click in the Server Behaviors panel, and then click **Paste** on the context menu. The Recordset behavior is pasted in the Database Details page.

3. Place the insertion point in the heading line after the heading text, press the **Right Arrow** key to move the insertion point past the heading text, and then press the **Enter** key to move the insertion point to the next line.

    Trouble? If Dreamweaver locks up, then you've encountered a bug in Dreamweaver that causes the program to lock up if you place the insertion point in the line below the heading and then press the Enter key when using server behaviors. End the program, restart the computer, and then repeat Steps 1 through 3.

4. Open the **database.asp** page in the Document window, right-click in the Server Behaviors panel, click **Paste** on the context menu to paste the Recordset behavior into the page, place the insertion point in the heading line, press the **Right Arrow** key to move the insertion point past the heading text, and then press the **Enter** key to move the insertion point to the next line.

5. Click the **Master Detail Page Set** button in the **Application** category on the Insert bar. The Insert Master-Detail Page Set dialog box opens. See Figure 9-36.

Figure 9-36 | Insert Master-Detail Page Set dialog box

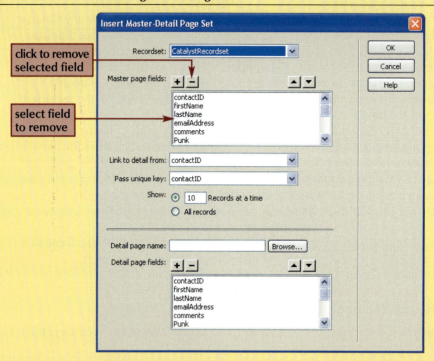

You will remove the fields from the Master Page Fields list that you do not want to display in the master page. You'll also change the field order so that the last name will appear in the first column.

▶ 6. Click **contactID** in the Master Page Fields list, and then click the **Remove Item** button ▬ above the Master Page Fields list. The selected field name is removed from the list.

▶ 7. Repeat Step 6 to delete the following field names: **comments**, **Punk**, **Alternative**, **Trance**, **Jazz**, **sloth_child**, **dizzied_connections**, **Life_In_Minor_Chords**, and **surface_suction**. Only the names of fields that will be visible in the Database page appear in the Master Page Fields list.

▶ 8. Click **lastName** in the Master Page Fields list, and then click the **Move Item Up** button ▲ located above the Master Page Fields list until the lastName field is at the top of the list. The fields will display in the page in the same order they appear in the list.

▶ 9. Click the **Link To Detail From** list arrow, and then click **lastName**. The data in the lastName field of the Database page is now linked to the record details, which will display in the Database Details page.

You'll set the record details to display in the database_details.asp page. As with the master page, you'll delete unneeded fields and change the field order for the details page.

To create the detail page:

1. Click the **Browse** button next to the Detail Page Name text box, click the **database_details.asp** page in the Select Detail Page dialog box, and then click the **OK** button. The page name appears in the Detail Page Name text box.
2. Click **contactID** in the Detail Page Fields list, and then click the **Remove Item** button. The field name is removed from the list and the field will not be displayed in the Database Details page.
3. Click the **Newsletter** field in the Detail Page Fields list, and then click the **Move Item Up** button until the field name is directly below the emailAddress field. See Figure 9-37.

Figure 9-41

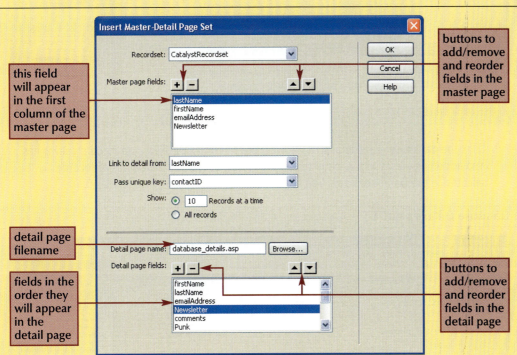

4. Click the **OK** button. The dialog box closes, and the master/detail pages are complete.

Dreamweaver adds elements to the pages that will enable you to view the data collected in the database as well as the details of selected records. Before continuing, you'll upload the pages to the remote server and preview the pages in the browser.

To view the Database Details page:

1. Save the Database page, and then upload the page to your remote server. Dreamweaver adds elements to the page that will enable you to view the data collected in the database. See Figure 9-38.

DRM 522 | Dreamweaver | Tutorial 9 Adding Database Functionality

Figure 9-38   **Database page**

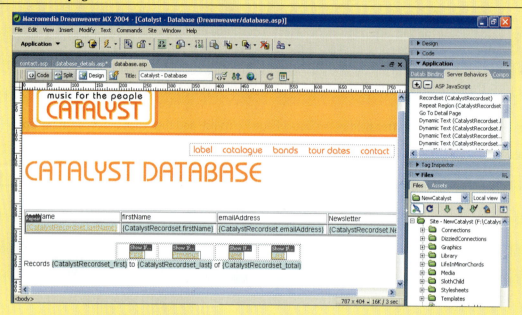

▶ 2. Click the **database_details.asp** tab to view the Database Details page. Dreamweaver has also added elements to this page that will enable you to view the details of records selected in the Database page. See Figure 9-39.

Figure 9-39   **Database Details page**

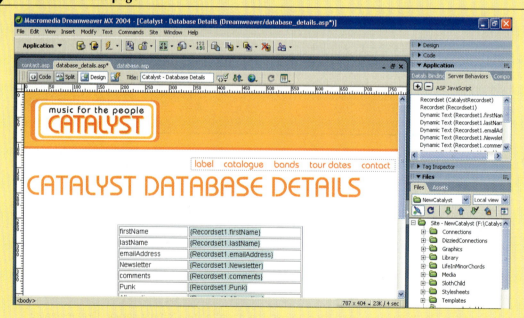

▶ 3. Save the page, and then upload the page to your remote server.

▶ 4. Click the **database.asp** tab, and then preview the page in a browser, clicking the **No** button when Dreamweaver asks you to upload the changes to the testing server because you have already done that (remember, your testing server and remote server are the same). The data you have collected from the form in the Contact page is displayed in the browser window. See Figure 9-40.

Figure 9-40

Database page previewed in a browser

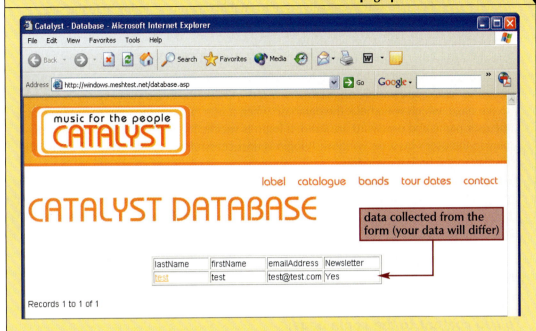

data collected from the form (your data will differ)

Trouble? If you see more than the one record you entered into the contact form, then you are sharing the database with classmates and the database will include all the entries that have been submitted. In a professional environment, this would probably not be the case.

5. Click a link to view the details of a record. The details are displayed in the Database Details page.

6. Click the **Back** button on the browser toolbar to return to the Database page, and then click another record if available.

7. Close the browser window, and then close all the pages.

Next, you will create a Login page to protect the data from unauthorized access.

Creating a Login Page to Protect Backend Pages

Data collected from a Web site and stored in a database is often displayed in Web pages. This convenience enables you to view the data from any computer that is connected to the Internet. However, most businesses do not want the general public to have access to this type of proprietary information. One way to restrict the access to Web pages is to require users to log in before they can view the pages. To add this functionality to pages you must:

- **Create a table in the database that holds user names and passwords.** The team that created the database included an administrative table with columns to collect user names and passwords. They also added one user name (catalyst) and one password (feelinit) in the table. You will use the user name and password included in the database to create and test the Login page. You will create additional pages that will enable users to create unique user names and passwords in the Review Assignments.
- **Create a page that enables users to create accounts by entering a unique user name and password.** Because only one member of the Catalyst staff is in charge of monitoring and reporting the information collected in the database, you won't create this page

now. The team member will use the supplied user name and password to log in to protected pages. Because you eventually want to enable other users to log in to the site, you will create additional pages that will enable users to create unique user names and passwords in the Review Assignments.

- **Create a page that enables users to log in to the site.** You have already created the Login page. Now you will create a form in the Login page that enables users to input their user name and password information. You will add the Log In User server behavior to the page, which will check the database when a user submits the form to ensure that the user name and password are valid. If login is successful, the Database page will display in the user's browser window. If login is unsuccessful, the Access Denied page will display in the browser window.
- **Restrict access to the pages.** You add the Restrict Access To Page server behavior to the pages that you want to protect, in this case, the Database and Database Details pages. Once this behavior is added to the pages, users who are not logged in will be sent to the Access Denied page.

You'll create the form in the Login page, and then add the Log In User server behavior to the page.

To add content to the Login page:

1. Open the **login.asp** page in the Document window, place the insertion point in the heading line, press the **Right Arrow** key until the insertion point is positioned at the right of the heading text, and then press the **Enter** key. The insertion point moves to the next line.

2. Click the **Form** button in the **Forms** category on the Insert bar. The code for a form is inserted into the page.

3. Type **loginform** in the Form Name text box in the Property inspector. For this form, it is not necessary to enter information for the other attributes in the Property inspector because you will add behaviors to control the form.

4. Click inside of the form area (the dotted red lines), and then click the **Table** button in the **Common** category on the Insert bar. The Table dialog box opens.

5. Type **3** in the Rows text box, type **2** in the Columns text box, type **80** percent in the Table Width text boxes, type **2** in the Cell Padding text box, type **2** in the Cell Spacing text box, and then click the **OK** button. The table is inserted into the form.

6. Select the left column, click the **Horz** list arrow in the Property inspector and click **Right**, click the **Vert** list arrow in the Property inspector and click **Top**, select the right column, click the **Horz** list arrow in the Property inspector and click **Left**, and then click the **Vert** list arrow in the Property inspector and click **Top**.

7. Click in the first cell of the table, type **User name:** (including the colon), press the **Tab** key to move the insertion point to the upper-right cell, and then click the **Text Field** button in the **Forms** category on the Insert bar to insert a text field.

8. Type **username** in the TextField text box, type **40** in the Char Width text box, and then type **20** in the Max Chars text box.

9. Click in the middle-left cell, type **Password:** (including the colon), and then press the **Tab** key to move the insertion point to the next cell.

10. Click the **Text Field** button in the **Forms** category on the Insert bar, type **password** in the TextField text box, type **40** in the Char Width text box, and then type **20** in the Max Chars text box.
11. Click in the bottom-right cell, click the **Button** button in the **Forms** category on the Insert bar, and then type **Login** in the Button Name and Label text boxes. See Figure 9-41.

Figure 9-41

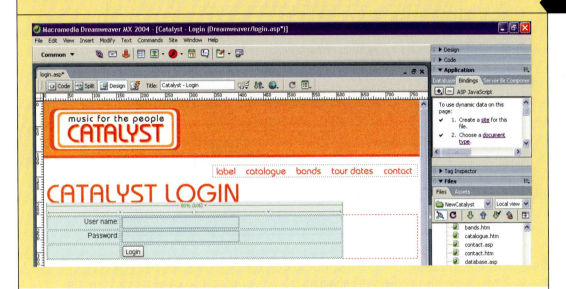

Next, you'll add the Log In User server behavior to the page, which will verify the submitted user name and password.

To add server behaviors to the Login page:

1. Select the **Login** button in the form, and then click **Log In User** in the **User Authentication** list in the **Application** category on the Insert bar. The Log In User dialog box opens.
2. Click **catalystdb** in the Validate Using Connection list, click **admin** in the Table list, if necessary, click **username** in the Username Column list, and then click **password** in the Password Column list.
3. Click the **Browse** button next to the If Login Succeeds, Go To text box, click the **database.asp** page in the Select File dialog box, and then click the **OK** button.
4. Click the **Browse** button next to the If Login Fails, Go To text box, click the **access_denied.htm** page in the Select File dialog box, and then click the **OK** button. This sets the Access Denied page to display in the browser window if the submitted user name and password are not listed in the database. See Figure 9-42.

Figure 9-42   Log In User dialog box

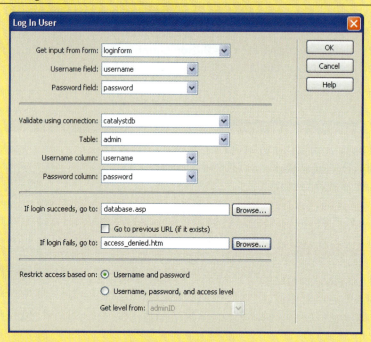

- 5. Click the **OK** button. The Log In User server behavior is added to the page.
- 6. If necessary, click the **Server Behaviors** tab in the Application panel group to see the server behaviors list.
- 7. Save the page, and then upload the page to your remote server.

You'll add text and a meta refresh tag to the Access Denied page, which tells the browser to automatically refresh the page (by reloading the current page or going to a different page) after a certain amount of time. You'll also add text to indicate that access was denied to that user.

To add content and a meta refresh tag to the Access Denied page:

- 1. Open the **access_denied.htm** page in the Document window.
- 2. Click the **Refresh** button in the **Head** list in the **HTML** category on the Insert bar. The Refresh dialog box opens.
- 3. Type **4** in the Delay text box, and then type **login.asp** in the Go To URL text box. See Figure 9-43.

Figure 9-43   Refresh dialog box

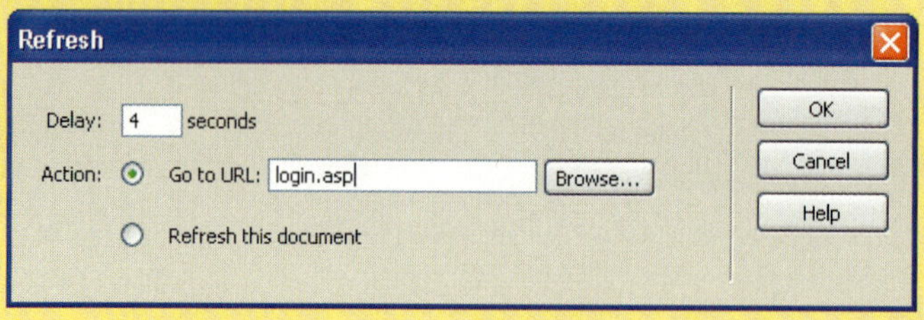

4. Click the **OK** button, place the insertion point after the heading, press the **Enter** key, and then type **Your access was denied. Please enter your login ID and password again.** (including the period).

5. Save the page, and then upload the page to your remote server.

Before you continue, you'll test the Login page and the behaviors you added to the Database and Access Denied pages.

To test the Login page:

1. Preview the login.asp page in a browser.

   The Update Copy on Testing Server dialog box opens.

2. Click the **Yes** button to ensure that the most recent copy of the page is on both the testing and remote servers. The Dependent Files dialog box opens.

3. Click the **Yes** button to ensure that all the dependent files are current on both the testing and remote servers. The Login page displays in the browser window.

   Trouble? If the message, "Warning: session_start():" followed by a file path and "failed: Permission denied" appears when you test the page on your remote server, you may need to adjust the permissions on your Web server's temporary directory (usually tmp) so that it is writable by the server. Contact your ISP or technical support person for assistance.

   You'll enter an invalid user name and password.

4. Type **test** in the User Name text box, type **test** in the Password text box, and then click the **Login** button. The login information is invalid, so the access_denied.htm page is displayed in the browser window. After four seconds, the Login page is redisplayed.

   Now, you'll enter a valid user name and password.

5. Type **catalyst** in the User Name text box, type **feelinit** in the Password text box, and then click the **Login** button. The Database page is displayed in the browser window.

6. Close the browser window, and then close the pages.

Finally, you will protect the Database and Database Details pages from unauthorized access by adding the Restrict Access server behavior to the page.

To restrict access to pages:

1. Open the **database.asp** page in the Document window.

2. Click the **Restrict Access To Page** button in the **User Authentication** list in the **Application** category on the Insert bar. The Restrict Access To Page dialog box opens.

3. Type **access_denied.htm** in the If Access Denied, Go To text box. See Figure 9-44.

Figure 9-44 Restrict Access To Page dialog box

4. Click the **OK** button, save the page, and then upload the page to your remote server.
5. Open the **database_details.asp** page in the Document window, and then repeat Steps 2 through 4 to restrict access to that page.

   Next, you'll test the behavior you added to the pages.
6. Preview the database.asp page in a browser. Because you are not logged in, the Database page will not display in the browser window. Instead, the Access Denied page is displayed for four seconds and then the Login page is displayed.

   Trouble? If the Database page does display, you did not close the browser window after you logged in and you are still logged in. Close any open browser windows and repeat Step 6.
7. Close the browser window, and then close the pages.

In this session, you created database-driven Web pages for the Catalyst site using Access and ASP for a Windows server. The database functionality will enable Sara and Brian to collect data about their customers' preferences. Analyzing this data will help them shape future marketing plans for Catalyst.

Review | Session 9.2 Quick Check

1. In addition to selecting a database, you must also select a(n) _____ that you will use to create server behaviors.
2. What language do you use to create server behaviors when you use an Access database?
3. What is a server behavior?
4. Why do you need the Recordset behavior?
5. Why would you create a Login page?
6. What is the purpose of the meta refresh tag?

Review | Tutorial Summary

In this tutorial, you learned about creating database-driven Web sites working with a Linux server and a Windows server. Then, you created database-driven Web pages for the Catalyst site using MySQL and PHP for a Linux server or using Access and ASP for a Windows server. To do this, you created the Web pages you needed, you placed or created the database on your remote server, you added server behaviors to connect the database to the form, you added server behaviors to Web pages to view the data collected in the database, you added content to the Login page, and then you set the Database and Database Details pages to display only when a user has logged in to the site with a valid user name and password.

Key Terms

connection string
database
database-driven Web site
dynamically generated
recordset
server behavior
SQL
Web site

Practice

Practice the skills you learned in the tutorial

Review Assignments

There are no Data Files needed for the Review Assignments.

Sara and Brian want you to create a Login Admin page that will enable users who already have user names and passwords to create new user accounts and create a page to display record details. You'll also create a master/details page set, using the Login Admin page as the master page so that you can view the user account information as soon as you create a new account. Finally, you will restrict access to the new pages so that only users that already have user accounts can enable other users to view the information.

If you are using MySQL and PHP on a Linux server, complete the following steps:

1. Open the NewCatalyst site you modified in the tutorial, right-click the login.php page in the Files panel, point to Edit on the context menu, and then click Duplicate.
2. Right-click the Copy of login.php page in the Files panel, click Rename on the context menu, type "login_admin.php" as the new filename, and then press the Enter key.
3. Open the login_admin.php page, and then type "Catalyst - Login Administration" in the Title text box on the Document toolbar.
4. Double-click the heading text to open the Insert Flash Text dialog box, type "CATALYST LOGIN ADMIN" in the Text text box, type "Media/HeadingLoginAdmin.swf" in the Save As text box, and then click the OK button.
5. Repeat Steps 1 through 4 to create an admin_details.php page, using "Catalyst - Login Administration Details" as the page title, "CATALYST LOGIN ADMIN DETAILS" as the page heading, and "Media/HeadingLoginAdminDetails.swf" as the page heading filename.
6. Select the form in the login_admin.php page, type "loginadminform" in the Form Name text box, and then press the Enter key.
7. Click the Login button, type "Add" in the Button Name text box, type "Add" in the Label text box, and then press the Enter key.
8. Click the Log In User server behavior in the Server Behaviors panel, and then click the Remove button to delete the behavior.
9. Click the Add Behavior button in the Server Behaviors panel, click Recordset to open the Recordset dialog box, type "loginadmin" in the Name text box, click CatalystDBconnection in the Connection list, click admin in the Table list, if necessary, and then click the OK button.
10. Click the Add Behavior button in the Server Behaviors panel, click Insert Record to open the Insert Record dialog box, click CatalystDBconnection in the Connection list, click admin in the Insert Table list, if necessary, type "login_admin.php" in the After Inserting, Go To text box (because you will display the results in this page), and then click the OK button.
11. Click the admin_details.php tab to display the page, click the Log In User server behavior in the Server Behaviors panel, click the Remove button to delete the

behavior, and then click the form to select it and press the Delete key. (*Hint:* The details table will be inserted in the blank line below the heading text where the insertion point is located in the page.)

12. Click the login_admin.php tab to display the page, click in the blank line below the form, and then click the Master Details Page Set button in the Application category on the Insert bar.

13. Click adminID in the Master Page Fields list, click the Remove Item button, type "admin_details.php" in the Detail Page Name text box, and then click the OK button. The admin_details.php page displays, and the details table and server behaviors have been added to the page. (*Hint:* If the admin_details.php page does not display, click the admin_details.php tab to view the page in the Document window.)

14. Save the page, and then upload the page to your remote server.

15. Click the login_admin.php tab to display the page and see an overview of the admin table content in the database below the loginadmin form.

16. Save the page, upload the page to your remote server, and then preview the page in a browser.

17. Type a user name and a password in the appropriate text boxes, click the Add button (your new user name and password appear in the table below the form), click your new user name to display the admin_details.php page, and then close the browser window.

18. Click Restrict Access To Page in the User Authentication list in the Application category on the Insert bar to open the Restrict Access To Page dialog box, type "access_denied.htm" in the If Access Denied, Go To text box, click the OK button, save the page, and then upload the page to your remote server. Users who do not already have user accounts cannot access this page.

19. Click the admin_details.php tab, and then repeat Step 18 to restrict access to that page.

20. Click the login_admin.php tab, place the insertion point to the right of the heading text, and press the Enter key to move the insertion point to the next line, type "To the database page," select the text, and then create a hyperlink to the database.php page. Save the page, upload the page to your remote server, and then close the page.

21. Open the database.php page, place the insertion point to the right of the heading text, press the Enter key to move the insertion point to the next line, type "To the login admin page," select the text, and then create a hyperlink to the login_admin.php page. Save the page, upload the page to your remote server, and then close the page.

22. In the admin_details.php page, place the insertion point to the right of the heading text, press the Enter key to move the insertion point to the next line, type "To the login admin page," select the text, and then create a hyperlink to the login_admin.php page. Save the page, upload the page to your remote server, and then close the page.

23. Preview the login.php page in a browser window, enter your user name and password in the appropriate text boxes, click the Login button, click the To login admin page link in the Database page, create a new user account by adding a new user name and password, and then close the browser window and any open pages.

If you are using Access and ASP on a Windows server, complete the following steps:

1. Open the NewCatalyst site you modified in the tutorial, right-click the login.asp page in the Files panel, point to Edit on the context menu, and then click Duplicate.

2. Right-click the Copy of login.asp page in the Files panel, click Rename on the context menu, type "login_admin.asp" as the new filename, and then press the Enter key.

3. Open the login_admin.asp page, and then type "Catalyst - Login Administration" in the Title text box on the Document toolbar.
4. Double-click the heading text to open the Insert Flash Text dialog box, type "CATALYST LOGIN ADMIN" in the Text text box, type "Media/HeadingLoginAdmin.swf" in the Save As text box, and then click the OK button.
5. Repeat Steps 1 through 4 to create an admin_details.asp page, using "Catalyst - Login Administration Details" as the page title, "CATALYST LOGIN ADMIN DETAILS" as the page heading, and "Media/HeadingLoginAdminDetails.swf" as the page heading filename.
6. Select the form in the login_admin.asp page, type "loginadminform" in the Form Name text box, and then press the Enter key.
7. Click the Login button, type "Add" in the Button Name text box, type "Add" in the Label text box, and then press the Enter key.
8. Click the Log In User server behavior in the Server Behaviors panel, and then click the Remove button to delete the behavior.
9. Click the Add Behavior button in the Server Behaviors panel, click Recordset to open the Recordset dialog box, type "loginadmin" in the Name text box, click catalystdb in the Connection list, click admin in the Table list, if necessary, and then click the OK button.
10. Click the Add Behavior button in the Server Behaviors panel, click Insert Record to open the Insert Record dialog box, click catalystdb in the Connection list, click admin in the Insert Into Table list, if necessary, type "login_admin.asp" in the After Inserting, Go To text box (because you will display the results in this page), and then click the OK button.
11. Click the admin_details.asp tab to display the page, click the Log In User server behavior in the Server Behaviors panel, click the Remove button to delete the behavior, and then select the form in the Document window and press the Delete key. (*Hint:* The details table will be inserted in the blank line below the heading text where the insertion point is located in the page.)
12. Click the login_admin.asp tab to display the page, click in the blank line below the form, and then click the Master Detail Page Set button in the Application category on the Insert bar.
13. Click adminID in the Master Page Fields list, click the Remove Item button, type "admin_details.asp" in the Detail Page Name text box, and then click the OK button. The admin_details.asp page displays and the details table and server behaviors have been added to the page.
14. Save the page, and then upload the page to your remote server.
15. Click the login_admin.asp tab to display the page and see an overview of the admin table content in the database below the loginadmin form.
16. Save the page, upload the page to your remote server, and then preview the page in a browser.
17. Type a user name and a password in the appropriate text boxes, click the Add button (your new user name and password appear in the table below the form), click your new user name to display the admin_details.asp page, and then close the browser window.
18. Click the Restrict Access To Page button in the User Authentication list in the Application category on the Insert bar to open the Restrict Access To Page dialog box, type "access_denied.htm" in the If Access Denied, Go To text box, click the OK button, save the page, and then upload the page to your remote server. Users who do not already have user accounts cannot access this page.
19. Click the admin_details.asp tab, and then repeat Step 18 to restrict access to that page.

20. Click the login_admin.asp tab, place the insertion point to the right of the heading text, press the Enter key to move the insertion point to the next line, type "To the database page," select the text, and then create a hyperlink to the database.asp page. Save the page, upload the page to your remote server, and then close the page.
21. Open the database.asp page, place the insertion point to the right of the heading text, press the Enter key to move the insertion point to the next line, type "To the login admin page," select the text, and then create a hyperlink to the login_admin.asp page. Save the page, upload the page to your remote server, and then close the page.
22. In the admin_details.asp page, place the insertion point to the right of the heading text, press the Enter key to move the insertion point to the next line, type "To the login admin page," select the text, and then create a hyperlink to the login_admin.asp page. Save the page, upload the page to your remote server, and then close the page.
23. Open the login.asp page in a browser window, enter your user name and password in the appropriate text boxes, click the Login button, click the To login admin page link in the Database page, create a new user account by adding a new user name and password, and then close the browser window and any open pages.

Case Problem 1

Challenge

Add database-driven pages to display social anthropologist Dr. Matt Hart's journal entries in a Web site on small rural communities in northern Vietnam.

Data Files needed for this Case Problem: hartdb.mdb or hartdb.sql

Hroch University Anthropology Department Dr. Matt Hart is reviewing his research on the rituals and practices of the small rural communities in northern Vietnam and has decided that site visitors would be interested in seeing some of his notes. He wants to be able to make ongoing journal entries that will automatically display in the Rituals and Practices page. You'll create database-driven pages to create a tool that will enable him to do this.

If you are using MySQL and PHP on a Linux server, complete the following steps:

1. Open the Hart site you modified in Tutorial 8, Case Problem 1.
2. Duplicate the contact.htm page in the Files panel, rename the copied page as "journal.php," and then update the links in the file.
3. Open the journal.php page in the Document window, select the heading text and type "Journal Entry," replace "Contact" in the Title text box on the Document toolbar with "Journal Entry," and then delete the content between the heading text and the footer in the page.
4. Insert a form in the page, enter "journalentry" as the form name, and then insert a table with 2 rows, 2 columns, 90% table width, 0 border thickness, 3 cell padding, and 0 cell spacing in the form.
5. Type "journal entry" in the upper-left cell, select the text, and then align the text to the Right and Top.

Explore

6. Insert a text field in the upper-right cell, name the field "journalentry," click the Multi Line option button, set the character width to 80 and the number of lines to 10, add a Submit button in the lower-right cell, and then save the page.
7. Modify the navigation bar to no longer display the Contact Information element in the Down state initially.
8. Ask your instructor for the information you need to connect to an existing database or create the database on your remote server using the **hartdb.sql** file located in the **Tutorial.09\Cases** folder included with your Data Files. (*Hint*: Obtain the information you need from your instructor or technical support person.)

9. Expand the Server Behaviors panel in the Application panel group, click the document type link in Step 2, select PHP as the document type, and then click the OK button.
10. Click the testing server link in Step 3, click PHP MySQL in the Server Model list, click FTP in the Access list, delete all the file path information from the URL Prefix text box, type the URL for your remote site, and then click the OK button.
11. Click the Add Behavior button in the Server Behaviors panel, click Recordset, type "HartRecordset" in the Name text box, click the Define button next to the Connection text box, click the New button, type "HartDBconnection" in the Connection Name text box, type "localhost" or the database server URL in the MySQL Server text box, type your user name and password in their respective text boxes, click the Select button to display a list of databases, click hartdb in the list, click the OK button, click the Done button, click HartDBconnection in the Connection list, click journal in the Table list, and then click the OK button. The Recordset behavior is added to the page and appears in the Server Behaviors panel.
12. Click the Add Behavior button in the Server Behaviors panel, click Insert Record, click journalentry in the Submit Values From list, if necessary, click HartDBconnection in the Connection list, click journal in the Insert Table list, click 'journal' Does Not Get a Value. in the Columns list, click FORM.journalentry in the Value list, click Text in the Submit As list if necessary, click the Browse button, click the rituals_and_practices.htm page in the site's local root directory, and then click the OK button in each dialog box. The Insert Record behavior is added to the page and appears in the Server Behaviors panel.
13. Save the page, upload the page to your remote server (include dependent files), preview the page in a browser, updating the page and the dependent files on the testing server if necessary, and then close the browser window.
14. Open the rituals_and_practices.htm page, click the document type link in the Server Behaviors panel, select PHP in the list, click the OK button, click the Update button to update the links in the pages, click the OK button in the message dialog box, and then update the Rituals & Practices element in the navigation bar in the rituals_and_practices.php page so that rituals_and_practices.php appears in the When Clicked, Go To URL text box.
15. Click the journalentry.php tab, right-click the Recordset behavior in the Server Behaviors panel, click Copy on the context menu, click the rituals_and_practices.php tab, right-click in the Server Behaviors panel, and then click Paste on the context menu to paste the Recordset behavior into the page.

Explore
16. Double-click the Recordset behavior in the Server Behaviors panel to open the Recordset dialog box, click the Selected option button in the Columns section, click journal in the Columns list box, and then click the OK button.

Explore
17. Delete the "Research in process, check back soon." text, click the Dynamic Table button in the Dynamic Data list in the Application category on the Insert bar, click the All Records option button, type "0" in the Border text box, type "3" in the Cell Padding text box, and then click the OK button.
18. Save the page, upload the rituals_and_practices.php page to your remote server (include dependent files), preview the journal.php page in a browser (updating the page and dependent files on the testing server if necessary), type a test entry in the form, and then click the Submit button to submit the form. The rituals_and_practices.php page with the new entry displays in the browser window. (*Hint*: If you are sharing a database with classmates, you may see additional entries in the database.)
19. Close the browser window and the pages.

If you are using Access and ASP on a Windows server, complete the following steps:

1. Open the Hart site you modified in Tutorial 8, Case Problem 1.
2. Duplicate the contact.htm page in the Files panel, rename the copied page as "journal.asp," and then update the links in the file.
3. Open the journal.asp page in the Document window, select the heading text and type "Journal Entry," replace "Contact" in the Title text box on the Document toolbar with "Journal Entry," and then delete the content between the heading text and the footer in the page.
4. Insert a form in the page, enter "journalentry" as the form name, and then insert a table with 2 rows, 2 columns, 90% table width, 0 border thickness, 3 cell padding, and 0 cell spacing in the form.
5. Type "journal entry" in the upper-left cell, select the text, and then align the text to the Right and Top.

Explore

6. Insert a text field in the upper-right cell, name the field "journalentry," click the Multi Line option button, set the character width to 80 and the number of lines to 10, add a Submit button in the lower-right cell, and then save the page.
7. Modify the navigation bar to no longer display the Contact Information element in the Down state initially.
8. Ask your instructor for the information you need to connect to an existing database or upload the database on your remote server using an FTP program and the **hartdb.mdb** file located in the **Tutorial.09\Cases** folder included with your Data Files. (*Hint*: Obtain the information you need from your instructor or technical support person.)
9. Expand the Server Behaviors panel in the Application panel group, click the document type link in Step 2, click ASP JavaScript in the list, if necessary, and then update the links.
10. Click the testing server link in Step 3, click ASP JavaScript in the Server Model list, click FTP in the Access list, delete all the file path information from the URL Prefix text box, type the URL for your posted site, and then click the OK button.
11. Click the Add Behavior button in the Server Behaviors panel, click Recordset, type "HartRecordset" in the Name text box, click the Define button, click the New button, click Custom Connection String, type "HartDBconnection" in the Connection Name text box, type "Driver={Microsoft Access Driver (*.mdb)};DBQ=" and the exact path to your database in the Connection String text box, click the Using Driver on Testing Server option button, if necessary, click the Test button, click the OK button to close the dialog box that indicates the connection was made successfully, click the Done button to close the Custom Connection String dialog box, click HartDBconnection in the Connection list, click journal in the Table list, and then click the OK button. The Recordset behavior is added to the page and appears in the Server Behaviors panel. (*Hint*: Do not put quotation marks around the connection string because Dreamweaver will do it. If you do not know the exact path to your database, ask your instructor or technical support person. If the test is unsuccessful, double-check the connection string and file path for your database or use an outside FTP program to upload the _mmServerScripts folder to the root folder on your remote server and your testing server if you're using a separate testing server.)
12. Click the Add Behavior button in the Server Behaviors panel, click Insert Record, click HartDBconnection in the Connection list, click journal in the Insert Into Table list, click the Browse button, click the rituals_and_practices.htm page in the site's local root folder, click the OK button, click journalentry in the Get Values From list, if necessary, click journal in the Column list, click journalentry inserts into column

"journal" (Text) in the Form Elements list, and then click the OK button. The Insert Record behavior is added to the page and appears in the Server Behaviors panel.

13. Save the page, upload the page to your remote server (include dependent files), and then preview the page in a browser.

14. Open the rituals_and_practices.htm page, click the document type link in the Server Behaviors panel, select ASP JavaScript in the list, click the OK button, click the Update button to update the links in the pages, click the OK button in the message dialog box, and then update the Rituals & Practices element in the navigation bar in the rituals_and_practices.asp page so that rituals_and_practices.asp appears in the When Clicked, Go To URL text box.

15. Click the journalentry.asp tab, right-click the Recordset behavior in the Server Behaviors panel, click Copy on the context menu, click the rituals_and_practices.asp tab, right-click in the Server Behaviors panel, and then click Paste on the context menu to paste the Recordset behavior into the page.

Explore

16. Double-click the Recordset behavior in the Server Behaviors panel to open the Recordset dialog box, click the Selected option button in the Columns section, click journal in the Columns list box, and then click the OK button.

Explore

17. Delete the "Research in process, check back soon." text, click the Dynamic Table button in the Dynamic Data list in the Application category on the Insert bar, click the All Records button, type "0" in the Border text box, type "3" in the Cell Padding text box, and then click the OK button.

18. Save the page, upload the rituals_and_practices.asp page to your remote server (include dependent files), preview the journal.asp page in a browser (updating the page and dependent files on the testing server if necessary), type a test entry in the form, and then submit the form. The rituals_and_practices.asp page with the new entry displays in the browser window. (*Hint*: If you are sharing a database with classmates, you may see additional entries in the database.)

19. Close the browser window and the pages.

Apply

Add database-driven pages to collect and display a tally of visitors' votes for favorite paintings in a Web site for an art museum.

Case Problem 2

Data Files needed for this Case Problem: museumdb.sql or museumdb.mdb

Museum of Western Art C. J. Strittmatter wants visitors to the Museum site to be able to vote for their favorite painting. You will create a form in the home page that enables visitors to vote for a painting. The form will be connected to a database that stores the votes, and the vote tally will be displayed below the form in the home page.

If you are using MySQL and PHP on a Linux server, complete the following steps:

1. Open the Museum site you modified in Tutorial 8, Case Problem 2, and then open the index.htm page in the Document window.
2. Insert a blank line after the last line of text, insert a form into the page, enter "voteform" as the form name, and then insert a table with 3 rows, 1 column, 40% table width, 0 border thickness, 2 cell padding, and 2 cell spacing in the form.
3. Type "Select your favorite painting" in the top row, select the text, and then align the selected text to the Left and Top.
4. Add a radio group in the second row, name the radio group "vote," replace "Radio" with "The Cow Puncher" in the first row of both the Label and Value columns, replace "Radio" with "A Figure of the Night" in the second row of both the Label and Value columns, click the Plus (+) button to add a new row, replace "Radio" with "A

Quiet Day in Utica" in the third row of both the Label and the Value columns, and then click the OK button.

5. Add a Submit button in the third row of the table, typing "Submit" as the button name and the label, if necessary, and then save the page.

6. Ask your instructor for the information you need to connect to an existing database or create the database on your remote server using the **museumdb.sql** file located in the **Tutorial.09\Cases** folder included with your Data Files. (*Hint*: Obtain the information you need from your instructor or technical support person.)

7. In the Server Behaviors panel, click the document type link in Step 2, click PHP in the list, if necessary, update the links, click the OK button to confirm that the index.php page could not be updated, save the index.php page, update the link for the MusuemLogoRollover to the index.php page, and then save the page again.

8. Click the testing server link in Step 3, click PHP MySQL in the Server Model list, click FTP in the Access list, delete all the file path information from the URL Prefix text box, type the URL for your posted site, and then click the OK button.

9. Click the Add Behavior button in the Server Behaviors panel, click Recordset, type "MuseumRecordset" in the Name text box, click the Define button, click the New button, type "MuseumDBconnection" in the Connection Name text box, type "localhost" or the database server URL in the MySQL Server text box, type your user name and password in their respective text boxes, click the Select button to display a list of databases, select the museumdb database from the list, click the OK button twice, click the Done button, click MuseumDBconnection in the Connection list, click vote in the Table list, click the Selected option button, click vote in the Columns list, and then click the OK button. The Recordset behavior is added to the page and appears in the Server Behaviors panel.

10. Click the Add Behavior button in the Server Behaviors panel, click Insert Record, click voteform in the Submit Values From list, if necessary, click MuseumDBconnection in the Connection list, click vote in the Insert Table list, click 'vote' Gets Value From 'FORM.vote' as 'Text' in the Columns list, click FORM.vote in the Value list, click Text in the Submit As list if necessary, click the Browse button, click the index.php page in the site's local root directory (because the totals will be displayed in this page), and click the OK button in each dialog box. The Insert Record behavior is added to the page and appears in the Server Behaviors panel.

11. Save the page, upload the page to your remote server (include dependent files), preview the page in a browser (update the page and dependent files on the testing server), and then close the browser window.

Explore 12. Double-click the Recordset behavior in the Server Behaviors panel to open the Recordset dialog box, click the Advanced button, delete all the text in the SQL text box, type the following code exactly as it appears, and then click the OK button to enter a query that will enable the vote tally to be displayed in a dynamic table.

  SELECT vote AS Painting, count(vote) AS Votes
  FROM vote
  GROUP BY vote
  ORDER BY vote

Explore 13. Place the insertion point in a blank line below the form, click Dynamic Table in the Dynamic Data list in the Application category on the Insert bar, click the All Records button, type "0" in the Border text box, type "3" in the Cell Padding text box, and then click the OK button.

14. Create a new CSS style for the table heading text, apply the style to the heading text in the form and the dynamic table, and then save and close the style sheet.

15. Save the index.php page, upload the page to your remote server (include dependent files), preview the page in a browser (update the page and the dependent files on the testing server if necessary), click an option button in the form, and then submit the form. The new vote tally appears below the form in the page. (*Hint*: If you are sharing a database with classmates, you may see additional entries in the database.)
16. Close the browser window and the page.

If you are using Access and ASP on a Windows server, complete the following steps:

1. Open the Museum site you modified in Tutorial 8, Case Problem 2, and then open the index.htm page in the Document window.
2. Insert a blank line after the last line of text, insert a form into the page, enter "voteform" as the form name, and then insert a table with 3 rows, 1 column, 40% table width, 0 border thickness, 2 cell padding, and 2 cell spacing in the form.
3. Type "Select your favorite painting" in the top row, select the text, and then align the selected text to the Left and Top.
4. Add a radio group in the second row, name the radio group "vote," replace "Radio" with "The Cow Puncher" in the first row of both the Label and Value columns, replace "Radio" with "A Figure of the Night" in the second row of both the Label and Value columns, click the Plus (+) button to add a new row, replace "Radio" with "A Quiet Day in Utica" in the third row of both the Label and the Value columns, and then click the OK button.
5. Add a Submit button in the third row of the table, typing "Submit" as the button name and the label, if necessary, and then save the page.
6. Ask your instructor for the information you need to connect to an existing database or upload the database to your remote server using an FTP program and the **museumdb.mdb** file located in the **Tutorial.09\Cases** folder included with your Data Files. (Hint: Obtain the information you need from your instructor or technical support person.)
7. In the Server Behaviors panel, click the document type link in Step 2, click ASP JavaScript in the list, click the OK button, update the links in the files, click the OK button to confirm that the index.asp page could not be updated, save the index.asp page, update the link for the MusuemLogoRollover to the index.asp page, and then save the page again.
8. Click the testing server link in Step 3, click ASP JavaScript in the Server Model list, click FTP in the Access list, delete all the file path information from the URL Prefix text box, type the URL for your posted site, and then click the OK button.
9. Click the Add Behavior button in the Server Behaviors panel, click Recordset, type "MuseumRecordset" in the Name text box, click the Define button, click the New button, click Custom Connection String, type "MuseumDBconnection" in the Connection Name text box, type "Driver={Microsoft Access Driver (*.mdb)};DBQ=" and then type the exact path to your database in the Connection String text box, click the Using Driver on Testing Server option button, if necessary, click the Test button, click the OK button to close the dialog box stating that the connection was made successfully, click the OK button to close the Custom Connection String dialog box, click the Done button, click MuseumDBconnection in the Connection list, click vote in the Table list, click the Selected option button, click vote in the Columns list, and then click the OK button. The Recordset behavior is added to the page and appears in the Server Behaviors panel. (*Hint*: Do not type quotation marks around the connection string because Dreamweaver will do it for you. If you do not know the exact path to your database, ask your instructor or technical support person. If the test is

unsuccessful, double-check the connection string and file path for your database or use an outside FTP program to upload the _mmServerScripts folder to the root folder on your remote server and your testing server if you're using a separate testing server.)

10. Click the Add Behavior button in the Server Behaviors panel, click Insert Record, click MuseumDBconnection in the Connection list, click vote in the Insert Into Table list, click the Browse button, click the index.asp page in the site's local root folder (because the totals will be displayed in this page), click the OK button, click voteform in the Get Values From list, if necessary, click vote in the Column list, click vote inserts into column "vote" (Text) in the Form Elements list, and then click the OK button. The Insert Record behavior is added to the page and appears in the Server Behaviors panel.

11. Save the page, upload the page to your remote server (include dependent files), and then preview the page in a browser.

Explore

12. Double-click the Recordset behavior in the Server Behaviors panel to open the Recordset dialog box, click the Advanced button, delete all the text in the SQL text box, type the following code exactly as it appears, and then click the OK button to enter a query that will enable the vote tally to be displayed in a dynamic table.

    SELECT vote AS Painting, count(vote) AS Votes
    FROM vote
    GROUP BY vote
    ORDER BY vote

Explore

13. Place the insertion point in a blank line below the form, click Dynamic Table in the Dynamic Data list in the Application category on the Insert bar, click the All Records button, type "0" in the Border text box, type "3" in the Cell Padding text box, and then click the OK button.

14. Create a new CSS style for the table heading text, apply the style to the heading text in the form and the dynamic table, and then save and close the style sheet.

15. Save the index.asp page, upload the page to your remote server (include dependent files), preview the index.asp page in a browser, click an option button in the form, and then submit the form. The new vote tally appears below the form in the page. (*Hint*: If you are sharing a database with classmates, you may see additional entries in the database.)

16. Close the browser window and the page.

Case Problem 3

Data Files needed for this Case Problem: normdb.sql or normdb.mdb

Apply

Display news items stored in a database in the home page of a Web site for an independent publisher of fringe writing.

NORM Mark Chapman asks you to create a section that displays news items at the bottom of the home page. You will create a News Admin page and then add a form in the page that enables NORM employees to enter content. The form will be connected to a database. Finally, you will add code at the bottom of the home page that will display content stored in the database.

If you are using MySQL and PHP on a Linux server, complete the following steps:

1. Open the NORM site you modified in Tutorial 8, Case Problem 3.
2. Duplicate the links.htm page in the Files panel, rename the copied page as "news.php," and then open the news.php page in the Document window.
3. Select the heading text, type "News Input," replace "Links" in the Title text box on the Document toolbar with "News Input," and then delete the content in the page.

4. Insert a form in the page, enter "newsform" as the form name, and then insert a table with 2 rows, 2 columns, 90% table width, 0 border thickness, 3 cell padding, and 0 cell spacing in the form.
5. Type "input news" in the upper-left cell, select the text, and then align the selected text to the Right and Top.
6. Insert a text area in the upper-right cell, enter "news" as the field name, set the character width to 80 and the number of lines to 10, add a Submit button in the lower-right cell, and then save the page.
7. Ask your instructor for the information you need to connect to an existing database or create the database on your remote server using the **normdb.sql** file located in the **Tutorial.09\Cases** folder included with your Data Files. (*Hint*: Obtain the information you need from your instructor or technical support person.)
8. In the Server Behaviors panel, select PHP as the document type in Step 2.
9. Set up the testing server in Step 3, selecting PHP MySQL as the server model and FTP as the access, and entering the URL for your posted site in the URL Prefix text box.
10. Click the Add Behavior button in the Server Behaviors panel, click Recordset, click the Simple button if necessary, type "normRecordset" in the Name text box, click the Define button, click the New button, type "normDBconnection" in the Connection Name text box, type "localhost" or your database server URL in the MySQL Server text box, type your user name and password in their respective text boxes, click the Select button to display a list of databases, double-click the normdb database in the list, click the OK button, click the Done button, click normDBconnection in the Connection list, click news in the Table list, click the Selected option button, click news_text in the Columns list, and then click the OK button. The Recordset behavior is added to the page and appears in the Server Behaviors panel.
11. Click the Add Behavior button in the Server Behaviors panel, click Insert Record, click newsform in the Submit Values From list, if necessary, click normDBconnection in the Connection list, click news in the Insert Table list, click 'news_text' Does Not Get a Value in the Columns list, click FORM.news in the Value list, click Text in the Submit As list, if necessary, click the Browse button, click the index.htm page in the site's local root folder, and click the OK button in each dialog box. The Insert Record behavior is added to the page and is visible in the Server Behaviors panel.
12. Save the page, upload the page to your remote server (include dependent files), and then preview the page in a browser (update the page and the dependent files on the testing server, if necessary).
13. Copy the Recordset behavior in the Server Behaviors panel, and then close the page.
14. Open the index.htm page, select PHP as the document type in Step 2 in the Server Behaviors panel, update the links in the file, paste the Recordset behavior into the Server Behaviors panel in the page, save the index.php page, update the Norm logo rollover to link to the index.php page, save the page again, and then upload the page to your remote server.

Explore
15. Select the first quote in the NEWS section, copy the text, delete the text from the page, open the news.php page in a browser window, paste the text into the input news text box, click the Submit button, repeat this process to copy the second quote in the NEWS section of the home page to the database, and then close the browser window.

Explore
16. Make sure the insertion point is below the NEWS heading in the home page, click the Dynamic Table button in the Dynamic Data list in the Application category on the Insert bar, click the All Records option button, set the border to 0, set the cell padding

to 5, click the OK button, and then delete the first row of the dynamic table (the row that shows "news_text").
17. Save the index.php page, upload the page to your remote server (include dependent files), preview the news.php page in a browser (update the files and dependent files on the testing server, if necessary), type a test entry in the form followed by your name, and then click the Submit button. The index.php page with the news entries displays in the browser window. (*Hint*: If you are sharing a database with classmates, you may see additional entries in the database.)
18. Close the browser window and the page.

If you are using Access and ASP on a Windows server, complete the following steps:

1. Open the NORM site you modified in Tutorial 8, Case Problem 3.
2. Duplicate the links.htm page in the Files panel, rename the copied page as "news.asp," and then open the news.asp page in the Document window.
3. Select the heading text, type "News Input," replace "Links" in the Title text box on the Document toolbar with "News Input," and then delete the content in the page.
4. Insert a form in the page, enter "newsform" as the form name, and then insert a table with 2 rows, 2 columns, 90% table width, 0 border thickness, 3 cell padding, and 0 cell spacing in the form.
5. Type "input news" in the upper-left cell, select the text, and then align the selected text to the Right and Top.
6. Insert a text area in the upper-right cell, enter "news" as the field name, set the character width to 80 and the number of lines to 10, add a Submit button in the lower-right cell, and then save the page.
7. Ask your instructor for the information you need to connect to an existing database or upload the database to your remote server using an FTP program and the **normdb.mdb** file located in the **Tutorial.09\Cases** folder included with your Data Files. (*Hint*: Obtain the information you need from your instructor or technical support person.)
8. In the Server Behaviors panel, select ASP JavaScript as the document type in Step 2.
9. Set up the testing server in Step 3, selecting ASP JavaScript as the server model list and FTP as the access, and entering the URL for your posted site in the URL Prefix text box.
10. Click the Add Behavior button in the Server Behaviors panel, click Recordset, click the Simple button in the Recordset dialog box, if necessary, type "NormRecordset" in the Name text box, click the Define button, click the New button, click Custom Connection String, type "normDBconnection" in the Connection Name text box, type "Driver={Microsoft Access Driver (*.mdb)};DBQ=" and then type the exact path to your database in the Connection String text box, click the Using Driver on Testing Server option button, click the Test button, click the OK button to confirm the connection was made successfully, click the OK button, click the Done button, click normDBconnection in the Connection list, click news in the Table list, click the Selected option button, click news in the Columns list, and then click the OK button. The Recordset behavior is added to the page and appears in the Server Behaviors panel. (*Hint*: Do not type quotation marks around the connection string because Dreamweaver will do it for you. If you do not know the exact path to your database, ask your instructor or technical support person. If the test is unsuccessful, double-check the connection string and file path for your database or use an outside FTP program to upload the _mmServerScripts folder to the root folder on your remote server and your testing server if you're using a separate testing server.)

11. Click the Add Behavior button in the Server Behaviors panel, click Insert Record, click normDBconnection in the Connection list, click news in the Insert Into Table list, click the Browse button, click the index.htm page in the site's local root folder, click the OK button, click newsform in the Get Values From list, if necessary, click news in the Columns list, click news inserts into column "news" (Text) in the Form Elements list, and then click the OK button. The Insert Record behavior is added to the page and appears in the Server Behaviors panel.
12. Save the page, upload the page to your remote server (include dependent files), and then preview the page in a browser.
13. Copy the Recordset behavior in the Server Behaviors panel, and then close the page.
14. Open the index.htm page, select ASP JavaScript as the document type in Step 2 in the Server Behaviors panel, update the links in the pages, click the OK button to confirm that the index.asp page could not be updated, paste the Recordset behavior into the Server Behaviors panel, save the index.asp page, update the Norm logo rollover to link to the index.asp page, save the page again, and then upload the page to your remote server (include dependent files).

Explore

15. Select the first quote in the NEWS section, copy the text, delete the text from the page, open the news.asp page in a browser window, paste the text into the input news text box, click the Submit button, repeat this process to copy the second quote in the NEWS section of the home page to the database, and then close the browser window.

Explore

16. Make sure the insertion point is below the NEWS heading in the home page, click the Dynamic Table button in the Dynamic Data list in the Application category on the Insert bar, click the All Records option button, set the border to 0, set the cell padding to 5, click the OK button, and then delete the first row of the dynamic table (the row that shows "news_text").
17. Save the index.asp page, upload the page to your remote server (include dependent files), preview the news.asp page in a browser (update the files and dependent files on the testing server, if necessary), type a test entry in the form followed by your name, and then click the Submit button form. The index.asp page with the news entries displays in the browser window. (*Hint*: If you are sharing a database with classmates, you may see additional entries in the database.)
18. Close the browser window and the page.

Create

Create database-driven pages to collect and display customer comments in a Web site for a newly opening sushi restaurant.

Case Problem 4

Data Files needed for this Case Problem: sushidb.sql or sushidb.mdb

Sushi Ya-Ya Mary O'Brien wants to add a form in the Contact page that includes a comments section. After you create the form, you will connect the form to a database and then add code to the home page that will enable the page to display customer comments.

1. Open the SushiYaYa site you modified in Tutorial 8, Case Problem 4, and then open the contact.htm page.
2. Create a form in the Contact page that enables customers to enter comments. The form should have a text area for comments and a Submit button for submission. (*Hint*: Use a table to create the form structure.)
3. If your instructor has not already done so, upload the database on the remote server using the **sushidb.sql** file (if you are using MySQL and PHP) or create the database on your remote server using the **sushidb.mdb** file (if you are using Access and ASP) located in the

Tutorial.09\Cases folder included with your Data Files. (*Hint*: Obtain the information you need from your instructor or technical support person.)
4. Connect the Web site to the database by completing Steps 2 and 3 in the Server Behaviors panel. (*Hint*: Remember to update the link on the contact.php page.)
5. Add the Recordset and the Insert Record server behaviors to the Contact page.
6. Copy the Recordset server behavior from the Contact page, open the index.htm page, and then paste the Recordset server behavior in the home page.

Explore

7. Add a customer comments heading below the existing page content, and then add a dynamic table that displays customer comments in the page. (*Hint*: To add a dynamic table, click the Dynamic Table button in the Dynamic Data list in the Application category on the Insert bar.)
8. Save the pages, upload the pages to your remote server, test the pages, and then close the browser window and the pages.

Quick Check Answers

Session 9.1

1. a collection of information that is arranged for ease and speed of search and retrieval.
2. MySQL and Access
3. language
4. PHP
5. a behavior that runs on the Web server before the Web page is sent to a user's browser and is written in PHP, ASP, JSP, or ColdFusion.
6. to specify which data you want to retrieve from the database and display in the Web page
7. to protect the data from unauthorized access
8. to tell the browser to automatically refresh the page (by reloading the current page or going to a different page) after a certain amount of time

Session 9.2

1. language
2. ASP
3. a behavior that runs on the Web server before the Web page is sent to a user's browser and is written in PHP, ASP, JSP, or ColdFusion.
4. to specify which data you want to retrieve from the database and display in the Web page
5. to protect the data from unauthorized access
6. to tell the browser to automatically refresh the page (by reloading the current page or going to a different page) after a certain amount of time

Dreamweaver | ADD 543

Additional Case 1

Building a Web Site with a Form

Case

Coffee Lounge

The Coffee Lounge is an all-night coffee bar located on Exposition Parkway, across from Fair Park, at the heart of the Dallas punk music scene. The lounge features live, alternative, and punk music on the weekends; an improvisational psychedelic jazz jam on Thursday nights; poetry slams on Wednesday nights; experimental film screenings on Tuesday nights; and a book club that discusses various titles in the cyberpunk genre on Monday nights. In addition, the Coffee Lounge encourages public art by allowing patrons and local artists to use the various pens, markers, and paints scattered throughout the club to add their mark to the walls and tables.

Coffee Lounge owner, Tommy Caddell, has decided that the lounge could benefit from a Web site. Tommy wants to use the site to inform patrons of upcoming and ongoing events, and as a marketing tool to promote featured events, the monthly special—a different coffee blend is featured each month—and sales. In addition, Tommy wants to include a page that features a different Dallas-based non-profit organization each month. The page should give a blurb about the organization, including contact information and, if possible, a link to the organization's Web site. He wants to be able to update this page himself.

Student Data Files

▼ **AddCases folder**

CoffeeLoungeFormTest.htm

1. Create a list of site goals; review the list for order of importance and wording.
2. Define a target audience, and create a user profile for the site. (*Hint:* Research the target audience as needed.)
3. Conduct market research to gather information about at least four competing Web sites or other Web sites that cater to the target audience, and then write a paragraph summarizing your findings.
4. Develop two end-user scenarios for the site.
5. Create an information category outline for the site.
6. Create a flowchart for the site.
7. Develop a site concept and a metaphor for the site. Write a paragraph explaining your choices.
8. Choose a color palette, fonts, and a graphic style for the site. Write a paragraph explaining your choices.
9. Create rough sketches of two layouts for the site. Write a paragraph explaining which layout you prefer and why.
10. Check the layout of the design you prefer for logic, and verify that your design reinforces the site goals and supports the site metaphor.
11. Create a local site definition and a remote site definition.
12. Create a main template for the site.
13. Add editable regions to the template and insert placeholder text as appropriate.
14. Add a background and colors to the template as appropriate based on your site plan.
15. Add an appropriate list of keywords to the head content of the template.
16. Add an appropriate description of the site to the head content of the template.
17. Create at least three CSS styles to format the text in the site; refer to your site plan for the appropriate colors, fonts, and so forth.
18. Insert a navigation bar into the template, and create appropriate elements. You will not create links in the navigation bar at this time because the pages have not yet been created; you will modify the template and add the links later. (*Hint:* If you do not have access to a graphics program, you can create a series of text links for site navigation instead of inserting a navigation bar.)
19. Create at least two library items for elements that you intend to reuse or update frequently, such as footers or an upcoming events list that will be displayed in more than one page.
20. Use the template to create a Web page.
21. Rename the Web page with a descriptive filename. (*Hint:* Remember to use index.htm or index.html as the filename for the home page.)
22. Set an appropriate page title for the Web page you created.
23. Open the Web page, type an appropriate page heading and text content, and then apply appropriate CSS styles, if necessary, to format the content.
24. Add at least one image to the Web page. (*Hint:* If you don't have an image file to insert, you can use any of the image files included with your Data Files.)
25. Save the page, and then preview the page in a browser.
26. Repeat Steps 20 through 25 to create a home page and at least three first-level pages for the site based on your site plan.
27. Once you have created all the pages for the site, open the template and modify the navigation bar, selecting each element and adding the link to the appropriate page.
28. Save the template, and then update the pages.
29. Create an image map in at least one Web page.
30. Copy the **CoffeeLoungeFormTest.htm** file located in the **AddCases** folder included with your Data Files to the site's local root folder. This will enable you to test the form.

31. Add a rollover button to at least one Web page.
32. Create a form in one Web page to collect appropriate data from visitors. Use a table to organize the form objects. Add at least four different types of form objects to the form.
33. Preview the form in a browser, and then test the form.
34. Insert a Flash movie, Flash text, Shockwave movie, video, or a sound into at least one page. (*Hint:* If you don't have one of these types of files to insert, you can use any of the files in the Tutorial.08 folders included with your Data Files as placeholders.)
35. Preview the site in a browser.
36. Upload the site to a remote server, and then preview the site over the Web.
37. Test each page of the site.

Building a Web Site with Database Functionality

Case

Tweetie

Sonia Orozco, known to most as Tweetie, is a band promoter of indie music. She has decided to create an online zine, called D-zine, that will be published monthly. Each issue will include band interviews, a calendar of local performances and events, reviews of local performances and new CD releases, as well as reader reviews and comments. The zine will also include a "wanted" section that will enable bands that are looking for new members to place ads at no cost and a section that features a local venue.

Student Data Files

▼ AddCases folder
 zine.mdb
 zine.sql

1. Create a list of site goals; review the list for order of importance and wording.
2. Define a target audience, and create a user profile for the site. (*Hint:* Research the target audience as needed.)
3. Conduct market research to gather information about at least four e-zine Web sites as well as two Web sites that promote local venues and bands, and then write a paragraph summarizing your findings.
4. Develop two end-user scenarios for the site.
5. Create an information category outline for the site.
6. Create a flowchart for the site.
7. Develop a site concept and a metaphor for the site. Write a paragraph explaining your choices.
8. Choose a color palette, fonts, and a graphic style for the site. Write a paragraph explaining your choices.
9. Create rough sketches of two layouts for the site. Write a paragraph explaining which layout you prefer and why.
10. Check the layout of the design you prefer for logic, and verify that your design reinforces the site goals and supports the site metaphor.
11. Create a local site definition and a remote site definition.
12. Create a main template for the site.
13. Add editable regions to the template and insert placeholder text as appropriate.
14. Add a background and colors to the template as appropriate based on your site plan.
15. Add an appropriate list of keywords to the head content of the template.
16. Add an appropriate description of the site to the head content of the template.
17. Create at least three CSS styles to format the text in the site; refer to your site plan for the appropriate colors, fonts, and so forth.
18. Insert a navigation bar into the template, and create appropriate elements. You will not create links in the navigation bar at this time because the pages have not yet been created; you will modify the template and add the links later. (*Hint:* If you do not have access to a graphics program, you can create a series of text links for site navigation instead of inserting a navigation bar.)
19. Create at least two library items for elements that you intend to reuse or update frequently, such as footers or an upcoming events list that will be displayed in more than one page.
20. Use the template to create a Web page.
21. Rename the Web page with a descriptive filename. (*Hint:* Remember to use index.htm or index.html as the filename for the home page.)
22. Set an appropriate page title for the Web page you created.
23. Open the Web page, type an appropriate page heading and text content, and then apply appropriate CSS styles, if necessary, to format the content. (*Hint:* You can use the Catalyst bands as featured bands.)
24. Add at least one image to the Web page. (*Hint:* If you don't have an image file to insert, you can use any of the image files included with your Data Files.)
25. Save the page, and then preview the page in a browser.
26. Repeat Steps 20 through 25 to create a home page and at least three first-level pages for the site based on your site plan.
27. Once you have created all the pages for the site, open the template and modify the navigation bar, selecting each element and adding the link to the appropriate page.
28. Save the template, and then update the pages.
29. Create an image map in at least one Web page.
30. Add a rollover button to at least one Web page.

31. Create a form in one Web page to collect comments from visitors. Use a table to organize the form objects and buttons. Don't forget to include a Submit button. (The zine database located in the AddCases folder included with your Data Files includes a name field, a comment field, and an email address field)
32. Upload the **zine** database file located in the **AddCases** folder included with your Data Files to your remote server if you are using ASP, or create the database on your remote server if you are using PHP.
33. Connect the site to the database, and then connect the form page to the database.
34. Add server behaviors to a Web page that will enable users to view the comments that are collected in the database.
35. Upload the site to your remote server, if necessary.
36. Preview the form in a browser, and then test the form by entering appropriate information and submitting the form.
37. Preview the Web page in which comments are displayed.
38. Insert a Flash movie, Flash text, Shockwave movie, video, or a sound into at least one page in the site. (*Hint:* If you don't have one of these types of files to insert, you can use any of the files in the Tutorial.08 folders included with your Data Files as placeholders.)
38. Preview the site in a browser.
39. Upload the site to a remote server, and then preview the site over the Web.
40. Test each page of the site.

Objectives

- Learn how to work with graphics using Fireworks MX 2004
- Create a Fireworks document
- Work with Selection, Bitmap, Vector, Web, Color, and View tools in the Tools panel
- Set options in the Property inspector
- Save and export files
- Work with the Optimize, Layers, and Assets panels

Introduction to Fireworks MX 2004

Knowing how to build HTML Web pages is very important. Integrating graphics into your pages is just as important. Many say the Internet's expanding popularity in the early 1990s was due to the visual appeal and easy navigation made possible by Web pages using graphics. Graphics can make a Web site more visually appealing to look at, causing the user to visit a site for a longer period of time. Graphics can also help users move through a Web site by showing them how to navigate with icons rather than having them read links. Many student Web sites are developed with "borrowed" graphics. If you are connected to the Internet and right-click most images, a pop-up menu will allow you to save the image on your hard drive. However, the images posted on the Web are copyrighted, unless otherwise stated. Knowing how to create your own images is essential to becoming a professional Web developer. This Appendix introduces you to **Fireworks MX 2004**, a Macromedia graphics package designed specifically for developing Web graphics.

Fireworks MX 2004 enables you to integrate graphics seamlessly into your Dreamweaver MX 2004 Web pages. The HTML and JavaScript code that is created by Fireworks MX 2004 is fully compatible with Dreamweaver MX 2004. This lets you work on graphics and Web design in an integrated development environment. In a single package, Fireworks MX 2004 offers various tools for creating and working with many different kinds of graphics files. For example, Fireworks allows you to create both bitmap and vector graphics and to scan and edit graphics, photographs, and files from many other graphics applications.

In this Appendix, you learn about the basic editing features of Fireworks, as well as the tools and effects that are available in Fireworks.

Student Data Files

▼**Appendix.A folder**
    britishdairy.jpg
    garnish.png
    layering.png
    lbclogo.png
    soaplogo.png
    tarts.jpg

Fireworks MX 2004 Editing Tools and File Creation

Fireworks MX 2004 lets you edit bitmap and vector graphics. A **bitmap graphic** is an image created from individual pixels of color. A scanned-in photograph is an example of a bitmap image. Photographs have complex variations of color. When digitized, a photograph is represented by a grid of pixels of these color variations, which together make up the image.

A **vector graphic** is one that uses mathematical formulas and vector paths to define shapes and figures. Because the image is defined mathematically, you do not see the pixel variations as you do with a bitmap image. Images created from scratch using tools such as those found in Fireworks are generally vector graphics. Fireworks MX 2004 lets you edit bitmap and vector images in one document. You will see examples of both bitmap and vector graphics in this Appendix.

When you first start Fireworks MX 2004, you may be a little intimidated by the number of elements displayed in the workspace. However, if you have worked with another drawing tool, some of what you see may be familiar to you. For example, the Paint Bucket tool for filling a shape or area with a specific color is used in many applications. Figure A-1 shows the Fireworks MX 2004 screen as it appears when you first open a blank document in the Fireworks MX 2004 application.

Figure A-1 Fireworks MX 2004 opening screen

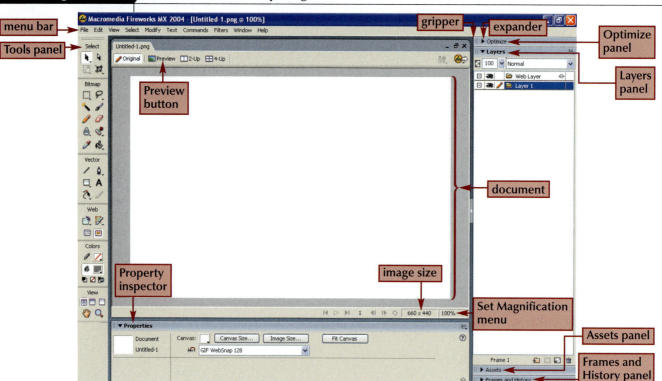

Most of the buttons on the screen offer tooltips to indicate what operation executes when you click the button. The blank, center area of the screen is your document, or canvas. At the top of the screen, you see a menu bar with ten options, which are described in Figure A-2.

Menu bar options Figure A-2

Option	Description
File	Provides options for opening, scanning, previewing, saving, and exporting files; also offers features for printing, preferences, HTML properties, and scripting
Edit	Provides standard Cut, Copy, and Paste editing tools; also offers features for inserting objects and using libraries
View	Contains controls for magnification, grids, edges, and rulers
Select	Allows you to control the selection of workspace areas by defining attributes of the selection marquee and by shrinking and expanding the marquee; you can also select everything or deselect objects
Modify	Provides options for modifying canvas and image properties and also makes controls for transforming and aligning objects available
Text	Provides options for basic text formatting of font, size, style, and alignment
Commands	Allows you to create your own commands by recording scriptlets (which are similar to macros) or by using the History file to create a command script
Filters	Contains effects that you can apply to selections or layers to make an image appear a specific way
Window	Allows you to open and close panels
Help	Provides online Help, a tutorial, and access to the Fireworks Product Support Center and product Web site

At the top of the document is a tab indicating the name of the file that you are working on (the file in Figure A-1 is untitled). Four buttons below the filename let you view your work in different ways:

- The Original button [Original] lets you view your original document.
- The Preview button [Preview] lets you see what your image will look like when loaded in a Web browser.
- The 2-Up button [2-Up] and the 4-Up button [4-Up] help you to compare settings when you optimize a document for the Web. To **optimize** a document (or graphic) means to obtain acceptable image quality with the smallest possible file size.

Below the document, the image size is shown, and the Set Magnification menu allows you to change the magnification of the image. At the bottom of the Fireworks screen is the **Property inspector**, which you use to edit attributes of objects in the canvas such as size, color, and effects.

By default, the workspace contains five panels:

- The two-column **Tools panel** provides drawing tools to help you create and modify artwork.
- The **Optimize panel** assists you with optimizing graphics for the Web, creating balance between file size and image quality.
- The **Layers panel** allows you to work in multiple layers, creating complex graphics, text, and effects.
- The **Assets panel** lets you use and manage styles, URLs, and library items for your Fireworks document.
- The **Frames and History panel** lets you use the Frames tab to create rollovers and animations and use the History tab to reverse and repeat commands.

You can navigate between the panels by clicking them or the tabs associated with them. You can minimize or expand the panels by clicking the expander to the left of the panel title. You can access any of the panels by clicking Window on the menu bar and selecting the desired panel from the menu. Panels can be moved, or undocked, to other locations in the workspace by dragging them with the gripper, located at the upper-left corner of the panel (see Figure A-1).

Previewing the Tools Panel

The Tools panel is divided into six categories: Select, Bitmap, Vector, Web, Colors, and View. The Tools panel and categories are shown in Figure A-3. You'll learn more about these tools as you apply them throughout this Appendix.

Figure A-3 Tools panel

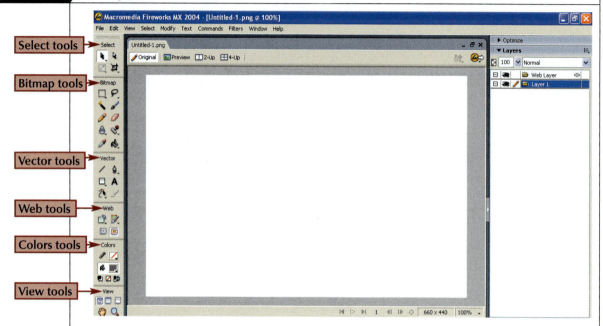

If you have used other drawing applications, these tools may be familiar to you. To use a tool, you click it and then apply it to the document in the workspace. If you see a small triangle at the lower-right corner of the tool, holding your mouse button down while the pointer is over the tool will reveal more tool options. Note that some tools will be grayed out, meaning that they are unavailable for use unless there is a shape drawn on the canvas.

The Main and Modify Toolbars

The Toolbars option on the Window menu gives you access to two additional toolbars—Main and Modify—which contain shortcut buttons for frequently used functions. The Main toolbar, shown in Figure A-4, is similar to that of many applications you may already use.

Figure A-4 Main and Modify toolbars

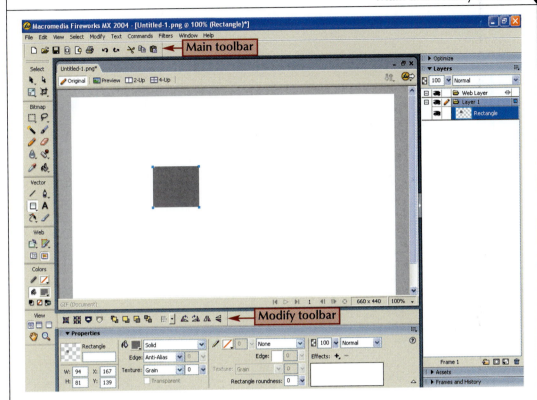

Using the Main toolbar, you can create a new document or open an existing one, save a file, import or export a file, and print. Two arrow buttons located near the center of the toolbar indicate options for edit undo and redo. Buttons for cut, copy, and paste are also available. The Modify toolbar, also shown in Figure A-4, contains buttons that allow you to orient objects in the workspace with respect to one another. For example, you can use these buttons to group, ungroup, rotate, and flip objects.

The Property Inspector

Every element you work with on the Fireworks canvas has properties associated with it. For example, if you draw a simple rectangle, it has width, height, color, and placement attributes that can all be defined and controlled. After you import or draw graphics and text on the canvas, you will see that the Property inspector, at the bottom of the workspace, changes depending on which object on the canvas is selected. It is much easier to manipulate attributes of an object through the Property inspector than it is to search through panels. Every time you select an object on the canvas, all of its attributes are displayed in the Property inspector and are easily modified via text boxes and slider bars. Figure A-5 shows the Property inspector for a rectangle.

Figure A-5 Property inspector for a rectangle

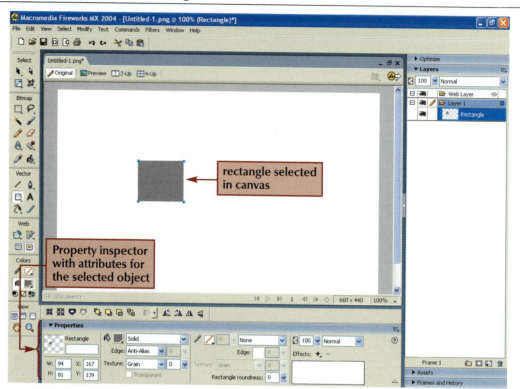

Creating a New Document

To create a new document, simply select the New command on the File menu. Using the New Document dialog box, shown in Figure A-6, you must specify the canvas size and resolution and select a canvas color. Most Web graphics are 72 dots per inch (dpi) because most monitors display graphics at this resolution. If you find working in inches or centimeters easier, you can click the list arrow next to the height and width text boxes and choose the setting you want.

Figure A-6 New Document dialog box

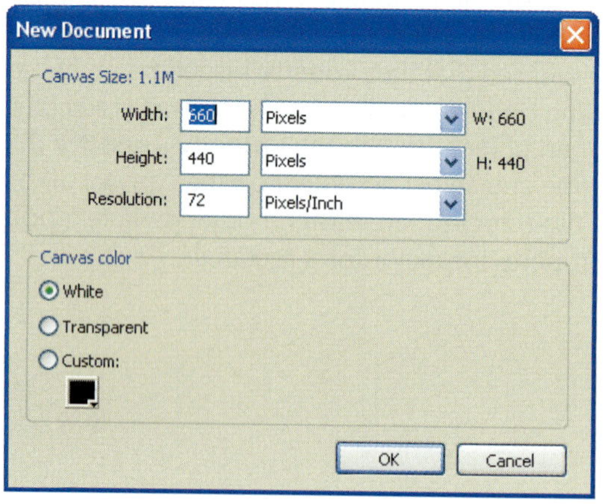

To determine the canvas size that you require, consider what you are trying to accomplish. Graphics for the Web come in many sizes; you need to consider who your target audience is and what you are trying to show:

- If you are designing individual rectangular buttons for a Web site, the pixel size of your canvas could be 100 pixels wide by 20 pixels high.
- If you are designing several buttons for a vertical navigation bar, then the height of the canvas would need to be greater.
- If you are designing a page for children, you may design large colorful buttons with graphics showing the button destination. In this case, the size of 100 pixels high by 100 pixels wide for an individual button may be more appropriate.

An image designed to be a banner across the top of a Web page can be 500 to 600 pixels wide and 100 to 200 pixels in height. You want to avoid images that are so large that they take too long to download or distract the user from scrolling to see other information on the Web page. It is useful to create a mock-up page and gain feedback before committing to a specific design concept. Doing so gives you a better understanding of your image size requirements. Remember that when using cropping, resizing, and scaling tools in Fireworks, you can modify the size of a graphic after you create it.

You can choose one of three options for the canvas color (see Figure A-6):

- White is the most popular background for a business Web page.
- Transparent displays a checkered background in the workspace that disappears (becomes transparent) when you save your graphics.
- Custom allows you to choose the background color from the Web-safe 216 color palette.

Modifying Properties for a New Document

After you create your workspace, you may decide that you need to modify the size of the canvas or image. To change any of these attributes, click Modify on the menu bar and then click Canvas. Figure A-7 shows the options for editing the canvas attributes.

Options for modifying the canvas — **Figure A-7**

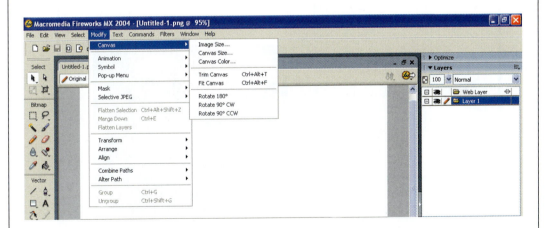

The options Image Size, Canvas Size, or Canvas Color let you edit the original settings for your document. Trim Canvas lets you reduce the canvas to fit the content. Fit Canvas does this too; however, if your content exceeds the canvas area, Fit Canvas will increase the canvas size. This can eliminate unnecessary white space and create more efficient graphics by ensuring that extraneous white space is not saved with your drawing. The Canvas submenu also provides options for rotating the entire canvas by 180 degrees, 90 degrees clockwise, or 90 degrees counterclockwise.

Saving and Exporting Files

To save your work in Fireworks, click File on the menu bar, and then click Save or Save As. Fireworks will automatically save your file in **Portable Network Graphic (PNG)** format. Many Web browsers do not support .png graphics without the use of a plug-in. Saving your graphics file in .png format maintains all the file's editable features as well as the layers created as part of the graphic so that you can continue editing the detail in the file. To save the file in .gif or .jpg format to be used with Dreamweaver, you must export the file.

Before exporting a file in a given format, Fireworks helps you preview and optimize it so you can see which format has optimal quality at minimal file size. As noted earlier, optimizing a graphic means to obtain acceptable image quality with the smallest possible file size. You can use the 2-Up and 4-Up buttons to optimize your graphic. The 2-Up button shows the original image and an additional panel in which you can alter the image characteristics to suit your needs. Similarly, the 4-Up button will show you four different panels of your image. The first is the original image, the next three can be altered using the Optimize panel, and a direct comparison can be made between the different images. Comparing the same image with different optimization characteristics lets you make the trade-off visually between image size and image quality.

After you've selected the optimized file, you can export just the image or the image and the HTML code. You can click Export Preview on the File menu to open the Export Preview dialog box, an example of which is shown in Figure A-8. You use this dialog box to preview changes to the file format, palette, transparency, and other formatting features.

Figure A-8   **Export Preview dialog box**

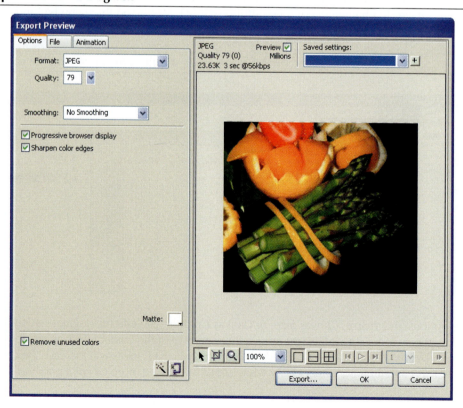

As mentioned, when you save an image for use on a Web page, it must have the .jpg or .gif format. The .gif format is better for line art and graphics with few colors. The .jpg format is better for photographs and complex pictures. The formats differ in the way that they compress image data. So, using .jpg for a photo will result in better quality and smaller file size than using .gif. Similarly, using .gif for text, a logo, or line art will result in a smaller file size than using .jpg.

In the following steps, you will open, optimize, and save a Web graphic.

To work with a Web graphic in Fireworks:

1. Start Fireworks. If this is the first time you've started Fireworks, an introductory screen will appear with options for opening an existing file or creating a new one. If this happens, select the option to open an existing file by clicking the Open file icon on the screen below Open a Recent Item. You may want to click the check box at the lower-left corner of the screen labeled "Don't show again." If you do this, you can open existing files and create new files using the File menu.

2. In the dialog box that opens, navigate to the **Appendix.A** folder included with your Data Files, and select the file **lbclogo.png**. Note that you can open many types of files in Fireworks, including .psd, .gif, .jpg, and .tif.

3. Click the **2-Up** button at the top of the document workspace. Two copies of the image appear: the original image and a preview image. If the Optimize panel is not visible, open it now by selecting it from the Window menu or by pressing the **F6** key. If the Optimize panel is visible but not open, you can open it by clicking the expander to the left of the panel.

    The image on the left is the original image. Note that it is 93.89K in size.

4. Click the second image at the right of the screen. An outline appears around the image, indicating it is selected. This image shows a smaller file size with a 1 second download time for a 56 kbps modem.

5. Click the **Settings** list arrow at the top of the Optimize panel, and then click **JPEG - Smaller File**. The file size is 10.95 K with a 1 second download time, but the image quality is highly degraded.

6. Click the **Settings** list arrow at the top of the Optimize panel, and then click **GIF Web 216**. Now the file size is 11.01 K with a 1 second download time, and the image quality is better.

7. Click the **No transparency** list arrow in the Optimize panel, and then click **Index Transparency**. A checkered grid should appear in the background of your image, indicating it has a transparent background.

8. Click **File** on the menu bar, and then click **Export**. The Export dialog box opens. Because the GIF file was selected in the Optimize panel, the .gif file format is automatically specified for the file.

9. Click the **Save as type** list arrow, and then click **HTML and Images** to save an HTML file and a .gif file from your Fireworks document.

10. In the Export dialog box, navigate to the **Appendix.A** folder. Note that the filename has changed to .htm file format. Type **lbclogo.htm** as the filename.

11. Click the **Save** button to export your .gif and .htm files. Click **File** on the menu bar, and then click **Save** to save your .png file.

12. Preview your Web page by opening **lbclogo.htm** in your Web browser. To do this, you can double-click the file, or you can click **File** on the menu bar and then click **Open** from the Web browser and navigate through your file structure to Appendix.A\lbclogo.htm. The lbclogo.gif image will appear on the Web page. When finished previewing, close the lbclogo.png file.

Using the Tools Panel

The Tools panel is located on the left of the Fireworks workspace. With it, you can create basic shapes, insert text, add color to shapes and text, and manipulate objects in the workspace. In this section, the major categories of the Tools panel are discussed.

Selection Tools

Selection tools are important for manipulating graphics and photographs in any graphics application. Being able to select shapes allows you to add colors to specific objects very precisely. Being able to select portions of drawings allows you to delete unneeded colors and backgrounds and to recolor photographs so that they fit any color scheme. Graphics applications usually give you several different ways to select elements of a drawing. The Fireworks tools that allow you to select objects and areas of the page are located at the top of the Tools panel. Figure A-9 describes these tools.

Figure A-9   Selection tools

Tool	Icon	Use
Pointer		Select objects and groups of objects by clicking or by clicking while holding down the Shift key
Select Behind		Select an object located behind another object in the workspace
Subselection		Select an object for the purpose of reshaping it; handles will appear so the object can be altered
Scale		Change an object's size and/or rotate the object
Skew		Stretch and/or rotate an object
Distort		Distort and/or rotate an object
Crop		Select only a portion of the document and discard the remainder
Export Area		Export a cropped area of the document

    The Pointer tool actually has two options: the Pointer tool and the Select Behind tool. Using the Pointer tool, you can select and reposition a shape any place on the canvas. A selected object has an outline around it. The Property inspector will display the attributes of that object for editing. To deselect an object, click elsewhere on the canvas, or click the object while holding down the Shift key. If you want to select multiple objects, hold the Shift key down and click each object you want to select.

    The Select Behind tool lets you perform the same action as the Pointer tool. However, if you have one object on top of another, it will enable you to select the object beneath by displaying red handles (dots) that outline that object. This is extremely useful for selecting and manipulating objects in a complex graphic.

    The Subselection tool is used to select an object for reshaping. When you select the tool and click an object, you will see several small handles—called **Bezier points**—around the object. With your mouse, you can drag these points into new positions and thus create new shapes. Figure A-10 shows how a Bezier point looks on the screen. In this figure, a polygon is being reshaped by dragging one of its points to another position.

Reshaping an object **Figure A-10**

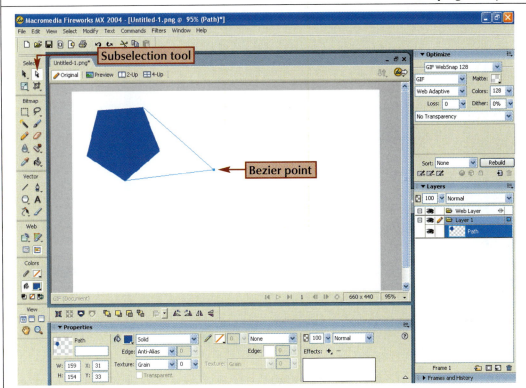

Pointer selection tools are useful for vector graphics because you can select an entire object and manipulate it. However, if you are editing a photograph, the Pointer tools cannot select a single object in the photograph because it is a bitmap image. For example, you cannot select someone's hair the same way that you would select a line or a rectangle. Clicking a photograph reveals no selectable shape, just a canvas of single colors. To select areas of a bitmap image, you need to use bitmap tools like the Marquee, Magic Wand, and Lasso (discussed later in this Appendix).

The Scale tool offers two additional tools in its pop-up menu: the Skew tool and the Distort tool. The Scale tool lets you change the size of an object, the Skew tool lets you stretch a selection along its vertical or horizontal axis, and the Distort tool lets you stretch a selection by dragging its sides with the mouse. All three tools let you rotate selections. To use these tools, you must select the shape you want to transform. After you use the tool, the selected shape changes. Handles appear around the shape, including a small circle handle in the center of the transformation selection. You can rotate a selected object when a curved arrow appears next to the selection, as shown in Figure A-11. You can grab the shape by the handles and drag or rotate it into the desired form. You can also scale an object by using the Property inspector. The inspector displays the object's width and height, which you can modify precisely by entering pixel numbers for these settings.

| Figure A-11 | Rotating an object |

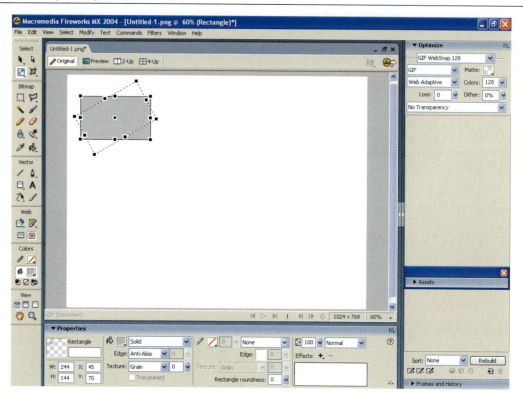

The Crop tool is used to select a portion of the document you are working on and discard the remainder of the document. This is a quick way to select part of a photograph or graphic that you want to use and immediately remove everything else. To use the Crop tool, drag the tool across the canvas to create a rectangular shape. Double-clicking the shape reduces the canvas size to the size of the selected, cropped area. Your original image will remain intact. The Crop tool provides one other option, the Export Area tool, which allows you to select a smaller portion of your graphic by dragging your mouse over that area. Double-clicking the area opens the Export Preview dialog box, which you can use to export that portion of your graphic into another file.

More selection options are available from the Select menu. These options are useful for different types of selecting or if you make a selection and then change it slightly to create a specific effect. For example, you might want to select an entire image, including all the layers. Using the Select All option on the Select menu is much quicker than clicking each object in the workspace individually. Another example is if you have an image you want to select that is on top of an entirely white background. Clicking the white background with the magic wand and then using the Select Inverse option lets you select only the image of interest.

In the following steps, you will modify a photograph of a decorative garnish using the Crop tool.

To modify a photograph using the Crop tool:

1. Open the file **garnish.png** located in the **Appendix.A** folder.
2. Click the **Crop** tool in the Tools panel. Place your mouse over the image. Notice the Crop icon over the canvas.

3. Drag the Crop tool over the asparagus garnish. In the Property inspector at the bottom of the workspace, enter the following values in the width, height, and coordinate boxes: W: **273**, H: **216**, X: **17**, and Y: **40**.

4. Double-click your mouse in the middle of the selection. Notice that the image has been cropped.

5. Click **File** on the menu bar, and then click **Save As**. In the Save dialog box, navigate to the **Appendix.A** folder, enter the filename **croppedgarnish.png**, and then click the **Save** button.

6. Close the croppedgarnish.png file.

Bitmap Tools

As discussed, a grid of pixels defines bitmap images. Each pixel has a color assigned to it. The combination of all the pixel colors makes up the image. The Bitmap tools in the Tools panel allow you to select and modify images based on selections of areas or selections of colors. Figure A-12 describes each of the Bitmap tools.

Figure A-12 Bitmap tools

Tool	Icon	Use
Marquee		Make a rectangular selection in the workspace
Oval Marquee		Make an oval selection in the workspace
Lasso		Make a free-form selection by dragging the mouse
Polygon Lasso		Make a polygon selection by dragging the mouse
Magic Wand		Select areas of a document that are similar in color
Brush		Draw paint lines (paths) freehand in the workspace
Pencil		Draw lines (paths) freehand in the workspace
Eraser		Erase portions of a graphic
Blur		Blur a selected area of an image
Sharpen		Sharpen a selected layer or area of an image
Dodge		Lighten a selected area of an image
Burn		Darken a selected area of an image
Smudge		Smudge an image by dragging color out from a selected area
Rubber Stamp		Copy a portion of a graphic and reproduce it somewhere else in the workspace
Replace Color		Select all areas of a specific color and replace them with a new color
Red Eye Removal		Remove red eyes from photographs
Eyedropper		Select a color from a pixel in the graphic to be placed in the fill color box
Paint Bucket		Fill areas with specified colors
Gradient		Create fills and effects that gradually change from one color to another

The Marquee and Lasso tools allow you to select an area of the canvas by drawing a shape around it. Using the Marquee tool, you can draw a fixed selection shape. The Marquee tool has one other option, the Oval Marquee tool, which you can view and select by holding down the mouse button over the tool. Both the Marquee and the Oval Marquee tools are used to draw a fixed shape over an area so that you can use or modify only the area selected. For example, if you wanted to copy the cherry on top of a photo of a sundae, you could drag the Marquee tool over the cherry and then copy it into another layer or canvas to use for some other purpose (such as making it a button). You can select an area of the canvas by dragging the marquee over the desired area. After a marquee is drawn, you can reposition it to select an area more accurately by dragging it on the canvas with your mouse. Figure A-13 shows a rectangular marquee drawn on a photograph to select a portion of the photograph.

Figure A-13 • Using the Marquee tool

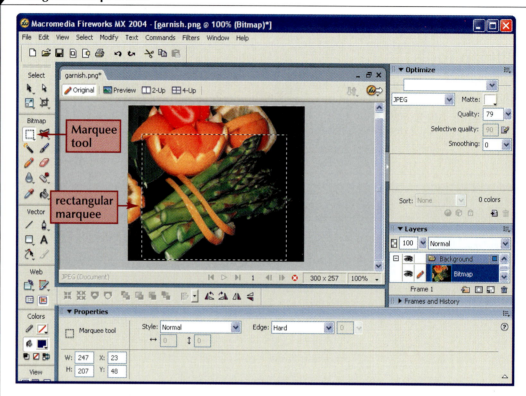

The Property inspector for the marquee lets you change attributes for width, height, X and Y locations on the canvas, style, and edge. The Style setting lets you set constraints for the marquee, if desired. For example, if you only want to select images 100 by 100 pixels, you can set the Style to Fixed Size. You can also select Fixed Ratio. The Edge setting provides the Hard, Anti-Alias, and Feathered options. A Hard edge creates a straight edge for the marquee, as if you were "cutting" something with a pair of scissors. The Anti-Alias option lets you create an edge that blends into the canvas color. This sometimes helps to make images appear cleaner on a Web page, reducing jagged edges. The Feathered option allows you to create a fuzzy effect where the marquee line cuts.

Using the Lasso tool, you can draw a customized selection shape. To use the Lasso tool, simply drag the mouse around a desired area, holding the mouse button down. The Lasso tool allows you to draw freely around a shape. The Lasso tool has one additional option, the Polygon Lasso tool, which enables you to select part of an image by clicking points around the desired area. So, the Polygon Lasso tool lets you select a shape without having to drag the mouse around by hand. Figure A-14 shows an area selected using the Polygon Lasso. As was the case with the Marquee tool, the Property inspector for the Lasso tool lets you change size, location, and edge options.

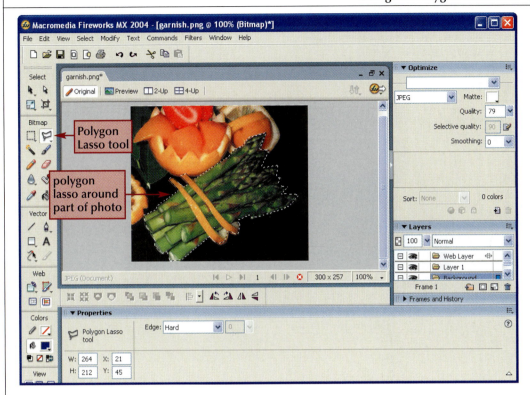

Figure A-14 Using the Polygon Lasso tool

Using the Magic Wand tool , you can select areas of a document that are all the same color. For example, if your photograph has a blue sky and you want a pink sky, you could use the Magic Wand tool to select the blue area and recolor it to a shade of pink. Figure A-15 shows how the Magic Wand selection would look in the workspace. In Figure A-15, the dark area behind the garnish was clicked using the Magic Wand tool. Notice that not all of the dark area in the image is selected. This is because the dark area to the left of the garnish is physically separated from the dark area to the right of the garnish. To select all of the dark area, you can hold down the Shift key and click the Magic Wand tool over the other dark areas. Additionally, in the Property inspector, you can set the tolerance of the Magic Wand to be more or less sensitive. A higher tolerance makes the tool less sensitive, selecting more of the picture.

Figure A-15 Using the Magic Wand tool

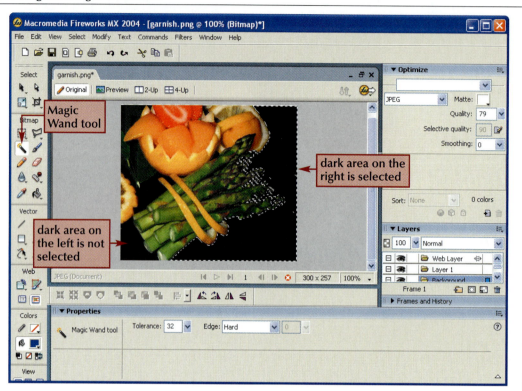

The Brush, Pencil, and Eraser tools operate in a similar way. To use them, you simply click the tool in the Tools panel and begin drawing on the document. You can use the Brush and Pencil tools to draw lines freehand by dragging them across the canvas. If you want to paint or draw a straight line, you can hold down the Shift key while dragging the brush or pencil in the desired direction.

The Property inspector for the Brush tool provides many options for changing the brush stroke. For example, you can alter the brush color, the tip size of the brush, the stroke category, the brush edge, the texture of the stroke, and how strongly it is applied to the canvas. The Texture pop-up menu lets you pick a style (grain, parchment, or sand) so that your stroke appears as a pattern instead of a solid fill. You can also change the opacity of the brush application and control how it will blend into the canvas. The Preserve Transparency option only lets you draw paths over existing pixels and will not draw on transparent areas of the image.

You can use the Property inspector for the Pencil tool to control color, anti-aliasing, auto erase, opacity, and blends. Checking the Anti-aliased check box will create a softer line that blends with the background color of the canvas. Figure A-16 shows a close-up of two lines drawn with the Pencil tool, one normal and one anti-aliased. Notice the blurred appearance of the anti-aliased line.

Figure A-16

Using the Pencil tool

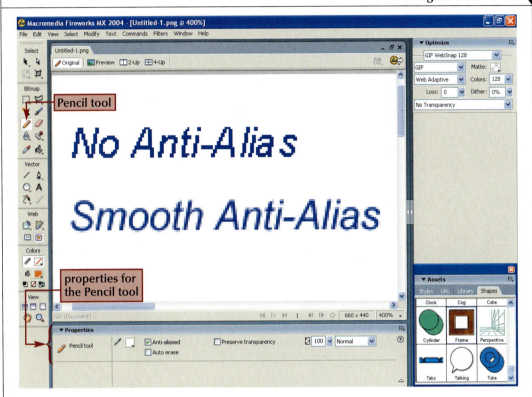

With a specified fill color, the Auto Erase option in the Property inspector lets you use the pencil in a manner that has the visual effect of erasing. The Preserve Transparency option only lets you draw paths over existing pixels. The Opacity option lets you control how transparent the line is, showing details of the image below the line. The Blend mode options let you control different blending options for a selection.

The Eraser tool in the Tools panel allows you to erase portions of your document by dragging an eraser over the canvas. Using the Property inspector for the Eraser tool, you can control the size, edge, shape, and opacity of the eraser.

The Blur tool, another Bitmap tool in the Tools panel, can distort the focus of selected areas of an image. By holding the mouse down and dragging the tool over the canvas, areas of a bitmapped image become less defined, in effect blurred. The Blur tool provides four additional tools: Sharpen, Dodge, Burn, and Smudge (refer back to Figure A-12). The Property inspectors for these tools are similar, allowing you to change the size, edge, and shape of the effect. These tools are used to touch-up small portions of bitmapped images.

Using the Rubber Stamp tool, you can copy a portion of a graphic and duplicate it over another area of the canvas. For example, if your graphic is an orange tree with only two oranges on it, you can create a rubber stamp of one orange and stamp the image to create a tree full of oranges. When you select the Rubber Stamp tool, you see a small indicator on the canvas. Clicking sets the beginning position for the rubber stamp. After you click, a blue circle appears on the canvas. Place the circle over the area you want to copy and drag it to fill in as much of the stamped area as you choose. The Rubber Stamp tool pastes copies of the stamped area over the canvas. In Figure A-17, the Rubber Stamp tool was used to eliminate the price card from a tray of tarts. The Property inspector for the Rubber Stamp tool lets you modify the size, edge, offset from cursor, source of pixels, opacity, and blend mode. The Rubber Stamp tool also provides two options: the Replace Color tool and the Red Eye Removal tool (refer back to Figure A-12 for descriptions of these tools).

Figure A-17 Using the Rubber Stamp tool

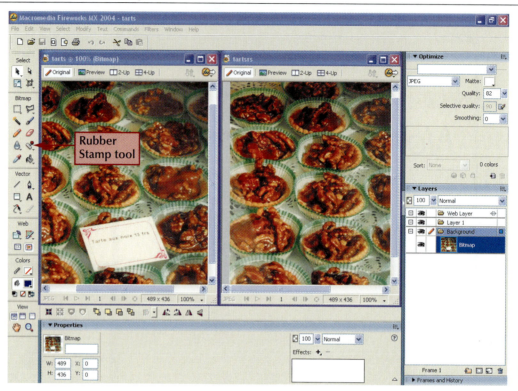

Sometimes when you edit a graphic or photograph, you want to use an exact color from one portion of the photo and apply it to another area. The Eyedropper tool lets you change the fill color in the Fill tool color box by clicking a pixel that contains the color you want to use. After the color is copied into the color box, you can use it as a fill color on other selections (similar to the Brush or Pencil tools). It may be easier to match a color exactly using the Eyedropper rather than trying to select it from a palette.

With the Paint Bucket tool, you can fill selections and areas with color. The Paint Bucket tool can be used in conjunction with the color box at the bottom of the Tools panel. When you click the Paint Bucket color box, a palette of colors is displayed. After you select a color, it is displayed in the color box. To apply that color, you simply click the Paint Bucket tool over a selected area to fill it with color. The Paint Bucket tool Property inspector, shown in Figure A-18, lets you change the tool's attributes, including edge, texture, tolerance, and opacity.

Using the Paint Bucket tool

Figure A-18

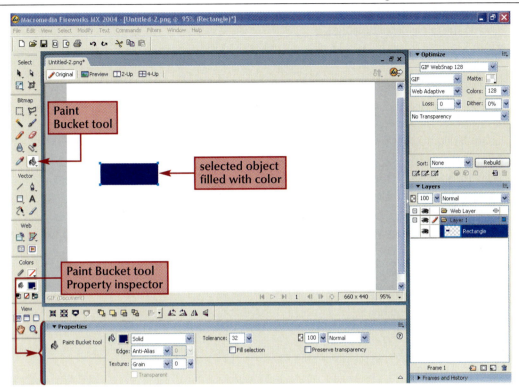

Holding the mouse down over the Paint Bucket tool reveals another option, the Gradient tool. This tool enables you to fill selections with a gradient fill rather than a solid fill. To apply the gradient, you click the Gradient tool, then click and drag your mouse in the fill area in the direction you want the gradient to be applied. To edit the appearance of the gradient, you can click the color box in the Gradient Property inspector. Dragging the color swatches lets you control how the gradient will appear; a preview is given so you can see if it is exactly the effect you want.

In the following steps, you'll use the Rubber Stamp tool to edit a price card out of a photograph of tarts at a bakery. To do this, you will copy an image of an unobscured tart and then stamp it over the tart with the price card.

To edit a photograph using the Rubber Stamp tool:

1. Open the file **tarts.jpg** located in the **Appendix.A** folder.
2. Click the **Rubber Stamp** tool in the Tools panel.
3. In the Property inspector for the Rubber Stamp tool, set the Size to **100** and the Edge to **25**.
4. Place the crosshairs in the center of the tart just above the tart that is covered by the card, and then click the mouse. A blue circle will appear. You have stamped the image of the tart that you want to use to cover the other tart.
5. Position the blue circle over the tart covered by the price card. You will stamp the copied tart image over the card. Click and hold the mouse, dragging it over the price card to replace the card with the new tart image. (Click **Edit** on the menu bar, and then click **Undo** if you have trouble covering the card.) Some of the card will still show once you have applied the rubber stamp.

The tart to the right of the one you just stamped has part of the price card still showing.

6. Repeat Step 5 to cover the price card on this tart, too.

   To cover the rest of the price card, you'll use the color from below the tarts and paint it onto the remaining card edges.

7. Click the **Stroke Color** box in the Tools panel in the Colors category to make sure it is selected.

8. Click the eyedropper on part of the white cloth beneath the tarts. Notice that the color from the image appears in the Stroke color box in the Tools panel. Selecting the color right below the price card edge (#8C9A69) gives a nice result because it is closest to what you are trying to cover.

9. Click the **Brush** tool in the Tools panel. Set the Brush Property inspector to a Tip Size of **10**, a Stroke category of **Soft rounded**, and an Edge of **50**. Drag the Brush tool over the remaining price card to blend it into the photograph.

   The image may not be perfect if you take a really close look. However, stamping, blurring, and filling elements of a photograph can give you images that more closely fit your design concept for the Web.

10. Click **File** on the menu bar, click **Save As**, and then save the file as **tarts.png** in the **Appendix.A** folder. The file should appear similar to the one shown in Figure A-17.

11. Close the tarts.png file.

Vector Tools

As mentioned earlier in this Appendix, vector images are defined by mathematical formulas and algorithms rather than by individual pixels. Codes that indicate color and scale, along with formulas for the shape or line, define the image. Vector lines and areas are often called paths and fills. This terminology reflects the fact that the images are defined mathematically. You use the Vector tools in the Tools panel to draw, select, and modify lines and shapes on the canvas. Each shape consists of strokes and fills that can be solid or patterned colors. Figure A-19 describes each of the Vector tools.

Figure A-19   Vector tools

Tool	Icon	Use
Line		Draw a straight line (path)
Pen		Draw lines
Vector Path		Draw lines as a series of editable segments (paths)
Redraw Path		Reshape selected segments of a path
Rectangle		Draw rectangular shapes
Rounded Rectangle		Draw rectangular shapes with rounded edges by entering the desired corner angle
Ellipse		Draw elliptical shapes
Polygon		Draw polygons by indicating a number of sides, and draw stars by indicating a number of sides and an angle
Text		Type text into a document
Freeform		Reshape a selected path by dragging points located on the path
Reshape Area		Reshape a selected area by dragging a selection circle located on the path

Figure A-19

Vector tools (continued)

Tool	Icon	Use
Path Scrubber Additive		Change/add speed and pressure-sensitive stroke effects (advanced tool)
Path Scrubber Subtractive		Change/remove speed and pressure-sensitive stroke effects (advanced tool)
Knife		Slice lines (paths) into more segments

While the Property inspector will change for each object you create using Vector tools, some of the more common attributes of these objects are identified in Figure A-20.

Figure A-20

Vector attributes in the Property inspector

Attribute	Description
Object Name box	Blank text box in which you can name the object you draw
W	Width of the object
H	Height of the object
X	Position coordinate; the X coordinate is the number of pixels from the left of the canvas
Y	Position coordinate; the Y coordinate is the number of pixels from the top of the canvas
Fill Color	Fill color of the object
Fill Options pop-up menu	Options for patterns, gradients, and effects for a filled object
Edge pop-up menu	Options for the fill edge: Hard, Anti-Alias, or Feathered
Edge Feather	Pixel amount of a feathered edge
Fill Texture pop-up menu	Options for various textures to apply to fills and strokes
Amount of Texture	How intensely the fill or stroke texture will be applied to an object
Transparent Texture	Transparent texture applied to the object
Stroke Color	Outline color of an object
Stroke Options	Variety of stroke styles such as Crayon, Water Color, and Felt Tip
Edge Softness	Softness of the stroke tip
Opacity	The degree to which an object is opaque or "see through"; 100% makes the object solid, and 0% makes the object invisible
Blend Mode	Attributes of an object defined with respect to the canvas, allowing you to control how an object blends with the document
Effects	Special effects, such as drop shadows, blurring, and beveling, applied to an object

To use the Line tool, you simply click the tool and then drag the crosshairs over the canvas to create a line. You can constrain the angles of the lines to 45 degrees if you hold down the Shift key while you drag the mouse.

The Pen tool is a bit more complex to operate. Again, you create the line (or path) by dragging the mouse over the canvas. However, this tool lets you define a path using anchor points and segments. You can draw straight lines in a series of segments by clicking the mouse to create anchor points. You can also draw curved lines by creating an anchor point and then holding the mouse button down as you drag it to create the desired curve. It takes some practice to get used to drawing curves. The Property inspector for the Pen tool has identical options to those of the Property inspector for the Line tool.

If you click and hold the solid rectangle in the Vector section of the Tools panel, you see a menu for 14 shapes. The first three shapes—rectangle, ellipse, and polygon—are frequently used. The additional 11 shapes make drawing specific shapes, such as a spiral or arrow, much easier than in earlier versions of Fireworks. To draw a rectangle, you click the Rectangle tool, position the mouse over the canvas, and then drag the crosshairs until the rectangle is the size you want, as shown in the example in Figure A-21. Releasing the mouse button draws the rectangle on the page. The object you draw will automatically apply the current color box selections. You can change stroke and fill colors in the Property inspector. Clicking the color box displays a palette of colors from which you can select the color you want.

Figure A-21   **Drawing a rectangle**

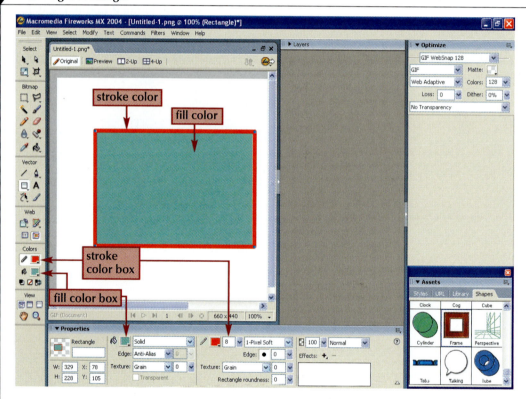

The Property inspector for the Rectangle tool is identical to the Property inspector for the Line tool, with one additional attribute: Rectangle Roundness. You can either enter a number between 0 and 100, or you can use the pop-up slider to open a slider bar and slide to the desired number. At 0%, there is no angle on the corners, and at 100%, the maximum angle, the rectangle will appear as an oval on the canvas. Alternatively, you could hold your mouse down over the Rectangle tool and select the Rounded Rectangle tool to draw a rectangle with rounded corners. To draw a shape of equal height and width, hold down the Shift key as you drag the mouse over the canvas to create the shape.

When you draw other shapes using the Shape tools available on the Rectangle tool pop-up menu, control points let you modify the shapes on the page. Figure A-22 shows an Arrow shape being modified to show a turn. Yellow diamonds mark the control points. By dragging the control points with the mouse, you can change several aspects of the shape you have selected. For the Arrow shape, you can change the Arrow Tip, Size, Thickness, and Roundness. The attributes will vary depending on which tool you select.

Appendix A Introduction to Fireworks MX 2004 | Dreamweaver | DRM 571

Modifying an Arrow shape

Figure A-22

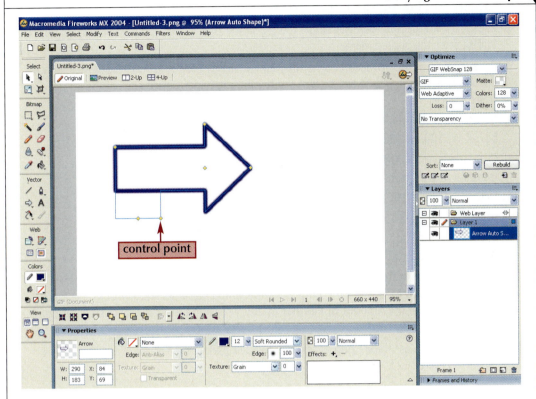

In the following steps, you'll create basic shapes using the appropriate Shape tools.

To create basic shapes:

1. Click **File** on the menu bar, and then click **New** to create a new document.

2. In the New Document dialog box, enter dimensions of **350 pixels** × **350 pixels** and **72-pixel resolution**. Click the **White** option if it is not already selected, and then click the **OK** button.

3. Click the **Rectangle** tool in the Tools panel, and then drag the crosshairs to draw a rectangle in the center of the canvas. Releasing the mouse will draw the rectangle onto the canvas. In the Property inspector for the rectangle, enter the following values in the width, height, and coordinate boxes: W: **100**, H: **100**, X: **30**, and Y: **30**.

4. With the rectangle still selected, click the **Fill Color** box in the Property inspector and then enter **#FF00FF** (pink). Click the **Stroke Color** box in the Property inspector, and then enter **#00FFFF** (blue). Enter **4** for Tip size.

5. Click and hold down the **Rectangle** tool, and then select the **Rounded Rectangle** tool from the pop-up menu.

6. Draw the rounded rectangle in the upper-right corner of your canvas by dragging your mouse on the workspace. Releasing the mouse draws the object. The object should have the same attributes you set for the previous object. In the Property inspector, enter the following values in the width, height, and coordinate boxes: W: **100**, H: **100**, X: **200**, and Y: **30**. Place your mouse over the yellow, diamond-shaped control point near the upper-left corner of the rounded rectangle. You will see a tooltip that says, "Click to switch corners." Click the control point and notice that the corners are inverted.

7. With the rounded rectangle still selected, click the **Fill Category**, click the **Fill Options** pop-up menu in the Property inspector, and then click **Pattern**. Click the **Fill Color** box

(instead of a palette of colors, you are supplied with a list of patterns), click the list arrow, and then click **Grass-Large**. Press the **Enter** key.

8. Click and hold the **Rounded Rectangle** tool in the Tools panel, and then select the **Ellipse** tool from the pop-up menu.

9. Draw a circle in the lower-left corner of your canvas by dragging the mouse and simultaneously pressing the **Shift** key so that the height and width dimensions of the ellipse remain equal.

10. In the Property inspector, enter the following values in the width, height, and coordinate boxes: W: **100**, H: **100**, X: **30**, and Y: **200**.

11. Click and hold the **Ellipse** tool in the Tools panel, and then select the **Polygon** tool from the pop-up menu.

12. Draw a polygon in the lower-right corner of your canvas by dragging the mouse over the workspace. Dragging will cause the polygon shape to form from the center outward.

13. In the Property inspector, enter the following values in the width, height, and coordinate boxes: W: **100**, H: **100**, X: **200**, and Y: **200**.

14. With the polygon still selected, click the **Stroke Color** box, and then select the **Transparent** button. Click the **Edge** pop-up menu under the Fill Color box, and then click **Feather**. Set the **Amount of Feather** to **20** by clicking the list arrow or by entering 20 into the text box.

15. Save your image as **shapes.png** in the **Appendix.A** folder. The results should appear as shown in Figure A-23.

Figure A-23	Basic shapes drawn on the canvas

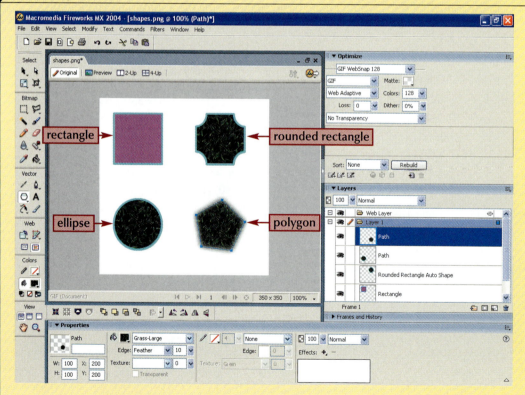

16. Close the shapes.png file.

The Text tool [A], another Vector tool, is useful for adding labels and text to your graphics. For example, if you are creating buttons or rollovers, you may need to add text to indicate the link destinations. You can click the Text tool and then click the canvas where you would like your text to appear. A blue rectangle will appear on the canvas and display the text as you type it. If you want text to wrap horizontally as you type it on the canvas, you can draw a text area where you would like the text to be displayed. The text area will grow vertically (not horizontally), wrapping the text.

Attributes in the Property inspector for the Text tool allow you to change the font type, size, color, and style. You can also control the text alignment and flow. Many of these text tools are probably familiar to you. What you may not have seen before are the following:

- With the **Kerning attribute**, you can control the amount of space between the characters of the text. A negative kerning value brings the text closer together, while a positive value adds more space. You can control the kerning value by using the slider, by typing a value directly into the text box, or by selecting the Auto Kern check box.
- The **Leading attribute** allows you to control the amount of space between multiple lines of text.
- Changing the **Horizontal Scale attribute** stretches or shrinks your text horizontally. A value of less than 100% shrinks the text, while values greater than 100% enlarge it.
- The **Baseline Shift attribute** is similar to superscript and subscript options you may have used in a word processing program for creating a degree sign or an exponent. When text is placed on the page, it has a natural baseline. The Baseline Shift attribute allows you to move the text either up or down from the natural baseline.
- The **Anti-Aliasing attribute** smoothes the edges between the path and the canvas. Without it, text and graphics can sometimes appear block-like. You can choose Crisp, Strong, Smooth, or Anti-Alias for this attribute.

In the following steps, you'll create stylized text with a drop shadow.

To create text with the Text tool:

1. Click **File** on the menu bar, and then click **New** to create a new document. In the New Document dialog box, enter these dimensions: Width: **500**, Height: **100**, and **72-pixel resolution**. Click the **White** option if it is not already selected, and then click the **OK** button.
2. Click the **Text** tool [A] on the Tools panel.
3. In the Property inspector, enter the following options: Font: **Comic Sans MS**, Size: **60**, Color: **#FF0000** (red), Anti-aliasing level: **Crisp Anti-Alias**.
4. Click your mouse to the left of the canvas, and then type **Culinary Tours**. You may need to reposition the text if it doesn't fit on the canvas.
5. In the Property inspector for the Text object, enter the following values in the coordinate boxes: X: **10** and Y: **10**.
6. Click the **Pointer** tool on the Tools panel.
7. With the Text object still selected, click **Add effects or choose a preset**, click **Shadow and Glow**, and then click **Drop Shadow**.
8. In the Drop Shadow dialog box, set the distance to **8**, the color to **#000068** (blue), opacity to **65%**, softness to **4**, and angle to **315 degrees**. Press the **Enter** key.
9. Preview your image in your Web browser by pressing the **F12** key. Close the browser. Preview your image in Fireworks by clicking the **Preview** button at the top of the canvas.
10. Click the **Original** button. Save your image as **culinarytours.png** in the **Appendix.A** folder, and then close the file.

You can use the Freeform tool to reshape a selected line. When you select a path and use the Freeform tool, a small s-shaped pull pointer appears next to the pointer. It indicates that you can stretch the line freely in whatever direction you choose. You can drag the line by its Bezier points or by a smooth segment of the line, where a Bezier point will be inserted for you. The Freeform tool provides three additional options in the pop-up menu: the Reshape Area tool, the Path Scrubber tool-additive, and the Path Scrubber tool-subtractive. The Reshape Area tool works similarly to the Freeform tool except that you drag a circled area, forcing portions of a path in a specific direction. Path Scrubber tools are advanced tools for working with vector drawings.

Using the Knife tool, you can cut vector paths into more than one path. As you use the Knife tool on a path in Fireworks, Bezier points appear indicating where the new break is in the path. After the cut is made, you can move and modify the newly created paths individually.

Web Tools

Fireworks lets you create hotspots and slices. **Hotspots** are areas defined on a graphic that a user can click, such as a hyperlink to go to another Web page. The three Hotspot tools—Rectangle, Circle, and Polygon—help you create the shape on a graphic that you want.

The Slice tool and Polygon Slice tool let you cut a graphic into several smaller graphics, or slices, and arrange them in a table using HTML. Slices reduce the time needed to load a large graphic and let you attach different behaviors to specific areas of the table. Slices are also the most productive way to create rollovers. The Hide Slices and Hotspots button lets you view your image free of hotspot or slice outlines. The Show Slices and Hotspots button displays hotspot or slice outlines for your image.

Colors Tools

In addition to being able to control stroke and fill color in the Property inspector, you can also set stroke and fill color using the Stroke Color box and the Fill Color box in the Tools panel. Figure A-24 shows the Stroke Color pop-up window displayed when you click the Stroke Color box in the Tools panel. You can select a color by choosing a swatch on the Stroke Color pop-up window or by entering a hexadecimal color code in the text box. Clicking the Transparent button makes the path invisible. Clicking the System Color Picker button opens the System Color Picker palette, where you can designate colors using another method. Clicking the list arrow on the right of the Stroke Color pop-up window lets you select other Color palettes available in Fireworks.

Figure A-24   **Stroke Color pop-up window**

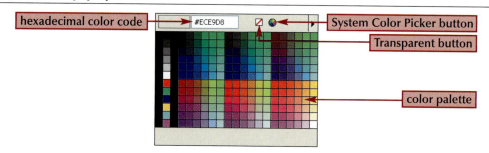

The Fill Color pop-up window looks and operates similarly to the Stroke Color pop-up window. Clicking the Fill Options button allows you to change fill attributes such as Fill Category, Edge, and Texture.

In the Tools panel, below the color boxes for strokes and fills, are three small buttons. The first, a black square over a clear square, is Set Default Stroke/Fill Colors. You can click it to set or restore default brush and fill colors. Next is the No Stroke or Fill option, which sets both color boxes to transparent or no colors. The third button, which appears as a double-sided curved arrow, is the Swap Stroke/Fill Colors option, which lets you instantly swap the color values for stroke and fill.

View Tools

The View tools are located at the very bottom of the Tools panel. The first three options let you quickly set how you will view the screen: Standard Screen mode, Full Screen with Menus mode, or Full Screen mode. You use the Hand tool to move around the workspace to view specific portions of documents that are bigger than your display. The Zoom tool is for magnifying a document so that you can edit a graphic more accurately. You can zoom into a graphic and edit it at the pixel level to achieve a perfect effect for your artwork. You can also use the View menu on the menu bar to zoom in to or out of a drawing. At the bottom of the canvas, you can also click the Set Magnification pop-up menu to open a list of different sizes in which to view your document.

Working with Panels

When you first open Fireworks, you see that several panels are available to assist you in editing your drawings. Refer back to Figure A-1, which shows the panels available when you first open Fireworks. This section of the Appendix describes the Optimize, Layers, and Assets panels in more detail.

The Optimize Panel

The Optimize panel lets you select export settings for the file you are working with. Earlier in this Appendix, you used the Optimize panel in conjunction with the 2-Up button to change the settings and export a graphic. Recall that the original file you work with is saved in .png format.

In the Preview, 2-Up, and 4-Up buttons, you can change the settings in the Optimize panel to preview how your image will look and what the file size is at different settings. This is an effective way to experiment with different file settings. The objective is to achieve the smallest possible file size with the highest acceptable image quality. As a rule, photographs compress well using JPEG format, and line art or images with fewer colors work well as GIF format.

The Optimize panel for the GIF format is different from the Optimize panel for the JPEG format because of file characteristics. Figure A-25 shows the Optimize panel for a GIF image, while Figure A-26 shows the Optimize panel for a JPEG image. Selecting fewer colors or less dithering can decrease your file size.

Figure A-25   **Optimize panel for GIF format**

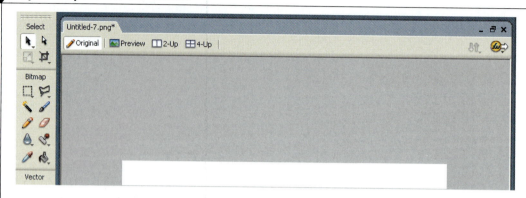

Figure A-26   **Optimize panel for JPEG format**

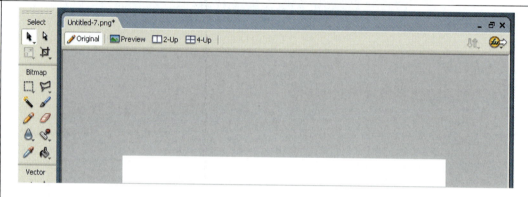

Dithering is a technique that widens your color options by placing pixels of two colors together to give the appearance of a third color. This is similar to the way a color printer works. If you look closely at your printout, you will see areas of color where two colors form a pattern, having the effect of creating a third color. Dithering gives you a wider selection of colors, but can also increase the file size of your graphic.

When working with JPEG images, you can decrease file size by reducing the Quality value. As you alter the settings in the Optimize panel, it is important to examine how the image degrades as the file size changes.

As an alternative to the Optimize panel, you can optimize your file using the Export Preview command available on the File menu. You can also select Export Wizard from the File menu to gain Fireworks suggestions for Export file type. After the wizard is finished, the Export Preview dialog box opens.

The Layers Panel

When you create a complex graphic, it is often necessary to work in layers. **Layers** are transparent canvases, stacked on top of one another. For example, an image that contains a boy with a ball playing in the grass plus some text might have a background layer containing the grass and sky, another layer containing the boy and the ball, and a third layer containing the text. Fireworks creates multiple objects in one layer, allowing you to edit the boy and ball and the background, for example, while working in the same layer.

The graphic formats available on the Web (.gif and .jpg) do not display layers. When you complete your drawing, you must flatten the layers or export your document so that the layers are flattened for you. Flattened layers cannot be separated again. The .png format in which you work in Fireworks preserves your layers. Saving the .png file is a good idea in case you decide later to change the document and need to alter the layers within it.

Figure A-27 shows the Layers panel for a food train graphic composed of several cropped images of various types of produce. Each object on the canvas occupies its own layer.

Layers panel **Figure A-27**

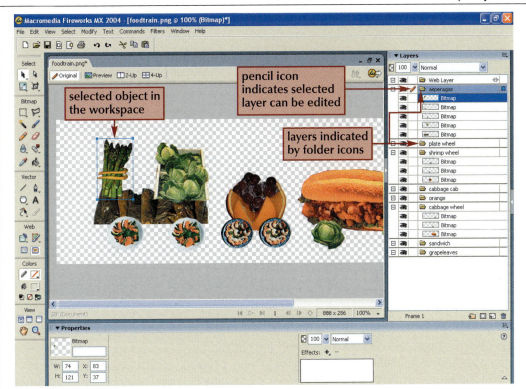

In the Layers panel, you can see each layer of the document (indicated by a folder) and the images that each layer contains. When an object is selected in the workspace, the layer is highlighted in the Layers panel. A pencil icon indicates that the layer is ready for editing. If you click the pencil icon, a lock will appear indicating that the layer cannot be edited. Clicking the eye icon will turn layers on and off in your graphic. This is useful for uncluttering the workspace so you can focus on a specific part of a document.

To rename a layer, you must click twice on the layer name in the Layers panel to type in your own custom layer name. To reposition layers with respect to one another, you can drag them in the Layers panel to the desired position, below or above another layer. The small squares on the left side of the panel let you contract or expand the layer, hiding or showing the layer objects. A square with a plus sign will appear, showing that the layer is contracted. Clicking the Options menu of the Layers panel opens an editing menu so you can add, delete, and perform other layer operations.

In the following steps, you'll use layers to create a logo for a company named La Bonne Cuisine. To do this, you'll reposition layers in the workspace with respect to one another. You will also add text to the file and create a drop shadow effect for the logo.

To create a logo:

1. Open the file **layering.png** located in the **Appendix.A** folder.
2. If it is not already open, open the Layers panel by pressing the **F2** key. In the layering.png file, the images in the layers are overlapping so you cannot see them all. You can see them in the Layers panel.
3. Use the **Pointer** tool to move the images to separate parts of the canvas so that you can see them all at once.
4. Click the **cabbage** image and observe that the corresponding layer in the Layers panel is highlighted. Double-click the text **Layer 2** in the Layers panel, and rename this layer **cabbage**. Press the **Enter** key. Rename the other layers the same way, naming them **orange**, **shrimp**, and **salad**.
5. Select the orange with the **Pointer** tool. Slide it around on the canvas and observe that it is located below the salad layer. (The Web layer at the top of the Layers panel is used for hotspots and sliced images.) Click and hold the **orange** layer name in the Layers panel and drag it to the top, above the Web layer. Drag the orange around the canvas to demonstrate that it now is on top of the shrimp and salad layers.
6. Click the **cabbage** object. In the Property inspector, enter the coordinates X: **4** and Y: **50**. Click the **salad** object. In the Property inspector, enter the coordinates X: **100** and Y: **4**. Click the **shrimp** object. In the Property inspector, enter the coordinates X: **10** and Y: **140**. Click the **orange** object. In the Property inspector, enter the coordinates X: **80** and Y: **115**.
7. Add a new layer to place text by clicking the **New/Duplicate Layer** button at the bottom of the Layers panel. Layer 2 is displayed in the Layers panel.
8. Double-click **Layer 2**. Rename the new layer as **Text**, and then press the **Enter** key.
9. Click the **Text** tool in the Tools panel, and position and click the mouse over the workspace. Create **#0000FF** (blue) bold text with a size of **50** and the **Arial** font by changing the attributes in the Property inspector. Type **La Bonne Cuisine**. Enter position coordinates of X: **70** and Y: **100**.
10. Click the **Pointer** tool on the Tools panel, and then click the text **La Bonne Cuisine** to select it. Click the **Fill Color** box in the Property inspector, and then move your mouse over the orange on the canvas. An eyedropper pointer will appear, adopting the color that the mouse is pointing to. Click the orange for a new text color or enter **#D17812**.
11. Click **Select** on the menu bar, and then click **Select All**. Click the **Add Effects** button in the Property inspector, select **Shadow and Glow**, and then select **Drop Shadow**. Press the **Enter** key. A black shadow appears beneath your image. Notice that the Drop Shadow effect is added to the Effects panel automatically. If you double-click the Drop Shadow text in the Effects panel, you can edit the attributes of the effect, changing the color, distance, and angle of the shadow.
12. Press the **F12** key to preview your image in your Web browser. It should look like Figure A-28.

Finished logo   Figure A-28

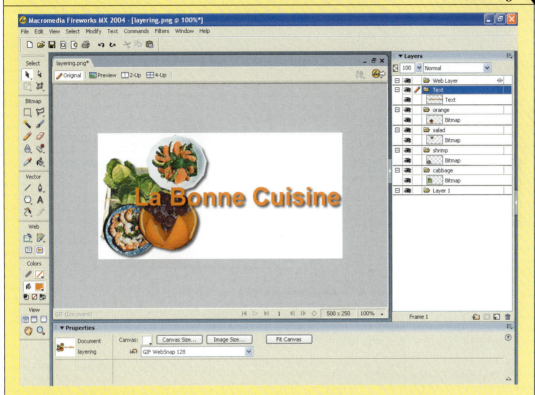

▶ **13.** Close your browser window, and then save the file as **lbcfoodlogo.png** in the **Appendix.A** folder.

The Assets Panel Group

The Assets panel group has four tabs: Styles, URLs, Library, and Shapes. The **Styles panel** lets you define a style for objects on your page and store it so you can reuse it again on other objects. The **URLs panel** lets you create hyperlinks from images. In the **Library panel**, you can define symbols and then use them throughout your document. The **Shapes panel** has Auto shapes not available in the Tools panel, such as a frame or a cylinder.

It can be overwhelming to work with so many options in Fireworks, and experimenting with them can be an unproductive way to approach your project. Often, it is better to plan your Web site's graphics in advance and to make modifications as you develop the site. Knowing what you are hoping to create ahead of time is much more effective than randomly seeking an effect that looks appealing.

Working with Images in Other Applications

Fireworks MX 2004 is integrated with Dreamweaver MX 2004 to enhance your Web development workflow. The ability to move between Fireworks and Dreamweaver with little effort makes it possible to develop a Web page in Dreamweaver, plus edit and optimize the graphics in Fireworks or by using the Fireworks Optimize panel.

Editing Options from the Dreamweaver Workspace

Dreamweaver has panels and tools similar to Fireworks MX 2004. At the top of the workspace are menus and an Insert bar to assist you in developing Web pages, to the right are panels, and at the bottom of the workspace is the Property inspector. In a Web page that contains an image, you can select the image by clicking it with your mouse. Figure A-29 shows the Property inspector for a selected image.

Figure A-29 **Dreamweaver Property inspector for images**

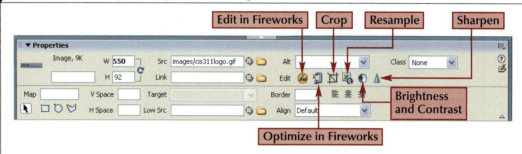

The editing options available in the Property inspector include:

- Edit. Opens the selected image in Fireworks MX 2004 for editing.
- Optimize. Opens the Fireworks Optimize panel.
- Crop. Cuts out unwanted parts of the image.
- Resample. Optimizes the color used in an image after it is resized.
- Brightness and Contrast. Changes the appearance of an image that is too dark.
- Sharpen. Makes an image appear more crisp.

The Edit and Optimize options allow you to change the image in Fireworks or using the Fireworks Optimize panel. The other options allow you to adjust the image within Dreamweaver. This is advantageous because you do not switch between two applications to achieve the desired results.

Working with Fireworks and Other Applications

Fireworks can open many different file formats including PSD files from Photoshop, Macromedia FreeHand, GIF, animated GIF, JPEG, WBMP, and CorelDraw. You can also use Fireworks to save some documents created in other applications in their original formats. Previously, everything edited with Fireworks was in a PNG format file. Now, you can open and edit files of Fireworks PNG, PNG created by other applications, GIF, animated GIF, JPG, BMP, WBMP, and TIF format and save them in their original format. This time-saving feature means that you no longer have to export a file to get the original format.

Fireworks files can be used in many other applications.

- To use graphics for the Web, you can export Fireworks PNG images as GIF or JPEG.
- To use Fireworks images with Adobe Photoshop, you can export the image into PSD file format. Photoshop does open PNG files; however, the layer information is lost. Saving the file in PSD format will preserve the layers so you can edit them in Photoshop.
- Microsoft FrontPage can be integrated with Fireworks. When installing Fireworks, you must select the option that allows you to edit graphics from within FrontPage.

Fireworks is compatible with many Macromedia products including Dreamweaver, Flash, FreeHand, and Director.

Working with the Quick Export Button

Another time-saving feature of Fireworks is the Quick Export button. Figure A-30 shows the drop-down menu for the Quick Export button. Notice that you can quickly export to Dreamweaver, Flash, FreeHand, or Director. You can preview an image in a Web browser. You can also select other applications such as Photoshop, GoLive, FrontPage, and Illustrator.

Figure A-30   **Quick Export button**

In the following steps, you use the Quick Export button in Fireworks to save a file in PSD (Photoshop) format.

To save a file in PSD format:

1. Open the **layering.png** file located in the **AppendixA** folder in Fireworks.
2. If necessary, press the **F2** key to open the Layers panel. In the layering.png file, the images in the layers overlap so you cannot see them all. You can see them in the Layers panel.
3. Click the **Quick Export** button, point to **Other**, and then click **Export to Photoshop**. A dialog box opens for you to save the image.
4. Save the file as "quickexport.psd" in the **Appendix.A** folder. PSD is the file extension for Photoshop. Fireworks should automatically fill in the correct extension for you. Notice that you are still using the layering.png file.
5. Open the **quickexport.psd** file, and then press the **F2** key to open the Layers panel, if necessary. Observe that the individual bitmap images are preserved, although they are combined into one layer.
6. Close the files.

Review

Quick Check

1. What is the Fireworks source file type?
2. What is the common resolution for a Web graphic?
   a. 72 dpi
   b. 100 dpi
   c. 200 dpi
   d. 350 dpi
3. What does it mean to optimize an image for the Web?
4. How do you draw a shape that maintains equal height and width?
5. Describe how you can create a rectangle with rounded edges.
6. True or False? Opaque refers to a fill texture for coloring an object.
7. What is a Bezier point?
8. What does the Kerning option in the Property inspector for the Text tool allow you to do?
9. True or False? Anti-aliasing softens lines and edges by blurring the edge with the background.
10. Describe the difference between a stroke and a fill.
11. A photograph is best saved as what file format for the Web?

Review

Appendix Summary

The Fireworks Tools panel allows you to create shapes and lines in a variety of colors, fills, and strokes. Selection tools include Pointer, Subselection, and Scale so that you can select, reshape, and resize images. You can apply a wide variety of strokes and fills to paths and objects using the Stroke and Fill options in the Property inspector for an object. Text tools are used to enter text on top of the canvas. You can alter text features including font, size, color, and style. You can also adjust alignment, kerning, and anti-aliasing. You can apply effects to text and other objects. Effects such as drop shadows and embossing can create appealing headlines and titles on a Web page. Paths, or lines, can be manipulated using the Property inspector. A wide variety of strokes create different pen styles, pen tip widths, and textures. The Optimize panel can be used with the preview of your graphic to experiment with different optimization properties. Layers are independent, stacked canvases in one document. Working with layers allows you to create a complex graphic with independent, editable objects on the different layers. The file you save in .png format will maintain layers. The file you export (for use on the Web) as a .gif or .jpg will not.

Key Terms

Anti-Aliasing attribute	hotspots	Portable Network Graphic (PNG)
Assets panel	Kerning attribute	Property inspector
Baseline Shift attribute	layers	Shapes panel
Bezier points	Layers panel	Slices
bitmap graphic	Leading attribute	Styles panel
dithering	Library panel	Tools panel
Fireworks MX 2004	optimize	URLs panel
Frames and History panel	Optimize panel	vector graphic
Horizontal Scale attribute		

Practice

Practice the skills you learned in the Appendix.

Review Assignments

Data Files needed for the Review Assignments: soaplogo.png and britishdairy.jpg

In these Review Assignments, you will open, optimize, and save a Web graphic. Then, working with a different file, you will crop a photograph and optimize a file, saving the HTML and image files when you export your work.

1. Open the file **soaplogo.png** located in the **Appendix.A** folder included with your data files.
2. Use the appropriate button to display two copies of the image: the original image and a preview image.
3. In the Optimize panel, specify the following setting for the preview image: JPEG - Smaller File. The file size should be 9.45 K with a 1 second download time, and the image quality should be highly degraded.
4. In the Optimize panel, select GIF Web 216. Now the file size is 11.17 K with a 1 second download time and the image quality is better.
5. Click the No Transparency pop-up menu on the Optimize panel, and then click Alpha Transparency. A checkered grid should appear in the background of your image, indicating that it has a transparent background.
6. Export the file as a GIF file named "soaplogo.gif."

7. Save an HTML file and a .gif file from your Fireworks document in the **Appendix.A** folder using the name "soaplogo.htm."
9. Save the .png file.
10. Preview your Web page by opening soaplogo.htm in your Web browser.
11. Close the browser window, and then close the **soaplogo.png** file.
12. Open the file **britishdairy.jpg** located in the **Appendix.A** folder.
13. In the photograph, select and crop the woman behind the counter of the dairy. In the Crop tool Property inspector, enter the following values in the width, height, and coordinate boxes: W: 80, H: 130, X: 175, and Y: 119. Crop the graphic.
14. Click File on the menu bar, and then click Export Wizard. Click Continue twice. Notice that Fireworks suggests either .gif or .jpg file types. Click Exit.
15. The Export dialog box opens with .jpg format selected. Click the Export button.
16. Save the file as "dairywoman.jpg" in the **Appendix.A** folder. (*Hint:* In the Save as Type box, click Images Only.)
17. Preview the file dairywoman.jpg in your Web browser.
18. Close the browser window, and then close the **britishdairy.jpg** file.

Review

Quick Check Answers

1. PNG
2. a. 72 dpi
3. to obtain acceptable image quality with the smallest possible file size
4. hold down the Shift key as you drag the mouse over the canvas to create the shape
5. hold the mouse over the Rectangle tool and then click the Rounded Rectangle tool
6. False; opaque is the degree to which an object is see-through
7. small handles around a selected object that can be dragged to reshape the object
8. control the amount of space between characters of text
9. True
10. stroke is the outline of an object; fill is the color or pattern inside the object
11. JPEG

Dreamweaver DRM 585

Appendix B

Guide to Using Dreamweaver on the Macintosh

The steps and figures in this book, *New Perspectives on Macromedia Dreamweaver MX 2004,* have been written for those users working in a Windows environment. However, you can easily complete the steps in a Macintosh environment with some minor modifications. These alternate steps will cover the major differences needed to perform the tutorials on a Macintosh so that you can apply different processes to the instructions. This presumes a basic knowledge of standard Mac OS X functions, such as file navigation, and opening and closing files and applications. As this is not a comprehensive guide, you may encounter some situations where you will need to determine the modifications for yourself.

Student Data Files

There are no Student Data Files needed for this appendix.

Global Alternate Instructions for Working on a Macintosh

There are a few instructions that you can apply globally to adapt the steps in the book to the Mac OS X environment.

Windows Instructions for Macintosh Users

When you see the following Windows instructions, substitute these corresponding Macintosh actions:

- Where it says to press the Enter key, press the return key.
- Where it says to right-click an item, control-click an item. The instruction control-click means that you should press and hold the control key and then click the object specified. This opens a context menu from which you can choose commands related to the object you clicked.
- Where it says to press Ctrl + (any other key), press ⌘ + (the other specified key). Please note that there are exceptions to this rule. If pressing ⌘ + (the other specified key) does not yield the correct result, try pressing the control key + (the other specified key).

There are some cases where the instructions will say to double-click an item and Macintosh users will only require a single click. Conversely, the instruction may say to click, and Macintosh users will need to double-click.

Previewing or Viewing Web Pages in a Browser

Frequently throughout the book, you will be instructed to preview the pages you are building in a browser. Sometimes the steps will instruct you to click the Close button to close the page and browser, sometimes the steps will instruct you to close the browser window, and sometimes the steps will instruct you to close or exit the browser. On the Macintosh, when you click the Close button in a browser window, you close the Web page you are viewing, but performing this action does not quit the browser. You do not need to exit the browser every time you preview a Web page, but you should quit the browser before ending your session at the computer. If you want to exit the browser immediately after closing the Web page or pages that you were viewing, click Explorer (or the name of your browser) on the menu bar, and then click Quit Explorer (or Quit *your browser name*). If you want to wait and quit the browser at the end of your session on the computer, you must first click your browser's icon on the Dock to activate it, then click Explorer (or the name of your browser) on the menu bar, and click Quit Explorer (or Quit *your browser name*).

File Navigation and Selection

Any time you are asked to navigate to a file, you will need to use Macintosh navigation, either through the Finder or by using Finder methods when asked to Open a new file or Import a file. In most cases, when importing or inserting a file into Dreamweaver, you will complete the operation by clicking the Choose button instead of the OK button specified for Windows users.

Using Dreamweaver MX 2004 on the Macintosh

Starting Dreamweaver

Although the process for starting Dreamweaver on your Macintosh may vary slightly depending on how your folders are arranged, this is the process for the default Macintosh folder structure.

To start Dreamweaver on the Macintosh:

1. Click **Finder** in the Dock to open the Finder window
2. Double-click the **Hard Drive** icon, double-click the **Applications** folder, double-click the **Macromedia Dreamweaver MX 2004** folder, and then double-click the **Dreamweaver MX 2004** icon.

When you are instructed in Tutorial 1 "To start Dreamweaver and select the Designer workspace environment," Windows users are instructed to click the Change Workspace button and then select the workspace environment (either Coder or Designer). For Macintosh users this option does not exist. There is only one workspace environment.

Importing a Word Document into Dreamweaver

When you are asked to Import a Word document in Dreamweaver, the Windows instructions are very simple: click File on the menu bar, point to Import, and then click Word Document. The purpose of this is to enable you to clean up Word-specific tags and other similar components. This particular function is not directly available in Mac OS X.

To import a Word document:

1. Open the Word .doc file in Word.
2. Click **File** on the menu bar, click **Save As Web Page**, select the folder in the site you wish to save the file to, and then click **Save**.
3. Open the .htm file you just saved in Dreamweaver.
4. Click **Commands** on the menu bar, and then click **Clean Up Word HTML**. The Clean Up Word HTML dialog box opens.
5. Click the **OK** button, then click the **OK** button on the dialog box that reports what has been cleaned up.
6. Cut and paste the text from the newly cleaned up file into the Dreamweaver page in which you need the text.

Dreamweaver Preferences

In Windows, the Preferences dialog box is found under Edit on the menu bar. In Macintosh, you will find Preferences under Dreamweaver on the menu bar.

Files Panel Menu Bar

In Windows, when you expand the Files panel, there is a small menu bar consisting of options of File, Edit, View, and Site. On the Macintosh, there is no menu bar. When the instructions ask you to select an item in one of the categories on the Files panel menu bar, click the Options button in the upper-right corner of the Files panel, and then point to the specified menu bar category (File, Edit, View, or Site) to open a drop-down menu from which you can choose the appropriate function.

Getting Help in Dreamweaver

Click Help on the menu bar, and then click Using Dreamweaver. This opens the Mac OS X Help Center, Help Viewer. You can then type in your question or a phrase in the Ask a Question box. You can also select a category from the Contents column or click Index and look for the category in question alphabetically. The Mac Help Viewer does not search for exact phrases if you put them in quotation marks. Regardless of whether you use quotation marks or not, your results will be the same. Additionally, the Mac Help Viewer does not highlight the search words or phrase.

Task Reference

TASK	PAGE #	RECOMMENDED METHOD
Alternate text, add to graphic or link	DRM 178	Select link or graphic, type text in Alt text box in Property inspector
Behavior, add to object with Behaviors panel	DRM 338	Select object to apply behavior, click ➕ in Behaviors panel, click action, click Event list arrow, click event
Behavior, delete	DRM 353	Select behavior in Behaviors panel, click ➖
Behavior, edit in Behaviors panel	DRM 353	Select object with behavior to edit, click behavior in Behaviors panel, click Events list arrow, click new event
Behaviors panel, display	DRM 344	Expand Tag Inspector panel group, click Behaviors tab
Browser window, close	DRM 14	See Reference Window: Closing the Browser Window
Cell attributes, modify in Layout mode	DRM 230	Select cell, set desired attributes in Property inspector
Cell, draw in Layout mode	DRM 219	Click ▦ in Layout category on Insert bar, drag ✚ to draw cell
Cell, select in Layout mode	DRM 223	Click perimeter of cell
Cell, select in Standard mode	DRM 198	Drag across table cell
Cells, merge	DRM 206	Select cells, click ▣ in Property inspector
Code view, display page in	DRM 27	Click <> Code on Document toolbar
Column, delete	DRM 209	Select column, right-click selected column, point to Table, click Delete Column
Column, insert	DRM 209	Select column to right of column you want to insert, right-click selected column, point to Table, click Insert Column
Column, resize	DRM 209	Drag column border
Column, select in Standard mode	DRM 199	Click in table, click list arrow above top border of column, click Select Column
Column span, adjust	DRM 207	Right-click cell in column, point to Table, click Increase Column Span or Decrease Column Span
Custom script, add to page	DRM 349	Click 🗇 in Script list in HTML category on Insert bar, select language, enter content, click OK
Custom style class, apply	DRM 126	Select text, click Style list arrow in Property inspector, click style name
Custom style class, create	DRM 125	See Reference Window: Creating a Custom Style Class
Database, connect Web site to	DRM 513	In Server Behaviors panel, click document type link to select document type, click testing server link to set testing server in site definition
Database, create on remote Linux server	DRM 488	Log into database management interface, run the SQL statements to create database
Database, upload to remote Windows server	DRM 510	Click Site, click Manage Sites, click New, click FTP & RDS Server, enter server information, click OK, click Done
Database-driven pages, create for Linux server	DRM 483	See Reference Window: Creating Database-Driven Pages for a Linux Server
Database-driven pages, create for Windows server	DRM 506	See Reference Window: Creating Database-Driven Pages for a Windows Server
Design view, display page in	DRM 26	Click Design on Document toolbar
Document window, change window size	DRM 30	Click ⬜ on Document window title bar, click Window Size menu on Document window status bar, click the desired size

REF 590 | Dreamweaver | Task Reference

TASK	PAGE #	RECOMMENDED METHOD
Dreamweaver, exit	DRM 39	See Reference Window: Exiting Dreamweaver
Dreamweaver, start	DRM 16	Click Start, point to All Programs, point to Macromedia, click Macromedia Dreamweaver MX 2004
Editable region, delete from template	DRM 452	Open template in Document window, select editable region, press Delete, save template, click Update, resolve inconsistent region names, click OK, click Close
E-mail link behavior, add to hotspot	DRM 348	Click hotspot, double-click Link text box in Property inspector, type "mailto:", type e-mail address, press Enter
Expanded Tables mode, switch to	DRM 200	Click Expanded Tables Mode button in Layout category on Insert bar
Extension for Dreamweaver, download	DRM 405	Click Help, click Dreamweaver Support Center, click Dreamweaver Exchange link, click Search Exchanges link, type RealMedia (or media type) in Search text box, click Dreamweaver Exchange in list, click Search, click Download next to extension, click Accept, click Open, click Accept, click OK, click ⊠, exit and restart Dreamweaver
External style sheet, attach to Web page	DRM 134	See Reference Window: Attaching an External Style Sheet to a Web Page
External style sheet, create	DRM 130	See Reference Window: Exporting Styles to an External Style Sheet
External style sheet, define new style in	DRM 135	See Reference Window: Defining a Style in an External Style Sheet
File list and site map, view in Files panel	DRM 22	See Reference Window: Viewing the File List and Site Map in the Files Panel
File, open in Document window	DRM 24	Double-click filename in Files panel
Files panel, expand or collapse	DRM 24	Click [icon] on Files panel toolbar
Flash button, add to Web page	DRM 383	Click [icon] ▼ in Media list in Common category on Insert bar, click button style in Style list, review button states in Sample box, click OK
Flash movie attributes, adjust	DRM 378	Select Flash movie, change attributes in Property inspector
Flash movies, add to Web page	DRM 376	See Reference Window: Adding a Flash Movie to a Web Page
Flash text, add to Web page	DRM 380	See Reference Window: Adding Flash Text a Web Page
Form, create	DRM 454	See Reference Window: Creating a Form
Form object, add to form	DRM 457	Click in form, click appropriate button in Forms category on Insert bar, type object name and set attributes in Property inspector
Formatting, remove from text	DRM 125	Select text, click Format list arrow in Property inspector, click None
Frame, adjust properties	DRM 271	Select frame, click Page Properties button in Property inspector, adjust properties as needed, click OK
Frame, create in Web page	DRM 262	See Reference Window: Creating a Web Page with Frames
Frame, save	DRM 269	See Reference Window: Saving a Frame
Frame borders, display	DRM 263	Click View, point to Visual Aids, click Frame Borders
Frame problems, find solutions to	DRM 291	Visit Macromedia Dreamweaver Support Center (www.macromedia.com/support/dreamweaver)
Frames panel, open	DRM 274	Click Window, click Frames
Frameset, adjust properties	DRM 278	Select frameset, adjust properties in Property inspector as needed
Frameset, save	DRM 270	See Reference Window: Saving a Frameset
Graphic, add to Web page	DRM 171	See Reference Window: Adding a Graphic to a Web Page

TASK	PAGE #	RECOMMENDED METHOD
Graphic, align to center	DRM 186	Select graphic, click ☰ in Property inspector
Graphic, apply CSS style to	DRM 175	Select graphic, click Class list arrow in Property inspector, click style
Graphic, change brightness and contrast	DRM 182	Select graphic, click ◐ in Property inspector, click OK, drag Brightness and/or Contrast slider, click OK
Graphic, crop	DRM 181	Select graphic, click ⌧ in Property inspector, click OK, drag resize handles to set crop area, press Enter
Graphic, resample	DRM 180	Select graphic, click 🖼 in Property inspector
Graphic, resize	DRM 179	Select graphic, drag resize handles or click ↻ in Property inspector
Graphic, sharpen	DRM 182	Select graphic, click △ in Property inspector, click OK, drag Sharpen slider, click OK
Grid, display or hide	DRM 331	Click View, point to Grid, click Show Grid
Header row, create	DRM 208	Select row, check Header check box in Property inspector
Help, get in Dreamweaver	DRM 35	See Reference Window: Getting Help in Dreamweaver
Hotspot, create	DRM 186	Click ▭, ○, or ⬠ in Property inspector, drag to create hotspot
HTML tag, modify	DRM 122	See Reference Window: Modifying an Existing HTML Tag
HTML tags, examine in Web pages	DRM 116	See Reference Window: Examining HTML Tags
Hyperlink, create from graphic	DRM 183	Select graphic, click 📁 next to Link text box in Property inspector, double-click file to which to link
Hyperlink, create from text	DRM 113	Select text, drag 🎯 from Property inspector to filename in Files panel to which to link
Hyperlink, customize appearance of	DRM 128	See Reference Window: Using the Advanced CSS Type for Hyperlinks
Hyperlink, delete	DRM 250	Select link, press Delete
Hyperlink, set target	DRM 284	Select link, click Target list arrow in Property inspector, click an option
Hyperlink, use	DRM 11	Click the link in browser window
Image map, create	DRM 184	See Reference Window: Creating an Image Map
Keywords, add to Web page	DRM 424	Click 🔑 in Head list in HTML category on Insert bar, type keywords in Keywords text box, click OK
Keywords, edit	DRM 425	Click in keywords list in Document window in Code view, make changes to keywords as needed in Property inspector or Document window
Layer, adjust properties	DRM 320	Select layer, set attributes in Property inspector
Layer, insert	DRM 310	Click 📄 in Layout category on Insert bar, drag in Document window to draw layer
Layer, make active	DRM 315	Click in layer
Layer, move	DRM 314	Select layer, drag with layer selection handle to new position
Layer, resize	DRM 312	Select layer, drag resize handle
Layer, select	DRM 312	Click layer border, click layer selection handle
Layer stacking order, adjust	DRM 325	Drag layer to new position in Layers panel
Layers panel, display	DRM 325	Expand Design panel group, click Layers tab
Layers, align	DRM 329	Select first layer, press and hold Shift, click layer to which you want to align, click Modify, point to Align, click desired alignment
Layers, convert to table	DRM 334	See Reference Window: Converting Layers to a Table

TASK	PAGE #	RECOMMENDED METHOD
Layout mode, switch to	DRM 218	Click Layout button in Layout category on Insert bar
Library item, add to Web page	DRM 432	Drag library item from library in Assets panel to desired location in page
Library item, create	DRM 430	See Reference Window: Creating a Library Item
Library item, delete from library	DRM 436	Select library item in library, drag selected library item to 🗑 in Assets panel
Library item, delete from page	DRM 436	Select library item in page, press Delete
Library item, edit	DRM 434	Open library item, make changes as needed, save the library item, click Update, click Close
Library item, open	DRM 434	Double-click library item in library in Assets panel
Local site definition, create	DRM 19	See Reference Window: Create a Local Site Definition
Local Web page, open in browser	DRM 9	See Reference Window: Opening a Local Web Page in a Browser
Meta description, add to Web page	DRM 427	Click 🗏 in Head list in HTML category on Insert bar, type description in Description text box, click OK
Meta description, edit	DRM 428	Click in description in Document window in Code view, make changes to description as needed in Property inspector or Document window
Navigation bar, copy	DRM 256	Select navigation bar, click Edit, click Copy HTML
Navigation bar, create	DRM 247	See Reference Window: Creating a Navigation Bar
Navigation bar, modify	DRM 257	See Reference Window: Modifying a Navigation Bar
Navigation bar, paste	DRM 256	Place insertion point at destination, click Edit, click Paste HTML
Nested layer, create	DRM 331	Select layer to nest in Layers panel, press and hold Ctrl, drag selected layer over parent layer
Nested table, remove	DRM 227	Select nested table, click 🗐 in Property inspector
Nested template, create	DRM 450	Create new page from main template, click 🗏 in Templates list in Common category on Insert bar, type template name, click Save, add or modify template content as needed, save page, click Yes, click Close
Netscape Resize Fix, add to Web site	DRM 333	See Reference Window: Adding the Netscape Resize Fix to a Web Site
NoFrames content, adding	DRM 282	See Reference Window: Adding NoFrames content
Nonbreaking space, insert	DRM 112	Click ⬇ in Characters category on Insert bar
Page properties, export to external style sheet	DRM 272	Click File, point to Export, click CSS Styles, navigate to Stylesheets folder, type filename, click Save
Page properties, set	DRM 82	Click Modify, click Page Properties, set desired properties, click OK
Page title, add	DRM 77	Type page title in Title text box on Document toolbar
Password, delete from remote site definition	DRM 91	Click Site, click Manage Sites, click Web site name in list, click Edit, click Remote Info in Category list, uncheck Save check box, click OK, click Done
Preview list, add browser to	DRM 87	Click File, point to Preview in Browser, click Edit Browser List, click ➕, type browser name in Name text box, click Browse, navigate to browser you want to add, click Open, check Primary Browser or Secondary Browser check box, click OK, click OK
Previously viewed Web pages, display in browser	DRM 13	Click ⬅ or ➡ on browser toolbar
RealVideo, add to Web page	DRM 407	See Reference Window: Adding a RealVideo Clip to a Web Page
Remote host, connect	DRM 90	Click 🔌 on Files panel toolbar
Remote host, disconnect	DRM 91	Click 🔌 on Files panel toolbar

TASK	PAGE #	RECOMMENDED METHOD
Remote site definition, create	DRM 72	See Reference Window: Creating a Remote Site Definition for FTP Access
Remote Web page, open in browser	DRM 7	See Reference Window: Opening a Remote Web Page in a Browser
Rollover, copy	DRM 190	Select rollover, click Edit, click Copy HTML
Rollover, insert	DRM 188	See Reference Window: Inserting a Rollover
Rollover, paste	DRM 190	Place insertion point at destination, click Edit, click Paste HTML
Row, delete	DRM 210	Select row, right-click selected row, point to Table, click Delete Row
Row, insert	DRM 209	Select row below row you want to insert, right-click selected row, point to Table, click Insert Row
Row, select in Standard mode	DRM 199	Click ➡ outside left border of row
Row span, adjust	DRM 207	Right-click cell in row, point to Table, click Increase Row Span or Decrease Row Span
Rulers, change to pixel measurement	DRM 203	Click View, point to Rulers, click Pixels
Rulers, show or hide	DRM 203	Click View, point to Rulers, click Show
Shockwave movie, add to Web page	DRM 389	See Reference Window: Adding a Shockwave Movie to a Web Page
Shockwave movie, attributes, adjust	DRM 393	Select Shockwave movie, change attributes in Property inspector
Show-Hide Layers behavior, add	DRM 338	See Reference Window: Adding the Show-Hide Layers Prewritten Behavior
Sound file, link to Web page	DRM 399	Select graphic, click Browse for File button next to Link text box in Property inspector, double-click sound file
Sound-only Flash movie attributes, adjust	DRM 399	Select sound-only Flash movie, change attributes in Property inspector
Sound-only Flash movie, embed in Web page	DRM 396	See Reference Window: Adding a Sound-only Flash Movie to a Web Page
Spelling, check in page	DRM 106	Click Text, click Check Spelling
Split view, display page in	DRM 28	Click Split on Document toolbar
Standard mode, switch to	DRM 201	Click Standard Mode button in Layout category on Insert bar
Style, define in external style sheet	DRM 135	See Reference Window: Defining a Style in an External Style Sheet
Style, delete	DRM 128	Select style in CSS Styles panel, click 🗑
Style, edit in CSS Styles panel	DRM 144	See Reference Window: Editing a Style
Style, edit with Tag inspector	DRM 146	Select text with style to edit in page, click ⬇ in Tag inspector, click value for attribute, enter new value, press Enter
Styles, delete from within document	DRM 132	Select <style> in CSS Styles panel, click 🗑 in CSS Styles panel
Styles, export to external style sheet	DRM 130	See Reference Window: Exporting Styles to an External Style Sheet
Table, convert to layers	DRM 334	Select Table, click Modify, point to Convert, click Table to Layers
Table, create in Layout mode	DRM 218	See Reference Window: Creating a Table in Layout Mode
Table, delete structure and content	DRM 205	Select table, press Delete
Table, format with preset designs	DRM 210	Click in table, click Commands, click Format Table, make selections, click OK
Table, insert in Standard mode	DRM 192	See Reference Window: Inserting a Table
Table, move in Layout mode	DRM 224	Drag Layout Table tab to new location
Table, move in page	DRM 204	Select table, drag with ⌖ from upper-left corner of table to new location
Table, resize in Layout mode	DRM 224	Select layout table, drag a resize handle

TASK	PAGE #	RECOMMENDED METHOD
Table, resize in Standard mode	DRM 204	Select table, drag a resize handle or type values in W and H text boxes in Property inspector
Table, select in Layout mode	DRM 222	Click Layout Table tab
Table, select in Standard mode	DRM 197	Right-click table, point to Table, click Select Table
Table attributes, modify in Layout mode	DRM 226	Select layout table, set desired attributes in Property inspector
Table attributes, modify in Standard mode	DRM 202	Select table, change desired attributes in Property inspector
Table tags, redefine using CSS styles	DRM 215	See Reference Window: Redefining Table Tags Using CSS Styles
Template, apply to existing Web page	DRM 447	Open Web page in Document window, select template in Assets panel, click Apply, designate in which regions to place existing content
Template, create	DRM 439	See Reference Window: Creating a Template
Template, delete	DRM 450	Select template in Assets panel, click 🗑
Template, edit	DRM 448	Open template in Document window, add, remove, and change elements as needed, save template, click Update, click Close
Text, align to right	DRM 112	Select text, click ▤ in Property inspector
Text, copy from text file and paste in Web page	DRM 281	Open text file, select text, press Ctrl+C, place insertion point in Web page in Dreamweaver, click Edit, click Paste Text
Text, find and replace in page	DRM 107	Click Text, click Find and Replace
Text, format using Property inspector	DRM 109	See Reference Window: Formatting Text Using the Property Inspector
Text, formatting in HTML mode	DRM 154	See Reference Window: Formatting Text in HTML Mode
Text, indent	DRM 281	Select text, click ▤
Video clip attributes, adjust	DRM 408	Select video clip, change attributes in Property inspector
Web page, create from template	DRM 445	See Reference Window: Creating a Template-Based Page
Web page, create new	DRM 74	Click HTML in Create New list on Start page
Web page, open in Document window	DRM 24	Double-click filename in Files panel
Web page, preview in browser	DRM 88	Open page to preview, click File, point to Preview in Browser, click browser name
Web page, save existing	DRM 77	Click File, click Save
Web page, save new	DRM 76	Click File, click Save As, select Save In location, type a filename in File Name text box, click Create
Web site, preview on Web from remote location	DRM 92	Start browser, type URL of remote site in Address bar, press Enter
Web site, upload to remote server	DRM 90	Click 🔗 on Files panel toolbar, select files and folder in Local view to upload to remote server, click ⬆, click Yes to upload dependent files if necessary, click 🔗
Web site, upload to remote server	DRM 154	See Reference Window: Uploading a Site to the Remote Server
Web site plan, create	DRM 48	See Reference Window: Creating a Plan for a New Web Site
Workspace environment, select	DRM 16	See Reference Window: Selecting a Workspace Environment

Glossary/Index

Note: Boldface entries include definitions.

A

Absolute font size A font size based on the standard default base size of 3. DRM 153

Absolute link A link that contains the complete URL of the page to which you are linking, which includes http://www.domainname.com/ plus the filename of the page to which you are linking; used to link to Web pages outside of a site. DRM 113

Absolute positioning Positioning that causes an object to stay exactly where you place it relative to the top and left margins of the page regardless of how a user resizes the browser window. DRM 310

Access, creating database-driven pages using, DRM 506–528

Access Denied page, DRM 503–504, DRM 526–527

Accessibility The quality and ease of use of a Web site by people who use assistive devices or people with disabilities. DRM 60–61, DRM 65

Action What you want to happen when the event is performed on the object in a behavior. DRM 337

Action attribute, DRM 456

Active cells, DRM 223

Active link A text hyperlink that is in the process of being clicked. DRM 66

Additive color system A system of color that uses red, green, and blue as its primary colors; also called RGB system. DRM 61

Advanced style A style used to redefine formatting for a group of tags or for all tags that contain a particular ID attribute; most commonly used to customize the appearance of text links. DRM 120

Align attribute
    Flash movie, DRM 379
    graphics, DRM 177
    table, DRM 202

Alignment attribute, DRM 381

Allow JavaScript Control attribute, DRM 408

Alt (Alternative) attribute
    graphics, DRM 177
    hotspot, DRM 184

Alternate Text, DRM 249

Amount of Texture attribute, DRM 569

Anchor tag An HTML tag used to crate hyperlinks in HTML. DRM 116–117, DRM 127–128

Animation. *See* Flash, Shockwave

Anti-Aliasing attribute In Fireworks, the smoothing of the edges between the path and the canvas. DRM 573

Anything Accept limit, DRM 468

Appearance category, DRM 80–81

Appearance page properties, setting, DRM 82–83

Apply All Attributes to TD Tags Instead of TR Tags feature, DRM 210

ASP, creating database-driven pages using, DRM 506–528

Asset An image, color, URL, Flash object, Shockwave object, movie, script, template, or library item that you use throughout a Web site. DRM 173

Assets panel Tools to use and manage assets, such as library items. DRM 551
    to add graphics, DRM 173–174
    tabs in group, DRM 579

Assistive device An apparatus that provide a disabled person with alternate means to experience electronic and information technologies. DRM 60

Attributes
    adding, to existing tag, DRM 141–142
    for CSS style, DRM 121
    cell, DRM 205–206, DRM 229–231
    editable tag, DRM 441
    Flash movie, DRM 378–379
    form, setting, DRM 455–457
    frame and frameset, adjusting, DRM 274–279
    graphics, DRM 176–177
    layer, DRM 320–323
    Shockwave movie, adjusting, DRM 393–394
    sound-only movie, adjusting, DRM 399
    table, modifying, DRM 201–203, DRM 225–227
    target, DRM 117
    Text tool, DRM 573
    vector, in Property inspector, DRM 569
    video clip, adjusting, DRM 408–409

Automatically Upload Files, DRM 73

Autoplay attribute, DRM 379

Auto-Start attribute, DRM 408

B

Backend pages
    creating, for viewing data in database, DRM 495–500, DRM 519–523
    creating login page to protect, DRM 500–505, DRM 523–528

Background settings, DRM 81

Background style attribute, DRM 121

Base font size, DRM 153

Base tag, DRM 422

Basefont tag, DRM 151

Baseline The imaginary line on which the text is sitting. DRM 177

Baseline Shift attribute In Fireworks, the shifting of text either up or down from the natural baseline, similar to superscript or subscript. DRM 573

Behaviors Codes added to a Web page that enable users to interact with various elements in the Web page, to alter the Web page in different ways, or to cause tasks to be performed. DRM 337–354
    adding, DRM 344–346
    editing and deleting, DRM 353–354
    testing, DRM 350–353
    Validate Form, DRM 468–472

Behaviors, server, DRM 482, DRM 491–495
    adding, DRM 514–518
    adding, to Login page, DRM 502–503, DRM 525–526

Behaviors panel, DRM 337–347

Bezier points Small handles that surround a selected object that can be dragged to new positions to reshape the object. DRM 558

Bg Color (Background Color) attribute
    cell, DRM 205, DRM 229
    Flash movie, DRM 379, DRM 381
    layers, DRM 321
    table, DRM 202, DRM 226

Bg Image (Background Image) attribute
    cell, DRM 205
    layers, DRM 321
    table, DRM 202

Bitmap graphic An image created from individual pixels of color. DRM 550

Bitmap tools, DRM 561–568

Blend Mode attribute, DRM 569

Block attribute, DRM 121

Blockquote tag, DRM 150

Blur tool, DRM 561, DRM 65

Body, DRM 79

Bold attribute, DRM 381

Bold tag, DRM 150

Border attribute
    frame, DRM 276
    graphics, DRM 177
    style, DRM 121

Border Color attribute, DRM 276

Borders The four lines that mark the edges of a cell; can be invisible or visible lines of a width you select.
    cell, DRM 192
    dragging, creating frames by, DRM 265–267

Box attribute, DRM 121

Bracketing tags HTML tags that consist of an opening tag and a closing tag that bracket the content to which they are applied. DRM 212

Brdr Color (Border Color) attribute
    cell, DRM 205
    table, DRM 202

Break tag, DRM 151

Brightness, DRM 179

Browser
    integrated file, DRM 22
    testing behaviors in, DRM 346–347
    viewing or previewing Web pages in, on Macintosh, DRM 586
    See also Web browser

Brush tool, DRM 561, DRM 564

Buffer To download the first 5 or 10 seconds of a video clip before it begins to play to Ensure continuous playback of the video clip. After the clip begins to play, the playback will continue without interruption as long as the current download is at or past the current clip playback location. DRM 402

Burn tool, DRM 561, DRM 565

Buttons, DRM 458
    adding, to form, DRM 466–468
    Flash, DRM 383–384

Quick Export, DRM 581

radio, adding, to form, DRM 463–464

for viewing Fireworks file, DRM 551

C

Cache A temporary local storage space in a computer. DRM 20

Cascading A series of stages, processes, operations, rules or selections that produce a cumulative effect. DRM 122

Cascading Style Sheets (CSS) A collection of styles that is either inserted in the head of the HTML of a Web page and used throughout that page (an internal style sheet) or is attached as an external document and used throughout the entire Web site (an external style sheet). DRM 119–121

See also CSS styles

Case problems
    Adding Database Functionality, DRM 532–542
    Adding and Formatting Text, DRM 158–164
    Adding Rich Media to a Web Site, DRM 416–419
    Adding Shared Site Elements, DRM 300–307
    Creating Dynamic Pages, DRM 358–366
    Creating Reusable Assets and Forms, DRM 475–478
    Introducing Dreamweaver, DRM 42–44
    Organizing Page Content and Layout, DRM 238–242
    Planning and Designing a Successful Web Site, DRM 95–100

Catalyst, DRM 103

Cell The container created by the intersection of a row and a column. DRM 192
    adding content to, DRM 195–196, DRM 231–233
    drawing, in Layout mode, DRM 218–220
    in Layout mode, DRM 221–223, DRM 228–233
    selecting, DRM 198, DRM 221–223
    working with, DRM 205–208

Cell attributes, modifying
    formatting and layout, DRM 205–206
    in Layout mode, DRM 229–231

Cell Padding attribute, DRM 226

Cell Spacing attribute, DRM 226

Cell tags, DRM 213

Char Width (Character Width) attribute, DRM 460

Check In/Out, DRM 73

Checkbox, DRM 457, DRM 462–463

Circle tool, DRM 574

Class attribute
    Flash movie, DRM 379
    graphics, DRM 177
    layers, DRM 321

Clear Row Height and Clear Column Width attribute, DRM 202, DRM 226

Client The person or persons for whom you are working. DRM 5–6, DRM 48

See also Web client

Clip attribute, DRM 321

Code, examining
    and adding keywords, DRM 424–425
    for CSS styles, DRM 137–144
    for layers, DRM 323–325
    for library item, DRM 432–433
    tables, DRM 212–215
    See also Hypertext Markup Language (HTML)

Code view, DRM 26
    adding meta description, DRM 427–428
    editing page in, DRM 80

CODEC (COmpressor/DECompressor) The software that converts sound to digital code, shrinks the code to the smallest possible size for faster transmission, and later expands the code for playback on the client computer. Several different popular CODECs are used for sound on the Web, including MP3, RealMedia, QuickTime, and Windows Media. DRM 395

Coder workspace environment, DRM 15

Color
    font, DRM 65
    selecting, DRM 61–64

Color attribute, DRM 381

Color tools, DRM 574–575

Column Crosses the table vertically. DRM 192
    selecting, DRM 199–200
    working with, DRM 208–210

Column span The width of the cell measured in columns.
    adjusting, DRM 207–208

Commands option, Fireworks MX 2004, DRM 551

Comment tag An unpaired tag that is used to add notes that do not appear in the page or affect the way the html is rendered, to the code. For example, the comment tag is nested within the style tag to hide the style definitions from older browsers that do not support CSS styles. DRM 433

Comp A comprehensive, fully developed, detailed drawing that provides a complete preview of what the final design will look like. DRM 68

Compression A process that shrinks a graphic's file size by using different types of encoding to remove redundant or less important information. The smaller a graphic's file size, the faster it will load in a browser.

    graphics and, DRM 168–170

Connection string All the information that a Web application server needs to connect to a database. DRM 515

Consistency, DRM 67

Content All the information that a Web application server needs to connect to a database. DRM 13

    dynamic page, exploring databases and, DRM 482–483

    head, DRM 422

Content, adding

    to cells, DRM 195–196
    to editable regions, DRM 446–447
    to frames, DRM 279–281
    to layer, DRM 315–320
    in Layout mode, DRM 231–233
    to Login page, DRM 501–502, DRM 524–525
    NoFrames, DRM 282–283

Contrast, DRM 179

Convert Table Widths to Percent and Convert Table Heights to Percent, DRM 202

Convert Table Widths to Pixels and Convert Table Heights to Pixels, DRM 202

Copy, navigation bar, DRM 255–257

Crop An image editing process that reduces the area of a graphic by deleting unwanted outer areas. DRM 178

Crop tool, DRM 558, DRM 560–561

CSS style A rule that defines the appearance of an element in a Web page either by redefining an existing HTML tag or by creating a custom style; also called a class style or a custom style class. DRM 119–121

    advanced, to customize anchor tag pseudoclasses, DRM 127–129
    editing, DRM 144–149
    examining code for, DRM 137–144
    and Property inspector, formatting graphics with, DRM 175–178
    redefining table tags with, DRM 215

CSS Style Definition dialog box, editing styles in, DRM 144–146

Custom scripting, DRM 337, DRM 348–350

Custom style (or custom style class) A style you create from scratch and apply to the element you have selected on the page. DRM 120

Custom style classes, DRM 120, DRM 125–127

D

Database A collection of information that is arranged for ease and speed of search and retrieval and usually associated with a specific software package, such as MySQL or Microsoft Access. It can be a simple list of people's names or can collect large quantities of complex information, such as a product inventory.

    connecting Web site to, DRM 489–491, DRM 512–514
    creating, on remote server, DRM 487–489
    exploring, and dynamic page content, DRM 482–483
    uploading, to remote server, DRM 510–512
    viewing data in, creating backend pages for, DRM 495–500, DRM 519–523

Database management interface, logging into, DRM 487–489

Database-driven Web site A Web site that uses a database to gather, display, or manipulate information. For example, e-commerce sites often use a database to store online orders and billing information, and weather sites often retrieve current weather conditions from a database and display it in a Web page. DRM 482

    creating pages using Access and ASP, DRM 506–528
    creating pages using MySQL and PHP, DRM 483–505

DBQ, DRM 515

Declaration The part of the CSS style (or rule) that defines the attributes that are included in the style. DRM 120

Deleting

    behaviors, DRM 353–354

    columns and rows, DRM 209–210
    library item, DRM 436–437
    table, DRM 205, DRM 227
    template, DRM 450

Dependent file A file that is used in a Web page. DRM 90

Deprecated Older HTML tags that are in the process of becoming obsolete. DRM 119

Description meta tag, DRM 422

Design, checking for logic, DRM 69

Design tools, DRM 14–15

Design view, DRM 26

Designer workspace environment, DRM 15

Details page, DRM 495–499, DRM 521–522

Digital video, DRM 402–404

Director A Macromedia program that is used to create comprehensive multimedia solutions deployable across multiple media including CD-ROM, DVD, Web, Kiosk, and so forth. Shockwave files are created in Director. DRM 385

Director projector A standalone executable file that does not need any software or plug-ins to run on a client computer. DRM 385

Disabilities, designing for people with, DRM 60–61

Distort tool, DRM 558–559

Dithering A technique that widens color options by placing pixels of two colors together to give the appearance of a third color. DRM 576

Div tag, DRM 150

Document

    new, Fireworks MX 2004, DRM 554–556
    Word, importing, into Dreamweaver, DRM 587
    See also Files

Document encoding Specifies how digital codes will display the characters in the Web page. The default Western [Latin1] setting is the setting for English and other Western European languages. DRM 82

Document relative link A link that specifies a path from the current Web page rather than the entire URL of the Web page to which you are linking; used to link to pages within a site. DRM 113

Document Size/Estimated Download Time, DRM 28

Document type, choosing, DRM 512–513

Document window The main workspace where you create and edit Web pages. DRM 26–30

Dodge tool, DRM 561, DRM 565

Domain name A name that identifies a Web site and is chosen by the site owner; combined with the top-level domain to create a unique name for the site. DRM 7

Down Image, DRM 249

Down state A navigation bar element or button after it has been clicked. DRM 246–247

Downloading
  RealMedia Suite Extension for Dreamweaver, DRM 404–406
  RealPlayer for Internet Explorer, DRM 409–412

Dreamweaver A Web site creation and management tool from Macromedia.
  editing graphics from within, DRM 178–183
  exiting, DRM 39
  exploring environment, DRM 22–35
  getting help in, DRM 35–39
  importing Word document into, DRM 587
  and Internet, DRM 4–14
  RealMedia Suite extension for, downloading, DRM 404–406
  starting, DRM 15–18, DRM 587
  using, on Macintosh, DRM 585–588
  workspace, editing options from, DRM 580

Dreamweaver Support Center The Dreamweaver Help section of the Macromedia Web site (www.macromedia.com) that provides the latest information on Dreamweaver, advice from experienced users, and advanced Help topics, as well as examples, tips, and updates. DRM 39, DRM 291–294

Driver, DRM 515

Dynamic HTML A combination of HTML enhancements and a scripting language that work together to add animation, interactive elements, and dynamic updating to Web pages. DRM 310

Dynamic page content, exploring databases and, DRM 482–483

Dynamically generated A Web page that displays data stored in a database. DRM 482

E

Edge Feather attribute, DRM 569

Edge pop-up menu attribute, DRM 569

Edge Softness attribute, DRM 569

Edit attribute, DRM 379

Edit option, Fireworks MX 2004, DRM 551

Editable optional region, DRM 441

Editable region An area that can be changed in the pages created from a template. DRM 440, DRM 437, DRM 446–447

Editable tag attribute, DRM 441

Editing
  behaviors, DRM 353–354
  in Code view, DRM 80
  CSS styles, DRM 144–149
  Fireworks MX 2004 tools for, DRM 550–557
  graphics, from within Dreamweaver, DRM 178–183
  keywords, DRM 423–426
  library item, DRM 434–436
  meta description, DRM 426–428
  options from Dreamweaver workspace, DRM 580
  photograph, with Rubber Stamp tool, DRM 567–568
  rollover, DRM 191
  template, DRM 448–450

Effects attribute, DRM 569

Element The name for each rollover object in a navigation bar; can have up to four states: Up, Over, Down, or Over While Down.
  positioning, using grid, DRM 330–331
  states of, DRM 246

Element name, DRM 249

Ellipse tool, DRM 568

E-mail Address Accept limit, DRM 468–469

E-mail link A link in a browser window that a user can click to start his or her default e-mail program, and open a blank message window with the e-mail address specified in the e-mail link already entered in the To field; also referred to as e-mail URL.
  adding, DRM 348

Embedded style sheet Another name for an internal style sheet because the styles in an internal style sheet are embedded (or placed) in the head of the Web page. DRM 138

Emphasis tag, DRM 150

Encryption The process of coding data so that only the sender and/or receiver can read it, preventing others from being able to understand it. DRM 6

Enctype (Encoding Type) attribute, DRM 456

End-user scenario An imagined situation in which the target audience might access a Web site. An end-user scenario is used to envision actual conditions that an end user will be in while experiencing the Web site.
  creating, DRM 54–55

Eraser tool, DRM 561, DRM 565

Event handler The code used to refer to the event in a behavior. DRM 337

Expanded Tables mode, DRM 200–201

Export Area tool, DRM 558, 560

Exporting, Fireworks files, DRM 556–557

Extensions, DRM 121
  See also File extensions

External style sheet A separate file that contains all the CSS styles connected with a Web site. The styles can be used in any page of the Web site to which you connect that style sheet. DRM 120, DRM 130–137

Eyedropper tool, DRM 561, DRM 566

F

Fields, hidden, DRM 457

File attribute, DRM 379

File extension A series of characters used by Windows to determine the file type. The file extension for HTML Web pages can be either .htm or .html. DRM 23
  Director, DRM 385
  Flash, DRM 373
  PHP, DRM 485
  video file formats, DRM 403

File field, DRM 458

File navigation and selection, on Macintosh, DRM 586

File option, Fireworks MX 2004, DRM 551

File Transfer Protocol (FTP) A common Internet protocol used to copy files from one computer to another. DRM 5

Filename The name under which a Web page (or other file) is saved; appears in parentheses to the right of the page title in the title bar. DRM 26

Files
    dependent, DRM 90
    Fireworks MX 2004, saving and exporting, DRM 556–557
    locked, DRM 385
    sound, creating links to, DRM 399–401
Files panel, DRM 22–25
Files panel menu bar, DRM 588
Fill Color attribute, DRM 569
Fill Color box, DRM 574
Fill Options pop-up menu attribute, DRM 569
Fill Texture pop-up menu attribute, DRM 569
Filters option, Fireworks MX 2004, DRM 551
Find and Replace tool, DRM 107–108
Firewall A hardware or software device that restricts access between the computer network and the Internet, thereby protecting the computer behind the firewall. DRM 72–73
Fireworks MX 2004 A Macromedia graphics package designed specifically for developing Web graphics.
    editing tools and file creation, DRM 550–557
    introduction to, DRM 549
    working with, and other applications, DRM 580
Flash One of the first widely used animation programs that used vector-based graphics. Because vector-based graphics can scale and compress to a very small file size without losing quality, Flash has become one of the premier solutions for creating and delivering interactive animations for display on the Web. DRM 372–375
    adding movies to Web pages, DRM 375–380
    adding text to Web pages, DRM 380–383
    adjusting movie attributes, DRM 378–379
    buttons, DRM 383–384
    embedding sound-only movie, DRM 396–399
Flowchart A diagram of geometric shapes connected by lines that shows steps in sequence. DRM 57–58
Font A set of letters, numbers, and symbols in a unified typeface.
    selecting, DRM 64–66
Font attribute, DRM 381
Font color The color that is applied to a font. DRM 65
Font size The size of a font. DRM 65, DRM 153–154

Font style The stylistic attributes that are applied to the font, which include bold, italic, and underline. DRM 65
Font tag An HTML tag that allowed designers to designate which font and which relative font size the Web page should be displayed in (as long as the designated font was installed on the user's computer); deprecated in HTML 4.01, their functions were replaced and expanded upon by Cascading Style Sheets. DRM 119
Form A means of collecting information from users. You can use forms to gather information about the user, create a user log in, gather user feedback, and so forth. Forms encourage user interaction because they enable the user to enter and send information over the Web without leaving the Web site. DRM 453–454
    adding buttons to, DRM 466–468
    adding lists to, DRM 465–466
    adding radio buttons to, DRM 463–464
    creating, DRM 454–457
    creating structure, DRM 458–459
    inserting checkboxes into, DRM 462–463
    inserting text fields and areas into, DRM 460–462
    modifying, DRM 484–485, DRM 506–508
    testing, DRM 470–472
Form attributes, setting, DRM 455–457
Form Name attribute, DRM 455
Form objects The mechanisms that enable users to input data into a form, such as text fields, text areas, hidden fields, checkboxes, radio buttons, radio groups, lists/menus, jump menus, image fields, file fields, and buttons. Each form object has a specific function. DRM 457–468
Formatting
    cell, and layout, modifying, DRM 205–206
    graphics, DRM 175–178
    with Property inspector, DRM 108–111
    removing, from text, DRM 125
Formatting, text
    in HTML mode, DRM 154–154
    in hyperlinks, DRM 111–112
4-Up button, DRM 551
Frame Divides one Web page into multiple HTML documents. Each frame contains a single HTML document with its own content and, if necessary, its own scroll bars. DRM 259–262
    adding content, DRM 279–281

    adjusting page properties for, DRM 271–274
    creating Web page that uses, DRM 262–271
    finding solutions to common problems, DRM 291–294
    reviewing HTML associated with, DRM 289–291
    selecting and saving, DRM 269
    using hyperlinks with, DRM 283–289
Frame, creating
    by dragging borders, DRM 265–267
    by splitting Web page, DRM 263–265
Frame attributes, adjusting, DRM 274–275, DRM 277–279
Frame Name attribute, DRM 275
Frame tag, DRM 289
Frames and History panel In Fireworks, Frame tools to create rollovers and animations and History tools to reverse and repeat commands. DRM 551
Frameset attributes, adjusting, DRM 274–279
Frameset A separate HTML document that defines the structure and properties of a Web page with frames. DRM 259–262, DRM 267–268
Frameset tags, DRM 289
Freeform tool, DRM 568, DRM 574
FTP Host, DRM 72

G

Generic font families The three categories of typefaces: serif, sans-serif, and mono (monospaced). DRM 64
GIF (Graphics Interchange Format) A graphics format invented by the CompuServe Company to provide its customers with a means to exchange graphics files online; usually used for line drawings or other graphics that have non-gradient colors. DRM 169, DRM 575–576
Gradient tool, DRM 561, DRM567
Graphic A visual representation, such as a drawing, painting, or photograph. DRM 11
    adding, to Web pages, DRM 171–174
    background layer, adding behavior to, DRM 346
    bitmap and vector, DRM 550
    choosing, DRM 66–68
    and compression, DRM 168–170
    editing, from within Dreamweaver, DRM 178–183

formatting, using CSS styles and Property inspector, DRM 175–178
for navigation bar, DRM 249–250
working with, in Fireworks, DRM 557
See also Fireworks MX 2004, Images

Graphic hyperlinks, creating, DRM 183–187

Graphic style The look of the graphic elements of the site.
choosing, DRM 66–68

Grid A series of parallel horizontal and vertical lines that overlap to create equal-sized squares in the background of the Document window; provides a guide for positioning or resizing layers or other elements.
positioning layers and other elements with, DRM 330–331

H

H (Height) attribute
cell, DRM 229
Flash movie, DRM 378
layers, DRM 321
graphics, DRM 176
table, DRM 201–202, DRM 226
vector, DRM 569

H Space (Horizontal Space) attribute
Flash movie, DRM 379
graphics, DRM 177

Hand tool, DRM 575

Head The portion of the HTML between the head tags in a Web page. DRM 79
reviewing content, DRM 422
Web page, DRM 137

Header attribute, cell, DRM 205

Header Cell tags, DRM 213

Headings, converting, to images, DRM 65

Headings category, DRM 80–82

Headings page properties, setting, DRM 84

Help
Dreamweaver, DRM 35–39, DRM 588
Fireworks MX 2004, DRM 551

Hexadecimal A number system that uses the digits 0 through 9 to represent the decimal values 0 through 9, plus the letters A through F to represent the decimal values 10 through 15. DRM 63–64

Hexadecimal color code Used instead of color names. A six-digit number in the form of #RRGGBB where RR is replaced by the hexadecimal color value for red, GG is replaced with the green value, and BB is replaced with the blue value. The specified amounts of each of these colors are mixed together by the system to create the color you specify. DRM 63

Hidden fields, DRM 457

Hide Logo attribute, DRM 408

Hide Slices and Hotspots button, DRM 574

Home page The main page of a Web site. DRM 10–11

HomeSite, DRM 15

Horizontal Scale attribute In Fireworks, the stretching or shrinking of text horizontally. DRM 573

Horz (Horizontal) attribute, cell, DRM 205, DRM 229

Host Directory, DRM 72

Hotspot An area of an image that a user can click with a mouse to cause an action, such as loading another Web page, to occur.
adding behaviors to, DRM 346
with image map, DRM 184
Web tools, DRM 574

HTML. *See* Hypertext Markup Language (HTML)

HTTP (Hypertext Transfer Protocol) The protocol that controls the transfer of Web pages over the Internet. DRM 5

HTTPS (Hypertext Transfer Protocol Secure) A protocol that encrypts data transferred between a browser and the server to keep the information secure. DRM 6

Hyperlink A node that provides the ability to cross-reference information within a document or a Web page and enable a user to move from one document or Web page to another; also called a link. DRM 11–13
adding and formatting text, DRM 111–112
creating, DRM 111–115
creating from text, DRM 112–115
exploring HTML tags for, DRM 115–118
graphic, creating, DRM 183–187
using, with frames, DRM 283–289
using advanced CSS type for, DRM 127–129

Hypertext Markup Language (HTML) The most common language that provides instructions for how to format Web pages for display.
examining code for layers, DRM 323–325
exploring table code, DRM 212–215
exploring tags for hyperlinks, DRM 115–118
exploring tags used with text, DRM 149–154
modifying tags, DRM 121–125
redefined tag, DRM 120
reviewing, associated with frames and targets, DRM 289–291
reviewing tags, DRM 78–80
See also Dynamic HTML

Hypertext Transfer Protocol *See* HTTP

Hypertext Transfer Protocol Secure *See* HTTPS

I

Image
converting headings to, DRM 65
as graphics attribute, DRM 176
linking, DRM 183
working with, in other applications, DRM 579–581

Image field, DRM 458

Image map A graphic that is divided into invisible regions, or hotspots.
creating, DRM 184–187

Information
creating categories for, DRM 56–57
gathering and organizing, DRM 59

Information architecture The process of determining what you need a site to do and then constructing the framework that will allow you to most effectively accomplish those goals.
creating, DRM 56–59

Inherit To receive from a parent object. DRM 122

Init Val (Initial Value), DRM 460

Inline Included within the actual code for the tag. DRM 323

Insert
behaviors, methods for, DRM 337
checkboxes, into form, DRM 462–463
columns and rows, DRM 209
elements, DRM 250

frames and NoFrames content, DRM 279–283
graphics, in Web pages, DRM 171–174
layers, DRM 310–311
navigation bar, DRM 249–255
new Web pages, DRM 74–75
text, in Web page, DRM 104–108
text fields and areas, into form, DRM 460–462

Insert bar A toolbar that contains buttons to create and insert objects. DRM 33–35, DRM 171–173

Insert Record, DRM 515, DRM 517–518

Insert Record behavior, DRM 492, DRM 494–495

Integrated file browser A program that enables you to browse files located outside of your site. DRM 22

Internal style sheet A file saved in the current document that embeds (or inserts) the styles in the head of the current Web page and applies them only throughout that document; also called an embedded style sheet. DRM 120, DRM 138–139

Internet A huge, global network made up of millions of smaller computer networks that are all connected together.
  adjusting RealMedia video clip to display over, DRM 412–413
  Dreamweaver and, DRM 4–14
  See also World Wide Web

Internet Explorer, downloading RealPlayer for, DRM 409–412

Internet service provider (ISP) A company that has direct access to the Internet and sells access to other smaller entities. DRM 6

ISP *See* Internet service provider

Italicize attribute, DRM 381

J

JavaScript A scripting language that works with HTML. DRM 188, DRM 348

JPEG A graphics format created by the committee from the Joint Photographic Experts Group to digitize photographic images; usually used on photographic images and graphics that have many gradient colors. DRM 169–170, DRM 575–576

Jump menu, DRM 458

K

Kerning attribute In Fireworks, the amount of space between the characters of the text. DRM 573

keyword A descriptive word or phrase that is placed in the meta tag with the attribute name="keywords"; one of the elements many search engines use to index Web pages.
  adding and editing, DRM 423–426

Keywords meta tag, DRM 422

Knife tool, DRM 569, DRM 574

L

L (Left) attribute, DRM 321

Lasso tool, DRM 561–562

Layer A transparent container you place in a Web page to hold different types of content; can be stacked on other layers. DRM 310–311, DRM 576
  adding, in Web page, DRM 390–392
  adding content to, DRM 315–320
  adjusting stacking order, DRM 325–329
  aligning, DRM 329–330
  converting, to tables, DRM 334–336
  drawing, and modifying attributes, DRM 342–343
  examining code for, DRM 323–325
  inserting Shockwave movie into, DRM 392
  modifying, DRM 325–333
  nested, DRM 331–333
  positioning, using grid, DRM 330–331
  selecting, resizing, and moving, DRM 311–315

Layer attributes, adjusting, DRM 320–323

Layer ID, DRM 320

Layers panel Tools for working with multiple layers. DRM 551, DRM 576–577

Layout The position of elements, in this case, on the screen.
  sketching, DRM 68–69

Layout mode
  creating table in, DRM 218–221
  planning table in, DRM 215–218
  selecting tables and cells in, DRM 221–223
  working with cells in, DRM 228–233
  working with tables in, DRM 223–228

Leading attribute In Fireworks, the amount of space between multiple lines of text. DRM 573

Left Col (Left Column) feature, DRM 210

Library A collection of library items that are located in the Library folder in the site's local root folder. DRM 429

Library item A page element (a piece of a Web page) saved as an .lbi file that can be inserted in more than one page of a site; useful for elements that you intend to reuse or update frequently. DRM 428–437

Library panel Tools to define symbols to use throughout a document. DRM 579

Line tool, DRM 568–569

Link
  colors for, DRM 66
  creating, to MP3 sound file, DRM 399–401
  e-mail, adding, to page, DRM 348
  See also Hyperlinks

Link attribute
  Flash movie, DRM 381
  hotspot, DRM 184

Link tag, DRM 422

Linked style sheet Another name for an external style sheet because a link tag appears within the head of the Web page and the styles are located in the external sheet, not in the head of the Web page. DRM 139

Links category, DRM 80–81

Links page properties, setting, DRM 83–84

Linux server, creating database-driven pages for, DRM 483–505

List attribute, style, DRM 121

List/menu, DRM 458

Lists, adding, to form, DRM 465–466

Local root folder The location where you store all the files used by the local version of the Web site. DRM 19

Local site definition The information stored on the computer that you are using that tells Dreamweaver the location of the site's local root folder. DRM 19–21, DRM 70–71

Locked file A file that cannot be opened in the authoring environment. DRM 385

Login, DRM 72

Login page
   creating, to protect backend pages, DRM 500–505, DRM 523–528
   testing, DRM 504, DRM 527

Logo A graphic used by a company for the purposes of brand identification. DRM 11, DRM 578–579

Loop attribute, DRM 379

Lossless compression A compression format in which no information is discarded when the file is compressed. DRM 170

Lossy A compression format that discards (or loses) information to compress an image. DRM 169

Low Src (Low Resolution Image Source File), as graphics attribute, DRM 177

M

Machine name A series of characters, often www, that a server administrator assigns to a Web site. The machine name is part of the URL. DRM 7

Macintosh, using Dreamweaver on, DRM 585–588

Macromedia Flash. *See* Flash

Macromedia Shockwave. *See* Shockwave

Magic Wand tool, DRM 61, DRM 563–564

Main toolbar, DRM 552–553

Make Widths Consistent attribute, DRM 226

Map hotspot attribute, DRM 184

Margin A measurement that specifies where page content is placed on the page. DRM 81

Margin Height attribute, DRM 276

Margin settings, DRM 81

Margin Width attribute, DRM 276

Market research The careful investigation and study of data about the target audience's preferences for a product or service. It also includes evaluating the products or services of competitors. DRM 52–54

Marquee tool, DRM 561

Master page, DRM 495–497, DRM 519–520

Max Chars (Maximum Characters)/Num Lines (Number of Lines), DRM 460

Media Any special configurable object you add to a Web page that needs a player or an application that is not part of the browser, such as plug-ins, ActiveX controls, or helper applications, to display within a browser. Some of the most useful media used in Web pages are Flash, Shockwave, sound, and video.
   adding, to Web site, DRM 372

Menu bar A categorized series of menus that provide access to all the tools and features available in Dreamweaver. DRM 18, DRM 550–551

Merges Selected Cells Using Spans, DRM 205

Meta description A short summary of the Web page that is placed in the meta tag with the attribute name="description". Many search engines use the meta description to index Web pages. DRM 426–428

Meta refresh tag, DRM 422, DRM 503–504, DRM 526–527

Meta tag A tag in the head content that holds information about the page, gives information to the server, or adds functionality to the page. DRM 422

Metafile attribute, DRM 408

Metaphor A comparison in which one object, concept, or idea is represented as another. DRM 59–60, DRM 67

Method attribute, DRM 456

Modify option, Fireworks MX 2004, DRM 551

Modify toolbar, DRM 552–553

Monospaced font A typface in which each letter takes exactly the same width in the line; for example, the letter i (a thin letter) would take the same amount of space as the letter m. Courier is a common monospaced font. DRM 64

Mood, creating, with color, DRM 62

Movies. *See* Flash, Shockwave

Moving
   cells in Layout mode, DRM 228–229
   layer, DRM 311–315
   table, DRM 203–205

MP3 A very commonly used sound format, because MP3 files can contain very high quality sound with a surprisingly small file size. This is perfect for sending sound over the Web, especially when the end user has a slow connection.
   creating link to, DRM 399–401

Multiple document interface (MDI) An interface that integrates all the Document windows and panels in one large application window. DRM 15

MySQL, creating database-driven pages using, DRM 483–505

N

Name attribute
   Flash movie, DRM 378
   video clip, DRM 408

Nav Bar Elements, DRM 249

Navigation bar A specific Dreamweaver item that consists of a series of rollover graphics that change state when specific browser actions occur, such as when the user places the pointer over a graphic. DRM 246, DRM 255–257
   creating, with targeted links, DRM 285–287
   inserting, DRM 249–255
   modifying, DRM 257–258, DRM 443

Navigation bar element *See* element

Navigation bar object, creating, DRM 246–257

Navigation system The interface that visitors use to move through a Web site. DRM 56

Nest To place one set of tags around another set of tags so that both sets apply to the text they surround. DRM 116

Nested frameset A frameset that is inside another frameset. DRM 267

Nested layer A layer contained within an outer (parent) layer similar to nested tables and nested frames. With layers, nesting does not refer to the physical position of the layers, but to the underlying code for the layers. This means that the nested layer does not have to touch its parent layer on-screen to be nested. Nesting is used to group layers. DRM 331–333

Nested table A table inside an existing table. DRM 216

Nested template A template created from the main template so that you can create a more defined structure for some pages of a site. Each nested template inherits all the features of the main template. In other words, each nested template contains the same editable and noneditable regions as the main template and is linked to the main template. DRM 450–453

Netscape Resize Fix JavaScript code that forces the page to reload every time the browser window is resized, thus eliminating display problems. DRM 333–334

Network A series of computers that are connected together to share information and resources. DRM 4

No Resize attribute, DRM 276

No Wrap attribute, cell, DRM 205, DRM 229

NoFrames, adding content, DRM 282–283

NoFrames content The content shown by browsers that cannot display frames. DRM 259

NoFrames tags, DRM 289

Nonbreaking space A special, invisible characters used to create more than one space between text and other elements. DRM 111

Nonbreaking Space tag, DRM 151

Noneditable region An area that can be changed in the template, but cannot be changed in the pages created from a template. DRM 437

Nongradient Color that is one shade and does not vary with subtle darkening or lightening. DRM 69

Nonlinear A process or event that does not occur in a straight line or a consecutive order. DRM 11

Number Accept limit, DRM 468

Number Form Accept limit, DRM 469

O

Object In Dreamweaver, anything that you create or insert into a page or attach a behavior to, such as a graphic or a layer. DRM 33, DRM 337

Object Name box attribute, DRM 569

Opacity attribute, DRM 569

Optimize To obtain acceptable image quality with the smallest possible file size. DRM 551

Optimize panel In Fireworks, tools for optimizing graphics for the Web, creating balance between file size and image quality. DRM 551, DRM 575

Optional region, DRM 440

Options, navigation bar, DRM 250

Ordered List tag, DRM 150

Original button, DRM 551

Oval Marquee tool, DRM 561

Over Image, DRM 249

Over state A navigation bar element or button when the pointer is positioned over the Up graphic. DRM 246

Over While Down Image, DRM 249

Over While Down state A navigation bar element or button when the pointer is placed over the Down graphic. DRM 247

Overflow attribute, DRM 321

P

Page element Either an object or text. DRM 30

Page properties Attributes that apply to an entire page rather than to only an element on the page.
    adjusting, for frames, DRM 271–274
    setting, DRM 80–86

Page title The name you give a Web page; appears in the browser's title bar when the Web page is displayed in a browser. DRM 26

Page-centric design An approach to design that concentrates on designing and creating Web pages individually and then linking them together, rather than concentrating on a Web site as a whole. DRM 15
    See also site-centric design

Paint Bucket tool, DRM 561, DRM 566–567

Panel A set of related commands, controls, and information about different aspects of working with Dreamweaver. DRM 18
    Assets, DRM 579
    Fireworks MX 2004, DRM 551
    tools, DRM 551–552, DRM 558–575
    working with, DRM 575–579

Panel group A collection of related panels. DRM 18

Paragraph tag, DRM 150

Parameters
    for table, DRM 192–193
    table tags, DRM 212–213

Parameters attribute, DRM 379

Parent frameset The frameset that holds the nested frameset. DRM 267

Passive FTP, DRM 72

Password, DRM 72, DRM 500, DRM 523–524

Path Scrubber Additive tool, DRM 569

Path Scrubber Subtractive tool, DRM 569

Pen tool, DRM 568–570

Pencil tool, DRM 561, DRM 564–565

Photograph, editing, with Rubber Stamp tool, DRM 567–568

PHP, creating database-driven pages using, DRM 483–505

Pixel Stands for picture element; the smallest adjustable unit on a display screen. DRM 28

Play attribute, DRM 379

Player, DRM 372

Plug-in, DRM 372

PNG. *See* Portable Network Graphic (PNG)

Pointer tool, DRM 558

Polygon Lasso tool, DRM 561–563

Polygon Slice tool, DRM 574

Polygon tool, DRM 568, DRM 574

Portable Network Graphic (PNG) A newer graphic compression format created by a group of designers who were frustrated by the limitations of existing compression formats. The source file format for Fireworks, which maintains all the file's editable features as well as the layers created as part of the graphic. DRM 170, DRM 556

Positioning, as style attribute, DRM 121

Pre tag, DRM 151

Predefined framset, DRM 267–268

Preset behavior tools, DRM 337–338

Preset table design list, DRM 210

Preview button, DRM 551

Properties, modifying, for new document, DRM 555–556

Property inspector A toolbar with buttons for examining or editing the attributes of any element that is currently selected in the page displayed in the Document window. DRM 30–33
    changing text appearance in, DRM 148–149
    creating targeted link with, DRM 287–289
    and CSS styles, formatting graphics with, DRM 175–178
    Fireworks MX 2004, DRM 551, DRM 553–554
    formatting text with, DRM 108–111
    vector attributes in, DRM 569

Proportional font A font in which each letter takes up a different width on the line proportional to the width of the letter—for example, the letter i takes less space than the letter m). Times New Roman and Helvetica are both proportional fonts. DRM 64

Protocol A set of technical specifications that define a format for sharing information. DRM 4

Pseudoclass Any class that is applied to entities other than HTML Specifications Standard tags; for example, the anchor tag has four pseudoclasses—a:link, a:hover, a:active, and a:visited. DRM 127–129

Q

Quality attribute, DRM 379
Quick Export button, DRM 581

R

Radio buttons
    adding, to form, DRM 463–464
    and radio group, DRM 458
RealMedia
    adding video clip to Web page, DRM 406–408
    adjusting video clip to display over Internet, DRM 412–413
    downloading, DRM 404–406
RealPlayer, downloading, DRM 409–412
Recordset A temporary collection of data retrieved from a database and stored on the application server that generates the Web page when that page is loaded in a browser window. DRM 491–493, DRM 514–517
Rectangle tool, DRM 568, DRM 570, DRM 574
Red Eye Removal tool, DRM 561, DRM 565
Redefined HTML tag An existing HTML tag that you modify to make the tag more useful. DRM 120
Redraw Path tool, DRM 568
Refresh tag. *See* Meta refresh tag
Regions
    adding, to template, DRM 440–444
    editable and noneditable, DRM 437
Relative font size A font size that adds or subtracts from the base font size. DRM 153
Remote location, uploading Web site to, DRM 89–92
Remote site definition A font size that adds or subtracts from the base font size.
    creating, DRM 71–74
Remove All Spacers attribute, table, DRM 226
Remove Nesting attribute, table, DRM 226
Repeating region, DRM 440
Replace Color tool, DRM 561, DRM 565

Resample An image editing process that adds or subtracts pixels from a graphic that has been resized. DRM 179
Reset button, adding, to form, DRM 467–468
Reset image size, as graphics attribute, DRM 177
Reset Size attribute, DRM 79
Reshape Area tool, DRM 568
Resizing
    cells, in Layout mode, DRM 228–229
    columns and rows, DRM 208–209
    graphic, DRM 180
    image, DRM 177
    layer, DRM 311–315
    in Layout mode, DRM 224–225
    table, DRM 203–205
    See also Netscape Resize Fix
Restrict Access to Page, DRM 504–505, DRM 527–528
RGB system A system of color that uses red, green, and blue as its primary colors (RGB stands for red, green, and blue); also called the additive color system. DRM 61–62
Robots Software that searches the Web and sends information back to the engine to compile information that is used to list pages in the search engines. DRM 423
Rollover An image that changes when the pointer moves across it.
    creating, DRM 187–191
Rollover Color attribute, DRM 381
Rounded Rectangle tool, DRM 568, DRM 570
Row Crosses the table horizontally. DRM 192
    selecting, DRM 199–200
    working with, DRM 208–210
Row Colors feature, DRM 210
Row span The height of the cell measured in rows.
    adjusting, DRM 207–208
Rubber Stamp tool, DRM 561, DRM 565–568
Rulers, turning on, DRM 250

S

Sans-serif typeface A typeface in which the lines, or serifs, are absent. (Sans means without in French, so sans-serif means without serif.) The most common sans-serif typeface is Helvetica. DRM 64
Save As attribute, DRM 381

Saving
    Fireworks files, DRM 556–557
    frames, DRM 269
    frameset, DRM 270–271
    Web pages in defined state, DRM 74–78
Scale attribute, DRM 379
Scale tool, DRM 558–559
Scroll attribute, DRM 276
Search engine A Web site whose primary function is to gather and report what information is available on the Web about specified keywords or phrases. DRM 53, DRM 422–423
Secure FTP (SFTP), DRM 73
Select Behind tool, DRM 558
Select option, Fireworks MX 2004, DRM 551
Selecting
    colors, DRM 61–64
    fonts, DRM 64–66
    frames, DRM 269
    frameset, DRM 70–271
    layer, DRM 311–315
    tables and cells in Layout mode, DRM 221–223
    tables and table elements, DRM 196–201
    workspace layout configuration, DRM 15–18
Selection tools, DRM 558–561
Selector The name of the CSS style. DRM 120
Serif typeface A typeface in which a delicate, horizontal line (called a serif) finishes off the main strokes of each character; an example would be the horizontal bars at the top and bottom of an uppercase M. The most common serif typeface is Times New Roman. DRM 64
Server The computer (or computers) that stores and distributes information to the other computers in a network. DRM 4
    and clients, DRM 5–6
    Linux, creating database-driven pages for, DRM 483–505
    testing, setting up, DRM 512–513
    Windows, creating database-driven pages for, DRM 506–528
Server, remote
    creating database on, DRM 487–489
    updating Web site on, DRM 154–155, DRM 233–234, DRM 294–296, DRM 354– 355, DRM 413–414, DRM 472
    uploading database to, DRM 510–512

Server behavior A behavior that runs on the Web server before the Web page is sent to a user's browser and is written in PHP, ASP, JSP, or ColdFusion. DRM 482, DRM 491–495, DRM 502–503, DRM 514–518, DRM 525–526

Shapes, basic, creating, DRM 571–572

Shapes panel In Fireworks, Auto shape tools not available in the Tools panel, such as a frame or cylinder. DRM 579

Sharpen, DRM 179

Sharpen tool, DRM 561, DRM 565

Shockwave The Macromedia solution for delivering interactive multimedia on the Web; used for more complex interactive media components such as games, interactive 3D, database-driven multimedia, multiuser applications, and educational materials. DRM 385–389
    adding movies to Web pages, DRM 389–394
    adjusting attributes of movie, DRM 393–394

Show Font attribute, DRM 381

Show Slices and Hotspots button, DRM 574

Simple Mail Transfer Protocol (SMTP) An agreed-upon format used by some e-mail software. DRM 4–5

Site concept A general underlying theme that unifies the various elements of a site and contributes to the site's look and feel. DRM 59–60, DRM 67

Site definition The information that tells Dreamweaver where to find the local and remote files for the Web site, along with other parameters that affect how the site is set up within Dreamweaver.
    creating, DRM 18–21

Site map A visual representation of how the pages in a Web site are interrelated. DRM 23–24

Site root relative link A link that specifies a path from the site root folder to the linked document; used in large sites with complex folder structures that change frequently. DRM 113

Site-centric design An approach to design that focuses on planning the Web site structure and design before creating any pages. DRM 15
    See also page-centric design

Size, of graphics, DRM 67

Size attribute, DRM 381

Skew tool, DRM 558–559

Slice A smaller graphic cut from a larger graphic; used to reduce the time needed to load a large graphic, to attach behaviors to specific areas of a graphic, and to create rollovers. DRM 574

Smudge tool, DRM 561, DRM 565

Sound, DRM 394–396

Sound files, creating links to, DRM 399–401

Sound formats The different types of compression used for sound; each sound format uses a different CODEC as the sound is compressed for delivery and decompressed for playback. DRM 395, DRM 399

Sound-only movie, embedding, DRM 396–399

Spacer image A one-pixel transparent image that is inserted into the fixed-width columns in a table created in Layout mode that contains an autostretch column to maintain the widths of the fixed width columns. DRM 226

Spelling, checking, DRM 106–107

Split Frame Down, DRM 264

Split Frame Left, DRM 263

Split Frame Right, DRM 263

Split Frame Up, DRM 264

Split view, DRM 6

Splits Cell into Rows or Columns, DRM 205

SQL (Structured Query Language) A specialized language used for working with databases. DRM 482

Src attribute
    Flash movie, DRM 379
    frame, DRM 275
    graphics, DRM 177
    video clip, DRM 408

Status bar A bar, located at the bottom of the Document window, that displays details about the Document window's content. DRM 28–30

Streaming Sound, video, or animation that begins to play on the end-user's computer after only a small portion downloads and will continue to play while the rest of the file is downloading. It is especially helpful to users with slow connections because they can begin to hear the sound or view the media without waiting for large files to download completely. DRM 395

Stroke Color attribute, DRM 569

Stroke Color box, DRM 574

Stroke Options attribute, DRM 569

Strong tag, DRM 150

Style sheets
    CSS, DRM 119–121, DRM 127–129, DRM 137–149, DRM 175–178, DRM 215
    external, DRM 120, DRM 130–137
    internal, DRM 120, DRM 138–139

Style tags, viewing, DRDM 141–144

Styles
    creating, in external style sheet, DRM 135–137
    deleting, from style sheet, DRM 132–133
    exporting, to external style sheet, DRM 130–132

Styles panel In Fireworks, tools to define and store styles for objects that you can reuse. DRM 579

Submit button, adding, to form, DRM 467–468

Subselection tool, DRM 558

Subtractive color system A system of color that uses cyan, magenta, and yellow as its primary colors; all other colors are created by mixing these primary colors. DRM 61

T

T (Top) attribute, layers, DRM 321

Table A grid structure that is divided into rows and columns.
    converting layers to, DRM 334–336
    creating, DRM 191–196, DRM 218–221
    exploring HTML code, DRM 212–215
    nested, DRM 216
    planning, in Layout mode, DRM 215–218
    repeating, creating, DRM 442–443
    selecting, in Layout mode, DRM 221–223
    and table elements, selecting, DRM 196–201
    using preset designs, DRM 210–212
    working with, in Layout mode, DRM 223–228
    working with entire, DRM 201–205
    See also Cell(s), Columns, Rows

Table attributes, modifying, in Layout mode, DRM 225–227

Table feature, DRM 210

Table ID attribute, DRM 201

Table Row tags, DRM 213

Table tags, DRM 212, DRM 215

Tag
  anchor, DRM 116, DRM 127–129
  bracketing, DRM 212
  font, DRM 119
  frameset, DRM 289
  meta refresh, adding, to Access Denied page, DRM 503–504, DRM 526–527
  style, DRM 141–144
Tag inspector, eding styles with, DRM 146–148
Tag selector, DRM 28
Tags, HTML, DRM 78–80
  exploring, for hyperlinks, DRM 115–118
  modifying, DRM 121–125
  redefined, DRM 120
  used with text, DRM 149–154
Target An anchor tab attribute that specifies where the link opens—in the current browser window or a new browser window. DRM 232, DRM 289–291
Target attribute
  with anchor link, DRM 117
  for Flash text, DRM 381
  form, DRM 456
  hotspot, DRM 184
Target audience The group of people whom you would most like to use your product or service.
  and color, DRM 62
  and graphics, DRM 67
  identifying, DRM 50–52
Template A special page that enables a designer to separate the look and layout of a page from the content by "locking" the page layout. The designer designates what is locked in a page by creating editable regions and noneditable regions. DRM 437–438
  applying, to existing Web page, DRM 447
  creating, DRM 438–440
  creating Web pages from, DRM 444–447
  editing, DRM 448–450
  nested, DRM 450–453
Testing server, setting up, DRM 512–513
Text
  applying custom style class to, DRM 142
  changing appearance, in Property inspector, DRM 148–149
  exploring HTML tags used with, DRM 149–154
  Flash, adding, to Web pages, DRM 380–383
  removing formatting from, DRM 125
Text, adding
  to table, DRM 195–196
  to Web page, DRM 104–108
Text, formatting
  in HTML mode, DRM 153–154
  using Property inspector, DRM 108–111
Text attribute, DRM 381
Text fields and text areas, DRM 457, DRM 460–462
Text link A hyperlink that has not yet been clicked. DRM 66
  creating, DRM 111–115
  eleting, DRM 250
Text option, Fireworks MX 2004, DRM 551
Text settings, DRM 80–81
Text tool, DRM 568, DRM 573
Title, DRM 79
Title bar A bar that displays the page title and the filename of the open Web page at the top of the Document window or the Dreamweaver window if the Document window is maximized, and displays the page title at the top of the browser window. DRM 26
Title/Encoding category, DRM 80, DRM 82
Toolbars, Main and Modify, DRM 552–553
Tools
  bitmap, DRM 561–568
  color, DRM 574–575
  selection, DRM 558–561
  vector, DRM 568–574
  view, DRM 575
  Web, DRM 574
Tools panel In Fireworks, drawing tools to help you create and modify artwork. DRM 551
  previewing, DRM 552
  using, DRM 558–575
Top Row feature, DRM 210
Top-level domain The highest category in the Internet naming system, it identifies the type of entity that owns the site or country of origin; combined with the domain name to create a unique name for the site. DRM 7
Transparent Texture attribute, DRM 569
2-Up button, DRM 551
Type, as style attribute, DRM 121
Type attribute, DRM 460

U

Uniform Resource Locator (URL) The unique address that Web browsers use to locate a Web page. DRM 6, DRM 579
Unordered List tag, DRM 150
Up Image, DRM 249
Up state A navigation bar element or button before the user clicks it. DRM 246
URLs panel In Fireworks, tools to create hyperlinks from images. DRM 579
Use Tables, DRM 250
User event What the user does to trigger the action in a behavior. DRM 337
User names, login page and, DRM 500, DRM 523–524
User profile The information about end users that you gather from a list of questions. DRM 50–52

V

V Space (Vertical Space) attribute
  Flash movie, DRM 379
  graphics, DRM 177
Validate Form behavior A behavior that enables you to create requirements/limits that check the form data before the form is submitted. DRM 468–472
Variable transparency The ability to make the background of the image transparent at different amounts. DRM 170
Vector attributes, in Property inspector, DRM 569
Vector graphic An image that uses mathematical formulas and vector paths to define shapes and figures. DRM 550
Vector Path tool, DRM 568
Vector tools, DRM 568–574
Vert (Vertical) attribute, cell, DRM 205, DRM 229
Video
  adding, to Web page, DRM 404–412
  digital, DRM 402–404
Video clip
  adding, to Web page, DRM 406–408
  adjusting attributes of, DRM 408–409
  RealMedia, adjusting, to display over Internet, DRM 412–413
Video file formats, reviewing, DRM 403–404
View option, Fireworks MX 2004, DRM 551

View tools, DRM 575
Views, DRM 26–28
Vis (Visibility) attribute, layers, DRM 321
Visited link A text hyperlink that has been clicked. DRM 66

W

W (Width) attribute
    cell, DRM 225, DRM 229
    layers, DRM 321
    Flash movie, DRM 378
    graphics, DRM 176
    vector, DRM 569
W and H attribute, DRM 408
Web. *See* World Wide Web
Web address, DRM 6–11
Web browser The software installed on a client computer that interprets and displays Web pages. DRM 6
    closing window, DRM 14
    previewing site in, DRM 87–89
Web clients The computer an individual uses to access information, via the Internet, that is stored on Web servers throughout the world.
    See Clients
Web page An electronic document of information on the Web. DRM 5
    adding Flash movies to, DRM 375–380
    adding Flash text to, DRM 380–383
    adding form to, DRM 454–457
    adding graphics to, DRM 171–174
    adding library item to, DRM 432
    adding new, DRM 74–75
    adding RealMedia video clip to, DRM 406–408
    adding Shockwave movies to, DRM 389–394
    adding text to, DRM 104–108
    adding video to, DRM 404–412
    attaching style sheet to, DRM 133–135
    backend, for viewing data in database, DRM 495–500, DRM 519–523
    creating new, for database-driven site, DRM 485–487, DRM 508–510
    creating and saving, in defined state, DRM 74–78
    checking spelling, DRM 106–107
    examining navigation bar in, DRM 248–249
    local, opening, in browser, DRM 9–11
    opening, in browser, DRM 8–9
    optimizing, for search engine placement, DRM 422–423
    resaving, DRM 77–78
    saving new, DRM 76
    setting titles, DRM 76–77
    splitting, creating frames by, DRM 263–265
    viewing or previewing, in browser, DRM 586
    and Web sites, DRM 6–14
Web pages, creating
    with frames, DRM 262–271
    from template, DRM 444–447
Web pages, database-driven, creating
    using Access and ASP, DRM 506–528
    using MySQL and PHP, DRM 483–505
Web Safe Color Palette A color palette of 216 colors that provides Web designers a reliable color palette to work with. The Web Safe Color Palette was created when many computers could display only 256 colors at a time. Because current computers can display 16+ million colors, many designers have disregarded the Web Safe Color Palette. DRM 63
Web server A specialized server that stores and distributes information to computers that are connected to the Internet.
    See Server
Web site A group of related and interconnected Web pages. DRM 5
    adding media to, DRM 372
    connecting, to database, DRM 489–491, DRM 512–514
    creating plan for, DRM 48–56
    database-driven, DRM 482
    designing, DRM 59–69
    determining goals, DRM 48–50
    new, creating, DRM 70–74
    previewing, in browser, DRM 87–89
    updating, on remote server, DRM 154–155, DRM 233–234, DRM 294–296, DRM 354–355, DRM 413–414, DRM 472
    uploading, to remote location, DRM 89–92
    and Web pages, DRM 6–14
Web tools, DRM 574
When Clicked, Go To URL, DRM 250

Window option, Fireworks MX 2004, DRM 551
Window Size menu, DRM 28
Windows, instructions for Macintosh users, DRM 586
Windows server, creating database-driven pages for, DRM 506–528
Word document, importing, into Dreamweaver, DRM 587
Workspace layout configuration, selecting, DRM 15–18
World Wide Web (WWW or Web) A subset of the Internet with its own protocol, HTTP, and its own document structure, called HTML. DRM 5
    evolving design tools, DRM 14–15
    previewing on, DRM 91–92
WWW. *See* World Wide Web
WYSIWYG (What You See Is What You Get) Software programs that display the element being created in the program window as it will appear to an end user and hide the underlying code from sight. Dreamweaver is a WYSIWYG program because it displays Web pages in the Document window as they will appear to an end user and hides the underlying HTML code from view. DRM 14

X

X attribute, DRM 569

Y

Y attribute, DRM 569

Z

Z-index attribute, DRM 321
Z-index number The z coordinate that determines a layer's stacking order; that is, the order in which the layer is stacked in the user's browser window when more than one layer is used on a page. DRM 312
Zoom tool, DRM 575

DATE DUE

Library Store #47-0108 Peel Off Pressure Sensitive